The Structure of Argument

Fifth Edition

Annette T. Rottenberg

Donna Haisty Winchell
CLEMSON UNIVERSITY

Bedford/St. Martin's
Boston ◆ New York

For Bedford/St. Martin's

Senior Developmental Editor: John E. Sullivan III
Production Editor: Deborah Baker
Production Supervisors: Yexenia Markland and Jennifer Wetzel
Senior Marketing Manager: Rachel Falk
Editorial Assistants: Christina Gerogiannis and Kaitlin Hannon
Copyeditor: Lisa Peachey Flanagan
Text Design: Gretchen Toles
Cover Design: Donna Lee Dennison
Cover Art: Victor Pesce, *Pile of Boxes 2002,* oil on canvas. Elizabeth Harris
  Gallery.
Composition: Pine Tree Composition
Printing and Binding: Haddon Craftsmen, Inc., an R.R. Donnelley & Sons
  Company

President: Joan E. Feinberg
Editorial Director: Denise B. Wydra
Editor in Chief: Karen S. Henry
Director of Marketing: Karen Melton Soeltz
Director of Editing, Design, and Production: Marcia Cohen
Managing Editor: Elizabeth M. Schaaf

Library of Congress Control Number: 2004118168

Manufactured in the United States of America.

0   9   8   7   6   5
f   e   d   c   b

For information, write: Bedford/St. Martin's, 75 Arlington Street, Boston, MA
02116 (617-399-4000)

ISBN: 0–312–45378–7
EAN: 978–0–312–45378–7

Acknowledgments

Charles Adams. "Lincoln's Logic." From *When In the Course of Human Events* by Charles Adams.
  Copyright © 2000 by Rowman & Littlefield Publishing. Reprinted by permission of the publisher.
Gordon Allport. "The Nature of Prejudice." From the 17th Claremont Reading Conference Yearbook, 1952. Reprinted by permission of Robert B. Allport.
Julia Álvarez. "A White Woman of Color." From *Half and Half: Writers on Growing Up Biracial and Bicultural,* edited by Claudine Chiawei O'Hearn. Copyright © 1998 by Julia Álvarez. Used by permission of Pantheon Books, a division of Random House, Inc.

*Acknowledgments and copyrights are continued at the back of the book on pages 566–69,
which constitute an extension of the copyright page. It is a violation of the law to reproduce
these selections by any means whatsoever without the written permission of the copyright
holder.*

PREFACE FOR INSTRUCTORS

PURPOSE

Argumentation as the basis of a composition course should need no defense, especially at a time of renewed pedagogical interest in critical thinking. A course in argumentation encourages practice in close analysis, use of supporting materials, and logical organization. It encompasses all the modes of development around which composition courses are often built. It teaches students to read and to listen with more than ordinary care. Not least, argument can engage the interest of students who have been indifferent or even hostile to required writing courses. Because the subject matter of argument can be found in every human activity — from the most trivial to the most elevated — both students and teachers can choose the materials that appeal to them.

Composition courses using the materials of argument are, of course, not new. But the traditional methods of teaching argument through mastery of the formal processes of reasoning cannot account for the complexity of arguments in practice. Even more relevant to our purposes as teachers of composition is the tenuous relationship between learning about induction and deduction, however helpful in analysis, and the actual process of student composition. The challenge has been to find a method of teaching argument that assists students in defending their claims as directly and efficiently as possible, a method that reflects the way people actually go about organizing and developing claims outside the classroom.

One such method, first adapted to classroom instruction by teachers of rhetoric and speech, uses a model of argument advanced by Stephen Toulmin in *The Uses of Argument*. Toulmin was interested in producing a description of the real process of argument. His model was the law.

"Arguments," he said, "can be compared with lawsuits, and the claims we make and argue for in extra-legal contexts with claims made in the courts."[1] Toulmin's model of argument was based on three principal elements: claim, evidence, and warrant. These elements answered the questions, "What are you trying to prove?" "What have you got to go on?" "How did you get from evidence to claim?" Needless to say, Toulmin's model of argument does not guarantee a classroom of skilled arguers, but his questions about the parts of an argument and their relationship are precisely the ones that students must ask and answer in writing their own essays and analyzing those of others. They lead students naturally into the formulation and development of their claims.

In this text we have adapted—and greatly simplified—some of Toulmin's concepts and terminology for first-year students. We have also introduced two elements of argument with which Toulmin is not directly concerned. Most rhetoricians consider them indispensable, however, to discussion of what actually happens in the defense or rejection of a claim. One is motivational appeals—warrants based on appeals to the needs and values of an audience, designed to evoke emotional responses. A distinction between logic and emotion may be useful as an analytical tool, but in producing or attacking arguments human beings find it difficult, if not impossible, to make such a separation. In this text, therefore, persuasion through appeals to needs and values is treated as a legitimate element in the argumentative process.

We have also stressed the significance of audience as a practical matter. In the rhetorical or audience-centered approach to argument, to which we subscribe in this text, success is defined as acceptance of the claim by an audience. Arguers in the real world recognize intuitively that their primary goal is not to demonstrate the purity of their logic but to win the adherence of their audiences. To gain this adherence, students need to be reminded of the necessity for establishing themselves as credible sources for their readers.

We hope *The Structure of Argument* will lead students to discover not only the practical and intellectual rewards of learning how to argue but the real excitement of engaging in civilized debate.

ORGANIZATION

In Part One, after two introductory chapters, a chapter each is devoted to the chief elements of argument—the definitions that lay a foundation for shared understanding, the claims that students make in their arguments, the support they must supply for their claims, and the warrants that underlie their arguments. Popular fallacies as well as induction and deduction are

---

[1] Stephen Toulmin, *The Uses of Argument* (Cambridge: Cambridge UP, 1958), p. 7.

treated in Chapter 7; because fallacies represent errors of reasoning, a knowl-edge of induction and deduction can make clear how and why fallacies occur. Chapter 8 deals with the power of word choice in arguing effectively.

We have provided examples, readings, discussion questions, and writ-ing suggestions that are, we hope, both practical and stimulating. The ex-amples include essays, articles, speeches, news reports, editorial opinions, letters to the editor, excerpts from online sources, cartoons, and adver-tisements. They reflect the liveliness and complexity of argumentation that exercises with no realistic context often suppress.

The fifty-four selections and seven advertisements in Part One sup-port in several ways the discussions of argumentation. First, they illus-trate the elements of argument; in each chapter, one or more essays have been analyzed to emphasize the principles of argument explained in the chapter. Second, they are drawn from current publications and cover as many different subjects as possible to convince students that argument is a pervasive force in the world they read about and live in. Third, some of the essays are obviously flawed and thus enable students to identify the kinds of weaknesses they should avoid in their own essays.

Part Two takes up the process of writing, researching, and presenting arguments. Chapter 9 explains how to find a topic, define the issues that it embraces, organize the information, and draft and revise an argument. Chapter 10 introduces students to the business of finding sources and using and documenting those sources effectively in research papers. The chapter concludes with two annotated student research papers: one that employs the Modern Language Association (MLA) documentation system; the other that represents research in the social and natural sciences and uses a modified American Psychological Association (APA) documentation style. Chapter 11 provides guidelines for presenting arguments orally.

The first appendix, Classic Arguments, reprints four selections that have stood the tests of both time and the classroom. They are among the arguments that teachers find invaluable in any composition course. The second, Arguing about Literature, provides an overview of the elements of fiction, drama, and poetry, plus a sample of each genre and a student paper based on the short story.

NEW TO THIS EDITION

This revision presented, as have earlier revisions of this text, both chal-lenges and opportunities. Previous users will notice that this is the first time that two authors have collaborated on *The Structure of Argument*. Our hope is that the union of two perspectives and our combined experience using the earlier editions in first-year classes will enrich the quality of the text that you use with your students. Donna Haisty Winchell, the new member of the team, comes to this revision having taught extensively with *The Structure of Argument* and having served as the composition director for several years at Clemson University. She learned from the experiences of others in her program and understood the challenges of revising a text used by instructors with diverse teaching styles and interests. By building on that knowledge of what works in the classroom, we have been able to gather many recent high-interest readings that will appeal to students.

Although the principles and concerns of the book have not changed, the new material in this edition should enhance the versatility of the text, deepen students' awareness of how pervasive argument is, and increase their ability to think critically and communicate persuasively. In short, we've added more help for students researching and writing argumentative papers, including new advice on finding, working with, and documenting sources. The new material first helps students understand *why* they should use sources and then helps students use them more effectively.

We have revised some of the Writer's Guides and have added eight others to offer students more writing instruction, and we have elaborated on how to smoothly incorporate quoted material into an essay. We have included two additional student essays and three additional professional models that illustrate correct documentation of sources. This edition incorporates a suggestion from past users that the definition chapter precede the chapters on claims, support, and warrant rather than breaking up that sequence. The number of selections in the fifth edition is now fifty-nine—thirty of them new.

For the short debates, we have retained one popular topic from the seventh edition—animal research—and have added five other timely ones: gay marriage, college costs, fast foods and obesity, stem-cell research, and gun control. Updated annotated Web links accompany these debates, encouraging students to conduct further research online.

The appendix of Classic Arguments now includes a provocative essay by Carrie Chapman Catt that investigates women as "assets" during World War I.

ANCILLARIES

The instructor's manual, *Resources for Teaching THE STRUCTURE OF ARGUMENT*, provides additional suggestions for using the book as well as for finding and using the enormous variety of materials available in a course on argument.

A companion Web site at <bedfordstmartins.com/rottenberg> includes annotated links for students and instructors looking for further information on controversial topics, online debates, and rhetorical theory. It also includes a sample syllabus and exercises for students on fallacies and warrants.

Mixed media and everyday arguments can be both more accessible and more challenging for students to examine. The i•claim CD-ROM offers a new way to visualize argument. It features six tutorials and an illustrated glossary. The i•claim CD-ROM can be packaged for free with *The Structure of Argument*. To see a sample tutorial, visit <bedfordstmartins .com/iclaim>. For ordering information, contact your local sales representative or e-mail us at sales_support@bfwpub.com.

Also available is *Teaching Argument in the Composition Course*, by Timothy Barnett. It offers a range of perspectives, from Aristotle to the present day, on argument and on teaching argument. The twenty-eight readings—many of them classic works in the field—present essential insights and practical information. For ordering information, contact your local sales representative or e-mail us at sales_support@bfwpub.com.

ALSO AVAILABLE

A longer edition, *Elements of Argument*, Eighth Edition, is available for instructors who prefer more readings. It presents not only Parts One and Two and the appendices, but also eight Multiple Viewpoints chapters, which include a total of fifty-nine selections and six cartoons, and an additional four selections in Classic Arguments.

ACKNOWLEDGMENTS

This book has profited by the critiques and suggestions of reviewers and instructors who responded to a questionnaire. We appreciate the thoughtful consideration given to previous editions by Kathryn Murphy Anderson, Kathryn Benander, Bill Bolin, Karen D. Bonnar, John Bradford, Kristina D. Busse, Alice Cleveland, Martha Goodman, Jean E. Graham, Jean E. Jost, Paul D. Knoke, David A. Kossy, Rebecca Lartigne, Madeleine Marchaterre, Judith Q. McMullen, Judith Mikesch, Don Miller, Rachel V. Mills, Theresa R. Mooney, John D. Musselman, William Provost, Karen L. Regal, Dr. Arthur T. Robinson, Diane Schlegel, Thomas F. Suggs, Elaine C. Theismeyer, and Jeffrey W. Vance. I would also like to thank those instructors who took the time to complete a questionnaire for the fourth edition: Lori Adolewski, Thomas Atwater, Victoria Lynn Ausland, Kim H. Baker, Kate Benzel, Edward H. Bloomfield, Ken A. Bugajski, Lisbeth Chapin, Patrick Clark, Irene P. Fass, Betsy Gwyn, Karen C. Holt, Steven R.

Mohr, Meg Morgan, L. J. Palumbo, Pedro Pence, Peggy L. Richards, Meisha Rosenberg, Joseph Sigalas, Micheline M. Soong, Kim Stallings, Arlo Stoltenberg, and Marguerite Tassi.

We are also grateful to Patricia DeMarco, Daniel Gonzalez, Laura Hope, David Kaufmann, Kimberly Manner, James Romesburg, Tracy Schrems, and Jennifer Stromer-Galley.

We would also like to thank those who have reviewed and responded to questionnaires about the longer text from which this one developed, *Elements of Argument,* through its previous four editions: Nancy E. Adams, Effrosini Piliouni Albrecht, Timothy C. Alderman, Yvonne Alexander, Kathleen Allison, John V. Andersen, Lucile G. Appert, William Arfin, Alison K. Armstrong, Karen Arnold, Angel M. Arzán, Mark Edward Askren, Michael Austin, David B. Axelrod, Jacquelyn A. Babush, Peter Banland, Carol A. Barnes, Tim Barnett, Marilyn Barry, Marci Bartolotta, Dr. Bonnie C. Bedford, Frank Beesley, Don Beggs, Martine Bellen, Bruce Bennett, Maureen Dehler Bennett, Chester Benson, Robert H. Bentley, Scott Bentley, Arthur E. Bervin, Patricia Bizzell, Don Black, Kathleen Black, Stanley S. Blair, Jim Bonnet, Nick Boone, Laurel Boyd, Mary Virginia Brackett, Robert J. Branda, Dianne Brehmer, Alan Brown, Megan Brown, Paul L. Brown, Bill Buck, W. K. Buckley, Alison A. Bulsterbaum, Eleanor Bunting, Clarence Bussinger, Deborah N. Byrd, Gary T. Cage, Karen Caig, Ruth A. Cameron, Dr. Rita Carey, Barbara R. Carlson, Eric W. Cash, Donna R. Chaney, Gail Chapman, Linda D. Chinn, Roland Christian, Gina Claywell, Dr. John O. Clemonts, Paul D. Cockeram, Tammy S. Cole, John Conway, Dr. Thomas S. Costello, Harry Costigan, Martha J. Craig, David J. Cranmer, Edward Crothers, Jennifer Cunningham, Sara Cutting, Jo Ann Dadisman, Sandra Dahlberg, Mimi Dane, Judy Davidson, Dr. Cynthia C. Davis, Philip E. Davis, Stephanie Demma, Loretta Denner, Cecile de Rocher, Julia Dietrich, Marcia B. Dinnech, Felicia A. Dixon, Jane T. Dodge, Ellen Donovan, L. Leon Duke, P. Dunsmore, Bernard Earley, Carolyn Embree, Carolyn L. Engdahl, Gwyn Enright, Stephen Ersinghaus, David Estes, Kristina Faber, Lester Faigley, Faridoun Farroth, B. R. Fein, Delia Fisher, Philip L. Fishman, Catherine Fitzgerald, Evelyn Flores, David D. Fong, Donald Forand, Mary A. Fortner, Alice R. France, Leslye Friedberg, Sondra Frisch, Richard Fulkerson, Maureen Furniss, Diane Gabbard, Donald J. Gadow, Eric Gardner, Frieda Gardner, Gail Garloch, Darcey Garretson, Victoria Gaydosik, E. R. Gelber-Beechler, Scott Giantralley, Michael Patrick Gillespie, Paula Gillespie, Wallace Gober, Sara Gogol, Stuart Goodman, Joseph Gredler, Lucie Greenberg, Mildred Buza Gronek, Marilyn Hagans, Linda L. Hagge, Lee T. Hamilton, Carolyn Han, Phillip J. Hanse, Pat Hardré, Susan Harland, A. Leslie Harris, Carolyn G. Hartz, Theresia A. Hartz, Fredrik Hausmann, Michael Havens, William Hayes, Ursula K. Heise, Anne Helms, Tena Lea Helton, Peter C. Herman, Diane Price Herndl, Heidi Hobbs, William S. Hochman, Sharon E. Hockensmith, Andrew J. Hoffman, Joyce Hooker, Richard S. Hootman, Laura Hope-Aleman, David Hulm, Clarence Hundley, Patrick Hunter, Richard Ice, Mary Griffith Jackson, Ann

S. Jagoe, Katherine James, Missy James, Ruth Jeffries, Owen Jenkins, Ruth Y. Jenkins, Iris Jennings, Linda Johnson, Richard M. Johnson, Janet Jubnke, E. C. Juckett, Catherine Kaikowska, George T. Karnezis, Richard Katula, Mary Jane Kearny, Joanne Keel, Patricia Kellogg-Dennis, N. Kesinger, Susan Kincaid, Jennifer Kirchoff, Joanne Kirkland, Judith Kirscht, Nancy Klug, John H. Knight, Paul D. Knoke, Frances Kritzer, George W. Kuntzman, Barbara Ladd, Jocelyn Ladner, M. Beardsley Land, Marlene J. Lang, Lisa Lebduska, Sara R. Lee, William Levine, Mary Levitt, Diana M. Liddle, Jack Longmate, Cynthia Lowenthal, Marjorie Lynn, Marcia MacLennan, Chantelle MacPhee, Kathryn McCormick, Nancy McGee, Patrick McGuire, Ray McKerrow, John McKinnis, Michael McKoski, Pamela J. McLagen, Suzanne McLaughlin, Patrick McMahon, Dennis McMillan, Donald McQuade, Christina M. McVay, D'Ann Madewell, Beth Madison, Susan Maloney, Dan M. Manolescu, Barbara A. Manrigue, Joyce Marks, Quentin E. Martin, Jim Matthews, Michael Matzinger, Charles May, Alan Merickel, Jean-Pierre Meterean, Ekra Miezan, Carolyn R. Miller, Lisa K. Miller, Amy Minervini, Logan D. Moon, Dennis D. Moore, Dan Morgan, Karen L. Morris, Curt Mortenson, Philip A. Mottola, Thomas Mullen, Charlotte A. Myers, Joan Naake, Michael B. Naas, Dana Nkana, Joseph Nassar, Byron Nelson, Elizabeth A. Nist, Jody Noerdlinger, Paralee F. Norman, Dr. Mary Jean Northcutt, Thomas O'Brien, James F. O'Neil, Mary O'Riordan, Arlene Okerland, Renee Olander, Elizabeth Oldfield, Amy Olsen, Richard D. Olson, Steven Olson, Lori Jo Oswald, Sushil K. Oswald, Roy Kenneth Pace II, Gary Pak, Linda J. Palumbo, Edna Parker, Jo Patterson, Laurine Paule, Leland S. Person, Betty Peters, Kelly S. Peterson, Nancy L. Peterson, Susan T. Peterson, Steve Phelan, Gail W. Pieper, Gloria Platzner, Rosanna Pronesti, Mildred Postar, Ralph David Powell, Jr., Teresa Marie Purvis, Nancy Raferty, Mark Razor, Barbara E. Rees, Karen L. Regal, Pat Regel, Charles Reinhart, Thomas C. Renzi, Janice M. Reynolds, Douglas F. Rice, G. A. Richardson, Beverly A. Ricks, James M. Ritter, Katherine M. Rogers, Marilyn Mathias Root, Judith Klinger Rose, Cathy Rosenfeld, Robert A. Rubin, Norma L. Rudinsky, Lori Ruediger, Cheryl W. Ruggiero, Richard Ruppel, Victoria Anne Sager, Joseph L. Sanders, Marlissa Santos, Irene Schiller, Suzette Schlapkohl, Sybil Schlesinger, Richard Schneider, Eileen Schwartz, Esther L. Schwartz, Eugene Senff, Jeffrey Seyall, Ron Severson, Lucy Sheehey, William E. Sheidley, Sallye J. Sheppeard, Sally Bishop Shigley, John Shout, Craig L. Shurtleff, Dr. Barbara L. Siek, Thomas Simmons, Michael Simms, Jacqueline Simon, Richard Singletary, Roger L. Slakey, Thomas S. Sloane, Beth Slusser, Denzell Smith, Rebecca Smith, Margaret Smolik, Katherine Sotol, Donald L. Soucy, Minoo Southgate, Linda Spain, Richard Spilman, Sarah J. Stafford, Jim Stegman, Martha L. Stephens, Deborah Steward, Arlo Stoltenberg, Elissa L. Stuchlik, Judy Szaho, Andrew Tadie, Fernanda G. Tate-Owens, R. Terhorst, Marguerite B. Thompson, Arline R. Thorn, Mary Ann Trevathan, Sandia Tuttle, Whitney G. Vanderwerff, Andrea Van Vorhis, Jennie VerSteeg, Les Wade, David L. Wagner, Jeanne Walker, Joseph Walker, James Wallace, Linda D. Warwick,

Carol Adams Watson, Roger D. Watson, Karen Webb, Raymond E. Whelan, Betty E. White, Julia Whitsitt, Toby Widdicombe, Mary Louise Willey, Heywood Williams, Matthew C. Wolfe, Alfred Wong, Bonnie B. Zitz, and Laura Zlogar.

We are also grateful to Kate Kiefer and Meg Morgan for their in-depth reviews.

We appreciate the contributions that Gail Stygall of the University of Washington made to the previous edition of the instructor's manual, which have been retained in this edition. We also thank once again Fred Kemp of Texas Tech University, who drafted the section on responding online in Chapter 2; Barbara Fister of Gustavus Adolphus College, who revised Chapter 10's discussion of information technologies; and Tim Barnett of Northeastern Illinois University, who enlarged and updated the sections on critical reading, evaluating electronic sources, note-taking, and summarizing, and for drafting the sample analysis of a Web site. All of their contributions have been retained in this edition.

We are grateful to those at Bedford/St. Martin's who have smoothed the process of bringing a new author on board and have helped in numerous ways large and small: Joan Feinberg, Elizabeth Schaaf, Denise Wydra, Karen Henry, Steve Scipione, Sandy Schechter, Coleen O'Hanley, Warren Drabek, Christina Gerogiannis, Gillian Speeth, Deborah Baker, and, most especially, John Sullivan.

CONTENTS

4. Claims 104

5. Support   *157*

SAMPLE ANNOTATED ESSAY

Single-Sex Education Benefits Men Too   *181*
CLAUDIUS E. WATTS III

The former president of the Citadel in South Carolina asserts that male students, like their female counterparts, deserve to reap the benefits of single-sex education.

SAMPLE ANALYSIS

The True Costs of SUVs   *185*
HAL R. VARIAN

A business professor from Berkeley compares car shopping to the arms race: "If other families buy bigger vehicles, then you will want to as well, if only in self-defense."

The True Confusion about SUV Costs   *189*
BETHANY ROYCE

A business instructor provides a critique of Varian's use of evidence.

STUDENT ESSAY

Safer? Tastier? More Nutritious?
The Dubious Merits of Organic Foods   *190*
KRISTEN WEINACKER

A student writer examines the claim that organic foods are more nutritious than conventionally grown ones.

READINGS FOR ANALYSIS

Connecting the Dots . . . to Terrorism   *194*
BERNARD GOLDBERG

A long-time television news reporter argues that television brings our nation together in moments of crisis, but that it should keep us better informed about where and why crises are developing.

A New Look, an Old Battle   *202*
ANNA QUINDLEN

A Pulitzer Prize–winning journalist and best-selling novelist writes that those who oppose abortion may support beneficial but controversial stem-cell research, which uses cells taken from human embryos.

8.   Language and Thought   *314*

Part Two
Writing, Researching, and Presenting Arguments   *371*

9. Writing an Argumentative Paper   *373*

11. Presenting an Argument Orally   *466*

Appendix: Classic Arguments   *481*

Appendix: Arguing about Literature 537

Part One

The Structure of Argument

CHAPTER 1

Understanding Argument

A conversation overheard in the school cafeteria:

> *"Hey, how come you didn't order the meat loaf special? It's pretty good today."*
> *"Well, I read this book about vegetarianism, and I've decided to give up meat. The book says meat's unhealthy and vegetarians live longer."*
> *"Don't be silly. Americans eat lots of meat, and we're living longer and longer."*
> *"Listen, this book tells how much healthier the Danes were during World War II because they couldn't get meat."*
> *"I don't believe it. A lot of these health books are written by quacks. It's pretty dumb to change your diet after reading one book."*

These people are having what most of us would call an argument, one that sounds dangerously close to a quarrel. There are, however, significant differences between the colloquial meaning of argument as a quarrel and its definition as a process of reasoning and advancing proof, although even the exchange reported above exhibits some of the characteristics of formal argument. The kinds of arguments we deal with in this text are not quarrels. They often resemble ordinary discourse about controversial issues. You may, for example, overhear a conversation like this one:

> "This morning while I was trying to eat breakfast I heard an announcer describing the execution of that guy in Texas who raped and murdered a teenaged couple. They gave him an injection, and it took him ten minutes to die. I almost lost my breakfast listening to it."
>
> "Well, he deserved it. He didn't show much pity for his victims, did he?"
>
> "Okay, but no matter what he did, capital punishment is really awful, barbaric. It's murder, even if the state does it."
>
> "No, I'd call it justice. I don't know what else we can do to show how we feel about a cruel, pointless murder of innocent people. The punishment ought to be as terrible as we can make it."

Each speaker is defending a value judgment about an issue that tests ideas of good and evil, right and wrong, and that cannot be decided by facts.

In another kind of argument the speaker or writer proposes a solution for a specific problem. Two men, both under twenty, are engaged in a conversation.

> "I'm going to be broke this week after I pay my car insurance. I don't think it's fair for males under twenty to pay such high rates. I'm a good driver, much better than my older sister. Why not consider driving experience instead of age or sex?"
>
> "But I always thought that guys our age had the most accidents. How do you know that driving experience is the right standard to apply?"
>
> "Well, I read a report by the Highway Commission that said it's really driving experience that counts. So I think it's unfair for us to be discriminated against. The law's behind the times. They ought to change the insurance laws."

In this case someone advocates a policy that appears to fulfill a desirable goal—making it impossible to discriminate against drivers just because they are young and male. Objections arise that the arguer must attempt to answer.

In these three dialogues, as well as in all the other arguments you will read in this book, human beings are engaged in explaining and defending their own actions and beliefs and opposing those of others. They do this for at least two reasons: to justify what they do and think both to themselves and to their opponents and, in the process, to solve problems and make decisions, especially those dependent on a consensus among conflicting views.

Unlike the examples cited so far, the arguments you will read and write will not usually take the form of dialogues, but arguments are implicit dialogues. Even when our audience is unknown, we write to persuade the unconvinced, to acquaint them with good reasons for changing their minds. As one definition has it, "Argumentation is the art of influencing others, through the medium of reasoned discourse, to believe or act as we wish them to believe or act."[1] This process is inherently dramatic; a good argument can create the kinds of tensions generated at sporting events. Who will win? What are the factors that enable a winner to emerge? One of the most popular and enduring situations on television is the courtroom debate, in which two lawyers (one, the defense attorney, the hero, unusually knowledgeable and persuasive; the other, the prosecuting attorney, bumbling and corrupt) confront each other before an audience of judge and jury that must render a heart-stopping verdict. Tensions are high because a life is in the balance. In the classroom the stakes are neither so intimidating nor so melodramatic, but even here a well-conducted argument can throw off sparks.

Of course, not all arguments end in clear victories for one side or another. Nor should they. In a democratic society of competing interests and values, a compromise between two or more extreme points of view may be the only viable solution to a vexing problem. Although formal debates under the auspices of a debating society, such as take place on many college campuses, usually end in winners and losers, real-life problems, both public and private, are often resolved through negotiation. Courtroom battles may result in compromise, and the law itself allows for exemptions and extenuating circumstances. Elsewhere in this book we speak of the importance of tradeoffs in social and political transactions, giving up one thing in return for another.

Keep in mind, however, that some compromises will not be morally defensible. In searching for a middle ground, the thoughtful arguer must determine that the consequences of a negotiated solution will contribute to the common good, not merely advance personal interests. (In Chapter 9 you will find a detailed guide for writing arguments in which you look for common ground.)

Most of the arguments in this book will deal with matters of public controversy, an area traditionally associated with the study of argument. As the word *public* suggests, these matters concern us as members of a community. "They are," according to one rhetorician, "the problems of war and peace, race and creed, poverty, wealth, and population, of democracy and communism. . . . Specific issues arise on which we must take decision from time to time. One day it is Suez, another Cuba. One week it is the Congo, another it is the plight of the American farmer or the railroads. . . . On these subjects the experts as well as the many take sides."[2] Today the issues are different from the issues that writers confronted more than twenty years ago. Today we are concerned about terrorism, the environment, privacy, and medical ethics, to name only a few.

---

[1] J. M. O'Neill, C. Laycock, and R. L. Scale, *Argumentation and Debate* (New York: Macmillan, 1925), p. 1.

[2] Karl R. Wallace, "Toward a Rationale for Teachers of Writing and Speaking," *English Journal*, September 1961, p. 386.

Clearly, if all of us agreed about everything, if harmony prevailed everywhere, the need for argument would disappear. But given what we know about the restless, seeking, contentious nature of human beings and their conflicting interests, we should not be surprised that many controversial questions, some of them as old as human civilization itself, will not be settled nor will they vanish despite the energy we devote to settling them. Unresolved, they are submerged for a while and then reappear, sometimes in another form, sometimes virtually unchanged. Capital punishment is one such stubborn problem; abortion is another. Nevertheless, we value the argumentative process because it is indispensable to the preservation of a free society. In *Areopagitica,* his great defense of free speech, John Milton, the seventeenth-century poet, wrote, "I cannot praise a fugitive and cloistered virtue, unexercised and unbreathed, that never sallies out and sees her adversary." How can we know the truth, he asked, unless there is a "free and open encounter" between all ideas? "Give me liberty to know, to utter, and to argue freely according to conscience, above all liberties."

WHY STUDY ARGUMENT?

Perhaps the question has already occurred to you: Why *study* argument? Since you've engaged in some form of the argumentative process all your life, is there anything to be learned that experience hasn't taught you? We think there is. If you've ever felt frustration in trying to decide what is wrong with an argument, either your own or someone else's, you might have wondered if there were rules to help in the analysis. If you've ever been dissatisfied with your attempt to prove a case, you might have wondered how good arguers, the ones who succeed in persuading people, construct their cases. Good arguers do, in fact, know and follow rules. Studying and practicing these rules can provide you with some of the same skills.

You will find yourself using these skills in a variety of situations, not only in arguing important public issues. You will use them, for example, in your academic career. Whatever your major field of study—the humanities, the social sciences, the physical sciences, business—you will be required to defend views about materials you have read and studied.

HUMANITIES Why have some of the greatest novels resisted translation into great films?

SOCIAL SCIENCE What is the evidence that upward social mobility continues to be a positive force in American life?

PHYSICAL SCIENCE What will happen to the world climate as the amount of carbon dioxide in the atmosphere increases?

BUSINESS Are the new tax laws beneficial or disadvantageous to the real estate investor?

For all these assignments, different as they may be, you would use the same kinds of analysis, research techniques, and evaluation. The conventions or rules for reporting results might differ from one field of study to another, but for the most part the rules for defining terms, evaluating evidence, and arriving at conclusions cross disciplinary lines. Many employers, not surprisingly, are aware of this. One sheriff in Arizona advertised for an assistant with a degree in philosophy. He had discovered, he said, that the methods used by philosophers to solve problems were remarkably similar to the methods used in law enforcement.

Whether or not you are interested in serving as a sheriff's assistant, you will encounter situations in the workplace that call for the same analytical and argumentative skills employed by philosophers and law enforcement personnel. Almost everywhere—in the smallest businesses as well as the largest corporations—a worker who can articulate his or her views clearly and forcefully has an important advantage in gaining access to positions of greater interest and challenge. Even when they are primarily informative, the memorandums, reports, instructions, questions, and explanations that issue from offices and factories obey the rules of argumentative discourse.

You may not anticipate doing the kind of writing or speaking at your job that you will practice in your academic work. It is probably true that in some careers, writing constitutes a negligible part of a person's duties. But outside the office, the studio, and the salesroom, you will be called on to exhibit argumentative skills as a citizen, as a member of a community, and as a consumer of leisure. In these capacities you can contribute to decision making if you are knowledgeable and prepared. By writing or speaking to the appropriate authorities, you can argue for a change in the meal ticket plan at your school or the release of pornographic films at the neighborhood theater or against a change in automobile insurance rates. Most of us are painfully aware of opportunities we lost because we were uncertain of how to proceed, even in matters that affected us deeply.

A course in argumentation offers another invaluable dividend: It can help you to cope with the bewildering confusion of voices in the world around you. It can give you tools for distinguishing between what is true and what is false, what is valid and what is invalid, in the claims of politicians, promoters of causes, newscasters, advertisers, salespeople, teachers, parents and siblings, employers and employees, neighbors, friends, and lovers, any of whom may be engaged at some time in attempting to persuade you to accept a belief or adopt a course of action. It can even offer strategies for arguing with yourself about a personal dilemma.

So far we have treated argument as an essentially pragmatic activity that benefits the individual. But choosing argument over force or evasion has clear moral benefits for society as well. We can, in fact, defend the study of argumentation for the same reasons that we defend universal education despite its high cost and sometimes controversial results. In a democracy, widespread literacy ultimately benefits all members of society, not only those who are the immediate beneficiaries of education, because only an informed citizenry can make responsible choices. One distinguished writer explains that "democracy depends on a citizenry that can reason for themselves, on men who know whether a case has been proved, or at least made probable."[3]

It is not too much to say that argument is a civilizing influence, the very basis of democratic order. In repressive regimes, coercion, which may express itself in a number of reprehensible forms—censorship, imprisonment, exile, torture, or execution—is a favored means of removing opposition to establishment "truth." In free societies, argument and debate remain the preeminent means of arriving at consensus.

Of course, rational discourse in a democracy can and does break down. Confrontations with police at abortion clinics, shouting and heckling at a meeting to prevent a speaker from being heard, student protests against university policies—such actions have become common in recent years. The demands of the demonstrators are often passionately and sincerely held, and the protesters sometimes succeed through force or intimidation in influencing policy changes. When this happens, however, we cannot be sure that the changes are justified. History and experience teach us that reason, to a far greater degree than other methods of persuasion, ultimately determines the rightness or wrongness of our actions.

A piece of folk wisdom sums up the superiority of reasoned argument as a vehicle of persuasion: "A man convinced against his will is of the same opinion still." Those who accept a position after engaging in a dialogue offering good reasons on both sides will think and act with greater willingness and conviction than those who have been coerced or denied the privilege of participating in the decision.

WHY WRITE?

If we agree that studying argumentation provides important critical tools, one last question remains: Why *write*? Isn't it possible to learn the rules by reading and talking about the qualities of good and bad arguments? Not quite. All writers, both experienced and inexperienced, will probably confess that looking at what they have written, even after long thought, can produce a startled disclaimer: But that isn't what I meant to say! They

[3]Wayne C. Booth, "Boring from Within: The Art of the Freshman Essay," adapted from a speech delivered to the Illinois Council of College Teachers of English in May 1963.

know that more analysis and more hard thinking are in order. Writers are also aware that words on paper have an authority and a permanency that invite more than casual deliberation. It is one thing to make an assertion, to express an idea or a strong feeling in conversation, and perhaps even to deny it later; it is quite another to write out an extended defense of your own position or an attack on someone else's that will be read and perhaps criticized by people unsympathetic to your views.

Students are often told that they must become better thinkers if they are to become better writers. It works the other way, too. In the effort to produce a clear and convincing argument, a writer matures as a thinker and a critic. The very process of writing calls for skills that make us better thinkers. Writing argumentative essays tests and enlarges important mental skills—developing and organizing ideas, evaluating evidence, observing logical consistency, expressing ourselves clearly and economically—that we need to exercise all our lives in our various social roles, whether or not we continue to write after college.

THE TERMS OF ARGUMENT

One definition of argument, emphasizing audience, has been given earlier: "Argumentation is the art of influencing others, through the medium of reasoned discourse, to believe or act as we wish them to believe or act." A distinction is sometimes made between argument and persuasion. Argument, according to most authorities, gives primary importance to logical appeals. Persuasion introduces the element of ethical and emotional appeals. The difference is one of emphasis. In real-life arguments about social policy, the distinction is hard to measure. In this book we use the term *argument* to represent forms of discourse that attempt to persuade readers or listeners to accept a claim, whether acceptance is based on logical or on emotional appeals or, as is usually the case, on both. The following brief definition includes other elements: *An argument is a statement or statements offering support for a claim.*

An argument is composed of at least three parts: the claim, the support, and the warrant.[4]

■ The Claim

The claim (also called a *proposition*) answers the question "What are you trying to prove?" It may appear as the thesis statement of your essay,

---

[4]Some of the terms and analyses used in this text are adapted from Stephen Toulmin's *The Uses of Argument* (Cambridge: Cambridge University Press, 1958).

although in some arguments it may not be stated directly. There are three principal kinds of claim (discussed more fully in Chapter 4): claims of fact, of value, and of policy. (The three dialogues at the beginning of this chapter represent these three kinds of claim respectively.) *Claims of fact* assert that a condition has existed, exists, or will exist and are based on facts or data that the audience will accept as being objectively verifiable:

> The present cocaine epidemic is not unique. From 1885 to the 1920s, cocaine was as widely used as it is today.
>
> Horse racing is the most dangerous sport.
>
> California will experience colder, stormier weather for the next ten years.

All these claims must be supported by data. Although the last example is an inference or an educated guess about the future, a reader will probably find the prediction credible if the data seem authoritative.

Claims of value attempt to prove that some things are more or less desirable than others. They express approval or disapproval of standards of taste and morality. Advertisements and reviews of cultural events are one common source of value claims, but such claims emerge whenever people argue about what is good or bad, beautiful or ugly.

> The opera *Tannhäuser* provides a splendid viewing as well as listening experience.
>
> Football is one of the most dehumanizing experiences a person can face.   —Dave Meggyesy
>
> Ending a patient's life intentionally is absolutely forbidden on moral grounds.   —Presidential Commission on Medical Ethics, 1983

Claims of policy assert that specific policies should be instituted as solutions to problems. The expression *should, must,* or *ought to* usually appears in the statement.

> Prisons should be abolished because they are crime-manufacturing concerns.
>
> Our first step must be to immediately establish and advertise drastic policies designed to bring our own population under control.
>   —Paul Ehrlich, biologist
>
> The New York City Board of Education should make sure that qualified women appear on any new list of candidates for Chancellor of Education.

Policy claims call for analysis of both fact and value. (A full discussion of claims follows in Chapter 4.)

■ The Support

Support consists of the materials used by the arguer to convince an audience that his or her claim is sound. These materials include *evidence* and *motivational appeals*. The evidence or data consist of facts, statistics, and testimony from experts. The motivational appeals are the ones that the arguer makes to the values and attitudes of the audience to win support for the claim. The word *motivational* points out that these appeals are the reasons that move an audience to accept a belief or adopt a course of action. For example, in his argument advocating population control, the claim of which is presented above, Paul Ehrlich first offered statistical evidence to prove the magnitude of the population explosion. But he also made a strong appeal to the generosity of his audience to persuade them to sacrifice their own immediate interests to those of future generations. (See Chapter 5 for detailed discussion of support.)

■ The Warrant

Certain assumptions underlie all the claims we make. In argument, the term *warrant* is used for such an assumption, a belief or principle that is taken for granted. It may be stated or unstated. If the arguer believes that the audience shares his assumption, he may feel it unnecessary to express it. But if he thinks that the audience is doubtful or hostile, he may decide to state the assumption to emphasize its importance or argue for its validity. The warrant, stated or not, allows the reader to make the same connection between the support and the claim that the author does.

This is how the warrant works. In the dialogue beginning this chapter, one speaker made the claim that vegetarianism was more healthful than a diet containing meat. As support he offered the evidence that the authors of a book he had read recommended vegetarianism for greater health and longer life. He did not state his warrant—that the authors of the book were trustworthy guides to theories of healthful diet. In outline form the argument looks like this:

CLAIM: Adoption of a vegetarian diet leads to healthier and longer life.

SUPPORT: The authors of *Becoming a Vegetarian Family* say so.

WARRANT: The authors of *Becoming a Vegetarian Family* are reliable sources of information on diet.

A writer or speaker may also need to offer support for the warrant. In the case cited above, the second speaker is reluctant to accept the unstated warrant, suggesting that the authors may be quacks. The first speaker will need to provide support for the assumption that the authors are trustworthy, perhaps by introducing proof of their credentials in science and medicine. Notice that although the second speaker accepts the evidence, he cannot agree that the claim has been proved unless he also accepts the warrant. If he fails to accept the warrant—that is, if he refuses to believe that the authors are credible sources of information about diet—then the evidence cannot support the claim.

The following example demonstrates how a different kind of warrant, based on values, can also lead an audience to accept a claim.

CLAIM: Laws making marijuana illegal should be repealed.

SUPPORT: People should have the right to use any substance they wish.

WARRANT: No laws should prevent citizens from exercising their rights.

Support for repeal of the marijuana laws often consists of medical evidence that marijuana is harmless. Here, however, the arguer contends that an important ethical principle is at work: Nothing should prevent people from exercising their rights, including the right to use any substance, no matter how harmful. Let us suppose that the reader agrees with the supporting statement, that individuals should have the right to use any substance. But to accept the claim, the reader must also agree with the principle expressed in the warrant—that government should not interfere with the individual's right. He or she can then agree that laws making marijuana illegal should be repealed. Notice that this warrant, like all warrants, certifies that the relationship between the support and the claim is sound.

One more important characteristic of the warrant deserves mention. In many cases, the warrant is a more general statement of belief than the claim. It can, therefore, support many claims, not only the one in a particular argument. For example, the warrant you have just read—"No laws should prevent citizens from exercising their rights"—is a broad assumption or belief that we take for granted and that can underlie claims about many other practices in American society. (For more on warrants, see Chapter 6.)

THE AUDIENCE

All arguments are composed with an audience in mind. We have already pointed out that an argument is an implicit dialogue or exchange. Often the writer of an argument about a public issue is responding to another writer or speaker who has made a claim that needs to be supported or opposed. In writing your own arguments, you should assume that there is a reader who may not agree with you. Throughout this book, we will continue to refer to ways of reaching such a reader.

Speechmakers are usually better informed than writers about their audience. Some writers, however, are familiar with the specific persons or groups who will read their arguments; advertising copywriters are a conspicuous example. They discover their audiences through sophisticated polling and marketing techniques and direct their messages to a well-targeted group of prospective buyers. Other professionals may be required to submit reports to persuade a specific and clearly defined audience of certain beliefs or courses of action: An engineer may be asked by an environmental interest group to defend his plans for the building of a sewage treatment plant; or a town planner may be called on to tell the town council why she believes that rent control may not work; or a sales manager may find it necessary to explain to his superior why a new product should be launched in the Midwest rather than the South.

In such cases the writer asks some or all of the following questions about the audience:

Why has this audience requested this report? What do they want to get out of it?

How much do they already know about the subject?

Are they divided or agreed on the subject?

What is their emotional involvement with the issues?

Providing abundant evidence and making logical connections between the parts of an argument may not be enough to win agreement from an audience. In fact, success in convincing an audience is almost always inseparable from the writer's credibility or the audience's belief in the writer's trustworthiness. Aristotle, the Greek philosopher who wrote a treatise on argument that has influenced its study and practice for more than two thousand years, considered credibility—what he called *ethos*—the most important element in the arguer's ability to persuade the audience to accept his or her claim.

Aristotle named "intelligence, character, and goodwill" as the attributes that produce credibility. Today we might describe these qualities somewhat differently, but the criteria for judging a writer's credibility remain essentially the same. First, the writer must convince the audience that he is knowledgeable, that he is as well informed as possible about the subject. Second, he must persuade his audience that he is not only truthful in the presentation of his evidence but also morally upright and dependable. Third, he must show that, as an arguer with good intentions, he has considered the interests and needs of others as well as his own.

As an example in which the credibility of the arguer is at stake, consider a wealthy Sierra Club member who lives on ten acres of a magnificent oceanside estate and who appears before a community planning board to argue against future development of the area. His claim is that more building will destroy the delicate ecological balance of the area. The board, acting in the interests of all the citizens of the community, will ask themselves: Has the arguer proved that his information about environmental impact is complete and accurate? Has he demonstrated that he sincerely desires to preserve the wilderness, not merely his own privacy and space? And has he also made clear that he has considered the needs and desires of those who might want to live in a housing development by the ocean? If the answers to all these questions are yes, then the board will hear the arguer with respect, and the arguer will have begun to establish his credibility.

A reputation for intelligence, character, and goodwill is not often won overnight. And it can be lost more quickly than it is won. Once a writer or speaker has betrayed an audience's belief in her character or judgment, she may find it difficult to persuade an audience to accept subsequent claims, no matter how sound her data and reasoning are. "We give no credit to a liar," said Roman statesman Cicero, "even when he speaks the truth."

Political life is full of examples of lost and squandered credibility. After it was discovered that President Lyndon Johnson had deceived the American public about U.S. conduct in the Vietnam War, he could not regain his popularity. After President Gerald Ford pardoned former President Richard Nixon for his complicity in the cover up of the bugging and burglary of the Democratic National Committee headquarters at the Watergate office complex, Ford was no longer a serious candidate for reelection. After proof that President Clinton had lied to a grand jury and the public about his sexual relationship with a young White House intern, public approval of his political record remained high, but approval of his moral character declined and threatened to diminish his influence.

We can see the practical consequences when an audience realizes that an arguer has been guilty of a deception—misusing facts and authority, suppressing evidence, distorting statistics, violating the rules of logic. But suppose the arguer is successful in concealing his or her manipulation of the data and can persuade an uninformed audience to take the action or adopt the idea that he or she recommends. Even supposing that the argument promotes a "good" cause, is the arguer justified in using evasive or misleading tactics?

The answer is no. To encourage another person to make a decision on the basis of incomplete or dishonestly used data is profoundly unethical. It indicates lack of respect for the rights of others—their right to know at least as much as you do about the subject, to be allowed to judge and compare, to disagree with you if they challenge your own interests. If the moral implications are still not clear, try to imagine yourself not as the perpetrator of the lie but as the victim.

There is also a danger in measuring success wholly by the degree to which audiences accept our arguments. Both as writers and readers, we must be able to respect the claim, or proposition, and what it tries to demonstrate. The English philosopher Stephen Toulmin has said: "To conclude that a proposition is true, it is not enough to know that this [person] or that finds it 'credible': the proposition itself must be *worthy* of credence."[5]

No matter what the subject, there are certain basic steps that a writer can take to insure that not only the proposition, or claim, but the whole argument, is worthy of credence. You are not yet an expert in many of the subjects you will deal with in assignments, although you are knowledgeable about many other things, including your cultural and social activities. But there are several ways in which you can develop confidence by your discussion of topics derived from academic disciplines, such as political science, psychology, economics, sociology, and art, on which most assignments will be based. The following steps that every writer of argumentative texts should follow will be the basis for Chapters 3 to 8.

■ Defining Key Terms (Chapter 3)

Many of the controversial questions you will read or write about are primarily arguments of definition. Such terms as *abortion, pornography, racism, poverty, freedom of speech,* and *terrorism* must be defined before useful solutions to the problems they represent can be formulated. Even if the primary purpose of your essay is not definition, you can successfully communicate with an audience only if that audience understands how you are using key terms.

■ Choosing an Appropriate Claim (Chapter 4)

It must be clear to the individual or group that constitutes your audience what change in thought or what action you hope to achieve by presenting your case. If you are seeking a change in your audience's thinking on a subject, you will have a much greater chance of accomplishing your goal if you consider the audience's current thinking on the subject and are realistic about the extent to which you might hope to change that thinking. If there is something you want your audience to do, that action must be realistically within the power of that audience.

■ Choosing and Documenting Appropriate Sources (Chapter 5)

You must submit evidence of careful research, demonstrating that you have been conscientious in finding the best authorities, giving credit, and attempting to arrive at the truth.

[5]*An Examination of the Place of Reason in Ethics* (Cambridge: Cambridge University Press, 1964), p. 71.

■ Analyzing Assumptions (Chapter 6)

You must consider the warrant or assumption on which your argument is based. A warrant need not be expressed if it is so widely accepted that you can assume any reasonable audience will not need proof of its validity. You must be prepared to defend any other warrant.

■ Avoiding Logical Errors (Chapter 7)

Understanding the ways in which inductive and deductive reasoning processes work can help you to determine the truth and validity of your arguments, as well as other arguments, and to identify and correct faulty reasoning.

■ Editing for Appropriate Language (Chapter 8)

Another important resource is the careful use of language, not only to define terms and express personal style but also to reflect clarity of thought, to avoid the clichés and outworn slogans that frequently substitute for fresh ideas, and to avoid word choices that would make your audience unwilling to consider your ideas.

Now let us turn to one of the most famous arguments in American history and examine its elements.

SAMPLE ANALYSIS

The Declaration of Independence

THOMAS JEFFERSON

When in the course of human events, it becomes necessary for one people to dissolve the political bands which have connected them with another, and to assume among the Powers of the earth, the separate and equal station to which the Laws of Nature and Nature's God entitle them, a decent respect to the opinions of mankind requires that they should declare the causes which impel them to the separation.

We hold these truths to be self-evident, that all men are created equal, that they are endowed by their Creator with certain unalienable Rights, that among these are Life, Liberty and the pursuit of Happiness.

That to secure these rights, Governments are instituted among Men, deriving their just powers from the consent of the governed.

Thomas Jefferson (1743–1826) served as governor of Virginia, minister to France, secretary of state, vice president under John Adams, and president from 1801 to 1809.

That whenever any Form of Government becomes destructive of these ends, it is the Right of the People to alter or to abolish it, and to institute a new Government laying its foundation on such principles and organizing its powers in such form, as to them shall seem most likely to effect their Safety and Happiness. Prudence, indeed, will dictate that Governments long established should not be changed for light and transient causes; and accordingly all experience hath shown that mankind are more disposed to suffer, while evils are sufferable, than to right themselves by abolishing the forms to which they are accustomed. But when a long train of abuses and usurpations pursuing invariably the same Object evinces a design to reduce them under absolute Despotism, it is their right, it is their duty, to throw off such government, and to provide new Guards for their future security.

Such has been the patient sufferance of these Colonies; and such is now the necessity which constrains them to alter their former Systems of Government. The history of the present King of Great Britain is a history of repeated injuries and usurpations, all having in direct object the establishment of an absolute Tyranny over these States. To prove this, let Facts be submitted to a candid world. 5

He has refused his Assent to Laws, the most wholesome and necessary for the public good.

He has forbidden his Governors to pass Laws of immediate and pressing importance, unless suspended in their operation till his Assent should be obtained; and when so suspended, he has utterly neglected to attend to them.

He has refused to pass other Laws for the accommodation of large districts of people, unless those people would relinquish the right of Representation in the Legislature, a right inestimable to them and formidable to tyrants only.

He has called together legislative bodies at places unusual, uncomfortable, and distant from the depository of their Public Records, for the sole purpose of fatiguing them into compliance with his measures.

He has dissolved Representative Houses repeatedly, for opposing with manly firmness his invasions on the rights of the people. 10

He has refused for a long time, after such dissolutions, to cause others to be elected; whereby the Legislative Powers, incapable of Annihilation, have returned to the People at large for their exercise; the State remaining in the mean time exposed to all the danger of invasion from without, and convulsions within.

He has endeavored to prevent the population of these States; for that purpose obstructing the Laws of Naturalization of Foreigners; refusing to pass others to encourage their migration hither, and raising the conditions of new Appropriations of Lands.

He has obstructed the Administration of Justice, by refusing his Assent to Laws for establishing Judiciary Powers.

He has made Judges dependent on his Will alone, for the tenure of their offices, and the amount and payment of their salaries.

He has erected a multitude of New Offices, and sent hither swarms of 15 Officers to harass our People, and eat out their substance.

He has kept among us, in time of peace, Standing Armies without the consent of our Legislature.

He has affected to render the Military independent of and superior to the Civil Power.

He has combined with others to subject us to jurisdictions foreign to our constitution, and unacknowledged by our laws; giving his Assent to their acts of pretended Legislation:

For quartering large bodies of armed troops among us:

For protecting them, by a mock Trial, from Punishment for any Mur- 20 ders which they should commit on the Inhabitants of these States:

For cutting off our Trade with all parts of the world:

For imposing Taxes on us without our Consent:

For depriving us in many cases, of the benefits of Trial by Jury:

For transporting us beyond Seas to be tried for pretended offenses:

For abolishing the free System of English Laws in a Neighbouring 25 Province, establishing therein an Arbitrary government, and enlarging its boundaries so as to render it at once an example and fit instrument for introducing the same absolute rule into these Colonies:

For taking away our Charters, abolishing our most valuable Laws, and altering fundamentally the Forms of our Governments:

For suspending our own legislatures, and declaring themselves invested with Power to legislate for us in all cases whatsoever.

He has abdicated Government here, by declaring us out of his Protection and waging War against us.

He has plundered our seas, ravaged our Coasts, burnt our towns and destroyed the Lives of our people.

He is at this time transporting large Armies of foreign Mercenaries to 30 compleat the works of death, desolation and tyranny, already begun with circumstances of Cruelty & perfidy scarcely paralleled in the most barbarous ages, and totally unworthy the Head of a civilized nation.

He has constrained our fellow Citizens taken Captive on the high Seas to bear Arms against their Country, to become the executioners of their friends and Brethren, or to fall themselves by their Hands.

He has excited domestic insurrections amongst us, and has endeavored to bring on the inhabitants of our frontiers, the merciless Indian Savages, whose known rule of warfare is an undistinguished destruction of all ages, sexes, and conditions.

In every stage of these Oppressions We Have Petitioned for Redress in the most humble terms. Our repeated petitions have been answered only by repeated injury. A Prince, whose character is thus marked by every act which may define a Tyrant, is unfit to be the ruler of a free People.

Not have We been wanting in attention to our British brethren. We have warned them from time to time of attempts by their legislature to extend an unwarrantable jurisdiction over us. We have reminded them of the circumstances of our emigration and settlement here. We have appealed to their native justice and magnanimity and we have conjured them by the ties of our common kindred to disavow these usurpations, which would inevitably interrupt our connections and correspondence. They too have been deaf to the voice of justice and of consanguinity. We must, therefore, acquiesce in the necessity, which denounces our Separation, and hold them, as we hold the rest of mankind, Enemies in War, in Peace Friends.

We, therefore, the Representatives of the United States of America, in 35 General Congress, Assembled, appealing to the Supreme Judge of the world for the rectitude of our intentions, do, in the Name, and by Authority of the good People of these Colonies, solemnly publish and declare, That these United Colonies are, and of Right ought to be, Free and Independent States; that they are Absolved from all Allegiance to the British Crown, and that all political connection between them and the State of Great Britain, is and ought to be totally dissolved; and that as Free and Independent States, they have full power to levy War, conclude Peace, contract Alliances, establish Commerce, and to do all other Acts and Things which Independent States may of right do. And for the support of this Declaration, with a firm reliance on the protection of Divine Providence, we mutually pledge to each other our lives, our Fortunes and our sacred Honor.

■ Analysis

The Declaration of Independence is addressed to several audiences: to the American colonists; to the British people; to the British Parliament; to the British king, George III; and to humanity or a universal audience. Not all the American colonists were convinced by Jefferson's argument. Large numbers remained loyal to the king and for various reasons opposed an independent nation. In the next-to-the-last paragraph, Jefferson refers to previous addresses to the British people. Not surprisingly, most of the British citizenry as well as the king also rejected the claims of the Declaration. But the universal audience, the decent opinion of humanity, found Jefferson's argument overwhelmingly persuasive. Many of the liberal reform movements of the eighteenth and nineteenth centuries were inspired by the Declaration. In basing his claim on universal principles of justice and equality, Jefferson was certainly aware that he was addressing future generations.

Definition: Several significant terms are not defined. Modern readers will ask for further definition of "all men are created equal," "Life, Liberty and the pursuit of Happiness," "Laws of Nature and Nature's God," among others. We must assume that the failure to explain these terms more strictly was deliberate, in part because Jefferson thought that his readers would understand the references—for example, to the eighteenth-century belief in freedom as the birthright of all human beings—and in part because he wished the terms to be understood as universal principles of justice, applicable in all struggles, not merely those of the colonies against the king of England. But a failure to narrow the terms of argument can have unpredictable consequences. In later years the Declaration of Independence would be used to justify other rebellions, including the secession of the South from the Union in 1861.

Claim: What is Jefferson trying to prove? *The American colonies are justified in declaring their independence from British rule.* Jefferson and his fellow signers might have issued a simple statement such as appears in the last paragraph, announcing the freedom and independence of these United Colonies. Instead, however, they chose to justify their right to do so.

Support: What does Jefferson have to go on? The Declaration of Independence bases its claim on two kinds of support: *factual evidence* and *motivational appeals* or appeals to the values of the audience.

FACTUAL EVIDENCE: Jefferson presents a long list of specific acts of tyranny by George III, beginning with "He has refused his Assent to Laws, the most wholesome and necessary for the public good." This list constitutes more than half the text. Notice how Jefferson introduces these grievances: "The history of the present King of Great Britain is a history of repeated injuries and usurpations, all having in direct object the establishment of an absolute Tyranny over these States. *To prove this, let Facts be submitted to a candid world*" (italics for emphasis added). Jefferson hopes that a recital of these specific acts will convince an honest audience that the United Colonies have indeed been the victims of an intolerable tyranny.

APPEAL TO VALUES: Jefferson also invokes the moral values underlying the formation of a democratic state. These values are referred to throughout. In the second and third paragraphs he speaks of equality, "Life, Liberty and the pursuit of Happiness," "just powers," "consent of the governed," and in the fourth paragraph, safety. In the last paragraph he refers to freedom and independence. Jefferson believes that the people who read his appeal will, or should, share these fundamental values. Audience acceptance of these values constitutes the most important part of the support. Some historians have called the specific acts of oppression cited by Jefferson trivial, inconsequential, or distorted. Clearly, however, Jefferson felt that the list of specific grievances was vital to definition of the abstract terms in which values are always expressed.

Warrant: How does Jefferson get from support to claim? *People have a right to revolution to free themselves from oppression.* This warrant is explicit:

"But when a long train of abuses and usurpations pursuing invariably the same Object evinces a design to reduce them under absolute Despotism, it is their right, it is their duty, to throw off such government, and to provide new Guards for their future security." Some members of Jefferson's audience, especially those whom he accuses of oppressive acts, will reject the principle that any subject people have earned the right to revolt. But Jefferson believes that the decent opinion of mankind will accept this assumption. Many of his readers will also be aware that the warrant is supported by seventeenth-century political philosophy, which defines government as a social compact between the government and the governed.

If Jefferson's readers do, in fact, accept the warrant and if they also believe in the accuracy of the factual evidence and share his moral values, then they will conclude that his claim has been proved—that Jefferson has justified the right of the colonies to separate themselves from Great Britain.

Logic: As a logical pattern of argument, the Declaration of Independence is largely *deductive.* Deduction usually consists of certain broad general statements which we know or believe to be true and which lead us to other statements that follow from the ones already laid down. The Declaration begins with such general statements, summarizing a philosophy of government based on the equality of men, the inalienable rights derived from the Creator, and the powers of the governed. These statements are held to be "self-evident"—that is, not needing proof—and if we accept them, then it follows that a revolution is necessary to remove the oppressors and secure the safety and happiness to which the governed are entitled. The particular grievances against the king are proof that the king has oppressed the colonies, but they are not the basis for revolution.

The fact that Jefferson emphasized the universal principles underlying the right of revolution meant that the Declaration of Independence could appeal to all people everywhere, whether or not they had suffered the particular grievances in Jefferson's list.

Language: Although some stylistic conventions of eighteenth-century writing would not be observed today, Jefferson's clear, elegant, formal prose—"a surprising mixture of simplicity and majesty," in the words of one writer—remains a masterpiece of English prose and persuades us that we are reading an important document. Several devices are worth noting:

1. *Parallelism,* or balance of sentence construction, gives both emphasis and rhythm to the statements in the introduction (first four paragraphs) and the list of grievances.

2. *Diction* (choice of words) supports and underlines the meaning: nouns that have positive connotations—*safety, happiness, prudence, right, duty, Supreme Judge, justice;* verbs and verbals that suggest

Writer's Guide: Learning the Key Terms

Claim — the proposition that the author or writer is trying to prove. The claim may appear as the thesis statement of an essay but may be implied rather than stated directly.

- *Claims of fact* assert that a condition has existed, exists, or will exist and are based on facts or data that the audience will accept as being objectively verifiable.

- *Claims of value* attempt to prove that some things are more or less desirable than others; they express approval or disapproval of standards of taste and morality.

- *Claims of policy* assert that specific plans or courses of action should be instituted as solutions to problems.

Support — the materials used by the arguer to convince an audience that his or her claim is sound; those materials include evidence and motivational appeals.

Warrant — an inference or assumption; a belief or principle that is taken for granted in an argument.

negative actions (taken by the king) — *refused, forbidden, dissolved, obstructed, plundered, depriving, abolishing.*

3. The *tone* suggests reason and patience on the part of the author or authors (especially paras. 5, 33, and 34).

ASSIGNMENTS FOR UNDERSTANDING ARGUMENT

1. Classify each of the following as a claim of fact, value, or policy.
   a. Congress should endorse the right-to-life amendment.
   b. Solar power can supply 20 percent of the energy needs now satisfied by fossil and nuclear power.
   c. Homosexuals should have the same job rights as heterosexuals.
   d. Rapists should be treated as mentally ill rather than depraved.
   e. Whale hunting should be banned by international law.
   f. Violence on television produces violent behavior in children who watch more than four hours a day.
   g. Both creationism and evolutionary theory should be taught in the public schools.
   h. Mentally defective men and women should be sterilized or otherwise prevented from producing children.

    i. History will pronounce Reggie Jackson a greater all-around baseball player than Joe DiMaggio.

    j. Bilingual instruction should not be permitted in the public schools.

    k. Some forms of cancer are caused by a virus.

    l. Dogs are smarter than horses.

    m. Curfews for teenagers will reduce the abuse of alcohol and drugs.

    n. The federal government should impose a drinking age of twenty-one.

    o. The United States should proceed with unilateral disarmament.

    p. Security precautions at airports are out of proportion to the dangers of terrorism.

    q. Bodybuilding cannot be defined as a sport; it is a form of exhibitionism.

2. Choose one of the more controversial claims in the previous list and explain the reasons it is controversial. Would it be difficult or impossible to support? Are the warrants unacceptable to many people? Try to go as deeply as you can, exploring, if possible, systems of belief, traditions, societal customs. You may confine your discussion to personal experience with the problem in your community or group. If there has been a change over the years in the public attitude toward the claim, offer what you think may be an explanation for the change.

3. Report on an argument you have heard recently. Identify the parts of that argument—claim, support, warrant—as they are defined in this chapter. What were the strengths and weaknesses in the argument you heard?

4. Discuss an occasion when a controversy arose that the opponents could not settle. Describe the problem, and tell why you think the disagreement was not settled.

5. In the following excerpt a student expresses his feelings about standard grading—that is, grading by letter or number on a scale that applies to a whole group.

> You go to school to learn, not to earn grades. To be educated, that's what they tell you. "He's educated, he graduated magna cum laude." What makes a magna cum laude man so much better than a man that graduates with a C? They are both still educated, aren't they? No one has a right to call someone less educated because they got a C instead of an A. Let's take both men and put them in front of a car. Each car has something wrong with it. Each man must fix his broken car. Our C man goes right to work while our magna cum laude man hasn't got the slightest idea where to begin. Who's more educated now?

Compare the preceding passage to the following one, written on the same subject by a student. Analyze the two pieces using the terminology introduced in this chapter and applied above to the Declaration of Independence.

> Grades are the play money in a university Monopoly game. As long as the tokens are offered, the temptation will be largely irresistible to play for them. Students are so busy taking notes, doing tests, and

getting tokens that they have forgotten to ask: Of what worth is all this? Or perhaps they ask and the grade is their answer.

One certainly learns something in the passive lecture-note-read-note-test process: how to do it all more efficiently next time (in the hope of eventually owning Boardwalk and Park Place). As Marshall McLuhan has said, we learn what we do. In this process most students come to view learning as studying and remembering what other people have learned. They assume that knowledge is logically and for practical reasons divided up into discrete pieces called "disciplines" and that the highest knowledge is achieved by specializing in a discipline. By getting good grades in a lot of disciplines they conclude they have learned a lot. They have indeed, and it is too bad.[6]

---

[6] Roy E. Terry in "Does Standard Grading Encourage Excessive Competitiveness?" *Change,* September 1974, p. 45.

CHAPTER 2

Responding to Argument

Most of us learn how to read, to listen, to write—and, with the increased use of computer technology, to view—arguments by attending critically to the arguments of those who have already mastered the important elements as well as those who have not. As we acquire skill in analyzing arguments, we learn to uncover the clues that reveal meaning and to become sensitive to the kinds of claims and support, language and visuals that experienced writers use in persuading their audiences. Listening, too, is a skill often underrated but increasingly important in an era when the spoken voice can be transmitted worldwide with astonishing speed. In becoming more expert listeners, we can engage in discussions with a wide and varied audience and gain proficiency in distinguishing between responsible and irresponsible speech. In becoming more expert users and viewers of electronic texts, we become part of a worldwide conversation that would have been inconceivable until recently.

A full response to any argument means more than understanding the message. It also means evaluating, deciding whether the message is successful and then determining *how* it succeeds or fails in persuading us. In making these judgments about the written, oral, and visual arguments of others, we learn how to deliver our own. We try to avoid what we perceive to be flaws in another's arguments, and we adapt the strategies that produce clear, honest, forceful arguments.

RESPONDING AS A CRITICAL READER

Critical reading is essential for mastery of most college subjects, but its importance for reading and writing about argument, where meaning is often complex and multilayered, cannot be overestimated. Reading arguments critically requires you to at least temporarily suspend notions of absolute "right" and "wrong" and to intellectually inhabit grey areas that do not allow for simple "yes" and "no" answers. Of course, even in these areas, significant decisions about such things as ethics, values, politics, and the law must be made, and in studying argument you shouldn't fall into the trap of simple relativism: the idea that all answers to a given problem are equally correct at all times. We must make decisions about arguments with the understanding that reasonable people can disagree on the validity of ideas. Read or listen to others' arguments carefully and consider how their ideas can contribute to or complicate your own. Also recognize that what appears to be a final solution will always be open to further negotiation as new participants, new historical circumstances, and new ideologies become involved in the debate.

The ability to read arguments critically is essential to advanced academic work—even in science and math—since it requires the debate of multifaceted issues rather than the memorization of facts. Just as important, learning to read arguments critically helps you develop the ability to *write* effective arguments, a process valued at the university, in the professional world, and in public life.

■ Critical Reading Strategies

The first step in the critical reading process is comprehension—understanding what an author is trying to prove. Comprehending academic arguments can be difficult, because they are often complex and often challenge accepted notions. Academic writing also sometimes assumes that readers already have a great deal of knowledge about a subject, and can require further research for comprehension.

Reading a text on its own terms means reading rhetorically. Imagine the initial context the author was writing in, the problem the author was trying to deal with, the author's ideal audience: Who would respond most favorably to the author's words and why? What values and ideals are shared by the author and the audience most likely to agree with the argument? How do these values and ideals help make sense of the content?

GENERAL READING STRATEGIES

Whether reading to comprehend or to evaluate any text, do the following:

1. Take prereading activities seriously. Clearly, the more information you have about an author and subject, the easier and more productive your reading

will be. However, you should learn to read in a way that allows you to discover not just meaning in the text itself but information about the author's point of view and background, the audience the author is writing for, and the author's motives and ideology. Such understanding comes from close analysis of texts, background reading on the author or the subject (a task made significantly easier by the Internet), and discussion with your classmates and instructors on the material.

2. Work hard to understand the kind of text you are reading. Was it published recently? Was it written for a specific or a general audience? Is it a textbook and therefore likely to cover the basic points of an issue but not to take a strong stance on anything? Does it come from a journal that publishes primarily conservative or liberal writers?

3. When reading an Internet site, carefully read the Web address or URL. This can provide clues about the author of the site (is it an individual or an organization?) and about the purpose of the Web site (for example, the domain suffix *.com* represents a business site, while *.edu* represents academic institutions). In addition, most Web material is not checked for factual accuracy, so you must learn to distinguish between Web writing that represents a free-for-all of ideas and Web writing that has certain standards of reliability, especially when dealing with new information (see the sections on Sample Analysis of a Web Site (p. 52) and Evaluating Web Sources (p. 407) for more information).

SAMPLE ANNOTATED ESSAY

The Pursuit of Whining: Affirmative Action circa 1776

JOHN PATRICK DIGGINS

Usually means that a second glance will show the opposite

At first glance, affirmative action appears to be consistent with America's commitment to egalitarianism, which derives from the Declaration of Independence and its ringing pronouncement that "all men are created equal" and are "endowed by their creator with certain unalienable rights." Actually affirmative action, as carried out, has little to do with equality and is so dependent on biology, ancestry, and history that it subverts the individualist spirit of the Declaration.

Means it's not what it seems

So he's against aff. action because it violates the D of I?

John Patrick Diggins teaches history at the Graduate Center of the City University of New York. This column appeared in the *New York Times* on September 25, 1995.

Seems to be his thesis; is group opportunity bad?

But the second part of the Declaration, which no one remembers, may affirm affirmative action as the politics of group opportunity.

The Declaration held rights to be equal and unalienable because in the state of nature, before social conventions had been formed, "Nature and Nature's God" (Jefferson's phrase) gave no person or class the authority to dominate over others. Aristocracy became such a class, and the idea of equality was not so much an accurate description of the human species as it was a protest against artificial privilege and hereditary right.

Reason for the Revolution

Today we have a new identity politics of entitlement, and who one is depends on ethnic categories and descriptions based on either ancestry or sex. This return to a pseudo-aristocratic politics of privilege based on inherited rights by reason of birth means that equality has been replaced by diversity as the criteri[on] of governmental decisions.

Interesting point — today's affirmative action is like yesterday's aristocracy (both claim privileges of birth).

Jefferson loved diversity, but he and Thomas   5
Paine trusted the many and suspected the few who saw themselves entitled to preferential treatment as an accident of birth. Paine was unsparing in his critique of aristocracy as a parasitic "noability." Speaking for the colonists, many of whom had worked their way out of conditions of indentured servitude, he insisted that hereditary privilege was "as absurd as an hereditary mathematician, or an hereditary wise man; and as ridiculous as an hereditary poet-laureate."

The founding fathers were against inherited privileges.

But if America's egalitarian critique of aristocratic privilege could be in conflict with affirmative action, the second part of the Declaration may be perfectly consistent with it. Here begins the art of protest as the Declaration turns to the colonists' grievances, and we are asked to listen to a long tale of woe. Instead of admitting that they simply had no desire to cough up taxes, even to pay for a war that drove the French out of North America and thus made possible a situation where settlers were now secure enough to demand self-government, the colonists blamed King George for every outrage conceivable.

So far, he's proved that first part of D of I argues against affirmative action.

But the second part, listing grievances, is consistent with it.

Thinks the colonists are crybabies!

Strong language

Even Jefferson gets a few lumps!

Help! I can't find it in the D of I! (Look it up?)

Wow!

Were any of their complaints justified?

"Paranoia" seems a bit much.
He's talking about blacks and women. Is he saying, "no justification for complaints against whites and males?" No way!

Explain a bit further

Our choices ◄

An ending that's all questions. I like it. But they're fake questions. He knows the answers and wants us to agree with him.

"He has erected . . . swarms of offices to harass our people and eat out their substance." Because the King, in response to the colonists' refusal to pay for the cost of protection, withdrew such protection, he is charged with abdicating "his allegiance and protection: he has plundered our seas, ravaged our coasts, burnt our towns, destroyed the lives of our people." Even Edmund Burke, the British parliamentarian and orator who supported the colonists, saw them as almost paranoid, "protestants" who protest so much that they would "snuff the approach of tyranny in every tainted breeze."

The ultimate hypocrisy comes when Jefferson accuses the King of once tolerating the slave trade, only "he is now exciting those very people to rise up in arms among us, and to purchase their liberty of which he has deprived them, by murdering the people upon whom he has obtruded them." The notion that slavery was forced upon the innocent colonists, who in turn only sought to be free of "tyranny," suggests the extent to which the sentiment of the Revolution grumbles with spurious charges.

The Declaration voiced America's first proclamation of victimology. Whatever the theoretical complexities embedded in the doctrine of equality, the Declaration demonstrated that any politics that has its own interests uppermost is best put forward in the language of victimization and paranoia.

The very vocabulary of the document ("harass," "oppress," and so on) is consistent with affirmative action, where white racists and male chauvinists have replaced King George as the specter of complaint. 10

Seeing themselves as sufferers to whom awful things happen, the colonists blamed their alleged oppressors and never acknowledged that they had any responsibility for the situation in which they found themselves.

What then is America's core value? Is it equality and civic virtue? Or is it the struggle for power that legitimizes itself in the more successful, and least demanding, shameless politics of whining?

COMPREHENDING ARGUMENTS

Readers sometimes fail to comprehend a text they disagree with or that is new to them, especially in dealing with essays or books making controversial, value-laden arguments. Some research even shows that readers will sometimes remember only those parts of texts that match their points of view.[1] The study of argument does not require you to accept points of view you find morally or otherwise reprehensible, but to engage with these views, no matter how strange or repugnant they might seem, on your own terms.

To comprehend difficult texts you should understand that reading and writing are linked processes, and use writing to help your reading. This can mean writing comments in the margins of the book or essay itself or in a separate notebook; highlighting passages in the text that seem particularly important; or freewriting about the author's essential ideas after you finish reading. For complex arguments, write down the methods the author uses to make the argument: Did the text make use of historical evidence or rely on the voice of experts? Were emotional appeals made to try to convince readers, or did the text rely on scientific or logical forms of evidence? Did the author use analogies or comparisons to help readers understand the argument? Was some combination of these or other strategies used? Writing down the author's methods for argumentation can make even the most complex arguments understandable.

STRATEGIES FOR COMPREHENDING ARGUMENTS

1. Skim the article or book for the main idea and overall structure. At this stage, avoid concentrating on details. As part of your prereading activities, try some or all of the following:

   a. Pay attention to the title, as it may state the purpose of the argument in specific terms, as in "Single-Sex Education Benefits Men Too" (p. 181). The title of the previous article, "The Pursuit of Whining" (p. 27), brings to mind the famous "pursuit of Happiness" phrase from the Declaration of Independence. The subtitle clinches the connection: "Affirmative Action circa 1776." Titles can also express the author's attitude toward the subject, and in the case of "The Pursuit of Whining," we realize that "whining," because it has negative connotations, will probably be attacked as a means of achieving happiness.

[1]See, for example, Patrick J. Slattery, "The Argumentative, Multiple-Source Paper: College Students Reading, Thinking, and Writing about Multiple Points of View," *Journal of Teaching Writing* 10, Fall/Winter 1991, 181–99.

b. Make a skeleton outline of the text in your mind or on paper. From this outline and the text itself, consider the relationship between the beginning, middle, and end of the argument. How has the author divided these sections? Are there subheadings in the body of the text? If you are reading a book, how are the chapters broken up? What appears to be the logic of the author's organization?

c. From your overview, what is the central claim or argument of the essay? What is the main argument against the author's central claim and how would the author respond to it?

2. Remember that the central argument — also known as the thesis statement or claim — is usually in one of the first two or three paragraphs (if it is an essay) or in the first chapter (if it is a book). The beginning of an argument can have other purposes, however; it may describe the position that the author will oppose, or provide background for the whole argument.

3. Pay attention to topic sentences. The topic sentence is usually but not always the first sentence of a paragraph. It is the general statement that controls the details and examples in the paragraph.

4. Don't overlook language signposts, especially transitional words and phrases that tell you whether the writer will change direction or offer support for a previous point — words and phrases like *but, however, nevertheless, yet, moreover, for example, at first glance, more important, the first reason,* and so on.

5. When it comes to vocabulary, you can either guess the meaning of an unfamiliar word from the context and go on, or look it up immediately. The first method makes for more rapid reading and is sometimes recommended by teachers, but guessing can be risky. Keep a good dictionary handy. If a word you don't understand seems crucial to meaning, look it up before going on.

6. If you use a colored marker to highlight main points, use it sparingly. Marking passages in color is meant to direct you to the major ideas and reduce the necessity for rereading the whole passage when you review. Look over the marked passages after reading and do a five-minute freewrite to sum up the central parts of the argument.

7. Once you are done reading, think again about the original context the text was written in: Why did the author write it and for whom? Why might an editor have published it in a book or journal and why did your instructor assign it for you to read?

EVALUATING ARGUMENTS

The second step in the critical reading of arguments involves evaluation — careful judgment of the extent to which the author has succeeded in making a point — which can be difficult because some readers who do not thoroughly engage with an author's point of view may immediately label an argument they disagree with as "wrong," and some readers believe they are incapable of evaluating the work of a published, "expert" author because they do not feel expert enough to make such judgments.

Evaluating arguments means moving beyond comprehending the context the author was writing within and starting to question it. One way to do this is to envision audiences the text was probably *not* written for, by considering, for example, whether an essay written for an academic audience takes into account the world outside the university. In addition, why is the problem significant to the author? For whom would it not be significant, and why?

When you evaluate an argument, imagine at least two kinds of audience for the text. Decide whose views would conflict most with the author's, and why. What ideology or values underlie the point of view most diametrically opposed to the author's argument? Then imagine yourself as a friend of the writer who simply wants him or her to succeed in clarifying and developing the argument. You could ask what additional methods the author should use to make the argument more effective or how the writer could more fully address opposing points of view. Are there any significant questions or issues the author has left unaddressed? How could he or she build on the strengths of the argument and downplay the weaknesses?

At this point, consider how you personally respond to the argument presented in the text, and your own response in light of the questions you've asked. Critically evaluating an argument means not simply reading a text and agreeing or disagreeing with it, but doing serious analytical work that addresses multiple viewpoints before deciding on the effectiveness of an argument.

STRATEGIES FOR EVALUATING ARGUMENTS

1. As you read the argument, don't be timid about asking questions of the text. No author is infallible, and some are not always clear. Disagree with the author if you feel confident of the support for your view, but first read the whole argument to see if your questions have been answered. If not, this may be a signal to read the article again. Be cautious about concluding that the author hasn't proved his or her point.

2. Reading an assigned work is usually a solitary activity, but what follows a reading should be shared. Talk about the material with classmates or others who have read it, especially those who have responded to the text differently than yourself. Consider their points of view. You probably know that discussion of a book or a movie strengthens both your memory of details and your understanding of the whole. And defending or modifying your evaluation will mean going back to the text and finding clues that you may have overlooked. Not least, it can be fun to discuss even something you didn't enjoy.

3. Consider the strengths of the argument, and examine the useful methods of argumentation, the points that are successfully made, (and those which help the reader to better understand the argument), and what makes sense about the author's argument.

4. Consider the weaknesses of the argument, and locate instances of faulty reasoning, unsupported statements, and the limitations of the author's assumptions about the world (the warrants that underlie the argument).

5. Consider how effective the title of the reading is, and whether it accurately sums up a critical point of the essay. Come up with an alternative title that would suit the reading better, and be prepared to defend this alternative title.

6. Evaluate the organizational structure of the essay. The author should lead you from idea to idea in a logical progression, and each section should relate to the ones before and after it and to the central argument in significant ways. Determine whether the writer could have organized things more clearly, logically, or efficiently.

7. Look at how the author follows through on the main claim, or thesis, of the argument. The author should stick with this thesis, and not waver throughout the text. If the thesis does waver, there could be a reason for the shift in the argument or perhaps the author is being inconsistent. The conclusion should drive home the central argument.

8. Evaluate the vocabulary and style the author uses. Is it too simple or too complicated? The vocabulary and sentence structure the author uses could relate to the audience the author was initially writing for.

SAMPLE ANALYSIS

The Gettysburg Address

ABRAHAM LINCOLN

Four score and seven years ago our fathers brought forth on this continent, a new nation, conceived in Liberty, and dedicated to the proposition that all men are created equal.

Now we are engaged in a great civil war, testing whether that nation, or any nation so conceived and so dedicated, can long endure. We are met on a great battle-field of that war. We have come to dedicate a portion of that field, as a final resting place for those who here gave their lives that that nation might live. It is altogether fitting and proper that we should do this.

Abraham Lincoln (1809–1865), the sixteenth president of the United States, delivered this speech at Gettysburg, Pennsylvania, on November 19, 1863.

But, in a larger sense, we can not dedicate—we can not consecrate—
we can not hallow—this ground. The brave men, living and dead, who
struggled here, have consecrated it, far above our poor power to add or
detract. The world will little note, nor long remember what we say here,
but it can never forget what they did here. It is for us the living, rather,
to be dedicated here to the unfinished work which they who fought here
have thus far so nobly advanced. It is rather for us to be here dedicated to
the great task remaining before us—that from these honored dead we
take increased devotion to that cause for which they gave the last full
measure of devotion—that we here highly resolve that these dead shall
not have died in vain—that this nation, under God, shall have a new
birth of freedom—and that government of the people, by the people, for
the people, shall not perish from the earth.

The following evaluation is by Charles Adams, whose stand on the Civil
War is clear from the title of the book from which the excerpt is taken:
When in the Course of Human Events: Arguing the Case for Southern Secession
(2000). Lincoln made his famous short speech in 1863 as a memorial to
the thousands who had died at Gettysburg, but in doing so, he was also
making an argument. The text in quotation marks is from the address itself. The rest is Adams's evaluation of it. As you read, consider what argument Lincoln is making but also whether or not you agree with
Adams's evaluation.

Lincoln's Logic

CHARLES ADAMS

Lincoln has become one of our national deities and a realistic examination of him is thus no longer possible.   —H. L. Mencken, 1931

At the Gettysburg Cemetery

Lincoln's mental processes and his logic have fascinated me ever since
my university days. In a class in logic, we studied his Gettysburg Address. The analysis showed that this famous speech didn't fit the real
world. It was good poetry, perhaps, but was it good thinking? It's chiseled

Charles Adams, a leading scholar on the history of taxation, is the author of *Fight,
Flight, Fraud* (1982); *Those Dirty Rotten Taxes* (1998); and *For Good and Evil* (1999). His
essay comes from *When in the Course of Human Events: Arguing the Case for Southern
Secession* (2000).

in stone in the Lincoln Memorial in Washington, and it ranks in the minds of most Americans with the Declaration of Independence and the Constitution. This oration was given to dedicate the cemetery at Gettysburg, where tens of thousands of young men died in a battle that was probably the turning point of the war. The address is reminiscent of the funeral oration of Pericles of Athens in the fifth century B.C. But Pericles's oration seemed to fit the real world of his day and the virtues of Athenian democracy. Lincoln's address did not fit the world of his day. It reflected his logic, which was based on a number of errors and falsehoods. That it has survived with such reverence is one of the most bizarre aspects of the war.

"Four Score and Seven Years Ago"

By simple arithmetic that would be 1776, when the Revolutionary War started and the Declaration of Independence was signed. That declaration was written with "decent respect for the opinions of mankind," to explain the reasons for the separation of the thirteen colonies from Great Britain. It contained no endowment of governmental power and created no government. The government came later in 1781 with the Articles of Confederation. The articles stated that this confederation was established by "sovereign states," like many of the leagues of states throughout history. To be accurate, Lincoln should have said "four score and two years ago," or better still, "three score and fourteen years ago." Even the Northern newspapers winced. The *New York World* sharply criticized this historical folly. "*This* United States" was not created by the Declaration of Independence but "the result of the ratification of a compact known as the Constitution," a compact that said nothing about equality. Others accused Lincoln of "gross ignorance or willful misstatement." Yet today, that gross ignorance is chiseled in stone as if it were some great truth like scripture, instead of a willful misstatement.

"Our Fathers Brought Forth on This Continent, a New Nation"

The federal compact among the former thirteen colonies, the new "sovereign states," as expressed in the Articles of Confederation in 1781, was not a nation as that term was then and is normally used. That was recently explained by Carl N. Degler, professor of American history at Stanford University, in a memorial lecture given at Gettysburg College in 1990: "The Civil War, in short, was not a struggle to save a failed union, but to create a nation that until then had not come into being."

Thus Lincoln's "new nation" really came into being by force of arms in the war between the states. Lincoln, according to Professor Degler, had a lot in common with Germany's Otto von Bismarck, who built a united Germany in the nineteenth century and believed that "blood and iron" were the main force for national policy. When it came to blood, Lincoln surpassed them all. The slaughter of Confederate men only matched, on a proportionate basis, the losses incurred by the Russians and the Germans in World War II.

In Lincoln's first inaugural address he used the word "Union" twenty   5
times but "nation" not at all. But once the South seceded, the term began
to disappear, and by the time of the Gettysburg Address, it was the American "nation" that was used, and the word "Union" had disappeared completely.

Thus the call from Northern peace Democrats—"the constitution as
it is; the Union as it was"—seems to make sense, but as Lincoln took over
control of the federal government, he soon wanted no part of it. Although he tried to trace the "new nation" back to 1776, he had to ignore
history and the intention and words of the Founders, and create a new
"gospel according to Lincoln" on the American commonwealth. Lincoln's new nation had no constitutional basis—no peaceful legal process.
It was created by war, by "blood and iron," like Bismarck's Germany, and
has survived to this day. In a sense, Lincoln did more to create America
than did the Founding Fathers. It is Lincoln who is the father of our present country, not George Washington. Lincoln's Gettysburg reference to
the Founders creating a new nation was not true. Just as Julius Caesar created an imperial order out of a republic, so Lincoln created a nation out
of a compact among states, and both used their military forces to do so.

"Conceived in Liberty"

A leading man of letters in Britain during the American Revolution,
Samuel Johnson, replied to the Americans' claims of tyranny in his book
Taxation Not Tyranny (1775). He said, "How is it that we hear the loudest
yelps for liberty among the drivers of negroes?"

The British are still chiding us for the absurdity of the Declaration of
Independence. Some years ago, while I was living in a British colony, we
Americans got together on the Fourth of July for a barbecue. One of my
older English friends asked me what the celebration was all about. I took
the bait and told him it was to celebrate the signing of the Declaration of
Independence. He replied, "Wasn't that document kind of a farce? All
that verbiage about equality of all men and liberty when over a million
black people were in bondage for life, and their children and children's
children?" Of course I had no answer, for the term "all men" meant all
white men. And to make matters worse, it really meant "white guys," as
white women weren't much better off. What is not known is that when
Lincoln issued his Emancipation Proclamation, many of the early
women's rights groups asked, How about us too? Thus the declaration
that Lincoln refers to in his address, of four score and seven years ago, was
not conceived in liberty *nor* was it dedicated to the proposition that all
men were created equal. So much for logic and reality.

Lincoln's logic at Gettysburg, as elsewhere, reveals a trial lawyer with
a tool of his craft—using the best logic he can muster to support his
client's (the North's) case, however bad that case may be. It is also, of
course, the craft of a politician, which may explain why so many politicians are lawyers.

"Today We Are Engaged in a Great Civil War"

Actually, it wasn't a civil war as that term was then, and is now, defined. 10
A civil war is a war that breaks out in a nation between opposing groups
for control of the state, for example, in Russia in 1917 with the Red
against the Whites or in China in the 1940s.

The War of Rebellion, as the war was called in the North, was really a
war for Southern independence. The Southern states had withdrawn from
the Union by democratic process—the same process they had followed to
join the Union initially. The Northern federation went to war to prevent
their secession from the Union just as Britain went to war in 1776 to prevent the colonies from seceding from the British nation. It was the fundamentals of the Revolutionary War, eighty-five years before. It was, if
you get down to the nuts and bolts of it, a war of conquest by the North
to destroy the Confederacy and to establish a new political leadership
over the conquered territories. Illiterate slaves were given the vote, and
the rest of the Southern society, the ruling groups, were not permitted to
vote. The poor, illiterate blacks were then told by Northern occupation
forces to vote as directed, and they did so, infuriating the conquered
people and creating a zeal for white supremacy that is only in our time
losing its grip on Southern society.

"Testing Whether That Nation . . . Can Long Endure"

That comment seems to presuppose that the South was out to conquer
the Northern federation. That is as absurd as saying that the revolting
colonies in 1776 were out to destroy the British nation. The thirteen
colonies' withdrawal from the British Empire in 1776 was the same as the
attempt of the Southern states to withdraw in 1861 from the 1789 federation. In reality, the 1789 federation was not in any danger. It would have
endured with secession. Unlike Grant, Lee was not out to conquer the
North. In reality, this logic was as absurd as the rest of Lincoln's funeral
oration.

"A Final Resting Place for Those Who Here Gave Their
Lives That That Nation Might Live"

Again, "that nation" was not in danger of dying—that was not Southern
Confederate policy and Lincoln knew it. But again, he was only being a
good lawyer, arguing his client's case as best he could, and with no rebuttal he was an easy winner.

"And That Government of the People, by the People
and for the People Shall Not Perish from the Earth"

Why did Lincoln even suggest that secession by the Southern states
would mean that democracy would perish from the earth—in America or
elsewhere? That was perfect nonsense, and Lincoln knew it, but again,
there was no one to rebut his argument.

Lincoln's repeated assertion that secession would amount to a 15
failure of the American experiment with democracy and liberty "just
is plain nonsense," wrote Professor Hummel in his refreshing book
on the Civil War, *Emancipating Slaves, Enslaving Free Men*.[2] The
London *Times* seems to have best understood what was going on in
America with the Northern invasion to prevent secession: "If North-
erners . . . had peaceably allowed the seceders to depart, the result
might fairly have been quoted as illustrating the advantages of Democracy, but when Republicans put empire above liberty, and resorted
to political oppression and war . . . It was clear that nature at Washington was precisely the same as nature at St. Petersburg. . . . Democracy
broke down. . . . when it was upheld, like any other Empire, by force of
arms."[3]

By 1860 democracy was strongly entrenched throughout Western civilization, and certainly in the American states. The democratic process
had emerged decades before in Europe—in Britain, France, the Netherlands, Switzerland, and so on. The war in America for Southern independence was in no way a danger to the concept of government "of the
people." Strange as it may seem, as it turned out, it was Lincoln who was
out to destroy governments of the people in the eleven Southern states.
The declaration's assertion that governments derive their "just powers
from the consent of the governed" was not an acceptable idea in Lincoln's mind so far as the South was concerned. Like a good lawyer he ignored it.

What makes Lincoln's ending so outrageous is that he didn't believe
in the self-determination of peoples, as British writers noted in 1861 and
a hundred years later in 1961.

Ordinances of secession had been adopted in the Southern states,
often with huge majorities. Their right to govern by consent was not acceptable to Lincoln's thinking—that would undermine his client's case.
Yet it was Lincoln who ended up destroying the Union as it was and substituting an all-powerful national government in which the states were
relegated to not much more than county status. There emerged the "imperial presidency" that is with us to this day, in which presidents can go
to war, without congressional approval, spend money without congressional approval; in fact, they can rule by decree like the consuls of Rome.
In other Western democracies, this is not so. Their chief executive must
have the permission and approval of their legislature to do such things.
Thus Lincoln did more to destroy the Union than preserve it. Is not this
irony at its best?

---

[2]Jeffrey Hummel, *Emancipating Slaves, Enslaving Free Men* (Chicago: Open Court
1997), p. 352.

[3]*Times* editorial, September 13, 1862, p. 8, cited in *Emancipating Slaves*, p. 352.

RESPONDING AS A WRITER

Notice the difference between the annotations a student made in response to the following essay and those another student made earlier in response to "The Pursuit of Whining" (p. 27). In the earlier example, the student was making marginal notes primarily on the ideas presented in the essay. Here the annotations focus on how the essay is written. In other words, the student is looking at the piece from a writer's perspective.

The essay is a claim of value in which, as the title suggests, the author claims that competitive sports are destructive. In arguments about values, the author may or may not suggest a solution to the problem caused by the belief or behavior. If so, the solution will be implicit—that is, unexpressed, or undeveloped—as is the case here, and the emphasis will remain on support for the claim.

Keep in mind that an essay of this length can never do justice to a complicated and highly debatable subject. It will probably lack sufficient evidence, as this one does, to answer all the questions and objections of readers who enjoy and approve of competitive games. What it can do is provoke thought and initiate an intelligent discussion.

SAMPLE ANNOTATED ESSAY

No-Win Situations

ALFIE KOHN

Intro: personal experience

I learned my first game at a birthday party. You remember it: X players scramble for X-minus-one chairs each time the music stops. In every round a child is eliminated until at the end only one is left triumphantly seated while everyone else is standing on the sidelines, excluded from play, unhappy . . . losers.

This is how we learn to have a good time in America.

This article by Alfie Kohn, author of *No Contest: The Case against Competition* (1986) and *The Case against Standardized Testing* (2000), appeared in *Women's Sports and Fitness Magazine* (July–August 1990).

Competition

Several years ago I wrote a book called *No Contest*, which, based on the findings of several hundred studies, argued that competition undermines self-esteem, poisons relationships, and holds us back from doing our best. I was mostly interested in the win/lose arrangement that defines our work-places and classrooms, but I found myself nagged by the following question: If competition is so de-structive and counterproductive during the week, why do we take for granted that it suddenly be-comes benign and even desirable on the week-end?

This is a particularly unsettling line of inquiry for athletes or parents. Most of us, after all, as-sume that competitive sports teach all sorts of useful lessons and, indeed, that games by defini-tion must produce a winner and a loser. But I've

come to believe that recreation at its best does not require people to try to triumph over others. Quite to the contrary.

Terry Orlick, a sports psychologist at the Uni-   5
versity of Ottawa, took a look at musical chairs and proposed that we keep the basic format of re-moving chairs but change the goal; the point be-

comes to fit everyone on a diminishing number of seats. At the end, a group of giggling children tries to figure out how to squish onto a single chair. Everybody plays to the end; everybody has a good time.

Orlick and others have devised or collected hundreds of such games for children and adults alike. The underlying theory is simple: All games involve achieving a goal despite the presence of an obstacle, but nowhere is it written that the ob-stacle has to be someone else. The idea can be for each person on the field to make a specified con-tribution to the goal, or for all the players to reach a certain score, or for everyone to work with her partners against a time limit.

Note the significance of an "opponent" be-coming a "partner." The entire dynamic of the game shifts, and one's attitude toward the other players changes with it. Even the friendliest game of tennis can't help but be affected by the game's inherent structure, which demands that each person try to hit the ball where the other can't get to it. You may not be a malicious person, but to play tennis means that you try to make the other person fail.

No advantages in competition

I've become convinced that not a single one of the advantages attributed to sports actually requires competition. Running, climbing, biking, swimming, aerobics—all offer a fine workout without any need to try to outdo someone else.

1) Some people point to the camaraderie that results from teamwork, but that's precisely the benefit of cooperative activity, whose very essence is that *everyone* on the field is working together for a common goal. By contrast, the distinguishing feature of team competition is that a given player works with and is encouraged to feel warmly toward only half of those present. Worse, a we-versus-they dynamic is set up, which George Orwell once called "war minus the shooting."

2) The dependence on sports to provide a sense of accomplishment or to test one's wits is similarly misplaced. One can aim instead at an objective standard (How far did I throw? How many miles did we cover?) or attempt to do better than last week. Such individual and group striving—like cooperative games—provides satisfaction and challenge without competition.

If large numbers of people insist that we can't   10 do without win/lose activities, the first question to ask is whether they've ever tasted the alternative. When Orlick taught a group of children non-competitive games, two-thirds of the boys and all of the girls preferred them to the kind that require opponents. If our culture's idea of fun requires beating someone else, it may just be because we don't know any other way.

It may also be because we overlook the
3) psychological costs of competition. Most people lose in most competitive encounters, and it's obvious why that causes self-doubt. But even winning doesn't build character. It just lets us gloat temporarily. Studies have shown that feelings of self-worth become dependent on external sources of evaluation as a result of competition. Your value is defined by what you've done and who you've beaten. The whole affair soon becomes a

vicious circle: The more you compete, the more you *need* to compete to feel good about yourself. It's like drinking salt water when you're thirsty. This process is bad enough for us; it's a disaster for our children.

4)   While this is going on, competition is having an equally toxic effect on our relationships. By definition, not everyone can win a contest. That means that each child inevitably comes to regard others as obstacles to his or her own success. Competition leads children to envy winners, to dismiss losers (there's no nastier epithet in our language than "loser!"), and to be suspicious of just about everyone. Competition makes it difficult to regard others as potential friends or collaborators; even if you're not my rival today, you could be tomorrow.

This is not to say that competitors will always detest one another. But trying to outdo someone is not conducive to trust — indeed it would be irrational to trust a person who gains from your failure. At best, competition leads one to look at others through narrowed eyes; at worst, it invites outright aggression.

Changing the Structure of Sports

But no matter how many bad feelings erupt during competition, we have a marvelous talent for

Conclusion

blaming the individuals rather than focusing on the structure of the game itself, a structure that makes my success depend on your failure. Cheating may just represent the logical conclusion of this arrangement rather than an aberration. And sportsmanship is nothing more than an artificial way to try to limit the damage of competition. If we weren't set against each other on the court or the track, we wouldn't need to keep urging people to be good sports; they might well be working *with* each other in the first place.

New idea that confirms his claim

As radical or surprising as it may sound, the 15 problem isn't just that we compete the wrong way or that we push winning on our children too early. The problem is competition itself. What we need to be teaching our daughters and sons is that it's possible to have a good time — a better time — without turning the playing field into a battlefield.

■ Analysis

The pattern of organization in this essay is primarily a *defense of the main idea*—that competitive sports are psychologically unhealthy. But because the author knows that competitive sports are hugely popular, not only in the United States but in many other parts of the world, he must also try to *refute the opposing view*—that competition is rewarding and enjoyable. In doing so, Kohn fails to make clear distinctions between competitive sports for children, who may find it difficult to accept defeat, and for adults, who understand the consequences of any competitive game and are psychologically equipped to deal with them. Readers may therefore share Kohn's misgivings about competition for children but doubt that his criteria apply equally to adults.

The *claim,* expressed as the *thesis statement* of the essay, appears at the end of paragraph 4: "recreation at its best does not require people to try to triumph over others. Quite to the contrary." The three-paragraph introduction recounts a relevant personal experience as well as the reasons that prompted Kohn to write his essay. Because we are all interested in stories, the recital of a personal experience is a popular device for introducing almost any subject (see "The Childswap Society," p. 343).

The rest of the essay, until the last two paragraphs, is devoted to summarizing the benefits of cooperative play and the disadvantages of competitive sport. The emphasis is overwhelmingly on the disadvantages as stated in the third paragraph: "competition undermines self-esteem, poisons relationships, and holds us back from doing our best." This is the *warrant,* the assumption that underlies the claim. In fact, here Kohn is referring to a larger study that he wrote about competition in workplaces and classrooms. We must accept this broad generalization, which applies to many human activities, before we can agree that the claim about competition in sports is valid.

Kohn relies for support on examples from common experience and on the work of Terry Orlick, a sports psychologist. The examples from experience are ones that most of us will recognize. Here we are in a position to judge for ourselves, without the mediation of an expert, whether the influence of competition in sports is as hurtful as Kohn insists. Orlick's research suggests a solution—adaptations of familiar games that will provide enjoyment but avoid competition. On the other hand, the results from studies by one psychologist whose work we aren't able to verify and the mention of "studies" in paragraph 3 without further attribution are probably not enough to answer all the arguments in favor of competition. Critics may also ask if Kohn has offered support for one of his contentions—that competition "holds us back from doing our best" (para. 3). (Support for this may appear in one of Kohn's books.)

The last two paragraphs sum up his argument that "The problem is competition itself" (para. 15)—the structure of the game rather than the people who play. Notice that this summary does not merely repeat the main idea. Like many thoughtful summaries, it also offers a new idea about good sportsmanship that confirms his conclusion.

The language is clear and direct. Kohn's article, which appeared in a women's sports magazine, is meant for the educated general reader, not the expert. This is also the audience for whom most student papers are written. But the written essay need not be unduly formal. Kohn uses contractions and the personal pronouns "I" and "you" to establish a conversational context. One of the particular strengths of his style is the skillful use of transitional expressions, words like "this" and "also" and clauses like "This is not to say that" and "Note the significance of" to make connections between paragraphs and new ideas.

The tone is temperate despite the author's strong feelings about the subject. Other authors, supporting the same argument, have used language that borders on the abusive about coaches and trainers of children's games. But a less inflammatory voice is far more effective with an audience that may be neutral or antagonistic.

You will find it helpful to look back over the essay to see how the examples we've cited and others work to fulfill the writer's purpose.

RESPONDING AS A CRITICAL LISTENER

Of course, not all public arguments are written. Oral arguments on radio and television now enjoy widespread popularity and influence. In fact, their proliferation means that we listen far more than we talk, read, or write. Today the art of listening has become an indispensable tool for learning about the world we live in. One informed critic predicts that the dissemination of information and opinions through the electronic media will "enable more and more Americans to participate directly in making the laws and policies by which they are governed."[4]

Because we are interested primarily in arguments about public issues—those that involve democratic decision making—we will not be concerned with the afternoon television talk shows that are largely devoted to personal problems. (Occasionally, however, *Oprah* introduces topics of broad social significance.) More relevant to the kinds of written arguments you will read and write about in this course are the television and radio shows that also examine social and political problems. The most intelligent and responsible programs usually consist of a panel of experts—politicians, journalists, scholars—led by a neutral moderator (or one who, at least, allows guests to express their views). Some of these programs are decades old; others are more recent—*Meet the Press, Face the*

---

[4]Lawrence K. Grossman, *The Electronic Republic: Reshaping Democracy in the Information Age* (New York: Viking, 1995).

Nation, Firing Line, The McLaughlin Group, The NewsHour with Jim Lehrer.
An outstanding radio show, *Talk of the Nation* on National Public Radio,
invites listeners, who are generally informed and articulate, to call in and
ask questions of, or comment on remarks made by, experts on the topic
of the day.

Several enormously popular radio talk shows are hosted by people
with strong, sometimes extreme ideological positions. They may use offensive language and insult their listeners in a crude form of theater.
Among the most influential shows are those of Don Imus and Howard
Stern. In addition, elections and political crises bring speeches and debates on radio and television by representatives of a variety of views.
Some are long and formal, written texts that are simply read aloud, but
others are short and impromptu.

Whatever the merits or shortcomings of individual programs, significant general differences exist between arguments on radio and television
and arguments in the print media. These differences include the degree
of organization and development and the risk of personal attacks.

First (excluding for the moment the long, prepared speeches), contributions to a panel discussion must be delivered in fragments, usually no
longer than a single paragraph, weakened by time constraints, interrup-
tions, overlapping speech, memory gaps, and real or feigned displays of
derision, impatience, and disbelief by critical panelists. Even on the best
programs, the result is a lack of both coherence—or connections between
ideas—and solid evidence that requires development. Too often we are
treated to conclusions with little indication of how they were arrived at.

The following brief passage appeared in a newspaper review of "Resolved: The flat tax is better than the income tax," a debate on *Firing Line*
by an impressive array of experts. It illustrates some of the difficulties that
accompany programs attempting to capture the truth of a complicated
issue on television or radio.

> "It is absolutely true," says a proponent. "It is factually untrue," coun-
> ters an opponent. "It's factually correct," responds a proponent. "I did
> my math right," says a proponent. "You didn't do your math right,"
> says an opponent. At one point in a discussion of interest income, one
> of the experts says, "Oh, excuse me, I think I got it backward."

No wonder the television critic called the exchange "disjointed and
at times perplexing."[5]

In the sensational talk shows the participants rely on personal experience and vivid anecdotes, which may not be sufficiently typical to prove
anything.

Second, listeners and viewers of all spoken arguments are in danger
of evaluating them according to criteria that are largely absent from

[5]Walter Goodman, "The Joys of the Flat Tax, Excluding the Equations," *New York
Times*, December 21, 1995, sec. C, p. 14.

GUIDELINES TO CRITICAL LISTENING

Listening is hearing with attention, a natural and immensely important human activity, which, unfortunately, many people don't do very well. The good news is that listening is a skill that can be learned and, unlike some other skills, practiced every day without big investments of money and effort.

Here are some of the characteristics of critical listening most appropriate to understanding arguments.

1. Above all, listening to arguments requires concentration. If you are distracted, you cannot go back as you do with the written word to clarify a point or recover a connection. Devices such as flow sheets and outlines can be useful aids to concentration. In following a debate, for example, judges and other listeners often use flow sheets — distant cousins of baseball scorecards — to record the major points on each side and their rebuttals. For roundtable discussions or debates you can make your own simple flow chart to fill out as you listen, with columns for claims, different kinds of support, and warrants. Leave spaces in the margin for your questions and comments about the soundness of the proof. An outline is more useful for longer presentations, such as lectures. As you listen, try to avoid being distracted by facts alone. Look for the overall pattern of the speech.

2. Listeners often concentrate on the wrong things in the spoken argument. We have already noted the distractions of appearance and delivery. Research shows that listeners are likely to give greater attention to the dramatic elements of speeches than to the logical ones. But you can enjoy the sound, the appearance, and the drama of a spoken argument without allowing these elements to overwhelm what is essential to the development of a claim.

3. Good listeners try not to allow their prejudices to prevent careful evaluation of the argument. This doesn't mean accepting everything or even most of what you hear. It means trying to avoid premature judgments about what is actually said. This precaution is especially relevant when the speakers and their views are well known and the listener has already formed an opinion about them, favorable or unfavorable.

evaluation of written texts. It is true that writers may adopt a persona or a literary disguise, which the tone of the essay will reflect. But many readers will not be able to identify it or recognize their own response to it. Listeners and viewers, however, can hardly avoid being affected by characteristics that are clearly definable: a speaker's voice, delivery, bodily mannerisms, dress, and physical appearance. In addition, listeners may be adversely influenced by clumsy speech containing more slang, colloquialisms, and grammar and usage errors than written texts that have had the benefit of revision.

But if listeners allow consideration of physical attributes to influence their judgment of what the speaker is trying to prove, they are guilty of an ad hominem fallacy — that is, an evaluation of the speaker rather than the argument. This is true whether the evaluation is favorable or unfavorable. (See p. 289 for a discussion of this fallacy.)

Talk shows may indeed be disjointed and perplexing, but millions of us find them both instructive and entertaining. Over time we are exposed to an astonishing variety of opinions from every corner of American life, and we also acquire information from experts who might not otherwise be available to us. Then there is the appeal of hearing the voices, seeing the faces of people engaged in earnest, sometimes passionate, discourse — a short, unrehearsed drama in which we also play a part as active listeners in a far-flung audience.

RESPONDING TO A VISUAL ARGUMENT

> Man has been communicating by pictures longer than he has been using words. With the development of photography in this century we are using pictures as a means of communication to such an extent that in some areas they overshadow verbal language.[6]

You've probably seen some of the powerful images in photographic journalism to which the author refers: soldiers in battle, destruction by weather disasters, beautiful natural landscapes, inhuman living conditions, the great mushroom cloud of early atomic explosions. These photographs and thousands of others encapsulate arguments of fact, value, and policy. We don't need to read their captions to understand what they tell us: *The tornado devastated the town. The Grand Canyon is our most stupendous national monument. We must not allow human beings to live like this.* The pictures stay with us long after we have forgotten the words that accompanied them.

Photographs, of course, function everywhere as instruments of persuasion. Animal-rights groups show pictures of brutally mistreated dogs and cats; children's rights advocates publish pictures of sick and starving children in desolate refugee camps. On a very different scale, alluring photographs from advertisers — travel agencies, restaurants, sporting goods manufacturers, clothiers, jewelers, movie studios — promise to fulfill our dreams of pleasure.

But photographs are not the only visual images we respond to. We are also susceptible to other kinds of illustrations and to signs and symbols which over the years have acquired connotations, or suggestive significance. The flag or bald eagle, the shamrock, the crown, the cross, the hammer and sickle, and the swastika can all rouse strong feelings for or against the ideas they represent. These symbols may be defined as

---

[6] Paul Wendt, "The Language of Pictures," in S. I. Hayakawa, ed., *The Use and Misuse of Language* (Greenwich, Conn.: Fawcett, 1962), p. 175.

abbreviated claims of value. They summarize the moral, religious, and po-litical principles by which groups of people live and often die. In com-mercial advertisements we recognize symbols that aren't likely to enlist our deepest loyalties but, nevertheless, have impact on our daily lives: the apple with a bite in it, the golden arches, the Prudential rock, the Nike swoosh, and a thousand others.

In fact, a closer look at commercial and political advertising, which is heavily dependent on visual argument and is something we are all famil-iar with, provides a useful introduction to this complex subject. We know that advertisements, with or without pictures, are short arguments, often lacking fully developed support, whose claims of policy urge us to take an action: Buy this product or service; vote for this candidate or issue. The claim may not be directly expressed, but it will be clearly implicit. In print, on television, or on the Internet, the visual representation of ob-jects, carefully chosen to appeal to a particular audience, can be as im-portant as, if not more important than, any verbal text.

In a political advertisement, for example, we often see a picture of the candidate surrounded by a smiling family. The visual image is by now a cliché, suggesting traditional values—love and security, the importance of home and children. Even if we know little or nothing about his or her platform, we are expected to make a sympathetic connection with the candidate.

In a commercial advertisement the image may be a picture of a real or fictitious person to whom we will react favorably. Consider the picture on a jar of spaghetti sauce. As a famous designer remarked, "When you think about it, sauce is mostly sauce. It's the label that makes the differ-ence."[7] And what, according to the designer, does the cheerful face of Paul Newman on jars of his spaghetti sauce suggest to the prospective buyer? "Paul Newman. Paul Newman. Paul Newman. Blue eyes. All the money goes to charity. It's humanitarian, funny, and sexy. Selling this is like falling off a log." Not a word about the quality of the sauce.

Even colleges, which are also selling a product, must think of appro-priate images to attract their prospective customers—students. Today the fact that more women than men are enrolled in college has caused some schools to rethink their images. One college official explained:

> We're having our recruiting literature redesigned, and we've been think-ing about what's a feminine look and what's a masculine look. We have a picture of a library with a lot of stained glass, and people said that was kind of a feminine cover. Now we're using a picture of the quadrangle.[8]

In addition to the emblem itself, the designer pays careful attention to a number of other elements in the ad: colors, light and shadow, fore-

[7] Tibor Kalman, "Message: Sweet-Talking Spaghetti Sauce," *New York Times Magazine,* December 13, 1998, p. 81.

[8] *New York Times,* December 6, 1998, p. 38.

ground and background, relative sizes of pictures and text, and placement of objects on the page or screen. Each of these contributes to the total effect, although we may be unaware of how the effect has been achieved. (In the ad that follows, you will be able to examine some of the psychological and aesthetic devices at work.)

When there is no verbal text, visual images are less subject to analysis and interpretation. For one thing, if we are familiar with the objects in the picture, we see the whole image at once, and it registers immediately. The verbal message is linear and takes far longer to be absorbed. Pictures, therefore, appear to need less translation. Advertisers and other arguers depend on this characteristic to provide quick and friendly acceptance of their claims, although the image may, in fact, be deceptive.

This expectation of easy understanding poses a danger with another visual ally of the arguer—the graph or chart. Graphics give us factual information at a glance. In addition to the relative ease with which they can be read, they are "at their best . . . instruments for reasoning about quantitative information. . . . Of all methods for analyzing and communicating statistical information, well-designed data graphics are usually the simplest and at the same time the most powerful."[9]

Nevertheless, they may mislead the quick reader. Graphics can lie. "The lies are told about the major issues of public policy—the government budget, medical care, prices, and fuel economy standards, for example. The lies are systematic and quite predictable, nearly always exaggerating the rate of recent change."[10]

Visual images, then, for all their apparent immediacy and directness, need to be read with at least the same attention we give to the verbal message if we are to understand the arguments they represent.

Consider these questions as you analyze images:

1. What does the arguer want me to do or believe? How important is the visual image in persuading me to comply?

2. Has the visual image been accompanied by sufficient text to answer questions I may have about the claim?

3. Are the visual elements more prominent than the text? If so, why?

4. Is the visual image representative of a large group, or is it an exception that cannot support the claim?

5. Does the arrangement of elements in the message tell me what the arguer considers most important? If so, what is the significance of this choice?

6. Can the validity of this chart or graph be verified?

[9]Edward R. Tufte, *The Visual Display of Quantitative Information* (Cheshire, Conn.: Graphics Press, 1983), introduction.
[10]Tufte, *The Visual Display,* p. 76.

7. Does the visual image lead me to entertain unrealistic expectations? (Can using this shampoo make hair look like that shining cascade on the television screen? Does the picture of the candidate for governor, shown answering questions in a classroom of eager, smiling youngsters, mean that he has a viable plan for educational reform?)

■ Sample Analysis of an Advertisement

We have pointed out that a commercial advertisement is a short argument that makes an obvious policy claim, which may or may not be explicit: *You should buy this product.* Depending on the medium — television, print, radio, or Internet — an ad may convey its message through language, picture, or sound.

Here is how one analyst of advertising sums up the goals of the advertiser: (1) attract attention, (2) arouse interest, (3) stimulate desire, (4) create conviction, and (5) get action.[11] Needless to say, not every ad successfully fulfills all these objectives. If you examine the ad reproduced on page 51, you can see how the advertiser brings language and visual image together in an attempt to support the claim.

The image in the ad appeals to our common knowledge as Americans. We have probably all heard the story of how George Washington, as a boy, chopped down a cherry tree. The clothes that the young boy in the ad is wearing — particularly the tricorner hat — along with the architecture, suggest a colonial setting. The hatchet hidden behind the boy's back combined with the exclamation "Oops!" calls to mind the specific story about Washington. Upon hearing the story, you may have envisioned a much smaller tree and less substantial damage, but it is critical to the ad's effect that in this rendering of the story of our first president's youth, the tree has fallen on someone's house, possibly the Washingtons'. The ad appears to have been reproduced on parchment, another detail that helps to place the incident historically, and each corner is subtly decorated with a cherry.

What has made the cherry tree story a classic for teaching morals is what the young Washington is said to have done after he chopped down the tree. All of us are familiar with the words "I can not tell a lie," Washington's response when questioned about what he had done. It was a fitting reply for a man who would later be chosen to lead the new nation. The largest text on the page — and the text most likely therefore to catch the attention of a reader casually flipping through *Newsweek* — is a play on this famous quote that changes *I* to *we*. The identification with Washington and his famous words is particularly critical for a company whose name may not be a household word. The designers of the ad, having captured the attention of the reader with the image and the quote, go on in the smaller text to build on the foundation they have established.

[11]J. V. Lund, *Newspaper Advertising* (New York: Prentice-Hall, 1947), p. 83.

Like most ads, this one is a claim of policy asking the audience to buy a product. In this case the product is Encompass Insurance. One of the frustrations of dealing with an insurance company is that not every possible type of loss is covered by the standard policy. Unfortunately, the homeowner often does not find this out until the damage has already been done. The ad is designed to sell the company's *Elite* policy, which "covers many of life's unexpected perils," unlike most insurance companies, which "only cover things that are specifically listed in your policy."

The text continues, "It covers pretty much everything that befalls your household, even if something like 'damage caused by child chopping down cherry tree' isn't specifically listed." Two examples of the sorts of damage that the company might cover are Worker's Compensation for an employee in your household and the recovery of lost computer data.

The support for the claim is not specific. The writer carefully avoided absolute statements, using instead such qualifiers as *many, pretty much*, and *most everything*. The last two are colloquial expressions that are designed to suggest that those who work for Encompass are simple folks with whom the average reader could identify. And if you want any more specifics about what the policy actually says—after all, the legal document that is an insurance policy can hardly use such qualifiers—you can call toll-free or visit the company's Web site.

The underlying warrant is that it is better to buy an insurance policy that covers you against damages that are not specifically listed on the policy than one that does not. A person in the market for insurance would certainly want to read the fine print and know the cost of the insurance compared to that offered by other companies before accepting the warrant and thus the claim.

The colloquial language and even the name of the policy—The Encompass Universal Security Policy—Elite—are designed to appeal to the reader's need to feel secure. The word choice also adds a subtle humor, from the cartoon-like "Oops!" to the final echo of the Pledge of Allegiance: "Liberty, Justice, and Really Good Insurance."

■ Sample Analysis of a Web Site

The Internet provides an important forum for individuals and organizations to make arguments. Through the Internet, anyone with access to a networked computer can potentially publish his or her ideas. While this ease of publication is exciting, it also means writers hoping to obtain reliable information from the Web need to read Web sites critically (see Critical Reading Strategies on page 26 for further insight into this issue).

With new genres being created daily, some researchers[12] have noted five major types of Web pages:

1. *Advocacy Web Pages:* Advocacy pages are typically created by not-for-profit organizations wishing to influence public opinion, and the URL for the site is likely to contain the domain suffix *.org* (organization).

2. *Business/Marketing Web Pages:* The majority of businesses in the United States have a Web presence today, and most business pages are either advertising or provide online opportunities to purchase

[12]See, for example, the Widener University Wolfgram Memorial Library Web site at http://www2.widener.edu/Wolfgram-Memorial-Library/webevaluation/webeval.htm.

goods and services. The addresses for such sites typically contain the domain suffix *.com* (for commercial).

3. *News Web Pages:* News pages provide current information on local, national, and international events. The addresses for news sites also contain the abbreviation *.com,* reflecting the fact that the news industry is also a business.

4. *Informational Web Pages:* Informational pages provide data such as that found in dictionaries or atlases. The addresses for these sites sometimes include *.edu* (university), *.k12* (primary or secondary school), or *.gov* (government) because they are often sponsored by academic institutions or government agencies.

5. *Personal Web Pages:* Personal pages are created by individuals, and can be intimate, entertaining, informative, bizarre, or some combination of these things. While the addresses for personal sites can end in *.com, .edu, .k12, .org,* or *.gov,* the presence of a tilde (~) in the address suggests that the page represents an individual.

On page 54 is a copy of the home page for *The Hunger Site* (a home page introduces and often provides a guide or table of contents for an entire site, which can consist of many pages). At first glance, *The Hunger Site* appears to be a combination informational page (because it contains facts about world hunger) and business/marketing page (because it advertises a variety of products). It is in fact both these things as well as a site for philanthropy (since advertisers' money pays for the food).

The significance of charitable giving to the site's mission is suggested by several things. Maybe most directly, a viewer's eye is immediately drawn to a gold icon reading "GIVE FREE FOOD: Click Here." This icon appears in the center of the home page and draws the eye immediately with its color and placement. It also presents an appealing prospect to readers: that they can be generous by supporting a significant cause and do so without spending money (the food is "free"). When you click on the icon, *The Hunger Site* donates two cups of food (or the financial equivalent) to the hungry.

The emphasis on giving is furthered by a link on the right side of the page that reads "Register Today & Give Up to 8 Extra Cups." As this suggests, readers can register as a member of *The Hunger Site* and donate additional food to hungry people. Directly underneath this is the announcement reading "More Ways To Help: Each purchase made gives up to 50 cups of food." Clicking here offers more opportunities to provide food for others, opportunities linked to purchases made from sponsoring companies.

It is this connection that links *The Hunger Site* to business interests, interests highlighted by the *.com* in the site's URL. Though donations can be given without spending money, the site also links consumer needs and desires to philanthropy by providing visitors the opportunity to support

The Hunger Site Home Page

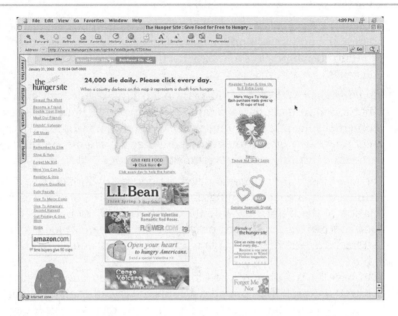

the hungry by purchasing a wide variety of goods—from clothing to flowers to seasonal gifts and decorations. Consumer givers, then, can feel good that the money they are spending is contributing to a valuable cause. In return, site sponsors, companies such as L.L. Bean who help subsidize the donations made to the hungry, receive advertising and gain new customers. In this way, viewers feel inspired to shop more, meaning that *The Hunger Site* has the potential to bind together corporate interests, consumer interests, and international benevolence.

In many ways, then, *The Hunger Site* reads like a traditional advertisement. It appeals to customers because it represents an easy way to do something socially responsible. To develop customer loyalty, businesses and organizations strive for "brand recognition," and *The Hunger Site* is no exception. It uses a golden strand of wheat as its logo. Gold, symbolizing both wheat and true value, is the color of the central icon that allows browsers to contribute food with a single click.

However, while *The Hunger Site* incorporates many traditional methods in appealing to its readers, it also makes use of Web technology. Directly above the "GIVE FREE FOOD" icon is a map that reflects deaths from hunger under the headline "24,000 die daily. Please click every day," and every few seconds a different country on the map darkens to represent a death from hunger. The print statistic that "24,000 die daily" is supplemented by this graphic reminder, of what it means for so many thousands to die every day. Viewers cannot help noticing the slow and steady stream of blackening countries, which make an abstract number more real.

The Hunger Site Thank You Page

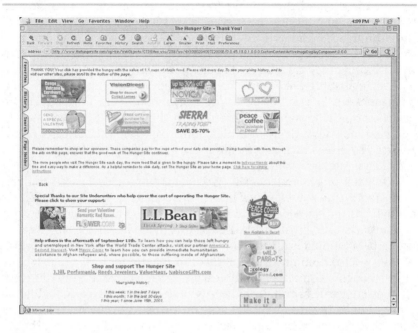

Interactivity is further displayed in the way the site acknowledges its readers' influence and importance. For example, the menu on the left-hand side of the home page begins with four links that directly involve visitor participation. The first, which reads "Spread the Word," opens onto a page that gives viewers the opportunity to e-mail friends an electronic form letter with prewritten statistics and information provided by *The Hunger Site.* However, viewers are also encouraged to personalize the e-mail with their own thoughts and ideas about the significance of *The Hunger Site.* In this way, viewers become coauthors of a letter with the authors of the site. Other icons acknowledge and celebrate "friends" of *The Hunger Site.* Becoming a friend of the site can be accomplished virtually instantaneously, and friends are then able to enter the "Friends' Gateway," which offers unique opportunities for both purchasing and giving. The value of this option is also made more real because it involves an actual locking out of those who have not attained the status of friends.

The emphasis on the immediacy of this interaction between reader and text can also be seen in the features that allow readers of the site to keep track of their giving by clicking on the link that reads "See your giving history at the bottom of our Thank You page." This displays up-to-the-minute statistics regarding the number of clicks the viewer has made, making the visitor feel like a carefully accounted for participant in the fight against hunger. In addition, the "Remember to Click" and "Forget Me Not" features bind viewers to the site. If viewers sign up for the

"Remember to Click" option, an e-mail reminder regularly reminds them to visit the site and click to give food. The "Forget Me Not" option reminds the computer user whenever he or she begins to shop online to shop through *The Hunger Site*. Visitors can choose these options, and they can always be dismantled once they are chosen, giving individuals control over how they are marketed to and connected to the Web site.

Distinguishing *The Hunger Site* from traditional print text is its embeddedness in a "web" of other pages. *The Hunger Site* links directly to pages that provide additional information about the site as well as sales and charitable giving opportunities. Some pages are official parts of *The Hunger Site;* others such as *Second Harvest,* which receives donations from *The Hunger Site,* are separate sites.

One aim of a comprehensive Web site is to provide answers to questions about the site. Unlike a print advertisement, *The Hunger Site* has enough space to provide, for example, information about the site owners and answers to frequently asked questions (FAQ) about the site. Readers interested in more information on *The Hunger Site* can do a general search of the Web to determine the legitimacy of the site.

Although it consists of multiple pages, *The Hunger Site* is also different from printed articles and books because it does not follow any traditional sense of order. Readers typically start on the site's home page, but from there they can go in multiple directions, each one equally logical. The authors of *The Hunger Site* have not determined a set path for readers to follow: Viewers can find information about world hunger, about hunger in the United States, about the owners of the site, about ways of providing food to the hungry, and about bargains at L.L. Bean or Patagonia. The reader is in control of the direction to be taken in the text, and the possible directions are numerous and cater to multiple needs.

RESPONDING ONLINE

You have learned that writers need the responses of readers and other writers to improve their writing. As the influence of computers permeates our society and more people rely on the Internet to send e-mail, it has become ever easier for writers to distribute their writing and for readers to respond to it. Only a decade ago, if you wanted feedback for your writing, you had to either read it aloud to others or copy and distribute it by hand or postal mail. Both methods were cumbersome and time-consuming, even expensive. Electronic networks now allow your writing to be distributed almost instantaneously to dozens or even thousands of readers with virtually no copying or mailing costs. Readers can respond to you just as quickly and cheaply. Even though there can be pitfalls and problems with communicating online, the overall ease of use encourages writers to seek, and readers to provide, editorial feedback.

■ Guidelines for Responding Online

You know that in face-to-face conversation the words themselves constitute only a part of your message. Much of what you say is communicated through your body language and tone of voice. Written words provide a much narrower channel of communication, which is why you must be more careful when you write to others than when you speak directly to them. Electronic writing, however, especially through e-mail, fosters a casualness and immediacy that often fools writers into assuming they are talking privately rather than writing publicly. Online you may find yourself writing quickly, carelessly, and intimately; without the help of your tone and body language, you may end up being seriously misunderstood. Words written hastily are often read much differently than intended; this is especially true when the writer attempts an ironic or sarcastic tone. For example, if a classmate walks up to you with a critical comment about one of your sentences and you respond by saying "I didn't realize you were so smart," the words, if unaccompanied by a placating smile and a pleasant, jocular tone, may come across as sarcastic or hostile. In e-writing, the same words appear without the mitigating body language and may be perceived as harsh, possibly insulting. You must keep this danger in mind as you respond online or risk alienating your reader.

Keep in mind, too, that e-mail may be read not only by your addressee but also by anyone with whom the addressee chooses to share your message. An intemperate or indiscreet message may be forwarded to other classmates or your instructor, or, depending on the limits of the system, to many other readers whom you do not know.

Experienced online communicators advocate a set of network etiquette guidelines called *Netiquette*. Here are some generally accepted Netiquette rules:

- Keep your sentences short and uncomplicated.

- Separate blocks of text—which should be no more than four or five lines long—by blank lines. For those rare occasions when a comment requires more than ten or fifteen consecutive lines of text, use subheadings on separate lines to guide your reader.

- Refer specifically to the text to which you are responding. You may want to quote directly from it, cutting and pasting phrases or sentences from the document to help show exactly what you are responding to.

- Greet the person(s) to whom you are writing politely and by name.

- Be wary about attempting to be funny. Humor, as just explained, often requires a context, tone of voice, and body language to emphasize that it is not to be taken seriously. Writing witty comments that are sure to be taken humorously calls for skill and care, and e-mail messages usually are written too quickly for either.

- Avoid profanity or invective, and be wary of brusque or abrupt statements. Consider how you would feel if someone wrote to you that way.

- Avoid discussion of politics or religion unless that is the specific topic of your message.

- Do not ridicule public figures. Your reader may not share your opinions of, say, Senator Edward Kennedy or radio talk show host Rush Limbaugh.

- Frame all comments in a helpful, not critical, tone. For instance, rather than beginning a critique with "I found a number of problems in your text," you may want to start out more like this: "You have some good ideas in this paper, and with a few changes I think it will do well."

DOCUMENTING YOUR SOURCES

Chapter 10 will explain in detail how to use both the Modern Language Association (MLA) and the American Psychological Association (APA) systems for citing publications. In the meantime, if you need to refer in your writing to one or more works that you have read, here is an overview of the basics.

Writer's Guide: Documenting Use of Summary, Paraphrase, and Quotation

1. The single most important thing to remember is why you need to inform your reader about your use of sources. Once it is clear from your writing that an idea or some language came from a source and thus is not your own original thought or language, full documentation provides the reader with a means of identifying and, if necessary, locating your source. If you do not indicate your source, your reader will naturally assume that the ideas and the language are yours. It is careless to forget to give credit to your sources. It is dishonest to intentionally take credit for what is not your own intellectual property.

2. One of the most common mistakes that student writers make is to think that material needs to be documented only if they use another author's own words. In fact, you must give credit for any *ideas* you get from others, not only for wording you get from them.

3. You must identify the author and the location of ideas that you summarize. A *summary* is the condensing of a longer passage into a shorter

one using your own words. You will use summary often in your academic writing when you want to report briefly on an idea covered at greater length in your source.

4. You must identify the author and the location of ideas that you paraphrase. A *paraphrase* is a rewording of another author's idea into your own words. A paraphrased passage is roughly the same length as the original.

5. You must identify the author and the location of the ideas that you quote. A *quotation* is the copying of the exact wording of your source and is placed in quotation marks. Remember that *exact* means just that. You cannot change anything inside quotation marks with these exceptions: (1) If there is a portion of the quotation that is not relevant to the point that you are trying to make and that can be omitted without distorting the author's meaning, you may indicate an omission of a portion of the quote with an ellipsis (. . .). If there is a sentence break within the portion you are omitting, you add a fourth period to the ellipsis to so indicate. (2) If you need to make a very slight change in the quote to make the quote fit grammatically into your own text or to avoid confusion and if the change does not distort the author's meaning, you may make that slight change and place the changed portion in brackets ([ ]). This method is used primarily to change the tense of a quoted passage to match that of your text or to identify a person identified in the quotation only by a pronoun.

6. Both the MLA and the APA system make use of in-text or parenthetical documentation. That means that while a complete bibliographical listing for each work summarized, paraphrased, or quoted in your text is included in a works cited list at the end of your paper, each is also identified exactly at the point in the text where you use the source. If you are using the MLA system of documentation, the system most commonly used in the humanities, immediately following the sentence in which you use material from a source you need to add in parentheses the author's name and the page number on which the material you are using appeared in the original source. However, since the credibility of your sources is critical in argumentative writing, it is even better to name the source in your own sentence and to identify the position or experience that makes that person a reliable source for the subject being discussed. In that case, you do not need to repeat the author's name in the parentheses. In fact, any time the author's name is clear from the context, you do not need to repeat it in the parentheses.

Acceptable: The mall has been called "a common experience for the majority of American youth" (Kowinski 117).

Better: According to William Severini Kowinski, author of *The Malling of America,* "The mall is a common experience for the majority of American youth" (Kowinski 117).

In the APA system, the system most commonly used in the social sciences, in-text or parenthetical documentation is handled a bit differently because the citation includes the year of publication. The most basic forms are these:

The mall has been called "a common experience for the majority of American youth" (Kowinski, 1985, p. 117).

Kowinski (1985) writes, "The mall is a common experience for the majority of American youth" (p. 117).

7. Remember that these examples show only the most basic form for documenting your sources. Some works will have more than one author. Sometimes you will be using more than one work by the same author. Usually Web sites do not have page numbers. Long quotations need to be handled differently from short ones. For all questions about documenting your use of sources not covered here, see Chapter 10.

Note: If you are writing about an essay in this book, you have a slightly more complicated situation than if you were looking at the essay in its original place of publication. Unless your instructor indicates otherwise, use the page numbers on which the essay appears in this textbook when summarizing, paraphrasing, or quoting from it instead of going back to the page numbers of the original. Also, unless your instructor indicates otherwise, use this model for listing in your works cited page an essay reprinted here:

Kowinski, William Severini. "Kids in the Mall: Growing Up Controlled." *The Malling of America: An Inside Look at the Great Consumer Paradise.* New York: Morrow, 1985. Rpt. in *Elements of Argument: A Text and Reader.* Annette T. Rottenberg and Donna Haisty Winchell. 8th ed. Boston: Bedford, 2006. 116–21.

ASSIGNMENTS FOR RESPONDING TO ARGUMENT

1. Choose an editorial of at least two paragraphs from your school paper or another newspaper on a controversial subject that interests you. The title will probably reveal the subject. Annotate the editorial as you read, questioning, agreeing, objecting, offering additional ideas. (The annotation of "The Pursuit of Whining," p. 27, will suggest ways of doing this, although your personal responses are what make the annotation useful.) Then read the editorial again. You should discover that annotating the article caused you to read more carefully, more critically, with greater comprehension and a more focused response.

2. Summarize the claim of the editorial in one sentence. Omit the supporting data and concentrate on the thesis. Then explain briefly your reaction to it. Has the author proved his or her point? Your annotation will show

you where you expressed doubt or approval. If you already know a good deal about the subject, perhaps you will be reasonably confident of your judgment. If not, you may find that your response is tentative and that you need to read further for more information about the subject and to consult guidelines for making evaluations about the elements of argument.

3. Summarize in one or two paragraphs one of the Classic Arguments. Include and document correctly at least one direct quotation from the reading. Remember to remain objective and not to interject your opinion into the summary.

4. People sometimes object to lectures as an educational tool. Think about some of the specific lectures you have listened to recently, and analyze the reasons that you liked or disliked them (or liked some aspects and disliked others). Do you think that you learned everything that the lecturer intended you to learn? If the results were doubtful, how much did your listening skills, good or bad, contribute to the result? Should the lecturer have done something differently to improve your response?

5. Watch (and *listen* to) one of the afternoon talk shows like *Oprah Winfrey* in which audiences discuss a controversial social problem. (The *TV Guide* and daily newspapers often list the subject. Past topics on *Oprah* include when parents abduct their children and when children kill children.) Write a critical review of the discussion, mentioning as completely as you can the major claims, the most important evidence, and the declared or hidden warrants. (Unspoken warrants or assumptions may be easier to identify in arguments on talk shows where visual and auditory clues can reveal what participants try to hide.) How much did the oral format contribute to success or failure of the argument(s)?

6. Listen to one of the television talk shows that feature invited experts. Write a review, telling how much you learned about the subject(s) of discussion. Be specific about the elements of the show that were either helpful or unhelpful to your understanding.

7. Listen with a friend or friends to a talk show discussion. Take notes as you listen. Then compare notes to discover if you agree on the outstanding points, the degree to which claims have been supported, and the part that seeing or hearing the discussion played in your evaluation. If there is disagreement about any of the elements, how do you account for it?

8. With three or four of your classmates select an argumentative essay in this book that all of you agree to read. Each of you should draft a response to the essay, either agreeing or disagreeing with the author's position, citing evidence to support your position. Then each of you prepare a letter soliciting a response to your draft from the members of your group. For example, you may want to state what your objective was, suggest what you think are the strengths and weaknesses of the draft, and ask what sort of revisions seem appropriate. E-mail the letter and the draft to each of your peer responders. Based on their comments, which should either be e-mailed to you or handwritten on a printed copy of your draft, revise your draft.

CHAPTER 3

Definition

Before we examine the other elements of argument, we need to consider definition, a component you may have to deal with early in writing an essay. Definition may be used in two ways: to clarify the meanings of vague or ambiguous terms or as a method of development for the whole essay. In some arguments your claims will contain words that need explanation before you can proceed with any discussion. But you may also want to devote an entire essay to the elaboration of a broad concept or experience that cannot be adequately defined in a shorter space.

The Roman statesman Cicero said, "Every rational discussion of anything whatsoever should begin with a definition in order to make clear what is the subject of dispute." You have probably already discovered the importance of definition in argument. If you have ever had a disagreement with your parents about using the car or drinking or dyeing your hair or going away for a weekend or staying out till three in the morning, you know that you were really arguing about the meaning of the term *adolescent freedom*.

Arguments often revolve around definitions of crucial terms. For example, how does one define *democracy*? Does a democracy guarantee freedom of the press, freedom of worship, freedom of assembly, and freedom of movement? In the United States, we would argue that such freedoms are essential to any definition of *democracy*. But countries in which these freedoms are nonexistent also represent themselves as democracies or governments of the people. In the words of Senator Daniel P. Moynihan, "For years now the most brutal totalitarian regimes have called themselves 'people's' or 'democratic' republics." Rulers in such governments are aware that defining their regimes as democratic may win the approval of people who would otherwise condemn them. In his formidable attack on totalitarianism, *1984,* George Orwell coined the slogans "War Is Peace" and "Slavery Is Freedom," phrases that represent the corrupt use of definition to distort reality.

But even where there is no intention to deceive, the snares of definition are difficult to avoid. How do you define *abortion*? Is it "termination of pregnancy"? Or is it "murder of an unborn child"? During a celebrated trial in 1975 of a physician who performed an abortion and was accused of manslaughter, the prosecution often used the word *baby* to refer to the fetus, but the defense referred to "the products of conception." These definitions of *fetus* reflected the differing judgments of those on opposite sides. Not only do judgments create definitions; definitions influence judgments. In the abortion trial, the definitions of *fetus* used by both sides were meant to promote either approval or disapproval of the doctor's action.

Definitions can indeed change the nature of an event or a "fact." How many farms are there in the state of New York? The answer to the question depends on the definition of *farm*. In 1979 the *New York Times* reported:

> Because of a change in the official definition of the word "farm," New York lost 20 percent of its farms on January 1, with numbers dropping from 56,000 to 45,000. . . .
> Before the change, a farm was defined as "any place from which $250 or more of agricultural products is sold" yearly or "any place of 10 acres or more from which $50 or more of agricultural products is sold" yearly. Now a farm is "any place from which $1,000 or more of agricultural products is sold" in a year.[1]

A change in the definition of *poverty* can have similar results. An article in the *New York Times*, whose headline reads, "A Revised Definition of Poverty May Raise Number of U.S. Poor," makes this clear.

> The official definition of *poverty* used by the Federal Government for three decades is based simply on cash income before taxes. But in a report to be issued on Wednesday, a panel of experts convened by the [National] Academy of Sciences three years ago at the behest of Congress says the Government should move toward a concept of poverty based on disposable income, the amount left after a family pays taxes and essential expenses.[2]

[1] *New York Times*, March 4, 1979, sec. 1, p. 40.
[2] *New York Times*, April 10, 1995, sec. A, p. 1.

The differences are wholly a matter of definition. But such differences can have serious consequences for those being defined, most of all in the disposition of billions of federal dollars in aid of various kinds. In 1992 the Census Bureau classified 14.5 percent of Americans as poor. Under the new guidelines, at least 15 or 16 percent would be poor, and, under some measures recommended by a government panel, 18 percent would be so defined.

In fact, local and federal courts almost every day redefine traditional concepts that can have a direct impact on our everyday lives. The definition of *family*, for example, has undergone significant changes that acknowledge the existence of new relationships. In January 1990 the New Jersey Supreme Court ruled that a family may be defined as "one or more persons occupying a dwelling unit as a single nonprofit housekeeping unit, who are living together as a stable and permanent living unit, being a traditional family unit or the *functional equivalent* thereof" (italics for emphasis added). This meant that ten Glassboro State College students, unrelated by blood, could continue to occupy a single-family house despite the objection of the borough of Glassboro.[3] Even the legal definition of maternity has shifted. Who is the mother—the woman who contributes the egg or the woman (the surrogate) who bears the child? Several states, acknowledging the changes brought by medical technology, now recognize a difference between the birth mother and the legal mother.

DEFINING THE TERMS IN YOUR ARGUMENT

In some of your arguments you will introduce terms that require definition. We've pointed out that a definition of *poverty* is crucial to any debate on the existence of poverty in the United States. The same may be true in a debate about the legality of euthanasia, or mercy killing. Are the arguers referring to passive euthanasia (the withdrawal of life-support systems) or to active euthanasia (the direct administration of drugs to hasten death)?

It is not uncommon, in fact, for arguments about controversial questions to turn into arguments about the definition of terms. If, for example, you wanted to argue in favor of the regulation of religious cults, you would first have to define *cult*. In so doing, you might discover that it is not easy to distinguish clearly between conventional religions and cults. Then you would have to define *regulation*, spelling out the legal restrictions you favored so as to make them apply only to cults, not to established religions. An argument on the subject might end almost before it began if writer and reader could not agree on definitions of these terms. While clear definitions do not guarantee agreement, they do ensure that all parties understand the nature of the argument.

[3] *New York Times*, February 1, 1990, sec. B, p. 5.

■ Defining Vague and Ambiguous Terms

You will need to define other terms in addition to those in your claim. If you use words and phrases that have two or more meanings, they may appear vague and ambiguous to your reader. In arguments of value and policy abstract terms such as *freedom, justice, patriotism*, and *equality* require clarification. Despite their vagueness, however, they are among the most important in the language because they represent the ideals that shape our laws. When conflicts arise, the courts must define these terms to establish the legality of certain practices. Is the Ku Klux Klan permitted to make disparaging public statements about ethnic and racial groups? That depends on the court's definition of *free speech*. Can execution for some crimes be considered cruel and unusual punishment? That, too, depends on the court's definition of *cruel and unusual punishment*. In addition, such terms as *happiness, mental health, success*, and *creativity* often defy precise definition because they reflect the differing values within a society or a culture.

The definition of *success*, for example, varies not only among social groups but also among individuals within the group. One scientist has postulated five signs by which to measure success: wealth (including health), security (confidence in retaining the wealth), reputation, performance, and contentment.[4] Consider whether all of these are necessary to your own definition of *success*. If not, which may be omitted? Do you think others should be added? Notice that one of the signs — reputation — is defined by the community; another — contentment — can be measured only by the individual. The assessment of performance probably owes something to both the group and the individual.

Christopher Atkins, an actor, gave an interviewer an example of an externalized definition of success — that is, a definition based on the standards imposed by other people:

> Success to me is judged through the eyes of others. I mean, if you're walking around saying, "I own a green Porsche," you might meet somebody who says, "Hey, that's no big deal. I own a green Porsche and a house." So all of a sudden, you don't feel so successful. Really, it's in the eyes of others.[5]

So difficult is the formulation of a universally accepted measure for success that some scholars regard the concept as meaningless. Nevertheless, we continue to use the word as if it represented a definable concept because the idea of success, however defined, is important for the identity and development of the individual and the group. It is clear, however, that when crossing subcultural boundaries, even within a small group, we need to be aware of differences in the use of the word. If contentment — that is, the satisfaction of achieving a small personal goal — is enough,

[4] Gwynn Nettler, *Social Concerns* (New York: McGraw-Hill, 1976), pp. 196–97.
[5] *New York Times*, August 6, 1982, sec. 3, p. 8.

then a person lying under a palm tree subsisting on handouts from pic-nickers may be a success. But you should not expect all your readers to agree that these criteria are enough to define *success.*

In arguing about aesthetic matters, whose vocabulary is almost al-ways abstract, the criteria for judgment must be revealed, either directly or indirectly, and then the abstract terms that represent the criteria must be defined. If you want to say that a film is distinguished by great acting, have you made clear what you mean by *great*? That we do not always un-derstand or agree on the definition of *great* is apparent, say, on the morn-ing after the Oscar winners have been announced.

Even subjects that you feel sure you can identify may offer surprising insights when you rethink them for an extended definition. One critic, defining *rock music,* argued that the distinguishing characteristic of rock music was noise—not beat, not harmonies, not lyrics, not vocal style, but noise, "nasty, discordant, irritating noise—or, to its practitioners, unfet-tered, liberating, expressive noise."[6] In producing this definition, the au-thor had to give a number of examples to prove that he was justified in rejecting the most familiar criteria.

Consider the definition of *race,* around which so much of American history has revolved, often with tragic consequences. Until recently, the only categories listed in the census were white, black, Asian-Pacific, and Native American, "with the Hispanic population straddling them all." But rapidly increasing intermarriage and ethnic identity caused a number of political and ethnic groups to demand changes in the classifications of the Census Bureau. Some Arab Americans, for example, prefer to be counted as "Middle Eastern" rather than white. Children of black-white unions are defined as black 60 percent of the time, while children of Asian-white unions are described as Asian 42 percent of the time. Re-search is now being conducted to discover how people feel about the terms being used to define them. As one anthropologist pointed out, "So-cially and politically assigned attributes have a lot to do with access to economic resources."[7]

METHODS FOR DEFINING TERMS

The following strategies for defining terms in an argument are by no means mutually exclusive. You may use all of them in a single argumen-tative essay.

---

[6]Jon Pareles, "Noise Evokes Modern Chaos for a Band," *New York Times*, March 9, 1986, sec. H, p. 26.

[7]*Wall Street Journal*, September 9, 1995, sec. B, p. 1.

■ Dictionary Definition

Giving a dictionary definition is the simplest and most obvious way to define a term. An unabridged dictionary is the best source because it usually gives examples of the way a word can be used in a sentence; that is, it furnishes the proper context.

In many cases, the dictionary definition alone is not sufficient. It may be too broad or too narrow for your purpose. Suppose, in an argument about pornography, you wanted to define the word *obscene*. *Webster's New International Dictionary* (third edition, unabridged) gives the definition of *obscene* as "offensive to taste; foul; loathsome; disgusting." But these synonyms do not tell you what qualities make an object or an event or an action "foul," "loathsome," and "disgusting." In 1973 the Supreme Court, attempting to narrow the definition of *obscenity,* ruled that obscenity was to be determined by the community in accordance with local standards. One person's obscenity, as numerous cases have demonstrated, may be another person's art. The celebrated trials in the early twentieth century about the distribution of novels regarded as pornographic—D. H. Lawrence's *Lady Chatterley's Lover* and James Joyce's *Ulysses*—emphasized the problems of defining obscenity.

Another dictionary definition may strike you as too narrow. *Patriotism,* for example, is defined in one dictionary as "love and loyal or zealous support of one's country, especially in all matters involving other countries." Some readers may want to include an unwillingness to support government policies they consider wrong.

■ Stipulation

In stipulating the meaning of a term, the writer asks the reader to accept a definition that may be different from the conventional one. He or she does this to limit or control the argument. Someone has said, "Part of the task of keeping definitions in our civilization clear and pure is to keep a firm democratic rein on those with the power, or craving the power, to stipulate meaning." Perhaps this writer was thinking of a term like *national security,* which can be defined by a nation's leaders in such a way as to sanction persecution of citizens and reckless military adventures. Likewise, a term such as *liberation* can be appropriated by terrorist groups whose activities often lead to oppression rather than liberation.

Religion is usually defined as a belief in a supernatural power to be obeyed and worshiped. But in an article entitled "Civil Religion in America," a sociologist offers a different meaning.

> While some have argued that Christianity is the national faith, and others that church and synagogue celebrate only the generalized religion of "the American way of life," few have realized that there actually exists alongside of and rather clearly differentiated from the churches an elaborate and well-institutionalized civil religion in America. This

article argues not only that there is such a thing, but also that this religion . . . has its own seriousness and integrity and requires the same care in understanding that any other religion does.[8]

When the author adds, "This religion—there seems no other word for it—was neither sectarian nor in any specific sense Christian," he emphasizes that he is distinguishing his definition of religion from definitions that associate religion and church.

Even the word *violence,* which the dictionary defines as "physical force used so as to injure or damage" and whose meaning seems so clear and uncompromising, can be manipulated to produce a definition different from the one normally understood by most people. Some pacifists refer to conditions in which "people are deprived of choices in a systematic way" as "institutionalized quiet violence." Even where no physical force is employed, this lack of choice in schools, in the workplace, in the black ghettos is defined as violence.[9]

In *Through the Looking-Glass* Alice asked Humpty Dumpty "whether you can make words mean so many different things."

"When *I* use a word," Humpty Dumpty said scornfully, "it means just what I choose it to mean—neither more nor less."[10]

A writer, however, is not free to invent definitions that no one will recognize or that create rather than solve problems between writer and reader.

■ Negation

To avoid confusion it is sometimes helpful to tell the reader what a term is *not.* In discussing euthanasia, a writer might say, "By euthanasia I do not mean active intervention to hasten the death of the patient."

A negative definition may be more extensive, depending on the complexity of the term and the writer's ingenuity. The critic of rock music quoted earlier in this chapter arrived at his definition of *noise* by rejecting attributes that seemed misleading. The former Communist party member Whittaker Chambers, in a foreword to a book on the spy trial of Alger Hiss, defined *communism* this way:

First, let me try to say what Communism is not. It is not simply a vicious plot hatched by wicked men in a subcellar. It is not just the writings of Marx and Lenin, dialectical materialism, the Politburo, the labor theory of value, the theory of the general strike, the Red Army

[8] Robert N. Bellah, "Civil Religion in America," *Daedalus,* Winter 1967, p. 1.

[9] Newton Garver, "What Violence Is," in James Rachels, ed., *Moral Choices* (New York: Harper and Row, 1971), pp. 248–49.

[10] Lewis Carroll, *Alice in Wonderland and Through the Looking-Glass* (New York: Grosset and Dunlap, 1948), p. 238.

secret police, labor camps, underground conspiracy, the dictatorship of the proletariat, the technique of the coup d'état. It is not even those chanting, bannered millions that stream periodically, like disorganized armies, through the heart of the world's capitals: Moscow, New York, Tokyo, Paris, Rome. These are expressions, but they are not what Communism is about.[11]

This, of course, is only part of the definition. Any writer beginning a definition in the negative must go on to define what the term *is*.

■ Examples

One of the most effective ways of defining terms in an argument is to use examples. Both real and hypothetical examples can bring life to abstract and ambiguous terms. The writer in the following passage defines *preferred categories* (classes of people who are meant to benefit from affirmative action policies) by invoking specific cases:

> The absence of definitions points up one of the problems with preferred categories. . . . These preferred categories take no account of family wealth or educational advantages. A black whose father is a judge or physician deserves preferential treatment over any nonminority applicant. The latter might have fought his way out of the grinding poverty of Appalachia, or might be the first member of an Italian American or a Polish American family to complete high school. But no matter.[12]

Insanity is a word that has been used and misused to describe a variety of conditions. Even psychiatrists are in dispute about its meaning. In the following anecdote, examples narrow and refine the definition.

> Dr. Zilboorg says that present-day psychiatry does not possess any satisfactory definition of mental illness or neurosis. To illustrate, he told a story: A psychiatrist was recently asked for a definition of a "well-adjusted person" (not even slightly peculiar). The definition: "A person who feels in harmony with himself and who is not in conflict with his environment." It sounded fine, but up popped a heckler. "Would you then consider an anti-Nazi working in the underground against Hitler a maladjusted person?" "Well," the psychiatrist hemmed, "I withdraw the latter part of my definition." Dr. Zilboorg withdrew the first half for him. Many persons in perfect harmony with themselves, he pointed out, are in "distinctly pathological states."[13]

■ Extended Definition

When we speak of an extended definition, we usually refer not only to length but also to the variety of methods for developing the definition.

---

[11]*Witness* (New York: Random House, 1952), p. 8.
[12]Anthony Lombardo, "Quotas Work Both Ways," *U.S. Catholic*, February 1974, p. 39.
[13]Quoted in *The Art of Making Sense*, p. 48.

Let's take the word *materialism*. A dictionary entry offers the following sentence fragments as definitions: "1. the doctrine that comfort, pleasure, and wealth are the only or highest goals or values. 2. the tendency to be more concerned with material than the spiritual goals or values." But the term *materialism* has acquired so many additional meanings, especially emotional ones, that an extended definition serves a useful purpose in clarifying the many different ideas surrounding our understanding of the term.

Below is a much longer definition of *materialism*, which appears at the beginning of an essay entitled "People and Things: Reflections on Materialism."[14]

> There are two contemporary usages of the term *materialism*, and it is important to distinguish between them. On the one hand we can talk about *instrumental materialism*, or the use of material objects to make life longer, safer, more enjoyable. By instrumental, we mean that objects act as essential means for discovering and furthering personal values and goals of life, so that the objects are instruments used to realize and further those goals. There is little negative connotation attached to this meaning of the word, since one would think that it is perfectly sensible to use things for such purposes. While it is true that the United States is the epitome of materialism in this sense, it is also true that most people in every society aspire to reach our level of instrumental materialism.
>
> On the other hand the term has a more negative connotation, which might be conveyed by the phrase terminal materialism. This is the sense critics use when they apply the term to Americans. What they mean is that we not only use our material resources as instruments to make life more manageable, but that we reduce our ultimate goals to the possession of things. They believe that we don't just use our cars to get from place to place, but that we consider the ownership of expensive cars one of the central values in life. Terminal materialism means that the object is valued only because it indicates an end in itself, a possession. In instrumental materialism there is a sense of directionality, in which a person's goals may be furthered through the interactions with the object. A book, for example, can reveal new possibilities or widen a person's view of the world, or an old photograph can be cherished because it embodies a relationship. But in terminal materialism, there is no sense of reciprocal interaction in the relation between the object and the end. The end is valued as final, not as itself a means to further ends. And quite often it is only the status label or image associated with the object that is valued, rather than the actual object.

In the essay from which this passage is taken, the authors distinguish between two kinds of materialism and provide an extended explanation, using contrast and examples as methods of development. They are aware that the common perception of materialism—the love of things for their

---

[14]Mihaly Csikszentmihalyi and Eugene Rochberg-Halton, "People and Things: Reflections on Materialism," *University of Chicago Magazine*, Spring 1978, pp. 7–8.

own sake—is a negative one. But this view, according to the authors, doesn't fully account for the attitudes of many Americans toward the things they own. There is, in fact, another more positive meaning that the authors call *instrumental materialism.* You will recognize that the authors are *stipulating* a meaning with which their readers might not be familiar. In their essay they distinguish between *terminal materialism,* in which "the object is valued only because it indicates an end in itself," and *instrumental materialism,* "the use of material objects to make life longer, safer, more enjoyable." Since *instrumental materialism* is the less familiar definition, the essay provides a great number of examples that show how people of three different generations value photographs, furniture, musical instruments, plants, and other objects for their memories and personal associations rather than as proof of the owners' ability to acquire the objects or win the approval of others.

THE DEFINITION ESSAY

The argumentative essay can take the form of an extended definition. An example of such an essay is the one from which we've just quoted, as well as the essays at the end of this chapter. The definition essay is appropriate when the idea under consideration is so controversial or so heavy with historical connotations that even a paragraph or two cannot make clear exactly what the arguer wants his or her readers to understand. For example, if you were preparing a definition of *patriotism,* you would probably use a number of methods to develop your definition: personal narrative, examples, stipulation, comparison and contrast, and cause-and-effect analysis.

Writer's Guide: Writing a Definition Essay

The following important steps should be taken when you write an essay of definition.

1. Choose a term that needs definition because it is controversial or ambiguous, or because you want to offer a personal definition that differs from the accepted interpretation. Explain why an extended definition is necessary. Or choose an experience that lends itself to treatment in an extended definition. One student defined *culture shock* as she had experienced it while studying abroad in Hawaii among students of a different ethnic background.

2. Decide on the thesis — the point of view you wish to develop about the term you are defining. If you want to define *heroism,* for example, you

> may choose to develop the idea that this quality depends on motivation and awareness of danger rather than on the specific act performed by the hero.
>
> 3. Begin by consulting the dictionary for the conventional definition. Make clear whether you want to elaborate on the dictionary definition or take issue with it because you think it is misleading or inadequate.
>
> 4. Distinguish wherever possible between the term you are defining and other terms with which it might be confused. If you are defining *love,* can you make a clear distinction between the different kinds of emotional attachments contained in the word?
>
> 5. Try to think of several methods of developing the definition — using examples, comparison and contrast, analogy, cause-and-effect analysis. However, you may discover that one method alone — say, use of examples — will suffice to narrow and refine your definition. See the sample essay "The Nature of Prejudice" on page 80 for an example of such a development.
>
> 6. Arrange your supporting material in an order that gives emphasis to the most important ideas.

SAMPLE ANNOTATED ESSAY

Cloning Misperceptions

LEE M. SILVER

Part of the confusion about cloning is confusion about definitions

Reason #1 for fear

Why do four out of five Americans think that human cloning is "against God's will" or "morally wrong"? Why are people so frightened by this technology? One important reason is that many people have a muddled sense of what cloning is. They confuse the popular meaning of the word *clone* and the specific meaning it takes on in the context of biology.

In its popular usage, *clone* refers to something that is a duplicate, or cheaper imitation, of a brand-name person, place, or thing. The British

---

Lee M. Silver is a professor of molecular biology at Princeton University. This essay is from *Remaking Eden: Cloning and Beyond in a Brave New World* (1997).

The popular image of cloning

politician Tony Blair has been called a clone of Bill Clinton, and an IBM PC clone is not only built like an IBM PC, it *behaves* like an IBM PC. It is this popular meaning of the word that caused many people to believe that human cloning would copy not just a person's body but a person's consciousness as well. This concept of cloning was at the center of the movie *Multiplicity,* which was released just months before the Dolly announcement. In it, a geneticist makes a clone of the star character played by Michael Keaton and explains that the clone will have "all of his feelings, all of his quirks, all of his memories, right up to the moment of cloning." The clone himself says to the original character, "You are me, I am you." It is this image that Jeremy Rifkin probably had in mind when he criticized the possible application of the sheep cloning technology to humans by saying, "It's a horrendous crime to make a Xerox (copy) of someone."

"Actual cloning technology"

But this popular image bears absolutely no resemblance to actual cloning technology, in either process or outcome. Scientists cannot make full-grown adult copies of any animal, let alone humans. All they can do is start the process of development over again, using genetic material obtained from an adult. Real biological cloning can only take place at the level of the cell — life *in the general sense.* It is only long after the cloning event is completed that a unique — and independent — life *in the special sense* could emerge in the developing fetus. Once again, it is the inability of many people to appreciate the difference between the two meanings of "life" that is the cause of confusion.

Different definitions of "life" are also a source of confusion

Reason #2 for fear

A second reason people fear cloning is based on the notion that a clone is an imperfect imitation of the real thing. This causes some people to think that — far from having the same soul as someone else — a clone would have no soul at all. Among the earliest popular movies to explore this idea was *Blade Runner,* in which synthetic people were produced that were just like humans in all respects but one — they had no empathy. (Coincidentally, *Blade Runner* was based on a 1968 book by Philip K. Dick entitled *Do Androids Dream of*

Examples of popular images of cloning

Electric Sheep?) And the same general idea of imperfection is explored in *Multiplicity* when a clone of the Michael Keaton character has himself cloned. The clone of the clone is a dimwitted clown because, as the original clone says, "Sometimes you make a copy of a copy and it's not as sharp as the original."

The Irvine, California, rabbi Bernard King was   5 seriously frightened by this idea when he asked, "Can the cloning create a soul? Can scientists create the soul that would make a being ethical, moral, caring, loving, all the things we attribute humanity to?" The Catholic priest Father Saunders suggested that "cloning would only produce humanoids or androids—soulless replicas of human beings that could be used as slaves." And Brent Staples, a member of the *New York Times* editorial board, warned that "synthetic humans would be easy prey for humanity's worst instincts."

Yet there is nothing synthetic about the cells used in cloning. They are alive before the cloning process, and they are alive after fusion has taken place. The newly created embryo can only develop inside the womb of a woman in the same way that all embryos and fetuses develop. Cloned children will be full-fledged human beings, indistinguishable in biological terms from all other

Attempt to dispel fear that clones would not have souls

members of the species. Thus, the notion of a soulless clone has no basis in reality.

His definition of a clone

When the misperceptions are tossed aside, it becomes clear what a cloned child will be. She, or he, will simply be a later-born identical twin—nothing more and nothing less. And while she may go through life looking similar to the way her progenitor-parent looked at a past point in time, she will be a unique human being, with a completely unique consciousness and a unique set of memories that she will build from scratch.

To many people, the mere word *clone* seems ominous, conjuring up images from movies like *The Boys from Brazil* with evil Nazis intent on ruling the world. How likely is it that governments or organized groups will use cloning as a tool to build future societies with citizens bred to fulfill a particular need?

A key question

The *Brave New World* Scenario

Quotation from
Huxley's novel Brave
New World

"Bokanovsky's Process," repeated the director. . . . One egg, one embryo, one adult—normality. But a bokanovskified egg will bud, will proliferate, will divide. From eight to ninety-six buds, and every bud will grow into a perfectly formed embryo, and every embryo into a full-sized adult. Making ninety-six human beings grow where only one grew before. Progress. . . . Identical twins—but not in piddling twos and threes as in the old viviparous days, when an egg would sometimes accidentally divide; actually by dozens, by scores at a time. . . . "But, alas," the Director shook his head, "we can't bokanovskify indefinitely." Ninety-six seemed to be the limit; seventy-two a good average.

Thus did Aldous Huxley present one of the technological underpinnings of his brave new world where cloning would be used "as one of the major instruments of social stability." With cloning, it was possible to obtain "standard men and women; in uniform batches. The whole of a factory staffed with the products of a single bokanovskified egg."

Brave New World evoked powerful feelings within people not only because they could see inklings of the rigid conformity of the brave new world society within their own, but because the science was presented in a hyperrealistic manner. Even the most minor technical details were carefully described.

Huxley, for one, was convinced that political forces would evolve in the direction he described. In the foreword to the 1946 edition, he wrote: "It is probable that all the world's governments will be more or less completely totalitarian even before the harnessing of atomic energy; that they will be totalitarian during and after the harnessing seems almost certain." It was the *science* that he was less certain of.

Yet, like so many other twentieth-century intellectuals, Huxley underestimated the power of technology to turn yesterday's fantasy into today's reality. Only sixty-four years after he speculated on the possibility of human cloning, it is on the verge of happening. But now that one aspect of science has caught up to *Brave New World,* what can we say about the politics? Will there be governments that choose to clone?

Definitely not in a democratic society for a very simple reason. Cloned children cannot appear out of the air. Each one will have to develop within the womb of a woman (for the time being). And in a free society, the state cannot control women's bodies and minds in a way that would be necessary to build an army of clones.

But what about a totalitarian government that wanted to produce clones to serve its own social needs: "Standard men and women; in uniform batches. The whole of a factory staffed with the products of a single bokanovskified egg."

This scenario is highly improbable. First, only   15 an extremely controlling totalitarian state would have the ability to enslave women en masse to act as surrogate mothers for babies that would be forcibly removed and raised by the state. Ruling governments this extreme are rare at the end of the twentieth century. But even if one did emerge, it is hard to imagine why it would want to clone people.

Would it be to produce an army of powerful soldiers? Any government that could clone would certainly get more fighting power out of high-tech weapons of destruction than even the most muscular and obedient soldier clones.

Would it be to produce docile factory workers? Cloning is not necessary for this objective, which has already been reached throughout many societies. And mind control could be achieved much more effectively with New Age drugs targeted at particular behaviors and emotions (another prediction made by Huxley).

Would it be to produce people with great minds? It is not clear how a government would choose a progenitor for such clones, or what it would do during the twenty years or so that it took for clones to mature into adults. After all that time, a new set of leaders might decide that the wrong characteristics had been chosen for cloning. A better approach would be to simply build a superior system of public education that allowed the brightest children to rise to the top, no matter where on society's ladder they began their lives.

In the end, one is hard-pressed to come up with a single strategic advantage that any government might get from breeding clones rather than allowing a population to regenerate itself naturally. Thus, the Huxleyan use of cloning as a means for building a stable society seems very unlikely. But there is an obvious exception—one that could occur in a state or society controlled by a single egomaniacal dictator with substantial financial and scientific resources.

Example of an exception

The example that comes to mind is that of the 20 Japanese cult leader Shoko Asahara. Asahara's group, Aum Shinrikyo, included well-educated chemists who produced nerve gas for the purpose of holding the Japanese government hostage. The group was exposed, and their leader was arrested and put on trial after a lethal gas attack on the Tokyo subway system in March 1995. Based on what we have learned about the group, it is possible that it might have had both the financial and technical resources required to put together the facility and equipment needed for cloning, as well as the power of persuasion required to convince skilled personnel to carry it out. And the aura that Asahara projected was such that he might well have succeeded in convincing women to become pregnant with his clones. Finally, Asahara himself seems to have been exactly the kind of egomaniac who would have preferred child clones over naturally conceived sons.

I doubt that we could stop people like Shoko Asahara from cloning themselves. But would it make any difference? Let us imagine that Asahara had cloned himself into a dozen children. It seems extremely unlikely that these children would have any greater effect on society, twenty years down the road, than sons conceived the old-fashioned way. It's not only that they wouldn't grow up in the same adverse environment that played an important role in turning Asahara into the cult leader that he became. It's also that they would grow up among different people who would be unlikely to respond to them

Another extreme example

in exactly the same way that people responded to Asahara. The same could be said for modern-day clones of Adolf Hitler. In both cases, the original men were catapulted into positions of leadership through chance personal or historical events that will never repeat themselves. An adult alive today with Adolf Hitler's mind, personality, and behavior would be more likely to find himself barricaded in a militia outpost or in jail than in the White House or the German Bundesrat.

Unstated claim of fact: It is highly unlikely that governments will ever make use of cloning to control the breeding of their citizens.

While Hitler's Third Reich and Asahara's Aum Shinrikyo were both short-lived phenomena, there are still examples of royal families—albeit with little real power today—that have handed down the crown from parent to child over hundreds of years. If after ascending to the throne, Prince Charles of Great Britain decided to place his clone—rather than his eldest son—next in line, would that upset the world order? On the contrary, I doubt if anyone would care.

■ Analysis

Although Silver is a professor of molecular biology, this essay is from a book published in 1997 with a lay audience rather than his fellow specialists in mind. The title of the book, *Remaking Eden: Cloning and Beyond in a Brave New World*, includes at the same time a reference to the Garden of Eden of Biblical fame and a reference to the 1932 novel *Brave New World* by Aldous Huxley. Silver later refers to Huxley's novel in a section heading and quotes from it. Readers familiar with that novel know that it is about a world gone awry due to man's tinkering with the natural human reproductive process. When a character named John the Savage, one of the few human beings allowed to develop naturally, without scientific intervention, cries out the quotation from Shakespeare "O brave new world, that has such people in it!" he is being ironic because he has had a glimpse of a world that no longer even knows that Shakespeare ever existed—a world supposedly without pain and suffering, but one that he loathes because it is also a world without feelings. On the other hand, the main title, *Remaking Eden*, suggests the possibility of rediscovering the idyllic life lived by the first man and woman before they disobeyed God's command and ate of the fruit of the Tree of the Knowledge of Good and Evil. There seems to be the suggestion that if humanity erred by wanting to know too much, it may yet be possible to attain once more—or remake—what was lost. The title of the essay, "Cloning Misperceptions," alerts Silver's readers to the fact that he feels that cloning is misunderstood. His goal in the essay is to correct some of the misperceptions to which the title refers. In his first sentence he acknowledges that 80 percent of his audience are likely to see cloning as wrong.

As any good arguer does, Silver makes clear how is he using his key term *clone*. In fact, he begins the essay by pointing out that many of the misperceptions about cloning come about because of the confusion between the popular meaning of the term and the more specialized one used by biologists. He also points out at the end of the third paragraph that people are often confused by two different meanings of the word *life*. To explain that cloning is not the same as Xeroxing a person, he writes, "Real biological cloning can only take place at the level of the cell—life *in the general sense*. It is only long after the cloning event is complete that a unique—and independent—life *in the special sense* could emerge in the developing fetus" [his italics].

In the opening paragraph of his extended definition, Silver is making use of a technique often used in definition: He is telling his readers what cloning is *not*. He is taking issue not with the dictionary definition of the term but with the popular notion of cloning. He makes use of examples from movies to show how the fictionalized images of cloning in them differ from the reality. What all of the examples have in common is that they show cloning in some way gone wrong.

The first section of Silver's extended definition is clearly organized around the two reasons he feels people fear cloning. Near the end of that section, he most clearly states his definition of a cloned child: "She, or he, will simply be a later-born identical twin—nothing more and nothing less." He ends that first section with a question which he attempts to answer in the next section, the one headed "The *Brave New World* Scenario": "How likely is it that governments or organized groups will use cloning as a tool to build future societies with citizens bred to fulfill a particular need?"

If Huxley believed that governments would use cloning to control citizens, Silver does not. If Huxley perhaps overestimated the willingness of governments to use cloning, he underestimated the ability of science to make such cloning possible. Silver's answer to the question whether there will be governments that choose to clone, however, is, "Definitely not in a democratic society." He is appealing to his readers' need to feel secure in their ability to maintain control of their own bodies when he points out that a cloned fetus cannot yet develop outside the body of the human female. (In Huxley's novel, it can.)

Much of the rest of Silver's essay is organized around a series of questions and answers. Here he is appealing to his readers' reason as he questions what advantage there could be for even the most totalitarian state in producing masses of identical clones. He concludes with the rare examples of two extreme individuals who might have been egomaniacal enough to try. He once again appeals to his readers' need for security when he points out how unlikely it would be for the conditions to be right for such extreme individuals to make their plan work.

Silver's unstated claim is a claim of fact: It is highly unlikely that governments will ever make use of cloning to control the breeding of their citizens.

READINGS FOR ANALYSIS

The Nature of Prejudice

GORDON ALLPORT

Before I attempt to define *prejudice,* let us have in mind four instances that I think we all would agree are prejudice.

The first is the case of the Cambridge University student who said, "I despise all Americans. But," he added, a bit puzzled, "I've never met one that I didn't like."

The second is the case of another Englishman, who said to an American, "I think you're awfully unfair in your treatment to Negroes. How *do* Americans feel about Negroes?" The American replied, "Well, I suppose some Americans feel about Negroes just the way you feel about the Irish." The Englishman said, "Oh, come now. The Negroes are human beings."

Then there's the incident that occasionally takes place in various parts of the world (in the West Indies, for example, I'm told). When an American walks down the street the natives conspicuously hold their noses till the American goes by. The case of odor is always interesting. Odor gets mixed up with prejudice because odor has great associative power. We know that some Chinese deplore the odor of Americans. Some white people think Negroes have a distinctive smell and vice versa. An intrepid psychologist recently did an experiment; it went as follows. He brought to a gymnasium an equal number of white and colored students and had them take shower baths. When they were nice and clean he had them exercise vigorously for fifteen minutes. Then he brought his judges in, and each went to the sheeted figures and sniffed. They were to say "white" or "black," guessing at the identity of the subject. The experiment seemed to prove that when we are sweaty we all smell the same way. It's good to have experimental demonstration of the fact.

Gordon Allport (1897–1967) was a psychologist who taught at Harvard University from 1924 until his death. He was the author of numerous books, among them *Personality: A Psychological Interpretation* (1937). Allport delivered "The Nature of Prejudice" at the Seventeenth Claremont Reading Conference in 1952. The speech was published as a paper in 1952 in the Seventeenth Claremont Reading Conference Yearbook.

The fourth example I'd like to bring before you is a piece of writing   5
that I quote. Please ask yourselves who, in your judgment, wrote it. It's a
passage about the Jews.

> The synagogue is worse than a brothel. It's a den of scoundrels. It's a
> criminal assembly of Jews, a place of meeting for the assassins of Christ,
> a den of thieves, a house of ill fame, a dwelling of iniquity. Whatever
> name more horrible to be found, it could never be worse than the syna-
> gogue deserves.
>
> I would say the same things about their souls. Debauchery and
> drunkenness have brought them to the level of lusty goat and pig. They
> know only one thing: to satisfy their stomachs and get drunk, kill, and
> beat each other up. Why should we salute them? We should not even
> have the slightest converse with them. They are lustful, rapacious,
> greedy, perfidious robbers.

Now who wrote that? Perhaps you say Hitler, or Goebbels, or one of
our local anti-Semites? No, it was written by Saint John Chrysostom, in
the fourth century A.D. Saint John Chrysostom, as you know, gave us the
first liturgy in the Christian church, still used in the Orthodox churches
today. From it all services of the Holy Communion derive. Episcopalians
will recognize him also as the author of that exalted prayer that closes the
offices of both matins and evensong in the *Book of Common Prayer*. I include this incident to show how complex the problem is. Religious people
are by no means necessarily free from prejudice. In this regard be patient
even with our saints.

What do these four instances have in common? You notice that all of
them indicate that somebody is "down" on somebody else—a feeling of
rejection, or hostility. But also, in all these four instances, there is indication that the person is not "up" on his subject—not really informed
about Americans, Irish, Jews, or bodily odors.

So I would offer, first a slang definition of prejudice: *Prejudice is being
down on somebody you're not up on*. If you dislike slang, let me offer the
same thought in the style of St. Thomas Aquinas. Thomists have defined
prejudice as *thinking ill of others without sufficient warrant*.

You notice that both definitions, as well as the examples I gave, specify two ingredients of prejudice. First there is some sort of faulty generalization in thinking about a group. I'll call this the process of
categorization. Then there is the negative, rejective, or hostile ingredient,
a *feeling* tone. "Being down on something" is the hostile ingredient; "that
you're not up on" is the categorization ingredient; "thinking ill of others"
is the hostile ingredient; "without sufficient warrant" is the faulty categorization.

Parenthetically I should say that of course there is such a thing as *pos-*   10
itive prejudice. We can be just as prejudiced *in favor of* as we are *against*.
We can be biased in favor of our children, our neighborhood, or our college. Spinoza makes the distinction neatly. He says that *love prejudice* is

"thinking well of others, through love, more than is right." *Hate prejudice,* he says, is "thinking ill of others, through hate, more than is right."

READING AND DISCUSSION QUESTIONS

1. This was a speech, obviously not delivered extemporaneously but read to the audience. What characteristics suggest an oral presentation? If you were to revise this essay into a paper, what changes would you make? Why?
2. Allport has arranged his anecdotes carefully. What principle of organization has he used?
3. Allport says that "'thinking ill of others' is the hostile ingredient; 'without sufficient warrant' is the faulty categorization" (para. 9). How would you define the word *warrant* in this part of Allport's definition? How is it related to the definition given on page 11?
4. This essay was written in 1952. Are there any references or examples that seem dated? Why or why not?

WRITING SUGGESTIONS

5. Some media critics claim that negative prejudice exists in the treatment of certain groups in movies and television: If you agree, select a group that seems to you to be the object of prejudice in these media, and offer evidence of the prejudice and the probable reasons for it. Or disagree with the media critics, and provide evidence that certain groups are *not* the object of prejudice.
6. Can you think of examples of what Allport calls *positive prejudice*? Perhaps you can find instances that are less obvious than the ones Allport mentions. Explain in what way these prejudices represent a love that is "more than is right" (para. 10).

Race by the Numbers

ORLANDO PATTERSON

In recent weeks, reporting and commentary that misinterpret early census results have been persistently misinforming the nation about its ethnic and racial composition. The misinformation is dangerous, since it fuels fears of decline and displacement among some whites, anxieties that are not only divisive but groundless. The Center for Immigration Studies, for example, a think tank in Washington, recently warned that by the middle of the century non-Hispanic whites will cease to be a majority and

Orlando Patterson is a professor of sociology at Harvard and the author of *Rituals of Blood*, the second volume of a trilogy on race relations.

that "each group in the new minority-majority country has longstanding grievances against whites."

Many articles have echoed the view that whites are fast becoming a minority in many areas of the country, largely because of the growth of the Hispanic population. The *New York Times* reported that seventy-one of the top 100 cities had lost white residents and made clear only in the third paragraph of the article that it is really "non-Hispanic whites" who are now a minority in these cities. Similarly, the *Miami Herald* reported that 20 cities and unincorporated communities in Miami-Dade county "went from majority to minority white, non-Hispanic." Left without commentary was the fact that the total white population—including Hispanic whites—of Miami, for example, is actually a shade under 70 percent.

These articles and too many others have failed to take account of the fact that nearly half of the Hispanic population is white in every social sense of this term; 48 percent of so-called Hispanics classified themselves as solely white, giving only one race to the census taker. Although all reports routinely note that "Hispanics can be of any race," they almost always go on to neglect this critical fact, treating Hispanics as if they were, in fact, a sociological race comparable to "whites" and "blacks."

In any case, the suggestion that the white population of America is fast on the way to becoming a minority is a gross distortion. Even if we view only the non-Hispanic white population, whites remain a robust 69.1 percent of the total population of the nation. If we include Hispanic whites, as we should, whites constitute 75.14 percent of the total population, down by only 5 percent from the 1990 census. And this does not take account of the 6.8 million people who identified in the census with "two or more races," 80 percent of whom listed white as one of these races.

Even with the most liberal of assumptions, there is no possibility that   5 whites will become a minority in this nation in this century. The most recent census projections indicate that whites will constitute 74.8 percent of the total population in 2050, and that non-Hispanic whites will still be 52.8 percent of the total. And when we make certain realistic sociological assumptions about which groups the future progeny of Hispanic whites, mixed couples, and descendants of people now acknowledging two or more races are likely to identify with, there is every reason to believe that the non-Hispanic white population will remain a substantial majority— and possibly even grow as a portion of the population.

Recent studies indicate that second-generation Hispanic whites are intermarrying and assimilating mainstream language and cultural patterns at a faster rate than second-generation European migrants of the late nineteenth and early twentieth centuries.

The misleading reports of white proportional decline are likely not only to sustain the racist fears of white supremacist groups but also to affect the views of ordinary white, nonextremist Americans. A false assumption that whites are becoming a minority in the nation their ancestors conquered and developed may be adding to the deep resentment of poor or struggling whites toward affirmative action and other policies aimed at righting the wrongs of discrimination.

How do we account for this persistent pattern of misinformation? Apart from the intellectually lazy journalistic tendency to overemphasize race, two influences are playing into the discussion.

One is the policy of the Census Bureau itself. Though on the one hand, the census has taken the progressive step of allowing citizens to classify themselves in as many racial ways as they wish, breaking up the traditional notion of races as immutable categories, on the other hand it is up to its age-old mischief of making and unmaking racial groups. As it makes a new social category out of the sociologically meaningless collection of peoples from Latin America and Spain, it is quietly abetting the process of demoting and removing white Hispanics from the "true" white race—native-born non-Hispanic whites.

There is a long history of such reclassification by federal agencies. In the early decades of the twentieth century, the Irish, Italians, and Jews were classified as separate races by the federal immigration office, and the practice was discontinued only after long and vehement protests from Jewish leaders. In 1930 Mexicans were classified as a separate race by the Census Bureau—which reclassified them as white in 1940, after protests. Between then and the 1960s, people from Latin America were routinely classified as whites; then, when vast numbers of poor immigrants began coming from Latin America, the Hispanic category emerged.

The first stage of racial classification, now nearly successfully completed for Hispanics, is naming and nailing them all together while disingenuously admitting that they can be "of any race." Next, the repeated naming and sociological classification of different groups under a single category inevitably leads to the gradual perception and reconstruction of the group as another race. Much the same process of racialization is taking place with that other enormous sociological nongroup, Asian Americans.

The other influence on perceptions of who is "white" originates among the so-called Hispanics. For political and economic reasons, including the benefits of affirmative action programs, the leadership of many Hispanic groups pursues a liberal, coalition-based agenda with African Americans and presses hard for a separate, unified Latino classification. This strategy is highly influential even though nearly half of Hispanics consider themselves white.

For African Americans, the nation's major disadvantaged minority, these tendencies are problematic, although African American leaders are too shortsighted to notice. Latino coalition strategies, by vastly increasing the number of people entitled to affirmative action, have been a major factor in the loss of political support for it. And any fear of a "white"

10

group that it might lose status tends to reinforce stigmatization of those Americans who will never be "white."

In this volatile transitional situation, where the best and worst are equally possible in our racial relations and attitudes, the very worst thing that journalists, analysts and commentators can do is to misinform the white majority that it is losing its majority status—something that recent surveys indicate it is already all too inclined to believe. We should stop obsessing on race in interpreting the census results. But if we must compulsively racialize the data, let's at least keep the facts straight and the interpretations honest.

READING AND DISCUSSION QUESTIONS

1. Where does Patterson state his claim?
2. What subtitles can you provide for the different parts of his argument? The topic sentences in several paragraphs offer clues to the organization.
3. According to Patterson, how is the matter of definition relevant to statistics about race?
4. Patterson's claim is strongly supported by statistics, history, and political analysis. Do you think these different kinds of support are equally persuasive? Which one is most susceptible to challenge? Why?
5. What is Patterson's objection to the definitions of *Hispanic* and *non-Hispanic* that are published by the Census Bureau and other agencies?

WRITING SUGGESTIONS

6. Narrate an experience you have had in which you felt you were either aided or hindered by the fact that you were defined as a member of a specific group. It could be a group such as those defined by gender, race, religious affiliation, or membership on a team or in a club.
7. Would adoption at the state level of a policy prohibiting classifying people by race, color, ethnicity, or national origin be beneficial or pernicious for the individual and for society? In other words, what is good or bad about classifying people?
8. Find a subject in which definition is critical to how statistics are interpreted and which can be argued successfully in a 750- to 1,000-word paper. Your essay should provide proof for a claim. (Patterson uses numbers to prove that whites need not fear that their numbers are declining.) Other subjects that depend on statistical support can be found throughout this book.

Family a Symbol of Love and Life, but Not Politics

ERIC ZORN

Family is one of our loveliest words. It speaks of a warm, enveloping, comforting, inspiring connection—a love relationship, a commitment, a safe harbor, a common enterprise.

Sometimes, sure, it's a messy and maddening entanglement. But even when it's imperfect, family is the foundation of identity and the cornerstone of success.

To many people—people of all faiths, orientations, and political beliefs—"family" is the word that expresses that which they hold most dear.

Not money. Not possessions. Not fame. Not career. Not country. Not friendship. Not romance. Not even freedom.

Family.   5

So it's time we took it back.

Sorry, Family PAC and Illinois Family Institute.

You, too, Focus on the Family, Family Research Council, Family Foundation, Pro-Family Network, American Family Association, and Culture and Family Institute.

Set that word down and back away slowly. It belongs to all of us.

You and other conservative organizations have monopolized it for 10 too long, turned it into shorthand for a social and political outlook that excludes rather than includes, and hectors those who don't, can't, or won't conform to your notions of morality.

"Family values" has come to mean the promotion of abstinence-only sex education, religion in the public sphere, education vouchers, traditional gender roles, and censorship. It's come to mean opposition to abortion rights and, particularly these days, resistance to the extension of full civil rights to gays and lesbians.

In covering the landmark beginning of legal gay marriages in Massachusetts last week, virtually every news organization featured the fulminations of officials from the Massachusetts Family Institute ("The piece of paper that says 'marriage' has been redefined and devalued!"), while Peter LaBarbera, executive director of the Illinois Family Institute ("A man marrying another man is a far cry from Rosa Parks!"), has become the go-to guy for local journalists seeking quotes from opponents of gay marriage.

The irony is that gay weddings mark an endorsement of family—of the power of that formal and lasting bond.

Eric Zorn is a columnist for the *Chicago Tribune*, where this essay was first published on May 23, 2004, and coauthor of *Murder of Innocence* (1990).

When two people get married, they are saying to society, "Yes! We believe in the fundamental importance of this institution in building and maintaining family ties. We want to join it and affirm that belief to the world."

And when a culture expands its definition of marriage to include the 15 expressions of lifelong commitment between two people of the same sex, it strengthens families by advancing the acceptance and tolerance of gay people.

Not every parent is as accepting of his gay child as Chicago Alderman Richard Mell, whose personal and political support for his daughter, who is a lesbian, has become a local legend. But the more our society loses its judgmental attitude about who loves whom and what sorts of unions are most normal, the closer we get to the day when extended families no longer are ripped apart by homosexuality.

I could argue that strengthening families is why we need to provide quality day care for working parents, why we need to work hard to maintain strict government neutrality in matters of faith, and why we should offer nonideological sex education to children and reproductive choice to women.

I could make the case that it reflects good family values to shift more of the tax burden to the rich, to support stem cell medical research and universal health care, to devote our energies to boosting public education, and to protect our natural environment against industrial polluters.

I could, but I won't.

"Family" is too important to too many of us to drag its name through 20 the muck of our bitter sociopolitical debates, let alone to yield it to one side or the other in the culture wars.

No one owns it. The left doesn't own peace and compassion, the right doesn't own the flag or the family.

The word "family" resonates profoundly in all of us—married, single, gay, straight, adopted, "biological," living alone or in crowded households bursting with the exuberant chaos of children. To have family, to be family with others, is to be fully human.

Mom always taught me to share. So, shall we?

READING AND DISCUSSION QUESTIONS

1. Where does Zorn most directly define the term *family*?
2. What does he mean when he says that we need to take family back? From whom?
3. How has the definition of the word *family* been politicized?
4. How do gay marriages expand the definition of family, according to Zorn?
5. What strategy is Zorn using when he tells his readers what he could argue, but won't?
6. What claim is Zorn supporting in the essay?

WRITING SUGGESTIONS

7. Even if you do not support same-sex marriage, do you believe that the definition of marriage is changing? Explain.

8. Explain whether or not you agree with this statement by Zorn: "And when a culture expands its definition of marriage to include the expressions of lifelong commitment between two people of the same sex, it strengthens families by advancing the acceptance and tolerance of gay people."

Don't Torture English to Soft-Pedal Abuse

GEOFFREY NUNBERG

"Torture is torture is torture," Secretary of State Colin Powell said this week in an interview on *Fox News Sunday* with Chris Wallace.

That depends on what papers you read. The media in France, Italy, and Germany have been routinely using the word "torture" in the headings of their stories on the abuses in the Abu Ghraib prison. And so have the British papers, not just the left-wing *Guardian* ("Torture at Abu Ghraib") but the right-wing *Express* ("Outrage at U.S. Torture of Prisoners") and Rupert Murdoch's *Times* ("Inside Baghdad's Torture Jail").

But the American press has been more circumspect, sticking with vaguer terms such as "abuse" and "mistreatment." In that, they may have been taking a cue from Defense Secretary Donald Rumsfeld. Asked about torture in the prison, he said, "What has been charged so far is abuse, which is different from torture. I'm not going to address the 'torture' word."

Some on the right have depicted the abuses even more mildly than that. In an opinion piece in the Los Angeles *Times*, Midge Decter called the treatment of detainees a "nasty hazing." Rush Limbaugh said it was "no different than what happens at the Skull and Bones initiation." On a San Francisco radio station, shock jocks were describing the prison as "Abu Grab-Ass" and talking about the treatment in a ribald way that made it sound like *Animal House III — Bluto Bonks Baghdad*.

Some American media have avoided "the 'torture' word" because   5
they want to play down the abuse of prisoners. Others are nervous about provoking attacks from the moral equivalence police: "Are you suggesting we're as bad as they are?"

Geoffrey Nunberg is a consulting professor in Stanford University's Department of Linguistics, the author of the book *Going Nucular* (2004), and a featured radio commentator. This essay was adapted from a piece he did on NPR's *Fresh Air*, that appeared in *Newsday* in May 2004.

But to a lot of Americans, *torture* and *torturer* don't seem quite the right words for the scenes in those photos. Torture may be familiar in the modern world, but it's also remote; we only see it up close in the movies. *Torture* suggests an aestheticized ritual. It doesn't seem odd that the torture scenes in *Battle of Algiers* should have a Bach chorale in the background.

In the movies, the torturer's cruelty is ironically counterpoised by a cosmopolitan and often effete manner—Laurence Olivier in *Marathon Man*, Gert Frobe in *Goldfinger*, or the Mohammed Khan character in *Lives of a Bengal Lancer* telling Gary Cooper, "We have ways of making men talk."

There are no middle-class middle-American torturers in our gallery, much less torturers with the pudding faces of those GIs who could have been working at McDonald's a year ago. And the humiliations they were inflicting didn't seem to have much in common with the rituals of pain and submission that *torture* brings to mind. The GIs went down another road, even if it fell off just as sharply.

That's what creates the sense of incongruity we feel when we see those photos. Those may have been far from Delta House high jinks, but you wouldn't know it from the clowning poses the GIs were striking.

True, "hazing" is a shamefully dishonest name for this. Leaving aside 10 the severity of the abuses, the prisoners weren't in a position to resign from the club, nor were they about to be given membership pins when pledge week was over. You may as well say that the Los Angeles police were hazing Rodney King.

But what went on in Abu Ghraib has at least this in common with

By Gary Varvel, *The Indianapolis Star,* Creators Syndicate

hazing: It's the sort of thing that any adolescent with a normal libido might be capable of—or worse, if the circumstances permit. As the Stanford psychologist Phil Zimbardo showed in a famous experiment more than thirty years ago, it doesn't take a lot to transform a group of well-mannered college students into sadistic prison guards, provided someone in authority seems to be giving them the nod.

Granted, what the Americans did in Abu Ghraib isn't remotely comparable to what went on there during Saddam Hussein's regime.

But it was torture, not just by the definitions of the Geneva Conventions, but by any ordinary standards of decency. Torture is torture is torture, as Secretary Powell put it—it isn't a place to be drawing fine semantic distinctions.

And it would be a good thing to acknowledge that "torture" is not quite as exotic an activity as the movies make it out to be. Looking at the unsettlingly familiar faces of the American soldiers in the Abu Ghraib photos, you realize that what can be most disturbing isn't the brutality that is inhuman so much as the brutality that is all too.

READING AND DISCUSSION QUESTIONS

1. Nunberg argues that the media control, to a certain extent at least, how the public perceive events. Besides the treatment of prisoners at Abu Ghraib prison in Iraq, how have the media exerted control over public perceptions?

2. What is Nunberg referring to when he makes this statement: "Others are nervous about provoking attacks from the moral equivalence police: 'Are you suggesting we're as bad as they are?'"

3. What is it that creates the sense of incongruity in the pictures from Abu Ghraib to which Nunberg refers?

4. In what sense was what went on at Abu Ghraib similar to hazing, although Nunberg calls hazing "a shamefully dishonest name for this"?

5. Explain what you believe Nunberg means by his last sentence.

WRITING SUGGESTIONS

6. Choose an event other than the Abu Ghraib scandal that was widely publicized and explain to what extent you feel the media controlled public perceptions of the event.

7. Write an essay in which you explain how governments sometimes hide the full truth behind euphemisms and other careful word choices. You may want to compare your ideas about language use with those expressed by George Orwell in his classic 1946 essay "Politics and the English Language."

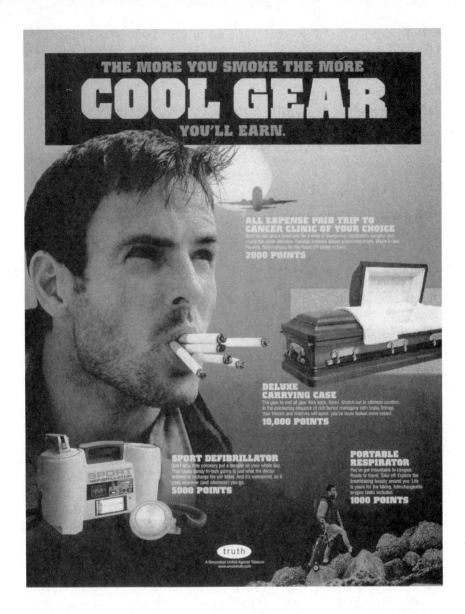

DISCUSSION QUESTIONS

1. The success of this advertisement depends largely on its play on the word *cool*. Why might the creators of this ad have decided to use that word in a prominent way in the ad? What other types of ads does this one recall?

2. What is the irony of the use of the word *cool* in this context?

3. How are the images in the ad used to make a point? Some of them, for instance, suggest a rugged outdoor lifestyle. Why?

4. How are the words in the smaller text accompanying each of the "prizes" used to reinforce the ad's intent?

5. What is this ad trying to "sell"?

Gay Marriage Shows Why We Need to Separate Church and State

HOWARD MOODY

If members of the church that I served for more than three decades were told I would be writing an article in defense of marriage, they wouldn't believe it. My reputation was that when people came to me for counsel about getting married, I tried to talk them out of it. More about that later.

We are now in the midst of a national debate on the nature of marriage, and it promises to be as emotional and polemical as the issues of abortion and homosexuality have been over the past century. What all these debates have in common is that they involved both the laws of the state and the theology of the church. The purpose of this writing is to suggest that the gay-marriage debate is less about the legitimacy of the loving relationship of a same-sex couple than about the relationship of church and state and how they define marriage.

In Western civilization, the faith and beliefs of Christendom played a major role in shaping the laws regarding social relations and moral behavior. Having been nurtured in the Christian faith from childhood and having served a lifetime as an ordained Baptist minister, I feel obligated first to address the religious controversy concerning the nature of marriage. If we look at the history of religious institutions regarding marriage we will find not much unanimity but amazing diversity—it is really a mixed bag. Those who base their position on "tradition" or "what the Bible says" will find anything but clarity. It depends on which "tradition" in what age reading from whose holy scriptures.

In the early tradition of the Jewish people, there were multiple wives and not all of them equal. Remember the story of Abraham's wives, Sara and Hagar. Sara couldn't get pregnant, so Hagar presented Abraham with a son. When Sara got angry with Hagar, she forced Abraham to send Hagar and her son Ishmael into the wilderness. In case Christians feel superior about their "tradition" of marriage, I would remind them that their scriptural basis is not as clear about marriage as we might hope. We have Saint Paul's conflicting and condescending words about the institution: "It's better not to marry." Karl Barth called this passage the Magna Carta of the single person. (Maybe we should have taken Saint Paul's advice more seriously. It might have prevented an earlier generation of parents from harassing, cajoling, and prodding our young until they were mar-

Reverend Howard Moody is minister emeritus of Judson Memorial Church in New York City. This article was published in July 2004 in the *Nation*.

ried.) In certain religious branches, the church doesn't recognize the licensed legality of marriage but requires that persons meet certain religious qualifications before the marriage is recognized by the church. For members of the Roman Catholic Church, a "legal divorce" and the right to remarry may not be recognized unless the first marriage has been declared null and void by a decree of the church. It is clear that there is no single religious view of marriage and that history has witnessed some monumental changes in the way "husband and wife" are seen in the relationship of marriage.

In my faith-based understanding, if freedom of choice means any-   5
thing to individuals (male or female), it means they have several options. They can be single and celibate without being thought of as strange or psychologically unbalanced. They can be single and sexually active without being labeled loose or immoral. Women can be single with child without being thought of as unfit or inadequate. If these choices had been real options, the divorce rate may never have reached nearly 50 percent.

The other, equally significant choice for people to make is that of lifetime commitment to each other and to seal that desire in the vows of a wedding ceremony. That understanding of marriage came out of my community of faith. In my years of ministry I ran a tight ship in regard to the performance of weddings. It wasn't because I didn't believe in marriage (I've been married for sixty years and have two wonderful offspring) but rather my unease about the way marriage was used to force people to marry so they wouldn't be "living in sin."

The failure of the institution can be seen in divorce statistics. I wanted people to know how challenging the promise of those vows was and not to feel this was something they had to do. My first question in premarital counseling was, "Why do you want to get married and spoil a beautiful friendship?" That question often elicited a thoughtful and emotional answer. Though I was miserly in the number of weddings I performed, I always made exceptions when there were couples who had difficulty finding clergy who would officiate. Their difficulty was because they weren't of the same religion, or they had made marital mistakes, or what they couldn't believe. Most of them were "ecclesiastical outlaws," barred from certain sacraments in the church of their choice.

The church I served had a number of gay and lesbian couples who had been together for many years, but none of them had asked for public weddings or blessings on their relationship. (There was one commitment ceremony for a gay couple at the end of my tenure.) It was as though they didn't need a piece of paper or a ritual to symbolize their lifelong commitment. They knew if they wanted a religious ceremony, their ministers would officiate and our religious community would joyfully witness.

It was my hope that since the institution of marriage had been used to exclude and demean members of the homosexual community, our church, which was open and affirming, would create with gays and lesbians a new kind of ceremony. It would be an occasion that symbolized, between two people of the same gender, a covenant of intimacy of two people to journey together, breaking new ground in human relationships—an alternative to marriage as we have known it.

However, I can understand why homosexuals want "to be married" 10 in the old-fashioned "heterosexual way." After all, most gays and lesbians were born of married parents, raised in a family of siblings; many were nourished in churches and synagogues, taught about a living God before Whom all Her creatures were equally loved. Why wouldn't they conceive their loving relationships in terms of marriage and family and desire that they be confirmed and understood as such? It follows that if these gays and lesbians see their relationship as faith-based, they would want a religious ceremony that seals their intentions to become lifelong partners, lovers and friends, that they would want to be "married."

Even though most religious denominations deny this ceremony to homosexual couples, more and more clergy are, silently and publicly, officiating at religious rituals in which gays and lesbians declare their vows before God and a faith community. One Catholic priest who defied his church's ban said: "We can bless a dog, we can bless a boat, but we can't say a prayer over two people who love each other. You don't have to call it marriage, you can call it a deep and abiding friendship, but you can bless it."

We have the right to engage in "religious disobedience" to the regulations of the judicatory that granted us the privilege to officiate at wedding ceremonies, and suffer the consequences. However, when it comes to civil law, it is my contention that the church and its clergy are on much shakier ground in defying the law.

In order to fully understand the conflict that has arisen in this debate over the nature of marriage, it is important to understand the difference between the religious definition of marriage and the state's secular and civil definition. The government's interest is in a legal definition of marriage—a social and voluntary contract between a man and woman in order to protect money, property, and children. Marriage is a civil union without benefit of clergy or religious definition. The state is not interested in why two people are "tying the knot," whether it's to gain money, secure a dynasty, or raise children. It may be hard for those of us who have a religious or romantic view of marriage to realize that loveless marriages are not that rare. Before the Pill, pregnancy was a frequent motive for getting married. The state doesn't care what the commitment of two people is, whether it's for life or as long as both of you love, whether it's sexually monogamous or an open marriage. There is nothing spiritual, mystical, or romantic about the state's license to marry—it's a legal contract.

Thus, George W. Bush is right when he says that "marriage is a sacred institution" when speaking as a Christian, as a member of his Methodist church. But as president of the United States and leader of all Americans, believers and unbelievers, he is wrong. What will surface in this debate as litigation and court decisions multiply is the history of the conflict between the church and the state in defining the nature of marriage. That history will become significant as we move toward a decision on who may be married.

After Christianity became the state religion of the Roman empire in 15 A.D. 325, the church maintained absolute control over the regulation of marriage for some 1,000 years. Beginning in the sixteenth century, English kings (especially Henry VIII, who found the inability to get rid of a wife extremely oppressive) and other monarchs in Europe began to wrest control from the church over marital regulations. Ever since, kings, presidents, and rulers of all kinds have seen how important the control of marriage is to the regulation of social order. In this nation, the government has always been in charge of marriage.

That is why it was not a San Francisco mayor licensing same-sex couples that really threatened the president's religious understanding of marriage but rather the Supreme Judicial Court of Massachusetts, declaring marriage between same-sex couples a constitutional right, that demanded a call for constitutional amendment. I didn't understand how important that was until I read an op-ed piece in the *Boston Globe* by Peter Gomes, professor of Christian morals and the minister of Memorial Church at Harvard University, that reminds us of a seminal piece of our history:

> The Dutch made civil marriage the law of the land in 1590, and the first marriage in New England, that of Edward Winslow to the widow Susannah White, was performed on May 12, 1621, in Plymouth by Governor William Bradford, in exercise of his office as magistrate.
>
> There would be no clergyman in Plymouth until the arrival of the Reverend Ralph Smith in 1629, but even then marriage would continue to be a civil affair, as these first Puritans opposed the English custom of clerical marriage as unscriptural. Not until 1692, when Plymouth Colony was merged into that of Massachusetts Bay, were the clergy authorized by the new province to solemnize marriages. To this day in the Commonwealth the clergy, including those of the archdiocese, solemnize marriage legally as agents of the Commonwealth and by its civil authority. Chapter 207 of the General Laws of Massachusetts tells us who may perform such ceremonies.

Now even though it is the civil authority of the state that defines the rights and responsibilities of marriage and therefore who can be married, the state is no more infallible than the church in its judgments. It wasn't until the mid-twentieth century that the Supreme Court declared antimiscegenation laws unconstitutional. Even after that decision, many mainline churches, where I started my ministry, unofficially discouraged interracial marriages, and many of my colleagues were forbidden to perform such weddings.

The civil law view of marriage has as much historical diversity as the church's own experience because, in part, the church continued to influence the civil law. Although it was the Bible that made "the husband the head of his wife," it was common law that "turned the married pair legally into one person—the husband," as Nancy Cott documents in her book *Public Vows: A History of Marriage and the Nation* (an indispensable resource for anyone seeking to understand the changing nature of marriage in the nation's history). She suggests that "the legal doctrine of marital unity was called coverture . . . [which] meant that the wife could not use legal avenues such as suits or contracts, own assets, or execute legal documents without her husband's collaboration." This view of the wife would not hold water in any court in the land today.

As a matter of fact, even in the religious understanding of President Bush and his followers, allowing same-sex couples the right to marry seems a logical conclusion. If marriage is "the most fundamental institution of civilization" and a major contributor to the social order in our society, why would anyone want to shut out homosexuals from the "glorious attributes" of this "sacred institution"? Obviously, the only reason one can discern is that the opponents believe that gay and lesbian people are not worthy of the benefits and spiritual blessings of "marriage."

At the heart of the controversy raging over same-sex marriage is the   20 religious and constitutional principle of the separation of church and state. All of us can probably agree that there was never a solid wall of separation, riddled as it is with breaches. The evidence of that is seen in the ambiguity of tax-free religious institutions, "in God we trust" printed on our money and "under God" in the Pledge of Allegiance to our country. All of us clergy, who are granted permission by the state to officiate at legal marriage ceremonies, have already compromised the "solid wall" by signing the license issued by the state. I would like to believe that my authority to perform religious ceremonies does not come from the state but derives from the vows of ordination and my commitment to God. I refuse to repeat the words, "by the authority invested in me by the State of New York, I pronounce you husband and wife," but by signing the license, I've become the state's "handmaiden."

It seems fitting therefore that we religious folk should now seek to sharpen the difference between ecclesiastical law and civil law as we beseech the state to clarify who can be married by civil law. Further evidence that the issue of church and state is part of the gay-marriage controversy is that two Unitarian ministers have been arrested for solemnizing unions between same-sex couples when no state licenses were involved. Ecclesiastical law may punish those clergy who disobey marital regulations, but the state has no right to invade church practices and criminalize clergy under civil law. There should have been a noisy outcry from all churches, synagogues, and mosques at the government's outrageous contravention of the sacred principle of the "free exercise of religion."

I come from a long line of Protestants who believe in a "free church in a free state." In the issue before this nation, the civil law is the determinant of the regulation of marriage, regardless of our religious views, and the Supreme Court will finally decide what the principle of equality means in our Constitution in the third century of our life together as a people. It is likely that the Commonwealth of Massachusetts will probably lead the nation on this matter, as the State of New York led to the Supreme Court decision to allow women reproductive freedom.

So what is marriage? It depends on whom you ask, in what era, in what culture. Like all words or institutions, human definitions, whether religious or secular, change with time and history. When our beloved Constitution was written, blacks, Native Americans, and, to some extent, women were quasi-human beings with no rights or privileges, but today they are recognized as persons with full citizenship rights. The definition of marriage has been changing over the centuries in this nation, and it will change yet again as homosexuals are seen as ordinary human beings.

In time, and I believe that time is now, we Americans will see that all the fears foisted on us by religious zealots were not real. Heterosexual marriage will still flourish with its statistical failures. The only difference will be that some homosexual couples will join them and probably account for about the same number of failed relationships. And we will discover that it did not matter whether the couples were joined in a religious ceremony or a secular and civil occasion for the statement of their intentions.

Will It Be Marriage or Civil Union?

JO ANN CITRON

This fall, while the right was still staggering from the U.S. Supreme Court's decision in *Lawrence v. Texas*, Massachusetts dealt conservatives another body blow when its highest court legalized same-sex marriage. In a 4–3 ruling authored by Chief Justice Margaret Marshall, the Supreme Judicial Court (SJC) held that denying marriage to homosexuals violates the Massachusetts Declaration of Rights, the state constitution. To remedy the violation, the court changed the common-law definition of civil marriage to eliminate its opposite-sex requirement and to compel the issuance of marriage licenses to qualified persons of the same sex. Civil marriage in Massachusetts now means "the voluntary union of two

Jo Ann Citron practices alternate family and civil rights law with the firm Altman & Citron and is a member of the Women's Studies Department at Wellesley College. The article was published in the *Gay and Lesbian Review Worldwide* in March–April 2004.

persons as spouses, to the exclusion of all others." The legislature, which was directed to "take such action as it may deem appropriate in light of this opinion," has been running for cover ever since.[1]

A friend recently asked me how important the Massachusetts decision is in the struggle to achieve marriage equality in the United States. I was struck, first of all, by the terms of the question because "marriage equality" is not the same as "marriage." The issue all along has been whether gays will get marriage or some equivalent formality that will make them equal to their heterosexual counterparts. There are those who say that civil union is marriage equality. It's what Vermont said and what many Massachusetts legislators are saying in their desperate search for an escape route from the SJC ruling. It's also what William Eskridge claimed in his 2002 book, *Equality Practice: Civil Union and the Future of Gay Rights*, where he argues that, while there is no principled basis for withholding marriage from gays and lesbians, the gay community should bow to the political will of the majority and move slowly, accepting the equality of civil union now and pressing for marriage later when it becomes more palatable to the majority. Eskridge views *Baker v. State*, the Vermont civil union decision, as the equivalent of *Brown v. Board of Education*, the 1954 landmark civil rights decision that opened the way to racial integration in this country. Marriage activist Evan Wolfson, on the other hand, views *Baker* as the gay rights version of *Plessy v. Ferguson*, the railway carriage case that authorized "separate but equal" status for disfavored minorities.

This essay is being written during the 180-day waiting period following the issuance of the decision, a period of either genuine confusion or deliberate obfuscation, depending on the degree of cynicism with which you view the political process. It might be useful at this point to summarize what the court said and how the legislature has responded. The court began by reminding everyone that the Massachusetts marriage statute is a licensing law. Because marriage has always been understood to mean the union of a man and a woman, the statute cannot be construed to authorize issuing a license to two people of the same sex. But to bar gay couples from all the benefits, protections, and obligations that accompany marriage violates the Massachusetts constitution, which means that the current marriage licensing law is unconstitutional. The remedy the court fashioned was to change the common law definition of civil marriage to eliminate its opposite-sex requirement, thereby removing the bar that excludes gay couples from obtaining marriage licenses.

Rather than declare that cities and towns must immediately begin to issue marriage licenses to gays, which would have created chaos, the court granted the legislature 180 days to revise state statutes so as to bring them into line with its ruling and to clean up a complicated domestic relations regulatory scheme that refers to husbands and wives. The court reminded the legislature that it retains "broad discretion to regulate marriage." This

---

[1] *Goodridge v. Department of Public Health.*

means that the Legislature can continue to impose certain restrictions upon persons who wish to marry. The legislature may refuse to authorize granting a marriage license to persons under a certain age, or to siblings, or to a parent and child. It may require a blood test or a birth certificate, or that applicants turn around three times and face north, or anything else that would be constitutional. But, as I read the decision, the legislature may not refuse to grant a license to otherwise qualified gay couples.

The SJC was perfectly clear in stating that the remedy for the consti-   5
tutional violation was the reformulation of the definition of civil marriage. Yet many legislators, together with the current attorney general, want to take a different view of the matter. They have seized upon the "protections, benefits, and obligations" language in the opinion in the hope that, by providing the benefits that marriage yields in our society, they can avoid providing marriage itself. The legislature has asked the SJC to render an advisory opinion about a civil union bill, and the SJC has invited interested parties to submit briefs. Meanwhile, the Massachusetts constitutional convention is scheduled to meet on February 11, 2004, to vote on a Defense of Marriage Act or DOMA that, in its present form, would not only prevent gay marriage but would also outlaw domestic partner benefits. If the legislature passes the DOMA in a second convention, the measure would appear on the ballot in November of 2006 and voters could, by a simple majority, amend the state constitution to make gay marriage, civil union, and domestic partnerships illegal. The political reality is that such a DOMA will probably not garner the necessary votes either in the legislature or among voters; however, a simple DOMA limiting itself to marriage is more likely to succeed, especially in the face of the SJC decision, which presents the right with what it would call a "clear and present danger." This means that gay marriage could become legal in Massachusetts on May 18, 2004, via the SJC decision and illegal in Massachusetts on November 14, 2006, via a voter referendum. No one knows what will happen to gay couples who marry in the interim. Let the courts sort through that one!

Massachusetts has a good track record when it comes to gay families: It permits second-parent adoption; it allows two women to appear as "parent" on a child's birth certificate; it protects the relationship between a child and her nonbiological parent. At the very least, *Goodridge* is going to yield "marriage equality" in some form of civil union. The problem, of course, is that there is no such thing as "marriage equality" for anyone who files federal income tax returns, bequeaths an estate, or travels outside of Massachusetts. When it comes to federal benefits or the tax-free transfer of marital property or the ability to have another state recognize your Massachusetts relationship, marriage is the only status that will do. This is why some are downplaying the SJC decision, pointing out that even if people are able to marry in Massachusetts, their status will not be recognized by the federal government or by any other state with a DOMA. In that respect, marriage is indeed no different from civil union.

In fact, it might even be worse for a while. We're beginning to see judges in some states accept the validity of a Vermont civil union. Even in states with a DOMA, it will be possible to find a judge who would give full faith and credit to a civil union because most DOMA laws have nothing to say about civil unions. Not so with marriage. For the time being, a Massachusetts marriage will be even less portable than a Vermont civil union.

But let there be no mistake: Whatever happens in Massachusetts is absolutely critical to how the gay marriage question will be answered in the rest of the United States. What happens here is even more important than what happened in Vermont. Here's why. The next marriage case with a reasonable likelihood of success is working its way through the courts in New Jersey, a state with a history of progressive court decisions. New Jersey will be looking very carefully at the way Vermont and Massachusetts have addressed the marriage question. If the Massachusetts SJC ratifies its decision and mandates the issuance of marriage licenses, New Jersey will look at its predecessor states and see two alternative models, marriage and civil union. New Jersey will choose one or the other. But the SJC could fail to confirm its marriage decision and approve instead some form of civil union. Coupled with the Vermont ruling, this will create a critical mass in favor of civil union, an outcome that will make it far more likely that New Jersey will opt for civil union over marriage. After that, the rest of the states will almost certainly fall into line with civil unions, and that will spell the end of gay marriage, probably forever.

Ironically, it may also mean the end of marriage in its present form, the one that the right is working so hard to preserve. Conservatives Andrew Sullivan and David Brooks have argued that the best way to protect marriage would be to open it to anyone who wants to vow fidelity and is willing to forego an easy exit from a supposedly permanent relationship. Marriage is, after all, a conservative institution, and persons who enter it with the blessing of the state may not leave it without the state's permission. Already, as a result of the marriage cases and their surrounding discourse, the very term "marriage" is being qualified. We now speak of "civil marriage" to distinguish it from the religious ceremonies that are but one of its aspects. Insofar as material benefits are concerned, marriage is a civil institution. Those material benefits can attach just as easily to any civil institution the state cares to identify. This is, after all, the point of wanting to offer gays something called "union" rather than something called "marriage." Nothing but prejudice prevents state and federal governments from offering to partners in a civil union the identical benefits, protections, and obligations that the state now offers to spouses.

William Eskridge is wrong in thinking that civil union is a step on the path towards marriage. Civil union and marriage are not sequential; they are alternatives to one another. There is no reason to think that the country will permit civil union now and confer marriage later. In fact, the reality is likely to be quite the reverse. Because of equal protection considerations, the civil union alternative will have to be available to straights as well as gays. And if my analysis is correct, it will become more widely available to everyone in the coming years. At the moment, there is little incentive for marriage-eligible couples to elect a civil union. But this will change.

It is not difficult to imagine a tacit compromise in which the right is 10 allowed to maintain its stranglehold on marriage in exchange for allowing the material benefits now associated with it to break free and accompany civil union. This is another reason why the Massachusetts decision in favor of marriage is strategically important. As long as even a single state has legalized marriage, civil union becomes more attractive to the right. And the gay community can leverage those few gay marriage licenses into a demand that marriage benefits attach to civil unions.

In my view, this would be a good outcome. I say this as someone who views marriage as a regressive institution that has never been good to women, that insidiously creates insiders and outsiders, and, most importantly, that violates the separation of church and state at the heart of our form of government. The state should not be in the business of attaching material benefits to a religious institution. The right to social security death benefits, the right to favorable tax treatment, the right to take your formalized relationship with you when you travel, should be detached from marriage altogether and should be awarded according to some other equitable system. To the extent that this becomes so, there will eventually be no material difference between the old form of marriage and the new form of civil unions. Traditional marriage will endure as a religious institution. Already there are hundreds of clergy willing to perform marriage ceremonies for gay congregants and thousands of gay couples who have participated in these ceremonies whose benefits are wholly spiritual. Over time, civil union and civil marriage will ultimately come to mean much the same thing. Whether the SJC ratifies its original position or abandons it, *Goodridge* brings us closer to a consensus around civil union. It is time for the gay community to turn its attention to winning for civil union all the rights, benefits, protections, and obligations of marriage. That is the truly revolutionary project.

DISCUSSION QUESTIONS

1. Why is definition a critical element in Moody's argument? Why is it a critical element in Citron's? Do the two of them agree on a definition of marriage?

2. What is Moody's attitude toward same-sex marriage? Why, in his opinion, do more serious problems arise when it comes to the laws of the state than the theology of the church?

3. Why does Moody feel that President Bush was wrong in saying, as president, that "marriage is a sacred institution"? Were you surprised by Moody's explanation of the history of marriage in our country?

4. When Citron published her essay, the nation was awaiting Massachusetts's decision on the legality of same-sex marriages. What was her biggest fear about the future of the legal standing of same-sex relationships?

5. Analyze Citron's analogy between decisions regarding same-sex unions and two Supreme Court decisions regarding racial integration, *Plessy v. Ferguson* and *Brown v. Board of Education*.

6. What is the author's claim in each of the two essays?

TAKING THE DEBATE ONLINE

For these and additional research URLs, see bedfordstmartins.com/rottenberg.

- **www.allianceformarriage.org**

  This site is maintained by the Alliance for Marriage (AFM), a nonprofit research and educational organization dedicated to promoting marriage and addressing the epidemic of fatherless families in the United States.

- **www.keepmedia.com/featuredtopics/gaymarriage**

  This site keeps updated lists of articles on gay marriage from a variety of publications.

- **www.now.org/issues/lgbi/marr-rep-2.html**

  The National Organization for Women's site keeps current on gay and lesbian issues as they impact the lives of women.

- **www.stateline.org/stateline**

  Stateline maintains recent information on the status of same-sex marriage, organized by state.

ASSIGNMENTS FOR UNDERSTANDING DEFINITION

1. Contrast the claims made by Jo Ann Citron in "Will It Be Marriage or Civil Union?" and Howard Moody in "Gay Marriage Shows Why We Need to Separate Church and State."

2. Contrast Citron's claim with that supported by Eric Zorn in "Family a Symbol of Love and Life, but Not Politics."

3. Use Orlando Patterson's "Race by the Numbers" as a starting point to discuss to what extent you feel you either are or are not defined by your racial identity.

4. Choose a print ad and analyze how the designer uses text and image to support the ad's claim.

5. Explain how the cartoon on page 89 illustrates how, in politics, the meaning of a term is relative. Or choose another cartoon and explain how different ways of defining a term can be the source of humor.

6. Use one or more cases to illustrate how, in a court of law, guilt or innocence can hinge on the matter of definition.

7. Many recent controversial movements and causes are identified by terms that have come to mean different things to different people. Choose one of the following and define it, explaining both the favorable and unfavorable connotations of the term. Use examples to clarify the meaning.

   a. abortion

   b. Palestinian homeland

   c. affirmative action

   d. assisted suicide

   e. the Patriot Act

8. Choose two words that are sometimes confused, and define them to make their differences clear. *Examples:* authoritarianism and totalitarianism, envy and jealousy, sympathy and pity, cult and established church, justice and equality, liberal and radical, agnostic and atheist.

9. Define *good parent, good teacher,* or *good husband* or *wife.* Try to uncover the assumptions on which your definition is based. (For example, in defining a good teacher, students sometimes mention the ability of the teacher to maintain order. Does this mean that the teacher alone is responsible for classroom order?)

10. Write about an important or widely used term whose meaning has changed since you first learned it. Such terms often come from the slang of particular groups: drug users, rock music fans, musicians, athletes, computer programmers, or software developers.

11. Define the differences between necessities, comforts, and luxuries. Consider how they have changed over time.

CHAPTER 4

Claims

Claims, or propositions, represent answers to the question: "What are you trying to prove?" Although they are the conclusions of your arguments, they often appear as thesis statements. Claims can be classified as *claims of fact, claims of value,* and *claims of policy.*

CLAIMS OF FACT

Claims of fact assert that a condition has existed, exists, or will exist and that their support consists of factual information—information such as statistics, examples, and testimony that most responsible observers assume can be verified.

Many facts are not matters for argument: Our own senses can confirm them, and other observers will agree about them. We can agree that a certain number of students were in the classroom at a particular time, that lions make a louder sound than kittens, and that apples are sweeter than potatoes.

We can also agree about information that most of us can rarely confirm for ourselves—information in reference books, such as atlases, almanacs, and telephone directories; data from scientific resources about the physical world; and happenings reported in the media. We can agree on the reliability of such information because we trust the observers who report it.

However, the factual map is constantly being redrawn by new data in such fields as history and science that cause us to reevaluate our conclusions. For example, the discovery of the Dead Sea Scrolls in 1947 revealed that some books of the Bible—Isaiah, for one—were far older than we had thought. Researchers at New York Hospital–Cornell Medical Center say that many symptoms previously thought inevitable in the aging process are now believed to be treatable and reversible symptoms of depression.[1]

In your conversations with other students you probably generate claims of fact every day, some of which can be verified without much effort, others of which are more difficult to substantiate.

CLAIM: Most of the students in this class come from towns within fifty miles of Boston.

To prove this the arguer would need only to ask the students in the class where they come from.

CLAIM: Students who take their courses pass/fail make lower grades than those who take them for specific grades.

In this case the arguer would need to have access to student records showing the specific grades given by instructors. (In most schools the instructor awards a letter grade, which is then recorded as a pass or a fail if the student has elected this option.)

CLAIM: The Red Sox will win the pennant this year.

This claim is different from the others because it is an opinion about what will happen in the future. But it can be verified (in the future) and is therefore classified as a claim of fact.

More complex factual claims about political and scientific matters remain controversial because proof on which all or most observers will agree is difficult or impossible to obtain.

CLAIM: Bilingual programs are less effective than English-only programs in preparing students for higher education.

CLAIM: The only life in the universe exists on this planet.

Not all claims are so neatly stated or make such unambiguous assertions. Because we recognize that there are exceptions to most generalizations, we often qualify our claims with words such as *generally, usually, probably,* and *as a rule.* It would not be true to state flatly, for example, "College graduates earn more than high school graduates." This statement is generally true, but we know that some high school graduates who are electricians or city bus drivers or sanitation workers earn more than college graduates who are schoolteachers or nurses or social workers. In

---

[1] *New York Times,* February 20, 1983, sec. 22, p. 4.

making such a claim, therefore, the writer should qualify it with a word that limits the claim.

To support a claim of fact, the writer needs to produce sufficient and appropriate data—that is, examples, statistics, and testimony from reliable sources. Provided this requirement is met, the task of establishing a factual claim would seem to be relatively straightforward. But as you have probably already discovered in ordinary conversation, finding convincing support for factual claims can pose a number of problems. Whenever you try to establish a claim of fact, you will need to ask at least three questions about the material you plan to use: *What are sufficient and appropriate data? Who are the reliable authorities?* and *Have I made clear whether my statements are facts or inferences?*

■ Sufficient and Appropriate Data

The amount and kind of data for a particular argument depend on the importance and complexity of the subject. The more controversial the subject, the more facts and testimony you will need to supply. Consider the claim "The murder rate in New York City is lower this year than last year." If you want to prove the truth of this claim, obviously you will have to provide a larger quantity of data than for a claim that says, "By following three steps, you can train your dog to sit and heel in fifteen minutes." In examining your facts and opinions, an alert reader will want to know if they are accurate, current, and typical of other facts and opinions that you have not mentioned.

The reader will also look for testimony from more than one authority, although there may be cases where only one or two experts who have achieved a unique breakthrough in their field will be sufficient. These cases would probably occur most frequently in the physical sciences. The Nobel Prize winners James Watson and Francis Crick, who first discovered the structure of the DNA molecule, are an example of such experts. However, in the case of the so-called Hitler diaries that surfaced in 1983, at least a dozen experts—journalists, historians, bibliographers who could verify the age of the paper and the ink—were needed to establish that they were forgeries.

■ Reliable Authorities

Not all those who pronounce themselves experts are trustworthy. Your own experience has probably taught you that you cannot always believe the reports of an event by a single witness. The witness may be poorly trained to make accurate observations—about the size of a crowd, the speed of a vehicle, his distance from an object. Or his own physical conditions—illness, intoxication, disability—may prevent him from seeing or hearing or smelling accurately. The circumstances under which he observes the event—darkness, confusion, noise—may also impair his observation. In addition, the witness may be biased for or against the outcome of the event, as in a hotly contested baseball game, where the observer sees the play that he wants to see. You will find the problems associated with the biases of witnesses to be relevant to your work as a reader and writer of argumentative essays.

You will undoubtedly want to quote authors in some of your arguments. In most cases you will not be familiar with the authors. But there are guidelines for determining their reliability: the rank or title of the experts, the acceptance of their publications by other experts, their association with reputable universities, research centers, or think tanks. For example, for a paper on euthanasia, you might decide to quote from an article by Paul R. McHugh, the Henry Phipps Professor of Psychiatry at the Johns Hopkins University School of Medicine and psychiatrist in chief at the Johns Hopkins Hospital in Baltimore. For a paper on crime by youth groups, you might want to use material supplied by Elizabeth Glazer, chief of Crime Control Strategies in the U.S. Attorney's office for the Southern District of New York, where she previously served as chief of both the Organized Crime Unit and Violent Gang Unit. Most readers of your arguments would agree that these authors have impressive credentials in their fields.

What if several respectable sources are in conflict? What if the experts disagree? After a preliminary investigation of a controversial subject, you may decide that you have sufficient material to support your claim. But if you read further, you may discover that other material presented by equally qualified experts contradicts your original claim. In such circumstances you will find it impossible to make a definitive claim. (On pp. 160–73 in the treatment of support of a claim by evidence, you will find a more elaborate discussion of this vexing problem.)

■ Facts or Inferences

We have defined a fact as a statement that can be verified. An inference is "a statement about the unknown on the basis of the known."[2] The difference between facts and inferences is important to you as the writer of an argument because an inference is an *interpretation,* or an opinion reached after informed evaluation of evidence. As you and your classmates wait in your classroom on the first day of the semester, a middle-aged woman wearing a tweed jacket and a corduroy skirt appears and stands in the front of the room. You don't know who this woman is. However, based on what you do know about the appearance of many

---

[2] S. I. Hayakawa, *Language in Thought and Action* (New York: Harcourt, Brace, Jovanovich, 1978), p. 35.

college teachers and the fact that teachers usually stand in front of the classroom, you may *infer* that this woman is your teacher. You will probably be right. But you cannot be certain until you have more information. Perhaps you will find out that this woman has come from the department office to tell you that your teacher is sick and cannot meet the class today.

You have probably come across a statement such as the following in a newspaper or magazine: "Excessive television viewing has caused the steady decline in the reading ability of children and teenagers." Presented this way, the statement is clearly intended to be read as a factual claim that has been or can be proved. But it is an inference. The facts, which can be and have been verified, are (1) the reading ability of children and teenagers has declined and (2) the average child views television for six or more hours a day. (Whether this amount of time is "excessive" is also an opinion.) The cause-and-effect relation between the two facts is an interpretation of the investigator, who has examined both the reading scores and the amount of time spent in front of the television set and *inferred* that one is the cause of the other. The causes of the decline in reading scores are probably more complex than the original statement indicates. Since we can seldom or never create laboratory conditions for testing the influence of television separate from other influences in the family and the community, any statement about the connection between reading scores and television viewing can only be a guess.

By definition, no inference can ever do more than suggest probabilities. Of course, some inferences are much more reliable than others and afford a high degree of probability. Almost all claims in science are based on inferences, interpretations of data on which most scientists agree. Paleontologists find a few ancient bones from which they make inferences about an animal that might have been alive millions of years ago. We can never be absolutely certain that the reconstruction of the dinosaur in the museum is an exact copy of the animal it is supposed to represent, but the probability is fairly high because no other interpretation works so well to explain all the observable data—the existence of the bones in a particular place, their age, their relation to other fossils, and their resemblance to the bones of existing animals with which the paleontologist is familiar.

Inferences are profoundly important, and most arguments could not proceed very far without them. But an inference is not a fact. The writer of an argument must make it clear when he or she offers an inference, an interpretation, or an opinion that it is not a fact.

Writer's Guide: Defending a Claim of Fact

Here are some guidelines that should help you to defend a factual claim. (We'll say more about support of factual claims in Chapter 5.)

1. Be sure that the claim — what you are trying to prove — is clearly stated, preferably at the beginning of your paper.

2. Define terms that may be controversial or ambiguous. For example, in trying to prove that "radicals" had captured the student government, you would have to define "radicals," distinguishing them from "liberals" or members of other ideological groups, so that your readers would understand exactly what you meant.

3. As far as possible, make sure that your evidence — facts and opinions, or interpretations of the facts — fulfills the appropriate criteria. The data should be sufficient, accurate, recent, typical; the authorities should be reliable.

4. Make clear when conclusions about the data are inferences or interpretations, not facts. For example, you might write, "The series of lectures titled Modern Architecture, sponsored by our fraternity, was poorly attended because the students at this college aren't interested in discussions of art." What proof could you offer that this *was* the reason and that your statement was a *fact*? Perhaps there were other reasons that you hadn't considered.

5. Emphasize your most important evidence by placing it at the beginning or the end of your paper (the most emphatic positions in an essay) and devoting more space to it.

SAMPLE ANNOTATED ESSAY: CLAIM OF FACT

A Reassuring Scorecard for Affirmative Action

MICHAEL M. WEINSTEIN

Introduction:
a) Review of the
attack on affirmative
action

Affirmative action — preferential treatment toward women and minority applicants as practiced by employers, university admissions officers, and government contractors — remains under attack thirty-two years after President

Michael M. Weinstein, Ph.D., is a senior fellow on the Council on Foreign Relations. He was on the editorial board of the *New York Times* when he wrote this October 17, 2000, article.

Johnson ordered federal contractors to seek female and minority employees. Two states have voted to wipe out the use of race- and gender-based preferences by state agencies. Parents have challenged the race-based admissions policies of public schools. Even Joseph Lieberman, the [2000] Democratic candidate for vice president, once opposed policies "based on group preference instead of individual merit."

b) Specific criticism

Some of affirmative action's critics contend that preferential hiring and admissions are always wrong in principle no matter how attractive the consequences. But other critics focus on affirmative action's alleged failings. According to this argument, the policy creates divisive workplaces, breeds cynicism and corruption, and hurts many of the individuals it is supposed to help. That debate should turn on the facts. Instead it has been fueled almost entirely by anecdotes—until now.

Refutation: authoritative source of new data

In the most recent issue of the *Journal of Economic Literature,* a publication of the American Economic Association, two respected economists provide an eighty-five page review of over two hundred serious scientific studies of affirmative action. Harry Holzer of Georgetown University and David Neumark of Michigan State University ferret out every statistic from the studies to measure the effects of affirmative action. Harsh critics of affirmative action will not find much comfort.

Claim: general benefits for women and minorities under affirmative action

The authors concede the evidence is sometimes murky. Yet they find that affirmative action produces tangible benefits for women, for minority entrepreneurs, students, and workers, and for the overall economy. Employers adopting the policy increase the relative number of women and minority employees by an average of between 10 and 15 percent. Affirmative action has helped boost the percentage of blacks attending college by a factor of three and the percentage of blacks enrolled in medical school by a factor of four since the early 1960s. Between 1982 and 1991 the number of federal contracts going to black-owned businesses rose by 125 percent, even though the total number of federal contracts rose by less than 25 percent during the period.

Support: a) Data about employment, education, business

To no one's surprise, the two economists rivet on economic performance. Here, the survey is in-   5 teresting for what it does *not* find. There is, the authors say, little credible evidence that affirmative action appointees perform badly or diminish the overall performance of the economy.

b) Data about credentials

Women hired under affirmative action, they say, largely match their male counterparts in credentials and performance. Blacks and Hispanics hired under affirmative action generally lag behind on credentials, such as education, but usually perform about as well as nonminority employees.

c) Data about worker performance

In a separate study, Mr. Holzer and Mr. Neumark interviewed thousands of supervisors and showed that they ranked most affirmative action hires roughly the same as ordinary hires. The authors find that companies undertaking affirmative action use extensive recruitment and training to bring workers who fall a notch below average on credentials up to the performance level of other workers.

d) Data about student performance

Critics have often pointed to the wide gap between SAT scores of black and white students admitted to selective universities as proof that they are lowering standards for minority students and putting them in settings they cannot handle. But the use of a test gap as a measure of reverse discrimination is misleading. Much of the gap would exist even if admissions were race-blind. Colleges pull applicants from a population that includes many more high-scoring whites than blacks.

A discrimination-free procedure would start by tapping the pool, largely white, of high scorers and then turn to the pool of lower-scoring whites and blacks. The average test scores for whites admitted to the college would thus exceed that of the blacks admitted.

To be sure, some selective universities add to 10 the test gap by giving preference to minority applicants. But, the data shows, black students at elite colleges graduate at greater rates than blacks at less demanding colleges, disproving claims that affirmative action disserves minority students.

e) Data about social benefits

The Holzer-Neumark survey shows that affirmative action in admissions has produced significant social benefits. For example, black doctors choose more often than their white medical school classmates to serve indigent or minority patients in inner cities and rural areas.

Conclusion: Contrary to criticism, evidence justifies affirmative action.

Though favorable, these findings hardly end the debate on affirmative action. The critics who refuse to accept government-sanctioned racial or gender preferences no matter what the benefit will continue to object. Affirmative action can be misused, as when whites running a company create a fiction of black ownership to qualify for credits in seeking government contracts. But the evidence marshaled by the authors largely vindicates affirmative action and should provide the ammunition for rebutting those critics who refuse to take facts into account.

■ Analysis

This article offers evidence that affirmative action provides benefits to women and minorities. A claim of fact often responds to some widely held belief that the author considers to be wrong—in this case, the failure of affirmative action. We need to ask three questions about a claim of fact: Are the data sufficient and appropriate? Are the authorities reliable? Are the distinctions between facts and inferences clear? Within its brief compass, this argument comes close to satisfying these criteria. In addition, its organization is straightforward, with clearly defined introduction, body, and conclusion.

The first three paragraphs constitute the introduction. First, the author reviews some of the claims of the opposition. At the end of the second paragraph, he makes clear his own emphasis: "That debate should turn on the facts." He then cites his source for the facts—a report in a respected professional journal by two university economists, who have examined the data on affirmative action in over two hundred serious scientific studies. This information reassures the reader that the first two criteria for judging a claim of fact will be met.

The body of the essay contains support for the claim, first in a short summary, then in substantial detail. Much of the data is statistical, a specific form of information that most readers find convincing and relatively easy to assimilate. (Of course, readers must regard the source as trustworthy.) The author has offered some interpretations—in paragraph 8, for example—to clarify what he considers a misunderstanding. Notice also the use of "To be sure," an expression that usually indicates that the writer recognizes an exception to his view. But the argument stands firmly on the facts. The ending is one often used by debaters—a modest challenge to the opposing side.

Unlike claims of fact, which attempt to prove that something is true and which can be validated by reference to the data, claims of value make a judgment. They express approval or disapproval. They attempt to prove that some action, belief, or condition is right or wrong, good or bad, beautiful or ugly, worthwhile or undesirable.

CLAIM: Democracy is superior to any other form of government.

CLAIM: Killing animals for sport is wrong.

CLAIM: The Sam Rayburn Building in Washington is an aesthetic failure.

Some claims of value are simply expressions of tastes, likes and dislikes, or preferences and prejudices. The Latin proverb "De gustibus non est disputandum" states that we cannot dispute about tastes. Suppose you express a preference for chocolate over vanilla. If your listener should ask why you prefer this flavor, you cannot refer to an outside authority or produce data or appeal to her moral sense to convince her that your preference is justified.

Many claims of value, however, can be defended or attacked on the basis of standards that measure the worth of an action, a belief, or an object. As far as possible, our personal likes and dislikes should be supported by reference to these standards. Value judgments occur in any area of human experience, but whatever the area, the analysis will be the same. We ask the arguer who is defending a claim of value: *What are the standards or criteria for deciding that this action, this belief, or this object is good or bad, beautiful or ugly, desirable or undesirable? Does the thing you are defending fulfill these criteria?*

There are two general areas in which people often disagree about matters of value: aesthetics and morality. They are also the areas that offer the greatest challenge to the writer. What follows is a discussion of some of the elements of analysis that you should consider in defending a claim of value in these areas.

Aesthetics is the study of beauty and the fine arts. Controversies over works of art — the aesthetic value of books, paintings, sculpture, architecture, dance, drama, and movies — rage fiercely among experts and laypeople alike. They may disagree on the standards for judging or, even if they agree about standards, may disagree about how successfully the art object under discussion has met these standards.

Consider a discussion about popular music. Hearing someone praise the singing of Manu Chao, a hugely popular European singer now playing to American crowds, you might ask why he is highly regarded. You expect Chao's fans to say more than "I like him" or "He's great." You expect them to give reasons to support their claims. They might show you a short review from a respected newspaper that says, "Mr. Chao's gift is simplicity. His music owes a considerable amount to Bob Marley . . . but Mr. Chao has a nasal, regular-guy voice, and instead of the Wailers' brooding, bass-heavy undertow, Mr. Chao's band delivers a lighter bounce. His tunes have the singing directness of nursery rhymes."[3] Chao's fans accept these criteria for judging a singer's appeal.

You may not agree that simplicity, directness, and a regular-guy voice are the most important qualities in a popular singer. But the establishment of standards itself offers material for a discussion or an argument. You may argue about the relevance of the criteria, or you may agree with the criteria but argue about the success of the singer in meeting them. Perhaps you prefer complexity to simplicity. Or even if you choose simplicity, you may not think that Chao has exhibited this quality to good effect.

It is probably not surprising then, that, despite wide differences in taste, professional critics more often than not agree on criteria and whether an art object has met the criteria. For example, almost all movie critics agree that *Citizen Kane* and *Gone with the Wind* are superior films. They also agree that *Plan 9 from Outer Space,* a horror film, is terrible.

Value claims about morality express judgments about the rightness or wrongness of conduct or belief. Here disagreements are as wide and deep as in the arts. The first two examples on page 113 reveal how controversial such claims can be. Although you and your reader may share many values—among them a belief in democracy, a respect for learning, and a desire for peace—you may also disagree, even profoundly, about other values. The subject of divorce, for example, despite its prevalence in our society, can produce a conflict between people who have differing moral standards. Some people may insist on adherence to absolute standards, arguing that the values they hold are based on immutable religious precepts derived from God and biblical scripture. Since marriage is sacred, divorce is always wrong, they say, whether or not the conditions of society change. Other people may argue that values are relative, based on the changing needs of societies in different places and at different times. Since marriage is an institution created by human beings at a particular time in history to serve particular social needs, they may say, it can also be dissolved when other social needs arise. The same conflicts between moral values might occur in discussions of abortion or suicide.

As a writer you cannot always know what system of values your reader holds. Yet it might be possible to find a rule on which almost all readers agree. One such rule was expressed by the eighteenth-century German philosopher Immanuel Kant: "Man and, in general, every rational being exists as an end in itself and not merely as a means to be arbitrarily used by this or that will." Kant's prescription urges us not to subject any creature to a condition that it has not freely chosen. In other words, we cannot use other creatures, as in slavery, for our own purposes.

---

[3]Jon Pareles, *New York Times,* July 10, 2001, p. B1.

Writer's Guide: Defending a Claim of Value

The following suggestions are a preliminary guide to the defense of a value claim. (We discuss value claims further in Chapter 5.)

1. Try to make clear that the values or principles you are defending are important and relatively more significant than other values. Keep in mind that you and your readers may differ about their relative importance. For example, although your readers may agree with you that brilliant photography is important in a film, they may think that a well-written script is even more crucial to its success. And although they may agree that freedom of the press is a mainstay of democracy, they may regard the right to privacy as even more fundamental.

2. Suggest that adherence to the values you are defending will bring about good results in some specific situation or bad results if respect for the values is ignored. You might argue, for example, that a belief in freedom of the press will make citizens better informed and the country stronger while a failure to protect this freedom will strengthen the forces of authoritarianism.

3. Since value terms are abstract, use examples and illustrations to clarify meanings and make distinctions. Comparisons and contrasts are especially helpful. If you use the term *heroism*, can you provide examples to differentiate between *heroism* and *foolhardiness* or *exhibitionism*?

4. Use testimony of others to prove that knowledgeable or highly regarded people share your values.

(Some philosophers would extend this rule to the treatment of animals by human beings.) This standard of judgment has, in fact, been invoked in recent years against medical experimentation on human beings in prisons and hospitals without their consent and against the sterilization of poor or mentally retarded women without their consent.

Nevertheless, even where people agree about standards for measuring behavior, a majority preference is not enough to confer moral value. If in a certain neighborhood a majority of heterosexual men decide to harass a few gay men and lesbians, that consensus does not make their action right. In formulating value claims, you should be prepared to ask and answer questions about the way in which your value claims and those of others have been arrived at. Lionel Ruby, an American philosopher, sums it up in these words: "The law of rationality tells us that we ought to justify our beliefs by evidence and reasons, instead of asserting them dogmatically."[4]

[4] *The Art of Making Sense* (New York: Lippincott, 1968), p. 271.

Of course, you will not always be able to persuade those with whom you argue that your values are superior to theirs and that they should therefore change their attitudes. Nor, on the other hand, would you want to compromise your values or pretend that they were different to win an argument. What you can and should do, however, as Lionel Ruby advises, is give *good reasons* that you think one thing is better than another. If as a child you asked why it was wrong to take your brother's toys, you might have been told by an exasperated parent, "Because I say so." Some adults still give such answers in defending their judgments, but such answers are not arguments and do nothing to win the agreement of others.

SAMPLE ANNOTATED ESSAY: CLAIM OF VALUE

Kids in the Mall: Growing Up Controlled

WILLIAM SEVERINI KOWINSKI

> Butch heaved himself up and loomed over the group. "Like it was different for me," he piped. "My folks used to drop me off at the shopping mall every morning and leave me all day. It was like a big free baby-sitter, you know? One night they never came back for me. Maybe they moved away. Maybe there's some kind of a Bureau of Missing Parents I could check with."
>
> —Richard Peck,
> *Secrets of the Shopping Mall,*
> a novel for teenagers

Introduction: interesting personal anecdote

From his sister at Swarthmore, I'd heard about a kid in Florida whose mother picked him up after school every day, drove him straight to the mall, and left him there until it closed—all at his insistence. I'd heard about a boy in Washington who, when his family moved from one suburb to another, pedaled his bicycle five miles every day to get back to his old mall, where he once belonged.

William Severini Kowinski is a freelance writer who has been the book review editor and managing arts editor of the *Boston Phoenix*. This excerpt is from his book *The Malling of America: An Inside Look at the Great Consumer Paradise* (1985).

Additional examples of
mall experience

These stories aren't unusual. The mall is a common experience for the majority of American youth; they have probably been going there all their lives. Some ran within their first large open space, saw their first fountain, bought their first toy, and read their first book in a mall. They may have smoked their first cigarette or first joint, or turned them down, had their first kiss or lost their virginity in the mall parking lot. Teenagers in America now spend more time in the mall than anywhere else but home and school. Mostly it is their choice, but some of that mall time is put in as the result of two-paycheck and single-parent households, and the lack of other viable alternatives. But are these kids being harmed by the mall?

Reasons for the
author's interest

I wondered first of all what difference it makes for adolescents to experience so many important moments in the mall. They are, after all, at play in the fields of its little world and they learn its ways; they adapt to it and make it adapt to them. It's here that these kids get their street sense, only it's mall sense. They are learning the ways of a large-scale, artificial environment; its subtleties and flexibilities, its particular pleasures and resonances, and the attitudes it fosters.

The presence of so many teenagers for so much time was not something mall developers planned on. In fact, it came as a big surprise. But kids became a fact of mall life very easily, and the International Council of Shopping Centers found it necessary to commission a study, which they published along with a guide to mall managers on how to handle the teenage incursion.

Expert opinion

The study found that "teenagers in suburban   5
centers are bored and come to the shopping centers mainly as a place to go. Teenagers in suburban centers spent more time fighting, drinking, littering and walking than did their urban counterparts, but presented fewer overall problems." The report observed that "adolescents congregated in groups of two to four and predominantly at locations selected by them rather than management." This probably had something to do with the decision to install game arcades, which allow management to channel these restless

adolescents into naturally contained areas away from major traffic points of adult shoppers.

The guide concluded that mall management should tolerate and even encourage the teenage presence because, in the words of the report, "The vast majority support the same set of values as does shopping center management." *The same set of values* means simply that mall kids are already preprogrammed to be consumers and that the mall can put the finishing touches to them as hard-core, lifelong shoppers just like everybody else. That, after all, is what the mall is about. So it shouldn't be surprising that in spending a lot of time there, adolescents find little that challenges the assumption that the goal of life is to make money and buy products, or that just about everything else in life is to be used to serve those ends.

Why the malls encourage adolescent presence

Growing up in a high-consumption society already adds inestimable pressure to kids' lives. Clothes consciousness has invaded the grade schools, and popularity is linked with having the best, newest clothes in the currently acceptable styles. Even what they read has been affected. "Miss [Nancy] Drew wasn't obsessed with her wardrobe," noted the *Wall Street Journal*. "But today the mystery in teen fiction for girls is what outfit the heroine will wear next." Shopping has become a survival skill and there is certainly no better place to learn it than the mall, where its importance is powerfully reinforced and certainly never questioned.

*Disadvantages:
a) Exposure to high-consumption society*

The mall as a university of suburban materialism, where Valley Girls and Boys from coast to coast are educated in consumption, has its other lessons in this era of change in family life and sexual mores and their economic and social ramifications. The plethora of products in the mall, plus the pressure on teens to buy them, may contribute to the phenomenon that psychologist David Elkind calls "the hurried child": kids who are exposed to too much of the adult world too quickly and must respond with a sophistication that belies their still-tender emotional development. Certainly the adult products marketed for children—form-fitting designer jeans, sexy tops for preteen girls—add to the social pressure to

b) Social pressures to buy

look like an adult, along with the home-grown need to understand adult finances (why mothers must work) and adult emotions (when parents divorce).

Kids spend so much time at the mall partly because their parents allow it and even encourage it. The mall is safe, doesn't seem to harbor any unsavory activities, and there is adult supervision; it is, after all, a controlled environment. So the temptation, especially for working parents, is to let the mall be their baby-sitter. At least the kids aren't watching TV. But the mall's role as a surrogate mother may be more extensive and more profound.

c) Mall as babysitter

Karen Lansky, a writer living in Los Angeles, 10 has looked into the subject, and she told me some of her conclusions about the effects on its teenaged denizens of the mall's controlled and controlling environment. "Structure is the dominant idea, since true 'mall rats' lack just that in their home lives," she said, "and adolescents about to make the big leap into growing up crave more structure than our modern society cares to acknowledge." Karen pointed out some of the elements malls supply that kids used to get from their families, like warmth (Strawberry Shortcake dolls and similar cute and cuddly merchandise), old-fashioned mothering ("We do it all for you," the fast-food slogan), and even home cooking (the "homemade" treats at the food court).

d) Mall as substitute for home

The problem in all this, as Karen Lansky sees it, is that while families nurture children by encouraging growth through the assumption of responsibility and then by letting them rest in the bosom of the family from the rigors of growing up, the mall as a structural mother encourages passivity and consumption, as long as the kid doesn't make trouble. Therefore all they learn about becoming adults is how to act and how to consume.

e) Encouragement of passivity

Kids are in the mall not only in the passive role of shoppers—they also work there, especially as fast-food outlets infiltrate the mall's enclosure. There they learn how to hold a job and take responsibility, but still within the same value context. When *CBS Reports* went to Oak Park Mall in suburban Kansas City, Kansas, to tape part of their

f) Undemanding jobs

hour-long consideration of malls, "After the Dream Comes True," they interviewed a teenaged girl who worked in a fast-food outlet there. In a sequence that didn't make the final program, she described the major goal of her present life, which was to perfect the curl on top of the ice-cream cones that were her store's specialty. If she could do that, she would be moved from the lowly soft-drink dispenser to the more prestigious ice-cream division, the curl on top of the status ladder at her restaurant. These are the achievements that are important at the mall.

Details

Other benefits of such jobs may also be over-rated, according to Laurence D. Steinberg of the University of California at Irvine's social ecology department, who did a study on teenage employment. Their jobs, he found, are generally simple, mindlessly repetitive and boring. They don't really learn anything, and the jobs don't lead anywhere. Teenagers also work primarily with other teenagers; even their supervisors are often just a little older than they are. "Kids need to spend time with adults," Steinberg told me. "Although they get benefits from peer relationships, without parents and other adults it's one-side socialization. They hang out with each other, have age-segregated jobs, and watch TV."

Advantages:
a) Time with other adolescents

Perhaps much of this is not so terrible or even so terribly different. Now that they have so much more to contend with in their lives, adolescents probably need more time to spend with other adolescents without adult impositions, just to sort things out. Though it is more concentrated in the mall (and therefore perhaps a clearer target), the value system there is really the dominant one of the whole society. Attitudes about curiosity, initiative, self-expression, empathy, and disinterested learning aren't necessarily made in the mall; they are mirrored there, perhaps a bit more intensely—as through a glass brightly.

b) Educational opportunities

Besides, the mall is not without its educational 15 opportunities. There are bookstores, where there is at least a short shelf of classics at great prices, and other books from which it is possible to learn more than how to do sit-ups. There are tools, from hammers to VCRs, and products, from clothes to records, that can help the young find and express themselves. There are older people with stories, and places to be alone or to talk one-on-one with a kindred spirit. And there is always the passing show.

The mall itself may very well be an education about the future. I was struck with the realization, as early as my first forays into Greengate, that the mall is only one of a number of enclosed and controlled environments that are part of the lives of today's young. The mall is just an extension, say, of those large suburban schools—only there's Karmelkorn instead of chem lab, the ice rink instead of the gym: It's high school without the impertinence of classes.

Conclusion and claim of value: mall as a controlled environment that teaches a few valuable lessons

Growing up, moving from home to school to the mall—from enclosure to enclosure, transported in cars—is a curiously continuous process, without much in the way of contrast or contact with unenclosed reality. Places must tend to blur into one another. But whatever differences and dangers there are in this, the skills these adolescents are learning may turn out to be useful in their later lives. For we seem to be moving inexorably into an age of preplanned and regulated environments, and this is the world they will inherit.

Still, it might be better if they had more of a choice. One teenaged girl confessed to *CBS Reports* that she sometimes felt she was missing something by hanging out at the mall so much. "But I'm here," she said, "and this is what I have."

■ Analysis

Kowinski has chosen to evaluate one aspect of an extraordinarily successful economic and cultural phenomenon—the commercial mall. He asks whether the influence of the mall on adolescents is good or bad. The answer seems to be a little of both. The good values may be described as exposure to a variety of experiences, a protective structure for adolescents who often live in unstable environments, and immersion in a world that may well serve as an introduction to adulthood. But the bad values, which Kowinski thinks are more influential (as the title suggests) are those of the shoppers' paradise, a society that believes in acquisition and consumption of goods as ultimate goals, and too much control over the choices available to adolescents. The tone of the judgment, however, is moderate and reflects a balanced, even scholarly, attitude. More than other arguments, the treatment of values requires such a voice, one which respects differences of opinion among readers. But serious doesn't mean heavy. His style is formal but highly readable, brightened by interesting examples and precise details. The opening paragraph is a strikingly effective lead.

Some of his observations are personal, but others are derived from studies by professional researchers, from *CBS Reports* to a well-known writer on childhood. These studies give weight and authority to his conclusions. Here and there we detect an appealing sympathy for adolescents who spend time in their controlled mall environments.

Like any thoughtful social commentator, Kowinski casts a wide net. He sees the mall not only as a hangout for teens but as a good deal more, an institution that offers insights into family life and work, the changing urban culture, the nature of contemporary entertainment, even glimpses of a somewhat forbidding future.

CLAIMS OF POLICY

Claims of policy argue that certain conditions should exist. As the name suggests, they advocate adoption of policies or courses of action because problems have arisen that call for solution. Almost always *should* or *ought to* or *must* is expressed or implied in the claim.

CLAIM: Voluntary prayer should be permitted in public schools.

CLAIM: A dress code should be introduced for all public high schools.

CLAIM: A law should permit sixteen-year-olds and parents to "divorce" each other in cases of extreme incompatibility.

CLAIM: Mandatory jail terms should be imposed for drunk driving violations.

In defending such claims of policy you may find that you must first convince your audience that a problem exists. This will require that, as part of your longer argument, you make a factual claim, offering data to prove that present conditions are unsatisfactory. You may also find it necessary to refer to the values that support your claim. Then you will be ready to introduce your policy, to persuade your audience that the solution you propose will solve the problem.

We will examine a policy claim in which all these parts are at work. The claim can be stated as follows: "The time required for an undergraduate degree should be extended to five years." Immediate agreement with this policy among student readers would certainly not be universal. Some

Writer's Guide: Defending a Claim of Policy

The following steps will help you organize arguments for a claim of policy.

1. Make your proposal clear. The terms in the proposal should be precisely defined.

2. If necessary, establish that there is a need for a change. When changes have been resisted, present reasons that explain this resistance. (It is often wrongly assumed that people cling to cultural practices long after their significance and necessity have eroded. But rational human beings observe practices that serve a purpose. The fact that you and I may see no value or purpose in the activities of another is irrelevant.)

3. Consider the opposing arguments. You may want to state the opposing arguments in a brief paragraph before answering them in the body of your argument.

4. Devote the major part of your essay to proving that your proposal is an answer to the opposing arguments and enumerating its distinct benefits for your readers.

5. Support your proposal with solid data, but don't neglect the moral considerations and the commonsense reasons, which may be even more persuasive.

students would not recognize a problem. They would say, "The college curriculum we have now is fine. There's no need for a change. Besides, we don't want to spend more time in school." First, then, the arguer would have to persuade a skeptical audience that there is a problem—that four years of college are no longer enough because the stock of knowledge in almost all fields of study continues to increase. The arguer would provide data to show that students today have many more choices in history, literature, and science than students had in those fields a generation ago. She would also emphasize the value of greater knowledge and more schooling compared to the value of other goods the audience cherishes, such as earlier independence. Finally, the arguer would offer a plan for implementing her policy. Her plan would have to consider initial psychological resistance, revision of the curriculum, costs of more instruction, and costs of lost production in the workforce. Most important, she would point out the benefits for both individuals and society if this policy were adopted.

In this example, we assumed that the reader would disagree that a problem existed. In many cases, however, the reader may agree that there is a problem but disagree with the arguer about the way to solve it. Most of us, no doubt, agree that we want to reduce or eliminate the following problems: misbehavior and vandalism in schools, drunk driving, crime on the streets, child abuse, pornography, pollution. But how should we go about solving those problems? What public policy will give us well-behaved, diligent students who never destroy school property? Safe streets where no one is ever robbed or assaulted? Loving homes where no child is ever mistreated? Some members of society would choose to introduce rules or laws that punish infractions so severely that wrongdoers would be unwilling or unable to repeat their offenses. Other members of society would prefer policies that attempt to rehabilitate or reeducate offenders through training, therapy, counseling, and new opportunities.

SAMPLE ANNOTATED ESSAY: CLAIM OF POLICY

Dependency or Death?
Oregonians Make a Chilling Choice

WESLEY J. SMITH

Introduction: misinterpretation of information in a new study of assisted suicide

Assisted suicide in Oregon has operated in a shroud of secrecy since the procedure was legalized by a 1997 referendum. But a new study, published in the *New England Journal of Medicine*, purports to shed light on the law's actual workings. Advocates of assisted suicide claim the report proves all is well. But a close reading reveals that many of the worries of assisted-suicide opponents are entirely justified.

Fifteen people in Oregon, we are told, legally committed suicide with the assistance of their doctors in 1998. According to the report, not one of them was forced into the act by intractable pain or suffering. Rather, those who died had strong personal beliefs in individual autonomy and chose suicide based primarily on fears of future dependence.

Refutation: a) Real reason for suicide

That isn't how assisted suicide was supposed to work. For many years, we have been told repeatedly by advocates that assisted suicide is to be a

Wesley J. Smith is an attorney and author or coauthor of eight books, including *Culture of Death: The Assault on Medical Ethics in America* (2001). Smith's writing and opinion columns on medical ethics, legal ethics, and public affairs have appeared in publications throughout the country, including *Newsweek,* the *New York Times,* and the *Wall Street Journal,* the source of this February 2, 1999, piece.

"last resort," applied only when nothing else can be done to alleviate "unrelenting and intolerable suffering." Yet pain wasn't a factor in a single one of the Oregon suicides. Thus, rather than being a limited procedure performed out of extreme medical urgency, legalization in Oregon has actually widened the category of conditions for which physician-hastened death is seen as legitimate.

b) Statement of the problem

Disability-rights advocates point out that allowing assisted suicide based upon fear of needing help going to the toilet, bathing, and performing other daily life activities will involve far more disabled and elderly people than terminally ill ones. They also note that dependency is an issue primarily for people who are not actually dependent and that like other difficulties in life dependency is a circumstance to which people adjust with time. To accept the notion that worry about the potential need for living assistance is a legitimate reason for doctors to write lethal prescriptions is to put disabled and elderly people at lethal risk. The dehumanizing message is that society regards such lives as undignified and not worth living. That is why nine national disability-rights organizations have come out strongly against legalizing assisted suicide and none support it.

Support:
a) Fears of the disabled and the elderly

Expression of values

The study also reports that the people who committed assisted suicide had "shorter" relationships with the doctors who prescribed lethally than did a control group of patients who died naturally. The exact time difference is not given, but we do know from earlier media reports that it may be quite short. The first woman to commit assisted suicide in Oregon had a two-and-a-half-week relationship with the doctor who wrote her lethal prescription. Her own doctor had refused to assist her suicide, as had a second doctor who diagnosed her with depression. So she went to an advocacy group, which referred her to a doctor willing to do the deed. Hers was not a unique case. The report states that six of the fifteen people sought lethal prescriptions from two or more doctors.

b) Hasty decisions of doctors

Example

5

Assisted suicide proponents told us this wouldn't happen either. They promised that assisted suicide would only occur after a deep exploration of values between patients and doctors who had long-term relationships. Thanks to the study, we now know that death decisions are being made by doctors the patients barely know. This isn't careful medical practice; it is rampant Kevorkianism.

c) Omission of data from the study

The study is as notable for what it omits as for what it includes. Information about the people who committed assisted suicide came from death-prescribing doctors. Treating doctors who did not participate in their patients' deaths—professionals who could have provided invaluable information about the health of the people who died—were not interviewed. Nor were the doctors who refused to write lethal prescriptions. Family members were not contacted either. Significantly, the investigators made no attempt to learn whether the prescribing doctors were affiliated with assisted-suicide advocacy groups, a matter of some importance if we are to judge whether the decisions to prescribe lethally were based on medicine or ideology. Moreover, none of the patients were autopsied to determine whether they were actually terminally ill.

Examples

d) Data from the Netherlands of unauthorized euthanasia

Near the end of the report, investigators admit that they do not know whether any unreported assisted suicides occurred. If history is any example, such deaths probably did happen. A recent *Journal of Medical Ethics* study about euthanasia in the Netherlands reveals that the Dutch policy is "beyond effective control" since 59 percent of doctors do not report euthanasia or assisted suicide to authorities as required by law. (In Oregon, there is no punishment for failing to report an assisted suicide.)

Examples

Moreover, killing by doctors in the Netherlands has expanded far beyond the rare case originally contemplated when euthanasia was first permitted in that country more than twenty years ago. Patients who are not terminally ill are routinely assisted in suicide. Depressed people can also be killed upon request even if they have no underlying organic disease. The lives of children born with birth defects are terminated by doctors based primarily on "quality of life" considerations. Most chilling, in one out of five euthanasia cases—nearly 1,000 per year—the patient has not asked to be killed.

Claim of policy: indictment of the present state of affairs, implying that it should be changed

The *New England Journal of Medicine* study is a 10 warning that Oregon has started down the same destructive path. Rather than alleviating concerns, the study reveals that assisted suicide is bad medicine and even worse public policy.

■ Analysis

In this claim of policy, the course of action is suggested in the last paragraph: Assisted suicide must be eliminated because it is "bad medicine and even worse public policy." That is, the law in Oregon that permits assisted suicide must be repealed. In the body of his argument, the author supports this claim with an array of facts and an appeal to deeply felt human values.

He begins, as many arguers do, with a brief reference to the situation he will attack. (It is summarized in the last section of the third paragraph.) The facts he provides come largely from a study in a distinguished professional journal that claims to establish the success of the Oregon law. But Smith interprets the facts of the study—and its omissions—to mean that the program is *not* fulfilling its humanitarian objective. Another study that is cited, from a journal of medical ethics, discusses the state of euthanasia in the Netherlands, where it is legal. This report appears at the end of Smith's article. Its position here emphasizes a disturbing conclusion—the dangerous future that the Oregon law may introduce. (In the Netherlands, says the report, "in one out of five euthanasia cases . . . the patient has not asked to be killed.")

An interesting and effective strategy in this argument is the author's reference to information which has been omitted from the debate on euthanasia. This lack of information is clearly spelled out in two paragraphs of the essay. In any debate, an accusation that the opposite side has failed to supply important data suggests that the data will prove damaging to the opponent's argument.

The most important element of this argument, however, is its appeal, both direct and implied, to the values of compassion and the natural desire to protect the helpless. All the examples are designed to heighten our sensitivity to the plight of those who have been victimized by death-prescribing doctors. But there is also an appeal to fear for readers who can imagine possible threats to their own welfare under such a law.

We don't, of course, expect neutrality from a lawyer for an antieuthanasia organization. Nevertheless, one of the strengths of this argument is its use of sober language, despite the emotionally charged subject matter. There are no vivid descriptions of suffering or maltreatment, and the author does not personalize his account. The absence of the pronoun *I,* in fact, lends his argument the formality of a legal brief. Undecided readers often find such restraint more persuasive than a passionate assault on the opposition.

Happiness Is a Warm Planet

THOMAS GALE MOORE

President Clinton convened a conference on global warming yesterday, as the White House agonizes over its posture at the forthcoming talks in Kyoto, Japan, on a worldwide global warming treaty. Mr. Clinton is eager to please his environmentalist supporters, but industry, labor and members of the Senate have told the administration that this treaty would wreck the economy, cost millions of jobs and provoke a flight of investment to more hospitable climes.

A crucial point gets lost in the debate: Global warming, if it were to occur, would probably *benefit* most Americans.

If mankind had to choose between a warmer or a cooler climate, we would certainly choose the former: Humans, nearly all other animals and most plants would be better off with higher temperatures. The climate models suggest, and so far the record confirms, that under global warming nighttime winter temperatures would rise the most, and daytime summer temperatures the least. Most Americans prefer a warmer climate to a colder one—and that preference is justified. More people die of the cold than of the heat; more die in the winter than the summer. Statistical evidence suggests that the climate predicted for the end of the next century might reduce U.S. deaths by about 40,000 annually.

In addition, less snow and ice would reduce transportation delays and accidents. A warmer winter would cut heating costs, more than offsetting any increase in air conditioning expenses in the summer. Manufacturing, mining and most services would be unaffected. Longer growing seasons, more rainfall and higher concentrations of carbon dioxide would benefit plant growth. Already there is evidence that trees and other plants are growing more vigorously. Although some locales may become too dry, too wet or too warm, on the whole mankind should benefit from an upward tick in the thermometer.

Thomas Gale Moore is a senior fellow at the Hoover Institution. His book *A Politically Incorrect View of Global Warming: Foreign Aid Masquerading as Climate Policy* was published in 1998 by the Cato Institute. This article appeared in the *Wall Street Journal* on October 7, 1997.

What about the economic effects? In the pessimistic view of the In-   5
tergovernmental Panel on Climate Change, the costs of global warming
might be as high as 1.5 percent of the U.S. gross domestic product by the
end of the next century. The cost of reducing carbon dioxide emissions,
however, would be much higher. William Cline of the Institute for International Economics has calculated that the cost of cutting emissions by
one-third from current levels by 2040 would be 3.5 percent of worldwide
GDP. The IPCC also reviewed various estimates of losses from stabilizing
emissions at 1990 levels, a more modest objective, and concluded that
the cost to the U.S. economy would be at least 1.5 percent of GDP by
2050, with the burden continuing to increase thereafter.

The forecast cost of warming is for the end of the next century, not
the middle. Adjusting for the time difference, the cost to the U.S. from a
warmer climate at midcentury, according to the IPCC, would be at most
0.75 percent of GDP, meaning that the costs of holding carbon dioxide to
1990 levels would be twice the gain from preventing any climate change.
But the benefit-cost calculus is even worse. The administration is planning to exempt Third World nations, such as China, India and Brazil,
from the requirements of the treaty. Under such a scheme, Americans
would pay a huge price for virtually no benefit.

And even if the developing countries agreed to return emissions to
1990 levels, greenhouse gas concentrations would not be stabilized. Since
for many decades more carbon dioxide would be added to the atmosphere than removed through natural processes, the buildup would only
slow; consequently temperatures would continue to go up. Instead of saving the full 0.75 percent of GDP by keeping emissions at 1990 levels, we
would be saving much less.

It is true that whatever dangers global warming may pose, they will
be most pronounced in the developing world. It is much easier for rich
countries to adapt to any long-term shift in weather than it is for
poor countries, which tend to be much more dependent on agriculture.
Poor countries lack the resources to aid their flora and fauna in adapting,
and many of their farmers earn too little to survive a shift to new conditions. But the best insurance for these poor countries is an increase in
their wealth, which would diminish their dependence on agriculture and
make it easier for them to adjust to changes in weather, including increases in precipitation and possible flooding or higher sea level. Subjecting Americans to high taxes and onerous regulations will help neither
them — we could buy less from them — nor us.

The optimal way to deal with potential climate change is not to embark on a futile attempt to prevent it, but to promote growth and prosperity so that people will have the resources to deal with the normal set
of natural disasters. Based on the evidence, including historical records,
global warming is likely to be good for most of mankind. The additional
carbon, rain and warmth should promote the plant growth necessary to
sustain an expanding world population. Global change is inevitable;
warmer is better; richer is healthier.

READING AND DISCUSSION QUESTIONS

1. This article is a claim of value in which the author tries to prove that something is good or bad—in this case, that a warmer climate would be better than a cold one. How many different reasons does he give to support his claim?

2. Moore offers a solution for the problems of a warm planet. Does this solution have shortcomings? If so, what are they?

3. Moore, an economist, spends the greater part of his argument on the economic consequences of global warming. Do you think he should have tried to develop other effects? Give examples of data that seem insufficient.

4. How much of the author's evidence comes from experts? If more testimony is needed, what kind should it be?

WRITING SUGGESTIONS

5. To ascertain whether Moore is right about the consequences of global warming, you will have to consult experts who disagree with him. They will not be hard to find. Most of those who have studied climatic changes think we are in trouble. Based on the testimony of other experts, write a paper that refutes some of Moore's claims.

6. Moore says that most of mankind would choose to live in a warm climate (para. 3). If you could choose, would you live in a tropical climate? A subtropical climate? In your answer, try to go beyond the most superficial reasons, like being tan all year long. Provide sufficient detail and personal background to bring to life the various reasons that would govern your choice.

A White Woman of Color

JULIA ÁLVAREZ

Growing up in the Dominican Republic, I experienced racism within my own family—though I didn't think of it as racism. But there was definitely a hierarchy of beauty, which was the main currency in our daughters-only family. It was not until years later, from the vantage point

Novelist and poet Julia Álvarez was raised in the Dominican Republic and immigrated to the United States at age ten with her parents. Her work includes the novels *How the García Girls Lost Their Accents* (1991), *In the Time of the Butterflies* (1994), *¡Yo!* (1997), and *In the Name of Salomé* (2000); two books of poems, *Homecoming: New and Collected Poems* (1996) and *The Woman I Kept to Myself* (2004); and a collection of nonfiction essays, *Something to Declare* (1998). She teaches literature and creative writing at Middlebury College. This essay appeared in *Half and Half: Writers on Growing Up Biracial and Bicultural*, edited by Claudine C. O'Hearn (1998).

of this country and this education, that I realized that this hierarchy of beauty was dictated by our coloring. We were a progression of whitening, as if my mother were slowly bleaching the color out of her children.

The oldest sister had the darkest coloring, with very curly hair and "coarse" features. She looked the most like Papi's side of the family and was considered the least pretty. I came next, with "good hair," and skin that back then was a deep olive, for I was a tomboy—another dark mark against me—who would not stay out of the sun. The sister right after me had my skin color, but she was a good girl who stayed indoors, so she was much paler, her hair a golden brown. But the pride and joy of the family was the baby. She was the one who made heads turn and strangers approach asking to feel her silken hair. She was white white, an adjective that was repeated in describing her color as if to deepen the shade of white. Her eyes were brown, but her hair was an unaccountable tow-headed blond. Because of her coloring, my father was teased that there must have been a German milkman in our neighborhood. How could *she* be *his* daughter? It was clear that this youngest child resembled Mami's side of the family.

It was Mami's family who were *really* white. They were white in terms of race, and white also in terms of class. From them came the fine features, the pale skin, the lank hair. Her brothers and uncles went to schools abroad and had important businesses in the country. They also emulated the manners and habits of North Americans. Growing up, I remember arguments at the supper table on whether or not it was proper to tie one's napkin around one's neck, on how much of one's arm one could properly lay on the table, on whether spaghetti could be eaten with the help of a spoon. My mother, of course, insisted on all the protocol of knives and forks and on eating a little portion of everything served; my father, on the other hand, defended our eating whatever we wanted, with our hands if need be, so we could "have fun" with our food. My mother would snap back that we looked like *jibaritas* who should be living out in the country. Of course, that was precisely where my father's family came from.

Not that Papi's family weren't smart and enterprising, all twenty-five brothers and sisters. (The size of the family in and of itself was considered very country by some members of Mami's family.) Many of Papi's brothers had gone to the university and become professionals. But their education was totally island—no fancy degrees from Andover and Cornell and Yale, no summer camps or school songs in another language. Papi's family still lived in the interior versus the capital, in old-fashioned houses without air conditioning, decorated in ways my mother's family would have considered, well, tasteless. I remember antimacassars on the backs of rocking chairs (which were the living-room set), garish paintings of flamboyant trees, ceramic planters with plastic flowers in bloom. They were *criollos*—creoles—rather than cosmopolitans, expansive, proud, colorful. (Some members had a sixth finger on their right—or was it their left hand?) Their features were less aquiline than Mother's family's, the skin darker, the hair coarse and curly. Their money still had the smell of the earth on it and was kept in a wad in their back pockets, whereas my mother's family had money in the Chase Manhattan Bank, most of it with George Washington's picture on it, not Juan Pablo Duarte's.

It was clear to us growing up then that lighter was better, but there   5 was no question of discriminating against someone because he or she was dark-skinned. Everyone's family, even an elite one like Mami's, had darker-skinned members. All Dominicans, as the saying goes, have a little black behind the ears. So, to separate oneself from those who were darker would have been to divide *una familia,* a sacrosanct entity in our culture. Neither was white blood necessarily a sign of moral or intellectual or political superiority. All one has to do is page through a Dominican history book and look at the number of dark-skinned presidents, dictators, generals, and entrepreneurs to see that power has not resided exclusively or even primarily among the whites on the island. The leadership of our country has been historically "colored."

But being black was something else. A black Dominican was referred to as a "dark Indian" (*indio oscuro*)—unless you wanted to come to blows with him, that is. The real blacks were the Haitians who lived next door and who occupied the Dominican Republic for twenty years, from 1822 to 1844, a fact that can still so inflame the Dominican populace you'd think it had happened last year. The denial of the Afro-Dominican part of our culture reached its climax during the dictatorship of Trujillo, whose own maternal grandmother was Haitian. In 1937, to protect Dominican race purity, Trujillo ordered the overnight genocide of thousands (figures range from 4,000 to 20,000) of Haitians by his military, who committed this atrocity using only machetes and knives in order to make this planned extermination look like a "spontaneous" border skirmish. He also had the Dominican Republic declared a white nation despite the evidence of the mulatto senators who were forced to pass this ridiculous measure.

So, black was not so good, kinky hair was not so good, thick lips not so good. But even if you were *indio oscuro con pelo malo y una bemba de aquí a Baní,* you could still sit in the front of the bus and order at the lunch counter—or the equivalent thereof. There was no segregation of races in the halls of power. But in the aesthetic arena—the one to which we girls were relegated as females—lighter was better. Lank hair and pale skin and small, fine features were better. All I had to do was stay out of the sun and behave myself and I could pass as a pretty white girl.

Another aspect of my growing up also greatly influenced my thinking on race. Although I was raised in the heart of a large family, my day-to-day caretakers were the maids. Most of these women were dark-skinned, some of Haitian background. One of them, Misiá, had been spared the machetes of the 1937 massacre when she was taken in and hidden from the prowling *guardias* by the family. We children spent most of the day with these women. They tended to us, nursed us when we were sick, cradled us when we fell down and scraped an elbow or knee (as a tomboy, there was a lot of this scraping for me), and most important, they told us stories of *los santos* and *el barón del cementerio*, of *el cuco* and *las ciguapas,* beautiful dark-skinned creatures who escaped capture because their feet were turned backwards so they left behind a false set of footprints. These women spread the wings of our imaginations and connected us deeply to the land we came from. They were the ones with the stories that had power over us.

We arrived in Nueva York in 1960, before the large waves of Caribbean immigrants created little Habanas, little Santo Domingos, and little San Juans in the boroughs of the city. Here we encountered a whole new kettle of wax—as my malapropping Mami might have said. People of color were treated as if they were inferior, prone to violence, uneducated, untrustworthy, lazy—all the "bad" adjectives we were learning in our new language. Our dark-skinned aunt, Tía Ana, who had lived in New York for several decades and so was the authority in these matters, recounted stories of discrimination on buses and subways. These Americans were so blind! One drop of black and you were black. Everyone back home would have known that Tía Ana was not black: she had "good hair" and her skin color was a light *indio.* All week, she worked in a *factoría* in the Bronx, and when she came to visit us on Saturdays to sew our school clothes, she had to take three trains to our nice neighborhood where the darkest face on the street was usually her own.

We were lucky we were white Dominicans or we would have had a 10 much harder time of it in this country. We would have encountered a lot more prejudice than we already did, for white as we were, we found that our Latino-ness, our accents, our habits and smells, added "color" to our complexion. Had we been darker, we certainly could not have bought our mock Tudor house in Jamaica Estates. In fact, the African American family who moved in across the street several years later needed police protection because of threats. Even so, at the local school, we endured the bullying of classmates. "Go back to where you came from!" they yelled at my sisters and me in the playground. When some of them started throwing stones, my mother made up her mind that we were not safe and began applying to boarding schools where privilege transformed prejudice into patronage.

"So where are you from?" my classmates would ask.

"Jamaica Estates," I'd say, an edge of belligerence to my voice. It was obvious from my accent, if not my looks, that I was not *from* there in the way they meant being from somewhere.

"I mean originally."

And then it would come out, the color, the accent, the cousins with six fingers, the smell of garlic.

By the time I went off to college, a great explosion of American cul- 15 ture was taking place on campuses across the country. The civil rights movement, the Vietnam War and subsequent peace movement, the women's movement, were transforming traditional definitions of American identity. Ethnicity was in: my classmates wore long braids like Native Americans and peasant blouses from Mexico and long, diaphanous skirts and dangly earrings from India. Suddenly, my foreignness was being celebrated. This reversal felt affirming but also disturbing. As huipils, serapes, and embroidered dresses proliferated about me, I had the feeling that my ethnicity had become a commodity. I resented it.

When I began looking for a job after college, I discovered that being a white Latina made me a nonthreatening minority in the eyes of these employers. My color was a question *only* of culture, and if I kept my cultural color to myself, I was "no problem." Each time I was hired for one of my countless "visiting appointments"—they were never permanent "invitations," mind you—the inevitable questionnaire would accompany my contract in which I was to check off my RACE: CAUCASIAN, BLACK, NATIVE AMERICAN, ASIAN, HISPANIC, OTHER. How could a Dominican divide herself in this way? Or was I really a Dominican anymore? And what was a Hispanic? A census creation—there is no such culture—how could it define who I was at all? Given this set of options, the truest answer might have been to check off other.

For that was the way I had begun to think of myself. Adrift from any Latino community in this country, my culture had become an internal homeland, periodically replenished by trips "back home." But as a professional woman on my own, I felt less and less at home on the island. My values, the loss of my Catholic faith, my lifestyle, my wardrobe, my hippy ways, and my feminist ideas separated me from my native culture. I did not subscribe to many of the mores and constraints that seemed to be an intrinsic part of that culture. And since my culture had always been my "color," by rejecting these mores I had become not only Americanized but whiter.

If I could have been a part of a Latino community in the United States, the struggle might have been, if not easier, less private and therefore less isolating. These issues of acculturation and ethnicity would have been struggles to share with others like me. But all my North American life I had lived in shifting academic communities—going to boarding schools, then college, and later teaching wherever I could get those yearly appointments—and these communities reflected the dearth of Latinos in the profession. Except for friends in Spanish departments, who tended to have come from their countries of origin to teach rather than being raised in this country as I was, I had very little daily contact with Latinos.

Where I looked for company was where I had always looked for company since coming to this country: in books. At first the texts that I read and taught were the ones prescribed to me, the canonical works which formed the content of the bread-and-butter courses that as a "visiting instructor" I was hired to teach. These texts were mostly written by white male writers from Britain and the United States, with a few women thrown in and no Latinos. Thank goodness for the occasional creative writing workshop where I could bring in the multicultural authors I wanted. But since I had been formed in this very academy, I was clueless where to start. I began to educate myself by reading, and that is when I discovered that there were others out there like me, hybrids who came in a variety of colors and whose ethnicity and race were an evolving process, not a rigid paradigm or a list of boxes, one of which you checked off.

This discovery of my ethnicity on paper was like a rebirth. I had been 20 going through a pretty bad writer's block: the white page seemed impossible to fill with whatever it was I had in me to say. But listening to authors like Maxine Hong Kingston, Toni Morrison, Gwendolyn Brooks, Langston Hughes, Maya Angelou, June Jordan, and to Lorna Dee Cervantes, Piri Thomas, Rudolfo Anaya, Edward Rivera, Ernesto Galarza (that first wave of Latino writers), I began to hear the language "in color." I began to see that literature could reflect the otherness I was feeling, that the choices in fiction and poetry did not have to be bleached out of their color or simplified into either/or. A story could allow for the competing claims of different parts of ourselves and where we came from.

Ironically, it was through my own stories and poems that I finally made contact with Latino communities in this country. As I published more, I was invited to read at community centers and bilingual programs. Latino students, who began attending colleges in larger numbers in the late seventies and eighties, sought me out as a writer and teacher "of color." After the publication of *How the García Girls Lost Their Accents,* I found that I had become a sort of spokesperson for Dominicans in this country, a role I had neither sought nor accepted. Of course, some Dominicans refused to grant me any status as a "real" Dominican because I was "white." With the color word there was also a suggestion of class. My family had not been among the waves of economic immigrants that left the island in the seventies, a generally darker-skinned, working-class group, who might have been the maids and workers in my mother's family house. We had come in 1960, political refugees, with no money but with "prospects": Papi had a friend who was the doctor at the Waldorf Astoria and who helped him get a job; Mami's family had money in the Chase Manhattan Bank they could lend us. We had changed class in America—from Mami's elite family to middle-class spics—but our background and education and most especially our pale skin had made mobility easier for us here. We had not undergone the same kind of race struggles as other Dominicans; therefore, we could not be "real" Dominicans.

What I came to understand and accept and ultimately fight for with my writing is the reality that ethnicity and race are not fixed constructs or measurable quantities. What constitutes our ethnicity and our race— once there is literally no common ground beneath us to define it— evolves as we seek to define and redefine ourselves in new contexts. My

Latino-ness is not something someone can take away from me or leave me out of with a definition. It is in my blood: it comes from that mixture of biology, culture, native language, and experience that makes me a different American from one whose family comes from Ireland or Poland or Italy. My Latino-ness is also a political choice. I am choosing to hold on to my ethnicity and native language even if I can "pass." I am choosing to color my Americanness with my Dominicanness even if it came in a light shade of skin color.

I hope that as Latinos, coming from so many different countries and continents, we can achieve solidarity in this country as the mix that we are. I hope we won't shoot ourselves in the foot in order to maintain some sort of false "purity" as the glue that holds us together. Such an enterprise is bound to fail. We need each other. We can't afford to reject the darker or lighter varieties, and to do so is to have absorbed a definition of ourselves as exclusively one thing or the other. And haven't we learned to fear that word "exclusive"? This reductiveness is absurd when we are talking about a group whose very definition is that of a mestizo race, a mixture of European, indigenous, African, and much more. Within this vast circle, shades will lighten and darken into overlapping categories. If we cut them off, we diminish our richness and we plant a seed of ethnic cleansing that is the root of the bloodshed we have seen in Bosnia and the West Bank and Rwanda and even our own Los Angeles and Dominican Republic.

As we Latinos redefine ourselves in America, making ourselves up and making ourselves over, we have to be careful, in taking up the promises of America, not to adopt its limiting racial paradigms. Many of us have shed customs and prejudices that oppressed our gender, race, or class on our native islands and in our native countries. We should not replace these with modes of thinking that are divisive and oppressive of our rich diversity. Maybe as a group that embraces many races and differences, we Latinos can provide a positive multicultural, multiracial model to a divided America.

READING AND DISCUSSION QUESTIONS

1. What is the meaning of the title of this essay? Is it an oxymoron?

2. Explain Álvarez's "hierarchy of beauty" (para. 1) in the Dominican Republic. What does she mean by "white in terms of race, and white also in terms of class" (para. 3)?

3. Does such a hierarchy of beauty have parallels in the United States? If it is not skin color, are other physical attributes rated as good or bad? How do you think such preferences arose?

4. Why did Álvarez think of herself as "adrift" (para. 17)? How does Álvarez explain the "discovery of my ethnicity" (para. 20)?

5. Álvarez ends her essay by summarizing what she has learned from her experience as a white woman "of color" (para. 21). How do the last three paragraphs differ in tone and content from the narrative that precedes it? Do you think they are effective? Would the essay have been stronger or weaker if she had ended it before the last three paragraphs?

WRITING SUGGESTIONS

6. Álvarez mentions a number of authors who inspired her with their views of otherness (para. 20). Perhaps you are familiar with their works or the works of other writers who explore ethnicity in America, such as *The Joy Luck Club, I Know Why the Caged Bird Sings, Native Son,* and *Reservation Blues.* Write a review of a book in which the author describes the experience of being different in the United States.

7. If you know any immigrants—in your own family or perhaps on campus—describe their attempts at acculturation. What aspects of American life have been most challenging for them? What aspects have been easiest to understand and accept?

College Life versus My Moral Code

ELISHA DOV HACK

Many people envy my status as a freshman at Yale College. My classmates and I made it through some fierce competition, and we are excited to have been accepted to one of the best academic and extracurricular programs in American higher education. I have an older brother who attended Yale, and I've heard from him what life at Yale is like.

He spent all his college years living at home because our parents are New Haven residents, and Yale's rules then did not require him to live in the dorms. But Yale's new regulations demand that I spend my freshman and sophomore years living in the college dormitories.

I, two other freshmen, and two sophomores have refused to do this because life in the dorms, even on the floors Yale calls "single sex," is contrary to the fundamental principles we have been taught as long as we can remember—the principles of Judaism lived according to the Torah and 3,000-year-old rabbinic teachings. Unless Yale waives its residence requirement, we may have no choice but to sue the university to protect our religious way of life.

Elisha Dov Hack was a member of the Yale College class of 2001. This article appeared on September 9, 1997, in the *New York Times.*

Bingham Hall, on the Yale quadrangle known as the Old Campus, is one of the dorms for incoming students. When I entered it two weeks ago during an orientation tour, I literally saw the handwriting on the wall. A sign titled "Safe Sex" told me where to pick up condoms on campus. Another sign touted 100 ways to make love without having sex, like "take a nap together" and "take a steamy shower together."

That, I am told, is real life in the dorms. The "freshperson" issue of 5 the *Yale Daily News* sent to entering students contained a "Yale lexicon" defining *sexile* as "banishment from your dorm room because your room-mate is having more fun than you." If you live in the dorms, you're expected to be part of the crowd, to accept these standards as the framework for your life.

Can we stand up to classmates whose sexual morality differs from ours? We've had years of rigorous religious teaching, and we've watched and learned from our parents. We can hold our own in the intellectual debate that flows naturally from exchanges during and after class. But I'm upset and hurt by this requirement that I live in the dorms. Why is Yale—an institution that professes to be so tolerant and open-minded—making it particularly hard for students like us to maintain our moral standards through difficult college years?

We are not trying to impose our moral standards on our classmates or on Yale. Our parents tell us that things were very different in college dormitories in their day and that in most colleges in the 1950s students who allowed guests of the opposite sex into their dorm rooms were subject to expulsion. We acknowledge that today's morality is not that of the 50s. We are asking only that Yale give us the same permission to live off campus that it gives any lower classman who is married or at least twenty-one years old.

Yale is proud of the fact that it has no "parietal rules" and that sexual morality is a student's own business. Maybe this is what Dean Richard H. Brodhead meant when he said that "Yale's residential colleges carry . . . a moral meaning." That moral meaning is, basically, "Anything goes." This morality is Yale's own residential religion, which it is proselytizing by force of its regulations.

We cannot, in good conscience, live in a place where women are permitted to stay overnight in men's rooms, and where visiting men can traipse through the common halls on the women's floors—in various stages of undress—in the middle of the night. The dormitories on Yale's Old Campus have floors designated by gender, but there is easy access through open stairwells from one floor to the next.

The moral message Yale's residences convey today is not one that our 10 religion accepts. Nor is it a moral environment in which the five of us can spend our nights, or a moral surrounding that we can call home.

Yale sent me a glossy brochure when it welcomed me as an entering student. It said, "Yale retains a deep respect for its early history and for the continuity that its history provides—a continuity based on constant reflection and reappraisal." Yale ought to reflect on and reappraise a policy that compels us to compromise our religious principles.

READING AND DISCUSSION QUESTIONS

1. Summarize Hack's "moral code" in a sentence or two. What examples of conduct does he give to make his definition clear?

2. What solution to his problem does the author propose? Why does Yale refuse to accept the solution? Are Yale's rules justified?

3. Hack says that religious students "may have no choice but to sue the university to protect our religious way of life" (para. 3). What support could he offer in a court of law for his claim that these students should be allowed to live off campus? If you can, ask a legal expert for ideas.

4. Many arguments, like this one between religious students and a university, arise out of a conflict not between good and evil but between two goods. Can you propose a compromise that would satisfy both sides in this case?

WRITING SUGGESTIONS

5. How do you think Yale could defend the sexual freedom that prevails on its campus? Write an argument setting out the philosophical principles and cultural values that justify tolerance for the practices Hack rejects.

6. Members of some minority groups on college campuses often insist on living together in separate dorms, taking their meals together, engaging in separate activities, etc. In light of today's emphasis on the multicultural experience, should the university allow such segregation?

Real Marriage, Real Life

E. J. GRAFF

L aughing at marriage, that age-old comedy staple, is trendy once again. *The Bachelor, The Bachelorette, Joe Millionaire,* and the "reality" genre's latest entry, *Married by America*: Watching what fools these mortals be is setting Nielsen records. And why not? Unlike the terrifyingly high-stakes disputes over Iraq, smallpox vaccinations, airport security, and secret detentions, marriage has an easy-to-follow storyline—one we're all sure we understand better than the players do.

But do these programs also reflect a new zeitgeist, a marrying mood? Are millions tuning in merely for distraction from the prospect of

E. J. Graff is a contributing editor to *The American Prospect* and to *Out* magazine, and is a visiting scholar at the Brandeis Women's Studies Research Center. Her book *What Is Marriage For? The Strange Social History of Our Most Intimate Institution* was published in 1999. This essay is from *The American Prospect*.

international thuggery? Or, given our scary times, are they ready to say goodbye to the commitment-free singles on *Seinfeld*, hoping to settle their own uncertain plotlines once and for all? If it's the latter, they'll be disappointed. Once upon a time, marriage could be life's answer. Because of capitalism, that can never be true again.

What's capitalism got to do with it? If you look closely, you'll find two ideas about marriage running through these reality shows. The first: The only moral reason to marry is for love. While that's the American philosophy of marriage today, it's a recent idea historically. The second: Money influences your choice of mate. That thought, currently taboo, is actually quite traditional.

With that in mind, consider *Joe Millionaire*. Twenty women competed to win the affections of a man they thought had inherited $50 million. But as the audience knew (and the women didn't during filming), "Joe" was actually Evan Marriott, a construction worker earning $19,000 a year, a fact he revealed only after choosing his prospective bride. Joe said he liked construction work better than college and would rather be poor than unhappy. In good fairy-tale fashion, our simple hero selected—from the seething pool of aspiring actresses and catty sophisticates hoping never to work again—another simple peasant, er, impoverished substitute teacher doing what she loved. Viewer faith in true love was renewed. But finances are what triumphed: These two are a perfect socioeconomic match.

Or consider *Married by America*, now under way. After having mates   5 chosen for them (first winnowed down by friends and families, final selections by viewer votes), five singles were "engaged" to five strangers on stage. Those couples who do marry after a month's onscreen cohabitation will win a list of consumer prizes, including that American dream, the single-family house—the payoff for making love and war in front of the nation. Here's my bet: Those couples best matched socioeconomically are most likely to win the real estate.

Tying marriage to money may sound crass, but it's more traditional than today's desperation dating. Ketubah, dowry, bride-price, breach-of-contract suits: In most eras and cultures, finances have been negotiated up front. Arranged marriages, in which a person's friends and family selected a prospect of equivalent socioeconomic "worth," worked out just as well as (if not better than) Match.com.

Today we still find love based on compatible finances. You can see it in the *New York Times* wedding pages: Marriages are financial mergers, although today's wealth comes in the form of a CV, a union card, or a string of degrees. What is a college education fund but an updated dowry, an investment in a child's financial future? And when was the last time you knew a corporate lawyer to marry a postal worker or (except in a J. Lo movie) a maid to wed a future U.S. senator?

Here's what's historically new: Few couples today are yoked together in daily labor. Traditionally, husbands and wives were business partners;

one brought in the fish, the other hawked them at the market. Working and sleeping together gave them a good shot at love—and a reason to stay together when love wasn't there.

But capitalism turned us into workers as mobile as cellular phones, able to make a living one by one. There's no FDIC guarantee on today's marital investment; we don't have to stay together to stay alive—even if, in these parlous times, it can seem as if we do.

After the international traumas of the 1930s and '40s, shell-shocked 10 young people raced down the aisle—and then, twenty years later, raced back out again. So far, almost no reality-show pair has made it more than a few minutes after the program's end. That's what makes it comedy. Don't you wish the mistakes in our international reality show could be so easily undone?

READING AND DISCUSSION QUESTIONS

1. What is Graff's strategy in opening with a reference to reality shows? What do those shows suggest about marriage today?

2. What claim is Graff supporting in the essay? Where does she state that claim most directly?

3. What sort of support does she offer? How effective do you find it to be?

4. Graff feels that tying marriage to money is actually a very old concept. What does she find new about today's marriages?

WRITING SUGGESTIONS

5. Like the marriages in the reality shows that Graff refers to, prenuptial agreements are often the target of humor. In all seriousness, do you feel that a prenuptial agreement is a good idea even if neither spouse is extremely wealthy?

6. Use examples from television and/or movies to argue that in the world of fiction, marriages between those of drastically different socioeconomic classes can and do succeed.

7. Attack or defend this statement by Graff: "Marriages are financial mergers, although today's wealth comes in the form of a CV, a union card, or a string of degrees" (para. 7).

Supersize Your Child?

RICHARD HAYES

In the late 1950s, soon after Watson and Crick had discovered DNA's structure, scientists began predicting that someday we'd be able to genetically engineer our children. We'd design them to be healthy, smart, and attractive, with life spans of 200 years, photographic memories, enhanced lung capacity for athletic endurance, and more. Our children would pass these modifications to their own children and add new ones as well. Humanity would take control of its own evolution and kick it into overdrive.

Few people took these speculations very seriously. Could this sort of genetic engineering really be done? Even if it could, would anyone really want to do it? If they did, wouldn't society step in and set limits? In any event, wouldn't it be decades before we'd have to worry about this?

Now it's 2004, and those decades have passed. The era of genetically modified humans is close upon us. Almost every day we read of new breakthroughs: cloning, artificial chromosomes and now high-tech sex selection. Scientists create genetically modified animals on an assembly-line basis. Biotech entrepreneurs discuss the potential market for genetically modified children at investors' conferences. For the most part, society has not stepped in and set limits.

Last year *Science* magazine reported that a variant of the human 5-HTT gene reduces the risk of depression following stressful experiences. Depression can be a devastating condition. Would it be wrong if a couple planning to start a family used in vitro fertilization procedures to have the 5-HTT gene variant inserted into the embryos of their prospective children? Taken as an isolated instance, many people would be hard-pressed to say that it was.

In 1993, University of California at San Francisco biochemist Dr.   5 Cynthia Kenyon discovered a variant of the DAF-2 gene that doubles the two-week life span of nematode worms. The university filed for patents based on knowledge of the metabolic pathway regulated by the human version of the DAF-2 gene. In 1999, Kenyon and others founded Elixir Pharmaceuticals, a biotech firm. In early 2003, Elixir licensed the university's patent rights to Kenyon's discoveries and secured $17 million in private financing. In an earlier interview with *ABC News*, Kenyon said she saw no reason humans might not be able to achieve 200-year life spans.

Richard Hayes is the executive director of the Center for Genetics and Society, a California-based nonprofit organization working for the responsible governance of genetic technologies. This piece was published on the TomPaine.com Web site in February 2004.

"Post-human" Nature

Last June at Yale University, the World Transhumanist Association held its first national conference. The Transhumanists have chapters in more than 20 countries and advocate the breeding of "genetically enriched" forms of "post-human" beings. Other advocates of the new techno-eugenics, such as Princeton University professor Lee Silver, predict that by the end of this century, "All aspects of the economy, the media, the entertainment industry, and the knowledge industry [will be] controlled by members of the GenRich class . . . Naturals [will] work as low-paid service providers or as laborers . . ."

What happens then? Here's Dr. Richard Lynn, emeritus professor at the University of Ulster, who, like Silver, supports human genetic modification: "What is called for here is not genocide, the killing off of the population of incompetent cultures. But we do need to think realistically in terms of the 'phasing out' of such peoples. . . . Evolutionary progress means the extinction of the less competent."

Notice that I've gone, in just four steps, from reducing susceptibility to depression, to extending the human life span, to the creation of a genetic elite, to proposals that genetically inferior people be "phased out."

When first presented with this scenario, people typically respond in one of two ways. Some say, "It's impossible." Others say, "It's inevitable." Notice what these otherwise diametrically different responses have in common: both counsel passivity. If the "post-human future" is impossible, there's no need to try to prevent it. If it's inevitable, such efforts would be in vain.

Will it actually be possible to genetically engineer our children? Most 10 scientists who have studied this question conclude that although the techniques need to be refined, there's no reason to believe it can't be done. Meanwhile, research on stem cells, cloning, artificial chromosomes and more continues to refine those techniques.

Many people believe that to suggest that manipulating genes can affect behavioral and cognitive traits in humans is to indulge discredited ideologies of "genetic determinism." It's true that the crude sociobiology of the 1970s has been discredited, as have simplistic notions that there exist "I.Q. genes" or "gay genes" that determine one's intelligence or sexual orientation. But to say that genes have no influence over traits is equally simplistic. Some genes have minimal influence, others have greater influence. Some have influence in the presence of certain environmental factors but no influence otherwise. Few genes determine anything; most confer propensities.

Deepening Inequality

Suppose scientists found a gene giving male children a 15 percent greater chance of growing one inch taller than they would have grown without that gene, all else equal. If fertility clinics offered to engineer embryos to include this gene, would there be customers? Yes. Couples would say, "In this competitive world, I want to do anything I can that might give my child an edge."

Once we allow children to be designed through embryo modification, where would we stop? If it's acceptable to modify one gene, why not two? If two, why not 20? Or 200? There are some 30,000 genes in the human genome. Each contributes, in smaller or larger proportions, to some propensity. Where would we stop? On what grounds?

Some suggest we allow embryo modification for certified medical conditions and prohibit it for cosmetic or enhancement purposes. It's unlikely that this would succeed. Prozac, Viagra, and Botox were all developed for medical purposes but in the blink of an eye became hugely profitable cosmetic and enhancement consumer products.

Will the use of genetic engineering to redesign our children exacer- 15 bate inequality? Amazingly, the neo-eugenic advocates don't deny that it will. As good libertarians, they celebrate free markets and social Darwinism, and counsel us to accept a rising tide of genetically enhanced inequality as the inevitable result of human ingenuity and desire.

But couldn't this be prevented? Wouldn't society step in? Several years ago, a team of health policy academics examined a range of proposals, including systems of national health insurance making eugenic engineering available to all, or preferentially to the poor, or by lottery. Despite their best efforts, they couldn't identify any realistic set of policies that would prevent the new eugenic technologies, once allowed at all, from generating unprecedented inequality.

And consider the international implications. What happens when some country announces an aggressive program of eugenic engineering explicitly intended to create a new, superior, omni-competent breed of human? What does the rest of the world do then?

We need to take a deep breath and realize what is going on here. The birth of the first genetically modified child would be a watershed moment in human history. It would set off a chain of events that would feed back upon themselves in ways impossible to control.

Unnatural Selection

Everything we experience, everything we know, everything we do is experienced, known and done by a species—homo sapiens—which evolved through natural selection over hundreds of thousands of years. We differ as individuals, but we are a single human species with a shared biology so fundamental to what we are that we are not even conscious of it, or of the manifold ways it unites us. What happens if we begin changing that fundamental shared biology?

Three hundred years ago the scientific and political leaders of that era 20 took as a self-evident fact the division of humanity into "superior" and "inferior" types, designed by Providence respectively as masters and slaves. Human beings were bred, bought and sold, like cattle or dogs.

After three hundred years of struggle and bloodshed we are on the verge—barely—of putting this awful legacy behind us.

Or maybe not. If left uncontrolled, the new human genetic technologies could set us on a trajectory leading to a new Dark Age in which people are once again regarded as little better than cattle or dogs. Here is "bioethicist" Gregory Pence, who has testified in support of human cloning before the U.S. Congress and elsewhere:

> [M]any people love their retrievers and their sunny dispositions around children and adults. Could people be chosen in the same way? Would it be so terrible to allow parents to at least aim for a certain type, in the same way that great breeders . . . try to match a breed of dog to the needs of a family?

The common initial responses to the prospect of the new techno-eugenics—"It's impossible," and "It's inevitable"—are incorrect and unhelpful. The response we need to affirm is at once more realistic and more challenging: The techno-eugenic future certainly is possible, and is certainly not inevitable.

Road to Regulation

In 1997, the Council of Europe negotiated an important international agreement, the Convention on Biomedicine and Human Rights. Thus far, it has been signed by more than two-thirds of the council's 45 member countries. The convention draws the lines on human genetic modification in just the right ways. It allows medical research, including stem cell research, to continue, and does not restrict abortion rights, but it bans genetic modifications that would open the door to high-tech eugenic engineering. Many countries in Asia, Africa, and Latin America have likewise begun to address these issues through legislation.

These efforts are encouraging, but we have a long way to go before such policies are implemented, as they must be, worldwide. In some countries, notably the United States, the politics of the new genetic technologies have become polarized to the point of gridlock. The religious right insists on total bans on nearly all human embryo research, while bio-research interests and the biotech industry insist on nearly total freedom from any meaningful social oversight and accountability.

In other countries, and at the international level, the challenge of a 25 new high-tech, free market eugenics, while worrisome, can seem remote in comparison with the real existing challenges of warfare, hunger, and disease.

What is to be done? More than anything, we need to realize the unprecedented nature of the challenges that the new human genetic technologies present. We need to distinguish benign applications of these technologies from pernicious ones, and support the former while opposing the latter. Concerned organizations and individuals need to engage these challenges and make their voices heard worldwide. National and international leaders in politics, the sciences and the arts need to declare that humanity is not going to let itself be split asunder by human genetic technology. The United Nations and other international bodies need to give these issues the highest attention. The hour is late. There is no greater challenge before us.

READING AND DISCUSSION QUESTIONS

1. Hayes alerts us that he is using the organization of his essay to help make his point. Explain where and how he does that. How does he appeal to his readers' need to feel secure? Why might his readers feel their sense of security being threatened?
2. Is Hayes supporting a claim of fact, value, or policy? Where does he state that claim most directly?
3. What types of support does Hayes offer to back up his opinion? How convincing do you find his support to be?
4. Can you identify the warrant underlying Hayes's argument? In order to accept his claim, what assumption of his must you agree with? Does he state his warrant explicitly anywhere in the essay?

WRITING SUGGESTIONS

5. Write an essay in which you either support or argue against Hayes's claim.
6. Write an essay in which you explain your own position on who should set limits on genetic engineering.
7. Choose an invention or scientific development that people once said was impossible and explain how those skeptics were proved wrong.
8. Choose an invention or scientific development and explain how it is now used, for good or ill, for purposes it was never intended to serve.

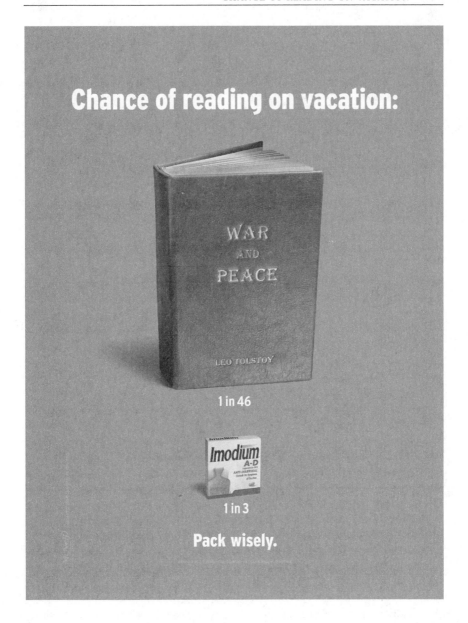

DISCUSSION QUESTIONS

1. What does the ad suggest about the intentions that people have when they go on vacation? What does it suggest about the reality of vacations?

2. What claim of policy is the ad supporting? Do you find it effective in supporting that claim? Why or why not?

3. What warrant underlies the ad? What general truth applied beyond this single ad does the ad seem to illustrate?

4. Is the choice of *War and Peace* as the featured book a good one, given that the ad was published in 2004 in *Newsweek*? Think of some different magazines that the ad could appear in. What book would be a better choice for each of the magazines you think of?

5. Since Imodium is the product being advertised, why is the image of the product so small?

DEBATE: Who is responsible for the college cost crisis?

Historical Perspective on College Cost Increases

JOHN A. BOEHNER AND HOWARD P. "BUCK" McKEON

College cost increases have dominated back to school stories in the media this fall, with tuitions jumping as much as 40 percent or more at both public and private colleges and universities across the nation. Although this disturbing trend is regularly blamed on the budget woes of the states facing difficult economic conditions, this analysis overlooks the long-term trends of college costs. America is facing a college cost crisis. This crisis is not the result of a bad economy and a few difficult years for institutions of higher education. The crisis exists because for decades, tuitions have been rising at a rate much more rapid than family income or student aid can keep pace with, and a boiling point has been reached in which students and families are losing out on the opportunity for higher education. Now, as higher education becomes increasingly important in a technologically dominated world, higher education should be more accessible, not less.

According to the College Board, in the 1970s there was little, if any, real growth in college prices. In the early 1980s, however, tuition and fees began to grow much more rapidly than consumer prices—in fact, during the 1980s, the cost of attending college rose over three times as fast as median family income. This trend of rapidly increasing college costs has

John A. Boehner is a Republican congressman from Ohio and chairman of the U.S. House Committee on Education and the Workforce. Howard P. "Buck" McKeon is a Republican congressman from California and chairman of the U.S. House Subcommittee on Twenty-First Century Competitiveness. This article is from their September 4, 2003, report "The College Cost Crisis: A Congressional Analysis of College Costs and Implications for America's Higher Education System."

continued through the 1990s. Over the ten-year period ending in 2002–2003, after adjusting for inflation, average tuition and fees at both public and private four-year colleges and universities rose 38 percent. . . . And according to information gathered from the College Board and the Census Bureau, over the last 22 years (since 1981), the cost of a public four-year college education has increased by 202 percent, while the CPI (Consumer Price Index) has gone up only 80 percent.

This year, average tuition and fees at a public four-year institution is over $4,000, an increase of 9.6 percent over last year. Average tuition and fees at a private college or university is over $18,000, an increase of 5.8 percent over last year's average. These increases exceeded the rise in the Consumer Price Index by 8.4 and 4.7 percent, respectively, and these figures do not include the additional costs associated with higher education, including room and board, books and supplies, lab fees and additional academic costs, transportation, and other personal expenses. Students attending four-year public colleges and universities in all 50 states will feel the squeeze of tuition hikes this fall, with every state in the nation increasing tuition to some degree.

The tuition increases facing students this year are not symptomatic of a single cause such as difficult economic circumstances, but are the culmination of years of disproportionate cost increases caused by a wide variety of influences and factors. . . .

Are Colleges Accountable Enough for Tuition Hikes?

Many observers believe the endlessly increasing tuition rates today's   5 parents and students have been forced to contend with are largely the result of a lack of accountability within the higher education system. Thanks to a combination of factors—including a shortage of easily compared information about tuition increases, and a willingness by government leaders to continue to subsidize higher education regardless of whether institutions make responsible decisions—consumers of higher education (parents and students) are denied the ability to exercise the kind of leverage they would normally expect to have in the marketplace.

A recent *Newsweek* article explores the college cost issue, interviewing a variety of individuals involved with higher education in an effort to identify the root of the problem for parents and students. While state funding cuts are taking a toll, the article notes, colleges are also increasing their expenditures, and they aren't always making the kind of sound economic decisions one might expect them to make in response to consumer unrest.

"Even as budgets are being squeezed, costs are escalating," the *Newsweek* account notes. "To compete in cutting-edge science and technology fields, for instance, universities are shelling out millions for research facilities. But because administrators can be more concerned about raising a college's profile than streamlining operations, says (National

Center for Public Policy and Higher Education president Patrick) Callan, they don't always act the way a private business might—like making all of a campus's divisions negotiate jointly with vendors for lower prices" (Arian Campo-Flores, "Why It Costs So Much; Tough Times Hurt Funding, but Schools Keep Spending," *Newsweek*, September 1, 2003).

Because parents and students keep coming back for more, there is "no market constraint to keep them from raising tuition," *Newsweek* quotes Ronald Ehrenberg, director of the Cornell Higher Education Research Institute, as saying. "People continue to knock on their doors." And, of course, the federal government continues to increase spending for higher education programs. A recent analysis appearing in Forbes suggests dramatic increases in federal spending for higher education programs have only made colleges and universities less accountable to parents and students.

"Over the past three decades the Federal Government has poured three-quarters of a trillion dollars into financial aid for college students," observes writer Ira Carnahan. "So why is college getting less—not more—affordable? One answer seems to be that all those federal dollars have given colleges more room to jack up tuition . . . The more cash the government pumps into parents' pockets, the more the schools siphon from them" ("Back to School: Why Federal College Aid Makes School More Expensive," Ira Carnahan, *Forbes*, September 1, 2003).

Greater competition in higher education, Carnahan's sources suggest, 10 would go a long way toward bringing college costs back down to Earth. Increasing competition among institutions would generate unforeseen savings that "would probably come out of frills like lavish recreational facilities and the salaries and generous perks that are paid to the tenured faculty and senior administrators" at many expensive institutions, Brown University economist Herschel Grossman is quoted as saying by *Forbes*.

"Academia loves Washington's financial aid but seldom feels any obligation to reciprocate," wrote Dr. David Hill in a recent op-ed (Hill, "College Costs become a GOP Issue," *The Hill*, July 30, 2003). But, Hill suggests, the public's tolerance for endless tuition increases may be wearing thin. "[With] even higher tuition rates being proposed, it is evident that widespread public revolt is possible," he observes.

"University officials say they need independence in setting tuition to build better programs, improve efficiencies and hire top rated faculty. But in doing so they must be careful . . . not to price students out of college," warned the *Houston Chronicle* in a July 28, 2003, editorial supporting congressional efforts to address the college cost crisis. "Our state must have more college educated citizens to grow and prosper . . . That will require sensible cost controls over college and university budgets and finding more effective ways to spend higher education dollars."

In the National Commission on the Cost of Higher Education's 1998 report to Congress entitled *Straight Talk about College Costs and Prices*, the Commission reported that, "Institutions of higher education, even to most people in the academy, are financially opaque. Academic institutions have made little effort, either on campus or off, to make themselves more transparent, to explain their finances. As a result, there is no readily available information about college costs and prices nor is there a common national reporting standard for either."

Students and Parents Take a Stand against Skyrocketing Tuition

"I have several friends who said they aren't going to be able to come back or they will have to cut back on their other activities, like clubs and student government, to take on another job."—a State University of New York junior, reacting to a 28 percent increase in tuition for the coming semester, as quoted by the Associated Press (Gormley, "Students, families deal with tuition bills," Associated Press, July 28, 2003).

The college cost crisis is having its most devastating impact on U.S. 15 students, who are most vulnerable to tuition hikes, since many are working their way through school on a shoestring budget.

On July 24, 2003, a group of University of California students filed a class action lawsuit in San Francisco Superior Court in an attempt to block university fee increases, which the student plaintiffs say were made without sufficient advance notice. "I don't know if I'll be able to enroll in school this semester," said Mo Kashmiri, a third-year law student at U.C. Berkeley, noting his bill for this fall will be $2,500 higher than last fall.

A May 1 article in the *Boston Globe* detailed the realities students encounter when faced with tuition increases. "Already working 48 hours a week at a laminating company to pay for his full-time course load at Framingham State College, freshman Brian Avery sighed and shook his head at the prospect of state budget cuts boosting his bill by as much as $1,000 next year. 'It just means more hours, more loans,' he said. 'It puts a damper on the mood around here. A lot of students here pay their own way, which is hard to do. This makes it harder.'" (Schworm, "Rising Costs Worry Students," *Boston Globe*, May 1, 2003).

Similarly, an Associated Press piece described the extreme measures students must undertake to make ends meet when facing tuition hikes. "Students such as (Brandon) Cox, an in-state philosophy major paying his way through college, have been particularly hard-hit. He is taking 20 credit hours per semester and expects his tuition to rise by $800 this year. 'It's almost come to the point of starvation a few times, but I've always managed to find something,' Cox said. 'The plasma center will pay you $20 a pint—if you're willing to bleed for two hours'" (AP, "Tuition Hikes slamming middle-class students," Associated Press, August 25, 2003).

Colleges Caught in Vise

STANLEY FISH

When a parent calls to complain about overcrowded classrooms or a reduction in courses and thinks to cinch the case by saying, "After all, I'm a taxpayer and I pay your salary," I respond by asking a question: What percentage of the university's operating costs do you guess are covered by public funds? Almost always, the answer is something on the order of 75 percent. When I say, no, the figure is just 25 percent and heading downward—and add that in some states the figure has dipped below 10 percent—the reaction is usually equal parts surprise and dismay.

I follow up with another question: What percentage of the cost to educate a student do you guess is covered by tuition? Again, the parent is usually shocked by the answer: If you include not just classroom education but the cost of everything that must be in place for that education to occur—a library, laboratories, computer centers, building maintenance, utilities, safety patrols and more—tuition covers only 26 percent. At this point in the conversation the unhappy parent is beginning to see what public universities are facing these days: "You're telling me that state funds are being withdrawn at the same time expenses are exceeding tuition by a factor of three to one. How can you stay in business?"

That's a good question. It is, however, one that two Republicans on the House education committee, John Boehner and Howard McKeon, do not seem to have spent much time considering. Rather, they have issued a report, "The College Cost Crisis," holding that "institutions of higher learning are not accountable enough to parents, students and taxpayers—the consumers of higher education." This conclusion is not backed by any analysis, except for a couple of references to "wasteful spending." But the message is clear: Universities should operate more like businesses and become more efficient. If they don't, Mr. McKeon has the answer, a bill that would cut federal financing to colleges whose tuition hikes are more than double the rate of inflation or the consumer price index.

But this remedy won't do anything except make the situation worse. If there is a crisis in college costs it has not been caused by price-gouging or bureaucratic incompetence on the part of universities; a better analogy would be the mass circulation magazines of the 1950s like *Collier's* and *Look*, which folded at the very point when they had more readers than ever. The problem was that production costs far outpaced the revenues

Stanley Fish is dean emeritus of the College of Liberal Arts and Sciences at the University of Illinois at Chicago. This essay was published in the *New York Times* on September 18, 2003, in response to Boehner and McKeon's September 4, 2003, report "The College Cost Crisis."

from subscriptions and advertisers, and every new reader actually cost them money.

This is just what is happening at many public universities. More people want the product—applications to my university are up 35 percent in the past two years—but as the demand for it rises the government support for delivering it is withdrawn. The result: Each new student we take increases the number on the debit side of the ledger. Moreover, the costs that neither tuition nor public dollars will cover are rising exponentially. Even if states impose salary and hiring freezes, they would be more than offset by increases no state government can control: raises mandated by union contracts, skyrocketing utility and insurance rates, the cost of replacing worn-out equipment, the cost of replacing equipment declared obsolete after three years, the cost of buying equipment that didn't exist 18 months ago, the cost of maintaining a crumbling physical plant, the cost of security measures deemed necessary after 9/11.

And now, on top of this, comes the threat of Mr. McKeon's bill. First of all, it seems curious to find members of the free-market Republican Party advocating price controls. In fact, it is downright unbusinesslike. Because if a business were to find itself with rising costs and falling revenues it would lop off unprofitable lines, close units, downsize the workforce, relax quality control and, of course, raise prices to whatever level the traffic would bear. In university terms, this would mean offering fewer courses, closing departments, sending students elsewhere, skimping on advising, hiring the pedagogical equivalent of migrant workers, eliminating remedial programs, ejecting the students for whom remedial programs are necessary, reducing health and counseling services, admitting fewer students and inventing fees for everything from registration to breathing.

Now, if a university were to offer this list as its plan to be more businesslike, Representatives Boehner and McKeon, the rest of Congress, America's parents and our other "consumers" would scream bloody murder. "That's not what we're paying for," all these aggrieved parties would complain. But, of course, that would be exactly what they were willing to pay for.

If the revenues sustaining your operation are sharply cut and you are prevented by law from raising prices, your only recourse is to offer an inferior product. Those who say, as the state has said to the University of Illinois, "We're taking $200 million from you but we expect you to do the job you were doing and do it even better," are trafficking either in fantasy or hypocrisy. I vote for hypocrisy.

DISCUSSION QUESTIONS

1. What claim are Boehner and McKeon trying to support? How effective do you feel they are in supporting that claim?

2. Fish's article was written in direct response to Boehner and McKeon's report. What weaknesses does he find in their reasoning? What analogy forms the basis for his disagreement with their argument? How effective would his argument be in convincing college students and their parents that higher education is worth the cost?

3. How successful are Boehner and McKeon in supporting the claim of fact that tuition costs have risen faster than family income and federal aid? Are they equally successful in supporting their view of why tuitions costs have risen? Fish refers to Boehner and McKeon's statement that "institutions of higher learning are not accountable enough to parents, students and taxpayers—the consumers of higher education." Is there any validity to Fish's claim that "[t]his conclusion is not backed by any analysis, except for a couple of references to 'wasteful spending'"? Explain.

4. Both articles raise the question of what the term "public" in public education means. Should colleges and universities really be called public institutions when less than 25 percent of their funding comes from public funds or, in some cases, when less than 10 percent does? Some schools whose state funding has been drastically cut have considered going private. What would be some of the advantages and disadvantages of a public institution's going private?

5. How creditable did you find the authors to be? Did you approach the two articles differently knowing that the first was written by two congressmen and the other by a dean at a university? In their formal report, Boehner and McKeon make more extensive use of sources than Fish does in his newspaper article. How reliable, in your opinion, are the sources they cite?

TAKING THE DEBATE ONLINE

For these and additional research URLS, see bedfordstmartins.com/rottenberg.

- *College Cost Central*
  www.house.gov/ed_workforce/issues/108th/education/ highereducation/collegecostcentral.htm

  This site, maintained by the Committee on Education and the Workforce of the U.S. House of Representatives, which is chaired by John A. Boehner, is designed as a resource for parents, students, and "taxpayers fed up with the high cost of higher education." A link from this site provides the full report in which "Historical Perspective on College Cost Increases" appears.

- *The Chronicle of Higher Education: The War on Higher Education*
  http://chronicle.com/jobs/2003/11/2003112601c.htm

  This article from Stanley Fish's regular column in the *Chronicle of Higher Education*, is a scathing critique of the College Cost Central site.

- *The Washington Dispatch: Collegiate Hypocrisy*
  www.washingtondispatch.com/printer_7558.shtml

  This article from the *Washington Dispatch*, written by Michael Tremoglie, responds to Fish's critique of the College Cost Central site.

- *American Association of Community Colleges: Costs—the Community College Perspective*
  www.statedirectors.org/Docs/college_costs.html

  This article is the response by the American Association of Community Colleges to what Boehner and McKeon term the "College Cost Crisis."

- *The Student Perspective: FSU Student Testifies to Congress on Tuition Increases*
  www.fsunews.com/vnews/display.v/ART/2003/10/06/3f808c7972c0a ?in_archive=1

  This article is a report from Florida State University's online news service about Jessica Hanson, the only student to testify before the U.S. House Subcommittee on Twenty-First Century Competitiveness in September, 2003, when testimony was heard on the issue of college tuition costs.

- *Cato Institute: The Tuition Aid Trap*
  www.cato.org/cgi-bin/scripts/printtech.cgi/dailys/10-09-03.html

  This article by Neal McCluskey, a policy analyst with the Center for Educational Freedom, argues that colleges and universities will have no incentive to control rising tuition as long as higher education is treated as a federally insured entitlement.

- *Washington Post: When States Pay Less, Guess Who Pays More?*
  http://faculty.wm.edu/dhfeld/washingtonpost_com%20When %20States%20Pay%20Less,%20Guess%20Who%20Pays%20More.htm

  In this article, Robert B. Archibald and David H. Feldman, professors of economics at the College of William and Mary, argue that a decline in political and financial support for affordable education for all is the source of the cost crisis rather than irresponsibility on the part of institutions of higher education.

ASSIGNMENTS FOR UNDERSTANDING CLAIMS

1. "I Like Colonel Sanders" is the title of an article that praises ugly architecture, shopping malls, laundromats, and other symbols of "plastic" America. The author claims that these aspects of the American scene have unique and positive values. Defend or refute his claim by pointing out some of the values of these things and giving reasons for your own assessments.

2. Write an essay in which you explain the function or functions that the mall or another gathering place has served for you and your peers.

3. In professional football and basketball, personality traits sometimes contribute as much to the fans' relationship with individual players as talent

on the field or court. Write an essay developing this idea as it applies to one or both sports and providing adequate evidence for your claim.

4. Write an analysis of the ad for Imodium A-D that appears on page 147. Consider how both text and visuals work to advance the claim.

5. Select a familiar ritual and argue for or against the value it represents. *Examples:* the high school prom, Christmas gift-giving, a fraternity initiation, a wedding, a confirmation or bar mitzvah, a funeral ceremony, a Fourth of July celebration.

8. Choose a recommended policy—from the school newspaper or elsewhere—and argue that it will or will not work to produce beneficial changes. *Examples:* expansion of core curriculum requirements, comprehensive tests as a graduation requirement, reinstitution of a physical education requirement, removal of junk food from vending machines.

9. Have you ever been a member of a group that tried but failed to solve a problem through discussion? Communication theorists talk about *interference*, defined by one writer as "anything that hinders or lessens the efficiency of communication."[5] Some of the elements of interference in the delivery of oral messages are fatigue, anger, inattention, vague language, personality conflict, and political bias. You will probably be able to think of others. Did any of these elements prevent the group from arriving at an agreement? Describe the situation and the kinds of interference that you noticed.

[5] Richard E. Crable, *One to Another* (New York: Harper and Row, 1981), p. 18.

CHAPTER 5

Support

All the claims you make—whether of fact, of value, or of policy—must
be supported. Sometimes you will use your own experience as support for
a claim. At other times you may conduct interviews, field research, lab experiments, or surveys to obtain support for your position. For the majority of your assignments, you will most likely turn primarily to print and
electronic sources. In your written assignments, you may already have
been using the readings from this text to support your ideas. The following, for instance, is the opening paragraph of a response to one of the
writing assignments at the end of Chapter 3. This writer chose to compare
the claims made by Jo Ann Citron and Howard Moody in their essays in
that chapter. To support her own claim, the writer quoted from each of
the authors, documenting by means of the page numbers in parentheses
exactly what page the quoted material came from:

> Although they were both writing during the time in 2004 when Massa-
> chusetts was about to make a critical decision about same-sex marriage
> and both for publications that are considered to be liberal, Jo Ann
> Citron and Howard Moody seem unlikely people to agree on anything.
> Citron is a lawyer writing for *The Gay and Lesbian Review Worldwide*, and
> Moody is a retired minister. They both, however, are compassionate to-
> ward people of the same sex who want to share a commitment to each

other. Surprisingly, Moody agrees with Citron that the definition of marriage is in the hands of the state. In his article "Gay Marriage Shows Why We Need to Separate Church and State," he claims that while both church and state can make mistakes, "it is the civil authority of the state that defines the rights and responsibilities of marriage and therefore who can be married" (95). Citron's claim in her essay is that the courts of Massachusetts should lead the other states in "winning for civil union all the rights, benefits, protections, and obligations of marriage" (101).

You will find that many of the readings included in this book are from newspapers and magazines. It has long been standard form for journalists not to use either footnotes or parenthetical documentation to identify their sources but rather to work their sources, when possible, into the text itself. (Sometimes all that their readers learn is that information is from "a source close to the White House.") In your academic writing, however, you will always be expected to give credit to any sources from which you get ideas or wording. Once you have learned the various types of support, you can find in Chapter 10 a detailed explanation of when and how to give credit to any sources you may use.

Support for a claim represents the answer to the question "What have you got to go on?"[1] There are two basic kinds of support in an argument: evidence and appeals to needs and values.

Evidence, as one dictionary defines it, is "something that tends to prove; ground for belief." When you provide evidence, you use facts, including statistics, and opinions, or interpretations of facts—both your own and those of experts. In the following conversation, the first speaker offers facts and the opinion of an expert to convince the second speaker that robots are exceptional machines.

> *"You know, robots do a lot more than work on assembly lines in factories."*
> *"Like what?"*
> *"They shear sheep, pick citrus fruit, and even assist in neurosurgery. And by the end of the century, every house will have a robot slave."*
> *"No kidding. Who says so?"*
> *"An engineer who's the head of the world's largest manufacturer of industrial robots."*

A writer often appeals to readers' needs (that is, requirements for physical and psychological survival and well-being) and values (or standards for right and wrong, good and bad). In the following conversation, the first speaker makes an appeal to the universal need for self-esteem and to the principle of helping others, a value the second speaker probably shares.

---

[1] Stephen Toulmin, *The Uses of Argument* (Cambridge: Cambridge University Press, 1958), p. 98.

"I think you ought to come help us at the nursing home. We need an extra hand."

"I'd like to, but I really don't have the time."

"You could give us an hour a week, couldn't you? Think how good you'd feel about helping out, and the old people would be so grateful. Some of them are very lonely."

Although they use the same kinds of support, conversations are less rigorous than arguments addressed to larger audiences in academic or public situations. In the debates on public policy that appear in the media and in the courts, the quality of support can be crucial in settling urgent matters. The following summary of a well-known court case demonstrates the critical use of both evidence and value appeals in the support of opposing claims.

On March 30, 1981, President Ronald Reagan and three other men were shot by John W. Hinckley Jr., a young drifter from a wealthy Colorado family. Hinckley was arrested at the scene of the shooting. In his trial the factual evidence was presented first: Dozens of reliable witnesses had seen the shooting at close range. Hinckley's diaries, letters, and poems revealed that he had planned the shooting to impress actress Jodie Foster. Opinions, consisting of testimony by experts, were introduced by both the defense and the prosecution. This evidence was contradictory. Defense attorneys produced several psychiatrists who defined Hinckley as insane. If this interpretation of his conduct convinced the jury, then Hinckley would be confined to a mental hospital rather than a prison. The prosecution introduced psychiatrists who interpreted Hinckley's motives and actions as those of a man who knew what he was doing and knew it was wrong. They claimed he was *not* insane by legal definition. The fact that experts can make differing conclusions about the meaning of the same information indicates that interpretations are less reliable than other kinds of support.

Finally, the defense made an appeal to the moral values of the jury. Under the law, criminals judged to be insane are not to be punished as harshly as criminals judged to be sane. The laws assume that criminals who cannot be held responsible for their actions are entitled to more compassionate treatment, confinement to a mental hospital rather than prison. The jury accepted the interpretive evidence supporting the claim of the defense, and Hinckley was pronounced not guilty by reason of insanity. Clearly the moral concern for the rights of the insane proved to be decisive.

In your arguments you will advance your claims, not unlike a lawyer, with these same kinds of support. But before you begin, you should ask two questions: Which kind of support should I use in convincing an audience to accept my claim? and How do I decide that each item of support is valid and worthy of acceptance? This chapter presents the different types of evidence and appeals you can use to support your claim and examines the criteria by which you can evaluate the soundness of that support.

■ Factual Evidence

In Chapter 4, we defined facts as statements possessing a high degree of public acceptance. In theory, facts can be verified by experience alone. Eating too much will make us sick; we can get from Hopkinton to Boston in a half hour by car; in the Northern Hemisphere it is colder in December than in July. The experience of any individual is limited in both time and space, so we must accept as fact thousands of assertions about the world that we ourselves can never verify. Thus we accept the report that human beings landed on the moon in 1969 because we trust those who can verify it. (Country people in Morocco, however, received the news with disbelief because they had no reason to trust the reporters of the event. They insisted on trusting their senses instead. One man said, "I can see the moon very clearly. If a man were walking around up there, wouldn't I be able to see him?")

Factual evidence appears most frequently as examples and statistics, which are a numerical form of examples.

Examples

Examples are the most familiar kind of factual evidence. In addition to providing support for the truth of a generalization, examples can enliven otherwise dense or monotonous prose.

In the following paragraph the writer supports the claim in the topic sentence by offering a series of specific examples.

> Americans expect the next century to bring some striking political and social changes, but people are discerning. Two-thirds believe gay marriages probably will be legal and over half think that fathers will spend as much time and energy with their kids as mothers. Half of the public also predicts that Social Security will probably die; that view is particularly prevalent among younger Americans. But a majority doubts that cigarette smoking will be illegal or that all racial and gender discrimination will disappear.[2]

Hypothetical examples, which create imaginary situations for the audience and encourage them to visualize what might happen under certain circumstances, can also be effective. The following paragraph illustrates

---

[2] Elizabeth Crowley, "Putting Faith in Technology for Year 3000." *The Wall Street Journal*, September 15, 2000, A10.

the use of hypothetical examples. (The author is describing megaschools, high schools with more than 2000 students.)

> And in schools that big there is inevitably a critical mass of kids who are neither jocks nor artists nor even nerds, kids who are nothing at all, nonentities in their own lives. . . . The creditable ballplayer who might have made the team in a smaller school is edged out by better athletes. The artist who might have had work hung in a smaller school is supplanted by abler talents. And the disaffected and depressed boy who might have found a niche, or a friend, or a teacher who noticed, falls between the cracks. Sometimes he quietly drops out. Sometimes he quietly passes through. And sometimes he comes to school with a gun.[3]

All claims about vague or abstract terms would be boring or unintelligible without examples to illuminate them. For example, if you claim that a movie contains "unusual sound effects," you will certainly have to describe some of the effects to convince the reader that your generalization can be trusted.

Statistics

Statistics express information in numbers. In the following example statistics have been used to express raw data in numerical form.

> Surveys have shown that almost half of all male high school seniors— and nearly 20 percent of all ninth grade boys—can be called "problem drinkers." . . . Over 5,000 teenagers are killed yearly in auto accidents due to drunken driving.[4]

These grim numbers probably have meaning for you, partly because you already know that alcoholism exists even among young teenagers and partly because your own experience enables you to evaluate the numbers. But if you are unfamiliar with the subject, such numbers may be difficult or impossible to understand. Statistics, therefore, are more effective in comparisons that indicate whether a quantity is relatively large or small and sometimes even whether a reader should interpret the result as gratifying or disappointing. For example, if a novice gambler were told that for every dollar wagered in a state lottery, 50 percent goes back to the players as prizes, would the gambler be able to conclude that the percentage is high or low? Would he be able to choose between playing the state lottery and playing a casino game? Unless he had more information, probably not. But if he were informed that in casino games, the return to the players is over 90 percent and in slot machines and racetracks the return is around 80 percent, the comparison would enable him to evaluate

---

[3] Anna Quindlen, "The Problem of the Megaschool," *Newsweek*, March 26, 2001, p. 68.
[4] "The Kinds of Drugs Kids Are Getting Into" (Spring House, Pa.: McNeil Pharmaceutical, n.d.).

the meaning of the 50 percent return in the state lottery and even to make a decision about where to gamble his money.[5]

Comparative statistics are also useful for measurements over time. A national survey by The Institute for Social Research of the University of Michigan, in which 17,000 of the nation's 2.7 million high school seniors were questioned about their use of drugs, revealed a continuing downward trend.

> 50.9 percent of those questioned in 1989 reported that they had at least tried an illicit drug like marijuana or cocaine, as against 53.9 percent in 1988 and 56.6 percent in 1987.[6]

Diagrams, tables, charts, and graphs can make clear the relations among many sets of numbers. Such charts and diagrams allow readers to grasp the information more easily than if it were presented in paragraph form. The bar graph[7] that is shown on page 163 summarizes the information produced by a poll on gambling habits. A pie chart[8] such as the one on page 164 can also clarify lists of data.

■ Opinions: Interpretations of the Facts

We have seen how opinions of experts influenced the verdict in the trial of John Hinckley. Facts alone were not enough to substantiate the claim that Hinckley was guilty of attempted assassination. Both the defense and the prosecution relied on experts—psychiatrists—to interpret the facts. Opinions or interpretations about the facts are the inferences discussed in Chapter 4. They are an indispensable source of support for your claims.

Suppose a nightclub for teenagers has opened in your town. That is a fact. What is the significance of it? Is the club's existence good or bad? What consequences will it have for the community? Some parents oppose the idea of a nightclub, fearing that it may allow teenagers to escape from parental control and engage in dangerous activities. Other parents approve of a club, hoping that it will serve as a substitute for unsupervised congregation in the streets. The importance of these interpretations is that they, not the fact itself, help people decide what actions they should take. If the community accepts the interpretation that the club is a source of delinquency, they may decide to revoke the owner's license and close it. As one writer puts it, "The interpretation of data becomes a struggle over power."

Opinions or interpretations of facts generally take four forms: (1) They may suggest the cause for a condition or a causal connection between two sets of data; (2) they may offer predictions about the future;

---

[5] Curt Suphee, "Lotto Baloney," *Harper's*, July 1983, p. 201.
[6] *New York Times*, February 14, 1990, sec. A, p. 16.
[7] *New York Times*, May 28, 1989, p. 24.
[8] *Wall Street Journal*, February 2, 1990, sec. B, p. 1.

Bar graph

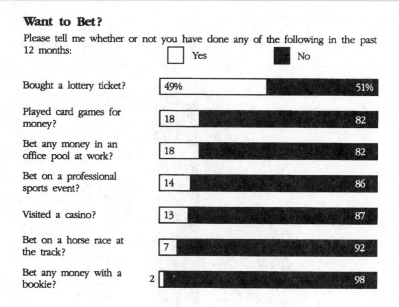

Want to Bet?

Please tell me whether or not you have done any of the following in the past 12 months:

☐ Yes   ■ No

	Yes	No
Bought a lottery ticket?	49%	51%
Played card games for money?	18	82
Bet any money in an office pool at work?	18	82
Bet on a professional sports event?	14	86
Visited a casino?	13	87
Bet on a horse race at the track?	7	92
Bet any money with a bookie?	2	98

(3) they may suggest solutions to a problem; (4) they may refer to the opinion of experts.

Causal Connection

Anorexia is a serious, sometimes fatal, disease characterized by self-starvation. It is found largely among young women. Physicians, psychologists, and social scientists have speculated about the causes, which remain unclear. A leading researcher in the field, Hilde Bruch, believes that food refusal expresses a desire to postpone sexual development. Another authority, Joan Blumberg, believes that one cause may be biological, a nervous dysfunction of the hypothalamus. Still others infer that the causes are cultural, a response to the admiration of the thin female body.[9]

Predictions about the Future

In the fall and winter of 1989 to 1990 extraordinary events shook Eastern Europe, toppling Communist regimes and raising more popular forms of government. Politicians and scholars offered predictions about future changes in the region. One expert, Zbigniew Brzezinski, former national security adviser under President Carter, concluded that the changes for the Soviet Union might be destructive.

[9] Phyllis Rose, "Hunger Artists," *Harper's*, July 1988, p. 82.

Pie chart

Plastic That Goes to Waste

Components of municipal solid waste, by volume

Types of plastic in municipal solid waste, by weight

Paper and cardboard

Plastics

38%

18%

13%

14%

4%

11%

Metals

Glass 2%

Yard waste

Food waste

Other

47% Polyethylene. Includes milk jugs, garbage bags, and most liquid soap and detergent bottles.

16% Polypropylene. Includes some electric appliances, videocassette cases, drinking straws, and screw-on tops.

16% Polystyrene. Includes foam cups, plates and hamburger containers; plastic utensils; and radio and TV cabinets.

6.5% Polyvinyl chloride. Includes plastic wrap and clear containers such as some peanut butter jars and dishwashing liquid bottles.

5% Polyethylene tereph- thalate. Includes soda bottles and other clear bottles such as some cooking oil containers.

5% Polyurethane. Includes foam for insulation and furniture.

4.5% Other plastics.

Source: Franklin Associates Ltd.

It would be a mistake to see the recent decisions as marking a break-through for democracy. Much more likely is a prolonged period of democratizing chaos. One will see the rise in the Soviet Union of in-creasingly irreconcilable conflicts between varying national political and social aspirations, all united by a shared hatred for the existing Communist nomenklatura. One is also likely to see a flashback of a na-tionalist type among the Great Russians, fearful of the prospective breakup of the existing Great Russian Empire.[10]

Solutions to Problems

How shall we solve the problems caused by young people in our cities "who commit crimes and create the staggering statistics in teenage preg-nancies and the high abortion rate"? The minister emeritus of the Abyssinian Baptist Church in New York City proposes establishment of a national youth academy with fifty campuses on inactive military bases. "It is a 'parenting' institution. . . . It is not a penal institution, not a prep school, not a Job Corps Center, not a Civilian Conservation Camp, but it borrows from them." Although such an institution has not been tried be-fore, the author of the proposal thinks that it would represent an effort "to provide for the academic, moral, and social development of young people, to cause them to become responsible and productive citizens."[11]

Expert Opinion

For many of the subjects you discuss and write about, you will find it nec-essary to accept and use the opinions of experts. Based on their reading of the facts, experts express opinions on a variety of controversial sub-jects: whether capital punishment is a deterrent to crime; whether legal-ization of marijuana will lead to an increase in its use; whether children, if left untaught, will grow up honest and cooperative; whether sex edu-cation courses will result in less sexual activity and fewer illegitimate births. The interpretations of the data are often profoundly important because they influence social policy and affect our lives directly and indirectly.

For the problems mentioned above, the opinions of people recog-nized as authorities are more reliable than those of people who have nei-ther thought about nor done research on the subject. But opinions may also be offered by student writers in areas in which they are knowledge-able. If you were asked, for example, to defend or refute the statement that work has advantages for teenagers, you could call on your own ex-perience and that of your friends to support your claim. You can also draw on your experience to write convincingly about your special interests.

---

[10]*New York Times*, February 9, 1990, sec. A, p. 13.
[11]Samuel D. Proctor, "To the Rescue: A National Youth Academy," *New York Times*, September 16, 1989, sec. A, p. 27.

One opinion, however, is not as good as another. The value of any opinion depends on the quality of the evidence and the trustworthiness of the person offering it.

EVALUATION OF EVIDENCE

Before you begin to write, you must determine whether the facts and opinions you have chosen to support your claim are sound. Can they convince your readers? A distinction between the evaluation of facts and the evaluation of opinions is somewhat artificial because many facts are verified by expert opinion, but for our analysis we discuss them separately.

■ Evaluation of Factual Evidence

As you evaluate factual evidence, you should keep in mind the following questions:

1. Is the evidence up to date? The importance of up-to-date information depends on the subject. If you are defending the claim that suicide is immoral, you will not need to examine new data. For many of the subjects you write about, recent research and scholarship will be important, even decisive, in proving the soundness of your data. "New" does not always mean "best," but in fields where research is ongoing—education, psychology, technology, medicine, and all the natural and physical sciences—you should be sensitive to the dates of the research.

In writing a paper a few years ago warning about the health hazards of air pollution, you would have used data referring only to outdoor pollution produced by automobile and factory emissions. But writing about air pollution today, you would have to take into account new data about indoor pollution, which has become a serious problem as a result of attempts to conserve energy. Because research studies in indoor pollution are continually being updated, recent evidence will probably be more accurate than past research.

2. Is the evidence sufficient? The amount of evidence you need depends on the complexity of the subject and the length of your paper. Given the relative brevity of most of your assignments, you will need to be selective. For the claim that indoor pollution is a serious problem, one example would obviously not be enough. For a 750- to 1,000-word paper, three or four examples would probably be sufficient. The choice of examples should reflect different aspects of the problem: in this case, different sources of indoor pollution—gas stoves, fireplaces, kerosene heaters, insulation—and the consequences for health.

Indoor pollution is a fairly limited subject for which the evidence is clear. But more complex problems require more evidence. A common fault in argument is generalization based on insufficient evidence. In a 1,000-word paper you could not adequately treat the causes of conflict in the Middle East; you could not develop workable proposals for healthcare reform; you could not predict the development of education in the next century. In choosing a subject for a brief paper, determine whether you can produce sufficient evidence to convince a reader who may not agree with you. If not, the subject may be too large for a brief paper.

3. Is the evidence relevant? All the evidence should, of course, contribute to the development of your argument. Sometimes the arguer loses sight of the subject and introduces examples that are wide of the claim. In defending a national health-care plan, one student offered examples of the success of health maintenance organizations, but such organizations, although subsidized by the federal government, were not the structure favored by sponsors of a national health-care plan. The examples were interesting but irrelevant.

Also keep in mind that not all readers will agree on what is relevant. Is the unsavory private life of a politician relevant to his or her performance in office? If you want to prove that a politician is unfit to serve because of his or her private activities, you may first have to convince some members of the audience that private activities are relevant to public service.

4. Are the examples representative? This question emphasizes your responsibility to choose examples that are typical of all the examples you do not use. Suppose you offered Vermont's experience to support your claim that same-sex marriage should be legal. Is the experience of Vermont typical of what is happening or may happen in other states? Or is Vermont, a small, mostly rural New England state, different enough from other states to make the example unrepresentative?

5. Are the examples consistent with the experience of the audience? The members of your audience use their own experiences to judge the soundness of your evidence. If your examples are unfamiliar or extreme, they will probably reject your conclusion. Consider the following excerpt from Jacob Neusner's hypothetical commencement speech (p. 351), which is meant to represent a faculty member's response to student apathy.

> For years we have created an altogether forgiving world, in which whatever slight effort you gave was all that was demanded. When you did not keep appointments, we made new ones. When your work came in beyond the deadline, we pretended not to care.
>
> Worse still, when you were boring, we acted as if you were saying something important. When you were garrulous and talked to hear yourself talk, we listened as if it mattered. When you tossed on our desks writing upon which you had not labored, we read it and even

responded, as though you earned a response. When you were dull, we pretended you were smart. When you were predictable, unimaginative, and routine, we listened as if to new and wonderful things. When you demanded free lunch we served it.

If most members of the audience find that such a description doesn't reflect their own attitudes or those of their friends, they will probably question the validity of the claim.

■ Evaluation of Statistics

The questions you must ask about examples also apply to statistics. Are they recent? Are they sufficient? Are they relevant? Are they typical? Are they consistent with the experience of the audience? But there are additional questions directed specifically to evaluation of statistics.

1. Do the statistics come from trustworthy sources? Perhaps you have read newspaper accounts of very old people, some reported to be as old as 135, living in the Caucasus or the Andes, nourished by yogurt and hard work. But these statistics are hearsay; no birth records or other official documents exist to verify them. Now two anthropologists have concluded that the numbers were part of a rural mythology and that the ages of the people were actually within the normal range for human populations elsewhere.[12]

Hearsay statistics should be treated with the same skepticism accorded to gossip or rumor. Sampling a population to gather statistical information is a sophisticated science; you should ask whether the reporter of the statistics is qualified and likely to be free of bias. Among the generally reliable sources are polling organizations such as Gallup, Roper, and Louis Harris and agencies of the U.S. government such as the Census Bureau and the Bureau of Labor Statistics. Other qualified sources are well-known research foundations, university centers, and insurance companies that prepare actuarial tables. Statistics from underdeveloped countries are less reliable for obvious reasons: lack of funds, lack of trained statisticians, lack of communication and transportation facilities to carry out accurate censuses.

2. Are the terms clearly defined? In an example in Chapter 3, the reference to poverty (p. 63) made clear that any statistics would be meaningless unless we knew exactly how *poverty* was defined by the user. *Unemployment* is another term for which statistics will be difficult to read if the definition varies from one user to another. For example, are seasonal workers employed or unemployed during the off-season? Are part-time workers employed? (In Russia they are unemployed.) Are workers on

---

[12] Richard B. Mazess and Sylvia H. Forman, "Longevity and Age Exaggeration in Vilcabamba, Ecuador," *Journal of Gerontology* (1979), pp. 94–98.

government projects employed? (During the 1930s they were considered employed by the Germans and unemployed by the Americans.) The more abstract or controversial the term, the greater the necessity for clear definition.

3. Are the comparisons between comparable things? Folk wisdom warns us that we cannot compare apples and oranges. Population statistics for the world's largest city, for example, should indicate the units being compared. Greater London is defined in one way, greater New York in another, and greater Tokyo in still another. The population numbers will mean little unless you can be sure that the same geographical units are being compared.

4. Has any significant information been omitted? *The Plain Truth,* a magazine published by the World-Wide Church of God, advertises itself as follows:

> *The Plain Truth* has now topped 5,000,000 copies per issue. It is now the fastest-growing magazine in the world and one of the widest circulated mass-circulation magazines on earth. Our circulation is now greater than *Newsweek.* New subscribers are coming in at the rate of around 40,000 per week.

What the magazine neglects to mention is that it is *free.* There is no subscription fee, and the magazine is widely distributed in drugstores, supermarkets, and airports. *Newsweek* is sold on newsstands and by subscription. The comparison therefore omits significant information.

■ Evaluation of Opinions

When you evaluate the reliability of opinions in subjects with which you are not familiar, you will be dealing almost exclusively with opinions of experts. Most of the following questions are directed to an evaluation of authoritative sources. But you can also ask these questions of students or of others with opinions based on their own experience and research. Keep them in mind when doing research on the Web.

1. Is the source of the opinion qualified to give an opinion on the subject? The discussion on credibility in Chapter 1 (pp. 13–15) pointed out that certain achievements by the interpreter of the data—publications, acceptance by colleagues—can tell us something about his or her competence. Although these standards are by no means foolproof (people of outstanding reputations have been known to falsify their data), nevertheless they offer assurance that the source is generally trustworthy. The answers to questions you must ask are not hard to find: Is the source qualified by education? Is the source associated with a reputable institution—a university or a research organization? Is the source credited with having made contributions to the field—books, articles, research studies? Suppose that in writing a paper on organ transplants you came across an article by Peter Medawar. He is identified as follows:

> Sir Peter Medawar, British zoologist, winner of the 1960 Nobel Prize in Physiology or Medicine, for proving that the rejection by the body of foreign organs can be overcome; president of the Royal Society; head of the National Institute for Medical Research in London; a world leader in immunology.

These credentials would suggest to almost any reader that Medawar was a reliable source for information about organ transplants.

If the source is not so clearly identified, you should treat the data with caution. Such advice is especially relevant when you are dealing with popular works about such subjects as miracle diets, formulas for instant wealth, and sightings of monsters and UFOs. Do not use such data until you can verify them from other, more authoritative sources.

In addition, you should question the identity of any source listed as "spokesperson" or "reliable source" or "an unidentified authority." The mass media are especially fond of this type of attribution. Sometimes the sources are people in public life who plant stories anonymously or off the record for purposes they prefer to keep hidden.

Even when the identification is clear and genuine, you should ask if the credentials are relevant to the field in which the authority claims expertise. So specialized are areas of scientific study today that scientists in one field may not be competent to make judgments in another. William Shockley is a distinguished engineer, a Nobel Prize winner for his contribution to the invention of the electronic transistor. But when he made the claim, based on his own research, that blacks are genetically inferior to whites, geneticists accused Shockley of venturing into a field where he was unqualified to make judgments. Similarly, advertisers invite stars from the entertainment world to express opinions about products with which they are probably less familiar than members of their audience. All citizens have the right to express their views, but this does not mean that all views are equally credible or worthy of attention.

2. Is the source biased for or against his or her interpretation? Even authorities who satisfy the criteria for expertise may be guilty of bias. Bias arises as a result of economic reward, religious affiliation, political loyalty, and other interests. The expert may not be aware of the bias; even an expert can fall into the trap of ignoring evidence that contradicts his or her own intellectual preferences. A British psychologist has said:

> The search for meaning in data is bound to involve all of us in distortion to greater or lesser degree. . . . Transgression consists not so much in a clear break with professional ethics, as in an unusually high-

handed, extreme or self-deceptive attempt to promote one particular view of reality at the expense of all others.[13]

Before accepting the interpretation of an expert, you should ask: Is there some reason why I should suspect the motives of this particular source?

Consider, for example, an advertisement claiming that sweetened breakfast cereals are nutritious. The advertisement, placed by the manufacturer of the cereal, provides impeccable references from scientific sources to support its claims. But since you are aware of the economic interest of the company in promoting sales, you may wonder if they have reproduced only facts that favor their claims. Are there other facts that might prove the opposite? As a careful researcher you would certainly want to look further for data about the advantages and disadvantages of sugar in our diets.

It is harder to determine bias in the research done by scientists and university members even when the research is funded by companies interested in a favorable review of their products. If you discover that a respected biologist who advocates the use of sugar in baby food receives a consultant's fee from a sugar company, should you conclude that the research is slanted and that the scientist has ignored contrary evidence? Not necessarily. The truth may be that the scientist arrived at conclusions about the use of sugar legitimately through experiments that no other scientist would question. But it would probably occur to you that a critical reader might ask about the connection between the results of the research and the payment by a company that profits from the research. In this case you would be wise to read further to find confirmation or rejection of the claim by other scientists.

The most difficult evaluations concern ideological bias. Early in our lives we learn to discount the special interest that makes a small child brag, "My mother (or father) is the greatest!" Later we become aware that the claims of people who are avowed Democrats or Republicans or supply-side economists or Yankee fans or zealous San Franciscans or joggers must be examined somewhat more carefully than those of people who have no special commitment to a cause or a place or an activity. This is not to say that all partisan claims lack support. They may, in fact, be based on the best available support. But whenever special interest is apparent, there is always the danger that an argument will reflect this bias.

3. Has the source bolstered the claim with sufficient and appropriate evidence? In an article attacking pornography, one author wrote, "Statistics prove that the recent proliferation of porno is directly related

---

[13]Liam Hudson, *The Cult of the Fact* (New York: Harper and Row, 1972), p. 125.

to the increasing number of rapes and assaults on women."[14] But the author gave no further information—neither statistics nor proof that a cause-effect relation exists between pornography and violence against women. The critical reader will ask, "What are the numbers? Who compiled them?"

Even those who are reputed to be experts in the subjects they discuss must do more than simply allege that a claim is valid or that the data exist. They must provide facts to support their interpretations.

■ When Experts Disagree

Authoritative sources can disagree. Such disagreement is probably most common in the social sciences. They are called the "soft" sciences precisely because a consensus about conclusions in these areas is more difficult to arrive at than in the natural and physical sciences. Consider the controversy over what determines the best interests of the child where both biological and foster parents are engaged in trying to secure custody. Experts are deeply divided on this issue. Dr. Daniel J. Cohen, a child psychologist and director of the Yale Child Study Center, argues that the psychological needs of the child should take precedence. If the child has a stable and loving relationship with foster parents, that is where he should stay. But Bruce Bozer and Bernadine Dohrn of the Children and Family Justice Center at Northwestern University Law School insist that "such a solution may be overly simplistic." The child may suffer in later life when he learns that he has been prevented from returning to biological parents "who fought to get him back."[15]

But even in the natural and physical sciences, where the results of observation and experiment are more conclusive, we encounter heated differences of opinion. A popular argument concerns the extinction of the dinosaurs. Was it the effect of an asteroid striking the earth? Or widespread volcanic activity? Or a cooling of the planet? All these theories have their champions among the experts.

Environmental concerns also produce lively disagreements. Scientists have lined up on both sides of a debate about the importance of protecting the tropical rain forest as a source of biological, especially mammalian, diversity. Dr. Edward O. Wilson, a Harvard biologist, whose books have made us familiar with the term *biodiversity,* says, "The great majority of organisms appears to reach maximum diversity in the rain forest. There is no question that the rain forests are the world's headquarters of diversity." But in the journal *Science* another biologist, Dr. Michael Mares, a professor of zoology at the University of Oklahoma, argues that "if one could choose only a single South American habitat in which to preserve

[14]Charlotte Allen, "Exploitation for Profit," *Daily Collegian* [University of Massachusetts], October 5, 1976, p. 2.
[15]*New York Times,* September 4, 1994, sec. E, p. 3.

the greatest mammalian diversity, it would be the dry lands. . . .The dry lands are very likely far more highly threatened than the largely inaccessible rain forests."[16] A debate of more immediate relevance concerns possible dangers in genetically modified foods, as distinguished from foods modified by traditional breeding practices. Dr. Louis Pribyl, a U.S. Food and Drug Administration microbiologist, has accused the agency of claiming "that there are no unintended effects that raise the FDA's level of concern. But . . . there are no data to back up this contention." On the other hand, Dr. James Marjanski, the FDA's biotechnology coordinator, maintains that "as long as developers of these foods follow agency guidelines, genetically engineered foods are as safe as any on the market."[17]

How can you choose between authorities who disagree? If you have applied the tests discussed so far and discovered that one source is less qualified by training and experience or makes claims with little support or appears to be biased in favor of one interpretation, you will have no difficulty in rejecting that person's opinion. If conflicting sources prove to be equally reliable in all respects, then continue reading other authorities to determine whether a greater number of experts support one opinion rather than another. Although numbers alone, even of experts, don't guarantee the truth, nonexperts have little choice but to accept the authority of the greater number until evidence to the contrary is forthcoming. Finally, if you are unable to decide between competing sources of evidence, you may conclude that the argument must remain unsettled. Such an admission is not a failure; after all, such questions are considered controversial because even the experts cannot agree, and such questions are often the most interesting to consider and argue about.

APPEALS TO NEEDS AND VALUES

Good factual evidence is usually enough to convince an audience that your factual claim is sound. Using examples, statistics, and expert opinion, you can prove, for example, that women do not earn as much as men for the same work. But even good evidence may not be enough to convince your audience that unequal pay is wrong or that something should be done about it. In making value and policy claims, an appeal to the needs and values of your audience is absolutely essential to the success of your argument. If you want to persuade the audience to change their minds or adopt a course of action—in this case, to demand legalization of equal pay for equal work—you will have to show that assent to your claim will bring about what they want and care deeply about.

[16] *New York Times,* April 7, 1992, sec. C, p. 4.
[17] *New York Times,* December 1, 1999, A15.

As a writer, you cannot always know who your audience is; it's impossible, for example, to predict exactly who will read a letter you write to a newspaper. Even in the classroom, you have only partial knowledge of your readers. You may not always know or be able to infer what the goals and principles of your audience are. You may not know how they feel about big government, the draft, private school education, feminism, environmental protection, homosexuality, religion, or any of the other subjects you might write about. If the audience concludes that the things you care about are very different from what they care about, if they cannot identify with your goals and principles, they may treat your argument with indifference, even hostility, and finally reject it. But you can hope that decent and reasonable people will share many of the needs and values that underlie your claims.

■ Appeals to Needs

Suppose that you are trying to persuade Joan Doakes, a friend who is still undecided, to attend college. In your reading you have come across a report about the benefits of a college education written by Howard Bowen, a former professor of economics at Claremont (California) Graduate School, former president of Grinnell College, and a specialist in the economics of higher education. Armed with his testimony, you write to Joan. As support for your claim that she should attend college, you offer evidence that (1) college graduates earn more throughout their lifetime than high school graduates; (2) college graduates are more active and exert greater influence in their communities than high school graduates; and (3) college graduates achieve greater success as partners in marriage and as thoughtful and caring parents.[18]

Joan writes back that she is impressed with the evidence you've provided—the statistics, the testimony of economists and psychologists—and announces that she will probably enroll in college instead of accepting a job offer.

How did you succeed with Joan Doakes? If you know your friend pretty well, the answer is not difficult. Joan has needs that can be satisfied by material success; more money will enable her to enjoy the comforts and luxuries that are important to her. She also needs the esteem of her peers and the sense of achievement that political activity and service to others will give her. Finally, she needs the rootedness to be found in close and lasting family connections.

Encouraged by your success with Joan Doakes, you write the same letter to another friend, Fred Fox, who has also declined to apply for admission to college. This time, however, your argument fails. Fred, too, is

[18] "The Residue of Academic Learning," *Chronicle of Higher Education,* November 14, 1977, p. 13.

impressed with your research and evidence. But college is not for him, and he repeats that he has decided not to become a student.

Why such a different response? The reason, it turns out, is that you don't know what Fred really wants. Fred Fox dreams of going to Alaska to live alone in the wilderness. Money means little to him, influence in the community is irrelevant to his goals, and at present he feels no desire to become a member of a loving family.

Perhaps if you had known Fred better, you would have offered different evidence to show that you recognized what he needed and wanted. You could have told him that Bowen's study also points out that "college-educated persons are healthier than are others," that "they also have better ability to adjust to changing times and vocations," that "going to college enhances self-discovery" and enlarges mental resources, which encourage college graduates to go on learning for the rest of their lives. This information might have persuaded Fred that college would also satisfy some of his needs.

As this example demonstrates, you have a better chance of persuading your reader to accept your claim if you know what he or she wants and what importance he or she assigns to the needs that we all share. Your reader must, in other words, see some connection between your evidence and his or her needs.

The needs to which you appealed in your letters to Joan and Fred are the requirements for physiological or psychological well-being. The most familiar classification of needs was developed by the psychologist Abraham H. Maslow in 1954.[19] These needs, said Maslow, motivate human thought and action. In satisfying our needs, we attain both long- and short-term goals. Because Maslow believed that some needs are more important than others, he arranged them in hierarchical order from the most urgent biological needs to the psychological needs that are related to our roles as members of a society.

PHYSIOLOGICAL NEEDS Basic bodily requirements: food and drink; health; sex

SAFETY NEEDS Security; freedom from harm; order and stability

BELONGINGNESS AND LOVE NEEDS Love within a family and among friends; roots within a group or a community

ESTEEM NEEDS Material success; achievement; power, status, and recognition by others

SELF-ACTUALIZATION NEEDS Fulfillment in realizing one's potential

For most of your arguments you won't have to address the audience's basic physiological needs for nourishment or shelter. The desire for health, however, now receives extraordinary attention. Appeals to buy

[19]*Motivation and Personality* (New York: Harper and Row, 1954), pp. 80–92.

health foods, vitamin supplements, drugs, exercise and diet courses, and health books are all around us. Many of the claims are supported by little or no evidence, but readers are so eager to satisfy the need for good health that they often overlook the lack of facts or authoritative opinion. The desire for physical well-being, however, is not so simple as it seems; it is strongly related to our need for self-esteem and love.

Appeals to our needs to feel safe from harm, to be assured of order and stability in our lives are also common. Insurance companies, politicians who promise to rid our streets of crime, and companies that offer security services all appeal to this profound and nearly universal need. (We say "nearly" because some people are apparently attracted to risk and danger.) At this writing those who monitor terrorist activity are attempting both to arouse fear for our safety and to suggest ways of reducing the dangers that make us fearful.

The last three needs in Maslow's hierarchy are the ones you will find most challenging to appeal to in your arguments. It is clear that these needs arise out of human relationships and participation in society. Advertisers make much use of appeals to these needs.

BELONGINGNESS AND LOVE NEEDS

"Whether you are young or old, the need for companionship is universal." (ad for dating service)

"Share the Fun of High School with Your Little Girl!" (ad for a Barbie Doll)

ESTEEM NEEDS

"Enrich your home with the distinction of an Oxford library."

"Apply your expertise to more challenges and more opportunities. Here are outstanding opportunities for challenge, achievement, and growth." (Perkin-Elmer Co.)

SELF-ACTUALIZATION NEEDS

"Be all that you can be." (former U.S. Army slogan)

"Are you demanding enough? Somewhere beyond the cortex is a small voice whose mere whisper can silence an army of arguments. It goes by many names: integrity, excellence, standards. And it stands alone in final judgment as to whether we have demanded enough of ourselves and, by that example, have inspired the best in those around us." (*New York Times*)

Of course, it is not only advertisers who use these appeals. We hear them from family and friends, from teachers, from employers, from editorials and letters to the editor, from people in public life.

■ Appeals to Values

Needs give rise to values. If we feel the need to belong to a group, we learn to value commitment, sacrifice, and sharing. And we then respond to arguments that promise to protect our values. It is hardly surprising that values, the principles by which we judge what is good or bad, beautiful or ugly, worthwhile or undesirable, should exercise a profound influence on our behavior. Virtually all claims, even those that seem to be purely factual, contain expressed or unexpressed judgments. When Michael M. Weinstein in Chapter 4 (pp. 109–12) quotes evidence that affirmative action does not promote unqualified candidates, he does so not because he is doing research for academic reasons but because he hopes to persuade people that affirmative action is good social policy.

For our study of argument, we will speak of groups or systems of values because any single value is usually related to others. People and institutions are often defined by such systems of values. We can distinguish, for example, between those who think of themselves as traditional and those who think of themselves as modern by listing their differing values. One writer contrasts such values in this way:

> Among the values of traditionalism are merit, accomplishment, competition, and success; self-restraint, self-discipline, and the postponement of gratification; the stability of the family; and a belief in certain moral universals. The modernist ethos scorns the pursuit of success; is egalitarian and redistributionist in emphasis; tolerates or encourages sensual gratification; values self-expression as against self-restraint; accepts alternative or deviant forms of the family; and emphasizes ethical relativism.[20]

Systems of values are neither so rigid nor so distinct from one another as this list suggests. Some people who are traditional in their advocacy of competition and success may also accept the modernist values of self-expression and alternative family structures. Values, like needs, are arranged in a hierarchy; that is, some are clearly more important than others to the people who hold them. Moreover, the arrangement may shift over time or as a result of new experiences. In 1962, for example, two speech teachers prepared a list of what they called "Relatively Unchanging Values Shared by Most Americans."[21] Included were "puritan and pioneer standards of morality" and "perennial optimism about the future." More than forty years later, an appeal to these values might fall on a number of deaf ears.

You should also be aware of not only changes over time but also different or competing value systems that reflect a multitude of subcultures

---

[20]Joseph Adelson, "What Happened to the Schools," *Commentary,* March 1981, p. 37.

[21]Edward Steele and W. Charles Redding, "The American Value System: Premises for Persuasion," *Western Speech,* 26 (Spring 1962), pp. 83–91.

in our country. Differences in age, sex, race, ethnic background, social environment, religion, even in the personalities and characters of its members define the groups we belong to. Such terms as *honor, loyalty, justice, patriotism, duty, responsibility, equality, freedom,* and *courage* will be interpreted very differently by different groups.

All of us belong to more than one group, and the values of the several groups may be in conflict. If one group to which you belong—say, peers of your own age and class—is generally uninterested in and even scornful of religion, you may nevertheless hold to the values of your family and continue to place a high value on religious belief.

How can a knowledge of your readers' values enable you to make a more effective appeal? Suppose you want to argue in favor of a sex education program in the middle school you attended. The program you support would not only give students information about contraception and venereal disease but also teach them about the pleasures of sex, the importance of small families, and alternatives to heterosexuality. If the readers of your argument are your classmates or your peers, you can be fairly sure that their agreement will be easier to obtain than that of their parents, especially if their parents think of themselves as conservative. Your peers are more likely to value experimentation, tolerance of alternative sexual practices, freedom, and novelty. Their parents are more likely to value restraint, conformity to conventional sexual practices, obedience to family rules, and foresight in planning for the future.

Knowing that your peers share your values and your goals will mean that you need not spell out the values supporting your claim; they are understood by your readers. Convincing their parents, however, who think that freedom, tolerance, and experimentation have been abused by their children, will be a far more challenging task. In one written piece you have little chance of changing their values, a result that might be achieved only over a longer period of time. So you might first attempt to reduce their hostility by suggesting that, even if a community-wide program were adopted, students would need parental permission to enroll. This might convince some parents that you share their values regarding parental authority and primacy of the family. Second, you might look for other values to which the parents subscribe and to which you can make an appeal. Do they prize maturity, self-reliance, responsibility in their children? If so, you could attempt to prove, with authoritative evidence, that the sex education program would promote these qualities in students who took the course.

But familiarity with the value systems of prospective readers may also lead you to conclude that winning assent to your argument will be impossible. It would probably be fruitless to attempt to persuade a group of lifelong pacifists to endorse the use of nuclear weapons. The beliefs, attitudes, and habits that support their value systems are too fundamental to yield to one or two attempts at persuasion.

EVALUATION OF APPEALS TO NEEDS AND VALUES

If your argument is based on an appeal to the needs and values of your audience, the following questions will help you evaluate the soundness of your appeal.

1. Have the values been clearly defined? If you are appealing to the patriotism of your readers, can you be sure that they agree with your definition? Does patriotism mean "Our country, right or wrong!" or does it mean dissent, even violent dissent, if you think your country is wrong? Because value terms are abstractions, you must make their meaning explicit by placing them in context and providing examples.

2. Are the needs and values to which you appeal prominent in the reader's hierarchy at the time you are writing? An affluent community, fearful of further erosion of quiet and open countryside, might resist an appeal to allow establishment of a high-technology firm, even though the firm would bring increased prosperity to the area.

3. Is the evidence in your argument clearly related to the needs and values to which you appeal? Remember that the reader must see some connection between your evidence and his or her goals. Suppose you were writing an argument to persuade a group of people to vote in an upcoming election. You could provide evidence to prove that only 20 percent of the town voted in the last election. But this evidence would not motivate your audience to vote unless you could provide other evidence to show that their needs were not being served by such a low turnout.

Writer's Guide: Using Effective Support

1. In deciding how much support you need for your claim, it is always a good idea to assume that you are addressing an audience that may be at least slightly hostile to that claim. Those who already agree with you do not need convincing.

2. Keep a mental, if not a written, list of the different types of support you use in an essay. Few essays will use all of the different types of support, but being aware of all the possibilities will prevent you from forgetting to draw on one or more types of support that may advance your argument.

3. In that checklist of types of support, don't forget that there are two main categories: evidence and appeals to needs and values. Appeals to needs and values will generally need the reinforcement that comes from more objective forms of evidence, but the two in combination can often

provide the strongest case for your claim. Aristotle explained that in an ideal world, arguers could depend on logic alone, but we live in a world that is far from ideal.

4. Use the following questions about the evaluation of evidence as a check-list to analyze the support you use in your argumentative essays:

Factual evidence:

- Is the evidence up to date?
- Is the evidence sufficient?
- Is the evidence relevant?
- Are the examples representative?
- Are the examples consistent with the experience of the audience?

Statistics:

- Do the statistics come from trustworthy sources?
- Are the terms clearly defined?
- Are the comparisons between comparable things?
- Has any significant information been omitted?

Opinion:

- Is the source of the opinion qualified to give an opinion on the subject?
- Is the source biased for or against his or her interpretation?
- Has the source bolstered the claim with sufficient and appropriate evidence?

5. Also check your essays against the list of questions regarding appeals to needs and values:

- Have the values been clearly defined?
- Are the needs and values to which you appeal prominent in the reader's hierarchy at the time you are writing?
- Is the evidence in your argument clearly related to the needs and values to which you appeal?

Single-Sex Education Benefits Men Too

CLAUDIUS E. WATTS III

Introduction: background of the problem

The values that the author will defend

Claim of policy: to preserve single-sex education for men

Support: expert opinion, appeal to values

Last week Virginia Military Institute, an all-male state college, got the good news from a federal judge that it can continue its single-sex program if it opens a leadership program at Mary Baldwin College, a nearby private women's school. But it is likely that the government will appeal the decision. Meanwhile, the Citadel, another such institution in Charleston, S.C., remains under attack. Unwittingly, so are some fundamental beliefs prevalent in our society: namely, the value of single-sex education, the need for diversity in education, and the freedom of choice in associating with, and not associating with, whomever one chooses.

When Shannon Faulkner received a preliminary injunction to attend day classes with the Citadel's Corps of Cadets, she was depicted as a nineteen-year-old woman fighting for her constitutional rights, while the Citadel was painted as an outdated and chauvinistic Southern school that had to be dragged into the twentieth century.

But the Citadel is not fighting to keep women out of the Corps of Cadets because there is a grandiose level of nineteenth-century machismo to protect. Rather, we at the Citadel are trying to preserve an educational environment that molds young men into grown men of good character, honor, and integrity. It is part of a single-sex educational system that has proven itself successful throughout history.

The benefits of single-sex education for men are clear: Says Harvard sociologist David Riesman, not only is single-sex education an optimal means of character development, but it also

---

Lieutenant General Claudius E. Watts III, retired from the U.S. Air Force, is a former president of the Citadel in South Carolina. This selection is from the May 3, 1995, edition of the *Wall Street Journal*.

removes the distractions of the "mating-dating" game so prevalent in society and enables institutions to focus students on values and academics.

In short, the value of separate education is, simply, the fact it is separate.   5

In October 1992, a federal appeals court ruled that "single-sex education is pedagogically justifiable." Indeed, a cursory glance at some notable statistics bears that out. For instance, the Citadel has the highest retention rate for minority students of any public college in South Carolina: 67 percent of black students graduate in four years, which is more than 2½ times the national average. Additionally, the Citadel's four-year graduation rate for all students is 70 percent, which compares with 48 percent nationally for all other public institutions and 67 percent nationally for private institutions. Moreover, many of the students come from modest backgrounds. Clearly, the Citadel is not the bastion of male privilege that the U.S. Justice Department, in briefs filed by that agency, would have us all believe.

While the Justice Department continues to reject the court's ruling affirming the values of single-sex education, others continue to argue that because the federal military academies are coeducational, so should the Citadel be. However, it is not the Citadel's primary mission to train officers for the U.S. armed forces. We currently commission approximately 30 percent of our graduates, but only 18 percent actually pursue military careers. At the Citadel, the military model is a means to an end, not the end itself.

Today there are eighty-four women's colleges scattered throughout the United States, including two that are public. These colleges defend their programs as necessary to help women overcome intangible barriers in male-dominated professions. This argument has merit; women's colleges produce only 4.5 percent of all female college graduates but have produced one-fourth of all women board members of Fortune 500 companies and one-half of the women in Congress. However, the educational benefits of men's colleges are equally clear; and to allow women alone to benefit from single-sex education seems to per-

Support: statistics

Support: facts, statistics

Support: facts, statistics

Support: causal connection

petuate the very stereotypes that women—including Ms. Faulkner—are trying to correct.

Warrant: men should enjoy the same freedom of choice

If young women want and need to study and learn in single-sex schools, why is it automatically wrong for young men to want and need the same? Where is the fairness in this assumption?

Support: causal connection

"At what point does the insistence that one individual not be deprived of choice spill over into depriving countless individuals of choice?" asks Emory University's Elizabeth Fox Genovese in an article by Jeffrey Rosen published in the February 14 *New Republic*.

Support: appeal to values

Yet so it is at the Citadel. While one student maintains that she is protecting her freedom to associate, we mustn't forget that the Citadel's cadets also have a freedom—the freedom not to associate. While we have read about one female student's rights, what hasn't been addressed are the rights of the 1,900 cadets who chose the Citadel—and the accompanying discipline and drill—because it offered them the single-sex educational experience they wanted. Why do one student's rights supersede all theirs?

Support: predictions about the future

One might be easily tempted to argue on the grounds that Ms. Faulkner is a taxpayer and the Citadel is a tax-supported institution. But if the taxpayer argument holds, the next step is to forbid all public support for institutions that enroll students of only one sex. A draconian measure such as this would surely mean the end of private—as well as public—single-gender colleges.

Backing for warrant: tax-supported education should be equal for men and women

Most private colleges—Columbia and Converse, the two all-female schools in South Carolina, included—could not survive without federal financial aid, tax exemptions, and state tax support in the form of tuition grants. In fact, nearly 900 of Columbia and Converse's female students receive state-funded tuition grants, a student population that is almost half the size of the Corps of Cadets. In essence, South Carolina's two private women's colleges may stand or fall with the Citadel.

Carried to its logical conclusion, then, the effort to coeducate the Citadel might mean the end of all single-sex education—for women as well as men, in private as well as public schools.

■ **Analysis: Support**

In 1993 Shannon Faulkner, a woman, was rejected for admission to the Citadel, an all-male state-supported military academy in South Carolina. In 1995, after a long court battle, she was admitted but resigned after a week of physical and emotional stress. The Court was asked to decide if an education equal to that of the Citadel could be provided for women at a nearby school.

Claudius Watts III tackles a subject that is no longer controversial in regard to women's colleges: the virtues of single-sex education. But in this essay he argues that colleges for men only deserve the same right as women's colleges to exclude the opposite sex.

The author has taken care in the limited space available to cover all the arguments that have emerged in the case of Shannon Faulkner. At the end of the opening paragraph he lays out the three ideas he will develop—the value of single-sex education, the need for diversity in education, and freedom of choice. In paragraphs 3 through 6 he supports his case for the benefits of separate education by first quoting a prominent sociologist and then offering statistics to prove that the Citadel population is both diverse and successful. In paragraph 7 he refutes a popular analogy—that since the service academies, like West Point and the Naval Academy, admit women, so should the Citadel. The goals of the Citadel, he says, are broader than those of the service academies. But he does more. In paragraph 8 he provides data that women's colleges produce successful graduates. This reinforces his claim that separate education has advantages over coed schooling. Perhaps it also helps to make friends of opponents who might otherwise be hostile to arguments favoring male privileges.

Notice the transition in paragraph 10. This leads the author to the defense of his last point, the far more elusive concept of freedom of choice and the rights of individuals, ideas whose validity cannot be measured in numbers. He introduces this part of his argument by quoting the words of a supporter of single-sex education, a woman professor at Emory University. He makes a strong appeal to the reader's sense of fairness and belief in the rights of the majority, represented here by the male students at the Citadel. There is also an obvious appeal to fear, an implied threat of the danger to women's colleges, in the next-to-last sentence of the essay. Finally, he invokes logic. If single-sex education cannot be defended for males, neither can it be defended for females. He assumes that against logic there can be no real defense.

Some leading advocates for women's rights have, in fact, agreed with General Watts's arguments for that reason. But those who support both Shannon Faulkner's admission to the Citadel and the sanctity of women's colleges will claim that women, as a disadvantaged group, deserve special consideration, while men do not. (One writer even insisted that the

Citadel *needed* women as a civilizing influence.) General Watts's argument, however, should go some distance toward reopening the dialogue.

SAMPLE ANALYSIS

At times, assignments may ask you to analyze or evaluate the evidence and appeals to needs and values offered in support of a claim. At other times, you will have to discover your own support for use in an argument that you are writing. After the following essay about sport utility vehicles and its reading and discussion questions, you will first find an example of an essay of the type you might write if you were asked to evaluate an author's use of support. It is followed by a student essay that illustrates effective use of support.

The True Costs of SUVs

HAL R. VARIAN

Traffic fatalities in the United States fell steadily from 54,600 in 1972 to 34,900 in 1992. But then they started to rise again, and by 2002 there were 38,300 traffic deaths a year.

Our performance compared with other countries has also deteriorated. America's ranking has fallen from first to ninth over the last thirty years, with Australia, Britain, and Canada all having better records.

A big part of the difference between the United States and other countries seems to be the prevalence of sport utility vehicles and pickups on American highways. Sales of light trucks—SUVs, pickups, and minivans—were about a fifth of total automobile sales thirty years ago. Now they account for more than half.

But aren't large vehicles supposed to be safer than small cars? Yes, they are safer for their occupants in collisions, but their design makes them all the more dangerous for anyone they hit.

Michelle White, an economist at the University of California, San   5
Diego, estimates that for each fatality that light-truck drivers avoid for themselves and their passengers, they cause four fatalities involving car occupants, pedestrians, bicyclists, and motorcyclists. "Safety gains for

---

A professor in the School of Information Management and Systems at the University of California at Berkeley, Hal R. Varian has written economics textbooks as well as columns for the *New York Times*. This piece appeared in the *Times* as the "Economic Scene" article on December 12, 2003.

those driving light trucks," Ms. White said, "come at an extremely high cost to others."

Being larger than ordinary vehicles, SUVs and light trucks cause more damage to upper bodies and heads in collisions. Furthermore, their bumpers do not always align with automobile bumpers, and their body structure is stiffer, transferring more force to other vehicles during impact.

A few weeks ago, the auto industry announced a voluntary plan to deal with some of these design problems. They intend to make side-impact airbags standard to help protect heads and upper bodies better in collisions, and they intend to standardize bumper heights.

These will no doubt be helpful improvements, but do they go far enough?

Recently Ms. White examined the econometrics of traffic accidents in an attempt to measure the benefits and costs of changing the number of light trucks on the road. Professor White's paper can be downloaded from http://econ.ucsd.edu/~miwhite/suv-revision.pdf.

Ms. White notes that changing average vehicle size could, in prin- 10 ciple, increase or decrease the cost of accidents.

The results of an accident in New York involving a sport utility vehicle and a smaller car. Traffic fatalities are on the rise, apparently linked to the increase of SUVs.

G. Paul Burnett/*The New York Times*

Suppose the cost of a small vehicle–large vehicle collision is $50, the cost of a small vehicle–small vehicle collision is $45, and the cost of a large vehicle–large vehicle collision is $40.

If all vehicles are small, and there are 10 accidents a year, the total cost of the accidents is $450. But if 10 percent of the small vehicles are replaced by large ones, the average cost of collisions becomes $458.50, since more collisions will be between large and small vehicles. On the other hand, if 60 percent of the vehicles on the road are large, the average cost of a collision is only $456, since more collisions are between large vehicles.

Think about a safety-conscious soccer mom choosing a vehicle. If there are mostly small cars in her town, she can reduce the risk to her and her family in the event of a collision by buying an SUV.

The unfortunate side effect is that the large SUV would cause significant damage to smaller cars if she was involved in an accident.

The laudable private incentive to choose a safe vehicle could, per- 15 versely, reduce overall safety.

In addition, Ms. White finds that people involved in single-vehicle crashes are more likely to be killed or seriously injured if they are in SUVs or light trucks rather than cars. This may be a result of the increased likelihood of rollovers.

On the other hand, suppose everybody in town drives an SUV. Then the soccer mom will definitely want to purchase one for herself, since it would both increase her family's safety and reduce the overall costs of collisions.

In this case, private incentives and social incentives are aligned.

The dynamics involved is the same as that of an arms race: If other families buy bigger vehicles, then you will want to as well, if only in self-defense.

To see where we are in this arms race, Ms. White examined crash data 20 maintained by the National Highway Safety Administration at www .nass.nhtsa.dot.gov/nass.

Using this data, Ms. White was able to estimate how the probability of fatalities or serious injury varied with the types of vehicles involved in collisions.

For example, in a two-car accident, the probability of a fatality in the car is 38 percent less than in a car–light truck accident. However, in car–light truck accidents, the probability of fatalities in the light truck is 55 percent less than it would be in a truck–truck accident.

If a light truck hits a pedestrian or a cyclist, the probability of fatalities is about 82 percent greater than if a car is involved.

Ms. White then asked what the impact would be of replacing a million light trucks with cars. She considered two models for driver behavior. In the first, she assumed that the former drivers of light trucks would have the same number of accidents as they did when driving trucks. In the second, she assumed that the former drivers of light trucks would have the same accident probabilities as other car drivers.

Using conventional methods for value-of-life calculations, she finds   25
that each light-truck owner who switches to a car saves about $447 in total expected costs of accidents.

Ms. White examines various policies that might persuade drivers to adopt such changes, including changes in liability rules, traffic rules and insurance rules.

Unfortunately, each of these policies has its problems, so there are no easy solutions.

One interesting way to reduce the arms race problem would be to link automobile liability insurance to gasoline taxes. This means drivers whose cars use more gasoline and those who drive a lot would pay more for their insurance—not unreasonable, since, on average, they impose more costs in accidents.

Aaron Edlin, a professor of economics and law at the University of California, Berkeley, has argued that such "pay at the pump" insurance premiums would have many other benefits (www.bepress.com/ aaronedlin/contribution5/). So this type of payment scheme is worth considering for a variety of reasons.

READING AND DISCUSSION QUESTIONS

1. For the purposes of his article, how is Varian defining *light truck*?

2. What relationship does he see between light trucks and number of traffic fatalities?

3. What type of support does Varian use in the three opening paragraphs? Does he use that type of support anywhere else in the essay?

4. What other types of support does Varian make use of in his essay? What types of support do you find most effective in making his argument? What types do you find least effective?

5. What claim is Varian supporting in the essay?

6. How does Varian document his sources? How does he try to establish that his sources are reliable?

The True Confusion about SUV Costs

BETHANY ROYCE

Hal R. Varian entitled his December 18, 2003, *New York Times* piece on sport utility vehicles "The True Costs of SUVs." A more accurate title might have been "The Confusing Costs of SUVs." While Varian turns to the right type of support for his subject—statistics—his use of that support is more confusing than enlightening.

Varian made a wise choice in appealing to his readers' need to feel safe and secure. His statistics are most appealing when he points out that for twenty years the number of traffic fatalities in our country went down and that parents can feel secure knowing that they can make their children safer by buying light trucks (SUVs, pickups, or minivans) instead of cars. In each case, however, there is a negative side. The number of fatalities started rising again between 1992 and 2002, in part because of the increase in the number of sales of light trucks during that time. And Varian tells us that in making their families safer by buying light trucks, they are increasing the risk of doing more harm to others should they be involved in accidents.

For the rest of his support, Varian draws primarily on research done by Michelle White, whom he identifies only "as an economist at the University of California, San Diego" (185). She may have done excellent work, but the way that Varian explains it is confusing and unconvincing. White tries to predict how the cost of accidents would change depending on the size of the vehicles involved. Instead of using realistic cost estimates, however, she arbitrarily assigns the cost of $50 to a small vehicle–large vehicle collision, the cost of $45 to a small vehicle–small vehicle collision, and the cost of $40 to a large vehicle–large vehicle collision. Varian summarizes what this hypothetical scenario reveals:

> If all vehicles are small, and there are 10 accidents a year, the total cost of the accidents is $450. But if 10 percent of the small vehicles are replaced by large ones, the average cost of collisions becomes $458.50, since more collisions will be between large and small vehicles. On the other hand, if 60 percent of the vehicles on the road are large, the average cost of a collision is only $456, since more collisions are between large vehicles. (187)

Average Americans are left wondering what all of this means to them. The hypothetical situation cannot be easily applied to any individual driver and certainly not to any specific accident. How should a reader evaluate the information in attempting to make the decision regarding what size

---

Bethany Royce teaches business courses and introductory economics at a two-year college in Florida and writes a consumer advice column for a local newspaper.

vehicle to buy? The driver who just paid $3000 in car repairs is going to find any of the numbers Varian cites attractive.

There are a lot of "ifs" in Varian's argument. If you live in a town with lots of SUVs, it is safer to drive one yourself. If you live in a town where there are few SUVs, you should drive a car so that you would not be as likely to hurt someone else in a wreck. If you have a single-vehicle accident in an SUV, you are more likely to be killed. If you hit a pedestrian while driving one, you are more likely to kill that person.

There are also few clear conclusions to be drawn from the support   5 that Varian offers. After Ms. White examines "various policies that might persuade drivers to adopt such changes, including changes in liability rules, traffic rules and insurance rates," the unfortunate conclusion is that "each of these policies has its problems, so there are no easy solutions" (188). The only solution that Varian advances as "worth considering" is one by a colleague of his at the University of California, Berkeley, that would link a vehicle owner's liability insurance to gas taxes (188). Overall the article succeeds more in revealing the complexities involved in the increased use of SUVs than in clarifying any of those complexities.

STUDENT ESSAY

Safer? Tastier? More Nutritious?
The Dubious Merits of Organic Foods

KRISTEN WEINACKER

Organic foods are attractive to some consumers because of the principles behind them and the farming techniques used to produce them. There is a special respect for organic farmers who strive to maintain the ecological balance and harmony that exist among living things. As these farmers work in partnership with nature, some consumers too feel a certain attachment to the earth (Wolf 1–2). They feel happier knowing that these foods are produced without chemical fertilizers, pesticides, and additives to extend their shelf life (Pickerell; Agricultural Extension Service 5). They feel that they have returned to nature by eating organic foods that are advertised as being healthy for maintaining a vigorous lifestyle. Unfortunately, research has not provided statistical evidence that organic foods are more nutritious than conventionally grown ones.

The debate over the nutritional benefits has raged for decades. Defenders of the nutritional value of organic foods have employed excellent

At the time she wrote this essay Kristen Weinacker was an undergraduate at Clemson University.

marketing and sales strategies. First, they freely share the philosophy behind their farming and follow up with detailed descriptions of their management techniques. Second, organic farmers skillfully appeal to our common sense. It seems reasonable to believe that organic foods are more nutritious since they are grown without chemical fertilizers and pesticides. Third, since the soil in which these crops are grown is so rich and healthy, it seems plausible that these crops have absorbed and developed better nutrients. As Lynda Brown asserts in her book *Living Organic,* "Organic farmers believe that growing crops organically provides the best possible way to produce healthy food" (26). Brown provides beautifully illustrated and enlarged microscopic photographs to show the more developed structure of organic foods compared to conventional products to convince the consumer to believe that organic foods are more nutritious (27). Fourth, many consumers view the higher price tags on organic foods and assume that they must be more nutritious. Generalizations permeate the whole world of organic foods. These marketing strategies persuade the consumer that organic foods are healthier than conventional foods without providing any factual comparisons.

In their book *Is Our Food Safe?* Warren Leon and Caroline Smith Dewaal compare organic and conventionally produced foods. They strongly suggest that consumers buy organic foods to help the environment (68). They believe that organic foods are healthier than conventional ones. However, statistics supporting this belief are not provided. The authors even warn consumers that they need to read product labels because some organic foods may be as unhealthy as conventional ones (68–69). An interesting poll involving 1,041 adults was conducted by ABC News asking, "Why do people buy organic?" Analyst Daniel Merkle concluded that 45% of the American public *believes* that organic products are more nutritious than conventionally grown ones. Also, 57% of the population maintains that organic farming is beneficial for the environment. According to the pollsters, the primary reason why people bought organic foods is the belief that they are healthier because they have less pesticide residue. However, there has never been any link established between the nutritional value of organic foods and the residue found on them. Clever marketing strategies have made the need for concrete data really not of prime importance for the consumer to join the bandwagon promoting organic foods.

This pervasive belief among the American public that organic foods are probably healthier than conventionally grown foods was reiterated in my telephone interview with Mr. Joseph Williamson, an agricultural county extension agent working with Clemson University. When asked if organically grown foods are more nutritious than those grown conventionally, he replied that they probably were for two reasons. First, organic crops tend to grow more slowly. Therefore, the nutrients have more time to build up in the plants. Second, organic plants are usually grown locally. The fruits and vegetables are allowed to stay on the plants for a longer period of time. They ripen more than those picked green and transported across miles. He contends that these conditions promote a better nutrient buildup. Unfortunately, the extension agent acknowledges that statistical evidence is not available to support the claim that organic products are more nutritious.

An article entitled "Effects of Agricultural Methods in Nutritional $\quad$ 5 Quality: A Comparison of Organic with Conventional Crops" reports on conclusions drawn by Dr. Virginia Worthington, a certified nutrition specialist. Worthington examines why it is so difficult to ascertain if organic foods are more nutritious. First, "the difference in terms of health effects is not large enough to be readily apparent." There is no concrete evidence that people are healthier eating organic foods or, conversely, that people become more ill eating conventionally grown produce. Second, Dr. Worthington notes that variables such as sunlight, temperature, and amount of rain are so inconsistent that the nutrients in crops vary yearly. Third, she points out that the nutrient value of products can be changed by the way products are stored and shipped. After reviewing at least thirty studies dealing with the question if organic foods are more nutritious than conventionally grown ones, Dr. Worthington concludes that there is too little data available to substantiate the claim of higher nutritional value in organic foods. She also believes that it is an impossible task to make a direct connection between organic foods and the health of those people who consume them.

After being asked for thirty years about organic foods by her readers and associates, Joan Dye Gusson, writer for *Eating Well* magazine, firmly concludes that there is "little hard proof that organically grown produce is reliably more nutritious." Reviewing seventy years' worth of studies on the subject, Gusson has no doubt that organic foods should be healthier because of the way they are produced and cultivated. Gusson brings up an interesting point about chemical and pesticide residue. She believes that the fact that organic foods have been found to have fewer residues does not make them automatically more nutritious and healthier for the consumer. As scientific technologies advance, Gusson predicts that research will someday discover statistical data that will prove that organic foods have a higher nutritional value compared to conventionally grown ones.

In order to provide the public with more information about the nature of organic foods, the well-known and highly regarded magazine *Consumer Reports* decided to take a closer look at organic foods in their January, 1998, magazine, in an article entitled "Organic Foods: Safer? Tastier? More nutritious?" By conducting comparison tests, their researchers discovered that organic foods have less pesticide residue, and that their flavors are just about the same as conventionally grown foods. These scientists came to the conclusion that the "variability within a given crop is greater than the variability between one cropping system and another." *Consumer Reports* contacted Professor Willie Lockeretz from the Tufts University School of Nutrition Science and Policy. He told researchers that "the growing system you use probably does affect nutrition. . . . But it does it in ways so complex you might be studying the problem forever." Keeping in mind these comments made by Dr. Lockeretz, *Consumer Reports* believes it would be an impossible task to compare the nutritional values of organic and conventional foods. Therefore, researchers at *Consumer Reports* decided not to carry out that part of their comparison testing.

Although statistical evidence is not available at this time to support the claim that organic foods are more nutritious than conventionally grown ones, there is a very strong feeling shared by a majority of the general public that they are. We are called back to nature as we observe the love that organic farmers have for the soil and their desire to work in partnership with nature. We are easily lured to the attractive displays of organic foods in the grocery stores. However, we must keep in mind the successful marketing techniques that have been used to convince us that organic foods are more nutritious than conventionally grown ones. Although common sense tells us that organic foods should be more nutritious, research has not provided us with any statistical data to prove this claim.

Works Cited

Agricultural Extension Service. *Organic Vegetable Gardening.* The University of Tennessee. PB 1391.

Brown, Lynda. *Organic Living.* New York: Dorling Kindersley Publishing, Inc., 2000.

Gussow, Joan Dye. "Is Organic Food More Nutritious? *Eating Well* (May/June 1997). 27 March 2003. <http://www.prnac.net/rodmap - nutrition.html>.

"Effect of Agricultural Methods on Nutritional Quality: A Comparison of Organic with Conventional Crops." *Alternative Therapies* 4 (1998): 58–69. 18 Feb. 2003. <http://www.purefood.org/healthier101101.cfm>.

Leon, Warren, and Caroline Smith DeWaal. *Is Our Food Safe?* New York: Three Rivers Press, 2002.

Merkle, Daniel. "Why Do People Buy Organic?" ABCNews.com. 3 Feb. 2000. 27 March 2003.

"Organic Foods: Safer? Tastier? More Nutritious?" *Consumer Reports.* Jan. 1998. 24 Feb. 2003. <http://www.consumerreports.org/main/detailsv2.jsp?content%3%ecnt_id +18959&f>.

Pickrell, John. "Federal Government Launches Organic Standards." *Science News* 162.17 (Nov. 2002). <http://www.sciencenews.org/20021102/food.asp._17_March 2003>.

Williamson, Joseph. Telephone interview. 28 Feb. 2003.

Wolf, Ray, ed. *Organic Farming: Yesterday's and Tomorrow's Agriculture.* Philadelphia: Rodale Press, 1977.

Connecting the Dots . . . to Terrorism

BERNARD GOLDBERG

Most of the time television is nothing more than a diversion—proof, as the old quip goes, that we would rather do anything than talk to each other. We'd also rather watch a bad sitcom than read a good book. Bad sitcoms get millions of viewers; good books get thousands. In an "entertainment culture," even the news is entertainment. Certainly too much local news has been pure fluff for some time now, with their Ken and Barbie anchors who have nothing intelligent to say but look great while they're saying it. And because network news is losing viewers every year, executives and producers are trying to figure out ways to hold on to the ones they still have. They think cosmetics will work, so they change the anchor desk or they change the graphics. They get the anchor to stand instead of sit. They feature more "news you can use." They put Chandra Levy[22] on all over the place, hoping they can concoct a ratings cocktail by mixing one part missing intern with ten parts sex scandal.

And then something genuinely big and really important happens that shakes us to our core, and all those producers who couldn't get enough of Chandra are through with her. Only in the fickle world of television news can someone who has disappeared without a trace disappear a second time.

And it's when that history-making story comes along that Americans—no matter what their politics, religion, age, race, or sex—turn to television, not just for information, but also for comfort and for peace of mind. It doesn't happen often, but when it does, television becomes a lot more than just a diversion.

It happened when John Kennedy was assassinated. We all turned to Walter Cronkite and Huntley and Brinkley, not just for facts, but also for reassurance—that despite the terrible tragedy, America was going to be okay.

It happened when *Challenger* blew up. And it happened again on September 11, 2001, when a band of religious lunatics declared war on the United States of America to punish us for not wanting to dwell in the fourteenth century, where they currently reside, and, of course, to show   5

---

[22] *Chandra Levy*: A government intern whose disappearance was widely covered in the press in 2001. —Eds.

Bernard Goldberg was a reporter and producer for CBS for more than thirty years. He has won seven Emmy awards and was once rated by *TV Guide* as one of the ten most interesting people on television. This chapter is from his 2002 book *Bias: A CBS Insider Exposes How the Media Distort the News*, written after he left the network.

the world that their intense hatred of Israel—*and of Israel's friends*—knows no bounds. On September 11, they not only killed as many innocent Americans as they could in the most dramatic way they knew how, but, as the *Wall Street Journal* put it, they also "wiped out any remaining illusions that America is safe from mass organized violence."

On that day we all turned to television. We turned to Dan Rather and Peter Jennings and Tom Brokaw and the others. And they did a fine job, as they often do when covering tragedy. They showed empathy. They were fair and accurate, and the information they passed along to us wasn't filtered through the usual liberal political and social sensibilities. They gave us the news on that day the way they should give us the news *all the time*, whether the story is about race or feminism or taxes or gay rights or anything else. *For a change, they gave it to us straight.*

On the night of September 11, 2001, Peter Jennings made a point about how, in times of danger and tragedy, television serves the function that campfires used to serve in the old days when Americans migrated westward in covered wagons. Back then, they would sit around the campfire and get the news from other travelers about what they should look out for down the road. "Some people pulled the wagons around," Peter said, "and discussed what was going on and tried to understand it." But the campfire was more than just a meeting place where families could pick up important information. The campfire also provided a sense of community, a sense that *we're all in this together*. That's what television was on September 11.

As I listened to Peter tell that story, I thought about another American tragedy that shocked us six years earlier, when Timothy McVeigh—another true believer who cared nothing about killing innocent Americans—blew up the federal building in Oklahoma City. I thought about how it took some of the media elites only a few days before they started to play one of their favorite games—connect the dots. What they found back then—or more accurately, what they convinced themselves they found—was a line stretching from Oklahoma City to the Republican Party to conservatives in general and finally to Rush Limbaugh.

Dan Rather said, "Even after Oklahoma City, you can turn on your radio in any city and still dial up hate talk: extremist, racist, and violent from the hosts and those who call in."

Time senior writer Richard Lacayo put it this way: "In a nation that 10 has entertained and appalled itself for years with hot talk on radio and the campaign trail, the inflamed rhetoric of the '90s is suddenly an unindicted coconspirator in the blast."

Nina Easton wrote in the *Los Angeles Times*, "The Oklahoma City attack on federal workers and their children also alters the once-easy dynamic between charismatic talk show host and adoring audience. Hosts who routinely espouse the same antigovernment themes as the militia movement now must walk a fine line between inspiring their audience—and inciting the most radical among them."

On *Face the Nation*, Bob Schieffer asked this question: "Mr. Panetta, there's been a lot of antigovernment rhetoric, it comes over talk radio, it comes from various quarters. Do you think that that somehow has led these people to commit this act, do they feed on that kind of rhetoric, and what impact do you think it had?"

Carl Rowan, the late columnist, was quoted in a *Washington Post* story saying that, "Unless Gingrich and Dole[23] and the Republicans say 'Am I inflaming a bunch of nuts?' you know we're going to have some more events. I am absolutely certain the harsher rhetoric of the Gingriches and the Doles . . . creates a climate of violence in America."

And David Broder had this to say in the *Washington Post*: "The bombing shows how dangerous it really is to inflame twisted minds with statements that suggest political opponents are enemies. For two years, Rush Limbaugh described this nation as 'America held hostage' to the policies of the liberal Democrats, as if the duly elected president and Congress were equivalent to the regime in Tehran. I think there will be less tolerance and fewer cheers for that kind of rhetoric."

The message was clear: Conservative talk radio and conservative 15 politicians created an antigovernment atmosphere in America that spawned Timothy McVeigh and therefore were at least partially to blame for his terrorism. It's true, of course, that the atmosphere in which we live contributes to everything that happens in our culture. Calling people "kikes" or "niggers" makes it easier to see them as less than human and to treat them as something less than human. But to point fingers at talk radio for somehow encouraging Timothy McVeigh strikes me as a stretch at best; more likely it's just another opportunity for liberal journalists to blame conservatives for one more evil. And if this kind of connecting the dots is fair game, then should we also accuse Americans who spoke out loudly and forcefully against the war in Vietnam—including many journalists—of contributing to the 1972 bombing of the Pentagon and to other sometimes deadly terrorism, perpetuated by fanatics on the Left? According to the media elites' rulebook, when liberals rant it's called free speech; when conservatives rant it's called incitement to terrorism.

As I watched the coverage of the attacks on the Pentagon and the World Trade Center, I wondered why I hadn't seen more stories on television news, long before these zealots flew their hijacked planes into American buildings, about the culture of anti-American hate that permeates so much of the Middle East—stories that might help explain how little Arab children can grow up to become fanatical suicide bombers.

If the media found it so important to discuss the malignant atmosphere created by "hot" conservative talk radio, then why didn't they find it important to delve into this malignant atmosphere that seems to have

[23]*Gingrich and Dole:* Newt Gingrich (b. 1943) was Speaker of the House of Representatives from 1995 to 1999. Robert Dole (b. 1923) was a Senate majority leader and served in the Senate from 1968 to 1996. —EDS.

bred such maniacal killers? Why would journalists, so interested in connecting the dots when they thought they led to Rush Limbaugh, be so uninterested in connecting the dots when there might actually be dots to connect—*from hateful, widely held popular attitudes in much of the Arab world straight to the cockpits of those hijacked jetliners?*

One of the networks put an American Muslim woman on the news who said that no one blamed Christianity when McVeigh killed all those people. Why blame Islam now? The reporter interviewing this woman let her have her say, never bothering to point out that Timothy McVeigh didn't kill all those people in the name of Christianity. Suicide airplane hijackers, on the other hand, are people who actually believe their murderous acts will earn them a one-way ticket to Paradise.

Was what happened on September 11 a subversion of Islam, as pundits and journalists on network and cable TV told us over and over again? Or was it the result of an *honest* reading of the Koran? It's true, of course, that if taken too literally by uncritical minds, just about any holy book can lead to bad things. Still, why are there no Christian suicide bombers, or Jewish suicide bombers, or Hindu suicide bombers, or Buddhist suicide bombers, but no apparent shortage of Muslim suicide bombers? If Islam is "a religion of peace" as so many people from President Bush on down were telling us (and, for what it's worth, I'm prepared to believe that it is), then what exactly is it in the Koran that so appeals to these Islamic fanatics? Don't look for that answer on the network news. A Lexis-Nexis search going back to 1991 linking the words "Koran" and "terrorist" produced absolutely nothing that told us what the Koran actually says which *might* encourage a Muslim, no matter how misguided, to commit acts of terrorism.

I understand that even to ask questions about a possible connection 20 between Islam and violence is to tread into politically incorrect terrain. But it seems to me that the media need to go there anyway. And any network that can put thousands of stories on the air about sex and murder should be able to give us a few on the atmosphere that breeds religious zealotry. It might have helped us see what was coming on September 11.

In fact, I learned much more about the atmosphere that breeds suicide bombers from one short article in *Commentary* magazine than I have from watching twenty years of network television news. In its September 2001 issue (which came out before the attack on America), there was an article by Fiamma Nirenstein, an Italian journalist based in Israel, entitled "How Suicide Bombers Are Made." In it, she tells about a "river of hatred" that runs through not just the most radical of Arab nations but also much of what we like to think of as the "moderate" Arab world.

She tells us about a series of articles that ran in the leading government-sponsored newspaper in Egypt, *Al Ahram*, about how Jews supposedly use the blood of Christians to make matzah for Passover.

She tells us about a hit song in Cairo, Damascus, and the West Bank with the catchy title "I Hate Israel."

Why didn't I know this? A computer check soon answered my question. On television, only CNN reported the "I Hate Israel" story. On radio, NPR did a piece. So did the *Christian Science Monitor* and the *Chicago Tribune*. The *Los Angeles Times* ran a short wire service story that said "'I Hate Israel' . . . made an overnight singing sensation of a working-class crooner."

Can you imagine if the big hit song in Israel was "I Hate Palestine" or 25 "I Hate Arabs"? The *New York Times* would have put the story on page one and then run an editorial just to make sure we all got the message—that the song is indecent and contributes to an atmosphere of hate. And since the *Times* sets the agenda for the networks, Dan Rather, Tom Brokaw, and Peter Jennings would have all fallen into line and run big stories on their evening newscasts, too, saying the exact same thing. A week later, Mike Wallace would have landed in Tel Aviv looking absolutely mortified that those Jews would do such a thing.

And that's part of the problem. Despite the liberalism of the media, there is a subtle form of racism at work here. As Fiamma Nirenstein writes, "The Arabs, it is implicitly suggested, are a backward people, not to be held to civilized standards of the West." Of the Israelis, however, the American media expect much more. That is why a song called "I Hate Israel" becomes a big hit, and yet is not a news story. And it is why a series of stories in a government-sponsored newspaper—in a supposedly moderate country—about Jews killing Christians for their blood holds almost no interest for American journalists.

It's true that not long after the twin towers of the World Trade Center came tumbling down, the networks showed us pictures of Palestinians in East Jerusalem honking their horns, firing their guns into the air, and generally having a good old time celebrating the death of so many Americans in New York and Washington. They cheered "God is great" while they handed out candy, which is a tradition in the Arab world when something good happens.

It's not that there's been a total news blackout of anti-American hate in the Middle East—*Nightline* has done some good, intelligent work in this area—it's just that we need more than pictures of happy Palestinians reveling in the death of thousands of Americans. And we need more than what has become a staple of Middle East television news coverage: young children throwing stones at Israeli soldiers—the perfect made-for-television David and Goliath story. What we need are stories that connect the dots, not just back to Afghanistan and its backward and repressive Taliban government, but also between the fanatics in New York and Washington and a cultural environment in the Arab world where even "moderates" hand out candy to celebrate the massacre of Americans.

But here the media—apparently feeling squeamish about stories that put the "underdogs" in a bad light—keep us virtually in the dark. And it's not just little tidbits like "I Hate Israel" and articles about Jews taking Christian blood that I—and almost all Americans—knew nothing about.

Here's a quick rundown of what goes on in much of the Middle East as reported by Ms. Nirenstein in *Commentary*—news that is virtually ignored on the big American TV networks:

> In Egypt and Jordan, news sources have repeatedly warned that Israel has distributed drug-laced chewing gum and candy, intended (it is said) to kill children and make women sexually corrupt. . . .
>
> [Palestinian television] recently asserted that, far from being extermination camps, Chelmo, Dachau, and Auschwitz were in fact mere "places of disinfection."
>
> On April 13—observed in Israel as Holocaust Remembrance Day— the official Palestinian newspaper *Al-Hayat al-Jadida* featured a column . . . entitled "The Fable of the Holocaust."
>
> A columnist in Egypt's government-sponsored Al-Akhbar thus expressed his "thanks to Hitler, of blessed memory, who on behalf of the Palestinians took revenge in advance on the most vile criminals on the face of the earth. Still, we do have a complaint against [Hitler], for his revenge on them was not enough."

In addition to these examples, Ms. Nirenstein cites a textbook for Syr- 30 ian tenth graders which teaches them that "the logic of justice obligates the application of the single verdict [on the Jews] from which there is no escape: namely, that their criminal intentions be turned against them and that they be exterminated." And she notes that in June 2001, two weeks after the fatal collapse of a Jewish wedding hall in Jerusalem, Palestinian television broadcast a sermon by a Muslim imam praying that "this oppressive Knesset [Israel's parliament] will [similarly] collapse over the heads of the Jews."

I did not know any of that because it's simply not the kind of news that we normally get from the Middle East—certainly not from network evening newscasts or from *Dateline, 20/20,* or *48 Hours,* three news magazine programs that are usually too busy peddling the trivial and sensational to bother with more significant stories. And besides, that kind of news makes liberal journalists uneasy. After all, these are the same people who bend over backwards to find "moral equivalence" between Palestinian terrorists who blow up discos in Tel Aviv filled with teenagers, on the one hand, and Israeli commandos who *preemptively* kill terrorist ringleaders *before* they send their suicide bombers into Israel on a mission to kill Jews, on the other.

On September 11, right after the networks showed us the pictures of Palestinians celebrating American deaths, they also showed us Yasser Arafat expressing his condolences and giving blood for the American victims. This, in its way, represented a kind of moral equivalence: while some Palestinians celebrate, the news anchors were suggesting, their leader does not; he is somber and, we're led to believe, absolutely shocked. But we could have done with a little less moral equivalence on the part of the press and a little more tough journalism. Someone should have asked the leader of the Palestinian people if he understood that the cultures that he and other "moderate" Arab leaders preside over "carefully nurture and inculcate resentments and hatreds against America and the non-Arab world," as a *Wall Street Journal* editorial put it. And if that's asking too much of a field reporter covering a seemingly shaken and distraught Arafat in the wake of September 11, then an anchor back in New York should have wondered out loud about that very connection.

But to have asked such a question might have been viewed as anti-Arab (and therefore pro-Israeli), and reporters and anchors would rather be stoned by an angry mob in Ramallah than be seen in that light. So we didn't learn that day if Chairman Arafat quite understood his role in the celebration he so deplored. Nor did we get an explanation on the news about why there were not thousands of other Arabs in the streets — on the West Bank or in Jerusalem or in the "moderate" Arab countries — expressing their *condolences*. Was it because they are afraid to show support for American victims of terrorism? Or was it because they, like the Palestinians we saw with great big smiles, didn't feel that bad about what happened?

If the networks can give us months and months of Chandra and Jon-Benet and Lorena Bobbitt and Joey Buttafuoco, then they can give us more than they do about the river of hatred that breeds suicide bombers.

But this is where journalists — given their liberal tendency to empathize with, and sometimes even root for, the "underdog" — run into a big problem: if they start to connect those ideological and religious dots, they may not like what they find.   35

American journalists who covered the civil rights struggle recognized the pathology of racism and rightly made no allowance for it. They understood that in order for evil to flourish in places throughout the South, all it took was a few fundamentally bad people — while everybody else sat around making believe it wasn't happening, either because they were afraid or because they just didn't want to get involved.

The Middle East, of course, is a place with a long and troubled history. But it should be obvious that a place that turns "I Hate Israel" into a hit, that runs stories in its most important newspaper about Jews killing Christians for their blood, that faults Hitler *only because he did not kill more Jews*, and that celebrates the murder of thousands of innocent Americans is a place populated by many nasty people. Perhaps it has many good people, too, who just don't want to get involved. The point is, a story about all of this is at least as important as a story about Anne Heche and her sex life, even if sex does better in the ratings than disturbing news about raw, ignorant hatred in the world of Islam.

None of this is an argument that the media are intentionally pro-Arab. Rather, like the U.S. State Department, they are pro "moral equivalence." If they connect the dots with stories on the news about hit songs called "I Hate Israel" and all the rest, the Arab world will accuse the "Jewish-controlled" American media of being sympathetic to "Israeli oppression." If journalists — who were so willing to connect the dots when there was a belief that they led to Rush Limbaugh — connected *these* dots, they might find that there are a lot fewer moderates in those moderate places than they keep telling us about.

So they look the other way, which, as Ms. Nirenstein tells us, is not that easy. One has to turn "a determinedly blind eye to this river of hatred . . . [and] to be persuaded that, after all, 'everybody' in the Middle East really wants the same thing."

Obviously, there are legitimate issues about which there are differing 40 viewpoints in the Middle East: Should Israel blow up the houses that belong to the families of terrorists? Should Israel allow the construction of new settlements on the West Bank? These are two that come quickly to mind.

But moral equivalence and the quest for evenhanded journalism should not stop the media from telling us more — much more in my view — about the kind of backwardness and hatred that is alive and well, *not just in places like Kabul and Baghdad*, but in "moderate" cities and villages all over the Arab world. Even if it means going against their liberal sensibilities and reporting that sometimes even the underdog can be evil.

READING AND DISCUSSION QUESTIONS

1. How does Goldberg support his claim that television draws Americans together in times of crisis?

2. How does he feel the news is different during times of crisis from how it usually is?

3. Explain the title that Goldberg chose for this piece. What does he claim the "media elites" have "connected the dots" to find?

4. What does Goldberg feel the news media are *not* telling Americans? What sort of support does he offer for that part of his argument?

5. What type or types of support that Goldberg uses do you find most effective? Why?

WRITING SUGGESTIONS

6. Analyze the types of support that Goldberg makes use of in his essay.

7. Evaluate the effectiveness of the major types of support that he uses in his essay.

8. Attack or defend the claim that Goldberg is advancing in his essay.

9. What is your personal opinion of the media coverage of the tragedies of September 11?

10. Do you feel that your education has exposed you to recent history as well as the more distant past? Explain.

A New Look, an Old Battle

ANNA QUINDLEN

Public personification has always been the struggle on both sides of the abortion battle lines. That is why the people outside clinics on Saturday mornings carry signs with photographs of infants rather than of zygotes, why they wear lapel pins fashioned in the image of tiny feet and shout, "Don't kill your baby," rather than, more accurately, "Don't destroy your embryo." Those who support the legal right to an abortion have always been somewhat at a loss in the face of all this. From time to time women have come forward to speak about their decision to have an abortion, but when they are prominent, it seems a bit like grandstanding, and when they are not, it seems a terrible invasion of privacy when privacy is the point in the first place. Easier to marshal the act of presumptive ventriloquism practiced by the opponents, pretending to speak for those unborn unknown to them by circumstance or story.

But the battle of personification will assume a different and more sympathetic visage in the years to come. Perhaps the change in the weather was best illustrated when conservative Sen. Strom Thurmond invoked his own daughter to explain a position opposed by the antiabortion forces. The senator's daughter has diabetes. The actor Michael J. Fox has Parkinson's disease. Christopher Reeve is in a wheelchair because of a spinal-cord injury, Ronald Reagan locked in his own devolving mind by Alzheimer's. In the faces of the publicly and personally beloved lies enormous danger for the life-begins-at-conception lobby.

The catalytic issue is research on stem cells. These are versatile building blocks that may be coaxed into becoming any other cell type; they could therefore hold the key to endless mysteries of human biology, as well as someday help provide a cure for ailments as diverse as diabetes, Parkinson's, spinal-cord degeneration, and Alzheimer's. By some estimates, more than 100 million Americans have diseases that scientists suspect could be affected by research on stem cells. Scientists hope that the astonishing potential of this research will persuade the federal government to help fund it and allow the National Institutes of Health to help oversee it. This is not political, researchers insist. It is about science, not abortion.

And they are correct. Stem-cell research is typically done by using frozen embryos left over from in vitro fertilization. If these embryos were placed in the womb, they might eventually implant, become a fetus, then a child. Unused, they are the earliest undifferentiated collection of cells made by the joining of the egg and sperm, no larger than the period at

---

Anna Quindlen is a Pulitzer Prize–winning journalist and best-selling novelist. This piece appeared in the April 9, 2001, issue of *Newsweek* magazine.

QUINDLEN • A NEW LOOK, AN OLD BATTLE **203**

the end of this sentence. One of the oft-used slogans of the anti-abortion movement is "abortion stops a beating heart." There is no heart in this preimplantation embryo, but there are stem cells that, in the hands of scientists, might lead to extraordinary work affecting everything from cancer to heart disease.

All of which leaves the anti-abortion movement trying desperately to 5
hold its hard line, and failing. Judie Brown of the American Life League can refer to these embryos as "the tiniest person," and the National Right to Life organization can publish papers that refer to stem-cell research as the "destruction of life." But ordinary people with family members losing their mobility or their grasp on reality will be able to be more thoughtful and reasonable about the issues involved.

The anti-abortion activists know this, because they have already seen the defections. Some senators have abandoned them to support fetal-tissue research, less promising than stem-cell work but still with significant potential for treating various ailments. Elected officials who had voted against abortion rights found themselves able to support procedures that used tissue from aborted fetuses; perhaps they were men who had fathers with heart disease, who had mothers with arthritis and whose hearts resonated with the possibilities for alleviating pain and prolonging life. Senator Thurmond was one, Senator McCain another. Former senator Connie Mack of Florida recently sent a letter to the president, who must decide the future role of the federal government in this area, describing himself "as a conservative pro-life now former member" of Congress, and adding that there "were those of us identified as such who supported embryonic stem-cell research."

When a recent test of fetal tissue in patients with Parkinson's had disastrous side effects, the National Right to Life Web site ran an almost gloating report: "horrific," "rips to shreds," "media cheerleaders," "defy description." The tone is a reflection of fear. It's the fear that the use of fetal tissue to produce cures for debilitating ailments might somehow launder the process of terminating a pregnancy, a positive result from what many people still see as a negative act. And it's the fear that thinking—really thinking—about the use of the earliest embryo for life-saving research might bring a certain long-overdue relativism to discussions of abortion across the board.

The majority of Americans have always been able to apply that relativism to these issues. They are more likely to accept early abortions than later ones. They are more tolerant of a single abortion under exigent circumstances than multiple abortions. Some who disapprove of abortion in theory have discovered that they can accept it in fact if a daughter or a girlfriend is pregnant.

And some who believe that life begins at conception may look into the vacant eyes of an adored parent with Alzheimer's or picture a paralyzed child walking again, and take a closer look at what an embryo really is, at what stem-cell research really does, and then consider the true cost of a cure. That is what Senator Thurmond obviously did when he looked at his daughter and broke ranks with the true believers. It may be an over-simplification to say that real live loved ones trump the imagined un-born, that a cluster of undifferentiated cells due to be discarded anyway is a small price to pay for the health and welfare of millions. Or perhaps it is only a simple commonsensical truth.

READING AND DISCUSSION QUESTIONS

1. Understanding Quindlen's argument requires understanding of the terms she uses. In her introductory paragraph, she refers to "public personifica-tion," "grandstanding," and "presumptive ventriloquism." Explain these terms in the context of her argument.

2. Why are anti-abortion activists opposed to the use of stem-cell research? How does Quindlen defend her own position?

3. What does Quindlen mean when she says that stem-cell research "might bring a certain long-overdue relativism to discussions of abortion" (para. 7)? (The meaning of *relativism* is the key.)

4. Although this essay clearly suggests a policy, it is primarily a claim of value: Stem-cell research is vital because it will contribute to the life and health of our loved ones. Point out places in the essay where Quindlen makes an emotional appeal to our compassion.

WRITING SUGGESTIONS

5. The debate about stem-cell research in the Congress, the media, and the medical and scientific professions, expanded after a speech by President Bush on August 9, 2001, in which he agreed to permit limited research on stem cells. Look up some of the news stories, editorials, and letters to the editors that followed his speech, and summarize the opposition to the president's proposal.

6. Quindlen explores the possible influence of stem-cell research on in-creased acceptance of abortion. Write an essay that argues for or against the right of a woman to an abortion. If you have reservations, make clear what circumstances would govern your judgment.

Marriage-Plus

THEODORA OOMS

The public has been concerned about "family breakdown" for a long time, but it was not until the passage of welfare reform in 1996 that the federal government decided to get into the business of promoting marriage. Although it was little noticed at the time, three of the four purposes of the welfare legislation refer directly or indirectly to marriage and family formation. The law exhorts states to promote "job preparation, work and marriage," to "prevent and reduce the incidence of out-of-wedlock pregnancies," and to "encourage the formation and maintenance of two-parent families."

The Bush administration, as it contemplates this year's extension of welfare legislation, plans to make marriage even more central. The administration's reauthorization proposal, announced February 27, includes $300 million for demonstration grants to focus on promoting healthy marriages and reducing out-of-wedlock births.[24] Meanwhile, Oklahoma Governor Frank Keating has launched a $10 million, multisector marriage initiative, and other smaller-scale government-sponsored initiatives have been enacted in Arizona, Florida, Louisiana, Michigan, and Utah. The federal government is primarily concerned with reducing out-of-wedlock births, which it views as a principal cause of welfare dependency and a host of other social problems. By contrast, state marriage initiatives are most concerned about the effects of high divorce rates and father absence on children.[25]

This new emphasis on marriage as a panacea for social problems is troubling to many liberals. For one thing, it risks being dismissive of children who happen to find themselves in single-parent families. It also can be seen as disparaging single mothers and ignoring the fact that many women have left abusive marriages for good reasons.

That said, it's hard to dismiss an overwhelming consensus of social-science research findings that children tend to be better off, financially and emotionally, when their parents are married to each other. Around 50 percent of all first marriages are expected to end in divorce, and 60 percent of all divorces involve children. One-third of all births are out of

---

[24]See *Working Toward Independence: The President's Plan to Strengthen Welfare Reform*, February 2002. http://www.whitehouse.gov/news/releases/2002/02/welfare-reform-announcement-book.pdf.
[25]Theodora Ooms, "The Role of the Federal Government in Strengthening Marriage," in *Virginia Journal of Social Policy and the Law*, Fall 2002. To be posted on www.clasp.org.

Theodora Ooms is a senior policy analyst at the Center for Law and Social Policy. Her article is an annotated version of one that originally appeared in a special issue of *The American Prospect* on "The Politics of the American Family," April 8, 2002.

wedlock, nearly 40 percent of children do not live with their biological fathers, and too many nonresident fathers neither support nor see their children on a regular basis.

Children living with single mothers are five times as likely to be poor   5 as those in two-parent families. Growing up in a single-parent family also roughly doubles the risk that a child will drop out of school, have difficulty finding a job, or become a teen parent. About half of these effects appear to be attributable to the reduced income available to single parents, but the other half is due to non-economic factors.[26] It's not just the presence of two adults in the home that helps children, as some argue. Children living with cohabiting partners and in stepfamilies generally do less well than those living with both married biological parents.[27]

Marriage also brings benefits to husbands and wives. Married adults are more productive on the job, earn more, save more, have better physical and mental health, and live longer, according to an extensive review of research, conducted by scholar Linda Waite. Although Waite admits that these findings partly reflect the selection of better-adjusted people into marriage, she finds that when people marry, they act in more health promoting and productive ways.[28]

Conservatives are prone to exaggerate these research findings and underplay the importance of economics. If married people are more likely (other things being equal) to produce thriving children, other things are not, in fact, equal. It's not just the case that single mothers find themselves poor because they are unmarried; they find themselves unmarried because they are poor. Successful marriages are more difficult when husbands and wives are poorly educated, lack access to jobs that pay decently, and cannot afford decent child care. Economic hardship and other problems associated with poverty can wreak havoc on couples' relationships.

The controversy mostly isn't about research, however, but about values.[29] Most people regard decisions to marry, divorce, and bear children as intensely private. Any policy proposals that hint at coercing

[26]Sara McLanahan and Julien Teitler, "The Consequences of Father Absence," in *Parenting and Child Development in "Non-Traditional" Families*, ed. Michael E. Lamb (Mahwah, NJ: Lawrence Erlbaum, 1998). Also see Sara McLanahan and Gary Sanderfur, *Growing Up with a Single Parent: What Hurts, What Helps* (Cambridge, MA: Harvard UP, 1994).

[27]See McLanahan and Teitler; Susan L. Brown, "Child Well-Being in Cohabiting Unions" and Wendy D. Manning, "The Implications of Cohabitation for Children's Well-Being," in *Just Living Together: Implications of Cohabitation for Children, Families and Social Policy*, eds. Alan Booth and Ann C. Crouter (Mahwah, NJ: Lawrence Erlbaum, 2002).

[28]Linda J. Waite and Maggie Gallagher, *The Case for Marriage: Why Married People Are Happier, Healthier and Better Off Financially* (New York: Doubleday, 2000).

[29]Theodora Ooms, *Toward More Perfect Unions: Putting Marriage on the Public Agenda* (Washington, DC: Family Impact Seminar, 1998). Available from tooms@clasp.org.

people to marry, reinforcing Victorian conceptions of gender roles, or limiting the right to end bad marriages are viewed as counter to American values of individual autonomy and privacy. Some worry about the existence of hidden agendas that threaten to put women back into the kitchen, ignore domestic violence, and eliminate public assistance for low-income families. Others fear that holding out marriage as the ideal blames single parents, many of whom do a terrific job under difficult circumstances. Use of the term "illegitimate" is especially offensive because it stigmatizes children (and, in fact, is legally inaccurate, as children born outside of marriage now have virtually the same legal rights as those born within marriage).[30] And some worry that the pro-marriage agenda discriminates against ethnic and sexual minorities and their children, particularly gays and lesbians.

There are also more pragmatic concerns. Skeptics of the pro-marriage agenda observe that the decline in marriage is worldwide, a result of overwhelming social and economic forces that cannot be reversed. In their view, attempts to change family formation behavior are largely futile; we should instead just accept and help support the increasing diversity of family forms. For others, the concern is less about the value of promoting marriage and more about whether government, rather than individuals, communities, or faith institutions, should lead the charge.

Finally, marriage per se is too simplistic a solution to the complex 10 problems of the poor. Marrying a low-income, unmarried mother to her child's father will not magically raise the family out of poverty when the parents often have no skills, no jobs, terrible housing, and may be struggling with depression, substance abuse, or domestic violence. Advocates also worry that funds spent on untested marriage-promotion activities will be taken away from programs that provide desperately needed services for single parents, such as child care.

In response to some of these concerns—as well as research showing that serious parental conflict harms children—some marriage advocates respond that marriage per se should not be the goal but rather voluntary, "healthy" marriages.[31] They also agree that protections should be built into programs to guard against domestic violence. But this only raises doubts about how "healthy" will be defined, and by whom, and whether we even know how to help people create better relationships.

There also are some plainly foolish ideas in the marriage movement. West Virginia currently gives married families an extra $100 a month in welfare payments as a "marriage incentive." Robert Rector of the Heritage Foundation has proposed giving a $4,000 government bounty to welfare

[30]Ruth-Arlene W. Howe, "Legal Rights and Obligations: An Uneven Evolution," in *Young Unwed Fathers: Changing Roles and Emerging Policies*, eds. Robert I. Lerman and Theodora Ooms (Philadelphia: Temple UP, 1993), pp. 141–69.

[31]See, for example, Robin Toner, "Welfare Chief Is Hoping to Promote Marriage," *New York Times*, February 19, 2002, sec. A, p. 1.

recipients who marry before they have a child and stay married for two years.[32] Charles Murray wants to end public assistance altogether and has proposed eliminating all aid to *unmarried* mothers under 21 in one state to test the idea. This proposal is especially egregious and surely would harm children of single mothers.[33]

Progressives and others thus are placed in a quandary. They don't want to oppose marriage—which most Americans still value highly—but are skeptical of many pro-marriage initiatives. Given that healthy marriage is plainly good for children, however, one can envision a reasonable agenda—one that would gain broad support—that we might call marriage-plus. This approach puts the well-being of children first by helping more of them grow up in married, healthy, two-parent families. However, for many children, the reality is that marriage is not a feasible or even a desirable option for their parents. Thus, a secondary goal is to help these parents—whether unmarried, separated, divorced, or remarried—cooperate better in raising their children. These are not alternative strategies. Children need us to do both.

A marriage-plus agenda does not promote marriage just for marriage's sake. It acknowledges that married and unmarried parents, mothers and fathers, may need both economic resources and non-economic supports to increase the likelihood of stable, healthy marriages and better co-parenting relationships. In addition, a marriage-plus agenda focuses more on the front end—making marriage better to be in—rather than the back end—making marriage more difficult to get out of.

Here are some elements of this agenda.   15

Strengthen "fragile families" at the birth of a child. For many poor families, relationship-education programs may be helpful but not enough. A new national study finds that at the time of their child's birth, one-half of unmarried parents (so-called "fragile families") are living together, and another third are romantically attached but not cohabiting.[34] The majorities of these parents are committed to each other and to their child and have high hopes of eventual marriage and a future together—although these hopes too often are not realized. We should reach out to young parents to help them achieve their desire to remain together as a family. A helpful package of services to offer these young families might include a combination of "soft" services—relationship-skills and

[32]Robert Rector, *A Plan to Reduce Illegitimacy*, memorandum handed out at a meeting on Capitol Hill in early 2001.

[33]Charles Murray, "Family Formation," in *The New World of Welfare*, eds. Rebecca M. Blank and Ron Haskins (Washington, DC: Brookings Institution Press, 2001), pp. 137–68.

[34]Sara McLanahan et al., *The Fragile Families and Child Wellbeing Study Baseline Report*, August 2001, http://crcw.princeton.edu/fragilefamilies/nationalreport.pdf; and Sara McLanahan, Irwin Garfinkel, and Ronald B. Mincy, "Fragile Families, Welfare Reform, and Marriage," *Welfare Reform and Beyond Policy Brief*, No. 10, November, 2001. http://www.brookings.edu/dybdocroot/wrb/publications/pb/pb10.htm. For additional papers from the Fragile Families study, see http://crcw.princeton.edu/fragilefamilies/index.htm.

marriage-education workshops, financial-management classes, and peer-support groups—and "hard" services, such as job training and placement, housing, medical coverage, and substance-abuse treatment, if necessary. At present, all we do is get the father to admit paternity and hound him for child support.

Reduce economic stress by reducing poverty. Poverty and unemployment can stress couples' relationships to their breaking point. Results of a welfare-to-work demonstration program in Minnesota suggest that enhancing the income of the working poor can indirectly promote marriage. The Minnesota Family Investment Program (MFIP), which subsidized the earnings of employed welfare families, found that marriage rates increased for both single-parent long-term recipients and two-parent families. Married two-parent families were significantly more likely to remain married. MFIP also reduced the reported incidence of domestic abuse.[35]

Provide better-paying jobs and job assistance for the poor. The inability of low-skilled, unemployed men to provide income to their families is a major reason for their failure to marry the mothers of their children. Better employment opportunities help low-income fathers, and men in general, to become responsible fathers and, perhaps, more attractive and economically stable marriage partners.[36] There is also growing support for making changes in the child-support system to ensure that more support paid by fathers goes to the children (rather than being used to recoup government program costs).[37]

Invest more in proven programs that reduce out-of-wedlock childbearing. Teen pregnancy and birth rates have fallen by over 20 percent since the early 1990s, and there is now strong evidence that a number of prevention programs are effective. A related strategy is enforcement of child support. States that have tough, effective child support systems have been found to have lower nonmarital birth rates, presumably because men are beginning to understand there are serious costs associated with fathering a child.[38]

Institute workplace policies to reduce work/family conflict and stress on couples. Stress in the workplace spills over into the home. Persistent

[35]Virginia Knox, Cynthia Miller, and Lisa A. Gennetian, *Reforming Welfare and Rewarding Work: A Summary of the Final Report on the Minnesota Family Investment Program* (New York: Manpower Demonstration Research Corporation, September, 2000).

[36]See Chapter 4, "The Fading Inner-City Family," in William Julius Wilson, *When Work Disappears: The World of the New Urban Poor* (New York: Alfred A. Knopf, 1996), pp. 87–110; Kathy Edin, "Few Good Men: Why Poor Mothers Don't Marry or Remarry," *The American Prospect*, January 3, 2000.

[37]See Vicki Turetsky, Testimony Given to the Social Security and Family Policy Subcommittee of the U.S. Senate Finance Committee, October 11, 2001, and Vick Turetsky, *What If All the Money Came Home?* (Washington, DC: Center for Law and Social Policy, June, 2000). Both available on line at www.clasp.org.

[38]Robert D. Plotnick, Inhoe Ku, Irwin Garfinkel, and Sara S. McLanahan, *The Impact of Child Support Enforcement Policy on Nonmarital Childbearing.* Paper presented at the Association for Public Policy Analysis and Management, Year 2000 Research Conference in Seattle, WA.

overtime, frequent travel, and inflexible leave policies place great strain on couples at all income levels. Employers are increasingly demanding nonstandard work schedules. A recent study found that married couples with children who work night and rotating shifts are at higher risk of separation and divorce.[39] The absence of affordable and reliable child care forces many parents who would prefer a normal workday to working split shifts solely to make sure that a parent is home with children.

Reduce tax penalties and other disincentives to marriage. There has always been strong support for reducing marriage tax penalties for many two-earner families. This is a complicated task because the majority of married couples, in fact, receive tax bonuses rather than penalties.[40] A positive step was taken in 2001 to reduce significantly the marriage penalty affecting low-income working families in the Earned Income Tax Credit program. While there is uncertainty about the extent to which these tax-related marriage penalties affect marital behavior, there is broad general agreement that government has a responsibility to "first do no harm" when it comes to marriage.

Similarly, there is near unanimous agreement that government should not make it harder for eligible two-parent families to receive welfare benefits and assistance. In the past, the old welfare program, Aid to Families with Dependent Children, was much criticized for offering incentives to break up families. At least 33 states already have removed the stricter eligibility rules placed on two-parent families,[41] and the President's welfare reauthorization proposal encourages the other states to do the same. In addition, it proposes to end the higher work participation rate for two-parent families, a federal rule that has been criticized widely by the states. Another needed reform would forgive accumulated child-support debt owed by noncustodial fathers if they marry the mothers of their children. (Currently, such debt is owed to the state if the mothers and children are receiving welfare benefits.)[42]

Educate those who want to marry and stay married about how to have healthy relationships and good marriages. A vast industry is devoted to helping couples plan a successful wedding day—wedding planners, 500-page bridal guides, specialty caterers, the list goes on. But where do young people go to learn about how to sustain good, lifelong marriages? In fact,

[39]Harriet B. Presser, "Nonstandard Work Schedules and Marital Instability," *Journal of Marriage and the Family* (February, 2000).

[40]Congressional Budget Office, *For Better or For Worse: Marriage and the Federal Income Tax* (Washington, DC: Congress of the United States, Congressional Budget Office, June, 1997).

[41]Gene Falk and Jill Tauber, *Welfare Reform: TANF Provisions Related to Marriage and Two-Parent Families* (Washington, DC: Congressional Research Service, Library of Congress, October 30, 2001).

[42]Paul Roberts, *An Ounce of Prevention and a Pound of Cure: Developing State Policy on the Payment of Child Support Arrears by Low Income Parents.* (Washington, DC: Center for Law and Social Policy, May, 2001). Available online at www.clasp.org.

we now know a lot about what makes contemporary marriages work. With the transformation of gender roles, there now are fewer fixed rules for couples to follow, meaning they have to negotiate daily about who does what and when. In the absence of the legal and social constraints that used to keep marriages together, there's now a premium on developing effective relationship skills. Building on three decades of research, there are a small but rapidly growing number of programs (both religious and secular) that help people from high school through adulthood understand the benefits of marriage for children and for themselves, develop realistic expectations for healthy relationships, understand the meaning of commitment, and learn the skills and attitudes needed to make marriage succeed.[43] Other programs help married couples survive the inevitable ups and downs that occur in most marriages, and remarried couples with the additional challenges of step-parenting. Oklahoma, Utah, and Michigan have begun using government funds to make these relationship- and marriage-education programs accessible to low-income couples. The Greater Grand Rapids Community Marriage Policy initiative is urging area businesses to include marriage education as an Employee Assistance Program benefit, arguing that it's more cost-effective to prevent marital distress than incur the costs of counseling and lost productivity involved when employees' marriages break up.[44]

A marriage-plus agenda that includes activities such as these is not just the responsibility of government. Some of the strategies proposed here are being implemented by private and religious groups, some by governments, and some by partnerships between these sectors. The approach adopted in Oklahoma, Greater Grand Rapids, and Chattanooga, for example, mobilizes the resources of many sectors of the community— government, education, legal, faith, business, and media—in a comprehensive effort to create a more marriage-supportive culture and to provide new services to promote, support, and strengthen couples and marriage and reduce out-of-wedlock childbearing and divorce. This "saturation model" seems particularly promising because it takes into account the many factors that influence individuals' decisions to marry, to divorce, or to remain unmarried. We should proceed cautiously, trying out and evaluating new ideas before applying them widely.

Ironically, in the midst of this furor about government's role in marriage, it's worth noting that the federal government recently has begun to shirk a basic responsibility: counting the numbers of marriages and divorces in the United States. Since budget cuts in 1995, the government   25

[43]See Scott Stanley, "Making a Case for Premarital Education," in *Family Relations* (July 2001). Also see *Directory of Couples and Marriage Education Programs* at www .smartmarriages.com.

[44]Personal communication with Mark Eastburg, Ph.D., director of Pine Rest Family Institute, Grand Rapids, Michigan. See Web site for the Greater Grand Rapids Community Marriage Initiative, www.ggrcmarriagepolicy.org.

has been unable to report on marriage and divorce rates in the states or for the nation as a whole.[45] And, for the first time in the history of the Census, Americans were not asked to give their marital status in the 2000 survey. What kind of pro-marriage message from the government is that?

If liberals and conservatives are serious about strengthening families for the sake of helping children, liberals ought to acknowledge that noncoercive and egalitarian approaches to bolstering marriage are sound policy. Conservatives, meanwhile, should admit that much of what it takes to make marriage work for the benefit of spouses and children is not just moral but economic.

READING AND DISCUSSION QUESTIONS

1. What does Ooms mean when she says in the first paragraph that in 1996 "the federal government decided to get into the business of promoting marriage"?

2. How does Ooms support her belief that children are better off in a two-parent home?

3. What type of support does she use in the sixth paragraph to argue that "[m]arriage also brings benefits to husbands and wives"?

4. What are some of the problems that arise when government gets involved in promoting marriage?

5. What claim is Ooms supporting? How effective is she in supporting that claim? Are some types of support that she uses more effective than others, in your opinion?

6. This essay, unlike the others in the Readings for Analysis, provides a list of works cited. What effect, if any, does that have on the strength of Ooms's argument?

WRITING SUGGESTIONS

7. Write an essay in which you oppose or support Ooms's marriage-plus plan.

8. Analyze the primary types of support that Ooms uses. If you wish, you may go a step further and evaluate the effectiveness of her support.

---

[45]Stephanie Ventura, "Vital Statistics from the National Center for Health Statistics," in *Data Needs for Measuring Family and Fertility Change after Welfare Reform*, ed. Douglas Besharov (College Park, MD: Maryland School of Public Affairs, Welfare Reform Academy).

one **reason** barbara whittaker

GM has purchased more than $44.3 billion in goods and services from minority suppliers over the last 36 years. One reason? Barbara Whittaker. As Executive Director of Machinery & Equipment and Indirect Purchasing, Barbara works directly with GM suppliers from all over the globe, including more than 600 certified minority suppliers like The Bartech Group. Formed under the sponsorship of GM in 1976, The Bartech Group is now a $200 million company, and one of the largest staffing companies in the nation. Which means that they not only help Barbara diversify GM's supplier base, they help to diversify GM's workforce as well.

GM awards more than $7 billion in purchasing and contracts annually to minority firms. Barbara Whittaker is just one reason GM is committed to increasing that number each and every year. For information about GM's Supplier Diversity Program visit www.gmsupplypower.com.

GM

CHEVROLET   SAAB   PONTIAC   GMAC   OLDSMOBILE   SATURN   BUICK   CADILLAC   HUMMER   GMC   gm.com
© 2004 GM Corp. All rights reserved.

DISCUSSION QUESTIONS

1. For what audience does the GM ad seem to have been designed?
2. What claim is the ad supporting?
3. What different types of support are used in the ad? How effective is the support?
4. How does the picture work with the text to advance the argument made by the ad?

Animal Research Saves Human Lives

HELOISA SABIN

That scene in *Forrest Gump* in which young Forrest runs from his schoolmate tormentors so fast that his leg braces fly apart and his strong legs carry him to safety may be the only image of the polio epidemic of the 1950s etched in the minds of those too young to remember the actual devastation the disease caused. Hollywood created a scene of triumph far removed from the reality of the disease.

Some who have benefited directly from polio research, including that of my late husband, Albert, think winning the real war against polio was just as simple. They have embraced a movement that denounces the very process that enables them to look forward to continued good health and promising futures. This "animal rights" ideology—espoused by groups such as People for the Ethical Treatment of Animals, the Humane Society of the United States and the Fund for Animals—rejects the use of laboratory animals in medical research and denies the role such research played in the victory over polio.

The leaders of this movement seem to have forgotten that year after year in the early fifties, the very words *infantile paralysis* and *poliomyelitis* struck great fear in young parents that the disease would snatch their children as they slept. Each summer public beaches, playgrounds, and movie theaters were places to be avoided. Polio epidemics condemned millions of children and young adults to lives in which debilitated lungs could no longer breathe on their own and young limbs were left forever wilted and frail. The disease drafted tiny armies of children on crutches and in wheelchairs who were unable to walk, run, or jump. In the United States, polio struck down nearly 58,000 children in 1952 alone.

Unlike the braces on Forrest Gump's legs, real ones would be replaced only as the children's misshapen legs grew. Other children and young adults were entombed in iron lungs. The only view of the world these patients had was through mirrors over their heads. These memories, however, are no longer part of our collective cultural memory.

Albert was on the front line of polio research. In 1961, thirty years 5 after he began studying polio, his oral vaccine was introduced in the United States and distributed widely. In the nearly forty years since, polio has been eradicated in the Western Hemisphere, the World Health Organization reports, adding that, with a full-scale effort, polio could be eliminated from the rest of the world by the year 2000.

Heloisa Sabin is honorary director of Americans for Medical Progress in Alexandria, Virginia. This essay appeared in the *Wall Street Journal* on October 18, 1995.

Without animal research, polio would still be claiming thousands of lives each year. "There could have been no oral polio vaccine without the use of innumerable animals, a very large number of animals," Albert told a reporter shortly before his death in 1993. Animals are still needed to test every new batch of vaccine that is produced for today's children.

Animal activists claim that vaccines really didn't end the epidemic — that, with improvements in social hygiene, polio was dying out anyway, before the vaccines were developed. This is untrue. In fact, advanced sanitation was responsible in part for the dramatic *rise* in the number of paralytic polio cases in the fifties. Improvements in sanitation practices reduced the rate of infection, and the average age of those infected by the polio virus went up. Older children and young adults were more likely than infants to develop paralysis from their exposure to the polio virus.

Every child who has tasted the sweet sugar cube or received the drops containing the Sabin vaccine over the past four decades knows polio only as a word, or an obscure reference in a popular film. Thank heavens it's not part of their reality.

These polio-free generations have grown up to be doctors, teachers, business leaders, government officials, and parents. They have their own concerns and struggles. Cancer, heart disease, strokes, and AIDS are far more lethal realities to them now than polio. Yet, those who support an "animal rights" agenda that would cripple research and halt medical science in its tracks are slamming the door on the possibilities of new treatments and cures.

My husband was a kind man, but he was impatient with those who 10 refused to acknowledge reality or to seek reasoned answers to the questions of life.

The pioneers of polio research included not only the scientists but also the laboratory animals that played a critical role in bringing about the end of polio and a host of other diseases for which we now have vaccines and cures. Animals will continue to be as vital as the scientists who study them in the battle to eliminate pain, suffering, and disease from our lives.

That is the reality of medical progress.

Why We Don't Need Animal Experimentation

PEGGY CARLSON

The issue of animal experimentation has become so polarized that rational thinking seems to have taken a back seat. Heloisa Sabin's October 18 editorial-page article "Animal Research Saves Lives" serves only to further misinform and polarize. She does a great disservice to science to incorrectly portray the debate about animal experimentation as occurring between "animal rights activists" and scientists. The truth is, the value of animal experimentation is being questioned by many scientists.

Mrs. Sabin uses the example of the polio vaccine developed by her husband to justify animal experimentation. However, in the case of the polio vaccine, misleading animal experiments detoured scientists away from reliable clinical studies thereby, according to Dr. Sabin himself, delaying the initial work on polio prevention. It was also unfortunate that the original polio vaccine was produced using monkey cells instead of available human cells as can be done today. The use of monkey cells resulted in viruses with the potential to cause serious disease being transferred to humans when the polio vaccine was administered.

The polio vaccine example cannot logically be used to justify the current level of animal experimentation—several billion dollars and about 30 million animals yearly. Although most people would prefer to believe that the death and suffering of all these animals is justified, the facts do not support that conclusion.

Nearly everything that medicine has learned about what substances cause human cancer and birth defects has come from human clinical and epidemiological studies because animal experiments do not accurately predict what occurs in humans. Dr. Bross, the former Director of Biostatistics at the Roswell Institute for Cancer Research states, "While conflicting animal results have often delayed and hampered advances in the war on cancer, they have never produced a single substantial advance either in the prevention or treatment of cancer." A 1990 editorial in *Stroke* notes that none of the twenty-five compounds "proven" efficacious for treating stroke in animal experiments over the preceding ten years had been effective for use in humans. From human studies alone we have learned how to lessen the risk of heart attacks. Warnings to the public that smoking cigarettes leads to an increased risk of cancer were delayed as researchers sought, unsuccessfully, to confirm the risk by using animals.

Animal tests for drug safety, cancer-causing potential, and toxicity are 5 unreliable, and science is leading us to more accurate methods that will

Peggy Carlson, M.D., was the research director of the Physicians Committee for Responsible Medicine in Washington, D.C., at the time her letter appeared in the *Wall Street Journal* on November 7, 1995.

offer greater protection. But if we refuse to acknowledge the inadequacies of animal tests we put a stranglehold on the very progress that will help us. Billions of precious health-care dollars have been spent to fund animal experiments that are repetitious or that have no human relevance.

An uncritical acceptance of the value of animal experiments leads to its overfunding, which, in turn, leads to the underfunding of other more beneficial areas.

DISCUSSION QUESTIONS

1. Sabin uses the vaccine against polio as the principal example in her support of animal research. Does this limit her argument? Should she have been more specific in her references to other diseases?
2. What is the significance of Sabin's repeated references to "reality"?
3. List all the kinds of support that Carlson provides. Which of the supporting materials is most persuasive?
4. Does Carlson refute all the arguments in Sabin's article? Be specific.
5. Sabin makes strong emotional appeals. Describe them, and decide how large a part such appeals play in her argument. Does Carlson appeal to the emotions of her readers?

TAKING THE DEBATE ONLINE

For these and additional research URLs, see bedfordstmartins.com/rottenberg.

- *University of Colorado at Boulder: Frequently Asked Questions*
  www.colorado.edu/Research/animal_resources/faqs.html

  This multilayered site examines animal resources at the university and explores many ethical questions on animal research.
- *National Institutes of Health*
  www.nih.gov/

  This institute investigates America's premier medical research facilities for their treatment of animals.
- *People for the Ethical Treatment of Animals Online*
  www.peta.org

  This association unequivocally condemns animal research.
- *Medical Research Modernization Committee*
  www.mrmcmed.org/Critical_Look.pdf

  The MRMC is a nonprofit health advocacy organization promoting "efficient, reliable, and cost-effective research methods."
- *Scientific American*
  www.sciam.com/

This site contains links to featured stories about animal experimentation in the February 1997 issue of the magazine.

- *Fund for the Replacement of Animals in Medical Experiments* **www.frame.org.uk/**

This association promotes the researching of alternatives to animal testing.

ASSIGNMENTS FOR UNDERSTANDING SUPPORT

1. In the summer of 1983, after an alarming rise in the juvenile crime rate, the mayor of Detroit instituted a curfew for young people under the age of eighteen. Explain the pros and cons of using a curfew as a way to cut down on juvenile crime.

2. Write a full-page advertisement to solicit support for a project or cause in which you believe.

3. How do you account for the large and growing interest in fantasy films and books? In addition to their entertainment value, are there other less obvious reasons for their popularity?

4. According to some researchers soap operas are influential in transmitting values, lifestyles, and sexual information to youthful viewers. Do you agree? If so, what values and information are being transmitted? Be specific.

5. Choose one of the following stereotypical ideas and argue that it is true or false or partly both. Discuss the reasons for the existence of the stereotype.

    a. Jocks are stupid.

    b. The country is better than the city for bringing up children.

    c. Television is justly called "the boob tube."

    d. Politicians are dishonest.

    e. Beauty contests are degrading to women.

6. Defend or refute the view that star high school basketball players should be allowed to go directly to the pros.

7. The philosopher Bertrand Russell said, "Most of the work that most people have to do is not in itself interesting, but even such work has certain advantages." Defend or refute this assertion. Use your own experience as support.

8. Choose a product advertised on television by many different makers. (Cars, pain relievers, fast food, cereals, and soft drinks are some of the most popular products.) What kinds of support do the advertisers offer? Why do they choose these particular appeals? Would the support be significantly different in print?

9. From time to time advocates of causes speak on campus. The causes may be broadly based—minority rights, welfare cuts, abortion, foreign aid—or they may be local issues, having to do with harassment policy, course requirements, or tuition increases. Attend a meeting or a rally at which a speaker argues his or her cause. Write an evaluation of the speech, paying particular attention to the kinds of support. Did the speaker provide sufficient and relevant evidence? Did he or she make emotional appeals? What signs, if any, reflected the speaker's awareness of the kind of audience he or she was addressing?

10. Choose one of the Readings for Analysis and write an essay explaining the primary types of support used in it.

11. Choose one of the Readings for Analysis and write an essay evaluating the author's use of support.

12. Write a letter to the editor of your local newspaper encouraging its readers not to buy light trucks. Use information from Varian's essay to support your position. You will not document your letter as you would an academic paper, but in the text of your letter you must make clear that you are drawing on information provided by Varian.

13. Find a subject that might be defended or opposed with the use of statistics but modest enough to be argued successfully in a 750- to 1,000-word essay. Sports, both professional and amateur, for example, offer topics for research: the decline of attendance at big-league baseball games, the high salaries of professional players, injuries and death suffered by high school athletes. Your essay should provide proof for a claim. Other subjects that depend on statistical support can be found throughout this book.

CHAPTER 6

Warrants

We now come to the third element in the structure of the argument—the warrant. Claim and support, the other major elements we have discussed, are more familiar in ordinary discourse, but there is nothing mysterious or unusual about the warrant. All our claims, both formal and informal, are grounded in warrants or assumptions that the audience must share with us if our claims are to prove to be acceptable.

The following exercise provides a good starting point for this chapter. Do the assigned task by yourself or in a small group.

■ Who Should Survive?

Task: A series of environmental catastrophic events has virtually wiped out human life on earth. The only known survivors in your vicinity are the eleven listed below. There are resources to sustain only seven. Choose seven of the following people to survive. List them in the order in which you would choose them and be prepared to explain the reasons for your selection; that is, why you chose these particular persons and why you placed them in this certain order.

- Dr. Dane—thirty-seven, white, no religious affiliation, Ph.D. in history, college professor, in good health (jogs daily), hobby is botany, enjoys politics, married with one child (Bobby).

- Mrs. Dane—thirty-eight, white, Jewish, rather obese, diabetic, MA in psychology, counselor in a mental health clinic, married to Dr. Dane, has one child.

- Bobby Dane—ten, white, Jewish, mentally retarded with IQ of 70, healthy and strong for his age.

- Mrs. Garcia—twenty-three, Spanish American, Catholic, ninth-grade education, cocktail waitress, worked as a prostitute, married at age sixteen, divorced at age eighteen, one son (Juan).

- Juan Garcia—three months old, Spanish American, healthy.

- Mary Evans—eighteen, black, Protestant, trade school education, wears glasses, artistic.

- Mr. Newton—twenty-five, black power advocate, starting last year of medical school, suspected homosexual activity, music as a hobby, physical fitness buff.

- Mrs. Clark—twenty-eight, black, Protestant, daughter of a minister, college graduate, electronics engineer, single now after a brief marriage, member of Zero Population Growth.

- Mr. Blake—fifty-one, white, Mormon, BS in mechanics, married with four children, enjoys outdoors, experienced in construction, quite handy, sympathizes with antiblack views.

- Father Frans—thirty-seven, white, Catholic priest, active in civil rights, former college athlete, farming background, often criticized for liberal views.

- Dr. Gonzales—sixty-six, Spanish American, Catholic, doctor in general practice, two heart attacks in the past five years, loves literature and quotes extensively.

Obviously this is an exercise with no right answer. What it can teach us, however, is to consider the assumptions on which our beliefs are based. There are reasons you might have chosen certain individuals to survive that could be stated as general principles: Those who are in the best physical condition should be allowed to survive. Those with the most useful skills should be allowed to survive. Those who are mentally deficient should not be allowed to survive. Those who are most likely to reproduce should be allowed to survive.

There may have been a great deal of disagreement as to who the survivors should be. If so, different members of your group or your class as a whole were operating under different assumptions or basing their decisions on different warrants. Some of you may have chosen not to let Mrs. Garcia survive because she seemed to have nothing particularly vital to offer to the survival of the group as a whole. Others of you may have felt that she should be allowed to survive along with her son, the infant in the group. Some of you, whether you acknowledge it or not, may have opposed letting Mrs. Garcia survive because she was once a prostitute. Think about the warrant that would underlie the claim that Mrs. Garcia should not be one of the seven allowed to survive. What assumption—what generalized principle—would a person who made that claim be accepting about women who were once prostitutes? What assumption would underlie the claim that Bobby Dane should be allowed to live (or die)?

Fortunately, this is merely an intellectual exercise. Whenever you take a stand in a real-life situation, though, you do so on the basis of certain general principles that guide your choices. Those general principles that you feel most strongly about exist as part of your intellectual and moral being because of what you have experienced in your life thus far. They have been shaped by your observations, your personal experience, and your participation in a culture. But because these observations, experiences, and cultural associations will vary, the audience may not always agree with the warrants or assumptions of the writer.

What does this have to do with argumentation? Any time you support an argumentative claim, you have to analyze the assumptions behind the argument and consider whether the members of your audience share the same assumptions. Some warrants are so widely accepted that you do not need to state them or to offer any proof of their validity. If you argue that every new dorm on campus should have a sprinkler system, you probably do not even need to state your warrant. If you did, it would be something like this: Measures that would increase the likelihood that dorm residents would survive a fire should be implemented in all dorms.

What about claims that are more controversial? Why is it so difficult for those who oppose abortion, for example, to communicate with those who favor it and vice versa? Anyone who believes that abortion is the murder of an unborn child is basing that argument on the warrant that a fetus is a child from conception. Many on the other side of the debate do not accept that warrant and thus do not accept the claim. Obviously disagreements on such emotionally charged issues are very difficult to resolve because the underlying warrants are based on firmly held beliefs that are difficult to change. It is always better to be aware of your opponent's warrants, however, than to simply dismiss them as irrelevant.

The British philosopher Stephen Toulmin, who developed the concept of warrants, dismissed more traditional forms of logical reasoning in favor of a more audience-based, courtroom-derived approach to argumentation. He refers to warrants as "general, hypothetical statements, which can act as bridges" and "entitle one to draw conclusions or make claims."[1] The word *bridges* to denote the action of the warrant is crucial. One dictionary defines warrant as a "guarantee or justification." We use the word *warrant* to emphasize that in an argument it guarantees a connecting link—a

---

[1] Stephen Toulmin, *The Uses of Argument* (Cambridge: Cambridge University Press, 1958), p. 98.

bridge—between the claim and the support. This means that even if a reader agrees that the support is sound, the support cannot prove the validity of the claim unless the reader also agrees with the underlying warrant. Recall the sample argument outlined in Chapter 1 (p. 3):

CLAIM: Adoption of a vegetarian diet leads to healthier and longer life.

SUPPORT: The authors of *Becoming a Vegetarian Family* say so.

WARRANT: The authors of *Becoming a Vegetarian Family* are reliable sources of information on diet.

Notice that the reader must agree with the assumption that the testimony of experts is trustworthy before he or she arrives at the conclusion that a vegetarian diet is healthy. Simply providing evidence that the authors say so is not enough to prove the claim.

The following dialogue offers another example of the relationship between the warrant and the other elements of the argument.

> *"I don't think that Larry can do the job. He's pretty dumb."*
> *"Really? I thought he was smart. What makes you say he's dumb?"*
> *"Did you know that he's illiterate—can't read above third-grade level? In my book that makes him dumb."*

If we put this into outline form, the warrant or assumption in the argument becomes clear.

CLAIM: Larry is pretty dumb.

EVIDENCE: He can't read above third-grade level.

WARRANT: Anybody who can't read above third-grade level must be dumb.

We can also represent the argument in diagram form, which shows the warrant as a bridge between the claim and the support.

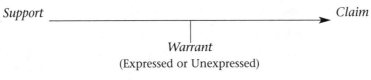

Support ⎯⎯⎯⎯⎯⎯⎯⎯⎯⎯⎯⎯⎯⎯⎯⎯⎯→ *Claim*

Warrant
(Expressed or Unexpressed)

The argument above can then be written like this:

Support ⎯⎯⎯⎯⎯⎯⎯⎯⎯⎯⎯⎯→ *Claim*
Larry can't read above   He's pretty dumb.
third-grade level.

Warrant
Anybody who can't read above third-grade
level must be pretty dumb.

Is this warrant valid? We cannot answer this question until we consider the *backing*. Every warrant or assumption rests on something else that gives it authority; this is what we call backing. Backing or authority for the warrant in this example would consist of research data that prove a relationship between stupidity and low reading ability. This particular warrant, we would discover, lacks backing because we know that the failure to learn to read well may be due to a number of things unrelated to intelligence. So if the warrant is unprovable, the claim—that Larry is dumb—is also unprovable, even if the evidence is true. In this case, then, the evidence does not guarantee the soundness of the claim.

Now consider this example of a somewhat more complicated warrant: The beautiful and unspoiled Eastern Shore of Maryland is being discovered by thousands of tourists, vacationers, and developers who will, according to the residents, change the landscape and the way of life, which is now based largely on fishing and farming. In a few years the Eastern Shore may become a noisy, crowded string of resorts. Mrs. Walkup, the Kent County commissioner, says,

> Catering to the wealthy puts property back on the tax rolls, but it's going to make the Eastern Shore look like the rest of the country. Everything that made our way of life so special is being eroded. We are a fragile area. The Eastern Shore is still special, but it is feeling pressure from all directions. Lots of people don't seem to appreciate the fact that God made us to need a little peace and quiet now and then.[2]

In simplified form the argument of those opposed to development would be outlined this way:

CLAIM: Development will bring undesirable changes to the present way of life on the Eastern Shore, a life of farming and fishing, peace and quiet.

SUPPORT: Developers will build express highways, condominiums, casinos, and nightclubs.

WARRANT: A pastoral life of fishing and farming is superior to the way of life brought by expensive, fast-paced modern development.

Notice that the warrant is a broad generalization that can apply to a number of different situations, while the claim is about a specific place and time. It should be added that in other arguments the warrant may not be stated in such general terms. However, even in arguments in which the warrant makes a more specific reference to the claim, the reader can infer an extension of the warrant to other similar arguments. In the vegetarian diet example (p. 3, outlined on p. 11), the warrant mentions a specific book. But it is clear that such warrants can be generalized to apply to

[2]Michael Wright, "The Changing Chesapeake," *New York Times Magazine*, July 10, 1983, p. 27.

other arguments in which we accept a claim based on the credibility of the sources.

To be convinced of the validity of Mrs. Walkup's claim, you must first find that the support is true, that the developers plan to introduce drastic changes that will destroy the pastoral life of the Eastern Shore. You may, however, believe that the support is not entirely sound, that the development will be much more modest than residents fear, and that the Eastern Shore will not be seriously altered. Next, you may want to see more justification for the warrant. Is pastoral life superior to the life that will result from large-scale development? Perhaps you have always thought that a life of fishing and farming means poverty and limited opportunities for the majority of the residents. Although the superiority of a way of life is largely a matter of taste and therefore difficult to prove, Mrs. Walkup may need to produce backing for her belief that the present way of life is more desirable than one based on developing the area for new residents and summer visitors. If you find either the support or the warrant unconvincing, you cannot accept the claim.

Remember that a claim is often modified by one or more qualifiers, which limit the claim. Mrs. Walkup might have said, "Development will *probably* destroy *some aspects of* the present way of life on the Eastern Shore." Warrants can also be modified or limited by *reservations*, which remind the reader that there are conditions under which the warrants will not be relevant. Mrs. Walkup might have added, "unless increased prosperity and exposure to the outside world brought by development improve some aspects of our lives."

A diagram of Mrs. Walkup's argument shows the additional elements:

Support ⟶ *Claim*

The developers will build highways, condos, casinos, nightclubs.	Development will bring undesirable changes to life on the Eastern Shore.

Warrant — *Qualifier*

A way of life devoted to farming and fishing is superior to a way of life brought by development.	Development will *most likely* bring undesirable changes.

Backing
We have experienced crowds, traffic, noise, rich strangers, and high-rises, and they destroy peace and quiet.

Reservation
But increased development might improve some aspects of our lives.

Claim and support (or lack of support) are relatively easy to uncover in most arguments. One thing that makes the warrant different is that it is often unexpressed and therefore unexamined by both writer and reader because they take it for granted. In the argument about Larry's intelligence, the warrant was stated. But in the argument about development on the Eastern Shore, Mrs. Walkup did not state her warrant directly, although her meaning is perfectly clear. She probably felt that it was not necessary to be more explicit because her readers would understand and supply the warrant.

We can make the discovery of warrants even clearer by examining another argument, in this case a policy claim. We've looked at a factual claim (that Larry is dumb) and a value claim (that Eastern Shore development is undesirable). Now we examine a policy claim that rests on one expressed and one unexpressed warrant. Policy claims are usually more complicated than other claims because the statement of policy is preceded by an array of facts and values. In addition, such claims may represent chains of reasoning in which one argument is dependent on another. These complicated arguments may be difficult or impossible to summarize in a simple diagram, but careful reading, asking the same kinds of questions that the author may have asked about his claim, can help you to find the warrant or chain of warrants that must be accepted before evidence and claim can be linked.

In a familiar argument that appeared a few years ago,[3] the author argues for a radical reform in college sports—the elimination of subprofessional intermural team sports, as practiced above all in football and basketball. The claim is clear, and evidence for the professional character of college sports not hard to find: the large salaries paid to coaches, the generous perquisites offered to players, the recruitment policies that ignore academic standing, the virtually full-time commitment of the players, the lucrative television contracts. But can this evidence support the author's claim that such sports do not belong on college campuses? Advocates of these sports may ask, Why not? In the conclusion of the article the author states one warrant or assumption underlying his claim.

> Even if the money to pay college athletes could be found, though, a larger question must be answered—namely, why should a system of professional athletics be affiliated with universities at all? For the truth is that the requirements of athletics and academics operate at cross purposes, and the attempt to play both games at once serves only to reduce the level of performance of each.

In other words, the author assumes that the goals of an academic education on the one hand and the goals of big-time college sports on the other hand are incompatible. In the article he develops the ways in which each enterprise harms the other.

[3] D. G. Myers, "Why College Sports?" *Commentary*, December 1990, pp. 49–51.

But the argument clearly rests on another warrant that is not expressed because the author takes for granted that his readers will supply it: The academic goals of the university are primary and should take precedence over all other collegiate activities. This is an argument based on an authority warrant, the authority of those who define the goals of the university—scholars, public officials, university administrators, and others. (Types of warrants are discussed in the following section.)

This warrant makes clear that the evidence of the professional nature of college sports cited above supports the claim that they should be eliminated. If quasiprofessional college sports are harmful to the primary educational function of the college or university, then they must go. In the author's words, "The two are separate enterprises, to be judged by separate criteria. . . . For college sports, the university is not an educational institution at all; it is merely a locus, a means of coordinating the different aspects of the sporting enterprise."

This argument may be summarized in outline form as follows:

CLAIM: Intermural college team sports should be abolished.

SUPPORT: College sports have become subprofessional.

WARRANT: The goals of an academic education and big-time college sports are incompatible.

BACKING
FOR THE
WARRANT: Academic education is the primary goal of the college and must take precedence over athletic activity.

The next essay, by student writer Stuart Glenn, also examines what activities deserve a place in schools. As you read, consider on what warrant or warrants his argument is based. Remember that a warrant provides a necessary bridge between the support and the claim. Consider how different the essay would have been without the material that Stuart drew from his sources. Stuart's essay makes use of the MLA style of documenting sources.

SAMPLE ESSAY

Musical Reasoning

STUART GLENN

Music has been around for centuries and has functioned mainly as a form of entertainment and artistic expression. It has evolved from simple whistled tunes and percussion to complex arrangements for symphonies and opera. Music has also had various effects on its listeners. Certain types of music calm people while other types generate excitement.

People listen to light jazz, for instance, to relax because that music creates a calm atmosphere for the listener. This could be because light jazz relies heavily on harmony and every note played fits smoothly with others in the tune. Rock, on the other hand, will often evoke excitement in the listener. Rock music has very aggressive musical elements such as dissonant melodic phrasing and the overdriven, distorted tone of the instruments. Some employers use music in training their employees because they have found that music's calming effect can increase productivity (M.D. 1). A person's favorite song can send shivers down the spine, which seems to relate music to the physical nervous system. Studies of this effect suggest that music may trigger nerve responses in a way similar to memories that trigger goose bumps ("Brain Health" 1). Scientists are studying why music is able to achieve all of these diverse effects and have found interesting results. Music is tied to the human brain in some way, and current studies have been investigating what exactly creates the link.

A music study published by Temple Grandin, Matthew Peterson, and Gordon Shaw has given proof that music is somehow able to affect the brain and its ability to perform certain tasks (1). The team investigated how certain types of music can increase the brain's capacity to understand certain concepts. The findings suggest that music can in fact help a person to grasp specific types of concepts. If music has that effect on people, it is reasonable to assume that early and regular music training will have an effect on students. It is widely known that the minds of young children are more susceptible to influence and training than those of older students. Based on the results of music's effect on the brain, it would be beneficial to investigate the implementation of musical training in education ranging from kindergarten through high school.

The results of the study were very interesting and are still being investigated in order to use them to their full potential. The study found a definite link between music and the mind, specifically the area of the brain that can solve tasks known as spatial-temporal tasks. The research team planned a study that would test a control group's performance on spatial-temporal tasks after having listened to a certain type of music for a short amount of time. The team chose Mozart's "Sonata in D major for two pianos" for the control group (Grandin, Peterson, and Shaw 2). The team chose this particular piece because of its complexity and its use of regular patterns and sequences (Reimer 4). Mozart was chosen because he was a child prodigy himself and the team hoped that his music would stimulate some of the same spatial-temporal advances that he had demonstrated in his youth (Grandin, Peterson, and Shaw 2). Mozart's music is filled with patterns and scales. These aspects of music have a strong tie to mathematics in the sense that they are both ordered, repeating sequences. Recent studies have also shown that the mind functions in a manner that can be predicted by math, specifically logarithms ("Can you hum . . ." 2). The brain was mapped by its response to logarithmic sequences, and this map highlights the relationship of the brain to mathematics (Simpson 1). If the brain is related to math and music is related to math as well, then it is reasonable to investigate a relationship between the brain and music. Shaw's research team investigated this by predicting what area of the brain would be affected by Mozart's music and giving tests accordingly. They isolated a group of college students and let them listen to Mozart before taking a spatial-temporal task test (Simpson 1). The effect of the music seemed to last only as long as the study, but the results were very encouraging to the scientists ("Can you hum . . ." 2). These results indicate that music can improve brain function on certain levels. Gordon Shaw of the research team believes that after careful study "specific music could enhance how we think, reason, and create" (Grandin, Peterson, and Shaw 1).

Music training can assist educators in the teaching of spatial-temporal concepts. The current education system does not focus as much on spatial-temporal tasks as it does on language-analytical tasks. Spatial-temporal tasks are those tasks that involve "the transforming and relating of mental images in space and time" (Grandin, Peterson, and Shaw 1). These tasks include many applications that are being taught in schools today. In math, basic patterns and diagrams are examples of spatial-temporal problems. Art and architecture applications also involve spatial-temporal analysis. If music programs are put into place in schools today, the spatial-temporal-based lessons in other subjects will be enhanced. Shaw feels that this would be a much needed improvement since "the current educational system concentrates on developing language-analytical reasoning skills and neglects the complementary spatial-temporal form of reasoning" (Grandin, Peterson, and Shaw 3).

The studies have produced interesting results in how music affects young children. The basis of this research is the fact that infants have shown an understanding of music before they can comprehend language and other stimuli. Music is understood by infants, before language, and could be a way to "train" young minds (Grandin, Peterson, and Shaw 3). This theory prompted further research into the effects of music on pre-school children. These children are still subject to heavy suggestion from educators due to their young age. Their minds are still able to go through easy transformation, and the music training will have a substantial effect (Grandin, Peterson, and Shaw 2). Studies have followed preschool students through different musical training programs. Children who have been through six months of musical training have shown improvement in spatial-temporal tasks (Grandin, Peterson, and Shaw 1). This training could be implemented in school programs. Schools should put basic music theory and keyboarding classes into place for preschool and elementary students. These courses can be made simple enough for preschool age children to understand, but they would also help the children in their other courses. The students in the study showed improvement in reproducing mental images and manipulating them (Grandin, Peterson, and Shaw 3). The benefits of music training will not only be seen in the individual's respect for and greater exposure to the arts, but also in mathematics and higher learning.

The program would also benefit students if it were carried through to graduation. A twelve-year exposure to music education has a good chance of enhancing a student's ability to work spatial-temporal problems in the future. These music programs should not be forced on students, but should be readily available. As a student progresses through high school, the level of difficulty rises sharply in mathematics. Students progress through geometry, trigonometry, and calculus. Each of these mathematics courses requires a strong understanding of spatial-temporal reasoning. Higher mathematics requires students to visualize objects and points without the aid of pen and paper. A student with a background in music education has an advantage in this area, according to the results of the "Mozart" studies. The music education will provide a greater grasp of mental reasoning. The benefits of music will also be helpful in higher learning and in adult life. Higher learning will produce new mathematical challenges in new areas. Students who major in engineering, architecture, programming, or even music will all benefit from an early emphasis on the arts. As these students graduate from college and continue into the work force, they will be valuable to employers that are looking for creative and sharp minds.

The implementation of a music education program in schools will be advantageous to students of all fields of study. The benefits of this program will not end with just school. The students will carry their understanding through to their careers for the rest of their lives. As a bonus, students will also be more exposed to music in general. The benefits of improved spatial-temporal reasoning are enough to justify the implementation of a music program. Yet these students will also grow up with a sense of the history of music as an art form. Music will improve their intelligence while still remaining a form of relaxation and entertainment. Music's use as a tool for increasing reasoning is the next step in its continuing evolution.

Works Cited

"Brain Health: Music and the Mind." *Harvard Health Letter* 27.2 (Dec. 2001): 1–2.

"Can You Hum Your Way to Math Genius?" *Forbes* 163.8 (19 April 1999): 176.

Delahoussaye, Martin. "Requiem for a Trainer." *Training* 39.6 (June 2002): 28.

Grandin, Temple, Matthew Peterson, and Gordon Shaw. "Spatial-Temporal Versus Language-Analytical Reasoning: The Role of Music Training." *Arts Education Policy Review* 99.6 (July–August 1998): 11–14.

Reimer, Bennett. "Facing the Risks of the 'Mozart Effect.'" *Phi Delta Kappan* 81.4 (Dec. 1999: 278.

Simpson, Marion. "Will Listening to Mozart Make You Smarter?" *Student BMJ* (March 2002): 64

Arguers will often neglect to state their warrants for one of two reasons: First, like Mrs. Walkup, they may believe that the warrant is obvious and need not be expressed; second, they may want to conceal the warrant in the hope that the reader will overlook its weakness.

What kinds of warrants are so obvious that they need not be expressed? Here are a few that will probably sound familiar:

Mothers love their children.

The more expensive the product, the more satisfactory it will be.

A good harvest will result in lower prices for produce.

First come, first served.

These statements seem to embody beliefs that most of us would share and that might be unnecessary to make explicit in an argument. The last statement, for example, is taken as axiomatic, an article of faith that we seldom question in ordinary circumstances. Suppose you hear someone make the claim, "I deserve to get the last ticket to the concert." If you ask why he is entitled to a ticket that you also would like to have, he may answer in support of his claim, "Because I was here first." No doubt you accept his claim without further argument because you understand and agree with the warrant that is not expressed: "If you arrive first, you deserve to be served before those who come later." Your acceptance of the warrant probably also takes into account the unexpressed backing that is based on a belief in justice: "It is only fair that those who sacrifice time and comfort to be first in line should be rewarded for their trouble."

In this case it may not be necessary to expose the warrant and examine it. Indeed, as Stephen Toulmin tells us, "If we demanded the credentials of all warrants at sight and never let one pass unchallenged, argument could scarcely begin."[4]

But even those warrants that seem to express universal truths invite analysis if we can think of claims for which these warrants might not, after all, be relevant. "First in line," for example, may justify the claim of a person who wants a concert ticket, but it cannot in itself justify the claim of someone who wants a vital medication that is in short supply. Moreover, offering a rebuttal to a long-held but unexamined warrant can often produce an interesting and original argument. If someone exclaims, "All this buying of gifts! I think people have forgotten that Christmas celebrates the birth of Christ," she need not express the assumption—that the buying of gifts violates what ought to be a religious celebration. It goes unstated by the speaker because it has been uttered so often that she knows the hearer will supply it. But one writer, in an essay titled "God's Gift: A Commercial Christmas," argued that, contrary to popular belief, the purchase of gifts, which means the expenditure of time, money, and thought on others rather than oneself, is not a violation but an affirmation of the Christmas spirit.[5]

[4] *The Uses of Argument* (Cambridge: Cambridge University Press, 1958), p. 106.
[5] Robert A. Sirico, *Wall Street Journal*, December 21, 1993, sec. A, p. 12.

The second reason for refusal to state the warrant lies in the arguer's intention to disarm or deceive the reader, although the arguer may not be aware of this. For instance, failure to state the warrant is common in advertising and politics, where the desire to sell a product or an idea may outweigh the responsibility to argue explicitly. The following advertisement is famous not only for what it says but for what it does not say:

> In 1918 Leona Currie scandalized a New Jersey beach with a bathing suit cut above her knees. And to irk the establishment even more, she smoked a cigarette. Leona Currie was promptly arrested.
> Oh, how Leona would smile if she could see you today.
> You've come a long way, baby. *Virginia Slims.* The taste for today's woman.

What is the unstated warrant? The manufacturer of Virginia Slims hopes we will agree that being permitted to smoke cigarettes is a significant sign of female liberation. But many readers would insist that proving "You've come a long way, baby" requires more evidence than women's freedom to smoke (or wear short bathing suits). The shaky warrant weakens the claim.

Politicians, too, conceal warrants that may not survive close scrutiny. In the 1983 mayoral election in Chicago, one candidate revealed that his opponent had undergone psychiatric treatment. He did not have to state the warrant supporting his claim. He knew that many in his audience would assume that anyone who had undergone psychiatric treatment was unfit to hold public office. This same assumption contributed to the withdrawal of a vice-presidential candidate from the 1972 campaign.

TYPES OF WARRANTS

Arguments may be classified according to the types of warrants offered as proof. Because warrants represent the reasoning process by which we establish the relationship between support and claim, analysis of the major types of warrants enables us to see the whole argument as a sum of its parts.

Warrants may be organized into three categories: *"authoritative, substantive,* and *motivational."*[6] We have already given examples of these types of warrants in this chapter and in Chapter 1. The *authoritative warrant* (see p. 223) is based on the credibility or trustworthiness of the source. If we assume that the source of the data is authoritative, then we find that the support justifies the claim. A *substantive warrant* is based on beliefs about reliability of factual evidence. In the example on page 223 the speaker assumes, although mistakenly, that the relationship between

[6]D. Ehninger and W. Brockriede, *Decision by Debate* (New York: Dodd, Mead, 1953).

low reading level and stupidity is a verifiable datum, one that can be proved by objective research. A *motivational warrant*, on the other hand, is based on the needs and values of the audience. For example, the warrant on page 12 reflects a preference for individual freedom, a value that would cause a reader who held it to agree that laws against marijuana should be repealed.

Each type of warrant requires a different set of questions for testing its soundness. The following list of questions will help you to decide whether a particular warrant is valid and can justify a particular claim.

1. *Authoritative* (based on the credibility of the sources)

   Is the authority sufficiently respected to make a credible claim?

   Do other equally reputable authorities agree with the authority cited?

   Are there equally reputable authorities who disagree?

2. *Substantive* (based on beliefs about the reliability of factual evidence)

   Are sufficient examples given to convince us that a general statement is justified? That is, are the examples given representative of the whole community?

   If you have argued that one event or condition can bring about another (a cause-and-effect argument), does the cause given seem to account entirely for the effect? Are other possible causes equally important as explanations for the effect?

   If you have used comparisons, are the similarities between the two situations greater than the differences?

   If you have used analogies, does the analogy explain or merely describe? Are there sufficient similarities between the two elements to make the analogy appropriate?

3. *Motivational* (based on the values of the arguer and the audience)

   Are the values ones that the audience will regard as important?

   Are the values relevant to the claim?

The Case for Torture

MICHAEL LEVIN

Introduction:
statement of
opposing view

It is generally assumed that torture is impermissible, a throwback to a more brutal age. Enlightened societies reject it outright, and regimes suspected of using it risk the wrath of the United States.

Claim of policy:
rebuttal of opposing
view

I believe this attitude is unwise. There are situations in which torture is not merely permissible but morally mandatory. Moreover, these situations are moving from the realm of imagination to fact.

Support: hypothetical
example to test the
reader's belief

Suppose a terrorist has hidden an atomic bomb on Manhattan Island which will detonate at noon on July 4 unless . . . (here follow the usual demands for money and release of his friends from jail). Suppose, further, that he is caught at 10 A.M. of the fateful day, but — preferring death to failure — won't disclose where the bomb is. What do we do? If we follow due process — wait for his lawyer, arraign him — millions of people will die. If the only way to save those lives is to subject the terrorist to the most excruciating possible pain, what grounds can there be for not doing so? I suggest there are none. In any case, I ask you to face the question with an open mind.

Torturing the terrorist is unconstitutional? Probably. But millions of lives surely outweigh constitutionality. Torture is barbaric? Mass murder is far more barbaric. Indeed, letting millions of innocents die in deference to one who flaunts his guilt is moral cowardice, an unwillingness to dirty one's hands. If *you* caught the terrorist, could you sleep nights knowing that millions died because you couldn't bring yourself to apply the electrodes?

Once you concede that torture is justified in 5 extreme cases, you have admitted that the deci-

---

Michael Levin is a professor of philosophy at the City College of New York. This essay is reprinted from the June 7, 1982, issue of *Newsweek*.

sion to use torture is a matter of balancing inno- cent lives against the means needed to save them. You must now face more realistic cases involving more modest numbers. Someone plants a bomb on a jumbo jet. He alone can disarm it, and his de- mands cannot be met (or if they can, we refuse to set a precedent by yielding to his threats). Surely we can, we must, do anything to the extortionist to save the passengers. How can we tell 300, or 100, or 10 people who never asked to be put in danger, "I'm sorry, you'll have to die in agony, we just couldn't bring ourselves to . . ."

Here are the results of an informal poll about a third, hypothetical, case. Suppose a terrorist group kidnapped a newborn baby from a hospi- tal. I asked four mothers if they would approve of torturing kidnappers if that were necessary to get their own newborns back. All said yes, the most "liberal" adding that she would administer it herself.

I am not advocating torture as punishment. Punishment is addressed to deeds irrevocably past. Rather, I am advocating torture as an accept- able measure for preventing future evils. So un- derstood, it is far less objectionable than many extant punishments. Opponents of the death penalty, for example, are forever insisting that ex- ecuting a murderer will not bring back his victim (as if the purpose of capital punishment were supposed to be resurrection, not deterrence or ret- ribution). But torture, in the cases described, is intended not to bring anyone back but to keep innocents from being dispatched. The most pow- erful argument against using torture as a punish- ment or to secure confessions is that such prac- tices disregard the rights of the individual. Well, if the individual is all that important — and he is — it is correspondingly important to protect the rights of individuals threatened by terrorists. If life is so valuable that it must never be taken, the lives of the innocents must be saved even at the price of hurting the one who endangers them.

Better precedents for torture are assassination and preemptive attack. No Allied leader would have flinched at assassinating Hitler, had that been possible. (The Allies did assassinate Heydrich.)

Support: hypothetical example

Support: informal poll

Defense of the claim a) Not punishment but protection of the innocent

Hypothetical examples: b) Analogies with World War II

Americans would be angered to learn that Roosevelt could have had Hitler killed in 1943—thereby shortening the war and saving millions of lives—but refused on moral grounds. Similarly, if nation A learns that nation B is about to launch an unprovoked attack, A has a right to save itself by destroying B's military capability first. In the same way, if the police can by torture save those who would otherwise die at the hands of kidnappers or terrorists, they must.

c) Denial that terrorists have rights

There is an important difference between terrorists and their victims that should mute talk of the terrorists' "rights." The terrorist's victims are at risk unintentionally, not having asked to be endangered. But the terrorist knowingly initiated his actions. Unlike his victims, he volunteered for the risks of his deed. By threatening to kill for profit or idealism, he renounces civilized standards, and he can have no complaint if civilization tries to thwart him by whatever means necessary.

Just as torture is justified only to save lives (not 10 extort confessions or recantations), it is justifiably administered only to those *known* to hold innocent lives in their hands. Ah, but how can the authorities ever be sure they have the right malefactor? Isn't there a danger of error and abuse? Won't We turn into Them?

d) Easy identification of terrorists

Questions like these are disingenuous in a world in which terrorists proclaim themselves and perform for television. The name of their game is public recognition. After all, you can't very well intimidate a government into releasing your freedom fighters unless you announce that it is your group that has seized its embassy. "Clear guilt" is difficult to define, but when 40 million people see a group of masked gunmen seize an airplane on the evening news, there is not much question about who the perpetrators are. There will be hard cases where the situation is murkier. Nonetheless, a line demarcating the legitimate use of torture can be drawn. Torture only the obviously guilty, and only for the sake of saving innocents, and the line between Us and Them will remain clear.

Conclusion warrant: "Paralysis in the face of evil is the greater danger."

There is little danger that the Western democracies will lose their way if they choose to inflict pain as one way of preserving order. Paralysis in the face of evil is the greater danger. Some day soon a terrorist will threaten tens of thousands of lives, and torture will be the only way to save them. We had better start thinking about this.

■ Analysis

Levin's controversial essay attacks a popular assumption that most people have never thought to question—that torture is impermissible under any circumstances. Levin argues that in extreme cases torture is morally justified to bring about a greater good than the rights of the individual who is tortured.

Against the initial resistance that most readers may feel, Levin makes a strong case. Its strength lies in the backing he provides for the warrant that torture is sometimes necessary. This backing consists in the use of two effective argumentative strategies. One is the anticipation of objections. Unprecedented? No. Unconstitutional? No. Barbaric? No. Second, and more important, are the hypothetical examples that compel readers to rethink their positions and possibly arrive at agreement with the author. Levin chooses extreme examples—kidnapping of a newborn child, planting a bomb on a jumbo jet, detonating an atomic bomb in Manhattan— that draw a line between clear and murky cases and make agreement easier. And he bolsters his moral position by insisting that torture is not to be used as punishment or revenge but only to save innocent lives.

To support such an unpopular assumption the writer must convey the impression that he is a reasonable man, and this Levin attempts to do by a searching definition of terms, the careful organization and development of his argument, including references to the opinions of other people, and the expression of compassion for innocent lives.

Another strength of the article is its readability—the use of contractions, informal questions, conversational locutions. This easy, familiar style is disarming; the reader doesn't feel threatened by heavy admonitions from a writer who affects a superior, moral attitude.

Writer's Guide: Recognizing Warrants

1. Locate in your essay the one sentence that best states your claim, or if there is no single sentence that does so, try to express your claim in a single sentence.

2. If you have not already done so, think about for what audience you are writing. How is that audience likely to respond to your claim? The most important question to ask about your audience regarding warrants is this one: What assumption or assumptions must my audience make to be able to accept my claim? The answer to that question will be the warrant or warrants on which your essay is based.

3. The support you offer will make it easier for your audience to accept your claim. Remember that the warrant is the link between claim and support. It may help to use the formula used in this chapter to think systematically through your argument. Ask yourself what the claim is, what support you are offering, and what warrant connects the two. Do that for each major supporting statement that you make.

4. You may not need to state your warrant directly if it is a universally accepted truth that most reasonable readers would agree with it. You should be able to do so, however, in order to check your own logic.

5. If you are asking the members of your audience to accept a warrant that they are not likely to accept, you must offer backing for that warrant or consider restating your claim in a way that does not ask them to agree to an assumption that they will not be willing to agree with.

READINGS FOR ANALYSIS

A Proposal to Abolish Grading

PAUL GOODMAN

Let half a dozen of the prestigious universities—Chicago, Stanford, the Ivy League—abolish grading, and use testing only and entirely for pedagogic purposes as teachers see fit.

Anyone who knows the frantic temper of the present schools will understand the transvaluation of values that would be effected by this modest innovation. For most of the students, the competitive grade has come to be the essence. The naive teacher points to the beauty of the subject and the ingenuity of the research; the shrewd student asks if he is responsible for that on the final exam.

Paul Goodman (1911–1972) was a college professor and writer whose outspoken views were popular with students during the 1960s. This essay is from *Compulsory Miseducation* (1964).

Let me at once dispose of an objection whose unanimity is quite fascinating. I think that the great majority of professors agree that grading hinders teaching and creates a bad spirit, going as far as cheating and plagiarizing. I have before me the collection of essays, *Examining in Harvard College*, and this is the consensus. It is uniformly asserted, however, that the grading is inevitable; for how else will the graduate schools, the foundations, the corporations *know* whom to accept, reward, hire? How will the talent scouts know whom to tap?

By testing the applicants, of course, according to the specific task requirements of the inducting institution, just as applicants for the Civil Service or for licenses in medicine, law, and architecture are tested. Why should Harvard professors do the testing *for* corporations and graduate schools?

The objection is ludicrous. Dean Whitla, of the Harvard Office of   5 Tests, points out that the scholastic-aptitude and achievement tests used for *admission* to Harvard are a superexcellent index for all-around Harvard performance, better than high-school grades or particular Harvard course-grades. Presumably, these college-entrance tests are tailored for what Harvard and similar institutions want. By the same logic, would not an employer do far better to apply his own job-aptitude test rather than to rely on the vagaries of Harvard section-men? Indeed, I doubt that many employers bother to look at such grades; they are more likely to be interested merely in the fact of a Harvard diploma, whatever that connotes to them. The grades have most of their weight with the graduate schools — here, as elsewhere, the system runs mainly for its own sake.

It is really necessary to remind our academics of the ancient history of Examination. In the medieval university, the whole point of the grueling trial of the candidate was whether or not to accept him as a peer. His disputation and lecture for the Master's was just that, a masterpiece to enter the guild. It was not to make comparative evaluations. It was not to weed out and select for an extramural licensor or employer. It was certainly not to pit one young fellow against another in an ugly competition. My philosophic impression is that the medievals thought they knew what a good job of work was and that we are competitive because we do not know. But the more status is achieved by largely irrelevant competitive evaluation, the less will we ever know.

(Of course, our American examinations never did have this purely guild orientation, just as our faculties have rarely had absolute autonomy; the examining was to satisfy Overseers, Elders, distant Regents — and they as paternal superiors have always doted on giving grades, rather than accepting peers. But I submit that this set-up itself makes it impossible for the student to *become* a master, to *have* grown up, and to commence on his own. He will always be making A or B for some overseer. And in the present atmosphere, he will always be climbing on his friend's neck.)

Perhaps the chief objectors to abolishing grading would be the students and their parents. The parents should be simply disregarded; their anxiety has done enough damage already. For the students, it seems to me that a primary duty of the university is to deprive them of their props, their dependence on extrinsic valuation and motivation, and to force them to confront the difficult enterprise itself and finally lose themselves in it.

A miserable effect of grading is to nullify the various uses of testing. Testing, for both student and teacher, is a means of structuring, and also of finding out what is blank or wrong and what has been assimilated and can be taken for granted. Review—including high-pressure review—is a means of bringing together the fragments, so that there are flashes of synoptic insight.

There are several good reasons for testing, and kinds of test. But if the   10 aim is to discover weakness, what is the point of down-grading and punishing it, and thereby inviting the student to conceal his weakness, by faking and bulling, if not cheating? The natural conclusion of synthesis is the insight itself, not a grade for having had it. For the important purpose of placement, if one can establish in the student the belief that one is testing *not* to grade and make invidious comparisons but for his own advantage, the student should normally seek his own level, where he is challenged and yet capable, rather than trying to get by. If the student dares to accept himself as he is, a teacher's grade is a crude instrument compared with a student's self-awareness. But it is rare in our universities that students are encouraged to notice objectively their vast confusion. Unlike Socrates, our teachers rely on power-drives rather than shame and ingenuous idealism.

Many students are lazy, so teachers try to goad or threaten them by grading. In the long run this must do more harm than good. Laziness is a character-defense. It may be a way of avoiding learning, in order to protect the conceit that one is already perfect (deeper, the despair that one *never* can be). It may be a way of avoiding just the risk of failing and being down-graded. Sometimes it is a way of politely saying, "I won't." But since it is the authoritarian grown-up demands that have created such attitudes in the first place, why repeat the trauma? There comes a time when we must treat people as adult, laziness and all. It is one thing courageously to fire a do-nothing out of your class; it is quite another thing to evaluate him with a lordly F.

Most important of all, it is often obvious that balking in doing the work, especially among bright young people who get to great universities, means exactly what it says: The work does not suit me, not this subject, or not at this time, or not in this school, or not in school altogether. The student might not be bookish; he might be school-tired; perhaps his development ought now to take another direction. Yet unfortunately, if such a student is intelligent and is not sure of himself, he *can* be bullied into passing, and this obscures everything. My hunch is that I am describing a common situation. What a grim waste of young life and teacherly effort! Such a student will retain nothing of what he has "passed" in. Sometimes he must get mononucleosis to tell his story and be believed.

And ironically, the converse is also probably commonly true. A student flunks and is mechanically weeded out, who is really ready and eager to learn in a scholastic setting, but he has not quite caught on. A good teacher can recognize the situation, but the computer wreaks its will.

READING AND DISCUSSION QUESTIONS

1. Goodman divides his argument into several parts, each of which develops a different idea. How would you subtitle these parts?

2. Are some parts of the argument stronger than others? Does Goodman indicate what points he wants to emphasize?

3. Why do you think Goodman calls on "half a dozen of the prestigious universities" (para. 1) instead of all universities to abolish grading?

4. Where does the author reveal the purposes of his proposal?

5. Most professors, Goodman argues, think that grading hinders teaching. Why, then, do they continue to give grades? How does Goodman reply to their objections?

6. What does Goodman think the real purpose of testing should be? How does grading "nullify the various uses of testing" (para. 9)?

WRITING SUGGESTIONS

7. Do you agree that grading prevents you from learning? If so, write an essay in which you support Goodman's thesis by reporting what your own experience has been.

8. If you disagree with Goodman, write an essay that outlines the benefits of grading.

9. Is there a better way than grading to evaluate the work of students—a way that would achieve the goals of education Goodman values? Suggest a method, and explain why it would be superior to grading.

An Unjust Sacrifice

ROBERT A. SIRICO

An appeals court in London has made a Solomonic ruling, deciding that eight-week-old twins joined at the pelvis must be separated. In effect, one twin, known as Mary, is to be sacrificed to save the other, known as Jodie, in an operation the babies' parents oppose.

The judges invoked a utilitarian rationale, justified on the basis of medical testimony. The specialists agreed that there is an 80 to 90 percent

Robert A. Sirico, a Roman Catholic priest, is president of the Acton Institute for the Study of Religion and Liberty in Grand Rapids, Michigan. This article appeared in the September 28, 2000, *New York Times*.

chance that the strong and alert Jodie could not survive more than a few months if she continued to support the weak heart and lungs of Mary, whose brain is underdeveloped.

This is a heartbreaking case, and the decision of the court was not arrived at lightly. But even the best of intentions, on the part of the state or the parents, is no substitute for sound moral reasoning. Utilitarian considerations like Mary's quality of life are not the issue. Nor should doctors' expert testimony, which is subject to error, be considered decisive.

Here, as in the case of abortion, one simple principle applies: There is no justification for deliberately destroying innocent life. In this case, the court has turned its back on a tenet that the West has stood by: Life, no matter how limited, should be protected.

While this case is so far unique, there are guidelines that must be fol- 5 lowed. No human being, for instance, can be coerced into donating an organ—even if the individual donating the organ is unlikely to be harmed and the individual receiving the organ could be saved. In principle, no person should ever be forced to volunteer his own body to save another's life, even if that individual is a newborn baby.

To understand the gravity of the court's error, consider the parents' point of view. They are from Gozo, an island in Malta. After being told of their daughters' condition, while the twins were in utero, they went to Manchester, England, seeking out the best possible medical care. Yet, after the birth on August 8, the parents were told that they needed to separate the twins, which would be fatal for Mary.

They protested, telling the court: "We cannot begin to accept or contemplate that one of our children should die to enable the other one to survive. That is not God's will. Everyone has a right to life, so why should we kill one of our daughters to enable the other one to survive?"

And yet, a court in a country in which they sought refuge has overruled their wishes. This is a clear evil: coercion against the parents and coercion against their child, justified in the name of a speculative medical calculus.

The parents' phrase "God's will" is easily caricatured, as if they believed divine revelation were guiding them to ignore science. In fact, they believe in the merit of science, or they would not have gone to Britain for help in the first place.

But utilitarian rationality has overtaken their case. The lawyer ap- 10 pointed by the court to represent Jodie insisted that Mary's was "a futile life." That is a dangerous statement—sending us down a slippery slope where lives can be measured for their supposed value and discarded if deemed not useful enough.

Some might argue that in thinking about the twins, we should apply the philosophical principle known as "double effect," which, in some circumstances, permits the loss of a life when it is an unintended consequence of saving another. But in this case, ending Mary's life would be a deliberate decision, not an unintended effect.

Can we ever take one life in favor of another? No, not even in this case, however fateful the consequences.

READING AND DISCUSSION QUESTIONS

1. Underlying the author's claim that the parents of the twins should not separate them is the warrant—a broad assumption about life, in this case. What sentences express that warrant?

2. If you do not agree with Sirico's argument, point out what you think are flaws in his reasoning, based on your own understanding of moral principles.

3. In the fifth paragraph, Sirico cites another kind of medical dilemma as an analogy to that of the twins. How effective is it in supporting his claim?

4. The author condemns "utilitarianism" (para. 2). This ethical doctrine holds, as one dictionary defines it, "that conduct should be directed toward the greatest happiness of the greatest number of persons." Find statements in this essay that might explain why this philosophy is unacceptable to Sirico.

WRITING SUGGESTIONS

5. The author's conclusion is expressed as an absolute—a rule of behavior for which there are no exceptions. Can you think of any rules of human conduct which ought to be obeyed without exception? Reviewing the Ten Commandments might be a place to start. If so, define the rule, and tell why it must be so observed. If not, explain why some rules of behavior are subject to exception.

6. Peter Singer, a philosopher at Princeton University who subscribes to the utilitarian doctrine, has said that if the parents of a handicapped infant decide to kill him before he is two months old because his death would increase their happiness and decrease the infant's suffering, they have a right to do so. In another case he has argued that instead of spending money to reduce the suffering of a family member, a person should "send the same sum to ease the suffering of ten Sudanese."[7] Write an argument for or against the practice of utilitarianism in one of these cases or any other in which the sacrifice of life is an issue.

---

[7] George F. Will, "Life and Death at Princeton," *Newsweek*, September 13, 1999, p. 82. This article is critical of Singer's philosophy.

Computers and the Pursuit of Happiness

DAVID GELERNTER

In recent years we have been notified almost continuously that we are living in an "information age." Mankind (it is suggested) has completed a sort of phase shift: the solid agricultural age was replaced two centuries ago by the liquid industrial age, which has now given way to the gaseous (so to speak) age of information. Everyone says so, but is it true? *Has* an old age ended, and are we, thanks to computers and the Internet, living in a new one? A related question: computers have been around for roughly a half-century; have they been good or bad for mankind? And finally: are they likely to do good or bad over the next half-century?

1

We are *not* in an information age, and computers and the Internet are not a revolutionary development in human history.

In the old industrial age (people say) coal, steel, and concrete mattered; in the new age, information counts. Yet it is obvious that coal, steel, and concrete still count just as much as they ever did. We have always needed food, clothing, shelter, possessions, and above all each other. We always *will* need those things, and the "information revolution" will never lessen our needs by half a hair's breadth. So whom are we kidding? What nouveau cyber-billionaire ever used his billions to buy *information?* Who ever worried about poverty because he would be unable to keep his family well-informed?

Not long ago I saw a rented U-Haul trailer with the inevitable Web address in big letters on the side, "uhaul.com"—the information age in nine easy characters. Yes, it is convenient to check a Web site for information about trailers for rent; but the Internet will never (*can* never) change our need for physical stuff, or for trailers to haul it around in. Fifty years from now, it may be possible to download artistically designed experiences and beam them via trick signals into your brain. (To many people this will sound like a junior grade of hell, but some technologists think of it as a Coming Attraction.) The interesting fact remains: virtual gourmet food will make you feel full but will not keep you from starving. Virtual heat will make you feel warm but will not keep you from freezing. Virtual sex will make you feel satisfied in the sense that a pig feels satisfied.

About computers in particular, believers in a new information age 5
make three arguments. They say it is a new age because we now have so-

---

David Gelernter is a professor of computer science at Yale. In addition to the books on computer technology mentioned in this essay, he is the author of the memoir *Drawing Life: Surviving the Unabomber* (1997), and *1939: The Lost World of the Fair* (1996). This essay appeared in the January, 2001 issue of *Commentary*.

phisticated machines to create, store, and deliver information; because computer networks can overcome geography; and because machines (in their own special areas) can act intelligently. All three claims are wrong. Computers have done marvelous deeds—but in each case, their great deeds are in keeping with the long-established patterns of the industrial age. Computation today is a dusting of snow that makes everything look different—on the surface.

Fancy machines to create, move, and store information were a main preoccupation of the whole twentieth century, not just the computerized part of it. Movies, phonographs, color photography and color printing, the electronic transmission of photos, the invention of radio and radio networks and international radio hookups, newsreels, television, transistorized electronics, long-distance phone networks, communication satellites, fax machines, photocopiers, audio and video tapes, compact disks, cell phones, cable TV—and then, with the emergence of PC's and the Internet, suddenly we are in an information age? The twentieth century was one information-gusher after another; information pouring into people's lives through more and more stuck-open faucets.

The defeat of geography? In *Cyberspace and the American Dream* (1994), distributed electronically by the Progress and Freedom Foundation, a distinguished group of authors argued that "we constitute the final generation of an old civilization and, at the very same time, the first generation of a new one." Their claim centered on the idea that, thanks to computer networks, geography had (in effect) been overcome; henceforth, shared interests and not physical proximity would shape community and society.

But using technology to defeat distance has been another goal of the industrial revolution from the start, from railroads through the Panama Canal and onward. Rail networks, telegraph networks, air and phone and highway and radio and TV networks—the Internet is the latest in a long line.

The twentieth century teemed with smart machines, too, long before the computer showed up—simple ones like the thermostat or a car's electrical system (with automatic spark-advance); complex, sophisticated ones like automatic transmissions or the Norden bombsight in World War II. Granted, computers are a huge advance over the machines that came before, but huge advances are the stuff of the industrial age. The Web is a big deal, but flying machines were a pretty big deal, too. Radio and TV changed the nature of American democracy. The electric-power industry turned society inside out.

The cost of not knowing history is not ignorance so much as arro- 10 gance. A popular book about the Internet and the Web begins with this "personal note" from the author:

> The Internet is, by far, the greatest and most significant achievement in the history of mankind. What? Am I saying that the Internet is more impressive than the pyramids? More beautiful than Michelangelo's

David? More important to mankind than the wondrous inventions of the industrial revolution? Yes, yes, and yes.

That sort of statement suggests that technologists are fundamentally unserious. By the way: a useful and interesting book. But the author protests too much. It is hard to picture comparable statements greeting the airplane's or the electric-power industry's emergence; they were too big and too obviously important to need this sort of cheerleading. What the author is really announcing is not a new age of information but a new age of hype, a new age of new ages.

Computers and the Internet *have* made a revolution in science and engineering. Studying computational models of reality can be cheaper and better than studying reality. Sometimes reality is impossible to measure or too steep to scale, and computational models are the only way to get any purchase on it. Those are the *actual* computer revolutions; the others are mostly potential and not real, locked up in awe-inspiring icebergs that just float around eliciting admiration and making trouble. The computer revolution is still frozen, latent, waiting to happen.

As for the information age, it must have begun at least a hundred years ago if it exists at all. *Are* we better informed than we used to be? I doubt it. Is anyone prepared to assert that the U.S. electorate is better informed today than it was at the time of (say) the 1960 presidential election? That our fifth graders are better informed about reading, writing, history, or arithmetic? That our fifth-grade *teachers* are better informed? (Recently my fifth-grade son learned from his English teacher that "incredible" and "incredulous" are synonyms. That's the information age for you.)

2

Have computers been good or bad for mankind since they were invented roughly fifty years ago?

Other things being equal, information is good. Wealth is good. Computers have supplied lots of information, and generated much wealth.

But we are marvelously adaptable. We can take miserable conditions 15 in stride and triumph over them; we can take wonderful conditions in stride and triumph over *them*. Humanity in any given age has a wealth threshold and an information threshold. If you are below either one, living in poverty or ignorance, you need more wealth or information. But once you are over the threshold, only the rate of change matters. Acquire more wealth or information, and presumably you will be happier; then you stabilize at your new, higher level, and chances are you are no happier than before. It is not exactly a deep or novel observation that money doesn't buy happiness. Neither does information.

In this country, the majority—obviously not everyone, but most of us—have been over-threshold in wealth and information for several generations, roughly since the end of World War II. That is a remarkable achievement; it ought to make us proud and thankful. But it follows that increasing our level of wealth or information is unlikely to count terribly much in the larger scheme of things. The increase itself will feel good, but the substance of our new wealth or information won't matter much.

Here is a small case in point. My two boys, who are ten and thirteen, love playing with computers, like most children nowadays. The computer is their favorite toy, and unquestionably it makes them happy. Computer play as it is practiced in real life, at least at our house, is a mindless activity; like many families, we have to limit the time our boys are allowed at it or they would spend all day wrecking pretend Porsches and blowing up enemy airplanes. But mindless activities are fine in reasonable doses. It's good for children to have fun, and I'm glad ours have so much fun with computers.

When my wife and I were children, we didn't have computers to play with. We lacked these wonderful, happiness-generating devices. But—so what? Other things made us happy. We never felt deprived on account of our lack of computer power. It would be crazy to deny that computers are great toys, but it would be equally crazy to argue that they have made children any happier, on the whole, than children used to be. Fifty years from now, the computer-based toys will make today's look pathetic, and children will love all their snazzy new stuff—just as much, probably, as children loved their bats and balls and blocks and trains and jump-ropes and dollhouses in 1900.

What we ordinarily fail to take into account when we are adding up the score is the nature of technological change. Technology is a tool for building social structures. Granted, each new technology is better than the one it replaces. But new technologies engender new social structures, and the important question is not whether the new technology is better but whether the new structure is better. Except in the case of medical technologies, the answer will nearly always be debatable; nearly always *must* be debatable. We can easily show that, with each passing generation, paints have improved. It is much harder to show that art has improved.

Human nature does not change; human needs and wants remain ba- 20 sically the same. Human ingenuity dreams up a new technology, and we put it to use—doing in a new way something we have always done in some other way. In years past, many towns had shared public wells. They were communal gathering places: you met neighbors, heard the news, checked out strangers, sized up the competition, made deals, dates, matches. Plumbing was a great leap forward, which few of us (certainly not me) would be willing to trade in. The old system was a nuisance, especially if *you* were the one carrying the water; but it was neighborly. The new, plumbing-induced social structure was far more convenient, not to say healthier. It was also lonelier. The old and new structures excelled in different ways and cannot be directly compared.

The Web is an improvement much like plumbing, without the health benefits. Fifty years ago, most shopping was face to face. In the Internet age, face-to-face stores will not survive long, any more than communal wells survived the advent of plumbing. To our great-grandchildren, shopping will mean "online," as it meant "face to face" to our great-grandparents. Future generations will look back wistfully but probably not unhappily. On the whole, their happiness and their ancestors' will probably be about the same. To the extent future generations *are* happier or unhappier than we—and "national happiness" does change, it's hard to doubt that America in 1950 was a happier country than America today—we can be fairly sure of one thing. The net change will have nothing to do with technology.

A major new technology remakes society—picks up the shoebox, shakes it hard, puts it back. The new social structures we build almost always incorporate less human labor than the old ones. The old structures (in other words) have a larger "human ingredient," the new ones a larger "machine ingredient." It is nearly always impossible to compare the two directly. And in the meantime the old ones have disappeared. Where technology is concerned, we demolish the past and live in a permanent present.

In the lush technology future, we will be kids in a candy store. The old zero-sum economics of Malthus and his modern disciples has long since been discredited; we will swagger into that Candy Store of the Future with more money all the time, and find more and fancier candy in there every day. Our inventiveness, productivity, and potential wealth are all unlimited. Only our appetite for candy is not.

3

If mankind were somehow prevented from continuing to develop computers and software—that would be a tragedy, and the world would suffer. Nothing comes more naturally to us than building and playing with machines. Inventing technology is the intellectual equivalent of breathing.

Is breathing helpful? Yes. Will it conduce to a better world in 2050? 25 Right again! But only in a certain sense.

In 1991 I published a book called *Mirror Worlds;* in a way, it was a celebration of computing technology (although it was ambivalent about computers in the end). It predicted the emergence of software versions of real-world institutions that you would "tune in" by means of a global network. It claimed that this would be a good development: you would be able to tour the world "without changing out of your pajamas." These mirror worlds would be "the new public square," would "monopolize the energy and attention of thousands . . . broadcast an aesthetic and a worldview to millions, mold behavior and epitomize the age."

Talk about modest claims—although in looking back at the Web boom that began in 1994 they seem, if anything, too modest. In predicting that "the software revolution hasn't begun yet, but it will soon," I was basically right. The industrial age ushered in new categories and possibilities, and computers and software are creating new possibilities, too: new types of structures that are just as unprecedented as the Eiffel Tower.

Consider an online school. Such a school might offer guided nature walks through teeming, chattering, blossoming rain forests of the intellect where your guide knows exactly what you are capable of, can make the path expand or shrink to suit you, can point out the biggest vistas or the tiniest orchid—and the whole structure can be moored in cyberspace, where anyone who likes can climb aboard. Instead of merely reteaching the same class year after year, we could make the path better every year. As a student follows a trail, we could turn that trail into his personal diary, for review or revisiting whenever he likes; he could keep his whole school career in his back pocket. We could plant pictures or maps at the center of lessons if they belonged there, instead of pasting them in as afterthoughts.

And these new software structures could be world-spanning switch-boards, connecting the right student to the right teacher. If Mrs. Feinstein is the English teacher for little Kate Smith, then wherever Mrs. Feinstein lives (Auckland, Nome, Passaic), whatever hours she keeps, whatever her formal qualifications, we could patch her into the system.

I would rather put Kate in an actual school where actual teachers 30 could look her in the face when they are trying to teach her something. But American education is in desperate trouble—and under the circumstances, software-based teaching is probably our best hope. In the future we will compare our ubiquitous software schools to the face-to-face education of the pre-1970s the way we compare online shopping to long-ago Main Streets: we will be wistful, as usual, but not wistful enough to do anything about it. On the whole we will be content.

Of course, we are talking about new software *structures*—not mere computers, not mere information. And we are talking about something that *could* happen, but hasn't yet.

Human beings are mainly interested in human beings. If computers do good in the next fifty years, the good they are most likely to do lies in helping mankind know itself better.

A large part of cognitive science is built on a famous analogy, the analogy that did so much for the functionalist school of philosophy in the 1950s and 60s and that many researchers still believe today: mind is to brain as software is to computer. This analogy is fundamentally wrong.

Just the fact that software is portable (it can be moved from one computer to another) and minds are not (they cannot be moved from one brain to another) should have told us at the very start that the analogy was fishy. There is no reason to believe that you will ever be able to off-load Joe Schwartz's mind and run it on Melissa Clark's brain. It is not even clear what this would mean in principle, because *part* of Schwartz's mind is the fact that it belongs to Schwartz. "Porting a mind" is not only impossible, but in principle meaningless.

In *The Muse in the Machine* (1994) I argued that you cannot under- 35 stand human thought unless you understand the "cognitive spectrum" that exists in every mind. That spectrum ranges from highly focused, highly aware-of-the-environment "analytic" thought all the way down to "low-focus," oblivious-of-the-environment thought—all the way down, in other words, to the kind of hallucinatory thought that happens routinely when we are asleep and dreaming. We will never get a computer to think until we have figured out how to make one hallucinate. To reproduce thought on a computer, we will need to reproduce the whole cognitive spectrum and not just one narrow slice of it.

For many years, the biggest challenge in cognitive science and philosophy has been to understand how we discover analogies, where we get our amazing capacity to notice that two things—objects, situations, events—that *seem* completely unrelated in fact have deep, hidden similarities. This capacity to draw analogies underlies human creativity and our useful knack of discovering and inventing new things. How does it work?

The evidence suggests, it seems to me, that analogy is driven by emotion. The remarkable thing about human emotion is that two wholly different-*seeming* scenes or memories or circumstances can make us *feel* exactly the same way. Emotion lets us make spectacularly nonobvious connections; in so doing, it lets us discover new analogies, lets us create.

Now, human emotions obviously depend not only on the mind but on the body. You don't think them, you feel them. So we cannot hope to simulate thought on a computer unless we can simulate the discovery of analogies. We cannot hope to do *that* unless we can simulate emotions on a machine. And we cannot hope to do *that* unless we can simulate not merely abstract mental processes but the complex, nuanced physical reality of the human body.

Eventually, this will be done. Certainly not soon (and certainly not by me)—but it will be done. But even at the end of this enormously difficult, complex task, when humanity has achieved the technological marvel of a machine that can accurately fake human emotions and (therefore) can realistically fake human thought, where exactly will we be?

The human body and its brain have the "emergent property"—or   40 "ensemble property"—of consciousness. When you put exactly the right pieces together in exactly the right way . . . consciousness emerges.

There is no reason, in principle, why computers and software could not have this property as well, and thus lead us to a deeper appreciation of what consciousness means and what it represents. It could be that we will wind up with a "thinking machine" that does not merely talk about daffodils, identify them, draw pictures of them; we might in principle end up with a machine that actually knows what a daffodil *is*. That actually experiences fragrance as we do, color as we do, form as we do—or at least experiences fragrance, color, and form in *some* way; or at least experiences *something* in some way. In other words, that is actually conscious.

All this *could* be. But we have no good reason to think it ever will be. It could be that consciousness will emerge from exactly the right combination of electronics and software; it could be that consciousness will emerge from exactly the right combination of mozzarella and tomato sauce, or bricks and mortar, or cardboard and rubber cement. None of these things is (in principle) impossible, but none of them is terribly likely, either.

Machines can move faster than we do; so it cannot be that the important thing (the distinguishing thing) about humans is how fast we are. Cannot be how strong we are. Cannot be how well we do arithmetic. It might easily be that in fifty years, machines will be smarter than we are, too. . . .

But I do not think we will conclude that to be human is no big deal after all. I have heard one of technology's most honored, distinguished men tell a large audience how he wished human beings would stop thinking that they are somehow different from animals; it pained him to hear the old canard about man's "uniqueness." He is offering us an easy out: it is simple to be an animal and complicated (Lord knows) to be a man. Should we stop trying, call it a day, and relocate to the barnyard?

Not yet. Most of us are not quite ready to toss out the scraps of moral- 45 ity and sanctity we have pieced together over the long, hard centuries; they may look shabby but they are the best clothes we own. They might even be as important as the Internet. I think we will decide not that we are merely animals after all but that our uniqueness lies beyond strength, speed *and* intellect.

People have said so for a long time, of course. Jews and Christians have long believed it. Chances are that, fifty years from now—thanks to computers—many more people will believe it. Chances are that, fifty years from now, we will be grateful to computer technology for showing us what marvelously powerful machines we can build—and how little they mean after all.

READING AND DISCUSSION QUESTIONS

1. State the warrant underlying the author's claim that computers cannot guarantee happiness. Look for it in the last part of the essay, although it is not stated directly.

2. Summarize Gelernter's responses to the three questions asked in the first paragraph. Do you find all of his arguments equally persuasive? Explain your answer.

3. Gelernter uses history, psychology, and personal experiences to support his claim. Point out some specific examples of these forms of support. Did any of his evidence surprise you? Does your own experience with computers confirm his insights?

4. The use of language in this essay is worth noting. The author has a highly readable style that encompasses both the formal and the informal. Find places where he speaks directly to the reader, using conversational language—colloquial in both grammar and vocabulary—to reach his audience.

5. The ending of this essay resembles one in a short story (and, in fact, Gelernter writes fiction, too). There is no explicit summing up. The meaning of the ending is indirect: It must be inferred from all that has been said before. (Contrast, for example, the closing statements of "An Unjust Sacrifice.") Why does Gelernter say that computers will not mean much, after all? What is the significance of the reference to Jews and Christians? Do you find the ending inspiring, as the author clearly intends? Or too elusive?

WRITING SUGGESTIONS

6. Write an essay elaborating on some of the ways in which the use of the computer has changed your life, for better or worse. You might want to refute or confirm one or more of the issues raised by Gelernter.

7. A few years ago a student took first prize in an essay contest in which she argued the superiority of printed books over books on the computer. The writer ended her essay this way: "It all boils down to which definition of communication you prefer: interpersonal or technological. A library of empty bookshelves would be a travesty." What is the difference between "interpersonal" and "technological"? Write a response to the student's comment, spelling out some advantages of the electronic book.

DISCUSSION QUESTIONS

1. What is the significance of the name of the product?
2. What assumptions underlie the remaining text in the ad?
3. How do the visual elements reinforce the text?
4. Can you think of other ads that make use of celebrities? What are some of the warrants that underlie the use of celebrities to sell products?

Do We Need the Census Race Question?

NATHAN GLAZER

A FEW years ago, when I was asked to comment on the controversy over how best to handle the demand of so-called multiracial advocacy groups for a "multiracial" category in the census, I made a brash and wildly unrealistic proposal.[1] Before describing my proposal, however, I should explain what concerned me about the existing questions on race, Hispanicity, and ancestry in the census. These questions had evolved by the 1980 and 1990 censuses in a way that was to my mind false to American racial and ethnic reality and incapable of getting coherent responses, to the degree that that is possible and that is normally expected in a census.

The census short form is the piece of official government paper that is probably seen by more Americans than any other, surpassing in the extent of its distribution the income tax forms. It is a message to the American people, and like any message it educates them to some reality: This is what the government needs, this what it wants, this is what it thinks is important. The census tells the American people that the government thinks the most important thing about them is to get them classified by race and ethnicity—ethnicity, that is, only if it qualifies as something called "Hispanic"; otherwise, the government is not interested. The census asks Americans first for the kinds of information that almost any form does, whether for a credit card or a driver's license—name, sex, age, family status—but then it turns out the main thing the government is interested in is their "race," described in the greatest detail, down to distinctions between Samoan and Guamanian and, if the respondent is Hispanic, between Argentinean, Colombian, Dominican, Nicaraguan, and even Spanish.

The government, in this message sent to all of us, apparently considers these matters more important than how educated we are, or whether we are citizens, or whether we are foreign born, or whether we voted in the last election. Scholars and researchers who follow the matter closely know why these questions are there, so prominently, so fully detailed. Do the American people in general know? If they do not—and it is hardly likely they are fully briefed on the legislation and regulations and politics

---

Nathan Glazer is a professor emeritus at the Graduate School of Education at Harvard University and past professor of sociology at the University of California at Berkeley. He is a former assistant editor for *Commentary* magazine and is a contributing editor of the *New Republic*. His books include *Beyond the Melting Pot* (with Daniel Patrick Moynihan; 1970), *We Are All Multiculturalists Now* (1997), and *The Lonely Crowd* (with David Riesman; rev. ed. 2001). He has served on presidential task forces on education and urban policy and on National Academy of Science committees on urban policy and minority issues.

and the pressures that have made the census form, with respect to race and Hispanicity, what it is today—what are they to conclude?

The census is supposed to give us a portrait of America. Is this what America looks like? Is the matter of race so important that it deserves this prominence and degree of detail?

A further problem is evident: that these questions are trying to im-   5
pose on identities in flux—not all, of course, but many—a categorization scheme that will inevitably confuse many people. It is a scheme in which many cannot place themselves, and one that requires all sorts of manipulations by the census professionals to put the results into a form in which it can be presented to Congress, the press, and the American people. There is bound to be a substantial degree of error in these final figures, which are never rounded to indicate their uncertainty nor presented with any indication of their degree of error—in contrast with public opinion polls. Yet asking about race and ethnicity has many similarities to public opinion polls about attitudes, compared with questions about age, or amount of schooling, or a number of other topics on which respondents are pretty clear.

Finally, there is simply the irrationality of the categories. Why does Hispanicity include people from Argentina and Spain but not those from Brazil or Portugal? Are there really all those races in Asia, where each country seems to consist of a single and different race, compared with simply "white" for all of Europe and the Middle East? Why, indeed, do people of Spanish origin rate special treatment, as against people from Italy, Poland, or Greece?

All this is familiar. And so I made my proposal. I confess that underlying my proposal was an ideological or political position—just as ideological and political positions underlie the present census arrangements. My position was that it is necessary and desirable to recognize and encourage the ongoing assimilation of the many strands that make the American people into a common culture. It is, I realize, a delicate task to draw a line between "recognize"—which is what the census should do—and "encourage," which it should not see as part of its task. Any form of recognition or nonrecognition is also, however, a form of encouragement or dissuasion. One encourages what one recognizes and dissuades what one does not. My proposal also responded to my interest as a social scientist in recording the progress of this change, which has been continuous in American history, affecting all groups in different degree but tragically leaving aside, for most of our history, one major group.

So then, my brash and unrealistic proposal: I proposed reducing the mishmash of race, Hispanicity, and ancestry to basically two questions. One question would determine whether a person considered himself or herself black or African American. That would remain the only race for which the census requested information. A second question or group of questions would ask in which country the respondent was born and in which country his or her parents were born and could be extended to ask where that person's grandparents were born. These questions on the country of birth of parents and grandparents would be filled in by respondents rather than presented in a multiple-choice format with predetermined options.

Why the interest in only one race? The census has counted blacks, slave and free, since the first enumeration of 1790. History alone and the virtues of continuity would make a claim that that determination be continued. There are, of course, far more potent reasons. This is the group that has suffered from prejudice, discrimination, and a lower-caste status since the origins of the Republic. In law, all this is now overcome and does not exist, but African Americans, we know, despite their presence in large numbers from our origins as a group of British colonies on the Atlantic shore, are less integrated in American society than any other large group. They are more segregated residentially. The rate of intermarriage with others outside the group, even if rapidly increasing, is still the lowest for any large group. They have a clear sense of their identity. One can depend on a high degree of reliability in the answers they give to the race question, as census research has shown.

The second question or group of questions replaces the "ancestry" 10 question because of the rapid rate of assimilation of all groups except blacks or African Americans. The limitation of these questions to the parental generation, and possibly the grandparental, is first a response to the reality that by the third generation and certainly by the fourth, the mix of ethnicities is extensive; second, it serves as an indication that the census and the government are not interested in group characteristics in the third generation and beyond.[2] With intermarriage rates in new non-black immigrant groups of 30 percent or thereabouts, we assume that by the third generation assimilation has progressed to the point at which identity is mixed and fluctuating and its ethnic character has become largely symbolic. We leave the question of what that identity consists of to the excellent sociologists, such as Richard Alba and Mary Waters, who have studied the nature of ethnic identification in these later generations. The census thereby gets out of the business of trying to affix an ancestry to each American.

If one thinks that each of the peoples of Asia forms a distinct race, this question will be able to encompass all the immigrants from that country and their children. There are not many yet in the third generation. By the time there is a substantial third generation of the post-1960s wave of immigrants, many will be of mixed ancestry, and the question of their identity will be left to them. Intermarriage statistics suggest the same for Hispanics, the great majority of whom are now immigrants and the children of immigrants. The only distinct group for which the census will try to get statistics on all those identified with it is the black or African American, for historical reasons we all know but also because black or African American identity does not fade after a few generations in this country but maintains itself in a varying but full form generation after generation.

I realize that problems remain regarding American Indians, Alaska Natives, Hawaiians, and part-Hawaiians. All these groups have a legal status, and there are means for determining who does and does not belong to each of these groups. I can see the virtue of specific questions beyond those I have suggested for Hawaii and Alaska, but I do not think 280 million Americans have to be troubled to determine the numbers of these very small groups.

Questions on birthplace and parental birthplace as posed today, as against the same questions during the last great wave of immigration, have one virtue: during that earlier wave, immigrants came from Europe, where many ethnic groups could be found within the boundaries of great multiethnic empires, and thus birthplace said little about ethnicity. In addition, the boundaries of eastern Europe have been radically recast three times in a century, and European immigrants and their children could be properly confused as to the country of their birth. What was the birthplace of a person born in Bukowina? If the census asks, "what country were you born in?" there are at least four reasonable candidates. Most of today's immigrants, in contrast, come from countries whose boundaries have been stable for a century or more, and their birthplaces and those of their parents permit us to make reasonable judgments as to their ethnic group.

This, I argued, was all that was needed in place of the present questions on race, Hispanicity, and ancestry. These two questions would provide less detailed data but more accurate data. They would also be more responsive to what America was like, and what it was becoming.

I knew the proposal was politically naive, but I was not aware of how 15 powerful and steady were the forces that created the present unsatisfactory situation until I went further into the history of the creation of the present categories (Skerry 2000; Nobles 2000; Anderson and Fienberg 1999; Bryant and Dunn 1995; Mitroff, Mason, and Barabba 1983). This research underlines the somewhat utopian character of my proposals today.

The experts seem to agree that when it comes to the census, the political outweighs the scientific, and this is a reality we have to live with. The word "political" can, of course, refer to many things, from the more to the less noble. What we have today in the census is political in all these senses. Some of it is, in part, the result of major civil rights legislation, which, to my mind, falls on the noble side. That legislation had to be interpreted by the courts and by the administrative agencies, however, under the pressure of ethnic groups. As we follow this process further into the details that shaped the form of the census questions, the element of nobility in the political process declines. I am not sure the legislation itself, which was concerned with the right to vote, required what the census has done in its effort to respond to the demand for small-area data on

Hispanics and Asian Americans. One could make a case that questions on birthplace and parental birthplace alone and the language question could give us the data to satisfy the legislation. But it would not give us the data in a form that satisfies proponents of distinct group interests and activists.

There are also the less noble political interventions. The census questions, whatever we think of their incongruity and irrationality, are the direct result of powerful pressures from the ethnic groups concerned, from Congress, and from the Executive Office of the President. These are political, alas, not only in the sense that political actors are involved but also in the narrower and less respectable sense that they are often motivated by narrow partisan political considerations.

Thus, Peter Skerry informs us, the unfortunate "ancestry" question was "criticized by social scientists for being vague and uninformative" in comparison with the question on birthplace of respondent's parents that it replaced. The Census Bureau also opposed it. "So why did the ancestry question end up on the questionnaire?" Skerry asks. "According to former deputy census director Louis Kincannon, who was working at the Statistical Policy Division of OMB when the decision was made, 'the ethnic desk' in the [Carter] White House insisted that the ancestry question go on the census . . . . It is evident that in the period leading up to the 1980 Presidential campaign, politics overrode the objections of both the OMB and the Census Bureau" (Skerry 2000, 37).

Democrats are understandably more responsive than Republicans to ethnic-group pressures, but Skerry tells us that Republican administrations have been no help, either. Concerning the origins of the Hispanic question, he notes that:

> the finalized questionnaires for the 1970 census were already at the printers when a Mexican American member of the U.S. Interagency Committee on Mexican American Affairs demanded that a specific Hispanic-origin question be included. . . . Over the opposition of Census Bureau officials, who argued against inclusion of an untested question so late in the process, Nixon ordered the secretary of commerce and the census director to add the question. . . . So it was hastily added to the long form. As former bureau official Conrad Taeuber recalls, "The order came down that we were to ask a direct question, have the people identify themselves as Hispanic." (Skerry 2000, 37–38)

The pressures initially come from the ethnic groups involved or their 20 leaders. Although there is only an uncertain relation between the numbers and the benefits that members of a group might get from one affirmative action program or another, undoubtedly the notion that one will in some way benefit from being counted as a distinct group plays a role in these pressures. At one time, Asian Indians were divided as to whether they should be "Caucasian" or yet another Asian race. Melissa Nobles reports on the discussion in the 1970s of the Federal Interagency Committee on Education on devising racial and ethnic categories for various federal programs. "The committee debated whether persons from India should be categorized under the 'Asian and Pacific Islander' category or under the 'White/Caucasian' category. . . . In the trial directive, they were classified as Caucasian, but they were reclassified as Asian in the final version (most likely in response to Asian Indian lobbying to ensure racial minority status)" (Nobles 2000, 79).

At the time, many in the Asian Indian community, taking into account their relatively high educational and economic position in the United States, rejected the idea that they should be eligible for benefits. Alas, the possibility of getting preferences for Indians under affirmative action programs for government contracts outweighed other considerations, and Indians—or at least some leadership groups—decided it was best to join the Chinese, Japanese, Koreans, and the rest as an "Asian race." I recall a report in an Indian newspaper that President Ronald Reagan's Small Business Administration (SBA) director had announced to an Indian conference that the SBA had decided to include South Asians among the groups that were considered qualified for preference in bidding for government contracts—this despite the fact that President Reagan was publicly an opponent of affirmative action programs. No doubt the administration hoped to garner a few Indian contributions or votes.

Congressional intervention can go into a level of detail that boggles the mind. Congress intervened in the wording of the 1990 race question when the Census Bureau shortened it to include only seven categories. Representative Robert Matsui introduced legislation "in which the formatting of the . . . race question was spelled out, even to the point of stipulating that 'Taiwanese' be one of the subgroups." Both houses passed it. "It was only President Reagan's pocket veto that blocked this extraordinary degree of congressional involvement in what is ordinarily considered the technical side of questionnaire design" (Skerry 2000, 41).

Social scientists deal with levels of irrationality—irrationality, that is, from the point of view of social science—that cannot be much affected by reasoned argument. Stanley Lieberson describes what happened when he attended a conference preparatory to the 1990 census. "I naively suggested that there was no reason to have a Hispanic question separate from the ethnic ancestry question since the former—as far as I could tell—could be classified as a subpart of the latter. Several participants from prominent Hispanic organizations were furious with such a proposal. They were furious, by the way, not at me (just a naive academic), rather it was in the form of a warning to census personnel of the consequences that would follow were this proposal to be taken seriously" (Lieberson 1993, 30).

So, what else is new? Undoubtedly the degree of political intervention, however we understand the term "political," is now at a peak, and to propose changes in the race, Hispanicity, and ancestry questions is probably an exercise in futility. (I wonder whether Reynolds Farley's excellent suggestion that the three questions be combined into one—

"What is this person's primary identity?" — followed by the five "official" group designations, with write-ins permitted under each, has ever gotten any public discussion.)

In the longer view, we know that politics has always played a signifi-   25
cant role in the census. Melissa Nobles tells us the fascinating history of the use of "mulatto" in the census — a term that was included in censuses from 1850 until 1920 (Nobles 2000). It was originally introduced to support slaveholders' arguments that freedom and intermixture was bad for blacks. The abolition of slavery did not end the use of the category — it could still be used, its proponents believed, to argue that races were best off separated and that intermixture produced an inferior human being. In 1888, a member of Congress from Alabama, having decided that it was necessary to go into more detail on this thesis, introduced legislation — which passed both houses and became law — directing the census to "take such steps as may be necessary to ascertain . . . the birth rate and death rate among pure whites, and among negroes, Chinamen, Indians, and half-breeds or hybrids of any description . . . as well as of mulattoes, quadroons, and octoroons" (quoted in Nobles 2000, 56). Indeed, so directed, the census did have categories for quadroons and octoroons in the 1890 census — however useless may have been the results.

The mulattoes, quadroons, and octoroons are gone. What are the longterm prospects for that astonishing list of races in the census and that equally astonishing list of "Hispanics"? Will the lists get longer in the future, or shorter, and what factors might affect their future?

This is an interesting exercise in forecasting and prediction. It is possible that the pressures that derive from affirmative action and the hope for benefits from it, for example, will decline as affirmative action itself is restricted. It has already been banned, by public referendum, judicial action, or administrative action, in the public colleges and universities of four states. One effect of this ban has been an increase in the number of students giving no racial or ethnic identity to university authorities. There has been a substantial increase in the number of such students at the University of California at Berkeley. Why identify oneself if there is no longer a benefit in doing so? Is there an incipient revolt one can detect against the degree of racial and ethnic categorization that has been institutionalized, a revolt that will reduce further the reliability of these questions?

Much of the institutionalization of these categories in the census can be traced to the Voting Rights Act, and the ill-advised extension of this act in 1975 to "language minorities," persons of Spanish heritage, American Indians, and Asian Americans. I do not know what evidence there was, even in 1975, that these groups were prevented from voting because of lack of knowledge of English. This act requires hundreds of jurisdictions to produce voting materials in various languages — itself an irritation in various parts of the country. I wonder whether there is any evidence this has increased voting among members of these groups.

(I would guess there is not.) These provisions require the census to tabulate and distribute census small-area data on the groups protected in the Voting Rights Act very rapidly after a census has been taken.

There is an inherent contradiction between the assumptions of this act and the requirement that one know English to be naturalized as a citizen. When a large number of Jewish immigrants spoke Yiddish and read only Yiddish-language newspapers, they had no trouble voting in substantial numbers equivalent to their English-speaking neighbors—even electing Socialist legislators. Are matters very different for current immigrants speaking foreign languages? Will these provisions survive, even to the census of 2010? Note that whenever a measure to declare English the "official language" gets on the ballot, as it has in a number of states, it passes. This suggests a popular hostility to these Voting Rights Act provisions. How long would they survive if submitted to a popular vote? The original point of the act was to overcome barriers to voting by blacks in the South, which were indeed great, were enforced by white officials, and had little to do with knowledge of English. The bilingual voting assistance provisions come up for renewal in 2007. Is it possible that some bold member of Congress will suggest that they are no longer needed?

All this suggests that the present distribution of political forces is not 30 eternal, and the time may come when the questions now used for race and Hispanicity will seem as outlandish as the 1890 attempt to count quadroons and octoroons. The powerful assimilatory forces in American life are at work—working more slowly, it is true, for blacks than for other groups but still working to an end that will change how the census asks about race, Hispanicity, and ancestry. I hope that change comes about not because of some xenophobic revolt against this excessive census involvement in racial and ethnic categorization but because the members of the groups so marked out themselves no longer see any reason for the U.S. government to inquire officially into an ever murkier and indeterminate racial and ethnic identity.

Notes

1. My proposal is most easily found in Hartman 1997. It originally appeared in *Poverty and Race*, the newsletter of the Poverty and Race Research Action Council.

2. On the mix of ethnicities, see the impressive demonstration in Perlmann 2000. It is also evident in the analysis of responses to the ancestry question presented in Lieberson and Waters 1998.

References

Anderson, Margo J., & Fienberg, Stephen E. (1999). *Who Counts? The Politics of Census-Taking in Contemporary America*. New York: Russell Sage Foundation.

Bryant, Barbara Everitt, & Dunn, William. (1995). *Moving Power and Money: The Politics of Census Taking*. Ithaca: New Strategist Publications.

Hartman, Chester. (Ed.) (1997). *Double Exposure: Poverty and Race in America*. Armonk: M. E. Sharpe.

Lieberson, Stanley. (1993). "The Enumeration of Ethnic and Racial Groups in the Census: Some Devilish Principles." In *Challenges of Measuring an Ethnic World*. Proceedings of the Joint Canada-United States Conference on the Measurement of Ethnicity. Washington: U.S. Department of Commerce, U.S. Bureau of the Census.

Lieberson, Stanley, & Waters, Mary. (1988). *From Many Strands*. New York: Russell Sage Foundation.

Mitroff, Ian I., Mason, Richard O., & Barabba, Vincent P. (1983). *The 1980 Census: Policymaking Amid Turbulence*. Lexington: Lexington Books.

Nobles, Melissa. (2000). *Shades of Citizenship*. Stanford: Stanford University Press.

Perlmann, Joel. (2000). "Demographic Outcomes of Ethnic Intermarriage in American History: Italian-Americans Through Four Generations." Working Paper 312. Annandale-on-Hudson: Jerome Levy Economics Institute.

Skerry, Peter. (2000). *Counting on the Census: Race, Group Identity, and the Evasion of Politics*. Washington: Brookings Institution.

READING AND DISCUSSION QUESTIONS

1. Glazer is discussing a change in the census form that he suggested "a few years ago." (The article was published in 2002.) What was his proposal?

2. Why does he feel his proposal offers an improvement over the current census form's questions about race and ethnicity?

3. What warrant or warrants underlie his argument?

4. Does his proposal seem to be reasonable? Does it seem to be an improvement on the current form?

5. This article by Glazer appeared on the Web before it was published in print form in a collection of essays. In the online article, Glazer had no documentation. He did have a note, however, that explained that a version with documentation was forthcoming in print. Is there less need for documentation when a piece of writing appears in electronic form? Why add documentation only when the piece moves into print?

WRITING SUGGESTIONS

6. Write an essay in which you either agree or disagree with Glazer's proposed change.

7. Glazer argues that ethnic and racial lines become blurred quickly after a short time in America. Do you feel that is a positive or a negative result of immigration to America?

8. Why do so many forms that we fill out ask for our race or national origin? Are there some situations in which race and national origin are relevant and others in which they are not? Explain. (Can you think of situations in which it is unlawful to ask such a question?)

Absolutely. Government Has No Business Interfering with What You Eat

RADLEY BALKO

Nutrition activists are agitating for a panoply of initiatives that would bring the government between you and your waistline. President Bush earmarked $125 million in his budget for the encouragement of healthy lifestyles. State legislatures and school boards have begun banning snacks and soda from school campuses and vending machines. Several state legislators and Oakland, California, Mayor Jerry Brown, among others, have called for a "fat tax" on high-calorie foods. Congress is considering menu-labeling legislation that would force chain restaurants to list fat, sodium and calories for each item.

That is precisely the wrong way to fight obesity. Instead of intervening in the array of food options available to Americans, our government ought to be working to foster a personal sense of responsibility for our health and well-being.

We're doing just the opposite. For decades, America's health-care system has been migrating toward nationalized medicine. We have a law that requires some Americans to pay for other Americans' medicine, and several states bar health insurers from charging lower premiums to people who stay fit. That removes the financial incentive for making healthy decisions. Worse, socialized health care makes us troublingly tolerant of government trespasses on our personal freedom. If my neighbor's heart attack shows up on my tax bill, I'm more likely to support state regulation of what he eats—restrictions on what grocery stores can put on their shelves, for example, or what McDonald's can put between its sesame-seed buns.

The best way to combat the public-health threat of obesity is to remove obesity from the realm of "public health." It's difficult to think of a matter more private and less public than what we choose to put in our bodies. Give Americans moral, financial and personal responsibility for their own health, and obesity is no longer a public matter but a private one—with all the costs, concerns, and worries of being overweight borne only by those people who are actually overweight.

Let each of us take full responsibility for our diet and lifestyle. We're 5 likely to make better decisions when someone else isn't paying for the consequences.

Radley Balko is a policy analyst with the Cato Institute and a columnist for FoxNews.com. This article first appeared in *Time* on June 7, 2004.

Not If Blaming the Victim Is Just an Excuse to Let Industry Off the Hook

KELLY BROWNELL AND MARION NESTLE

The food industry, like any other, must grow to stay in business. One way it does so is by promoting unhealthy foods, particularly to children. Each year kids see more than 10,000 food ads on TV alone, almost all for items like soft drinks, fast foods and sugared cereals. In the same year that the government spent $2 million on its main nutrition-education program, McDonald's spent $500 million on its We Love to See You Smile campaign. It can be no surprise that teenagers consume nearly twice as much soda as milk (the reverse was true twenty years ago) and that 25 percent of all vegetables eaten in the United States are french fries.

To counter criticism, the food industry and pro-business groups use a public relations script focused on personal responsibility. The script has three elements: (1) if people are overweight, it is their own fault; (2) industry responds to consumer demand but does not create it; and (3) insisting that industry change—say, by not marketing to children or requiring restaurants to reveal calories—is an attack on freedom.

Why quarrel with the personal-responsibility argument?

First, it's wrong. The prevalence of obesity increases year after year. Were people less responsible in 2002 than in 2001? Obesity is a global problem. Is irresponsibility an epidemic around the world?

Second, it ignores biology. Humans are hardwired, as a survival strategy, to like foods high in sugar, fat, and calories. 5

Third, the argument is not helpful. Imploring people to eat better and exercise more has been the default approach to obesity for years. That is a failed experiment.

Fourth, personal responsibility is a trap. The argument is startlingly similar to the tobacco industry's efforts to stave off legislative and regula-

Kelly D. Brownell is professor and chair of psychology at Yale University and also serves as professor of epidemiology and public health and as director of the Yale Center for Eating and Weight Disorders. He has written numerous books, and one of his articles, "Understanding and Preventing Relapse," published in the *American Psychologist*, is one of the most frequently cited articles in the field of psychology.

Marion Nestle is Paulette Goddard Professor in the Department of Nutrition, Food Studies, and Public Health at New York University. Her degrees include a Ph.D. in molecular biology and an M.P.H. in public health nutrition, both from the University of California, Berkeley. She is the author of *Food Politics: How the Food Industry Influences Nutrition and Health* (2002) and *Safe Food: Bacteria, Biotechnology, and Bioterrorism* (2003), both from University of California Press.

tory interventions. The nation tolerated personal-responsibility arguments from Big Tobacco for decades, with disastrous results.

Governments collude with industry when they shift attention from conditions promoting poor diets to the individuals who consume them. Government should be doing everything it can to create conditions that lead to healthy eating, support parents in raising healthy children, and make decisions in the interests of public health rather than private profit.

DISCUSSION QUESTIONS

1. In his first paragraph, Balko mentions some specific initiatives that would involve some governmental control over Americans' eating habits. Which of them, if any, do you support?
2. What does Balko favor instead of such initiatives?
3. According to Balko, what mistakes have Americans made in the way they have tried to fight obesity?
4. Why do Brownell and Nestle feel that the government must bear some of the blame for obesity?
5. What does the food industry offer in its defense?
6. How did the practice of making health the personal responsibility of the consumer work when it came to smoking?
7. Whose argument do you find more convincing and why?

TAKING THE DEBATE ONLINE

For these and additional research URLs, see bedfordstmartins.com/rottenberg.

- *American Obesity Association*
  www.obesity.org
  The "leading organization for advocacy and education on obesity" presents "the most comprehensive site on obesity" on the Internet.

- *National Association to Advance Fat Acceptance*
  www.naafa.org
  This is the Web site where "fat is not a four-letter word."

- *Understanding Adult Obesity*
  www.niddk.nih.gov/health/nutrit/pubs/unders.htm
  This site, from the National Institute of Diabetes & Digestive & Kidney Diseases, considers the causes and consequences of obesity.

- *Action to Help Fight Obesity*
  http://banzhaf.net/obesitylinks

  This site, maintained by John F. Banzhaf III, Professor of Public Interest Law at George Washington University Law School, contains links to the latest developments in using the court system to fight obesity.

- *National Restaurant Association*
  http://restaurant.org

  This site is devoted to "representing, educating, and promoting the restaurant/hospitality industry"; its position on obesity is that "the emphasis should be on education, personal responsibility, moderation, and healthier lifestyles," not on holding restaurants responsible.

ASSIGNMENTS FOR UNDERSTANDING WARRANTS

1. What are some of the assumptions underlying the preference for *natural* foods and medicines? Can *natural* be clearly defined? Is this preference part of a broader philosophy? Try to evaluate the validity of the assumption.

2. Is plagiarism wrong? What assumptions about education are relevant to the issue of plagiarism? (Some students defend it. What kinds of arguments do they provide?)

3. Choose an advertisement, and examine the warrants on which the advertiser's claim is based.

4. "Religious beliefs are (or are not) necessary to a satisfactory life." Explain the warrants underlying your claim. Define any ambiguous terms.

5. Should students be given a direct voice in the hiring of faculty members? On what warrants about education do you base your answer?

6. Discuss the validity of the warrant in this statement from *The Watch Tower* (a publication of the Jehovah's Witnesses) about genital herpes: "The sexually loose are indeed 'receiving in themselves the full recompense, which was due for their error' (Romans 1:27)."

7. Read the following passage about suicide by the Greek philosopher Aristotle (adapted from his *Ethics*). Then defend or attack his argument, being careful to make clear both Aristotle's and your own warrants.

   Just as a murderer does not have the right to take a mother from her family or a child from her parents and simultaneously to deny society the use of a productive citizen, so the suicide, even though he or she freely chooses to be his or her own victim, does not possess the right to thus diminish the welfare of so many others.

8. In view of increasing interest in health in general, and nutrition and exercise in particular, do you think that universities and colleges should impose physical education requirements? If so, what form should they take? If not, why not? Defend your reasons.

9. Both state and federal governments have been embroiled in controversies concerning the rights of citizens to engage in harmful practices. In Massachusetts, for example, a mandatory seat-belt law was repealed by rebellious voters who considered the law an infringement of their freedom. What principles do you think ought to guide government regulation of dangerous practices?

10. The author of the following passage, Katherine Butler Hathaway, became a hunchback as a result of a childhood illness. Here she writes about the relationship between love and beauty from the point of view of someone who is deformed. Discuss the warrants on which the author bases her conclusion.

    I could secretly pretend that I had a lover . . . but I could never risk showing that I thought such a thing was possible for me . . . with any man. Because of my repeated encounters with the mirror and my irrepressible tendency to forget what I had seen, I had begun to force myself to believe and to remember, and especially to remember, that I would never be chosen for what I imagined to be the supreme and most intimate of all experience. I thought of sexual love as an honor that was too great and too beautiful for the body in which I was doomed to live.

11. People often complain that they aren't listened to. Children complain about parents, patients about doctors, wives about husbands, citizens about government. Are the complaints to be taken literally? Or are they based on unexpressed warrants or assumptions about communication? Choose a specific familiar situation, and explain the meaning of the complaint.

12. Barbara Ehrenreich, in a *Time* essay, defends "talk shows of the *Sally Jessy Raphael* variety" as highly moralistic. Listen to a couple of these shows—*Ricki Lake, Jerry Springer*—and determine what moral assumptions about personal relationships and behavior underlie the advice given to the participants by the host and the audience. Do you think Ehrenreich is correct?

13. Explain which argument you find more convincing, Balko's or Brownell and Nestle's.

CHAPTER 7

Induction, Deduction, and Logical Fallacies

Throughout the book we have pointed out the weaknesses that cause arguments to break down. In the vast majority of cases these weaknesses represent breakdowns in logic or the reasoning process. We call such weaknesses *fallacies*, a term derived from the Latin. Sometimes these false or erroneous arguments are deliberate; in fact, the Latin word *fallere* means "to deceive." But more often these arguments are either carelessly or unintentionally constructed. Thoughtful readers learn to recognize them; thoughtful writers learn to avoid them.

The reasoning process was first given formal expression by Aristotle, the Greek philosopher, almost 2,500 years ago. In his famous treatises, he described the way we try to discover the truth—observing the world, selecting impressions, making inferences, generalizing. In this process Aristotle identified two forms of reasoning: *induction* and *deduction*. Both forms, he realized, are subject to error. Our observations may be incorrect or insufficient, and our conclusions may be faulty because they have violated the rules governing the relationship between statements. The terms we've introduced may be unfamiliar, but the processes of reasoning, as well as the fallacies that violate these processes, are not. Induction and deduction are not reserved only for formal arguments about important problems; they also represent our everyday thinking about the most ordinary matters. As for the fallacies, they, too, unfortunately, may crop up anywhere, whenever we are careless in our use of the reasoning process.

In this chapter we examine some of the most common fallacies. First, however, a closer look at induction and deduction will make clear what happens when fallacies occur.

INDUCTION

Induction is the form of reasoning in which we come to conclusions about the whole on the basis of observations of particular instances. If you notice that prices on the four items you bought in the campus bookstore are higher than similar items in the bookstore in town, you may come to the conclusion that the campus store is a more expensive place to shop. If you also noticed that all three of the instructors you saw on the first day of school were wearing faded jeans and running shoes, you might say that your teachers are generally informal in their dress. In both cases you have made an *inductive leap*, reasoning from what you have learned about a few examples to what you think is true of a whole class of things.

How safe are you in coming to these conclusions? As we've noticed in discussing data and generalization warrants, the reliability of your conclusion depends on the quantity and quality of your observations. Were four items out of the thousands available in the campus store a sufficiently large sample? Would you come to the same conclusion if you chose fifty items? Might another selection have produced a different conclusion? As for the casually dressed instructors, perhaps further investigation would disclose that the teachers wearing jeans were all teaching assistants and that associate and full professors usually wore business clothes. Or the difference might lie in the academic discipline; anthropology teachers might turn out to dress less formally than business school teachers.

In these two situations, you could come closer to verifying your conclusions by further observation and experience—that is, by buying more items at both stores over a longer period of time and by coming into contact with a greater number of professors during a whole semester. Even without pricing every item in both stores or encountering every instructor on campus, you would be more confident of your generalization as the quality and quantity of your samples increased.

In some cases you can observe all the instances in a particular situation. For example, by acquiring information about the religious beliefs of all the residents of the dormitory, you can arrive at an accurate assessment of the number of Buddhists. But since our ability to make definitive observations about everything is limited, we must also make an inductive leap about categories of things that we ourselves can never encounter in their entirety. For some generalizations, as we have learned about evidence, we rely on the testimony of reliable witnesses who report that they have experienced or observed many more instances of the phenomenon. A television documentary may give us information about unwed teenage mothers in a city neighborhood; four girls are interviewed and followed for several days by the reporter. Are these girls typical of thousands of others? A sociologist on the program assures us that, in fact, they are. She herself has consulted with hundreds of other young mothers and can vouch for the fact that a conclusion about them, based on our observation of the four, will be sound. Obviously, though, our conclusion can only be probable, not certain. The sociologist's sample is large, but she can account only for hundreds, not thousands, and there may be unexamined cases that will seriously weaken our conclusions.

In other cases, we may rely on a principle known in science as "the uniformity of nature." We assume that certain conclusions about oak trees in the temperate zone of North America, for example, will also be true for oak trees growing elsewhere under similar climatic conditions. We also use this principle in attempting to explain the causes of behavior in human beings. If we discover that institutionalization of some children from infancy results in severe emotional retardation, we think it safe to conclude that under the same circumstances all children would suffer the same consequences. As in the previous example, we are aware that certainty about every case of institutionalization is impossible. With rare exceptions, the process of induction can offer only probability, not certain truth.

SAMPLE ESSAY: AN INDUCTIVE ARGUMENT

True or False: Schools Fail Immigrants

RICHARD ROTHSTEIN

A common indictment of public schools is that they no longer offer upward mobility to most immigrants. It is said that in the first half of the twentieth century, children learned English, went to college, and joined the middle class but that many of today's immigrants are more likely to drop out, take dead-end jobs, or end up in prison.

Many true accounts reinforce these beliefs. But less noticed are equally valid anecdotes pointing to an opposite claim.

Policy by anecdote is flawed because too often we notice only what confirms our preconceptions. California's recent experience with Mexican immigrants provides ample material for stories about school failure. But on a day to celebrate the American promise, we might also turn to anecdotes of another kind.

Richard Rothstein is a research associate of the Economic Policy Institute, a senior correspondent of the *American Prospect*, and the national education columnist of the *New York Times*, where this article appeared on July 4, 2001. He is the author of *The Way We Were: Myths and Realities of America's Student Achievement* (1997).

Recent college commencements across California featured many immigrants from impoverished families whose first language was Spanish, who came through much-maligned bilingual education programs, learned English, and now head for graduate schools or professions.

At California State University at Fresno, for example, about 700 of   5
4,000 graduates this spring were Latino, typically the first in their families to attend college. Top-ranked were Pedro Nava and Maria Rocio Magaña, Mexican-born children of farm laborers and cannery workers.

Mr. Nava did not settle in the United States until the third grade. Before that, he lived in migrant labor camps during harvests and in Mexico the rest of the year. His California schooling was in Spanish until the fifth grade, when he was moved to English instruction. Now, with a college degree, he has enrolled in management and teacher training courses.

Ms. Magaña did not place into English classes until the second half of the eleventh grade. Now fluent in both academic and conversational English, she will soon begin a Ph.D. program in anthropology at the University of Chicago.

Their achievements are not unique. Both credit success to their mothers' emphasis on education. Both mothers enrolled in English and high school equivalency courses at the local community college.

Across California, these two-year institutions play an especially important role for immigrants.

Lourdes Andrade just finished her junior year at Brown University,   10
having transferred there after getting associate of arts degrees in history and liberal arts at Oxnard Community College, about forty miles northwest of Los Angeles.

Ms. Andrade arrived here at the age of four and all through elementary school worked with her mother making beds and cleaning bathrooms in hotels. Ms. Andrade, too, attributes her success to her mother's strong academic pressure and also to mentoring she received in a federally financed program to give extra academic support to migrant children.

The program's director, Lorenzo Moraza, also grew up speaking only Spanish. Now a school principal, Mr. Moraza estimates that about 30 percent of the immigrant children he has worked with acquired public school records that led them to college. Those who receive bachelor's degrees are many fewer, but Mr. Moraza says he thinks most drop out of college for economic reasons, not academic ones.

At the Fresno campus, nearly two-thirds of the immigrants and children of immigrants who enter as freshmen eventually graduate. The university operates special support services to help them do so.

You cannot spend time in California without noticing an extensive middle class of Latino schoolteachers, doctors, lawyers, and small-business people. Not all are recent immigrants, but many are. Some attended Catholic schools, but most are products of the public system.

Many had bilingual education in the 1970s, 80s, and 90s. California has now banned such instruction, assuming it failed.

There are plenty of anecdotes to support a claim that schools fail im- 15 migrant children or an equally persuasive claim that schools serve them well. Getting better statistics should be a priority. Government numbers do not distinguish between students who are immigrants (or whose parents immigrated) from Hispanics with American roots for several generations.

To help interpret California's experience, the best federal data tell only that in 1996, there were 100,000 college students nationwide who were American citizens born in Mexico. This is less than 1 percent of all college students. But uncounted are even larger numbers of those born here to recent migrants.

Even a balanced collection of anecdotes that include successes as well as failures cannot determine whether California schools are less effective than we should expect, and whether wholesale change is needed to move more immigrants to the middle class. But the answer is certainly more complex than the stereotypes of systematic failure that pervade most accounts.

■ Analysis

An inductive argument proceeds by examining particulars and arriving at a generalization that represents a probable truth. The author of this article arrives at the truth he will defend—that public schools have been more successful than is often acknowledged in moving many immigrants into the middle class—by offering statistical data and a number of stories about immigrants from poor families who have entered graduate school or one of the professions.

Rothstein begins, as many arguers do, with a brief summary of the popular position with which he disagrees. At the end of the third paragraph, he announces that he will provide examples that point to a different conclusion.

The reader should ask three questions of an inductive argument: Is the evidence sufficient? Is it representative? Is it up-to-date? The evidence that Rothstein assembles consists of a series of anecdotes and statistical data about the performance of immigrant students. The success stories of five real persons are impressive, despite limitations imposed by the brevity of the essay, in part because they offer vivid examples of struggle that appeal to our emotions and bring to life an issue with which some of us may not be familiar. But five stories are hardly enough to prove a case; perhaps they are not representative. Rothstein, therefore, adds other data about the rate at which immigrant students graduate and the growing number of Latino professionals and businesspeople.

The reader has some reason to believe that the facts are up-to-date. First, Rothstein writes a regular column for a prestigious daily newspaper whose readers will be quick to find errors in arguments of which they're critical. Second, he refers to "recent college commencements," a graduation "this spring," bilingual education in the 1990s, and "the best federal data for California in 1996." At the same time, he does not claim that his argument is beyond debate, since the data are incomplete. Even the title suggests that the issue is still unsettled. Modesty in the arguer is always welcome and disposes the reader to view the argument more favorably.

DEDUCTION

While induction attempts to arrive at the truth, deduction guarantees sound relationships between statements. If each of a series of statements, called *premises*, is true, deductive logic tells us that the conclusion must also be true. Unlike the conclusions from induction, which are only probable, the conclusions from deduction are certain. The simplest deductive argument consists of two premises and a conclusion. In outline such an argument looks like this:

MAJOR PREMISE: All students with 3.5 averages and above for three years are invited to become members of Kappa Gamma Pi, the honor society.

MINOR PREMISE: George has had a 3.8 average for over three years.

CONCLUSION: Therefore, he will be invited to join Kappa Gamma Pi.

This deductive conclusion is *valid* or logically consistent because it follows necessarily from the premises. No other conclusion is possible. Validity, however, refers only to the form of the argument. The argument itself may not be satisfactory if the premises are not true—if Kappa Gamma Pi has imposed other conditions or if George has only a 3.4 average. The difference between truth and validity is important because it alerts us to the necessity for examining the truth of the premises before we decide that the conclusion is sound.

One way of discovering how the deductive process works is to look at the methods used by Sherlock Holmes, that most famous of literary detectives, in solving his mysteries. His reasoning process follows a familiar pattern. Through the inductive process—that is, observing the particulars of the world—he came to certain conclusions about those particulars. Then he applied deductive reasoning to come to a conclusion about a particular person or event.

On one occasion Holmes observed that a man sitting opposite him on a train had chalk dust on his fingers. From this observation Holmes deduced that the man was a schoolteacher. If his thinking were outlined, it would take the form of the syllogism, the classic form of deductive reasoning:

MAJOR PREMISE: All men with chalk dust on their fingers are schoolteachers.

MINOR PREMISE: This man has chalk dust on his fingers.

CONCLUSION: Therefore, this man is a schoolteacher.

One dictionary defines *syllogism* as "a formula of argument consisting of three propositions." The first proposition is called the major premise and offers a generalization about a large group or class. This generalization has been arrived at through inductive reasoning or observation of particulars. The second proposition is called the minor premise, and it makes a statement about a member of that group or class. The third proposition is the conclusion, which links the other two propositions, in much the same way that the warrant links the support and the claim.

If we look back at the syllogism that summarizes Holmes's thinking, we see how it represents the deductive process. The major premise, the first statement, is an inductive generalization, a statement arrived at after observation of a number of men with chalk on their fingers. The minor premise, the second statement, assigns a particular member, the man on the train, to the general class of those who have dust on their fingers.

But although the argument may be logical, it is faulty. The deductive argument is only as strong as its premises. As Lionel Ruby pointed out, Sherlock Holmes was often wrong.[1] Holmes once deduced from the size of a large hat found in the street that the owner was intelligent. He obviously believed that a large head meant a large brain and that a large brain indicated intelligence. Had he lived one hundred years later, new information about the relationship of brain size to intelligence would have enabled him to come to a different and better conclusion.

In this case, we might first object to the major premise, the generalization that all men with chalk dust on their fingers are schoolteachers. Is it true? Perhaps all the men with dusty fingers whom Holmes had so far observed had turned out to be schoolteachers, but was his sample sufficiently large to allow him to conclude that all dust-fingered men, even those with whom he might never have contact, were teachers? Were there no other vocations or situations that might require the use of chalk? Draftsmen or carpenters or tailors or artists might have fingers just as white as those of schoolteachers. In other words, Holmes may have ascertained that all schoolteachers have chalk dust on their fingers, but he

---

[1] *The Art of Making Sense* (Philadelphia: Lippincott, 1954), ch. 17.

had not determined that *only* schoolteachers can be thus identified. Sometimes it is helpful to draw circles representing the various groups in their relation to the whole.

If a large circle (see the figure below) represents all those who have chalk dust on their fingers, we see that several different groups may be contained in this universe. To be safe, Holmes should have deduced that the man on the train *might* have been a schoolteacher; he was not safe in deducing more than that. Obviously, if the inductive generalization or major premise is false, the conclusion of the particular argument is also false or invalid.

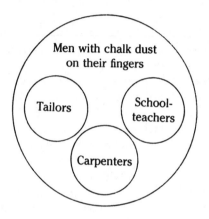

The deductive argument may also go wrong elsewhere. What if the minor premise is untrue? Could Holmes have mistaken the source of the white powder on the man's fingers? Suppose it was not chalk dust but flour or confectioner's sugar or talcum or heroin? Any of these possibilities would weaken or invalidate his conclusion.

Another example, closer to the kinds of arguments you will examine, reveals the flaw in the deductive process.

MAJOR PREMISE: All Communists oppose organized religion.

MINOR PREMISE: Robert Roe opposes organized religion.

CONCLUSION: Therefore, Robert Roe is a Communist.

The common name for this fallacy is "guilt by association." The fact that two things share an attribute does not mean that they are the same thing. The following diagram makes clear that Robert Roe and Communists do not necessarily share all attributes. Remembering that Holmes may have misinterpreted the signs of chalk on the traveler's fingers, we may also want to question whether Robert Roe's opposition to organized religion has been misinterpreted.

An example from history shows us how such an argument may be used. In a campaign speech during the summer of 1952, Senator Joseph McCarthy, who had made a reputation as a tireless enemy of communism, said, "I do not tell you that Schlesinger, Stevenson's number one man, number one braintrust, I don't tell you he's a Communist. I have no information on that point. But I do know that if he were a Communist he would also ridicule religion as Schlesinger has done."[2] This is an argument based on a sign warrant. Clearly the sign referred to by Senator McCarthy, ridicule of religion, would not be sufficient to characterize someone as a Communist.

Some deductive arguments give trouble because one of the premises, usually the major premise, is omitted. As in the warrants we examined in Chapter 6, a failure to evaluate the truth of the unexpressed premise may lead to an invalid conclusion. When only two parts of the syllogism appear, we call the resulting form an *enthymeme*. Suppose we overhear the following snatch of conversation:

> *"Did you hear about Jean's father? He had a heart attack last week."*
> *"That's too bad. But I'm not surprised. I know he always refused to go for his annual physical checkups."*

The second speaker has used an unexpressed major premise, the cause-and-effect warrant "If you have annual physical checkups, you can avoid heart attacks." He does not express it because he assumes that it is unnecessary to do so. The first speaker recognizes the unspoken warrant and may agree with it. Or the first speaker may produce evidence from reputable sources that such a generalization is by no means universally true, in which case the conclusion of the second speaker is suspect.

---

[2]Joseph R. McCarthy, "The Red-Tinted Washington Crowd," speech delivered to a Republican campaign meeting at Appleton, Wisconsin, November 3, 1952.

A knowledge of the deductive process can help guide you toward an evaluation of the soundness of your reasoning in an argument you are constructing. The syllogism is often clearer than an outline in establishing the relations between the different parts of an argument.

Suppose you wanted to argue that your former high school should introduce a dress code. You might begin by asking these questions: What would be the purpose of such a regulation? How would a dress code fulfill that purpose? What reasons could you provide to support your claim?

Then you might set down part of your argument like this:

> Dressing in different styles makes students more aware of social differences among themselves.
>
> The students in this school dress in many different styles.
>
> Therefore, they are more aware of differences in social status among the student body.

As you diagram this first part of the argument, you should ask two sets of questions:

1. Is the major premise true? Do differences in dress cause awareness of differences in social status? Has my experience confirmed this?

2. Is the minor premise true? Has my observation confirmed this?

The conclusion, of course, represents something that you don't have to observe. You can deduce with certainty that it is true if both the major and minor premises are true.

So far the testing of your argument has been relatively easy because you have been concerned with the testing of observation and experience. Now you must examine something that does not appear in the syllogism. You have determined certain facts about perceptions of social status, but you have not arrived at the policy you want to recommend: that a dress code should be mandated. Notice that the dress code argument is based on acceptance of a moral value.

> Reducing awareness of social differences is a desirable goal for the school.
>
> A uniform dress code would help to achieve that goal.
>
> Therefore, students should be required to dress uniformly.

The major premise in this syllogism is clearly different from the previous one. While the premise in the previous syllogism can be tested by examining sufficient examples to determine probability, this statement, about the desirability of the goal, is a value judgment and cannot be proved by counting examples. Whether equality of social status is a desirable goal depends on an appeal to other, more basic values.

Setting down your own or someone else's argument in this form will not necessarily give you the answers to questions about how to support your claim, but it should clearly indicate what your claims are and, above all, what logical connections exist between your statements.

SAMPLE ANNOTATED ESSAY: A DEDUCTIVE ARGUMENT

Divorce and Our National Values

PETER D. KRAMER

Introduction: The problem: a marital crisis caused by opposing views of marriage

How shall we resolve a marital crisis? Consider an example from the advice column of Ann Landers. An "Iowa Wife" wrote to ask what she should do about her husband's habit, after thirty years of marriage, of reading magazines at table when the couple dined out. Ann Landers advised the wife to engage her husband by studying subjects of interest to him.

Examples of opposing views

Readers from around the country protested. A "Fourteen-Year-Old Girl in Pennsylvania" crystallized the objections: "You told the wife to read up on sports or business, whatever he was interested in, even though it might be boring to her. Doesn't that defeat the basic idea of being your own self?" Chastened, Ann Landers changed course, updated her stance: Reading at table is a hostile act, perhaps even grounds for divorce.

When it comes to marriage, Ann Landers seems a reasonable barometer of our values. In practical terms, reading the sports pages might work for some Iowa wife — but we do not believe that is how spouses ought to behave. Only the second response, consider divorce, expresses our overriding respect for autonomy, for the unique and separate self.

Claim of fact or thesis statement: Divorce expresses respect for the separate self.
A proposed solution to the problem: "covenant marriage"

Look south now from Iowa and Pennsylvania to Louisiana, where a new law allows couples to opt for a "covenant marriage" — terminable only

---

Peter D. Kramer, a clinical professor of psychiatry at Brown University, is the author of *Listening to Prozac* (1993), *Should You Leave?* (1997), and the novel *Spectacular Happiness* (2001). This article appeared on the op-ed page of the *New York Times* on August 29, 1997.

after a lengthy separation or because of adultery, abandonment, abuse, or imprisonment. The law has been praised by many as an expedient against the epidemic of divorce and an incarnation of our "traditional values."

Whether the law will lower the divorce rate is   5
an empirical question to be decided in the future, but it is not too soon to ask: Does covenant marriage express the values we live by?

Questioning the covenant marriage Development and support: (1) history and philosophy of autonomy

History seems to say no. American literature's one great self-help book is *Walden,* a paean to self-reliance and an homage to Henry David Thoreau's favorite preacher, Ralph Waldo Emerson, who declaimed: "Say to them, O father, O mother, O wife, O brother, O friend, I have lived with you after appearances hitherto. Hence-forward, I am the truth's. . . . I must be myself. I cannot break my self any longer for you, or you."

The economic philosophy we proudly export, fundamentalist capitalism, says that society functions best when members act in a self-interested manner. The nation's founding document is a bill of divorcement. Autonomy is the characteristic American virtue.

(2) autonomy as a goal of psychotherapy

As a psychiatrist, I see this value embedded in our psychotherapy, the craft that both shapes and expresses the prevailing common sense. In the early 1970s, Carl Rogers, known as the "Psychologist of America," encapsulated the post–World War II version of our ideals: A successful marriage is one that increases the "self-actualization" of each member. Of a failed union, he wrote: "If Jennifer had from the first insisted on being her true self, the marriage would have had much more strife and much more hope."

Rogers was expressing the predominant viewpoint; for most of the past fifty years, enhanced autonomy has been a goal of psychotherapy. Erik Erikson began the trend by boldly proclaiming that the search for identity had become as important in his time as the study of sexuality was in Freud's. Later, Murray Bowen, a founder of family therapy, invoked a scale of maturity whose measure is a person's ability to maintain his or her beliefs in the face of family pressures. The useful response to crises within couples, Bowen suggested, is to hold fast to your values and challenge your partner to rise to meet your level of maturity.

But autonomy was a value for men only, and 10 largely it was pseudoautonomy, the successful man propped up by the indentured wife and overburdened mother. (No doubt Thoreau sent his clothes home for laundering.)

(3) autonomy extended to women

The self-help movement, beginning in the 1970s, extended this American ideal to women. Once both partners are allowed to be autonomous, the continuation of marriage becomes more truly voluntary. In this sense, an increase in divorce signals social progress.

It signals social progress, except that divorce is itself destructive. So it seems to me the question is whether any other compelling value counterbalances the siren song of self-improvement.

Another opposing view: mutuality as a preferable value

Turning again to psychotherapy, we do hear arguments for a different type of American value. Answering Erikson's call for individual identity, Helen Merrell Lynd, a sociologist at Sarah Lawrence College, wrote, "Nor must complete finding of oneself . . . precede finding oneself in and through other persons."

Her belief entered psychiatry through the writings of her pupil, Jean Baker Miller. A professor of psychiatry at Boston University, Dr. Miller faults most psychotherapy for elevating autonomy at the expense of qualities important to women, such as mutuality. To feel connected (when there is genuine give-and-take) is to feel worth. Miller wants a transformed culture in which mutuality "is valued as highly as, or more highly than, self-enhancement."

Refutation (the warrant): Americans do not value mutuality.

Mutuality is an ideal the culture believes it 15 should honor but does not quite. Ours is a society that does a half-hearted job of inculcating compromise, which is to say that we still teach these skills mainly to women. Much of psychotherapy addresses the troubles of those who make great efforts at compromise only to be taken advantage of by selfish partners.

Often the more vulnerable spouse requires rescue through the sort of move Ann Landers recommends, vigorous self-assertion, and even divorce.

Backing for the warrant: Self-assertion in school, office, and marketplace

Mutuality is a worthy ideal, one that might serve as a fit complement and counterbalance to our celebration of the self. But if we do not reward it elsewhere — if in the school and office and marketplace, we celebrate self-assertion — it seems worrisome to ask the institution of marriage to play by different rules.

What is insidious about Louisiana's covenant marriage is that, contrary to claims on its behalf, it is out of touch with our traditional values: self-expression, self-fulfillment, self-reliance.

The Louisiana law invites couples to lash themselves to a morality the broader culture does not support, an arrangement that creates a potential for terrible tensions.

Conclusion: restatement of the claim: Divorce reflects our national values.

Though we profess abhorrence of divorce, I 20 suspect that the divorce rate reflects our national values with great exactness, and that conventional modern marriage — an eternal commitment with loopholes galore — expresses precisely the degree of loss of autonomy that we are able to tolerate.

■ Analysis

A deductive argument proceeds from a general statement that the writer assumes to be true to a conclusion that is more specific. Deductive reasoning is commonplace, although seldom so pure as the definition suggests. In Kramer's article the conclusion appears at the end of paragraph 3: "the second response, consider divorce, expresses our overriding respect for autonomy, for the unique and separate self." The major premise or general statement may be summed up as "Self-actualization is an important American value," and the minor premise as "Divorce is an expression of self-actualization."

Kramer's defense of the major premise is admirable. Despite its brevity, the article brims with significant quotations and instructive examples from literature, psychiatry, and social and economic history that began, as he reminds us, with a "bill of divorcement" (para. 7) from England in 1776.

Finding support for the minor premise is a more difficult exercise because the reader here confronts a *specific* consequence of self-fulfillment — divorce. In all arguments, details and examples test the strength of our generalizations, and while self-actualization is suitably vague, divorce is not. We know that it does not always represent liberation for both partners. Kramer is aware of the problem. In the same paragraph he has insisted both that divorce "signals social progress" and that it is "destructive" (para. 12). He knows that his critics will call on him to reconcile this contradiction.

So far Kramer's argument has been largely factual, proof of the existence of the American ideal. Now he advances onto shakier ground in an examination of values: "the question is whether any other compelling value counterbalances the siren song of self-improvement" (para. 12).

Kramer then responds to those therapists who value a different ideal—that of mutuality, cooperation, and compromise rather than self-assertion. He admires such virtues but finds them unlikely to prevail against the ideal of self-fulfillment that pervades all areas of American life. Divorce, he believes, is simply one expression of that ideal, and he rejects the proposition that we should "ask the institution of marriage to play by different rules" (para. 17).

In deductive argument the conclusion must be true. Questions of social behavior, however, are not so easily proved. We accept the conclusions in such cases if they are plausible—well supported and consistent with experience. Within the limits of this brief essay, Kramer's findings are convincing.

One other element is worth noting: Kramer's objectivity, his role as observer rather than advocate. For the most part, he has excluded himself from the argument. We suspect that, as a psychiatrist, he supports values of self-expression, but in this article he is describing not his own views but those of most Americans. He does not explicitly defend divorce; he explains it. On the whole, this is an effective strategy. We do not need to agree on the morality of self-fulfillment to accept his conclusion.

A NOTE ON THE SYLLOGISM AND THE TOULMIN MODEL

In examining the classical deductive syllogism, you may have noticed the resemblance of its three-part outline to the three-part structure of claim, support, and warrant that we have used throughout the text to illustrate the elements of argument. We mentioned that the syllogism was articulated over two thousand years ago by the Greek philosopher Aristotle. By contrast, the claim-support-warrant structure is based on the model of argument proposed by the modern British philosopher Stephen Toulmin.

Now, there is every reason to think that all models of argument will share some similarities. Nevertheless, the differences between the formal syllogism and the informal Toulmin model suggest that the latter is a more effective instrument for writers who want to know which questions to ask, both before they begin and during the process of developing their arguments.

The syllogism is useful for laying out the basic elements of an argument, as we have seen in several examples. It lends itself more readily to simple arguments. The following syllogism summarizes a familiar argument.

MAJOR PREMISE: Advertising of things harmful to our health should be legally banned.

MINOR PREMISE: Cigarettes are harmful to our health.

CONCLUSION: Therefore, advertising of cigarettes should be legally banned.

Cast in the form of a Toulmin outline, the argument looks like this:

CLAIM: Advertising of cigarettes should be legally banned.

SUPPORT (EVIDENCE):   Cigarettes are harmful to our health.

WARRANT: Advertising of things harmful to our health should be legally banned.

or in diagram form:

Support ————————————————▶ *Claim*
Cigarettes are harmful   Advertising of cigarettes
to our health.   should be legally banned.

Warrant
Advertising of things harmful to our
health should be legally banned.

In both the syllogism and the Toulmin model the principal elements of the argument are expressed in three statements. You can see that the claim in the Toulmin model is the conclusion in the syllogism—that is, the proposition that you are trying to prove. The evidence (support) in the Toulmin model corresponds to the minor premise in the syllogism. And the warrant in the Toulmin model resembles the major premise of the syllogism.

But the differences are significant. One difference is the use of language. The syllogism represents an argument "in which the validity of the assumption underlying the inference 'leap' is uncontested."[3] That is, the words "major premise" seem to suggest that the assumption has been proved. They do not emphasize that an analysis of the premise—"Advertising of things harmful to our health should be legally banned"—is nec-

[3] Wayne E. Brockenreide and Douglas Ehninger, "Toulmin on Argument: An Interpretation and Application," *Contemporary Theories of Rhetoric: Selected Readings*, ed. Richard L. Johannesen (New York: Harper and Row, 1971), p. 245. This comparative analysis is indebted to Brockenreide and Ehninger's influential article.

essary before we can decide that the conclusion is acceptable. Of course, a careful arguer will try to establish the truth and validity of all parts of the syllogism, but the terms in which the syllogism is framed do not encourage him or her to examine the real relationship among the three elements. Sometimes the enthymeme (see p. 277), which uses only two elements in the argument and suppresses the third, makes analyzing the relationship even more difficult.

In the Toulmin model, the use of the term *warrant* indicates that the validity of the proposition must be established to *guarantee* the claim or make the crossing from support to claim. It makes clear that the arguer must ask *why* such advertising must be banned.

Nor is the term *minor premise* as useful to the arguer as "support." The word *support* instructs the arguer that he or she must take steps to provide the claim with factual evidence or an appeal to values.

A second difference is that while the syllogism is essentially static, with all three parts logically locked into place, the Toulmin model suggests that an argument is a *movement* from support to claim by way of the warrant, which acts as a bridge. Toulmin introduced the concept of warrant by asking "How do you get there?" (His first two questions, introducing the claim and support, were, "What are you trying to prove?" and "What have you got to go on?")

Lastly, recall that in addition to the three basic elements, the Toulmin model offers supplementary elements of argument. The *qualifier,* in the form of words like "probably" or "more likely," shows that the claim is not absolute. The *backing* offers support for the validity of the warrant. The *reservation* suggests that the validity of the warrant may be limited. These additional elements, which refine and expand the argument itself, reflect the real flexibility and complexity of the argumentative process.

COMMON FALLACIES

In this necessarily brief review it would be impossible to discuss all the fallacies listed by logicians, but we can examine the ones most likely to be found in the arguments you will read and write. Fallacies are difficult to classify, first, because there are literally dozens of systems for classifying, and second, because under any system there is always a good deal of overlap. Our discussion of the reasoning process, however, tells us where faulty reasoning occurs.

Inductive fallacies, as we know, result from the wrong use of evidence: That is, the arguer leaps to a conclusion on the basis of an insufficient sample, ignoring evidence that might have altered his or her conclusion. Deductive fallacies, on the other hand, result from a failure to follow the logic of a series of statements. Here the arguer neglects to make a clear connection between the parts of his or her argument. One of the commonest strategies is the introduction of an irrelevant issue, one that has little or no direct bearing on the development of the claim and serves only to distract the reader.

It's helpful to remember that, even if you cannot name the particular fallacy, you can learn to recognize it and not only refute it in the arguments of others but avoid it in your own as well.

■ 1. Hasty Generalization

In Chapter 5 (see pp. 166–67) we discussed the dangers in drawing conclusions on the basis of insufficient evidence. Many of our prejudices are a result of hasty generalization. A prejudice is literally a judgment made before the facts are in. On the basis of experience with two or three members of an ethnic group, for example, we may form the prejudice that all members of the group share the characteristics that we have attributed to the two or three in our experience. (See Gordon Allport, "The Nature of Prejudice," on p. 80.)

Superstitions are also based in part on hasty generalization. As a result of a very small number of experiences with black cats, broken mirrors, Friday the thirteenth, or spilled salt, some people will assume a cause-and-effect relation between these signs and misfortunes. *Superstition* has been defined as "a notion maintained despite evidence to the contrary." The evidence would certainly show that, contrary to the superstitious belief, in a lifetime hundreds of such "unlucky" signs are not followed by unfortunate events. To generalize about a connection is therefore unjustified.

■ 2. Faulty Use of Authority

Faulty use of authority—the attempt to bolster claims by citing the opinions of experts—was discussed in Chapter 5. Both writers and readers need to be especially aware of the testimony of authorities who may disagree with those cited. In circumstances where experts disagree, you are encouraged to undertake a careful evaluation and comparison of credentials.

■ 3. Post Hoc or Doubtful Cause

The entire Latin term for this fallacy is *post hoc, ergo propter hoc,* meaning, "After this, therefore because of this." The arguer infers that because one event follows another event, the first event must be the cause of the second. But proximity of events or conditions does not guarantee a causal relation. The rooster crows every morning at 5:00 and, seeing the sun rise immediately after, decides that his crowing has caused the sun to rise. A month after A-bomb tests are concluded, tornadoes damage the area where the tests were held, and residents decide that the tests caused the tornadoes. After the school principal suspends daily prayers in the class-room, acts of vandalism increase, and some parents are convinced that failure to conduct prayer is responsible for the rise in vandalism. In each of these cases, the fact that one event follows another does not prove a causal connection. The two events may be coincidental, or the first event may be only one, and an insignificant one, of many causes that have pro-duced the second event. The reader or writer of causal arguments must determine whether another more plausible explanation exists and whether several causes have combined to produce the effect. Perhaps the suspension of prayer was only one of a number of related causes: a decline in disciplinary action, a relaxation of academic standards, a change in school administration, and changes in family structure in the school community.

In the previous section we saw that superstitions are the result not only of hasty generalization but also of the willingness to find a cause-and-effect connection in the juxtaposition of two events. A belief in as-trological signs also derives from erroneous inferences about cause and effect. Only a very few of the millions of people who consult the astrol-ogy charts every day in newspapers and magazines have submitted the predictions to statistical analysis. A curious reader might try this strategy: Save the columns, usually at the beginning or end of the year, in which astrologers and clairvoyants make predictions for events in the coming year, allegedly based on their reading of the stars and other signs. At the end of the year evaluate the percentage of predictions that were fulfilled. The number will be very small. But even if some of the predictions prove true, there may be other less fanciful explanations for their accuracy.

In defending simple explanations against complex ones, philoso-phers and scientists often refer to a maxim called *Occam's razor,* a prin-ciple formulated by the medieval philosopher and theologian William of Occam. A modern science writer says this principle "urges a preference for the simplest hypothesis that does all we want it to do."[4] Bertrand Russell, the twentieth-century British philosopher, explained it this way:

> It is vain to do with more what can be done with fewer. That is to say, if everything in some science can be interpreted without assuming this or that hypothetical entity, there is no ground for assuming it. I have my-self found this a most fruitful principle in logical analysis.[5]

In other words, choose the simpler, more credible explanation wherever possible.

We all share the belief that scientific experimentation and research can answer questions about a wide range of natural and social phenom-ena: evolutionary development, hurricanes, disease, crime, poverty. It is

[4]Martin Gardner, *The Whys of a Philosophical Scrivener* (New York: Quill, 1983), p. 174.

[5]*Dictionary of Mind, Matter and Morals* (New York: Philosophical Library, 1952), p. 166.

true that repeated experiments in controlled situations can establish what seem to be solid relations suggesting cause and effect. But even scientists prefer to talk not about cause but about an extremely high probability that under controlled conditions one event will follow another.

In the social sciences cause-and-effect relations are especially susceptible to challenge. Human experiences can seldom be subjected to laboratory conditions. In addition, the complexity of the social environment makes it difficult, even impossible, to extract one cause from among the many that influence human behavior.

■ 4. False Analogy

Many analogies are merely descriptive and offer no proof of the connection between the two things being compared. In recent years a debate has emerged between weight-loss professionals about the wisdom of urging overweight people to lose weight for health reasons. Susan Wooley, director of the eating disorders clinic at the University of Cincinnati and a professor of psychiatry, offered the following analogy in defense of her view that dieting is dangerous.

> We know that overweight people have a higher mortality rate than thin people. We also know that black people have a higher mortality rate than white people. Do we subject black people to torturous treatments to bleach their skin? Of course not. We have enough sense to know skin-bleaching will not eliminate sickle-cell anemia. So why do we have blind faith that weight loss will cure the diseases associated with obesity?"[6]

But it is clear that the false analogy between black skin and excessive weight does not work. The color of one's skin does not cause sickle-cell anemia, but there is an abundance of proof that excess weight influences mortality.

Historians are fond of using analogical arguments to demonstrate that particular circumstances prevailing in the past are being reproduced in the present. They therefore feel safe in predicting that the present course of history will follow that of the past. British historian Arnold Toynbee argues by analogy that humans' tenure on earth may be limited.

> On the evidence of the past history of life on this planet, even the extinction of the human race is not entirely unlikely. After all, the reign of man on the Earth, if we are right in thinking that man established his present ascendancy in the middle paleolithic age, is so far only about 100,000 years old, and what is that compared to the 500 million or 900 million years during which life has been in existence on the surface of this planet? In the past, other forms of life have enjoyed reigns

[6]*New York Times*, April 12, 1992, sec. C, p. 43.

which have lasted for almost inconceivably longer periods—and which yet at last have come to an end.[7]

Toynbee finds similarities between the limited reigns of other animal species and the possible disappearance of the human race. For this analogy, however, we need to ask whether the conditions of the past, so far as we know them, at all resemble the conditions under which human existence on earth might be terminated. Is the fact that human beings are also members of the animal kingdom sufficient support for this comparison?

■ 5. Ad Hominem

The Latin term *ad hominem* means "against the man" and refers to an attack on the person rather than on the argument or the issue. The assumption in such a fallacy is that if the speaker proves to be unacceptable in some way, his or her statements must also be judged unacceptable. Attacking the author of the statement is a strategy of diversion that prevents the reader from giving attention where it is due—to the issue under discussion.

You might hear someone complain, "What can the priest tell us about marriage? He's never been married himself." This ad hominem accusation ignores the validity of the advice the priest might offer. In the same way an overweight patient might reject the advice on diet by an overweight physician. In politics it is not uncommon for antagonists to attack each other for personal characteristics that may not be relevant to the tasks they will be elected to perform. They may be accused of infidelity to their partners, homosexuality, atheism, or a flamboyant social life. Even if certain accusations should be proved true, voters should not ignore the substance of what politicians do and say in their public offices.

This confusion of private life with professional record also exists in literature and the other arts. According to their biographers, the American writers Thomas Wolfe, Robert Frost, and William Saroyan—to name only a few—and numbers of film stars, including Charlie Chaplin, Joan Crawford, and Bing Crosby, made life miserable for those closest to them. Having read about their unpleasant personal characteristics, some people find it hard to separate the artist from his or her creation, although the personality and character of the artist are often irrelevant to the content of the work.

Ad hominem accusations against the person do *not* constitute a fallacy if the characteristics under attack are relevant to the argument. If the politician is irresponsible and dishonest in the conduct of his or her personal life, we may be justified in thinking that the person will also behave irresponsibly and dishonestly in public office.

---

[7] *Civilization on Trial* (New York: Oxford University Press, 1948), pp. 162–63.

■ 6. False Dilemma

As the name tells us, the false dilemma, sometimes called the *black-white fallacy,* poses an either-or situation. The arguer suggests that only two alternatives exist, although there may be other explanations of or solutions to the problem under discussion. The false dilemma reflects the simplification of a complex problem. Sometimes it is offered out of ignorance or laziness, sometimes to divert attention from the real explanation or solution that the arguer rejects for doubtful reasons.

You may encounter the either-or situation in dilemmas about personal choices. "At the University of Georgia," says one writer, "the measure of a man was football. You either played it or worshiped those who did, and there was no middle ground."[8] Clearly this dilemma—"Love football or you're not a man"—ignores other measures of manhood.

Politics and government offer a wealth of examples. In an interview with the *New York Times* in 1975, the Shah of Iran was asked why he could not introduce into his authoritarian regime greater freedom for his subjects. His reply was, "What's wrong with authority? Is anarchy better?" Apparently he considered that only two paths were open to him—authoritarianism or anarchy. Of course, democracy was also an option, which, perhaps fatally, he declined to consider.

■ 7. Slippery Slope

If an arguer predicts that taking a first step will lead inevitably to a second, usually undesirable step, he or she must provide evidence that this will happen. Otherwise, the arguer is guilty of a slippery slope fallacy.

Asked by an inquiring photographer on the street how he felt about censorship of a pornographic magazine, a man replied, "I don't think any publication should be banned. It's a slippery slope when you start making decisions on what people should be permitted to read. . . . It's a dangerous precedent." Perhaps. But if questioned further, the man should have offered evidence that a ban on some things leads inevitably to a ban on everything.

Predictions based on the danger inherent in taking the first step are commonplace:

> Legalization of abortion will lead to murder of the old and the physically and mentally handicapped.
> The Connecticut law allowing sixteen-year-olds and their parents to divorce each other will mean the death of the family.
> If we ban handguns, we will end up banning rifles and other hunting weapons.

[8]Phil Gailey, "A Nonsports Fan," *New York Times Magazine,* December 18, 1983, sec. 6, p. 96.

Distinguishing between probable and improbable predictions — that is, recognizing the slippery-slope fallacy — poses special problems because only future developments can verify or refute predictions. For example, in 1941 the imposition of military conscription aroused some opponents to predict that the draft was a precursor of fascism in this country. Only after the war, when 10 million draftees were demobilized, did it become clear that the draft had been an insufficient sign for a prediction of fascism. In this case the slippery-slope prediction of fascism might have been avoided if closer attention had been paid to other influences pointing to the strength of democracy.

More recently, the debate about cloning has raised fears of creation of genetic copies of adults. The *New York Times* reported that

> Many lawmakers today warned that if therapeutic cloning went forward, scientists would step onto a slippery slope that would inevitably lead to cloning people.[9]

Most scientists, however, reject this possibility for the foreseeable future.

Slippery slope predictions are simplistic. They ignore not only the dissimilarities between first and last steps but also the complexity of the developments in any long chain of events.

■ 8. Begging the Question

If the writer makes a statement that assumes that the very question being argued has already been proved, the writer is guilty of begging the question. In a letter to the editor of a college newspaper protesting the failure of the majority of students to meet the writing requirement because they had failed an exemption test, the writer said, "Not exempting all students who honestly qualify for exemption is an insult." But whether the students are honestly qualified is precisely the question that the exemption test was supposed to resolve. The writer has not proved that the students who failed the writing test were qualified for exemption. She has only made an assertion *as if* she had already proved it.

In an effort to raise standards of teaching, some politicians and educators have urged that master teachers be awarded higher salaries. Opponents have argued that such a proposal begs the question because it assumes that the term *master teachers* can be or has already been defined.

Circular reasoning is an extreme example of begging the question: "Women should not be permitted to join men's clubs because the clubs are for men only." The question to be resolved first, of course, is whether clubs for men only should continue to exist.

[9] August 1, 2001, p. A11.

■ 9. Straw Man

The straw-man fallacy consists of an attack on a view similar to but not the same as the one your opponent holds. It is a familiar diversionary tactic. The name probably derives from an old game in which a straw man was set up to divert attention from the real target that a contestant was supposed to knock down.

One of the outstanding examples of the straw-man fallacy occurred in the famous Checkers speech of Senator Richard Nixon. In 1952 during his vice-presidential campaign, Nixon was accused of having appropriated $18,000 in campaign funds for his personal use. At one point in the radio and television speech in which he defended his reputation, he said:

> One other thing I probably should tell you, because if I don't they will probably be saying this about me, too. We did get something, a gift, after the election.
>
> A man down in Texas heard Pat on the radio mention the fact that our two youngsters would like to have a dog, and, believe it or not, the day before we left on this campaign trip we got a message from Union Station in Baltimore saying they had a package for us. We went down to get it. You know what it was?
>
> It was a little cocker spaniel dog, in a crate that he had sent all the way from Texas, black and white, spotted, and our little girl, Tricia, the six-year-old, named it Checkers.
>
> And, you know, the kids, like all kids, loved the dog, and I just want to say this, right now, that regardless of what they say about it, we are going to keep it.[10]

Of course, Nixon knew that the issue was the alleged misappropriation of funds, not the ownership of the dog, which no one had asked him to return.

■ 10. Two Wrongs Make a Right

The two-wrongs-make-a-right fallacy is another example of the way in which attention may be diverted from the question at issue.

After President Jimmy Carter in March 1977 attacked the human rights record of the Soviet Union, Russian officials responded:

> As for the present state of human rights in the United States, it is characterized by the following facts: millions of unemployed, racial discrimination, social inequality of women, infringement of citizens' personal freedom, the growth of crime, and so on.[11]

---

[10] Radio and television address of Senator Nixon from Los Angeles on September 23, 1952.

[11] *New York Times,* March 3, 1977, p. 1.

The Russians made no attempt to deny the failure of *their* human rights record; instead they attacked by pointing out that the Americans are not blameless either.

■ 11. Non Sequitur

The Latin term *non sequitur,* which means "it does not follow," is another fallacy of irrelevance. An advertisement for a book, *Worlds in Collision,* whose theories about the origin of the earth and evolutionary development have been challenged by almost all reputable scientists, states:

> Once rejected as "preposterous"! Critics called it an outrage! It aroused incredible antagonism in scientific and literary circles. Yet half a million copies were sold and for twenty-seven years it remained an outstanding bestseller.

We know, of course, that the popularity of a book does not bestow scientific respectability. The number of sales, therefore, is irrelevant to proof of the book's theoretical soundness—a non sequitur.

Other examples sometimes appear in the comments of political candidates. Donald Trump, the wealthy real-estate developer, in considering a run for president of the United States in 2000, told an interviewer:

> My entire life, I've watched politicians bragging about how poor they are, how they came from nothing, how poor their parents and grandparents were. And I said to myself, if they can stay so poor for so many generations, maybe this isn't the kind of person we want to be electing to higher office. How smart can they be? They're morons. . . . Do you want someone who gets to be president and that's literally the highest paying job he's ever had?[12]

As a brief glance at U.S. history shows, it does not follow that men of small success in the world of commerce are unfit to make sound decisions about matters of state.

■ 12. Ad Populum

Arguers guilty of the *ad populum* fallacy make an appeal to the prejudices of the people (*populum* in Latin). They assume that their claim can be adequately defended without further support if they emphasize a belief or attitude that the audience shares with them. One common form of ad populum is an appeal to patriotism, which may allow arguers to omit evidence that the audience needs for proper evaluation of the claim. In the following advertisement the makers of Zippo lighters made such an appeal in urging readers to buy their product.

[12] *New York Times,* November 28, 1999, p. 11.

It's a grand old lighter. Zippo—the grand old lighter that's made right here in the good old U.S.A.

We truly make an all-American product. The raw materials used in making a Zippo lighter are all right from this great land of ours.

Zippo windproof lighters are proud to be Americans.

■ 13. Appeal to Tradition

In making an appeal to tradition, the arguer assumes that what has existed for a long time and has therefore become a tradition should continue to exist *because* it is a tradition. If the arguer avoids telling his or her reader *why* the tradition should be preserved, he or she may be accused of failing to meet the real issue.

The following statement appeared in a letter defending the membership policy of the Century Club, an all-male club established in New York City in 1847 that was under pressure to admit women. The writer was a Presbyterian minister who opposed the admission of women.

> I am totally opposed to a proposal which would radically change the nature of the Century. . . . A club creates an ethos of its own over the years, and I would deeply deplore a step that would inevitably create an entirely different kind of place.
>
> A club like the Century should surely be unaffected by fashionable whims. . . .[13]

■ 14. Faulty Emotional Appeals

In some discussions of fallacies, appeals to the emotions of the audience are treated as illegitimate or "counterfeit proofs." All such appeals, however, are *not* illegitimate. As we saw in Chapter 5 on support, appeals to the values and emotions of an audience are an appropriate form of persuasion. You can recognize fallacious emotional appeals if (1) they are irrelevant to the argument or draw attention from the issues being argued or (2) they appear to conceal another purpose. Here we treat two of the most popular appeals—to pity and to fear.

Appeals to pity, compassion, and natural willingness to help the unfortunate are particularly hard to resist. The requests for aid by most charitable organizations—for hungry children, victims of disaster, stray animals—offer examples of legitimate appeals. But these appeals to our sympathetic feelings should not divert us from considering other issues in a particular case. It would be wrong, for example, to allow a multiple murderer to escape punishment because he or she had experienced a wretched childhood. Likewise, if you are asked to contribute to a charitable cause, you should try to learn how many unfortunate people or animals are being helped and what percentage of the contribution will be

---

[13]David H. C. Read, letter to the *New York Times,* January 13, 1983, p. 14.

allocated to maintaining the organization and its officers. In some cases the financial records are closed to public review, and only a small share of the contribution will reach the alleged beneficiaries.

Appeals to fear are likely to be even more effective. But they must be based on evidence that fear is an appropriate response to the issues and that it can move an audience toward a solution to the problem. (Fear can also have the adverse effect of preventing people from taking a necessary action.) Insurance companies, for example, make appeals to our fears of destitution for ourselves and our families as a result of injury, unemployment, sickness, and death. These appeals are justified if the possibilities of such destitution are real and if the insurance will provide relief. It would also be legitimate to arouse fear of the consequences of drunk driving, provided, again, that the descriptions were accurate. On the other hand, it would be wrong to induce fear that fluoridation of public water supplies causes cancer without presenting sound evidence of the probability. It would also be wrong to instill a fear of school integration unless convincing proof were offered of undesirable social consequences.

An emotional response by itself is not always the soundest basis for making decisions. Your own experience has probably taught you that in the grip of a strong emotion like love or hate or anger you often overlook good reasons for making different and better choices. Like you, your readers want to be given the opportunity to consider all the available kinds of support for an argument.

Writer's Guide: Avoiding Logical Fallacies

1. If you are making use of induction, that is, drawing a conclusion based on a number of individual examples, do you have enough examples with variety to justify the conclusion? In other words, will your readers be able to make the inductive leap from examples to the conclusion you are asking them to make?

2. If you are making use of deduction, is your conclusion a logical one based on the premises underlying it? To be sure, write out your argument in the form of a syllogism. Also avoid wording your thesis in absolute terms like *all, every, everyone, everybody,* and *always.*

3. It is relatively easy — and sometimes humorous — to notice other writers' logical fallacies. It is harder to notice your own. Use the list of fallacies in this chapter as a checklist as you read the draft of each of your essays with a critical eye, looking for any breakdown in logic. It may be useful to read your essay aloud to someone because if that listener cannot follow your logic, you may need to clarify your points.

On Nation and Race

ADOLF HITLER

There are some truths which are so obvious that for this very reason they are not seen or at least not recognized by ordinary people. They sometimes pass by such truisms as though blind and are most astonished when someone suddenly discovers what everyone really ought to know. Columbus's eggs lie around by the hundreds of thousands, but Columbuses are met with less frequency.

Thus men without exception wander about in the garden of Nature; they imagine that they know practically everything and yet with few exceptions pass blindly by one of the most patent principles of Nature's rule: the inner segregation of the species of all living beings on this earth.

Even the most superficial observation shows that Nature's restricted form of propagation and increase is an almost rigid basic law of all the innumerable forms of expression of her vital urge. Every animal mates only with a member of the same species. The titmouse seeks the titmouse, the finch the finch, the stork the stork, the field mouse the field mouse, the dormouse the dormouse, the wolf the she-wolf, etc.

Only unusual circumstances can change this, primarily the compulsion of captivity or any other cause that makes it impossible to mate within the same species. But then Nature begins to resist this with all possible means, and her most visible protest consists either in refusing further capacity for propagation to bastards or in limiting the fertility of later offspring; in most cases, however, she takes away the power of resistance to disease or hostile attacks.

This is only too natural.   5

Any crossing of two beings not at exactly the same level produces a medium between the level of the two parents. This means: The offspring will probably stand higher than the racially lower parent, but not as high as the higher one. Consequently, it will later succumb in the struggle against the higher level. Such mating is contrary to the will of Nature for a higher breeding of all life. The precondition for this does not lie in associating superior and inferior, but in the total victory of the former. The stronger must dominate and not blend with the weaker, thus sacrificing his own greatness. Only the born weakling can view this as cruel, but he after all is only a weak and limited man; for if this law did not prevail, any conceivable higher development of organic living beings would be unthinkable.

Adolf Hitler (1889–1945) became the Nazi dictator of Germany in the mid-1930s. "On Nation and Race" (editor's title) begins Chapter 11 of *Mein Kampf* (*My Struggle*), vol. 1, published in 1925.

The consequence of this racial purity, universally valid in Nature, is not only the sharp outward delimitation of the various races, but their uniform character in themselves. The fox is always a fox, the goose a goose, the tiger a tiger, etc., and the difference can lie at most in the varying measure of force, strength, intelligence, dexterity, endurance, etc., of the individual specimens. But you will never find a fox who in his inner attitude might, for example, show humanitarian tendencies toward geese, as similarly there is no cat with a friendly inclination toward mice.

Therefore, here, too, the struggle among themselves arises less from inner aversion than from hunger and love. In both cases, Nature looks on calmly, with satisfaction, in fact. In the struggle for daily bread all those who are weak and sickly or less determined succumb, while the struggle of the males for the female grants the right or opportunity to propagate only to the healthiest. And struggle is always a means for improving a species' health and power of resistance and, therefore, a cause of its higher development.

If the process were different, all further and higher development would cease and the opposite would occur. For, since the inferior always predominates numerically over the best, if both had the same possibility of preserving life and propagating, the inferior would multiply so much more rapidly that in the end the best would inevitably be driven into the background, unless a correction of this state of affairs were undertaken. Nature does just this by subjecting the weaker part to such severe living conditions that by them alone the number is limited, and by not permitting the remainder to increase promiscuously, but making a new and ruthless choice according to strength and health.

No more than Nature desires the mating of weaker with stronger in- 10 dividuals, even less does she desire the blending of a higher with a lower race, since, if she did, her whole work of higher breeding, over perhaps hundreds of thousands of years, might be ruined with one blow.

Historical experience offers countless proofs of this. It shows with terrifying clarity that in every mingling of Aryan blood with that of lower peoples the result was the end of the cultured people. North America, whose population consists in by far the largest part of Germanic elements who mixed but little with the lower colored peoples, shows a different humanity and culture from Central and South America, where the predominantly Latin immigrants often mixed with the aborigines on a large scale. By this one example, we can clearly and distinctly recognize the effect of racial mixture. The Germanic inhabitant of the American continent, who has remained racially pure and unmixed, rose to be master of the continent; he will remain the master as long as he does not fall a victim to defilement of the blood.

The result of all racial crossing is therefore in brief always the following:

(a) Lowering of the level of the higher race;

(b) Physical and intellectual regression and hence the beginning of a slowly but surely progressing sickness.

To bring about such a development is, then, nothing else but to sin 15
against the will of the eternal creator.

And as a sin this act is rewarded.

When man attempts to rebel against the iron logic of Nature, he
comes into struggle with the principles to which he himself owes his existence as a man. And this attack must lead to his own doom.

Here, of course, we encounter the objection of the modern pacifist, as
truly Jewish in its effrontery as it is stupid! "Man's role is to overcome
Nature!"

Millions thoughtlessly parrot this Jewish nonsense and end up by
really imagining that they themselves represent a kind of conqueror of
Nature; though in this they dispose of no other weapon than an idea, and
at that such a miserable one, that if it were true no world at all would be
conceivable.

But quite aside from the fact that man has never yet conquered Na- 20
ture in anything, but at most has caught hold of and tried to lift one or
another corner of her immense gigantic veil of eternal riddles and secrets,
that in reality he invents nothing but only discovers everything, that he
does not dominate Nature, but has only risen on the basis of his knowledge of various laws and secrets of Nature to be lord over those other living creatures who lack this knowledge—quite aside from all this, an idea
cannot overcome the preconditions for the development and being of humanity, since the idea itself depends only on man. Without human beings there is no human idea in this world; therefore, the idea as such is
always conditioned by the presence of human beings and hence of all the
laws which created the precondition for their existence.

And not only that! Certain ideas are even tied up with certain men.
This applies most of all to those ideas whose content originates, not in an
exact scientific truth, but in the world of emotion, or, as it is so beautifully and clearly expressed today, reflects an "inner experience." All these
ideas, which have nothing to do with cold logic as such, but represent
only pure expressions of feeling, ethical conceptions, etc., are chained to
the existence of men, to whose intellectual imagination and creative
power they owe their existence. Precisely in this case the preservation of
these definite races and men is the precondition for the existence of these
ideas. Anyone, for example, who really desired the victory of the pacifistic
idea in this world with all his heart would have to fight with all the means
at his disposal for the conquest of the world by the Germans; for, if the
opposite should occur, the last pacifist would die out with the last German, since the rest of the world has never fallen so deeply as our own
people, unfortunately, has for this nonsense so contrary to Nature and
reason. Then, if we were serious, whether we liked it or not, we would
have to wage wars in order to arrive at pacifism. This and nothing else was
what Wilson, the American world savior, intended, or so at least our German visionaries believed—and thereby his purpose was fulfilled.

In actual fact the pacifistic-humane idea is perfectly all right perhaps
when the highest type of man has previously conquered and subjected

the world to an extent that makes him the sole ruler of this earth. Then this idea lacks the power of producing evil effects in exact proportion as its practical application becomes rare and finally impossible. Therefore, first struggle and then we shall see what can be done. Otherwise mankind has passed the high point of its development and the end is not the domination of any ethical idea but barbarism and consequently chaos. At this point someone or other may laugh, but this planet once moved through the ether for millions of years without human beings and it can do so again some day if men forget that they owe their higher existence, not to the ideas of a few crazy ideologists, but to the knowledge and ruthless application of Nature's stern and rigid laws.

Everything we admire on this earth today—science and art, technology and inventions—is only the creative product of a few peoples and originally perhaps of *one* race. On them depends the existence of this whole culture. If they perish, the beauty of this earth will sink into the grave with them.

However much the soil, for example, can influence men, the result of the influence will always be different depending on the races in question. The low fertility of a living space may spur the one race to the highest achievements; in others it will only be the cause of bitterest poverty and final undernourishment with all its consequences. The inner nature of peoples is always determining for the manner in which outward influences will be effective. What leads the one to starvation trains the other to hard work.

All great cultures of the past perished only because the originally cre- 25 ative race died out from blood poisoning.

The ultimate cause of such a decline was their forgetting that all culture depends on men and conversely; hence that to preserve a certain culture the man who creates it must be preserved. This preservation is bound up with the rigid law of necessity and the right to victory of the best and stronger in this world.

Those who want to live, let them fight, and those who do not want to fight in this world of eternal struggle do not deserve to live.

Even if this were hard—that is how it is! Assuredly, however, by far the harder fate is that which strikes the man who thinks he can overcome Nature, but in the last analysis only mocks her. Distress, misfortune, and diseases are her answer.

The man who misjudges and disregards the racial laws actually forfeits the happiness that seems destined to be his. He thwarts the triumphal march of the best race and hence also the precondition for all human progress, and remains, in consequence, burdened with all the sensibility of man, in the animal realm of helpless misery.

It is idle to argue which race or races were the original representative of 30 human culture and hence the real founders of all that we sum up under the word *humanity*. It is simpler to raise the question with regard to the present, and here an easy, clear answer results. All the human culture, all the results of art, science, and technology that we see before us today, are almost exclusively the creative product of the Aryan. This very fact admits of the not unfounded inference that he alone was the founder of all higher humanity, therefore representing the prototype of all that we understand by the word *man*. He is the Prometheus of mankind from whose bright forehead the divine spark of genius has sprung at all times, forever kindling anew that fire of knowledge which illumined the night of silent mysteries and thus caused man to climb the path to mastery over the other beings of this earth. Exclude him — and perhaps after a few thousand years darkness will again descend on the earth, human culture will pass, and the world turn to a desert.

READING AND DISCUSSION QUESTIONS

1. Find places in the essay where Hitler attempts to emphasize the scientific objectivity of his theories.

2. Are some passages difficult to understand? (See, for example, para. 11.) How do you explain the difficulty?

3. In explaining his ideology, how does Hitler misinterpret the statement that "Every animal mates only with a member of the same species" (para. 3)? How would you characterize this fallacy?

4. Hitler uses the theory of evolution and his interpretation of the "survival of the fittest" to justify his racial philosophy. Find the places in the text where Hitler reveals that he misunderstands the theory in its application to human beings.

5. What false evidence about race does Hitler use in his assessment of the racial experience in North America? Examine carefully the last sentence of paragraph 11: "The Germanic inhabitant of the American continent, who has remained racially pure and unmixed, rose to be master of the continent; he will remain the master as long as he does not fall a victim to defilement of the blood."

6. What criticism of Jews does Hitler offer? How does this criticism help to explain Hitler's pathological hatred of Jews?

7. Hitler believes that pacifism is a violation of "Nature and reason" (para. 21). Would modern scientists agree that the laws of nature require unremitting struggle and conflict between human beings — until the master race conquers?

WRITING SUGGESTION

8. Use your responses to the Reading and Discussion Questions as the basis of an essay evaluating Hitler's logic in "On Nation and Race."

9. Do some research in early human history to discover the degree of truth in this statement: "All the human culture, all the results of art, science, and technology that we see before us today, are almost exclusively the creative product of the Aryan" (para. 30). You may want to limit your discussion to one area of human culture.

CHERYL SILAS had a highway collision, was hit twice from behind, and then sold three cars for us.

When Cheryl unbuckled her shoulder harness and lap belt, it took her a moment to realize her Saturn coupe was really a mess. And that, remarkably, she wasn't. That's when she decided to get another SC.

Several other people arrived at similar conclusions. A policeman at the accident scene came in soon after and ordered himself a sedan. As did a buddy of his, also on the force. Then Cheryl's brother, glad he still had a sister, bought yet another Saturn in Illinois.

Now, good referrals are important to any product. And we're always glad to have them. But we'd be more than happy if our customers found less dramatic ways to help spread the word.

A DIFFERENT KIND of COMPANY. A DIFFERENT KIND of CAR.

DISCUSSION QUESTIONS

1. What example of inductive reasoning does the advertiser use? How would you evaluate the probability of the conclusion?

2. To what extent does the use of an alleged real person in a narrative contribute to the effectiveness of the advertiser's pitch? Should the ad have contained more factual information?

Show Biz Encourages Looser Teen Sex Habits

SHERYL McCARTHY

As the high school prom season winds down, we are learning more than we ever wanted to know about the social and sexual mores of today's teenagers.

Such as how they're avoiding "dating," opting instead to attend the prom with groups of friends. Everybody has a blast without suffering the angst of waiting for some guy to ask you to be his date, or worrying that the girl you ask will reject you.

This seems a lot healthier than it was when I went to my high school prom. I was lucky enough to have a great date and a wonderful prom night. But I've heard countless women complain thirty years later about missing their prom because nobody invited them. Going as a group takes the power to decide who gets to go out of the boys' hands, and takes the pressure of having to find a date off everybody.

Some of the other recent trends aren't so hot. A newspaper reporter who attended several local proms this year was shocked by the highly sexualized dancing that went on. When I was in school, the occasional guy put you in a back-breaking full-body lock that lasted the duration of a song. But now, virtually all the males and females engage in "freaking" and "backing up"—which amounts to simulating sex on the dance floor.

And there's the growing phenomenon of "hooking up." Having 5 steady boyfriends or girlfriends has been replaced by kids who travel in packs, breaking away to have casual sexual encounters with friends or mere acquaintances. These encounters range from kissing to petting, masturbating each other to oral sex—all without emotional strings. And they say they like it that way.

I find this retreat from intimacy rather depressing. My classmates weren't into sex, by and large. But there was something nice about the boyfriend-girlfriend thing. In endless phone calls or Sunday night sofa-sitting, we achieved a certain emotional intimacy, along with our sexual gropings. The guys may have been thinking mostly about sex, but there was at least an idealized notion of what it meant to be a couple.

The current teenage social scene strikes me as rather aimless. Those who work with teenagers attribute the surge in dirty dancing to the music videos in which young musical stars like Britney Spears, Christina Aguilera, and Beyonce Knowles provocatively shake their scantily-clad booties, and legions of gorgeous females swarming over ordinary-looking

Sheryl McCarthy is on the faculty of the Graduate School of Journalism of Columbia University. She has been a reporter for the *Boston Globe*, the *Baltimore Evening Sun*, and the New York *Daily News* and a national correspondent for ABC News. She is now a columnist for *Newsday*, where this article appeared on June 24, 2004.

men seem to define what relations between males and females are supposed to be.

Tamar Rothenberg, editor of *New Youth Connections*, a newspaper put out by New York City high school students, says she worries about the message the videos give to teenagers trying to figure out what they're supposed to be doing in relationships.

"Hooking-up" apparently results from teenagers wanting to avoid being tied down in relationships that can cause pain and disappointment. Teenage girls may also be rebelling against the old sexual double standard and wanting to have the same freedom as boys. But the girls are often on the giving end of the casual sex, and teens often don't realize that they can catch diseases from oral sex.

The moguls of MTV and BET and the video producers and the titans 10 of hip-hop deserve a lot of the blame for this, and deserve to be booed off any stage where they are hypocritical enough to lament the high rate of teen pregnancy and the social fallout from irresponsible male sexual behavior.

But so do the spineless politicians and educators and the squeamish parents who are far more obsessed with keeping teenagers chaste than with helping them to have responsible relationships.

That's why I applaud groups like Planned Parenthood and *New Youth Connections* that treat teenagers like the semi-adults they are, and try to be helpful instead of self-righteous.

"I'm cool with kids having sex if they're being careful," says Rothenberg. "But they have to understand the possible emotional consequences and the health consequences."

Yeah, it was nice having prom dates who made no sexual demands, and having boyfriends instead of sexual hookups. But times have changed, and, to be helpful to teens living in a more sexualized world, the adults have to change too.

READING AND DISCUSSION QUESTIONS

1. Did McCarthy choose to use an inductive or a deductive approach to her subject?

2. Do you find the conclusions that McCarthy has drawn about today's teens convincing? Are they discredited by your own observations of teens?

3. Do you feel that there are any logical fallacies in McCarthy's argument? If so, what type of fallacies are they?

WRITING SUGGESTIONS

4. Examine how teen dating and/or sex habits are characterized on at least one current television show.

5. How do you respond to McCarthy's indictment of teens' sexual mores?

Food for Thought (and for Credit)

JENNIFER GROSSMAN

Want to combat the epidemic of obesity? Bring back home economics. Before you choke on your 300-calorie, trans-fat-laden Krispy Kreme, consider: Teaching basic nutrition and food preparation is a far less radical remedy than gastric bypass surgery or fast-food lawsuits. And probably far more effective. Obesity tends to invite such drastic solutions because it is so frustratingly difficult to treat. This intractability, coupled with the sad fact that obese children commonly grow up to be obese adults, argues for a preventative approach. As the new school year begins, we need to equip kids with the skills and practical knowledge to take control of their dietary destinies.

Despite its bad rep as Wife Ed 101, home economics has progressive roots. At the turn of the century it "helped transform domesticity into a vehicle to expand women's political power," according to Sarah Stage in *Rethinking Home Economics: Women and the History of a Profession.* In time, focus shifted from social reform to the practical priorities of sanitation and electrification, and then again to an emphasis on homemaking after World War II—giving ammunition to later critics like Betty Friedan who charged home ec with having helped foster the "feminine mystique."

Banished by feminists, Becky Home-ecky was left to wander backwater school districts. For a while it seemed that mandating male participation might salvage the discipline while satisfying political correctness. By the late 1970s one-third of male high school graduates had some home-ec training, whereas they comprised a mere 3.5 percent of home-ec students in 1962. Since then, "home economics has moved from the mainstream to the margins of American high school," according to the United States Department of Education, with even female participation—near universal in the 1950s—plummeting by 67 percent.

What has happened since? Ronald McDonald and Colonel Sanders stepped in as the new mascots of American food culture, while the number of meals consumed outside the home has doubled—from a quarter in 1970 to nearly half today. As a result, market economics has increasingly determined ingredients, nutrient content, and portion size. Agricultural surpluses and technological breakthroughs supplied the

Jennifer Grossman is director of the Dole Nutrition Institute, which distributes health information to the public through lectures and publications. Formerly, she was director of Education Policy at the Cato Institute and a speechwriter for President George H. W. Bush. She appears frequently as a commentator on shows such as *Larry King Live*, the *O'Reilly Factor*, the *Today Show*, and *Politically Incorrect*. She has written editorials for the *New York Times*, where this column appeared on September 2, 2003; the *Wall Street Journal*; the *Los Angeles Times*; the *New York Post*; the *Weekly Standard*; the *National Review*; and the *Women's Quarterly*.

cheap sweeteners and hydrogenated oils necessary for food to survive indefinitely on store shelves or under fast-food heat lamps.

Unsurprisingly, the caloric density of such foods soared relative to 5 those consumed at home. Good value no longer meant taste, presentation, and proper nutrition—but merely more-for-less. Thus, the serving of McDonald's French fries that contained 200 calories in 1960 contains 610 today. The lure of large was not limited to fast-food, inflating everything from snack foods to cereal boxes.

But the hunger for home economics didn't die with its academic exile. Martha Stewart made millions filling the void, vexing home-ec haters like Erica Jong for having "earned her freedom by glorifying the slavery of home." Home and Garden TV, the Food Network, and countless publications thrive on topics once taught by home ec.

All of which begs the question: If the free market has done such a good job of picking up the slack, why bring home ec back? Because much of the D.I.Y. (do-it-yourself) culture is divorced from the exigencies of everyday life. It's more like home rec: catering to pampered chefs with maids to clean up the kitchen.

The new home economics should be both pragmatic and egalitarian. Traditional topics—food and nutrition, family studies, home management—should be retooled for the twenty-first century. Children should be able to decipher headlines about the dangers of dioxin or the benefits of antioxidants. Subjects like home finance might include domestic problem-solving: How would you spend $100 to feed a family of four, including a diabetic, a nursing mother, and infant, for one week?

While this kind of training might most benefit those low-income minority children at highest risk of obesity, all children will be better equipped to make smart choices in the face of the more than $33 billion that food companies spend annually to promote their products. And consumer education is just part of the larger purpose: to teach kids to think, make, fix, and generally fend for themselves.

Some detractors will doubtless smell a plot to turn women back into 10 stitching, stirring Stepford Wives. Others will argue that schools should focus on the basics. But what could be more basic than life, food, home and hearth? A generation has grown up since we swept home ec into the dust heap of history and hung up our brooms. It's time to reevaluate the domestic discipline, and recapture lost skills.

READING AND DISCUSSION QUESTIONS

1. How would the students at the high school you attended have responded to a course such as the one Grossman describes?

2. Do you think that offering such a course would be a good idea? Why or why not?

3. How convincing is Grossman's argument that there is a need for consumer education? How convincing is her argument that it should be offered in school?

4. Do you feel there are any logical fallacies in her argument? If so, what type of fallacies are they?

WRITING SUGGESTIONS

5. Write a claim of policy essay arguing that the sort of course Grossman describes should be required of high school students.

6. Write an essay refuting what Grossman suggests.

7. Write an essay in which you argue that the majority of teenagers are responsible consumers or that they are not.

DEBATE: Should the federal government fund embryonic stem-cell research?

Use the Body's "Repair Kit": We Must Pursue Research on Embryonic Stem Cells

CHRISTOPHER REEVE

With the life expectancy of average Americans heading as high as 75 to 80 years, it is our responsibility to do everything possible to protect the quality of life of the present and future generations. A critical factor will be what we do with human embryonic stem cells. These cells have the potential to cure diseases and conditions ranging from Parkinson's and multiple sclerosis to diabetes and heart disease, Alzheimer's, Lou Gehrig's disease, even spinal-cord injuries like my own. They have been called the body's self-repair kit.

Their extraordinary potential is a recent discovery. And much basic research needs to be done before they can be sent to the front lines in the battle against disease. But no obstacle should stand in the way of responsible investigation of their possibilities. To that end, the work should be funded and supervised by the federal government through the National Institutes of Health. That will avoid abuses by for-profit corporations, avoid secrecy and destructive competition between laboratories, and en-

---

Christopher Reeve was a well-established actor when in 1995 he was paralyzed from the shoulders down in a riding accident. From that time until his death in 2004, he served as an outspoken and respected advocate for the sort of stem-cell research he believed would eventually help him and others like him. Through his personal example and his books *Still Me* (1999) and *Nothing Is Impossible: Reflections on a New Life* (2002), he offered hope and inspiration to the disabled and others. This article is from the May 1, 2000, edition of *Time*.

sure the widest possible dissemination of scientific breakthroughs. Human trials should be conducted either on the NIH campus or in carefully monitored clinical facilities.

Fortunately, stem cells are readily available and easily harvested. In fertility clinics, women are given a choice of what to do with unused fertilized embryos: they can be discarded, donated to research, or frozen for future use. Under NIH supervision, scientists should be allowed to take cells only from women who freely consent to their use for research. This process would not be open ended; within one to two years a sufficient number could be gathered and made available to investigators. For those reasons, the ban on federally funded human embryonic stem-cell research should be lifted as quickly as possible.

But why has the use of discarded embryos for research suddenly become such an issue? Is it more ethical for a woman to donate unused embryos that will never become human beings, or to let them be tossed away as so much garbage when they could help save thousands of lives?

Treatment with stem cells has already begun. They have been taken   5 from umbilical cords and become healthy red cells used as a potential cure for sickle-cell anemia. Stem-cell therapy is also being used against certain types of cancer. But those are cells that have significantly differentiated; that is, they are no longer pluripotent, or capable of transforming into other cell types. For the true biological miracles that researchers have only begun to foresee, medical science must turn to undifferentiated stem cells. We need to clear the path for them as rapidly as possible.

Controversy over the treatment of certain diseases is nothing new in this country: witness the overwhelming opposition to government funding of AIDS research in the early '80s. For years the issue was a political football—until a massive grass-roots effort forced legislators to respond. Today, the NIH is authorized to spend approximately $1.8 billion annually on new protocols, and the virus is largely under control in the United States.

While we prolong the stem-cell debate, millions continue to suffer. It is time to harness the power of government and go forward.

The Misleading Debate on Stem-Cell Research

MONA CHAREN

Addressing the Democratic National Convention, Ron Reagan told the delegates that in the debate over funding research on embryonic stem cells, we face a choice between "the future and the past; between reason and ignorance; between true compassion and mere ideology." Not satisfied with that contrast, he elaborated that "a few of these folks (who oppose funding this research) are just grinding a political axe, and they should be ashamed of themselves."

It is Reagan who ought to be ashamed. As the mother of a ten-year-old with juvenile diabetes, I yearn more than most for breakthroughs in scientific research. My son takes between four and six shots of insulin daily and must test his blood sugar by pricking his finger the same number of times. This disease affects every major organ system in the body and places him in the high-risk category for more problems than I care to name. When he settles down to sleep at night, I can never be entirely sure that he won't slip into a coma from a sudden low blood sugar. How happily I would take the disease upon myself if I could only spare him! So please don't lecture me about grinding a political axe.

But like millions of others, I am troubled by the idea of embryonic stem-cell research. It crosses a moral line that this society should be loath to cross—even for the best of motives. Taking the stem cells from human embryos kills them. Before turning to the arguments of the pro-research side, permit a word about the pro-life position. Too many pro-life activists, it seems to me, have argued this case on the wrong grounds. My inbox is full of missives about the scientific misfires that stem-cell research has led to, as well as breathless announcements that adult stem cells actually hold more promise.

This is neither an honest nor a productive line of argument. The reason pro-lifers oppose embryonic stem-cell research is because they hold life sacred at all stages of development. They ought not to deny this or dress it up in a lab coat to give it greater palatability. The moral case is an honorable one. Leave it at that.

Proponents of embryonic stem-cell research point out that some of the embryos currently sitting in freezers in fertility clinics around the world are going to be washed down the drain anyway—which surely kills them, and without any benefit to mankind. This is true. There are several

5

Mona Charen is a syndicated columnist whose column appears in over two-hundred newspapers nationwide and a political analyst who for six years was a regular on CNN's *Capital Gang* and *Capital Gang Sunday*. From 1984 to 1986, she worked at the White House as a speechwriter for Nancy Reagan and in the Public Affairs Office. This article appeared on townhall.com in August 2004.

answers to this. The first is that a society that truly honored each human life would take a different approach. Fertility clinics and the couples who use them would understand the moral obligation not to create more embryos than they can reasonably expect to transfer to the mother's uterus. In cases where this was impossible, the embryos could be placed for adoption with other infertile couples (this is already a widespread practice).

Once you begin to pull apart a human embryo and use its parts, you have thoroughly dehumanized it. You have justified taking one life to (speculatively) save another. Despite the rosy future painted by Ron Reagan and others, those of us who follow the field with avid interest have been disappointed by avenues of research that have failed, thus far, to pan out. Still, opponents of stem-cell research should not argue that the research is going to be fruitless. No one knows. The problem is that this kind of research is morally problematic. Germany, Italy, Portugal, Luxembourg, and Austria ban it. (The United States does not. We simply withhold federal funding.)

There is something else, as well. While the idea of growing spare parts — say, spinal nerves for a paraplegic — in a Petri dish seems wonderful, it may not be possible to do so from embryonic stem cells. As the *Wall Street Journal* reported on August 12 [2004], scientists have been frustrated by their inability to get stem cells to grow into endoderm (the cells that make up the liver, stomach, and pancreas), whereas they can coax them to become heart and nerve tissue.

"Scientists speculate," the *Journal* explained, "that might be because the embryo early on needs blood and nerve tissue to grow, while endoderm-based organs aren't needed until later." If we can use the stem cells of normal human embryos for research, by what logic would we shrink from allowing an embryo to reach a later stage of development in order to study better how endoderm forms?

These are treacherous moral waters we're setting sail in, and those who hesitate ought not to be scorned as ignorant, uncompassionate, or blinkered.

DISCUSSION QUESTIONS

1. Do both of these authors use both evidence and appeal to needs and values? Explain. How is your reading of each piece affected by the author's personal circumstances?

2. What is the effect of Reeve's choosing to call stem cells "the body's self-repair kit"? Give other examples of how his word choice either helps or hurts his argument.

3. Is the language that Reeve uses in discussing the embryos different from that used by Charen? How and why?

4. In what other ways does Charen's choice of words affect her argument?

5. Where does each author most directly state the claim of their piece?

TAKING THE DEBATE ONLINE

For these and additional research URLs, see bedfordstmartins.com/rottenberg.

- *NIH Stem Cell Information*
  http://stemcells.nih.gov/index.asp

  The official National Institutes of Health resource for stem-cell research.

- *Remarks by the President on Stem Cell Research*
  www.whitehouse.gov/news/releases/2001/08/20010809-2.html

  A transcript of a radio address given by President George W. Bush on August 9, 2001.

- *Stem Cell Research Foundation*
  www.stemcellresearchfoundation.org/

  The mission of the Stem Cell Research Foundation is to support research into the development of cell therapies to help find treatments and cures for a wide variety of diseases.

- *DoNoHarm: The Coalition of Americans for Research Ethics*
  www.stemcellresearch.org/

  The mission of DoNoHarm is to promote treatments that "do not require the destruction of human life, including the human embryo" and to "support continuation of federal laws prohibiting the federal funding of research that requires the destruction of human life, including the human embryo."

- *The International Society for Stem Cell Research*
  www.isscr.org/mission/index.htm

  The ISSSCR is an independent, nonprofit organization established to promote and foster the exchange and dissemination of information and ideas relating to stem cells.

ASSIGNMENTS FOR UNDERSTANDING INDUCTION, DEDUCTION, AND LOGICAL FALLACIES

1. For practice, decide whether the reasoning in the following examples is faulty. Explain your answers.

   1. The presiding judge of a revolutionary tribunal, on being asked why people were being executed without trial: "Why should we put them on trial when we know that they're guilty?"
   2. Since good nutrition is essential to the health of its citizens, the government should punish people who eat junk food.

3. Children who watch game shows rather than situation comedies receive higher grades in school. So it must be true that game shows are more educational than situation comedies.

4. The meteorologist predicted the wrong amount of rain for May. Obviously the meteorologist is unreliable.

5. Women ought to be permitted to serve in combat. Why should men be the only ones to face death and danger?

6. If Cher uses Equal, it must taste better than Sweet 'n Low.

7. People will gamble anyway, so why not legalize gambling in this state?

8. Because so much money was spent on public education in the last decade while educational achievement declined, more money to improve education can't be the answer to reversing the decline.

9. He's a columnist for the campus newspaper, so he must be a pretty good writer.

10. We tend to exaggerate the need for standard English. You don't need much standard English for most jobs in this country.

11. It's discriminatory to mandate that police officers must conform to a certain height and weight.

12. A doctor can consult books to make a diagnosis, so a medical student should be able to consult books when being tested.

13. Because this soft drink contains so many chemicals, it must be unsafe.

14. Core requirements should be eliminated. After all, students are paying for their education, so they should be able to earn a diploma by choosing the courses they want.

15. We should encourage a return to arranged marriages in this country since marriages based on romantic love haven't been very successful.

16. I know three redheads who have terrible tempers, and since Annabel has red hair, I'll bet she has a terrible temper, too.

17. Supreme Court Justice Byron White was an All-American football player while at college, so how can you say that athletes are dumb?

18. Benjamin H. Sasway, a student at Humboldt State University in California, was indicted for failure to register for possible conscription. Barry Lynn, president of Draft Action, an antidraft group, said, "It is disgraceful that this administration is embarking on an effort to fill the prisons with men of conscience and moral commitment."

19. James A. Harris, former president of the National Education Association: "Twenty-three percent of schoolchildren are failing to graduate, and another large segment graduate as functional illiterates. If 23 percent of anything else failed—23 percent of automobiles didn't run, 23 percent of the buildings fell down, 23 percent of stuffed ham spoiled—we'd look at the producer."

20. A professor at Rutgers University: "The arrest rate for women is rising three times as fast as that of men. Women, inflamed by the doctrines of feminism, are pursuing criminal careers with the same zeal as business and the professions."

21. Physical education should be required because physical activity is healthful.

22. George Meany, former president of the AFL-CIO, in 1968: "To these people who constantly say you have got to listen to these younger people, they have got something to say, I just don't buy that at all. They smoke more pot than we do and if the younger generation are the hundred thousand kids that lay around a field up in Woodstock, New York, I am not going to trust the destiny of the country to that group."

23. That candidate was poor as a child, so he will certainly be sympathetic to the poor if he's elected.

24. When the federal government sent troops into Little Rock, Arkansas, to enforce integration of the public school system, the governor of Arkansas attacked the action, saying that it was as brutal an act of intervention as Russia's sending troops into Hungary to squelch the Hungarians' rebellion. In both cases, the governor said, the rights of a freedom-loving, independent people were being violated.

25. Governor Jones was elected two years ago. Since that time constant examples of corruption and subversion have been unearthed. It is time to get rid of the man responsible for this kind of corrupt government.

26. Are we going to vote a pay increase for our teachers, or are we going to allow our schools to deteriorate into substandard custodial institutions?

27. You see, the priests were right. After we threw those virgins into the volcano, it quit erupting.

28. The people of Rome lost their vitality and desire for freedom when their emperors decided that the way to keep them happy was to provide them with bread and circuses. What can we expect of our own country now that the government gives people free food and there is a constant round of entertainment provided by television?

29. From Mark Clifton, "The Dread Tomato Affliction" (proving that eating tomatoes is dangerous and even deadly): "Ninety-two point four percent of juvenile delinquents have eaten tomatoes. Fifty-seven point one percent of the adult criminals in penitentiaries throughout the United States have eaten tomatoes. Eighty-four percent of all people killed in automobile accidents during the year have eaten tomatoes."

30. From Galileo, *Dialogues Concerning Two New Sciences*: "But can you doubt that air has weight when you have the clear testimony of Aristotle affirming that all elements have weight, including air, and excepting only fire?"

31. Robert Brustein, artistic director of the American Repertory Theatre, commenting on a threat by Congress in 1989 to withhold funding from an offensive art show: "Once we allow lawmakers to become art critics, we take the first step into the world of Ayatollah Khomeini, whose murderous review of *The Satanic Verses* still chills the heart of

everyone committed to free expression." (The Ayatollah Khomeini called for the death of the author, Salman Rushdie, because he had allegedly committed blasphemy against Islam in his novel.)

2. Find the printed text of a major political speech such as a state of the Union address, a major political convention speech, or an inaugural address and analyze its logic. Does it use an inductive approach, a deductive approach, or a combination? What types of support are used? Do you detect any logical fallacies? Write an essay about the speech that supports either a claim of fact or a claim of value.

3. Compare the argument made to Congress by President Roosevelt on the day after the attack on Pearl Harbor in 1941 and the one made by President Bush after the attacks on the World Trade Center and the Pentagon in 2001.

4. Write an essay explaining the logical fallacies in one of the essays from the Readings for Analysis portion of this chapter.

5. Explain in an essay whether you find Paige's or Weaver's argument more convincing and discuss why.

CHAPTER 8

Language and Thought

THE POWER OF WORDS

Words play such a critical role in argument that they deserve special treatment. An important part of successful writers' equipment is a large and active vocabulary, but no single chapter in a book can give this to you; only reading and study can widen your range of word choices. Even in a brief chapter, however, we can point out how words influence the feelings and attitudes of an audience, both favorably and unfavorably.

One kind of language responsible for shaping attitudes and feelings is *emotive language,* language that expresses and arouses emotions. Understanding it and using it effectively are indispensable to the arguer who wants to move an audience to accept a point of view or undertake an action.

Long before you thought about writing your first argument, you learned that words had the power to affect you. Endearments and affectionate and flattering nicknames evoked good feelings about the speaker and yourself. Insulting nicknames and slurs produced dislike for the speaker and bad feelings about yourself. Perhaps you were told, "Sticks and stones may break your bones, but words will never hurt you." But even to a small child it is clear that ugly words are as painful as sticks and stones and that the injuries are sometimes more lasting.

Nowhere is the power of words more obvious and more familiar than in advertising, where the success of a product may depend on the feelings that certain words produce in the prospective buyer. Even the names of products may have emotive significance. In recent years a new industry, composed of consultants who supply names for products, has emerged. Although most manufacturers agree that a good name won't save a poor product, they also recognize that the right name can catch the attention of the public and persuade people to buy a product at least once. According to an article in the *Wall Street Journal,* a product name not only should be memorable but also should "remind people of emotional or physical experiences." One consultant created the name Magnum for a malt liquor from Miller Brewing Company: "The product is aimed at students, minorities, and lower-income customers." The president of the consulting firm says that Magnum "implies strength, masculinity, and more bang for your buck."[1] This naming of products has been called the "Rumpelstiltskin effect," a phrase coined by a linguist. "The whole point," he said, "is that when you have the right name for a thing, you have control over it."[2]

Even scientists recognize the power of words to attract the attention of other scientists and the public to discoveries and theories that might otherwise remain obscure. A good name can even enable the scientist to visualize a new concept. One scientist says that "a good name," such as "quark," "black hole," "big bang," "chaos," or "great attractor," "helps in communicating a theory and can have substantial impact on financing."

It is not hard to see the connection between the use of words in conversation and advertising and the use of emotive language in the more formal arguments you will be writing. Emotive language reveals your approval or disapproval, assigns praise or blame—in other words, makes a judgment about the subject. Keep in mind that unless you are writing purely factual statements, such as scientists write, you will find it hard to avoid expressing judgments. Neutrality does not come easily, even where it may be desirable, as in news stories or reports of historical events. For this reason you need to attend carefully to the statements in your argument, making sure that you have not disguised judgments as statements of fact. Of course, in attempting to prove a claim, you will not be neutral. You will be revealing your judgment about the subject, first in the selection of facts and opinions and the emphasis you give to them and second in the selection of words.

Like the choice of facts and opinions, the choice of words can be effective or ineffective in advancing your argument, moral or immoral in the honesty with which you exercise it. The following discussions offer some insights into recognizing and evaluating the use of emotive language in the arguments you read, as well as into using such language in your own arguments where it is appropriate and avoiding it where it is not.

[1] *Wall Street Journal,* August 5, 1982, p. 19.
[2] *Harvard Magazine,* July–August 1995, p. 18.

CONNOTATION

The connotations of a word are the meanings we attach to it apart from its explicit definition. Because these added meanings derive from our feelings, connotations are one form of emotive language. For example, the word *rat* denotes or points to a kind of rodent, but the attached meanings of "selfish person," "evil-doer," "betrayer," and "traitor" reflect the feelings that have accumulated around the word.

In Chapter 3 we observed that definitions of controversial terms, such as *poverty* and *unemployment*, may vary so widely that writer and reader cannot always be sure that they are thinking of the same thing. A similar problem arises when a writer assumes that the reader shares his or her emotional response to a word. Emotive meanings originate partly in personal experience. The word *home*, defined merely as "a family's place of residence," may suggest love, warmth, and security to one person; it may suggest friction, violence, and alienation to another. The values of the groups to which we belong also influence meaning. Writers and speakers count on cultural associations when they refer to our country, our flag, and heroes and enemies we have never seen. The arguer must also be aware that some apparently neutral words trigger different responses from different groups—words such as *cult, revolution, police, beauty contest,* and *corporation*.

Various reform movements have recognized that words with unfavorable connotations have the power not only to reflect but also to shape our perceptions of things. The words *Negro* and *colored* were rejected by the civil rights movement in the 1960s because they bore painful associations with slavery and discrimination. Instead, the word *black,* which was free from such associations, became the accepted designation; more recently, the Reverend Jesse Jackson suggested another term, *African American,* to reflect ethnic origins. People of "Spanish/Hispanic/Latino" origin (as they are designated on the 2000 census) are now engaged in a debate about the appropriate term for a diverse population of more than 22 million American residents from Mexico, Puerto Rico, Cuba, and more than a dozen Central and South American countries. To some, the word *Hispanic* is unacceptable because it is an anglicization and recalls the colonization of America by Spain and Portugal.

The women's liberation movement also insisted on changes that would bring about improved attitudes toward women. The movement condemned the use of *girl* for a female over the age of eighteen and the use in news stories of descriptive adjectives that emphasized the physical appearance of women. And the homosexual community succeeded in reintroducing the word *gay,* a word current centuries ago, as a substitute for words they considered offensive. Now *queer,* a word long regarded as offensive, has been adopted as a substitute for *gay* by a new generation of gays and lesbians, although it is still considered unacceptable by many members of the homosexual community.

Members of certain occupations have invented terms to confer greater respectability on their work. The work does not change, but the workers hope that public perceptions will change if janitors are called custodians, if garbage collectors are called sanitation engineers, if undertakers are called morticians, if people who sell makeup are called cosmetologists. Events considered unpleasant or unmentionable are sometimes disguised by polite terms, called *euphemisms*. During the 1992 to 1993 recession new terms emerged that disguised, or tried to, the grim fact that thousands of people were being dismissed from their jobs: *skill-mix adjustment, workforce-imbalance correction, redundancy elimination, downsizing, indefinite idling,* even a daring *career-change opportunity.* Many people refuse to use the word *died* and choose *passed away* instead. Some psychologists and physicians use the phrase *negative patient care outcome* for what most of us would call *death*. Even when referring to their pets, some people cannot bring themselves to say *put to death* but substitute *put to sleep* or *put down*. In place of a term to describe an act of sexual intercourse, some people use *slept together* or *went to bed together* or *had an affair.*

Polite words are not always so harmless. If a euphemism disguises a shameful event or condition, it is morally irresponsible to use it to mislead the reader into believing that the shameful condition does not exist. In his powerful essay "Politics and the English Language" George Orwell pointed out that politicians and reporters have sometimes used terms like "pacification" or "rectification of frontiers" to conceal acts that result in torture and death for millions of people. An example of such usage was cited by a member of Amnesty International, a group monitoring human rights violations throughout the world. He objected to a news report describing camps in which the Chinese were promoting "reeducation through labor." This term, he wrote, "makes these institutions seem like a cross between Police Athletic League and Civilian Conservation Corps camps." On the contrary, he went on, the reality of "reeducation through labor" was that the victims were confined to "rather unpleasant prison camps." The details he offered about the conditions under which people lived and worked gave substance to his claim.[3] More recently, when news organizations referred to the expulsion of Romanian gypsies from Germany as part of a "deportation treaty," an official of Germany's press agency objected to the use of the word *deportation*. "You must know that by using words such as *deportation* you are causing great sadness. . . . We prefer that you use the term *readmission* or *retransfer*."[4]

Some of the most interesting changes in language usage occur in modern Bible translations. The vocabulary and syntax of earlier versions have been greatly simplified to make the Bible more accessible to that half of the American public who cannot read above eighth-grade level. Another change responds to arguments by feminists, environmentalists, and

---

[3] Letter to the *New York Times,* August 30, 1982, p. 25.
[4] *International Herald Tribune,* November 5, 1992.

multiculturalists for more "inclusive language." God is no longer the *Father,* human beings no longer have *dominion* over creation, and even the word *blindness* as a metaphor for sin or evil has been replaced by other metaphors.

Perhaps the most striking examples of the way that connotations influence our perceptions of reality occur when people are asked to respond to questions of poll-takers. Sociologists and students of poll-taking know that the phrasing of a question, or the choice of words, can affect the answers and even undermine the validity of the poll. In one case poll-takers first asked a selected group of people if they favored continuing the welfare system. The majority answered no. But when the poll-takers asked if they favored government aid to the poor, the majority answered yes. Although the terms *welfare* and *government aid to the poor* refer to essentially the same forms of government assistance, *welfare* has acquired for many people negative connotations of corruption and shiftless recipients.

In a *New York Times*/CBS poll conducted in January 1998, "a representative sample of Americans were asked which statement came nearer to their opinion: 'Is abortion the same thing as murdering a child, or is abortion not murder because the fetus really isn't a child?'" Thirty-eight percent chose "the fetus really isn't a child." But 58 percent, including a third of those who chose "abortion is the same thing as murdering a child," agreed that abortion "was sometimes the best course in a bad situation." The author of the report suggests an explanation of the fact that a majority of those polled seemed to have chosen "murder" as an acceptable solution to an unwanted pregnancy:

> These replies reveal, at least, a considerable moral confusion.
>
> Or maybe only verbal confusion? Should the question have asked whether abortion came closer, in the respondent's view, to "killing" rather than "murdering" a child? That would leave room for the explanation that Americans, while valuing life, are ultimately not pacifists: killing, they hold, may be justified in certain circumstances (self-defense, warfare, capital punishment).
>
> So one can challenge the wording of the question. Indeed, one can almost always challenge the wording of poll questions. . . . Poll takers themselves acknowledge the difficulty of wording questions and warn against relying too much on any single finding.[5]

This is also true in polls concerning rape, another highly charged subject. Dr. Neil Malamuth, a psychologist at the University of California at Los Angeles, says, "When men are asked if there is any likelihood they would force a woman to have sex against her will if they could get away with it, about half say they would. But if you ask them if they would rape a woman if they knew they could get away with it, only about 15 percent

---

[5] Peter Steinfels, "Beliefs," *New York Times,* January 24, 1998, sec. A, p. 15.

say they would." The men who change their answers aren't aware that "the only difference is in the words used to describe the same act."[6]

The wording of an argument is crucial. Because readers may interpret the words you use on the basis of feelings different from your own, you must support your word choices with definitions and with evidence that allows readers to determine how and why you made them.

SLANTING

Slanting, says one dictionary, is "interpreting or presenting in line with a special interest." The term is almost always used in a negative sense. It means that the arguer has selected facts and words with favorable or unfavorable connotations to create the impression that no alternative view exists or can be defended. For some questions it is true that no alternative view is worthy of presentation, and emotionally charged language to defend or attack a position that is clearly right or wrong would be entirely appropriate. We aren't neutral, nor should we be, about the tragic abuse of human rights anywhere in the world or even about less serious infractions of the law, such as drunk driving or vandalism, and we should use strong language to express our disapproval of these practices.

Most of your arguments, however, will concern controversial questions about which people of goodwill can argue on both sides. In such cases, your own judgments should be restrained. Slanting will suggest a prejudice—that is, a judgment made without regard to all the facts. Unfortunately, you may not always be aware of your bias or special interest; you may believe that your position is the only correct one. You may also feel the need to communicate a passionate belief about a serious problem. But if you are interested in persuading a reader to accept your belief and to act on it, you must also ask: If the reader is not sympathetic, how will he or she respond? Will he or she perceive my words as "loaded"— one-sided and prejudicial—and my view as slanted?

R. D. Laing, a Scottish psychiatrist, defined *prayer* in this way: "Someone is gibbering away on his knees, talking to someone who is not there."[7] This description probably reflects a sincerely held belief. Laing also clearly intended it for an audience that already agreed with him. But the phrases "gibbering away" and "someone who is not there" would be offensive to people for whom prayer is sacred.

The following remarks by one writer attacking another appeared in *Salon,* an online magazine:

[6] *New York Times,* August 29, 1989, sec. C, p. 1.
[7] "The Obvious," in David Cooper, ed. *The Dialectics of Liberation* (Penguin Books, 1968), p. 17.

> Urging the hyperbolic *Salon* columnist David Horowitz to calm down and cite facts instead of spewing insults seems as pointless as asking a dog not to defecate on the sidewalk. In either instance, the result is always and predictably the same: Somebody has to clean up a stinking pile.[8]

An audience, whether friendly or unfriendly, interested in a discussion of the issues, would probably be both embarrassed and repelled by this use of language in a serious argument.

In the mid-1980s an English environmental group, London Greenpeace, began to distribute leaflets accusing the McDonald's restaurants of a wide assortment of crimes. The leaflets said in part:

> McDollars, McGreedy, McCancer, McMurder, McDisease, McProfits, McDeadly, McHunger, McRipoff, McTorture, McWasteful, McGarbage.
>
> This leaflet is asking you to think for a moment about what lies behind McDonald's clean, bright image. It's got a lot to hide. . . .
>
> McDonald's and Burger King are two of the many U.S. corporations using lethal poisons to destroy vast areas of Central American rain forest to create grazing pastures for cattle to be sent back to the States as burgers and pet food. . . .
>
> What they don't make clear is that a diet high in fat, sugar, animal products and salt . . . and low in fiber, vitamins and minerals — which describes an average McDonald's meal — is linked with cancers of the breast and bowel, and heart disease. . . .[9]

Even readers who share the belief that McDonald's is not a reliable source of good nutrition might feel that London Greenpeace has gone too far, and that the name-calling, loaded words, and exaggeration have damaged the credibility of the attackers more than the reputation of McDonald's.

---

[8] July 6, 2000.

[9] *New York Times,* August 6, 1995, sec. E, p. 7. In 1990 McDonald's sued the group for libel. In June 1997, after the longest libel trial in British history, the judge ruled in favor of the plaintiff, awarding McDonald's £60,000. In March 1999 an appeal partially overturned the verdict, and reduced the damages awarded to McDonald's by approximately one-third.

Selection, Slanting, and Charged Learning

NEWMAN P. BIRK AND GENEVIEVE B. BIRK

A. THE PRINCIPLE OF SELCTION

Before it is expressed in words, our knowledge, both inside and outside, is influenced by the principle of selection. What we know or observe depends on what we notice; that is, what we select, consciously or unconsciously, as worthy of notice or attention. As we observe, the principle of selection determines which facts we take in.

Suppose, for example, that three people, a lumberjack, an artist, and a tree surgeon, are examining a large tree in the forest. Since the tree itself is a complicated object, the number of particulars or facts about it that one could observe would be very great indeed. Which of these facts a particular observer will notice will be a matter of selection, a selection that is determined by his interests and purposes. A lumberjack might be interested in the best way to cut the tree down, cut it up and transport it to the lumber mill. His interest would then determine his principle of selection in observing and thinking about the tree. The artist might consider painting a picture of the tree, and his purpose would furnish his principle of selection. The tree surgeon's professional interest in the physical health of the tree might establish a principle of selection for him. If each man were now required to write an exhaustive, detailed report on every thing he observed about the tree, the facts supplied by each would differ, for each would report those facts that his particular principle of selection led him to notice. . . .[1]

The principle of selection then serves as a kind of sieve or screen through which our knowledge passes before it becomes our knowledge. Since we can't notice everything about a complicated object or situation or action or state of our own consciousness, what we do notice is determined by whatever principle of selection is operating for us at the time we gain the knowledge. . . .

This selection first appeared in *Understanding and Using English* (1972). Together, the Birks also wrote *A Handbook of Grammar, Rhetoric, Mechanics, and Usage* (1976).

[1]Of course, all three observers would probalby report a good many facts in common— the height of the tree, for example, and the size of the trunk. The point we wish to make is that each observer would give us a different impression of the tree because of the different principle of selection that guided his observation. [All notes are the authors.]

B. THE PRINCIPLE OF SLANTING

When we put our knowledge into words, a second process of selection, the process of slanting, takes place. Just as there is something, a rather mysterious principle of selection, which chooses for us what we will notice, and what will then become our knowledge, there is also a principle which operates, with or without our awareness, to select certain facts and feelings from our store of knowledge, and to choose the words and emphasis that we shall use to communicate our meaning.[2] Slanting my be defined as the porcess of selecting (1) knowledge—factual and attitudinal; (2) words; and (3) emphasis, to achieve the intention of the communicator. Slanting is present in some degree in all communication: one may *slant for* (Favorable slanting), *slant against* (unfavorable slanting), or *slant both ways* (balanced shifting). . . .

C. SLANTING BY USE OF EMPHASIS

Slanting by use of the devices of emphasis is unavoidable,[3] for emphasis   5
is simply the giving of stress to subject matter, and so indicating what is important and what is less important. In speech, for example, if we say that Socrates was a wise old man, we can give several slightly different meanings, one by stressing wise, another by stressing old, another by giving equal stress to wise and old, and still another by giving chief stress to man. Each different stress gives a different slant (favorable or unfavorable or balanced) to the statement because it conveys a different attitude toward Socrates or a different judgement of him. Connectives and word order also slant by the emphasis they give: Consider the difference in slanting or emphasis produced *by old but wise, old and wise, wise but old.* In writing, we cannot indicate subtle stresses on words as clearly as in speech, but we can achieve our emphasis and so can slant by the use of more complex patterns of word order, by marks of punctuation that indicate short or long pauses and so give light or heavy emphasis. Question marks, quotation marks, and exclamation points can also contribute to slanting.[4] It is impossible either in speech or in writing to put two facts about a man, his awkwardness and his strength, we subtly slant those facts favorably or unfavorably in whatever way we may choose to join them.

---

[2] Notice that the "principle of selection" is at work as *we take in* knowledge, and that slanting occurs *as we express* our knowledge in words.

[3] When emphasis is present—and we can think of no instance in the use of language in which it is not—it necessarily influences the meaning by playing a part in the favorable, unfavorable, or balanced slant of the communicator. We are likely to emphasize by voice stress, even when we answer *yes* or *no* to simple questions.

[4] Consider the slanting achieved by punctuation in the following sentences: He called the Senator an honest man? *He* called the Senator an honest man? He called the Senator an honest man! He said one more such "honest" senator would corrupt the state.

More Favorable Slanting	*Less Favorable Slanting*
He is awkward and strong.	He is strong and awkward.
He is awkward but strong.	He is strong but awkward.
Although he is somewhat awkward, he is very strong.	He may be strong, but he's very awkward.

With more facts and in longer passages it is possible to maintain a delicate balance by alternating favorable emphasis and so producing a balanced effect

All communication, then, is in some degree slanted by the *emphasis* of the communicator.

D. SLANTING BY SELECTION OF FACTS

To illustrate the technique of slanting by selection of facts, we shall examine three passages of informative writing which achieve different effects simply by the selection and emphasis of material. Each passage is made up of true statements or facts about a dog, yet the reader is given three different impressions. The first passage is an example of objective writing or balanced slanting, the second is slanted unfavorably, and the third is slanted favorably.

1. Balanced Presentation

Our dog, Toddy, sold to us as a cocker, produces various reactions in various people. Those who come to the back door she usually growls and barks at (a milkman has said that he is afraid of her); those who come to the front door, she whines at and paws; also she tries to lick people's faces unless we have forestalled her by putting a newspaper in her mouth. (Some of our friends encourage these actions; others discourage them. Mrs. Firmly, one friend, slaps the dog with a newspaper and says, "I know how hard dogs are to train.") Toddy knows and responds to a number of words and phrases, and guests sometimes remark that she is a "very intelligent dog." She has fleas in the summer, and she sheds, at times copiously, the year round. Her blonde hairs are conspicuous when they are on people's clothing or on rugs or furniture. Her color and her large brown eyes frequently produce favorable comment. An expert on cockers would say that her ears are too short and set too high and that she is at least six ounds too heavy.

The passage above is made up of facts, verifiable facts,[5] deliberately selected and emphasized to produce a *balanced* impression. Of course not

[5] *Verifiable* facts are facts that can be checked and agreed upon and proved to be true by people who wish to verify them. That a particular theme received a failing grade is a verifiable fact; one needs merely to see the theme with the grade on it. That the instructor should have failed the theme or not, strictly speaking, a verifiable fact, but a matter of opinion. That women on the average live longer than men is a verifiable fact; that they live better is a matter of opinion, *a value judgement.*

all the facts about the dog have been given—to supply *all* the facts on any subject, even such a comparatively simple one, would be an almost impossible task. Both favorable and unfavorable facts are used, however, and an effort has been made to alternate favorable and unfavorable details so that neither will receive greater emphasis by position, proportion, or grammatical structure.

2. Facts Slanted Against

> That dog put her paws on my white dress as soon as I came in the door, and she made so much noise that it was two minutes before she had quieted down enough for us to talk and hear each other. Then the gas man came and she did a great deal of barking. And her hairs are on the rug and on the furniture. If you wear a dark dress they stick to it like lint. When Mrs. Firmly came in, she actually hit the dog with a newspaper to make it stay down, and she made some remark about training dogs. I wish the Birks would take the hint or get rid of that noisy, shorteared, overweight "cocker" of theirs.

This unfavorably slanted version is based on the same facts, but now these facts have been selected and given a new emphasis. The speaker, using her selected facts to give her impression of the dog, is quite possibly unaware of her negative slanting.

Now for a favorably slanted version:

3. Facts Slanted For

> What a lively and responsible dog! When I walked in the door, there she was with a newspaper in her mouth, whining and standing on her hind legs and wagging her tail all at the same time. And what an intelligent dog. If you suggest going for a walk, she will get her collar from the kitchen and hand it to you, and she brings Mrs. Birk's slippers whenever Mrs. Birk says she is "tired" or mentions slippers. At a command she catches balls, rolls over, "speaks," or stands on her hind feet and twirls around. She sits up and balances a piece of bread on her nose until she is told to take it; then she tosses it up and catches it. If you are eating something, she sits up in front of you and "begs" with those big dark brown eyes set in that light, buff-colored face of hers. When I got up to go and told her I was leaving, she rolled her eyes at me and sat up like a squirrel. She certainly is a lively and intelligent dog.

Speaker 3, like Speaker 2, is selecting from the "facts" summarized in balance version 1, and is emphasizing his facts to communicate his impression.

All three passages are examples of *reporting* (i.e., consist only of verifiable facts), yet they give three very different impressions of the same dog because of the different ways the speakers slanted the facts. Some people say that figures don't lie, and many people believe that if they have the "facts," they have the "truth," Yet if we carefully examine the ways of thought and language, we see that any knowledge that comes to us through words has been subjected to the double screening of the principle of selection and the slanting of language. . . .

Wise listeners and readers realize that the double screening that is produced by the principle of selection and by slanting takes place even when people honestly try to report the facts as they know them. (Speakers 2 and 3, for instance, probably thought of themselves as simply giving information about a dog and were not deliberately trying to mislead.) Wise listeners and readers know too that deliberate manipulators of language, by mere selection and emphasis, can make the slanted facts appear to support almost any cause.

In arriving at opinions and values we cannot always be sure that the facts that sift into our minds through language are representative and relevant and true. We need to remember that much of our information about politics, governmental activities, business conditions, and foreign affairs comes to us selected and slanted. More than we realize, our opinions on these matters may depend on what newspaper we read or what news commentator we listen to. Worthwhile opinions call for knowledge of reliable facts and reasonable arguments for and against—and such opinions include beliefs about morality and truth and religion as well as about public affairs. Because complex subjects involve knowing and dealing with many facts on both sides, reliable judgements are at best difficult to arrive at. If we want to be fairminded, we must be willing to subject our opinions to continual testing by new knowledge, and must realize that after all they *are* opinions, more or less trustworthy. Their trustworthiness will depend on the representativeness of our facts, on the quality of our reasoning, and on the standard of values that we choose to apply.

We shall not give here a passage illustrating the unscrupulous slanting of facts. Such a passage would also include irrelevant facts and false statements presented as facts, along with various subtle distortions of fact. Yet to the uninformed reader the passage would be indistinguisable from a passage intended to give a fair account. If two passages (2 and 3) of casual and unintentional slanting of facts about a dog can give such contradictory impressions of a simple subject, the reader can imagine what a skilled and designing manipulation of facts and statistics could do to mislead an uninformed reader about a really complex subject. An example of such manipulation might be the account of the United States that Soviet propaganda has supplied to the average Russian. Such propaganda, however, would go beyond the mere slanting of the facts: It would clothe the selected facts in charged words and would make use of the many other devices of slanting that appear in charged language.

E. SLANTING BY USE OF CHARGED WORDS

In the passages describing the dog Toddy, we were illustrating the tech- 15
nique of slanting by the selection and emphasis of facts. Though the facts
selected had to be expressed in words, the words chosen were as factual
as possible, and it was the selection and emphasis of facts and not of
words that was mainly responsible for the two distinctly different impressions of the dog. In the passages below we are demonstrating another
way of slanting—by the use of charged words. This time the accounts are
very similiar in the facts they contain; the different impressions of the
subject, Corlyn, are produced not by different facts but by the subtle selection of charged words.

The passages were written by a clever student who was told to choose
as his subject a person in action, and to write two descriptions, each using
the "same facts." The instructions required that one description be
slanted positively and the other negatively, so that the first would make
the reader favorably inclined toward the person and the action, and the
second would make him unfavorably inclined.

Here is the favorably charged description. Read it carefully and form
your opinion of the person before you go on to read the second description.

Corlyn

Corlyn paused at the entrance to the room and glanced about. A well-
cut black dress draped subtly about her slender form. Her long blonde
hair gave her chiseled features the simple frame they required. She
smiled an engaging smile as she accepted a cigarette from her escort. As
he lit it for her she looked over the flame and into his eyes. Corlyn had
that rare talent of making every male feel that he was the only man in
the world.

She took his arm and they descended the steps into the room. She
walked with an effortless grace and spoke with equal ease. They each took
a cup of coffee and joined a group of friends near the fire. The flickering
light danced across her face and lent an ethereal quality to her beauty.
The good conversation, the crackling logs, and the stimulating coffee
gave her a feeling of internal warmth. Her eyes danced with each leap of
the flames.

Taken by itself this passage might seem just a description of an attractive girl. The favorable slanting by use of charged words has been
done so skillfully that it is inconspicuous. Now we turn to the unfavorable slanted description of the "same" girl in the "same" actions:

Corlyn

Corlyn halted at the entrance to the room and looked around. A plain black dress hung on her thin frame. Her stringy bleached hair accentuated her harsh features. She smiled an inane smile as she took a cigarette from her escort. As he lit it for her she stared over the lighter and into his eyes. Corlyn had a habit of making every male feel that he was the last man on earth.

She grasped his arm and they walked down the steps and into the room. Her pace was fast and ungainly, as was her speed. They each reached for some coffee and broke into a group of acquaintances near the fire. The flickering light played across her face and revealed every flaw. The loud talk, the fire, and the coffee she had gulped down made her feel hot. Her eyes grew more red with each leap of the flames.

When the reader compares these two descriptions, he can see how charged words influence the reader's attitude. One needs to read the two descriptions several times to appreciate all the subtle differences between them. Words, some rather heavily charged, others innocent-looking but lightly charged, work together to carry to the reader a judgement of a person and a situation. If the reader had seen only the first description of Corlyn, he might well have thought that he had formed his "own judgement on the basis of the facts." And the examples just given only begin to suggest the techniques that may be used in heavily charged language. For one thing, the two descriptions of Corlyn contain no really good example of the use of charged abstraction; for another, the writer was obligated by the assignment to use the same set of facts and so could not slant by selecting his material.

F. SLANTING AND CHARGED LANGUAGE

. . . When slanting the facts, or words, or emphasis, or any combination of the three *significantly influences* feelings toward, or judgements about, a subject, the language used is charged language. . . . 20

Of course communications vary in the amount of charge they carry and in their effort on different people; what is very favorably charged for one person may have little or no charge, or may even be adversely charged, for others. It is sometimes hard to distinguish between charged and uncharged expression. But it is safe to say that whenever we wish to convey any kind of inner knowledge—feelings, attitudes, judgements, values—we are obliged to convey that attitudinal meaning through the medium of charged language; and when we wish to understand the inside knowledge of others, we have to interpret the charged language that they choose, or are obliged to use. Charged language, then, is the natural and necessary medium for the communication of charged or attitudinal meaning. At times we have difficulty in living with it, but we should have even greater difficulty in living without it.

Some of the difficulties in living with charged language are caused by its use in dishonest propaganda, in some editorials, in many political speeches, in most advertising, in certain kinds of effusive salesmanship, and in blatantly insincere, or exaggerated, or sentimental expressions of emotion. Other difficulties are caused by the misunderstandings and misinterpretations that charged language produces. A charged phrase misinterpreted in a love letter; a charged word spoken in haste or in anger; an acrimonious argument about religion or politics or athletics or fraternities; the frustating uncertainty produced by the effort to understand the complex attitudinal meaning in a poem or play or a short story—these troubles, all growing out of the use of charged language, may give us the feeling that Robert Louis Stevenson expressed when he said, "The battle goes sore against us to the going down of the sun. . . ."

READING AND DISCUSSION QUESTIONS

1. How do the Birks distinguish between the process of selection and the process of slanting?
2. Explain the three types of slanting described by the Birks and illustrate each with examples from your own experience.
3. According to the Birks, why is charged language unavoidable— and ultimately desirable?

WRITING SUGGESTIONS

4. Choose a printed ad and analyze the use of language, applying the Birks' terminology.
5. Choose one or more editorials or letters to the editor and show how word choice reveals a writer's attitude toward a subject.

We find slanting everywhere, not only in advertising and propaganda, where we expect to find it, but in news stories, which should be strictly neutral in their recounting of events, and in textbooks. In the field of history, for example, it is often difficult for scholars to remain impartial about significant events. Like the rest of us, they may approve or disapprove, and their choice of words will reflect their judgments.

The following passage by a distinguished Catholic historian describes the events surrounding the momentous decision by Henry VIII, king of England, to break with the Roman Catholic Church in 1534, in part because of the Pope's refusal to grant him a divorce from the Catholic princess Catherine of Aragon so that he could marry Anne Boleyn.

The *protracted* delay in receiving an annulment was very *irritating* to the *impulsive* English king. . . . Gradually Henry's former *effusive* loyalty to Rome gave way to a settled conviction of the tyranny of the papal power, and there *rushed* to his mind the recollections of efforts of earlier English rulers to restrict that power. A few *salutary* enactments against the Church might *compel* a favorable decision from the Pope.

Henry seriously opened his campaign against the Roman Church in 1531, when he *frightened* the clergy into paying a fine of over half a million dollars for violating an *obsolete* statute . . . and in the same year he *forced* the clergy to recognize himself as supreme head of the Church. . . .

His *subservient* Parliament then empowered him to stop the payments of annates to the Pope and to appoint bishops in England without recourse to the papacy. *Without waiting longer* for the decision from Rome, he had Cranmer, *one of his own creatures,* whom he had just named Archbishop of Canterbury, declare his marriage null and void. . . .

Yet Henry VIII encountered considerable *opposition* from the *higher clergy,* from the monks, and from many *intellectual leaders.* . . . A *popular uprising*—the Pilgrimage of Grace—was *sternly* suppressed, and such men as the *brilliant* Sir Thomas More and John Fisher, the *aged* and *saintly* bishop of Rochester, were beheaded because they retained their former belief in papal supremacy.[10] [Italics added]

In the first paragraph the italicized words help make the following points: that Henry was rash, impulsive, and insincere and that he was intent on punishing the church (the word *salutary* means healthful or beneficial and is used sarcastically). In the second paragraph the choice of words stresses Henry's use of force and the cowardly submission of his followers. In the third paragraph the adjectives describing the opposition to Henry's campaign and those who were executed emphasize Henry's cruelty and despotism. Within the limits of this brief passage the author has offered support for his strong indictment of Henry VIII's actions, both in defining the statute as obsolete and in describing the popular opposition. In a longer exposition you would expect to find a more elaborate justification with facts and authoritative opinion from other sources.

The advocate of a position in an argument, unlike the reporter or the historian, must express a judgment, but the preceding examples demonstrate how the arguer should use language to avoid or minimize slanting and to persuade readers that he or she has come to a conclusion after careful analysis. The careful arguer must not conceal his or her judgments by presenting them as if they were statements of fact, but must offer convincing support for his or her choice of words and respect the audience's feelings and attitudes by using temperate language.

---

[10]Carlton J. H. Hayes, *A Political and Cultural History of Modern Europe,* vol. 1 (New York: Macmillan, 1933), pp. 172–73.

Depending on the circumstances, *exaggeration* can be defined, in the words of one writer, as "a form of lying." An essay in *Time* magazine, "Watching Out for Loaded Words," points to the danger for the arguer in relying on exaggerated language as an essential part of the argument.

> The trouble with loaded words is they tend to short-circuit thought. While they may describe something, they simultaneously try to seduce the mind into accepting a prefabricated opinion about the something described.[11]

PICTURESQUE LANGUAGE

Picturesque language consists of words that produce images in the mind of the reader. Students sometimes assume that vivid picture-making language is the exclusive instrument of novelists and poets, but writers of arguments can also avail themselves of such devices to heighten the impact of their messages.

Picturesque language can do more than render a scene. It shares with other kinds of emotive language the power to express and arouse deep feelings. Like a fine painting or photograph, it can draw readers into the picture where they partake of the writer's experience as if they were also present. Such power may be used to delight, to instruct, or to horrify. In 1741 the Puritan preacher Jonathan Edwards delivered his sermon "Sinners in the Hands of an Angry God," in which people were likened to repulsive spiders hanging over the flames of Hell to be dropped into the fire whenever a wrathful God was pleased to release them. The congregation's reaction to Edwards's picture of the everlasting horrors to be suffered in the netherworld included panic, fainting, hysteria, and convulsions. Subsequently Edwards lost his pulpit in Massachusetts, in part as a consequence of his success at provoking such uncontrollable terror among his congregation.

Language as intense and vivid as Edwards's emerges from very strong emotion about a deeply felt cause. In an argument against abortion, a surgeon recounts a horrifying experience as if it were a scene in a movie.

> You walk toward the bus stop. . . . It is all so familiar. All at once you step on something soft. You feel it with your foot. Even through your shoe you may have the sense of something unusual, something marked by a special "give." It is a foreignness upon the pavement. Instinct pulls your foot away in an awkward little movement. You look down, and you see . . . a tiny naked body, its arms and legs flung apart, its head thrown back, its mouth agape, its face serious. A bird, you think, fallen from the nest. But there is no nest here on 73rd Street, no bird so big. It

---

[11] *Time*, May 24, 1982, p. 86.

is rubber, then. A model, a . . . a joke. And you bend to see. Because you must. And it is no joke. Such a gray softness can be but one thing. It is a baby, and dead. You cover your mouth, your eyes. You are fixed. Horror has found its chink and crawled in, and you will never be the same as you were. Years later you will step from a sidewalk to a lawn, and you will start at its softness and think of that upon which you have just trod.[12]

Here the use of the pronoun *you* serves to draw readers into the scene and intensify their experience.

The rules governing the use of picturesque language are the same as those governing other kinds of emotive language. Is the language appropriate? Is it too strong, too colorful for the purpose of the message? Does it result in slanting or distortion? What will its impact be on a hostile or indifferent audience? Will they be angered, repelled? Will they cease to read or listen if the imagery is too disturbing?

We expect strong language in arguments about life and death. For subjects about which your feelings are not so passionate, your choice of words will be more moderate. The excerpt below, from an article arguing against repeal of Sunday closing laws, creates a sympathetic picture of a market-free Sunday. Most readers, even those who oppose Sunday closing laws, would enjoy the picture and perhaps react more favorably to the argument.

Think of waking in the city on Sunday. Although most people no longer worship in the morning, the city itself has a reverential air. It comes to life slowly, even reluctantly, as traffic lights blink their orders to empty streets. Next, joggers venture forth, people out to get the paper, families going to church or grandma's. Soon the city is its Sunday self: People cavort with their children, discuss, make repairs, go to museums, gambol. Few people go to work, and any shopping is incidental. The city on Sunday is a place outside the market. Play dominates, not the economy.[13]

CONCRETE AND ABSTRACT LANGUAGE

Writers of argument need to be aware of another use of language—the distinction between concrete and abstract. Concrete words point to real objects and real experiences. Abstract words express qualities apart from particular things and events. *Beautiful roses* is concrete; we can see, touch, and smell them. *Beauty* in the eye of the beholder is abstract; we can

[12] Richard Selzer, *Mortal Lessons: Notes on the Art of Surgery* (New York: Simon and Schuster, 1974), pp. 153–54.

[13] Robert K. Manoff, "New York City, It Is Argued, Faces 'Sunday Imperialism,'" *New York Times,* January 2, 1977, sec. 4, p. 13.

speak of the quality of beauty without reference to a particular object or event. *Returning money found in the street to the owner, although no one has seen the discovery* is concrete. *Honesty* is abstract. In abstracting we separate a quality shared by a number of objects or events, however different from each other the individual objects or events may be.

Writing that describes or tells a story leans heavily on concrete language. Although arguments also rely on the vividness of concrete language, they use abstract terms far more extensively than other kinds of writing. Using abstractions effectively, especially in arguments of value and policy, is important for two reasons: (1) Abstractions represent the qualities, characteristics, and values that the writer is explaining, defending, or attacking; and (2) they enable the writer to make generalizations about his or her data. Equally important is knowing when to avoid abstractions that obscure the message.

In some textbook discussions of language, abstractions are treated as inferior to concrete and specific words, but such a distinction is misleading. Abstractions allow us to make sense of our experience, to come to conclusions about the meaning of the bewildering variety of emotions and events we confront throughout a lifetime. One writer summarized his early history as follows: "My elementary school had the effect of *destroying any intellectual motivation,* of *stifling* all *creativity,* of *inhibiting personal relationships* with either my teachers or my peers" (emphasis added). Writing in the humanities and in some social and physical sciences would be impossible without recourse to abstractions that express qualities, values, and conditions.

You should not, however, expect abstract terms alone to carry the emotional content of your message. The effect of even the most suggestive words can be enhanced by details, examples, and anecdotes. One mode of expression is not superior to the other; both abstractions and concrete detail work together to produce clear, persuasive argument. This is especially true when the meanings assigned to abstract terms vary from reader to reader.

In establishing claims based on the support of values, for example, you may use such abstract terms as *religion, duty, freedom, peace, progress, justice, equality, democracy,* and *pursuit of happiness.* You can assume that some of these words are associated with the same ideas and emotions for almost all readers; others require further explanation. Suppose you write, "We have made great progress in the last fifty years." One dictionary defines *progress* as "a gradual betterment," another abstraction. How will you define "gradual betterment" for your readers? Can you be sure that they have in mind the same references for progress that you do? If not, misunderstandings are inevitable. You may offer examples: supersonic planes, computers, shopping malls, nuclear energy. Many of your readers will react favorably to the mention of these innovations, which to them represent progress; others, for whom these inventions represent change but not progress, will react unfavorably. You may not be able to convince all of your readers that "we have made great progress," but all of them will now understand what you mean by "progress." And intelligent disagreement is preferable to misunderstanding.

Abstractions tell us what conclusions we have arrived at; details tell us how we got there. But there are dangers in either too many details or too many abstractions. For example, a writer may present only concrete data without telling readers what conclusions are to be drawn from them. Suppose you read the following:

> To Chinese road-users, traffic police are part of the grass . . . and neither they nor the rules they're supposed to enforce are paid the least attention. . . . Ignoring traffic-lights is only one peculiarity of Chinese traffic. It's normal for a pedestrian to walk straight out into a stream of cars without so much as lifting his head; and goodness knows how many Chinese cyclists I've almost killed as they have shot blindly in front of me across busy main roads.[14]

These details would constitute no more than interesting gossip until we read, "It's not so much a sign of ignorance or recklessness . . . but of fatalism." The details of specific behavior have now acquired a significance expressed in the abstraction *fatalism*.

A more common problem, however, in using abstractions is omission of details. Either the writer is not a skilled observer and cannot provide the details, or he or she feels that such details are too small and quiet compared to the grand sounds made by abstract terms. These grand sounds, unfortunately, cannot compensate for the lack of clarity and liveliness. Lacking detailed support, abstract words may be misinterpreted. They may also represent ideas that are so vague as to be meaningless. Sometimes they function illegitimately as short cuts (discussed on pp. 335–42), arousing emotions but unaccompanied by good reasons for their use. The following paragraph exhibits some of these common faults. How would you translate it into clear English?

> We respectively petition, request, and entreat that due and adequate provision be made, this day and the date hereinafter subscribed, for the satisfying of these petitioners' nutritional requirements and for the organizing of such methods of allocation and distribution as may be deemed necessary and proper to assure the reception by and for said petitioners of such quantities of baked cereal products as shall, in the judgment of the aforesaid petitioners, constitute a sufficient supply thereof.[15]

If you had trouble decoding this, it was because there were almost no concrete references—the homely words *baked* and *cereal* leap out of the paragraph like English signposts in a foreign country—and too many

---

[14] Philip Short, "The Chinese and the Russians," *The Listener*, April 8, 1982, p. 6.
[15] *New York Times*, May 10, 1977, p. 35.

long words or words of Latin origin when simple words would do: *requirements* instead of *needs, petition* instead of *ask*. An absence of concrete references and an excess of long Latinate words can have a depressing effect on both writer and reader. The writer may be in danger of losing the thread of the argument, the reader at a loss to discover the message.

The paragraph above, according to James B. Minor, a lawyer who teaches courses in legal drafting, is "how a federal regulation writer would probably write, 'Give us this day our daily bread.'" This brief sentence with its short, familiar words and its origin in the Lord's Prayer has a deep emotional effect. The paragraph composed by Minor deadens any emotional impact because of its preponderance of abstract terms and its lack of connection with the world of our senses.

That passage was invented to educate writers in the government bureaucracy to avoid inflated prose. But writing of this kind is not uncommon among professional writers, including academics. If the subject matter is unfamiliar and the writer an acknowledged expert, you may have to expend a special effort in penetrating the language. But you may also rightly wonder if the writer is making unreasonable demands on you.

> The human race is now entering upon a new phase of evolutionary consciousness and progress, a phase in which, impelled by the forces of evolution itself, it must converge upon itself and convert itself into one single human organism infused by a reconciliation of knowing and being in their inner unity and destined to make a qualitative leap into a higher form of consciousness as we know it, or otherwise destroy itself. For the entire universe is one vast field, potential for incarnation, and achieving incandescence here and there of reason and spirit. And in the whole world of *quality* with which by the nature of our minds we necessarily make contact, we here and there apprehend preeminent value. This can be achieved only if we recognize that we are unable to focus our attention on the particulars of the whole, without diminishing our comprehension of the whole, and of course, conversely, we can focus on the whole only by diminishing our comprehension of the particulars which constitute the whole.[16]

You probably found this paragraph even more baffling than the previous example. Although there is some glimmer of meaning here—that mankind must attain a higher level of consciousness, or perish—you should ask whether the extraordinary overload of abstract terms is justified. In fact, most readers would be disinclined to sit still for an argument with so little reference to the real world. One critic of social science prose maintains that if preeminent thinkers like Bertrand Russell can make themselves clear but social scientists continue to be obscure, "then you can justifiably suspect that it might all be nonsense."[17]

---

[16] Ruth Nanda Anshen, "Credo Perspectives," introduction to James Bryant Conant, *Two Modes of Thought* (New York: Simon and Schuster, 1964), p. x.

[17] Stanislav Andreski, *Social Sciences as Sorcery* (New York: St. Martin's Press, 1972), p. 86.

Finally, there are the moral implications of using abstractions that conceal a disagreeable reality. George Orwell pointed them out more than forty years ago in "Politics and the English Language." Another essayist, Joseph Wood Krutch, in criticizing the attitude that cheating "doesn't really hurt anybody," observed, "'It really doesn't hurt anybody' means it doesn't do that abstraction called society any harm." The following news story reports a proposal with which Orwell and Krutch might have agreed. His intention, says the author, is to "slow the hand of any President who might be tempted to unleash a nuclear attack."

> It has long been feared that a President could be making his fateful decision while at a "psychological distance" from the victims of a nuclear barrage; that he would be in a clean, air-conditioned room, surrounded by well-scrubbed aides, all talking in abstract terms about appropriate military responses in an international crisis, and that he might well push to the back of his mind the realization that hundreds of millions of people would be exterminated.
>
> So Roger Fisher, professor of law at Harvard University, offers a simple suggestion to make the stakes more real. He would put the codes needed to fire nuclear weapons in a little capsule, and implant the capsule next to the heart of a volunteer, who would carry a big butcher knife as he accompanied the President everywhere. If the President ever wanted to fire nuclear weapons, he would first have to kill, with his own hands, that human being.
>
> He has to look at someone and realize what death is—what an innocent death is. "It's reality brought home," says Professor Fisher.[18]

The moral lesson is clear: It is much easier to do harm if we convince ourselves that the object of the injury is only an abstraction.

SHORT CUTS

Short cuts are arguments that depend on readers' responses to words. Short cuts, like other devices we have discussed so far, are a common use of emotive language but are often mistaken for valid argument.

Although they have power to move us, these abbreviated substitutes for argument avoid the hard work necessary to provide facts, expert opinion, and analysis of warrants. Even experts, however, can be guilty of using short cuts, and the writer who consults an authority should be alert to that authority's use of language. Two of the most common uses of short cuts are clichés and slogans.

---

[18] *New York Times,* September 7, 1982, sec. C, p. 1.

■ Clichés

"I'm against sloppy, emotional thinking. I'm against fashionable think-ing. I'm against the whole cliché of the moment."[19] This statement by the late Herman Kahn, the founder of the Hudson Institute, a famous think tank, serves as the text for this section. A cliché is an expression or idea grown stale through overuse. Clichés in language are tired expressions that have faded like old photographs; readers no longer see anything when clichés are placed before them. Clichés include phrases like "cradle of civilization," "few and far between," "rude awakening," "follow in the footsteps of," "fly in the ointment."

But more important to recognize and avoid are clichés of thought. A cliché of thought may be likened to a formula, which one dictionary de-fines as "any conventional rule or method for doing something, espe-cially when used, applied, or repeated without thought." Clichés of thought represent ready-made answers to questions, stereotyped solu-tions to problems, "knee-jerk" reactions. Two writers who call these forms of expression "mass language" describe it this way: "Mass language is lan-guage which presents the reader with a response he is expected to make without giving him adequate reason for having this response."[20] These "clichés of the moment" are often expressed in single words or phrases. For example, the term "Generation Y" has been repeated so often that it has come to represent an undisputed truth about a huge age group from 12 to 18 who are supposed to share the same primitive tastes in enter-tainment. But, in fact, moviemakers attempting to capitalize on their al-leged preferences for horror and teen romance have discovered that "There is no way to program them." One of the teenagers says, "Our gen-eration is very diverse."[21]

Certain cultural attitudes encourage the use of clichés. The liberal American tradition has been governed by hopeful assumptions about our ability to solve problems. A professor of communications says that "we tell our students that for every problem there must be a solution."[22] But real solutions are hard to come by. In our haste to provide them, to prove that we can be decisive, we may be tempted to produce familiar responses that resemble solutions.

History teaches us that a solution to an old and serious problem is al-most always accompanied by unexpected drawbacks. As the writer quoted in the previous paragraph warns us, "Life is not that simple. There is no

---

[19]*New York Times,* July 8, 1983, sec. B, p. 1.

[20]Richard E. Hughes and P. Albert Duhamel, *Rhetoric: Principles and Usage* (Englewood Cliffs, N.J.: Prentice-Hall, 1962), p. 161.

[21]Bruce Orwall, "It's Hollywood's Turn to Scream," *Wall Street Journal,* August 10, 2001, Bi.

[22]Malcolm O. Sillars, "The New Conservatism and the Teacher of Speech," *Southern Speech Journal* 21 (1956), p. 240.

one answer to a given problem. There are multiple solutions, all with advantages and disadvantages." By solving one problem, we often create another. Automobiles, advanced medical techniques, industrialization, and liberal divorce laws have all contributed to the solution of age-old problems: lack of mobility, disease, poverty, domestic unhappiness. We now see that these solutions bring with them new problems that we nevertheless elect to live with because the advantages seem greater than the disadvantages. A well-known economist puts it this way: "I don't look for solutions; I look for trade-offs. I think the person who asks, 'What is the solution to this problem?' has a fundamental misconception of the way the world works. We have trade-offs, and that's all we have."[23]

This means that we should be skeptical of solutions promising everything and ignoring limitations and criticism. Such solutions have probably gone around many times. Having heard them so often, we are inclined to believe that they have been tried and proven. Thus they escape serious analysis.

Some of these problems and their solutions represent the fashionable thinking to which Kahn objected. They confront us everywhere, like the public personalities who gaze at us week after week from the covers of magazines and tabloid newspapers at the checkout counter in the supermarket. Alarms about the failures of public education, about drug addiction or danger to the environment or teenage pregnancy are sounded throughout the media continuously. The same solutions are advocated again and again: "Back to basics"; "Impose harsher sentences"; "Offer sex education." Their popularity, however, should not prevent us from asking: Are the problems as urgent as their prominence in the media suggests? Are the solutions workable? Does sufficient evidence exist to justify their adoption?

Your arguments will not always propose solutions. They will sometimes provide interpretations of or reasons for social phenomena, especially for recurrent problems. Some explanations have acquired the status of folk wisdom, like proverbs, and careless arguers will offer them as if they needed no further support. One object of stereotyped responses is the problem of juvenile delinquency, which liberals attribute to poverty, lack of community services, meaningless education, and violence on television. Conservatives blame parental permissiveness, decline in religious influence, lack of individual responsibility, lenient courts. Notice that the interpretations of the causes of juvenile delinquency are related to an ideology, to a particular view of the world that may prevent the arguer from recognizing any other way of examining the problem. Other stereotyped explanations for a range of social problems include inequality, competition, self-indulgence, alienation, discrimination, technology, lack of patriotism, excessive governmental regulation, and lack of sufficient

[23]Thomas Sowell, "Manhattan Report" (edited transcript of *Meet the Press*) (New York: International Center for Economic Policy Studies, 1981), p. 10.

governmental regulation. All of these explanations are worthy of consideration, but they must be defined and supported if they are to be used in a thoughtful, well-constructed argument.

Although formulas change with the times, some are unexpectedly hardy and survive long after critics have revealed their weaknesses. Overpopulation is often cited as the cause of poverty, disease, and war. It can be found in the writing of the ancient Greeks 2,500 years ago. "That perspective," says the editor of *Food Monitor*, a journal published by World Hunger Year, Inc., "is so pervasive that most Americans have simply stopped thinking about population and resort to inane clucking of tongues."[24] If the writer offering overpopulation as an explanation for poverty were to look further, he or she would discover that the explanation rested on shaky data. Singapore, the most densely populated country in the world (11,574 persons per square mile) is also one of the richest ($16,500 per capita income per year). Chad, one of the most sparsely populated (11 persons per square mile) is also one of the poorest ($190 per capita income per year).[25] Strictly defined, overpopulation may serve to explain some instances of poverty; obviously it cannot serve as a blanket to cover all or even most instances. "By repeating stock phrases," one columnist reminds us, "we lose the ability, finally, to hear what we are saying."

■ Slogans

> I have always been rather impressed by those people who wear badges stating where they stand on certain issues. The badges have to be small, and therefore the message has to be small, concise, and without elaboration. So it comes out as "I hate something" or "I love something," or ban this or ban that. There isn't space for argument, and I therefore envy the badge-wearer who is so clear-cut about his or her opinions.[26]

The word *slogan* has a picturesque origin. A slogan was the war cry or rallying cry of a Scottish or Irish clan. From that early use it has come to mean a "catchword or rallying motto distinctly associated with a political party or other group" as well as a "catch phrase used to advertise a product."

Slogans, like clichés, are short, undeveloped arguments. They represent abbreviated responses to often complex questions. As a reader you need to be aware that slogans merely call attention to a problem; they cannot offer persuasive proof for a claim in a dozen words or less. As a writer you should avoid the use of slogans that evoke an emotional re-

---

[24] Letter to the *New York Times*, October 4, 1982, sec. A, p. 18.

[25] *World Almanac and Book of Facts*, 1995 (New York: World Almanac, 1995), pp. 754, 818.

[26] Anthony Smith, "Nuclear Power—Why Not?" *The Listener*, October 22, 1981, p. 463.

sponse "without giving [the reader] adequate reason for having this response."

Advertising slogans are the most familiar. Some of them are probably better known than nursery rhymes: "Got milk?" "L'Oréal, because I'm worth it," "Nike, just do it." Advertisements may, of course, rely for their effectiveness on more than slogans. They may also give us interesting and valuable information about products, but most advertisements give us slogans that ignore proof—short cuts substituting for argument.

The persuasive appeal of advertising slogans heavily depends on the connotations associated with products. In Chapter 5 (see p. 173, under "Appeals to Needs and Values"), we discussed the way in which advertisements promise to satisfy our needs and protect our values. Wherever evidence is scarce or nonexistent, the advertiser must persuade us through skillful choice of words and phrases (as well as pictures), especially those that produce pleasurable feelings. "Let it inspire you" is the slogan of a popular liqueur. It suggests a desirable state of being but remains suitably vague about the nature of the inspiration. Another familiar slogan—"Noxzema, clean makeup"—also emphasizes a quality that we approve of, but what is "clean" makeup? Since the advertisers are silent, we are left with warm feelings about the word and not much more.

Advertising slogans are persuasive because their witty phrasing and punchy rhythms produce an automatic yes response. We react to them as we might react to the lyrics of popular songs, and we treat them far less critically than we treat more straightforward and elaborate arguments. Still, the consequences of failing to analyze the slogans of advertisers are usually not serious. You may be tempted to buy a product because you were fascinated by a brilliant slogan, but if the product doesn't satisfy, you can abandon it without much loss. However, ignoring ideological slogans coined by political parties or special-interest groups may carry an enormous price, and the results are not so easily undone.

Ideological slogans, like advertising slogans, depend on the power of connotation, the emotional associations aroused by a word or phrase. In the 1960s and 1970s, a period of well-advertised social change, slogans flourished; they appeared by the hundreds of thousands on buttons, T-shirts, and bumper stickers. One of them read, "Student Power!" To some readers of the slogan, distrustful of young people and worried about student unrest on campuses and in the streets, the suggestion was frightening. To others, mostly students, the idea of power, however undefined, was intoxicating. Notice that "Student Power!" is not an argument; it is only a claim. (It might also represent a warrant.) As a claim, for example, it might take this form: Students at this school should have the power to select the faculty. Of course, the arguer would need to provide the kinds of proof that support his or her claim, something the slogan by itself cannot do. Many people, whether they accepted or rejected the claim, supplied the rest of the argument without knowing exactly what the issues were and how a developed argument would proceed. They were accepting or rejecting the slogan largely on the basis of emotional reaction to words.

American political history is, in fact, a repository of slogans. Leaf through a history of the United States and you will come across "Tippecanoe and Tyler, too," "manifest destiny," "fifty-four forty or fight," "make the world safe for democracy," "the silent majority," "the domino theory," "the missile gap," "the window of vulnerability." Each administration tries to capture the attention and allegiance of the public by coining catchy phrases. Roosevelt's New Deal in 1932 was followed by the Square Deal and the New Frontier. Today, slogans must be carefully selected to avoid offending groups that are sensitive to the ways in which words affect their interests. In 1983 Senator John Glenn, announcing his candidacy for president, talked about bringing "old values and new horizons" to the White House. "New horizons" apparently carried positive connotations. His staff, however, worried that "old values" might suggest racism and sexism to minorities and women.

A professor of politics and international affairs at Princeton University explains why public officials use slogans, despite their obvious shortcomings:

> Officials long have tried to capture complicated events and to dominate public discussion of foreign policy by using simple phrases and slogans. They engage in phrase-making in order to reach wide audiences. . . .
> Slogans and metaphors often express the tendencies of officials and academics who have a common wish to be at once sweeping, unequivocal, easily understood, and persuasive. The desire to capture complicated phenomena through slogans stems also from impatience with the particular and unwillingness or inability to master interrelationships.[27]

Over a period of time slogans, like clichés, can acquire a life of their own and, if they are repeated often enough, come to represent an unchanging truth we no longer need to examine. "Dangerously," says the writer quoted above, "policy makers become prisoners of the slogans they popularize."

Following are two examples. The first is part of the second inaugural address of George C. Wallace, governor of Alabama, in 1971. The second is taken from an article in the *Militia News*, the organ of a group that believed the United States government was engaged in a "satanic conspiracy" to disarm the American people and then enslave them. Timothy McVeigh, who blew up the Oklahoma City federal building in 1995, was influenced by the group.

> The people of the South and those who think like the South, represent the majority viewpoint within our constitutional democracy, but they are not organized and do not speak with a loud voice. Until the day ar-

[27] Henry Bienen, "Slogans Aren't the World," *New York Times*, January 16, 1983, sec. 4, p. 19.

rives when the voice of the people of the South and those who think like us is, within the law, thrust into the face of the bureaucrats, only then can the "people's power" express itself legally and ethically and get results. . . . Too long, oh, too long, has the voice of the people been silenced by their own disruptive government—by governmental bribery in quasi-governmental handouts such as H.E.W. and others that exist in America today! An aroused people can save this nation from those evil forces who seek our destruction. The choice is yours. The hour is growing late![28]

Every gun owner who is the least bit informed knows that those who are behind this conspiracy—who now have their people well placed in political office, in the courts, in the media, and in the schools, are working for the total disarming of the American people and the surrender of our nation and our sovereignty. . . . The time is at hand when men and women must decide whether they are on the side of freedom and justice, the American republic, and Almighty God, or if they are on the side of tyranny and oppression, the New World Order, and Satan.[29]

Whatever power these recommendations might have if their proposals were more clearly formulated, as they stand they are collections of slogans and loaded words. (Even the language falters: Can the voice of the people be thrust into the face of the bureaucrats?) We can visualize some of the slogans as brightly colored banners: "Dislodge Big Money!" "Power to the People!" "Save This Nation from Evil Forces!" "The Choice Is Yours!" Do all the groups mentioned share identical interests? If so, what are they? Given the vagueness of the terms, it is not surprising that arguers on opposite sides of the political spectrum—loosely characterized as liberal and conservative—sometimes resort to the same clichés and slogans: the language of populism, or a belief in conspiracies against God-fearing people, in these examples.

Slogans have numerous shortcomings as substitutes for the development of an argument. First, their brevity presents serious disadvantages. Slogans necessarily ignore exceptions or negative instances that might qualify a claim. They usually speak in absolute terms without describing the circumstances in which a principle or idea might not work. Their claims therefore seem shrill and exaggerated. In addition, brevity prevents the sloganeer from revealing how he or she arrived at conclusions.

Second, slogans may conceal unexamined warrants. When Japanese cars were beginning to compete with American cars, the slogan "Made in America by Americans" appeared on the bumpers of thousands of American-made cars. A thoughtful reader would have discovered in this slogan several implied warrants: American cars are better than Japanese cars; the American economy will improve if we buy American; patriotism

---

[28] Second Inaugural Address as governor of Alabama, January 18, 1971.
[29] Chip Berlet and Matthew N. Lyons, *Right-Wing Populism in America* (New York: Guildford Press, 2000), p. 301.

can be expressed by buying American goods. If the reader were to ask a few probing questions, he or she might find these warrants unconvincing.

Silent warrants that express values hide in other popular and influential slogans. "Pro-life," the slogan of those who oppose abortion, assumes that the fetus is a living being entitled to the same rights as individuals already born. "Pro-choice," the slogan of those who favor abortion, suggests that the freedom of the pregnant woman to choose is the foremost or only consideration. The words *life* and *choice* have been carefully selected to reflect desirable qualities, but the words are only the beginning of the argument.

Third, although slogans may express admirable sentiments, they often fail to tell us how to achieve their objectives. They address us in the imperative mode, ordering us to take an action or refrain from it. But the means of achieving the objectives may be nonexistent or very costly. If the sloganeer cannot offer workable means for implementing his or her goals, he or she risks alienating the audience.

Sloganeering is one of the recognizable attributes of propaganda. Propaganda for both good and bad purposes is a form of slanting, of selecting language and facts to persuade an audience to take a certain action. Even a good cause may be weakened by an unsatisfactory slogan. The slogans of some organizations devoted to fundraising for people with physical handicaps have come under attack for depicting those with handicaps as helpless. According to one critic, the popular slogan "Jerry's kids" promotes the idea that Jerry Lewis is the sole support of children with muscular dystrophy. Perhaps increased sensitivity to the needs of people with disabilities will produce new words and new slogans. If you assume that your audience is sophisticated and alert, you will probably write your strongest arguments, devoid of clichés and slogans.

The Childswap Society

SANDRA FELDMAN

Introduction: reference to a sci-fi story that suggests her subject

Many years ago, when I was a teenager, I read a science fiction story that I've never been able to forget. It came back to me with special force this holiday season because I was thinking about this country's national shame—a child poverty rate of 25 percent—and about our lack of urgency in dealing with the problems this poverty creates.

The subject: the problem of child neglect

Development: the plot of the sci-fi story

The story described a society with a national child lottery which was held every four years. Every child's name was put into it—there were no exceptions—and children were randomly redistributed to new parents, who raised them for the next four years.

Babies were not part of this lottery. Parents got to keep their newborn children until the next lottery, but then they became part of the national childswap. The cycle was broken every third swap and kids were sent back to their original parents until the next lottery. So by the time you were considered an adult, at age twenty-six, the most time you could have spent with your birth parents was ten years. The other sixteen were simply a matter of chance.

The Luck of the Draw

Maybe one of your new parents would be the head of a gigantic multinational company and the most powerful person in the country or the president of a famous university. Or you might find yourself the child of a family living in a public housing project or migrant labor camp.

The whole idea sounded horrible to me, but 5 people in the childswap society took the lottery for granted. They didn't try to hide their children

Sandra Feldman is a former president of the American Federation of Teachers. This essay appeared in the *New York Times* on January 4, 1998, as part of an ongoing "Where We Stand" advertising campaign for the American Federation of Teachers.

343

or send them away to other countries; childswapping was simply part of their culture. And one thing the lottery did was to make the whole society very conscientious about how things were arranged for kids. After all, you never knew where your own child would end up after the next lottery, so in a very real sense everyone's child was—or could be—yours. As a result, children growing up under this system got everything they needed to thrive, both physically and intellectually, and the society itself was harmonious.

Virtues of the childswap society

What if someone wrote a story about what American society in the late twentieth century takes for granted in the arrangements for its children? We might not want to admit it, but don't we take for granted that some kids are going to have much better lives than others? Of course. We take for granted that some will get the best medical treatment and others will be able to get little or none. We take for granted that some kids will go to beautiful, well-cared-for schools with top-notch curriculums, excellent libraries, and computers for every child and others will go to schools where there are not enough desks and textbooks to go around—wretched places where even the toilets don't work.

Further development and support: contrast of the childswap society with American society

(Implicit warrant: All children are entitled to decent lives.)

We take for granted that teachers in wealthy suburban schools will be better paid and better trained than those in poor inner-city or rural schools. We take for granted, in so many ways, that the children whom the lottery of birth has made the most needy will get the least. "After all," we say to ourselves, "it's up to each family to look after its own. If some parents can't give their children what they need to thrive, that's *their* problem."

What Would Happen?

Transition to conclusion

Obviously I'm not suggesting that the United States adopt a childswap system. The idea makes me cringe, and, anyway, it's just a fable. But I like to imagine what would happen if we did.

Conclusion: claim of policy

We'd start with political figures and their children and grandchildren, with governors and mayors and other leaders. What do you suppose

We should treat all children as if they were our own.

would happen when they saw that their children would have the same chance as the sons and daughters of poor people—no more and no less? What would happen to our schools and health-care system—and our shameful national indifference to children who are not ours?

I bet we'd quickly find a way to set things straight and make sure *all* children had an equal chance to thrive. 10

■ Analysis

This essay concerns a serious educational challenge—equalizing opportunities for all children in this country, whatever their social or economic status. This subject might appear in a State of the Union address or another formal public-policy pronouncement before a large audience. In this essay the author has chosen to treat the subject as if she were engaged in a dialogue with the reader, speaking in familiar language that is neither technical, scholarly, nor literary. But despite its informality, it retains the patterns and grammar of written, not spoken, discourse.

Feldman begins with a kind of introduction that you've already encountered in other essays, an anecdote recounting a personal experience. Because this anecdote consumes a third of the essay, we know that the author considers it a crucial element in her appeal. Although no single personal experience unaccompanied by other evidence provides enough support to change public policy, it can gain our attention and arouse suspense. It can be effective in arguments about policies where personal feelings are relevant and where scientific research has little or no influence on the conclusion. And the use of the personal pronoun throughout ("I," "you," and "we")—even if the subject of the essay is not the author, as in this case—can often make a broad generalization seem more immediate.

Other stylistic devices contribute to the informality of the language. Feldman uses contractions such as "didn't," "can't," and "I've" to maintain the closeness to ordinary speech. In addition, she introduces expressions like "I bet" and the word "kids" for children and homely examples, like "even the toilets don't work." She also inserts rhetorical questions—to which she knows the answers—as a way of provoking thought about the issues. Even using "and" and "but" to begin sentences, a practice frowned on in technical and scientific papers, emphasizes the conversational style of the argument.

In a technical or scientific paper expression of the author's personality and feelings might divert attention from the objective research on which a sound conclusion rests. Feldman's language is appropriate for an article on the op-ed page of a newspaper or a column like "My Turn" in *Newsweek*. In an essay on the future of children or, for that matter, on any

Writer's Guide: Choosing Your Words Carefully

1. Be sure you have avoided language with connotations that might produce a negative reaction in your audience that would weaken your argument.
2. If you have used slanted language, consider whether it will advance your argument instead of weakening it.
3. Use picturesque language where appropriate for your purposes.
4. Replace abstract language with concrete language to be more effective.
5. Edit out any clichés or slogans from your early drafts.
6. Achieve a voice that is appropriate for your subject and audience.

subject about human welfare that stirs compassion, the language of personal concern can go far in persuading the reader to sympathize with the arguer and her claim.

READINGS FOR ANALYSIS

Americans Entitled to Cheap Gas—Right?

JOAN RYAN

Over the years, Americans have taken a lot of vicious abuse for being selfish and irresponsible. We are often portrayed as a nation that wants to have its cake and eat it too, which, as any American knows, is patently untrue. We also want our ice cream and maybe some Cool Whip.

I bring this up because, once again, we are the targets of international ridicule, this time for our anger over rising gas prices. Gas is up now to about $2 a gallon around the nation. It is averaging $2.31 in California. These prices are outrageous, as indicated by the newspaper and TV-news stories quoting motorists as saying, "These prices are outrageous."

The rest of the world, however, is not sympathetic. They think that because gas is $5.22 a gallon in England, $4.24 a gallon in Tokyo, and $4.92 a gallon in France, we are being piggy for complaining about per-gallon gas prices that, even with the recent spike, are still cheaper than a Starbucks Frappuccino.

Joan Ryan is a columnist for the *San Francisco Chronicle*, where this column appeared on May 20, 2004.

Apparently the rest of the world doesn't understand the underlying sociological reasons we react as we do to increases in gas prices. Unlike them, we drive cars the size of Paris apartments. They obviously don't realize how much gas cars like these consume! It apparently has come as something of a surprise to many of us, too.

When asked to rank the importance of 56 characteristics they considered when buying a new car, Americans ranked fuel economy 44th. This explains why sport utility vehicles, minivans, and light trucks accounted for 54 percent of all new cars bought last year.

"It's still more important to have the right number of cup holders than high fuel economy," said Art Spinella, director of CNW Marketing Research, which conducted the survey.

Peter Rennert sells cars at John Irish Jeep in San Rafael. He showed a gray Grand Cherokee to a woman one morning earlier this week. She took the slow stroll around the vehicle, opened the doors, checked out the cargo space, took it for a test drive.

"What kind of gas mileage does it get?" she asked Rennert. He showed her the manufacturer's sticker on the window: 17 to 21 miles per gallon highway.

"That was the last I ever heard about it," Rennert said. "People bring it up mostly because they believe they're supposed to." (The woman loved the car and said she'd be back soon with her husband to hammer out a deal.)

To understand Americans, it is essential for the rest of the world to remember that, underneath it all, we are socially responsible beings just like they are, except we like big things and lots of them. In the United States, there are now 204 million cars and 191 million drivers, more cars than we have people to operate them. Blueberry muffins here are the size of our heads. Soda cups are big enough to harbor small children. We build houses designed on the well-known scientific practice of multiplying the number of family members by pi to reach the appropriate number of bathrooms.

If the rest of the world wants to understand us better, I recommend they see the new movie, *Supersize Me!* It's a documentary about a guy who eats nothing but McDonald's food for a month. The movie reinforces what we Americans already know and have known for years: Fast food makes us fat and unhealthy. The movies shows, too, that this knowledge makes no difference whatsoever in our behavior. We still pull up to the golden arches, breathe in that great deep-fry aroma, and order a sack of cholesterol to go.

Why? For the same reasons we buy big cars despite our heartfelt concerns about saving the environment and weaning ourselves from Middle East oil: because it makes us feel good, and because everybody else is doing it.

Across the bay in Richmond, at the ARCO station on Cutting Boulevard and Harbor Way, Sandra Currier filled up her 1998 Chevy Blazer for

$42 the other day. "This is the most I've ever paid," she said of the $2.29 regular unleaded. "It's got to come down."

She is a mobile notary public from Castro Valley who sometimes has to travel as much as 200 miles in a day. She is considering charging more for her services to cover the rising price of gas, but gas is not yet expensive enough to consider trading in her Blazer for something smaller and more fuel-efficient. Maybe when it hits $2.75 a gallon, she said.

"I feel my daughter is safer in the SUV," Currier said. "I don't want to 15 be lower (than everybody else on the road), looking up and getting crunched."

In other words, if everybody else downsized, she would, too. Until then, she's not going to put herself in harm's way by being the poodle on a freeway of water buffalo.

How can the rest of the world blame her? They would do the same under the same circumstances, according to another CNW survey. In Western Europe, respondents said if gas prices were low enough, they would buy SUVs and big sedans, just like the Americans.

"It is kind of amusing," Spinella said. "When we do an international wish list, it's remarkable how similar people are in the kinds of things they would like to get their hands on."

See? There it is. We could be as responsible as the rest of the world if we had the benefit they do of high gas prices. The low price of gas in the United States enables our SUV indulgences. To put this complex social dynamic in the parlance of the latest psychological research: It is not our fault.

Therefore, since this situation is not of our own making, we should 20 not have to pay higher gas prices and give up the big-car life to which we have become accustomed. That would not be right.

And if there is one thing Americans believe in, it is doing what's right.

READING AND DISCUSSION QUESTIONS

1. In the first paragraph, how does Ryan reveal her attitude toward Americans' spending habits?
2. Does Ryan offer any support for her opinion other than her own emotional response to the values of other Americans?
3. How does Ryan's choice of language help her to make her point?
4. Is Ryan's use of sarcasm and exaggeration effective?

WRITING SUGGESTIONS

5. Rewrite Ryan's article using objective language.
6. Choose another one of America's "passions" and write an essay poking gentle fun at it. (Consider, for example, Americans' consumption of fast food.)
7. Compare Ryan's use of language in this piece with that used by Varian in "The True Cost of SUVs" in Chapter 5.

$hotgun Weddings

KATHA POLLITT

What would the government have to do to convince you to get married when you otherwise wouldn't? More than pay you $80 a month, I'll bet, the amount Wisconsin's much-ballyhooed "Bridefare" pilot program offered unwed teen welfare mothers beginning in the early nineties, which is perhaps why then-Governor Tommy Thompson, now Health and Human Services Secretary,[1] was uninterested in having it properly evaluated and why you don't hear much about Bridefare today. OK, how about $100 a month? That's what West Virginia is currently offering to add to a couple's welfare benefits if they wed. But even though the state has simultaneously cut by 25 percent the checks of recipients living with adults to whom they are not married (including, in some cases, their own grown children, if you can believe that!), results have been modest: Only around 1,600 couples have applied for the bonus and presumably some of these would have married anyway. With the state's welfare budget expected to show a $90 million shortfall by 2003, the marriage bonus is likely to be quietly abolished.

Although welfare reform was sold to the public as promoting work, the Personal Responsibility and Work Opportunity Reconciliation Act of 1996 actually opens with the declaration that "marriage is the foundation of a successful society." According to Charles Murray, Robert Rector, and other right-wing ideologues, welfare enabled poor women to rely on the state instead of husbands; forcing them off the dole and into the rigors of low-wage employment would push them into marriage, restore "the family," and lift children out of poverty. That was always a silly idea. For one thing, as any single woman could have told them, it wrongly assumed that whether a woman married was only up to her; for another, it has been well documented that the men available to poor women are also poor and often (like the women) have other problems as well: In one study, 30 percent of poor single fathers were unemployed in the week before the survey and almost 40 percent had been incarcerated; drugs, drink, violence, poor health, and bad attitudes were not uncommon. Would Murray want *his* daughter to marry a guy with even one of those strikes against him? Not surprisingly, there has been no upsurge of marriage among former welfare recipients since 1996. Of all births, the proportion that are to unwed mothers has stayed roughly where it was, at 33 percent.

[1]Thompson resigned on December 3, 2004.

Katha Pollitt has written about controversial moral and political issues for *The Nation*, *The New Yorker*, and the *New York Times*. This selection originally appeared in the February 4, 2002, edition of *The Nation*.

Since the stick of work and the carrot of cash have both proved ineffective in herding women to the altar, family values conservatives are calling for more lectures. Marriage promotion will be a hot item when welfare reform comes up for reauthorization later this year. At the federal level conservatives are calling for 10 percent of all TANF [Temporary Assistance for Needy Families] money to be set aside for promoting marriage; Utah, Arizona, and Oklahoma have already raided TANF to fund such ventures as a "healthy marriage" handbook for couples seeking a marriage license. And it's not just Republicans: Senator Joe Lieberman and Representative Ben Cardin, the ranking Democrat on the House Ways and Means Committee, are also interested in funding "family formation." In place of cash bonuses to individuals, which at least put money in the pockets of poor people, look for massive funding of faith-based marriage preparation courses (and never you mind that pesky separation of church and state), for fatherhood intervention programs, classes to instruct poor single moms in the benefits of marriage (as if they didn't know!), for self-help groups like Marriage Savers, abstinence education for kids and grownups alike and, of course, ingenious pilot projects by the dozen. There's even been a proposal to endow pro-marriage professorships at state universities — and don't forget millions of dollars for evaluation, follow-up, filing and forgetting.

There's nothing wrong with programs that aim to raise people's marital IQ — I love that journalistic evergreen about the engaged couple who take a quiz in order to qualify for a church wedding and call it off when they discover he wants seven kids and she wants to live in a tree. But remember when it was conservatives who argued against social engineering and micromanaging people's private lives and "throwing money at the problem"?

Domestic violence experts have warned that poor women may find   5
themselves pushed into marrying their abusers and staying with them — in a disturbing bit of Senate testimony, Mike McManus of Marriage Savers said domestic violence could usually be overcome with faith-based help. Is that the message women in danger should be getting? But there are even larger issues: Marriage is a deeply personal, intimate matter, involving our most private, barely articulated selves. Why should the government try to maneuver reluctant women into dubious choices just because they are poor? Even as a meal ticket wedlock is no panacea — that marriage is a cure for poverty is only true if you marry someone who isn't poor, who will share his income with you and your children, who won't divorce you later and leave you worse off than ever. The relation between poverty and marriage is virtually the opposite of what pro-marriage ideologues claim: It isn't that getting married gives feckless poor people middle-class values and stability; it's that stable middle-class people are the ones who can "afford" to be married. However marriage functioned a half-century ago, today it is a class marker. Instead of marketing marriage as a poverty program, how much better to invest in poor women — and

poor men—as human beings in their own right: with education, training for high-paying jobs, housing, mental health services, really good childcare for their kids. Every TANF dollar spent on marital propaganda means a dollar less for programs that really help people.

The very fact that welfare reformers are reduced to bribing, cajoling, and guilt-tripping people into marriage should tell us something. Or have they just not hit on the right incentive? As a divorced single mother, I've given some thought to what it would take for me to marry against my own inclination in order to make America great again. Here's my offer: If the government brings Otis Redding back to life and books him to sing at my wedding, I will marry the Devil himself. And if the Devil is unavailable, my ex-husband says he's ready.

READING AND DISCUSSION QUESTIONS

1. What claim is Pollitt supporting in the essay?
2. What does Pollitt reveal about the history of welfare reform as it relates to marriage? Where does Pollitt say the money for welfare reform is going? Where should it go?
3. Where does Pollitt's word choice reveal her bias? Does her own opinion keep her from being fair?

WRITING SUGGESTIONS

4. Write an essay in which you either support or refute Pollitt's claim.
5. If a monetary marriage bonus is not enough to entice many unwed Americans to get married, what might be enough?

The Speech the Graduates Didn't Hear

JACOB NEUSNER

We the faculty take no pride in our educational achievements with you. We have prepared you for a world that does not exist, indeed, that cannot exist. You have spent four years supposing that failure leaves no record. You have learned at Brown that when your work goes poorly, the painless solution is to drop out. But starting now, in the world to which you go, failure marks you. Confronting difficulty by quitting leaves you changed. Outside Brown, quitters are no heroes.

Jacob Neusner, formerly university professor at Brown University and distinguished professor of religious studies at the University of South Florida in Tampa, is now a research professor of religion and theology at Bard College. His speech appeared in Brown's *Daily Herald* on June 12, 1983.

With us you could argue about why your errors were not errors, why mediocre work really was excellent, why you could take pride in routine and slipshod presentation. Most of you, after all, can look back on honor grades for most of what you have done. So, here grades can have meant little in distinguishing the excellent from the ordinary. But tomorrow, in the world to which you go, you had best not defend errors but learn from them. You will be ill-advised to demand praise for what does not deserve it, and abuse those who do not give it.

For four years we created an altogether forgiving world, in which whatever slight effort you gave was all that was demanded. When you did not keep appointments, we made new ones. When your work came in beyond the deadline, we pretended not to care.

Worse still, when you were boring, we acted as if you were saying something important. When you were garrulous and talked to hear yourself talk, we listened as if it mattered. When you tossed on our desks writing upon which you had not labored, we read it and even responded, as though you earned a response. When you were dull, we pretended you were smart. When you were predictable, unimaginative, and routine, we listened as if to new and wonderful things. When you demanded free lunch, we served it. And all this why?

Despite your fantasies, it was not even that we wanted to be liked by you. It was that we did not want to be bothered, and the easy way out was pretense: smiles and easy Bs.

It is conventional to quote in addresses such as these. Let me quote someone you've never heard of: Professor Carter A. Daniel, Rutgers University (*Chronicle of Higher Education,* May 7, 1979):

> College has spoiled you by reading papers that don't deserve to be read, listening to comments that don't deserve a hearing, paying attention even to the lazy, ill-informed, and rude. We had to do it, for the sake of education. But nobody will ever do it again. College has deprived you of adequate preparation for the last fifty years. It has failed you by being easy, free, forgiving, attentive, comfortable, interesting, unchallenging fun. Good luck tomorrow.

That is why, on this commencement day, we have nothing in which to take much pride.

Oh, yes, there is one more thing. Try not to act toward your co-workers and bosses as you have acted toward us. I mean, when they give you what you want but have not earned, don't abuse them, insult them, act out with them your parlous relationships with your parents. This too we have tolerated. It was, as I said, not to be liked. Few professors actually care whether or not they are liked by peer-paralyzed adolescents, fools so shallow as to imagine professors care not about education but about popularity. It was, again, to be rid of you. So go, unlearn the lies we taught you. To Life!

READING AND DISCUSSION QUESTIONS

1. Neusner condemns students for various shortcomings. But what is he saying, both directly and indirectly, about teachers? Find places where he reveals his attitude toward them, perhaps inadvertently.

2. Pick out some of the language devices — connectives, parallel structures, sentence variety — that the author uses effectively.

3. Pick out some of the words and phrases — especially adjectives and verbs — used by Neusner to characterize both students and teachers. Do you think these terms are loaded? Explain.

4. Has the author chosen "facts" to slant his article? If so, point out where slanting occurs. If not, point out where the article seems to be truthful.

5. As a student you will probably object to Neusner's accusations. How would you defend your behavior as a student in answer to his specific charges?

WRITING SUGGESTIONS

6. Rewrite Neusner's article with the same "facts" — or others from your experience — using temperate language and a tone of sadness rather than anger.

7. Write a letter to Neusner responding to his attack. Support or attack his argument by providing evidence from your own experience.

8. Write your own short commencement address. Do some things need to be said that commencement speakers seldom or never express?

9. Write an essay using the same kind of strong language as Neusner uses about some aspect of your education of which you disapprove. Or write a letter to a teacher using the same form as "The Speech the Graduates Didn't Hear."

Tightening the Nuts and Bolts of Death by Electric Chair

A. C. SOUD JR., with TOM KUNTZ

No one doubts that things went wrong at the execution of Pedro Medina in Florida last March: as thousands of volts of electricity coursed through the murderer's body, flames burst from his face mask, startling the assembled witnesses and prompting a public outcry. But does this unsettling episode mean that execution in Florida's electric chair is cruel and unusual punishment?

A. C. Soud Jr. is a circuit court judge in Jacksonville, Florida. Tom Kuntz writes for the *New York Times,* where this article appeared on August 3, 1997.

No, a Florida circuit court judge ruled last month. In rejecting a death-row in-mate's constitutional challenge, Judge A. C. Soud Jr. provided many details of the mechanics and procedures of electrocution in Florida, along with the rea-soning behind his decision. Excerpts follow.

—Tom Kuntz

The judge upheld Florida's execution procedures, attributing the malfunction at the Medina execution to "unintentional human error" that caused a sponge used to conduct electricity to the inmate's head to ignite inside his headgear. A simi-lar problem was blamed in the fiery execution of Jesse Tafero in 1990. The judge gave details of execution procedures since then:

Findings of Fact

1. . . . There were sixteen executions carried out between the execu-tion of Tafero and the most recent execution of Pedro Medina. There were no changes made in the design to or the material used in the electric chair apparatus during that period of time. No malfunction of the electric chair occurred during the sixteen executions. . . .

2. The procedures used for testing the electric chair and its apparatus   5 have been consistently the same, through the Medina execution, for all seventeen executions since Tafero's execution. The testing procedures in-cluded the testing of the electrical equipment, the meters, the switches, the voltage output, and the amount of amperage created. Testing oc-curred three times before an execution: when the [death] warrant was signed, a week before the scheduled execution, and the day before an execution. . . .

The judge paid particular attention to the preparation of sponges:

3. The procedures for the preparation of the sponges used in an exe-cution have been employed consistently since the Tafero execution. . . . The preparation consisted of soaking one large and two smaller natural sea sponges in a container of water having a 9 percent saline content [salt-water]. The sponges were placed in the saline solution the night before the day of a scheduled execution. The large wet sponge is placed around the inmate's shaved right leg and the leg electrode is then placed on the inmate's right calf. The leg electrode is three-and-a-half inches high and eight inches long shaped in a semicircular fashion. The leg electrode was made of lead. The head piece is principally made of leather. The inside crown of the head piece consists of a brass screen secured by a nut to a high voltage wire, which enters the head piece from the outside. The brass screen is round and measures four inches in diameter. A dry natural sea sponge was laced into the bottom of the brass screen electrode. This component served as the head electrode. The head piece is turned over and one of the two smaller wet sponges is placed on top of the dry sponge in the head piece. The head piece is then turned back to an upright posi-

tion and placed on top of the inmate's head (the brass head electrode was, therefore, separated from the inmate's head by a dry sponge and a wet sponge, in that descending order). The second smaller soaked sponge is left in the soaking solution as a spare.

4. Preparation of inmate Medina was performed in all respects as was performed on the previous sixteen inmates who were executed since the execution of Tafero in 1990, and consisted of the shaving of Medina's head and the application of the normal amount of electroconductive gel to Medina's scalp. The gel is used to further reduce the normal amount of postmortem burning that occurs to the inmate's scalp during the electrocution process. . . .

5. Consistent with the previous sixteen executions, Medina was placed in the electric chair and straps were placed around Medina's chest, abdomen, arms, and legs. Medina's head was firmly secured to the back of the chair using a mouth and chin strap. A large wet (saline soaked) sponge was placed around Medina's right leg and the leg electrode was then strapped to his leg. The head piece, as previously described, was then placed over Medina's head.

6. Pursuant to the standard procedure used by the death chamber   10 team, death was brought on by activating the electrical system, which automatically—by a programmed controlled circuitry—administered three cycles of electricity in the following amounts and durations without interruption:

> First Cycle: High Voltage—2,200 to 2,350 volts—for eight seconds;
>
> Second Cycle: Low Voltage—750 to 1,000 volts—for twenty-two seconds;
>
> Third Cycle: High Voltage—2,200 to 2,350 volts—for eight seconds.

As with the sixteen previous executions, and according to the normal procedures used, the third cycle was manually shut down four seconds into the third cycle.

The switch at the panel box was activated at 7:04 A.M. Electricity was administered to Medina at 7:04.50 A.M. and cut off at 7:05.25 A.M. Electricity was administered continually for 35 seconds. Medina was pronounced dead at 7:10 A.M.

The judge then turned to what went wrong:

7. When Pedro Medina was executed on March 25, 1997, the following events occurred. When the electrical current was activated, within seconds, a little smoke emanated from under the right side of Medina's head piece, followed by a four- to five-inch yellow-orange flame, which lasted four to five seconds and then disappeared. After the flame went out, more smoke emanated from under the head piece to the extent that

the death chamber was filled with smoke—but the smoke was not dense enough to impair visibility. . . .

Although several witnesses to the execution tried to describe the odor 15 of the smoke, only one witness, Florida State prison Superintendent Ronald McAndrews, described the odor as burnt sponge. Mr. McAndrews was the only witness who was subsequently in attendance on April 8, 1997, when two experts appointed by the Governor [Lawton Chiles] were conducting tests on the electric chair apparatus and similarly ignited a dry sponge, resulting in smoke. Mr. McAndrews described both odors as being the same. This court finds that the odor smelled was burnt sponge, not burnt flesh. . . .

There was a further unsettling moment when a physician examined Mr. Medina just after the current was turned off.

Medina's chest was seen to move two or three times in a two- to four-minute period. A couple of witnesses thought Medina was trying to breathe. . . . A neurologist testified that this movement could be caused by the last vestiges of survival in the brain stem after the brain itself has died. . . .

The malfunction was widely reported (journalists are always included among the witnesses in an observation room), and the state ordered an autopsy of Mr. Medina's body:

[The pathologists] concluded in their testimony that Medina's death was instantaneous due to massive depolarization of Medina's brain and brain stem when the initial surge of 2,200 to 2,350 volts of electricity entered Medina's head. [One doctor] described it as "like turning the lights off." . . . Cause of death was further exacerbated by a dramatic rise in the brain's temperature to between 138 degrees Fahrenheit to 148 degrees Fahrenheit. . . .

But other expert witnesses called to testify on behalf of the death-row inmate 20 *seeking to avoid the chair theorized that Mr. Medina might have suffered an agonizing death. The appellant was Leo Alexander Jones, sentenced to death by Judge Soud for the 1981 slaying of a police officer. The judge rejected the alternate theories:*

He suffered no conscious pain. This can be said for all inmates who will be executed in Florida's electric chair hereafter. . . . The Florida electric chair—its apparatus, equipment, and electrical circuitry—is in excellent condition. Testimony in this regard is unrefuted. . . .

But the judge did recommend improvements:

1. The fire and smoke during the Medina execution was the result of the dry sponge laced onto the brass electrode in the head piece catching fire and burning almost completely due to a lack of saline solution in that sponge. The lack of saline solution in the dry sponge caused the dry

sponge to act as a resistor. The resistance produced heat which ignited and consumed the dry sponge.

2. Any future executions should be performed using only one wet sponge in the head piece. . . . The sponge should be thoroughly soaked in a saturated saline solution and not a 9 percent saline solution . . . [to] further reduce any possibility of a reoccurrence of a burning sponge. . . .

[In addition,] although the lead leg electrode was not defective . . . it 25 should be changed from lead to brass, as brass is a better conductor of electricity than lead. . . .

READING AND DISCUSSION QUESTIONS

1. What is your reaction to this objective description of an electrocution? Notice that this description appeared in a ruling by a judge that electrocution was not a violation of the Eighth Amendment's prohibition of cruel and unusual punishment. Does the description's lack of emotional language make the act itself seem less terrible? Explain the reason for your response.

2. Find the places in the report where specific language has been used to depersonalize the act of electrocution and remove emotional connotations. Is this strategy successful in distancing the reader from the actual event?

3. Why do you think the newspaper published this report?

4. If you were revolted by this description, do you think it would make any difference to know the details of the crime(s) that the murderer has committed? Theodore Kaczinski, the Unabomber, wrote in his diary about a secretary who opened a package containing a bomb he had mailed to her boss: "The bomb drove fragments of wood into her flesh. But no indication that she was permanently disabled. Frustrating that I can't seem to make a lethal bomb." Does such a specific reference make you more inclined to favor a death sentence for the bomber, or not?

WRITING SUGGESTIONS

5. Look up "A Hanging" by George Orwell (from *Shooting an Elephant and Other Essays*), a powerful description of an execution Orwell witnessed as an officer in the Indian Imperial Police in Burma. Compare Orwell's treatment of an execution with Soud's treatment in the report you have just read. Choose a claim that establishes the main difference between the two descriptions, and develop two or three points of difference in the language as support for your claim.

6. Write an essay about some incident in your life that taught you an important lesson. You might begin with a statement that summarizes what you learned. Use the language of description and emotion — rich vocabulary, details, metaphors — to make the experience vivid to the reader.

A gun in the home is much more likely to
kill a family member than to kill an intruder.

CEASE FIRE
Think about your family before you think about getting a handgun.

Cease Fire, Inc. P.O. Box 33424, Washington, D.C. 20033-0424.

DISCUSSION QUESTIONS

1. Would this claim of policy be just as successful if the note were excluded? Would additional facts about guns contribute to its effectiveness?

2. Why is the gun so much larger than the printed message?

3. What is the basis of the emotional appeal? Is there more than one? Does the note go too far in exploiting our emotions?

The Right to Bear Arms

WARREN E. BURGER

Our metropolitan centers, and some suburban communities of America, are setting new records for homicides by handguns. Many of our large centers have up to ten times the murder rate of all of Western Europe. In 1988, there were 9,000 handgun murders in America. Last year, Washington, D.C., alone had more than 400 homicides—setting a new record for our capital.

The Constitution of the United States, in its Second Amendment, guarantees a "right of the people to keep and bear arms." However, the meaning of this clause cannot be understood except by looking to the purpose, the setting, and the objectives of the draftsmen. The first ten amendments—the Bill of Rights—were not drafted at Philadelphia in 1787; that document came two years later than the Constitution. Most of the states already had bills of rights, but the Constitution might not have been ratified in 1788 if the states had not had assurances that a national Bill of Rights would soon be added.

People of that day were apprehensive about the new "monster" national government presented to them, and this helps explain the language and purpose of the Second Amendment. A few lines after the First Amendment's guarantees—against "establishment of religion," "free exercise" of religion, free speech and free press—came a guarantee that grew out of the deep-seated fear of a "national" or "standing" army. The same First Congress that approved the right to keep and bear arms also limited the national army to 840 men; Congress in the Second Amendment then provided:

> A well regulated Militia, being necessary to the security of a free State, the right of the people to keep and bear Arms, shall not be infringed.

In the 1789 debate in Congress on James Madison's proposed Bill of Rights, Elbridge Gerry argued that a state militia was necessary:

> to prevent the establishment of a standing army, the bane of liberty. . . . Whenever governments mean to invade the rights and liberties of the people, they always attempt to destroy the militia in order to raise an army upon their ruins.

We see that the need for a state militia was the predicate of the "right" guaranteed; in short, it was declared "necessary" in order to have 5

Warren E. Burger (1907–1995) was chief justice of the United States from 1969 to 1986. This article is from the January 14, 1990, issue of *Parade* magazine.

a state military force to protect the security of the state. That Second Amendment clause must be read as though the word "because" was the opening word of the guarantee. Today, of course, the "state militia" serves a very different purpose. A huge national defense establishment has taken over the role of the militia of 200 years ago.

Some have exploited these ancient concerns, blurring sporting guns — rifles, shotguns, and even machine pistols — with all firearms, including what are now called "Saturday night specials." There is, of course, a great difference between sporting guns and handguns. Some regulation of handguns has long been accepted as imperative; laws relating to "concealed weapons" are common. That we may be "overregulated" in some areas of life has never held us back from more regulation of automobiles, airplanes, motorboats, and "concealed weapons."

Let's look at the history.

First, many of the 3.5 million people living in the thirteen original Colonies depended on wild game for food, and a good many of them required firearms for their defense from marauding Indians — and later from the French and English. Underlying all these needs was an important concept that each able-bodied man in each of the thirteen independent states had to help or defend his state.

The early opposition to the idea of national or standing armies was maintained under the Articles of Confederation; that confederation had no standing army and wanted none. The state militia — essentially a part-time citizen army, as in Switzerland today — was the only kind of "army" they wanted. From the time of the Declaration of Independence through the victory at Yorktown in 1781, George Washington, as the commander in chief of these volunteer-militia armies, had to depend upon the states to send those volunteers.

When a company of New Jersey militia volunteers reported for duty 10 to Washington at Valley Forge, the men initially declined to take an oath to "the United States," maintaining, "Our country is New Jersey." Massachusetts Bay men, Virginians, and others felt the same way. To the American of the eighteenth century, his state was his country, and his freedom was defended by his militia.

The victory at Yorktown — and the ratification of the Bill of Rights a decade later — did not change people's attitudes about a national army. They had lived for years under the notion that each state would maintain its own military establishment, and the seaboard states had their own navies as well. These people, and their fathers and grandfathers before them, remembered how monarchs had used standing armies to oppress their ancestors in Europe. Americans wanted no part of this. A state militia, like a rifle and powder horn, was as much a part of life as the automobile is today; pistols were largely for officers, aristocrats — and dueling.

Against this background, it was not surprising that the provision concerning firearms emerged in very simple terms with the significant predicate—basing the right on the *necessity* for a "well regulated militia," a state army.

In the two centuries since then—with two world wars and some lesser ones—it has become clear, sadly, that we have no choice but to maintain a standing national army while still maintaining a "militia" by way of the National Guard, which can be swiftly integrated into the national defense forces.

Americans also have a right to defend their homes, and we need not challenge that. Nor does anyone seriously question that the Constitution protects the right of hunters to own and keep sporting guns for hunting game any more than anyone would challenge the right to own and keep fishing rods and other equipment for fishing—or to own automobiles. To "keep and bear arms" for hunting today is essentially a recreational activity and not an imperative of survival, as it was 200 years ago; "Saturday night specials" and machine guns are not recreational weapons and surely are as much in need of regulation as motor vehicles.

Americans should ask themselves a few questions. The Constitution 15 does not mention automobiles or motorboats, but the right to keep and own an automobile is beyond question; equally beyond question is the power of the state to regulate the purchase or the transfer of such vehicle and the right to license the vehicle and the driver with reasonable standards. In some places, even a bicycle must be registered, as must some household dogs.

If we are to stop this mindless homicidal carnage, is it unreasonable:

1. to provide that, to acquire a firearm, an application be made reciting age, residence, employment, and any prior criminal convictions?

2. to require that this application lie on the table for ten days (absent a showing for urgent need) before the license would be issued?

3. that the transfer of a firearm be made essentially as that of a motor vehicle?

4. to have a "ballistic fingerprint" of the firearm made by the manufacturer and filed with the license record so that, if a bullet is found in a victim's body, law enforcement might be helped in finding the culprit?

These are the kinds of questions the American people must answer if we are to preserve the "domestic tranquility" promised in the Constitution.

A God-Given Natural Right

ROGER D. McGRATH

I do not believe in unilateral disarmament: not for the nation; not for our citizens. Neither did the Founding Fathers. They were students of history, especially of classical antiquity. They knew the history of the Greek city-states and Rome as well as they knew the history of the American colonies. This led them to conclude that an armed citizenry is essential to the preservation of freedom and democracy. Once disarmed, populations either submit meekly to tyrants or fight in vain.

The ancient Greeks knew this. The Greek city-state of Laconia had a population that was five percent Spartan (the warrior aristocracy), one percent *perioeci* (small merchants and craftsmen), and 94 percent *helots* (serfs bound to the soil). It is no mystery how five percent of the population kept 94 percent of the people enslaved. The *helots* were kept disarmed and, if found in possession of a weapon, were put to death.

Meanwhile, most of the Greek city-states were bastions of democracy because they had developed strong middle classes of armed citizens known as *hoplites*. Supplying their own weapons and equipment, the *hoplites* went into battle not out of fear of punishment or in hopes of plunder and booty, as did subject peoples of the Oriental empires, but to defend their liberties and to protect hearth and home. They fought side by side with neighbors, brothers, fathers, sons, uncles, and cousins. They did their utmost to demonstrate courage, side by side with their comrades in arms. If they lost a battle to the armies of an Oriental despot, they stood to lose everything—property, freedom, democracy. A defeat for subject peoples usually meant nothing more than a change of rulers.

The ancient Romans also knew this. When Tarquin, the Etruscan king of Rome, issued an order—for the public good, for safety and security—that the Romans be disarmed, they rose in rebellion. Tarquin was driven from the city, and the early Roman Republic was established. For several hundred years, Rome was defended not by a professional army of mercenaries or subject peoples but by armed citizen-soldiers who left the farm from time to time to serve the republic. Once the system broke down, the Roman Republic was transformed into an empire similar to the despotic regimes of the East.

For fifteen years, Roger McGrath taught courses in the history of the American West, California, and the United States at UCLA. He now teaches at California State University, Northridge, and is a captain in the Naval Detachment of the California State Military Reserve. His articles have appeared in the *Wall Street Journal*, *American Guardian*, *Chronicles*, the *New York Times*, and *Harper's*, among others, and he appears extensively in documentaries about the West and has served as a consultant for television and movies. He is the author of *Gunfighters, Highwaymen, and Vigilantes* (1984) and coauthor of *Violence in America* (1989). This article appeared in the October 2003 issue of *Chronicles*.

Death and destruction commonly followed disarmament. England   5
did it to the Gaels—the Irish and Scots—and the consequences beggar
description. England had been fighting in Ireland for hundreds of years
by the time the English got Irish leader Patrick Sarsfield to sign the Treaty
of Limerick in 1691. The treaty guaranteed all Irish full civil, religious,
and property rights. In return, it required that Sarsfield and more than
20,000 of his soldiers leave Ireland for the Continent.

With the armed defenders of Ireland overseas, England began to ab-
rogate the rights supposedly guaranteed by the treaty. Beginning in 1709,
England passed the statutes that collectively became known as the Penal
Laws. One of the first of these laws declared that, for public safety, no
Irish Catholic could keep and bear arms. Then the Irish Catholic was denied the right to an education, to enter a profession, to hold public office,
to engage in trade or commerce, to own a horse of greater value than five
pounds, to purchase or lease land, to vote, to attend the worship of his
choice, to send his children abroad to receive an education. By the time
the last of the Penal Laws was enacted, the Irish, although they were not
chattel property, in many ways had fewer rights than black slaves in
America. The Irish were kept on a near starvation diet, and their life expectancy was the lowest in the Western world.

Things were not much better in the Highlands of Scotland. England
had subdued the Lowlands by the fourteenth century, but the Highlands,
the truly Gaelic portion of Scotland, continued to be troublesome well
into the eighteenth century. A major rebellion erupted in 1715; another,
in 1745. The end for the Highlanders came at the Battle of Culloden in
1746. Following the battle, the English built a series of forts across the
Highlands and passed laws for the Highlanders—who were originally
Irish, of course—similar to the Penal Laws. England made it a crime for
the Highlanders to wear kilts, play bagpipes, and keep and bear arms. A
Highlander found with a claymore or any other kind of sword or arm was
put to death. The English army, understanding that it is easier to starve a
fierce enemy into submission than to fight him, eagerly slaughtered the
cattle herds of the Highlands, precipitating a great starvation. Thousands
of Highlanders died or fled. The English later engaged in the infamous
"clearances" in which thousands more were driven from the land. Without arms, the Highlanders were helpless.

What the English did to the Irish and Scots was not lost on our
Founding Fathers or on the colonists in general. More than a quarter of
the colonists were Irish or Scottish or Scotch-Irish. When England tried to
disarm the American colonists, all under the guise of preserving public
order and peace, the colonists reacted violently. While it is rarely taught
in schools today, the reason the British army marched to Lexington and
Concord was to confiscate the arms caches of the local citizenry.

It is not by accident, then, that the Framers of the Constitution ensured that the government could not infringe on "the right of the people
to keep and bear arms." It is important to understand that the Second

Amendment grants no right to the people to keep and bear arms. This is a point misunderstood by most Americans today, even by most of those who are interested in keeping their guns.

The Second Amendment, like the First, recognizes a God-given, nat-   10
ural right of the people and guarantees that the government not interfere with the exercise of that right. Note the wording of the amendment. Nowhere does it say, "This Constitution grants the people the right to . . ." Instead, it says "the right of the people . . . shall not be infringed." The right to keep and bear arms, like that of freedom of speech, is known, constitutionally, as an inherent right. By contrast, the Sixth Amendment right to be represented by an attorney in a criminal case is a derivative right—a right that comes from the Constitution.

To understand this is critical to all arguments about guns, or about freedom of speech, or religion, or the press. These freedoms were not given to us by the Founding Fathers. They were recognized by the Founding Fathers as God-given, natural rights that existed long before the establishment of our republic. These rights are not granted to men by a benevolent government but given to man by God. They are not to be destroyed, suppressed, or even compromised. When they are, it is the duty of the citizens to rise in revolt, overthrow the government, and establish a government that will protect these unalienable rights. Sound familiar? It should. This was the philosophy of our Founding Fathers.

The most basic of the natural rights of man is the right to self-preservation, the right to self-defense. No one would deny that we have such a right. In debates at universities and at other public forums, in debates on radio, in debates on television, I have never seen anyone deny that man has a natural right to self-defense. It follows that, if man has a natural right to self-defense, then he has a right to the arms necessary for that self-defense. The right to be armed is a logical and inescapable corollary of the right to self-defense. We cannot have one without the other.

If we do not have the right to the arms necessary for self-defense, then the right of self-defense is purely theoretical—something like having freedom of the press but not being allowed access to a printing press. Can you imagine the National Rifle Association telling the *New York Times* that it has freedom of the press but it may not have printing presses, or that the *Times* can purchase only one printing press per month, or that its writers must undergo background checks by the government, or that it cannot buy ink for the presses in New York City, or that its presses have limits on their speed and capacity, or that its presses must meet certain design requirements? If any of this were suggested, the *Times* would squeal like a stuck pig, and well it should.

Some people, presumably well intentioned, argue that the right to arms (and, thus, the right to self-defense) should be compromised— compromised further than it already has been—in an effort to make society safer. Such a position is ironic on two counts.

First, many of the same people who make gun-restriction arguments, 15 such as the ACLU, would be apoplectic if it were suggested that freedom of speech be curtailed to ensure greater public safety. For example, we could have a two-week waiting period on expressing an opinion after the opinion was duly registered with a government agency. That way, the government could screen the opinion to ensure that it was politically correct.

The compromise-your-rights-for-safety argument is also ironic because the thousands of gun laws on the books—municipal, county, state, and federal—have done nothing to stop crime. In fact, they have done the opposite. The laws, for the most part, have disarmed, or made access to guns more difficult for, the law-abiding, peaceable citizen. Criminals do not turn in their guns. Murderers, rapists, and robbers do not obey gun laws. However, they do calculate the risks involved in committing crime. If they can assume that potential victims are unarmed, they are emboldened and are more likely to attack.

John Lott, in *More Guns Less Crime,* an exhaustive county-by-county study of rates of gun ownership and crime, concludes that the counties with the highest rates of gun ownership have the least crime and that those with the lowest rates of gun ownership have the most crime. For years, this has been obvious when looking at cities. Washington, D.C., and New York City, for example, with the most restrictive gun laws in the nation, have, for a generation, been cesspools of crime. Criminals there know that they can count on their victims being unarmed.

I suspect that even deeply disturbed killers, such as the teenage boys in Littleton, Colorado, understood that they could kill with impunity in the disarmed environment of the high school. The presence of a highly trained, armed security guard, with a reputation as an expert marksman, may have deterred them. If not, then the guard might have granted them their suicidal wish before they were able to commit mass murder. One or two key teachers, trained and armed, might also have made a difference. Certainly, gun laws did nothing to stop the killers. The two boys violated more than a dozen different gun laws, including one of the oldest on the books—possession of a sawed-off shotgun. Gun laws promise much and deliver little, because they affect only the law abiding, something like sheep passing resolutions requiring vegetarianism while wolves circle the flock.

I grew up in Los Angeles when gun laws were few and crime was low. Nearly everyone I knew had a 30.06, a couple of .22s, a shotgun, and a revolver or two sitting around their house. We could buy guns mail-order and pick up our ammunition at the local grocery store. A gun was a common companion to the road maps in the glove compartment of the car. Did this cause crime? In 1952, there were 81 murders in Los Angeles. In 1992, 40 years and many gun laws later, there were 1,092 murders. If the increase in murder had kept pace with the increase in population, there would have been 142 murders, a 75 percent increase. Instead, murder increased 1,350 percent. Other crimes had similar increases: robbery, 1,540 percent; auto theft, 1,100 percent.

The Los Angeles Police Department used to solve more than 90 percent of the murders committed in the city. Today, the figure is 60 percent. Detectives complain that the caseload is too great to conduct the kind of thorough investigations that were common in the '40s and '50s. It is far worse for lesser crimes. Merchants complain that customers brazenly walk out of their stores without paying for merchandise because they know that the police will not respond (at least in a timely fashion) to a call reporting shoplifting. Cars are stolen so often, some 200 per day, that the LAPD does nothing more than list the vehicle on a "hot sheet" and wish the victim good luck.

In the '50s, if your bicycle were stolen, the police would come out to your house and take a report. Try calling the LAPD today and telling them that your bike has been stolen! The police are simply overwhelmed by the sheer volume of crime and are kept fully occupied by murder, armed robbery, and rape—occupied, that is, by the aftermath of murder, armed robbery, and rape. When police arrive at the scene of a crime, the crime has already taken place—the victim has already been murdered, robbed, or raped.

"Carjacking" has become quite common in Los Angeles, because the carjackers know that California drivers cannot legally carry loaded firearms and will nearly always be unarmed. Occasionally, carjackers make poor choices. Three such carjackers followed my friend's son, Justin, as he drove home in his new car late one night. Little did they know that Justin was a reserve police officer. They did not know that he was well armed and an expert marksman.

When Justin pulled into the family driveway and got out of his car, one of the carjackers jumped out of his own vehicle and yelled at Justin, whose back was turned, "Freeze, motherf---er!" It was exactly what Justin had expected. Justin spun about and emptied the contents of his .45 into the carjacker. The carjacker's partners sped away as fast as their car would take them, leaving their good buddy very dead on my friend's front lawn.

Not long after Justin had sent the carjacker to the great salvage yard in the sky, I read of an off-duty police officer who had a similar encounter. On his way home and wearing plainclothes, he stopped to make a phone call. While he stood talking to his wife on an outdoor public phone, two muggers rushed up to him. One of them brandished a gun and said: "Your wallet!" Instead of pulling out his wallet, the cop drew a gun and sent the mugger to the morgue.

The *Los Angeles Times* noted that the mugger certainly picked on the wrong person. This is the same *Los Angeles Times* that regularly editorializes against an armed citizenry and has never seen a gun law that it did not like. Somehow, the newspaper thinks that disarming peaceable, law-abiding citizens will affect criminal behavior for the better. Disarming peaceable, law-abiding citizens *will* affect criminal behavior—but for the worse. Criminals will be emboldened because their chances of picking on the wrong person will be dramatically reduced. Shouldn't the opposite be the case? Shouldn't every person be the wrong person or, at least, potentially the wrong person?

Grandstanding politicians love to rail against the gun. Inanimate objects are good targets to beat up on. That way, politicians do not have to address the real problems in our society. We pay a price for this craven misdirection, though, in thousands of murders, muggings, rapes, robberies, and burglaries.

Yet that is not the greatest danger we face. The Founding Fathers knew that *governments* could turn criminal. That is the principal reason they wanted every man armed: An armed citizenry militates against the development of tyranny. The Founding Fathers did not want every man armed in order to shoot a burglar, although they had nothing against doing so. The Founding Fathers did not want every man armed in order to shoot Bambi or Thumper, although they had nothing against doing so. The Founding Fathers wanted every man armed in order to shoot soldiers or police of tyrannical regimes who suppress the rights of free men.

When governments become criminal, they disarm the populace. Then the numbers of deaths reach the tens of thousands, the hundreds of thousands, the millions. Can't happen? Ask the Irish and the Scots, or the Armenians, the Ukrainians, the Jews, the Chinese, the Cambodians.

In the Marine Corps, I was trained never to surrender my weapon. It was good advice then, and it is good advice now. I shall put my faith not in the goodwill of governments but in an armed citizenry—a band of brothers—steeped in the ideology of the Founding Fathers and the spirit of Patrick Henry, who said: "Is life so dear or peace so sweet as to be purchased at the price of slavery and chains? I know not what course others may take, but as for me, give me liberty or give me death."

DISCUSSION QUESTIONS

1. What does Burger understand the intent of the Second Amendment to have been, in context? How has history changed the way it should now be read?

2. What analogy does Burger make between guns and automobiles? Is his point a good one?

3. What questions does Burger feel Americans should be answering if we are to stop what he calls "this mindless homicidal carnage" (para. 15)?

4. Does McGrath make use of history in the same way and for the same purpose as Burger does? Explain.

5. What does McGrath mean when he says, "It is important to understand that the Second Amendment grants no right to the people to keep and bear arms" (para. 9)?

6. What is the warrant underlying Burger's essay? McGrath's?

7. What is McGrath's response to the claim that restrictions on guns would lead to a safer society?

8. Do you detect any logical fallacies in either essay?

9. Compare the authors' use of language. Do the authors use slanted or emotive language? Short cuts? Where in McGrath's essay is there a shift in the type of language used and why?

TAKING THE DEBATE ONLINE

For these and additional research URLs, see bedfordstmartins.com/rottenberg.

- *Handgun Control*
  www.handguncontrol.org/

  Handgun Control is "a non-partisan, not-for-profit organization that lobbies in favor of common-sense gun regulations at both a state and national level."

- *National Rifle Association of America*
  www.nra.org

  The objective of the National Rifle Association is to protect the right to bear arms. Click here to learn about the NRA's lobbying and legislative activities, youth programs and publications, relevant news articles, and firearms laws.

- *After Columbine*
  www.salon.com/news/special/littleton/

  Salon is an online magazine full of cultural criticism, book and film reviews, and political punditry. Click here for dozens of articles on gun control, the Columbine and Littleton shootings, and the culture of violence in America.

- *GunCite: Gun Control and Second Amendment Issues*
  www.guncite.com/

  GunCite has links to articles arguing against gun control.

- *The Bureau of Alcohol, Tobacco, and Firearms*
  www.atf.treas.gov/

  The Bureau of Alcohol, Tobacco, and Firearms (ATF) is a law enforcement organization within the United States Department of Treasury. Their Web site offers information about the use of firearms in violence, gangs, and youth crime.

ASSIGNMENTS FOR UNDERSTANDING LANGUAGE AND THOUGHT

1. Select one or two related bumper stickers visible in your town or city. Examine the hidden warrants on which they are based, and assess their validity.

2. For a slogan found on a bumper sticker or elsewhere, supply the evidence to support the claim in the slogan. Or find evidence that disproves the claim.

3. Examine a few periodicals from fifty or more years ago. Select either an advertising or a political slogan in one of them, and relate it to beliefs or events of the period. Or tell why the slogan is no longer relevant.

4. Discuss the origin of a cliché or slogan. Describe, as far as possible, the backgrounds and motives of its users.

5. Make up your own slogan for a cause that you support. Explain and defend your slogan.

6. Discuss the appeal to needs and values of some popular advertising or political slogan.

7. Choose a cliché, and find evidence to support or refute it. *Examples:* People were much happier in the past. Mother knows best. Life used to be simpler. Money can't buy happiness.

8. Choose one of the statements in Assignment 7 or another statement, and write a paper telling why you think such a statement remains in use.

9. Select a passage, perhaps from a textbook, written largely in abstractions, and rewrite it using simpler and more concrete language.

10. In watching television dramas about law, medicine, or criminal or medical investigation, do you find that the professional language, some of which you may not fully understand, plays a positive or negative role in your enjoyment of the show? Explain your answer.

11. Listen to a radio or television report of a sports event. Do the announcers use a kind of language, especially jargon, that would not be used in print reports? One critic thinks that sports broadcasting has had a "destructive effect . . . on ordinary American English." Is he right or wrong?

12. Whose argument about the right to bear arms do you find more convincing, Burger's or McGrath's? Explain.

Part Two

Writing, Researching, and Presenting Arguments

CHAPTER 9

Writing an Argumentative Paper

The person who understands how arguments are constructed has an important advantage in today's world. Television commercials, political speeches, newspaper editorials, and magazine advertisements, as well as many communications between individuals, all draw on the principles we have examined in the preceding chapters. By now you should be fairly adept at picking out claims, support, and warrants (explicit or unstated) in these presentations. The next step is to apply your skills to writing an argument of your own. The process of using what you have learned will enhance your ability to analyze critically the marketing efforts with which we are all bombarded every day. Mastering the writing of arguments also gives you a valuable tool for communicating with other people in school, on the job, and even at home.

In this chapter we move through the various stages involved in creating an argumentative paper: choosing a topic, defining the issues, organizing the material, writing the essay, and revising. We also consider the more general question of how to use the principles already discussed in order to convince a real audience. The more carefully you follow the guidelines set out here and the more thought you give to your work at each point, the better you will be able to utilize the art of argument when this course is over.

FINDING AN APPROPRIATE TOPIC

An old British recipe for jugged hare is said to begin, "First, catch your hare." To write an argumentative paper, you first must choose your topic. This is a relatively easy task for someone writing an argument as part of his or her job—a lawyer defending a client, for example, or an advertising executive presenting a campaign. For a student, however, it can be daunting. Which of the many ideas in the world worth debating would make a good subject?

Several guidelines can help you evaluate the possibilities. Perhaps your assignment limits your choices. If you have been asked to write a research paper, you obviously must find a topic on which research is available. If your assignment is more open-ended, you need a topic that is worth the time and effort you expect to invest in it. In either case, your subject should be one that interests you. Don't feel you have to write about what you know—very often finding out what you don't know will turn out to be more satisfying. You should, however, choose a subject that is familiar enough for you to argue about without fearing you're in over your head.

■ Invention Strategies

As a starting point, think of conversations you've had in the past few days or weeks that have involved defending a position. Is there some current political issue you're concerned about? Some dispute with friends that would make a valid paper topic? One of the best sources is controversies in the media. Keep your project in mind as you watch TV, read, or listen to the radio. You may even run into a potential subject in your course reading assignments or classroom discussions. Fortunately for the would-be writer, nearly every human activity includes its share of disagreement.

As you consider possible topics, write them down. One that looks unlikely at first glance may suggest others or may have more appeal when you come back to it later. Further, simply putting words on paper has a way of stimulating the thought processes involved in writing. Even if your ideas are tentative, the act of converting them into phrases or sentences can often help in developing them.

■ Evaluating Possible Topics

Besides interesting you, your topic must interest your audience. Who is the audience? For a lawyer it is usually a judge or jury; for a columnist, anyone who reads the newspaper in which his or her column appears. For the student writer, the audience is to some extent hypothetical. You should assume that your paper is directed at readers who are reasonably intelligent and well informed, but who have no specific knowledge of the subject. It may be useful to imagine you are writing for a local or school publication—this may be the case if your paper turns out well.

Be sure, too, that you choose a topic with two sides. The purpose of an argument is to defend or refute a thesis, which means the thesis must be debatable. In evaluating a subject that looks promising, ask yourself:

Can a case be made for the opposing view? If not, you have no workable ground for building your own case.

Finally, check the scope of your thesis. Consider how long your paper will be, and whether you can do justice to your topic in that amount of space. For example, suppose you want to argue in favor of worldwide nuclear disarmament. Is this a thesis you can support persuasively in a short paper? One way to find out is by listing the potential issues or points about which arguers might disagree. Consider the thesis: "The future of the world is in danger as long as nuclear weapons exist." Obviously this statement is too general. You would have to specify what you mean by the future of the world (the continuation of human life? of all life? of the earth itself?) and exactly how nuclear weapons endanger it before the claim would hold up. You could narrow it down: "Human beings are error-prone; therefore as long as nuclear weapons exist there is the chance that a large number of people will be killed accidentally." Though this statement is more specific and includes an important warrant, it still depends on other unstated warrants: that one human being (or a small group) is in the position to discharge a nuclear weapon capable of killing a large number of people; that such a weapon could, in fact, be discharged by mistake, given current safety systems. Can you expect to show sufficient evidence for these assumptions in the space available to you?

By now it should be apparent that arguing in favor of nuclear disarmament is too broad an undertaking. A more workable approach might be to defend or refute one of the disarmament proposals under consideration by the U.S. Congress, or to show that nuclear weapons pose some specific danger (such as long-term water pollution) that is sufficient reason to strive for disarmament.

Can a thesis be too narrow? Certainly. If this is true of the one you have chosen, you probably realized it when you asked yourself whether the topic was debatable. If you can prove your point convincingly in a paragraph, or even a page, you need a broader thesis.

At this preliminary stage, don't worry if you don't know exactly how to word your thesis. It's useful to write down a few possible phrasings to be sure your topic is one you can work with, but you need not be precise. The information you unearth as you do research will help you to formulate your ideas. Also, stating a thesis in final terms is premature until you know the organization and tone of your paper.

■ To This Point

Let's assume you have surveyed a range of possible topics and chosen one that provides you with a suitable thesis for your paper. Before you go on, check your thesis against the following questions:

1. Is this topic one that will interest both me and my audience?
2. Is the topic debatable?

3. Is my thesis appropriate in scope for a paper of this length?

4. Do I know enough about my thesis to have a rough idea of what ideas to use in supporting it and how to go about finding evidence to back up these ideas?

DEFINING THE ISSUES

■ Preparing an Initial Outline

An outline, like an accounting system or a computer program, is a practical device for organizing information. Nearly every elementary and high school student learns how to make an outline. What will you gain if you outline your argument? Time and an overview of your subject. The minutes you spend organizing your subject at the outset generally save at least double the time later, when you have few minutes to spare. An outline also enables you to see the whole argument at a glance.

Your preliminary outline establishes an order of priority for your argument. Which supporting points are issues to be defended, which are warrants, and which are evidence? Which supporting points are most persuasive? By constructing a map of your territory, you can identify the research routes that are likely to be most productive. You can also pinpoint any gaps in your reasoning.

List each issue as a main heading in your outline. Next, write below it any relevant support (or sources of support) that you are aware of. Then reexamine the list and consider which issues appear likely to offer the strongest support for your argument. You should number these in order of importance.

■ Computers in the Outlining Process

Word-processing software can make outlining simpler by providing an automatic outlining function. If you begin an outline with the roman numeral *I* followed by a period, many word-processing systems automatically supply *II* when you hit the enter key and move to the next line. If you have subtopics (marked by *A*s or *1*s), the outlining function will also automatically supply the next letters or numbers when you hit "Enter." This function is a simple but useful tool that can help you create hierarchies of ideas and skeletal texts.

Even more useful is the cut-and-paste function that is a part of all word-processing software because outlines are typically revised as writers discover new information and ideas or new connections between information and ideas. Revising outlines—experimenting with the order of ideas or with whether an idea should be a major or subpoint, for example—is easier with a computer, and the speed of cutting and pasting makes the revision process central to every part of the writing process, including outlining.

Finally, word-processing software also makes outlining done after a draft is completed much simpler. One way to see how a draft of a paper is working, for example, is to take the first (or topic) sentence of each paragraph and to put them in a list. Seeing how these individual sentences build from each other and connect to each other can help you see how the paper as a whole is working. If done with a pen, such a process can be time-consuming, but cutting and pasting by computer makes this helpful strategy easy.

■ Case Study: School Uniforms

To see how we raise and evaluate issues in a specific context, let's look at a controversy that has surfaced recently in many of our nation's public schools. Some schools are considering requiring school uniforms, but that proposal has not been met with unanimous support from students or their parents.

In one particular school district, those in favor of school uniforms raised these issues:

1. Other schools that initiated a uniform requirement experienced an improvement in discipline.
2. Buying uniforms is economical for parents.
3. Wearing uniforms takes away undesirable distinctions based on social and economic class.
4. Students who wear uniforms are not distracted by what they or others are wearing.
5. A uniform requirement does away with the need for increasingly detailed dress codes.

On the other side, those who opposed school uniforms introduced the following issues:

1. Requiring uniforms does not guarantee improved discipline.
2. A uniform requirement prevents parents from buying inexpensive clothing alternatives.
3. Students have the right to express themselves through their choice of clothing.
4. A dress code can eliminate fashions that are distracting to other students without taking away the student's choice of clothing completely.
5. Some students' weight, body shape, etc., may make them uncomfortable and self-conscious in the style of uniform chosen.

Now let's analyze these issues, comparing their strengths and weaknesses.

1. It is clear that not all the issues in this dispute were equally important. The arguers decided, therefore, to give greater emphasis to the issues most likely to be persuasive to their audiences and less attention to those difficult to prove or narrower in their appeal. At this time in some of the communities in the district, massive layoffs had forced parents out of work. Therefore, the cost of switching to uniforms was a major concern. If parents did not have to spend money on uniforms, they could shop for the most economic alternatives or let their younger children wear clothes their older children had outgrown. Within the district, there had been few problems with fashions that were extreme enough to be a distraction to other students, and those few could be addressed with minor additions to the dress code, certainly an easy accommodation to make. To those opposed to the uniform requirement, the economic concerns seemed to outweigh the use of uniforms as a means of establishing discipline, a goal they felt could be accomplished by other means.

2. It was also clear that, as in several of the other cases we have examined, the support on both sides consisted of both factual data and appeals to values. With regard to the factual data, each side reported evidence to prove that:

a. the wearing of uniforms leads or does not lead to a reduced number of discipline problems.

b. uniforms are or are not an economical alternative.

c. the majority of students favored or opposed wearing uniforms.

d. the majority of parents favored or opposed the uniform requirement.

The factual data were important. If opponents could prove that uniforms would place an increased financial burden on families already hurt by layoffs, the argument in favor of uniforms would be weakened. It would be weakened further if factual data from other similar districts showed no improvement in discipline.

Let us assume that the factual claims either were settled or remained in abeyance. We now turn our attention to a second set of issues, a contest over the values to be served.

3. Both sides in the dispute were concerned about the well-being of the students. Related to that, of course, was the well-being of their families. Improved discipline in the schools would benefit all students because the focus could be on education, not on policing student behavior. Beyond both of these concerns, however, were the issues of students' rights and their need to express themselves. If the majority of the students opposed uniforms, was that a strong enough concern to override the financial burden on their families? What about the minority who favored

uniforms and perhaps had felt stigmatized by being unable to afford the clothes in style among their peers? In such a situation, should a vote by the students play a major role in policy decisions? Students are not allowed to hire their own teachers or to choose their manner of instruction, their courses of study, their grades, or the rules of admission. In the school community, administrators argued, the experienced are required to lead and instruct the inexperienced.

In making our way through this debate, we have summarized a procedure for tackling the issues in any controversial problem.

1. Raise the relevant issues and arrange them in order of importance. Plan to devote more time and space to issues you regard as crucial.

2. Produce the strongest evidence you can to support your factual claims, knowing that the opposing side or critical readers may try to produce conflicting evidence.

3. Defend your value claims by finding support in the fundamental principles with which most people in your audience would agree.

4. Argue with yourself. Try to foresee what kinds of refutation are possible. Try to anticipate and meet the opposing arguments.

ORGANIZING THE MATERIAL

Once you are satisfied that you have identified all the issues that will appear in your paper, you should begin to determine what kind of organization will be most effective for your argument. Now is the time to organize the results of your thinking into a logical and persuasive form. If you have read about your topic, answered questions, and acquired some evidence, you may already have decided on ways to approach your subject. If not, you should look closely at your outline now, recalling your purposes when you began your investigation, and develop a strategy for using the information you have gathered to achieve those purposes.

The first point to establish is what type of thesis you plan to present. Is your intention to make readers aware of some problem? To offer a solution to the problem? To defend a position? To refute a position held by others? The way you organize your material will depend to a great extent on your goal. With that goal in mind, look over your outline and reevaluate the relative importance of your issues. Which ones are most convincing? Which are backed up by the strongest support? Which ones relate to facts, and which concern values?

With these points in mind, let us look at various ways of organizing an argumentative paper. It would be foolish to decide in advance how many paragraphs a paper ought to have; however, you can and should choose a general strategy before you begin writing. If your thesis presents an opinion or recommends some course of action, you may choose simply to state your main idea and then defend it. If your thesis argues against an opposing view, you probably will want to mention that view and then refute it. Both these organizations introduce the thesis in the first or second paragraph (called the *thesis paragraph*). You may decide that two or more differing positions have merit and that you want to offer a compromise between or among positions. A fourth possibility is to start establishing that a problem exists and then introduce your thesis as the solution; this method is called *presenting the stock issues*. Although these four approaches sometimes overlap in practice, examining each one individually can help you structure your paper. Let's take a look at each arrangement.

■ Defending the Main Idea

All forms of organization will require you to defend your main idea, but one way of doing this is simple and direct. Early in the paper state the main idea that you will defend throughout your argument. You can also indicate here the two or three points you intend to develop in support of your claim; or you can raise these later as they come up. Suppose your thesis is that widespread vegetarianism would solve a number of problems. You could phrase it this way: "If the majority of people in this country adopted a vegetarian diet, we would see improvements in the economy, in the health of our people, and in moral sensitivity." You would then develop each of the claims in your list with appropriate data and warrants. Notice that the thesis statement in the first (thesis) paragraph has already outlined your organizational pattern.

Defending the main idea is effective for factual claims as well as policy claims, in which you urge the adoption of a certain policy and give the reasons for its adoption. It is most appropriate when your thesis is straightforward and can be readily supported by direct statements.

■ Refuting the Opposing View

Refuting an opposing view means to attack it in order to weaken, invalidate, or make it less credible to a reader. Since all arguments are dialogues or debates—even when the opponent is only imaginary—refutation of the other point of view is always implicit in your arguments. As you write, keep in mind the issues that an opponent may raise. You will be looking at your own argument as an unsympathetic reader may look at it, asking yourself the same kinds of critical questions and trying to find its weaknesses in order to correct them. In this way every argument you write becomes a form of refutation.

How do you plan a refutation? Here are some general guidelines.

1. If you want to refute the argument in a specific essay or article, read the argument carefully, noting all the points with which you disagree. This advice may seem obvious, but it cannot be too strongly emphasized. If your refutation does not indicate scrupulous familiarity with your opponent's argument, he or she has the right to say, and often does, "You haven't really read what I wrote. You haven't really answered my argument."

2. If you think that your readers are sympathetic to the opposing view or are not familiar with it, summarize it at the beginning of your paper, providing enough information to give readers an understanding of exactly what you plan to refute. When you summarize, it's important to be respectful of the opposition's views. You don't want to alienate readers who might not agree with you at first.

3. If your argument is long and complex, choose only the most important points to refute. Otherwise the reader who does not have the original argument on hand may find a detailed refutation hard to follow. If the argument is short and relatively simple—a claim supported by only two or three points—you may decide to refute all of them, devoting more space to the most important ones.

4. Attack the principal elements in the argument of your opponent.

   a. Question the evidence. (See pp. 166–73 in the text.) Question whether your opponent has proved that a problem exists.

   b. Attack the warrants or assumptions that underlie the claim. (See pp. 232–33 in the text.)

   c. Attack the logic or reasoning of the opposing view. (Refer to the discussion of fallacious reasoning on pp. 285–95 in the text.)

   d. Attack the proposed solution to a problem, pointing out that it will not work.

5. Be prepared to do more than attack the opposing view. Supply evidence and good reasons in support of your own claim.

■ Finding the Middle Ground

Although an argument, by definition, assumes a difference of opinion, we know that opposing sides frequently find accommodation somewhere in the middle. As you mount your own argument about a controversial issue, you need not confine yourself to support of any of the differing positions. You may want to acknowledge that there is some justice on all sides and that you understand the difficulty of resolving the issue.

Consider these guidelines for an argument that offers a compromise between competing positions:

1. Early in your essay explain the opposing positions. Make clear the major differences separating the two (or more) sides.

2. Point out, whenever possible, that the opposing sides already agree to some exceptions to their stated positions. Such evidence may prove that the opposing sides are not so extreme as their advocates insist. Several commentators, writing about the budget conflict between Democrats and Republicans in late 1998, adopted this strategy, suggesting that compromise was possible because the differences were narrower than the public believed.

3. Make clear your own moderation and sympathy, your own willingness to negotiate. An example of this attitude appears in an essay on abortion in which the author infers how Abraham Lincoln might have treated the question of abortion rights.

> In this debate I have made my own position clear. It is a pro-life position (though it may not please all pro-lifers), and its model is Lincoln's position on slavery from 1854 until well into the Civil War: tolerate, restrict, discourage. Like Lincoln's, its touchstone is the common good of the nation, not the sovereign self. Like Lincoln's position, it accepts the legality but not the moral legitimacy of the institution that it seeks to contain. It invites argument and negotiation; it is a gambit, not a gauntlet.[1]

4. If you favor one side of the controversy, acknowledge that opposing views deserve to be considered. For example, in another essay on abortion, the author, who supports abortion rights, says,

> Those of us who are pro-choice must come to terms with those thoughtful pro-lifers who believe that in elevating the right to privacy above all other values, the most helpless form of humanity is left unprotected and is, in fact, defined away. They deserve to have their views addressed with sympathy and moral clarity.[2]

5. Provide evidence that accepting a middle ground can offer marked advantages for the whole society. Wherever possible, show that continued polarization can result in violence, injustice, and suffering.

6. In offering a solution that finds a common ground, be as specific as possible, emphasizing the part that you are willing to play in reaching a settlement. In an essay titled "Pro-Life and Pro-Choice? Yes!" the author concludes with this:

> Must those of us who abhor abortion, then, reconcile ourselves to seeing it spread unchecked? By no means. We can refuse to practice it ourselves—or, if we are male, beseech the women who carry our children to let them be born, and promise to sup-

[1] George McKenna, "On Abortion: A Lincolnian Position," *The Atlantic Monthly,* September 1995, p. 68. (A gauntlet or glove is flung down in order to challenge an opponent to combat; a gambit is the opening move in a chess game, or in the words of one dictionary, "a concession that invites discussion."—EDS.)

[2] Benjamin C. Schwarz, "Judge Ginsburg's Moral Myopia," *New York Times,* July 30, 1993, sec. A, p. 27.

port them, and mean it and do it. We can counsel and preach to others; those of us who are religious can pray. . . . What we must not do is ask the state to impose our views on those who disagree.[3]

On a different subject, a debate on pornography, the author, who is opposed to free distribution of obscene material, nevertheless refuses to endorse censorship.

I think that, by enlarging the First Amendment to protect, in effect, freedom of expression, rather than freedom of speech and of the press, the courts made a mistake. The courts have made other mistakes, but I do not know a better way of defining the interests of the community than through legislation and through the courts. So I am willing to put up with things I think are wrong in the hope that they will be corrected. I know of no alternative that would always make the right decisions.[4]

■ Presenting the Stock Issues

Presenting the stock issues, or stating the problem before the solution, is a type of organization borrowed from traditional debate format. It works for policy claims when an audience must be convinced that a need exists for changing the status quo (present conditions) and for introducing plans to solve the problem. You begin by establishing that a problem exists (need). You then propose a solution (plan), which is your thesis. Finally, you show reasons for adopting the plan (advantages). These three elements—need, plan, and advantages—are called the stock issues.

For example, suppose you wanted to argue that measures for reducing acid rain should be introduced at once. You would first have to establish a need for such measures by defining the problem and providing evidence of damage. Then you would produce your thesis, a means for improving conditions. Finally you would suggest the benefits that would follow from implementation of your plan. Notice that in this organization your thesis paragraph usually appears toward the middle of your paper, although it may also appear at the beginning.

■ Ordering Material for Emphasis

Whichever way you choose to work, you should revise your outline to reflect the order in which you intend to present your thesis and supporting ideas. Not only the placement of your thesis paragraph but also the wording and arrangement of your ideas will determine what points in your paper receive the most emphasis.

[3]George Church, *Time,* March 6, 1995, p. 108.
[4]Ernest van den Haag, *Smashing Liberal Icons: A Collection of Debates* (Washington, D.C.: Heritage Foundation, 1981), p. 101.

Suppose your purpose is to convince the reader that cigarette smoking is a bad habit. You might decide to concentrate on three unpleasant attributes of cigarette smoking: (1) it is unhealthy; (2) it is dirty; (3) it is expensive. Obviously, these are not equally important as possible deterrents. You would no doubt consider the first reason the most compelling, accompanied by evidence to prove the relationship between cigarette smoking and cancer, heart disease, emphysema, and other diseases. This issue, therefore, should be given greater emphasis than the others.

There are several ways to achieve emphasis. One is to make the explicit statement that you consider a certain issue the most important.

> Finally, and *most importantly,* human culture is often able to neutralize or reverse what might otherwise be genetically advantageous consequences of selfish behavior.[5]

This quotation also reveals a second way—placing the material to be emphasized in an emphatic position, either first or last in the paper. The end position, however, is generally more emphatic.

A third way to achieve emphasis is to elaborate on the material to be emphasized, treating it at greater length, offering more data and reasons for it than you give for the other issues.

■ Considering Scope and Audience

With a working outline in hand that indicates the order of your thesis and claims, you are almost ready to begin turning your notes into prose. First, however, it is useful to review the limits on your paper to be sure your writing time will be used to the best possible advantage.

The first limit involves scope. As mentioned earlier, your thesis should introduce a claim that can be adequately supported in the space available to you. If your research has opened up more aspects than you anticipated, you may want to narrow your thesis to one major subtopic. Or you could emphasize only the most persuasive arguments for your position (assuming these are sufficient to make your case) and omit the others. In a brief paper (three or four pages), three issues are probably all you have room to develop. On the other hand, if you suspect your thesis can be proved in one or two pages, look for ways to expand it. What additional issues might be brought in to bolster your argument? Alternatively, is there a larger issue for which your thesis could become a supporting idea?

Other limits on your paper are imposed by the need to make your points in a way that will be persuasive to an audience. The style and tone you choose depend not only on the nature of the subject but also on how you can best convince readers that you are a credible source. *Style* in this

---

[5] Peter Singer, *The Expanding Circle* (New York: New American Library, 1982), p. 171.

context refers to the elements of your prose—simple versus complex sentences, active versus passive verbs, metaphors, analogies, and other literary devices. *Tone* is the approach you take to your topic—solemn or humorous, detached or sympathetic. Style and tone together compose your voice as a writer.

Many students assume that every writer has only one voice. In fact, a writer typically adapts his or her voice to the material and the audience. Perhaps the easiest way to appreciate this is to think of two or three works by the same author that are written in different voices. Or compare the speeches of two different characters in the same story, novel, or film. Every writer has individual talents and inclinations that appear in most or all of his or her work. A good writer, however, is able to amplify some stylistic elements and diminish others, as well as to change tone, by choice.

It is usually appropriate in a short paper to choose an *expository* style, which emphasizes the elements of your argument rather than your personality. You may want to appeal to your readers' emotions as well as their intellects, but keep in mind that sympathy is most effectively gained when it is supported by believable evidence. If you press your point stridently, your audience is likely to be suspicious rather than receptive. If you sprinkle your prose with jokes or metaphors, you may diminish your credibility by detracting from the substance of your case. Both humor and analogy can be useful tools, but they should be used with discretion.

You can discover some helpful pointers on essay style by reading the editorials in newspapers such as the *New York Times,* the *Washington Post,* or the *Wall Street Journal.* The authors are typically addressing a mixed audience comparable to the hypothetical readers of your own paper. Though their approaches vary, each writer is attempting to portray himself or herself as an objective analyst whose argument deserves careful attention.

Again, remember your goals. You are trying to convince your audience of something; an argument is, by its nature, directed at people who may not initially agree with its thesis. Therefore, your voice as well as the claims you make must be convincing.

■ To This Point

The organizing steps that come between preparation and writing are often neglected. Careful planning at this stage, however, can save much time and effort later. As you prepare to start writing, you should be able to answer the following questions:

1. Is the purpose of my paper to persuade readers to accept a potentially controversial idea, to refute someone else's position, to find middle ground, or to propose a solution to a problem?

2. Can or should my solution also incorporate elements of compromise and negotiation?

3. Have I decided on an organization that is likely to accomplish this purpose?

4. Does my outline arrange my thesis and issues in an appropriate order to emphasize the most important issues?

5. Does my outline show an argument whose scope suits the needs of this paper?

6. What questions of style and tone do I need to keep in mind as I write to ensure that my argument will be persuasive?

WRITING

■ Beginning the Paper

Having found a claim you can defend and the voice you will adopt toward your audience, you must now think about how to begin. An introduction to your subject should consist of more than just the first paragraph of your paper. It should invite the reader to give attention to what you have to say. It should also point you in the direction you will take in developing your argument. You may want to begin the actual writing of your paper with the thesis paragraph. It is useful to consider the whole paragraph rather than simply the thesis statement for two reasons. First, not all theses are effectively expressed in a single sentence. Second, the rest of the paragraph will be closely related to your statement of the main idea. You may show why you have chosen this topic or why your audience will benefit from reading your paper. You may introduce your warrant, qualify your claim, and in other ways prepare for the body of your argument. Because readers will perceive the whole paragraph as a unit, it makes sense to approach it that way.

Consider first the kind of argument you intend to present. Does your paper make a factual claim? Does it address values? Does it recommend a policy or action? Is it a rebuttal of some current policy or belief? The answers to those questions will influence the way you introduce the subject.

If your thesis makes a factual claim, you may be able to summarize it in one or two opening sentences. "Whether we like it or not, money is obsolete. The currency of today is not paper or coin, but plastic." Refutations are easy to introduce in a brief statement: "Contrary to popular views on the subject, the institution of marriage is as sound today as it was a generation ago."

A thesis that defends a value is usually best preceded by an explanatory introduction. "Some wars are morally defensible" is a thesis that can be stated as a simple declarative opening sentence. However, readers who disagree may not read any further than the first line. Someone defending this claim is likely to be more persuasive if he or she first gives an example of a situation in which war is or was preferable to peace or presents the thesis less directly.

One way to keep such a thesis from alienating the audience is to phrase it as a question. "Are all wars morally indefensible?" Still better would be to prepare for the question:

> Few if any of us favor war as a solution to international problems. We are too vividly aware of the human suffering imposed by armed conflict, as well as the political and financial turmoil that inevitably result. Yet can we honestly agree that no war is ever morally defensible?

Notice that this paragraph gains appeal from use of the first person *we.* The author implies that he or she shares the readers' feelings but has good reasons for believing those feelings are not sufficient grounds for condemning all wars. Even if readers are skeptical, the conciliatory phrasing of the thesis should encourage them to continue reading.

For any subject that is highly controversial or emotionally charged, especially one that strongly condemns an existing situation or belief, you may sometimes want to express your indignation directly. Of course, you must be sure that your indignation can be justified. The author of the following introduction, a physician and writer, openly admits that he is about to make a case that may offend readers.

> Is there any polite way to introduce today's subject? I'm afraid not. It must be said plainly that the media have done about as sorry and dishonest a job of covering health news as is humanly possible, and that when the media do not fail from bias and mendacity, they fail from ignorance and laziness.[6]

If your thesis advocates a policy or makes a recommendation, it may be a good idea, as in a value claim, to provide a short background. The following paragraph introduces an argument favoring relaxation of controls in high schools.

> "Free the New York City 275,000" read a button worn by many young New Yorkers some years ago. The number was roughly the total of students enrolled in the City's high schools.
>
> The condition of un-freedom which is described was not, however, unique to the schools of one city. According to the Carnegie Commission's comprehensive study of American public education, *Crisis in the Classroom,* public schools across the country share a common characteristic, namely, "preoccupation with order and control." The result is that students find themselves the victims of "oppressive and petty rules which give their schools a repressive, almost prison-like atmosphere."[7]

[6]Michael Halberstam, "TV's Unhealthy Approach to Health News," *TV Guide,* September 20–26, 1980, p. 24.

[7]Alan Levine and Eve Carey, *The Rights of Students* (New York: Avon Books, 1977), p. 11.

There are also other ways to introduce your subject. One is to begin with an appropriate quotation.

> "Reading makes a full man, conversation makes a ready man, and writing makes an exact man." So Francis Bacon told us around 1600. Recently I have been wondering how Bacon's formula might apply to present-day college students.[8]

Or you may begin with an anecdote. In the following introduction to an article about the relation between cancer and mental attitude, the author recounts a personal experience.

> Shortly after I moved to California, a new acquaintance sat in my San Francisco living room drinking rose-hip tea and chainsmoking. Like so many residents of the Golden West, Cecil was "into" all things healthy, from jogging to *shiatsu* massage to kelp. Tobacco didn't seem to fit, but he told me confidently that there was no contradiction. "It all has to do with energy," he said. "Unless you have a lot of negative energy about smoking cigarettes, there's no way they can hurt you; you won't get cancer."[9]

Finally, you may introduce yourself as the author of the claim.

> I wish to argue an unpopular cause: the cause of the old, free elective system in the academic world, or the untrammeled right of the undergraduate to make his own mistakes.[10]

> My subject is the world of Hamlet. I do not of course mean Denmark, except as Denmark is given a body by the play; and I do not mean Elizabethan England, though this is necessarily close behind the scenes. I mean simply the imaginative environment that the play asks us to enter when we read it or go to see it.[11]

You should, however, use such introductions with care. They suggest an authority about the subject that you shouldn't attempt to assume unless you can demonstrate that you are entitled to it.

■ Guidelines for Good Writing

In general, the writer of an argument follows the same rules that govern any form of expository writing. Your style should be clear and readable, your organization logical, your ideas connected by transitional phrases

---

[8] William Aiken, "The Conversation on Campus Today Is, Uh . . . ," *Wall Street Journal,* May 4, 1982, p. 18.
[9] Joel Guerin, "Cancer and the Mind," *Harvard Magazine,* November–December 1978, p. 11.
[10] Howard Mumford Jones, "Undergraduates on Apron Strings," *Atlantic Monthly,* October 1955, p. 45.
[11] Maynard Mack, "The World of Hamlet," *Yale Review,* June 1952, p. 502.

and sentences, your paragraphs coherent. The main difference between an argument and expository writing, as noted earlier, is the need to persuade an audience to adopt a belief or take an action. You should assume your readers will be critical rather than neutral or sympathetic. Therefore, you must be equally critical of your own work. Any apparent gap in reasoning or ambiguity in presentation is likely to weaken the argument.

As you read the essays in this book and elsewhere, you will discover that good style in argumentative writing shares several characteristics:

- Variety in sentence structure: a mixture of both long and short sentences, different sentence beginnings

- Rich but standard vocabulary: avoidance of specialized terms unless they are fully explained, word choice appropriate to a thoughtful argument

- Use of details and examples to illustrate and clarify abstract terms, principles, and generalizations

You should take care to avoid the following:

- Unnecessary repetition: making the same point without new data or interpretation

- Exaggeration or stridency, which can create suspicion of your fairness and powers of observation

- Short paragraphs of one or two sentences, which are common in advertising and newspaper writing to get the reader's attention but are inappropriate in a thoughtful essay

In addition to these stylistic principles, seven general points are worth keeping in mind:

1. Although *you*, like *I*, should be used judiciously, it can be found even in the treatment of weighty subjects. Here is an example from an essay by the distinguished British mathematician and philosopher, Bertrand Russell.

> Suppose you are a scientific pioneer and you make some discovery of great scientific importance and suppose you say to yourself, "I am afraid this discovery will do harm": you know that other people are likely to make the same discovery if they are allowed suitable opportunities for research; you must therefore, if you do not wish the discovery to become public, either discourage your sort of research or control publication by a board of censors.[12]

Don't be afraid to use *you* or *I* when it is useful to emphasize the presence of the person making the argument.

---

[12]"Science and Human Life," in *What Is Science?* edited by James R. Newman (New York: Simon and Schuster, 1955), p. 12.

2. Don't pad. This point should be obvious; the word *pad* suggests the addition of unnecessary material. Many writers find it tempting, however, to enlarge a discussion even when they have little more to say. It is never wise to introduce more words into a paper that has already made its point. If the paper turns out to be shorter than you had hoped, it may mean that you have not sufficiently developed the subject or that the subject was less substantial than you thought when you selected it. Padding, which is easy to detect in its repetition and sentences empty of content, weakens the writer's credibility.

3. For any absolute generalization—a statement containing words such as *all* or *every*—consider the possibility that there may be at least one example that will weaken the generalization. Such a precaution means that you won't have to backtrack and admit that your generalization is not, after all, universal. A student who was arguing against capital punishment for the reason that all killing was wrong suddenly paused in her presentation and added, "On the other hand, if given the chance, I'd probably have been willing to kill Hitler." This admission meant that she recognized important exceptions to her rule and that she would have to qualify her generalization in some significant way.

4. When offering an explanation, especially one that is complicated or extraordinary, look first for a cause that is easier to accept, one that doesn't strain credibility. (In Chapter 8, we called attention to this principle. See pp. 286–88.) For example, years ago a great many people were bemused by reports about the mysterious Bermuda Triangle, which had apparently swallowed up ships and planes since the mid-nineteenth century. The forces at work were variously described as space-time warps, UFOs that transported earthlings to other planets, and sea monsters seeking revenge. But a careful investigation revealed familiar, natural causes. A reasonable person interested in the truth would have searched for more conventional explanations before accepting the bizarre stories of extraterrestrial creatures. He or she would also exercise caution when confronted by conspiracy theories that try to account for controversial political events, such as the assassination of John F. Kennedy.

5. Check carefully for questionable warrants. Your outline should specify your warrants. When necessary, these should be included in your paper to link claims with support. Many an argument has failed because it depended on an unstated warrant with which the reader did not agree. If you were arguing for a physical education requirement at your school, you might make a good case for all the physical and psychological benefits of such a requirement. But you would certainly need to introduce and develop the warrant on which your claim was based—that it is the proper function of a college or university to provide the benefits of a physical education. Many readers would agree that physical education is valuable, but they might question the assumption that an academic institution should introduce a nonintellectual enterprise into the curriculum. At any

point where you draw a controversial or tenuous conclusion, be sure your reasoning is clear and logical.

6. Avoid conclusions that are merely summaries. Summaries may be needed in long technical papers, but in brief arguments they create endings that are without force or interest. In the closing paragraph you should find a new idea that emerges naturally from the development of the whole argument.

7. Strive for a paper that is unified, coherent, and emphatic where appropriate. A *unified* paper stays focused on its goal and directs each claim, warrant, and piece of evidence toward that goal. Extraneous information or unsupported claims impair unity. *Coherence* means that all ideas are fully explained and adequately connected by transitions. To ensure coherence, give especially close attention to the beginnings and ends of your paragraphs: Is each new concept introduced in a way that shows it following naturally from the one that preceded it? *Emphasis,* as we have mentioned, is a function partly of structure and partly of language. Your most important claims should be placed where they are certain of receiving the reader's attention: key sentences at the beginning or end of a paragraph, key paragraphs at the beginning or end of your paper. Sentence structure can also be used for emphasis. If you have used several long, complex sentences, you can emphasize a significant point by stating it briefly and simply. You can also create emphasis with verbal flags, such as "The primary issue to consider . . ." or "Finally, we cannot ignore. . . ."

All clear expository prose will exhibit the qualities of unity, coherence, and emphasis. But the success of an argumentative paper is especially dependent on these qualities because the reader may have to follow a line of reasoning that is both complicated and unfamiliar. Moreover, a paper that is unified, coherent, and properly emphatic will be more readable, the first requisite of an effective argument.

REVISING

The final stage in writing an argumentative paper is revising. The first step is to read through what you have written for mistakes. Next, check your work against the guidelines listed under "Organizing the Material" and "Writing." Have you omitted any of the issues, warrants, or supporting evidence on your outline? Is each paragraph coherent in itself? Do your paragraphs work together to create a coherent paper? All the elements of the argument—the issues raised, the underlying assumptions, and the supporting material—should contribute to the development of the claim in your thesis statement. Any material that is interesting but irrelevant to that claim should be cut. Finally, does your paper reach a clear conclusion that reinforces your thesis?

Be sure, too, that the style and tone of your paper are appropriate for the topic and the audience. Remember that people choose to read an argument because they want the answer to a troubling question or the solution to a recurrent problem. Besides stating your thesis in a way that invites the reader to join you in your investigation, you must retain your audience's interest through a discussion that may be unfamiliar or contrary to their convictions. The outstanding qualities of argumentative prose style, therefore, are clarity and readability.

Style is obviously harder to evaluate in your own writing than organization. Your outline provides a map against which to check the structure of your paper. Clarity and readability, by comparison, are somewhat abstract qualities. Two procedures may be helpful. The first is to read two or three (or more) essays by authors whose style you admire and then turn back to your own writing. Awkward spots in your prose are sometimes easier to see if you get away from it and respond to someone else's perspective than if you simply keep rereading your own writing.

The second method is to read aloud. If you have never tried it, you are likely to be surprised at how valuable this can be. Again, start with someone else's work that you feel is clearly written, and practice until you achieve a smooth rhythmic delivery that satisfies you. And listen to what you are reading. Your objective is to absorb the patterns of English structure that characterize the clearest, most readable prose. Then read your paper aloud, and listen to the construction of your sentences. Are they also clear and readable? Do they say what you want them to say? How would they sound to a reader? According to one theory, you can learn the rhythm and phrasing of a language as you learn the rhythm and phrasing of a melody. And you will often *hear* a mistake or a clumsy construction in your writing that has escaped your eye in proofreading.

PREPARING THE MANUSCRIPT

Print your typed essay on one side of 8½-by-11-inch white computer paper, double-spacing throughout. Leave margins of 1 to 1½ inches on all sides, and indent each paragraph one-half inch or five spaces. Unless a formal outline is part of the paper, a separate title page is unnecessary. Instead, beginning about one inch from the top of the first page and flush with the left margin, type your name, the instructor's name, the course title, and the date, each on a separate line; then double-space and type the title, capitalizing the first letter of the words of the title except for articles, prepositions, and conjunctions. Double-space and type the body of the paper.

Writer's Guide: Checklist for Argumentative Papers

1. Present a thesis that interests both you and the audience, is debatable, and can be defended in the amount of space available.

2. Back up each statement offered in support of the thesis with enough evidence to give it credibility. Cite data from a variety of sources. Fully document all quotations and direct references to primary or secondary sources.

3. The warrants linking claims to support must be either specified or implicit in your data and line of reasoning. No claim should depend on an unstated warrant with which skeptical readers might disagree.

4. Present the thesis clearly and adequately introduce it in a thesis paragraph, indicating the purpose of the paper.

5. Organize supporting statements and data in a way that builds the argument, emphasizes your main ideas, and justifies the paper's conclusions.

6. Anticipate all possible opposing arguments and either refute or accommodate them.

7. Write in a style and tone appropriate for the topic and the intended audience. Your prose should be clear and readable.

8. Make sure your manuscript is clean, carefully proofed, and typed in an acceptable format.

Number all pages at the top right corner, typing your last name before each page number in case pages are mislaid. If an outline is included, number its pages with lowercase roman numerals.

Use the spell-check and grammar-check functions of your word-processing program, but keep in mind that correctness depends on context. A spell-check program will not flag a real word that is used incorrectly, such as the word *it's* used where the word *its* is needed. Also, a grammar-check function lacks the sophistication to interpret the meaning of a sentence and may flag as incorrect a group of words that is indeed correct while missing actual errors. It is ultimately up to you to proofread the paper carefully for other mistakes. Correct the errors, and reprint the pages in question.

CHAPTER 10

Researching an Argumentative Paper

The success of any argument, short or long, depends in large part on the quantity and quality of the support behind it. Research, therefore, can be crucial for any argument outside your own experience. Most papers will benefit from research in the library and elsewhere because development of the claim requires facts, examples, statistics, and informed opinions that are available only from primary and secondary research sources. This chapter offers information and advice to help you work through the steps of writing a research paper, from getting started to preparing the finished product.

GETTING STARTED

The following guidelines will help you keep your research on track:

1. Focus your investigation on building your argument, not merely on collecting information about the topic. Do follow any promising leads that turn up from the sources you consult, but don't be diverted into general reading that has no direct bearing on your thesis.

2. Look for at least two pieces of evidence to support each point you make. If you cannot find sufficient evidence, you may need to revise or abandon the point.

3. Use a variety of sources. Seek evidence from different kinds of sources (books, magazines, Web sites, government reports, even personal interviews with experts) and from different fields.

Writer's Guide: Why Use Sources?

1. You cannot be an authority on every subject. That means that you must turn to those who are authorities on subjects you know little about.

2. Because you may not yet have a name or credentials that are recognized for their authority, you may need to use those who are considered experts as sources of information and prestige.

3. The use of sources shows that you have taken the time do so some research on the subject at hand, including researching positions other than your own.

4. As in a court of law, the more evidence you can provide for your position, the stronger your case will be.

4. Be sure your sources are authoritative. We have already pointed out elsewhere the necessity for examining the credentials of sources. Although it may be difficult or impossible for those outside the field to conclude that one authority is more trustworthy than another, some guidelines are available. Articles and essays in scholarly journals are probably more authoritative than articles in college newspapers. Authors whose credentials include many publications and years of study at reputable institutions are probably more reliable than newspaper columnists and the so-called man in the street. However, we can judge reliability much more easily if we are dealing with facts and inferences than with values and emotions.

5. Don't let your sources' opinions outweigh your own. Your paper should demonstrate that the thesis and ideas you present are yours, arrived at after careful reflection and supported by research. The thesis need not be original, but your paper should be more than a collection of quotations or a report of the facts and opinions you have been reading. It should be clear to the reader that the quotations and other materials support *your* claim and that *you* have been responsible for finding and emphasizing the important issues, examining the data, and choosing between strong and weak opinions.

6. Prepare for research by identifying potential resources and learning how they work. Make sure you know how to use the library's catalog and other databases available either in the library or through the campus network. For each database that looks useful, explore how to execute a subject search, how to refine a search, and how to print out or download results. Make sure you know how to find books, relevant reference materials, and journals. Find out whether interlibrary loan is an option and how long it takes. If you plan to use government publications, find out if your library is a depository for federal documents. Identify relevant organizations using the *Encyclopedia of Associations* and visit their Web sites.

Finally, discuss your topic with a librarian at the reference desk to make sure you haven't overlooked anything.

MAPPING RESEARCH: A SAMPLE OUTLINE

To explore a range of research activities, let's suppose that you are preparing a research paper, six to ten pages long. You have chosen to defend the following thesis: *Conventional zoos should be abolished because they are cruel to animals and cannot provide the benefits to the public that they promise.* To keep your material under control and give direction to your reading, you would sketch a preliminary outline, which might look like this:

Why We Don't Need Zoos

I. Moral Objection: Animals have fundamental right to liberty
   A. Must prove animals are negatively affected by captivity
      1. research?
      2. research?
   B. Must refute claims that captivity is not detrimental to animals
      1. Brownlee's description of dolphin: "seeming stupor"; eating "half-heartedly"; not behaving like wild dolphins
      2. Personal experience: watching leopards running in circles in cages for hours
II. Practical Objection: Zoos can't accomplish what they claim to be their goals
   A. "Educational benefits" zoo provides are inaccurate at best: Public is not learning about wild animals at all but about domesticated descendants of same (support with research from [I.A] above)
   B. Conservation programs at zoos are ineffective
      1. It's difficult to breed animals in zoos
      2. Resultant offspring, when there is any, is victim of inbreeding. Leads to inferior stock that will eventually die out (research?)

Now you need to begin the search for the materials that will support your argument. There are two principal ways of gathering the materials — primary research and secondary research. Most writers will not want to limit themselves to one kind of research, but one method may work better than another for a particular project.

USING SOURCES: PRIMARY RESEARCH

Primary research involves looking for firsthand information. By *firsthand* we mean information taken directly from the original source, including field research (interviews, surveys, personal observations, or experiments). If your topic relates to a local issue involving your school or community, or if it focuses on a story that has never been reported by others, field research may be more valuable than anything available in the library. However, the library can be a source of firsthand information. Memoirs and letters written by witnesses to past events, photographs, contemporary news reports of historical events, or expert testimony presented at congressional hearings are all primary sources that may be available in your library. The Internet, too, can be a source of primary data. A discussion list, newsgroup, or chat room focused on your topic may give you a means to converse with activists and contact experts. Web sites of certain organizations provide documentation of their views, unfiltered by others' opinions. The text of laws, court opinions, bills, debates in Congress, environmental impact statements, and even selected declassified FBI files can be found through government-sponsored Web sites. Other sites present statistical data or the text of historical or political documents.

One of the rewards of primary research is that it often generates new information, which in turn produces new interpretations of familiar conditions. It is a favored method for anthropologists and sociologists, and most physical and natural scientists use observation and experiment at some point as essential tools in their research.

Consider the sample thesis that *zoos should be abolished.* Remember that you need to prove that *zoos are cruel to animals* and that *they cannot provide the benefits to the public that they promise.* It is possible to go directly to primary sources without consulting books or journals. For example:

- Phone the local area chapter of any animal rights group and ask to interview members on their opinions concerning zoos.

- Talk to the veterinarian on call at your local zoo and ask about animal injuries, illnesses, neuroses, and so forth.

- Search the World Wide Web for sites sponsored and developed by the groups associated with the animal rights movement. Many such informational sites will provide the text of current or proposed laws concerning this issue.

- Locate Internet newsgroups or discussion lists devoted to animal rights and identify experts in the field such as animal scientists who would be willing to provide authoritative opinions for your paper.

The information gleaned from primary research can be used directly to support your claim, or can provide a starting point for secondary research at the library.

Secondary research involves locating commentary and analysis of your topic. In addition to raw evidence found through primary research, secondary sources provide a sense of how others are examining the issues and can provide useful information and analysis. Secondary sources may be written for a popular audience, ranging from news coverage, to popular explanations of research findings, to social analysis, to opinion pieces. Or they may be scholarly publications—experts presenting their research and theories to other researchers. These sources might also come in the form of analytical reports written to untangle possible courses of action, such as a report written by staff members for a congressional committee or an analysis of an issue by a think tank that wants to use the evidence it has gathered to influence public opinion.

Whatever form it may take, be sure when you use a secondary source that you consider the author's purpose and the validity of the material presented to ensure that it is useful evidence for your argument. An opinion piece published in a small-town paper, for example, may be a less impressive source for your argument than an analysis written by a former cabinet member. A description of a scientific discovery published in a magazine will carry less weight as evidence than the article written by the scientists making the discovery, presenting their research findings in a scientific journal.

The nature of your topic will determine which route you follow to find good sources. If the topic is current, you may find it more important to use articles than books and might bypass the library catalog altogether. If the topic has to do with social policy or politics, government publications may be particularly useful, though they would be unhelpful for a literary paper. If the topic relates to popular culture, the Internet may provide more information than more traditional publications. Consider what kinds of sources will be most useful as you choose your strategy. If you aren't certain which approaches fit your topic best, consult with a librarian at the reference desk.

■ **Selecting and Searching Databases**

You will most likely use one or more *databases* (online catalogs of reference materials) to locate books and articles on your topic. The library catalog is a database of books and other materials owned by the library; other databases may cover articles in popular or specialized journals and may even provide the full text of articles. Some databases may be available only in the library; others may be accessible all over campus. Here are some common features that appear in many databases.

Keyword or Subject Searching. You might have the option of searching a database by *keyword*—using the words that you think are most relevant to your search—or by subject. Typically, a keyword search will search for any occurrence of your search term in titles, notes, or the descriptive headings provided by database catalogers or indexers. The advantage to keyword searching is that you can use terms that come naturally to you to cast your net as widely as possible. The disadvantage is that there may be more than one way to express your topic and you may not capture all the relevant materials unless you use the right keywords.

With *subject searching,* you use search terms from a list of subject headings (sometimes called *descriptors*) established by the creators of the database. To make searching as efficient as possible, they choose one word or phrase to express a subject. Every time a new source is entered into the database, the indexers describe it using words from the list of subject headings: When you use the list to search the database, you retrieve every relevant source. You might find that a database lists these subject headings through a thesaurus feature. The sophisticated researcher will always pay attention to the subject headings or descriptors generally listed at the bottom of a record for clues to terms that might work best and for related terms that might be worth trying.

Searching for More Than One Concept. Most database searches allow you to combine terms using the connectors *and, or,* and *not.* These connectors (also known as *Boolean operators*) group search terms in different ways. If you search for zoos *and* animal rights, for example, the resulting list of sources will include only those that deal with both zoos and animal rights, leaving out any that deal with only one subject and not the other. If you connect terms with *or,* your list will contain sources that deal with either concept: A search for dogs *or* cats will create a list of sources that cover either animal. *Not* excludes concepts from a search. A search for animal rights *not* furs will search for the concept animal rights and then cut out any sources that deal with furs.

Limiting a Search. Most databases have some options for limiting a search by a number of variables, such as publication date, language, or format. If you find a large number of sources in a database search, you might limit your search to sources published in English in the past three years. If you need a visual aid for a presentation, you might limit a search of the library's catalog to videos, and so on.

Truncating Search Terms with Wild Cards. At times you will search for a word that has many possible endings. A wild card is a symbol that, placed at the end of a word root, allows for any possible ending for a word. For example, *animal** will allow a search for *animal* or *animals.*

Options for Saving Records. You may have the opportunity to print, download to a disk, or e-mail to yourself the citations you find in a database. Many databases have a feature for marking just the records you want so you save only those of interest.

Help Screens. Most databases offer some kind of online help that explains how to use the database effectively. If you invest five minutes getting familiar with the basics of a database, it may save you twenty minutes later.

■ Types of Databases

The Library Catalog. If you want to search for books, videos, or periodical publications, the library catalog is the database to search. Most libraries now have computerized catalogs, but some still have a card catalog. In either case, the type of information provided is the same. Every book in the library has an entry in the catalog that gives its author, title, publisher, date, length, and subject headings and perhaps some notes about its contents. It also gives the call number or location on the shelf and often some indication as to whether it is currently available. You can search the catalog for an author, title, subject, or keyword. Most online catalogs have ways of combining and limiting searches and for printing results. Remember when searching the catalog, though, that entries are created for whole books and not for specific parts of them. If you use too narrow search terms, you may not find a book that has a chapter that includes exactly what you are looking for. Use broad search terms, and check the subject headings for search terms that will work best. Plan to browse the shelves and examine the tables of contents of the books that you find through the catalog to see which, in fact, are most helpful for your topic.

General Periodical Databases. If you want to search for articles, you can find a number of options at your library. Most libraries have a generalized database of periodical articles that may include citations, citations with abstracts (brief summaries), or the entire text of articles. *EBSCOhost, Infotrac, Searchbank, Readers' Guide Abstracts,* and *ProQuest* are all online indexes of this type. Ask a librarian what is available in your library. These are particularly good for finding current information in fairly nonspecialized sources, though they may include some scholarly journals. If you are looking for articles published before the 1980s — say, for news accounts published when the atomic bomb was dropped on Hiroshima — you would most likely need to use a print index such as the *Readers' Guide to Periodical Literature,* which began publication in 1900.

Specialized Databases. In addition to these general databases, you may find you need to delve deeper into a particular subject area. Every academic discipline has some sort of in-depth index to its research, and though the materials they cover tend to be highly specialized, they can provide more substantial support for your claims because they tend to cover sources written by experts in their fields. These resources may be available in electronic or print form:

Sample Online Catalog Record

You searched for the TITLE—animal rights movement

```
CALL #       Z7164.C45 M38 1994.
AUTHOR       Manzo, Bettina, 1943-
TITLE        The animal rights movement in the United States, 1975-
             1990 : an annotated bibliography / by Bettina Manzo.
IMPRINT      Metuchen, N.J. : Scarecrow Press, 1994.
PHYS DESCR   xi, 296 p. ; 23 cm.
NOTE         Includes indexes.
CONTENTS     Animal rights movement -- Activists and organizations --
             Philosophy, ethics, and religion -- Law and legislation
             -- Factory farming and vegetarianism -- Trapping and
             fur industry -- Companion animals -- Wildlife --
             Circuses, zoos, rodeos, dog
SUBJECT      Animal rights movement --United States --Bibliography.
             Animal rights --United States --Bibliography.
             Animal experimentation --United States --Bibliography.
OCLC #       30671149.
ISBN/ISSN    GB95-17241.
```

Art Index

Biological Abstracts (the online version is known as *Biosis*)

Business Periodicals Index

ERIC (focused on education research)

Index Medicus (*Medline* or *PubMed* online)

Modern Languages Association International Bibliography (*MLA Bibliography* online)

Psychological Abstracts (*PsychInfo* or *PsychLit* online)

Sociological Abstracts (*Sociofile* online)

Check with a librarian to find out which specialized databases or indexes that relate to your topic are available in your library.

Database Services. In addition to individual databases, many libraries subscribe to database services that provide access to a number of databases from one search screen. *FirstSearch,* for example, provides access to a variety of subject-specific databases as well as *WorldCat,* a massive database of library catalogs. *Lexis/Nexis* is a collection of databases to over a billion texts, most of them available in full text; it is a strong source for news coverage, legal research, and business information. These may be available to you through the Web anywhere on campus. Again, a visit with a librarian will help you quickly identify what your library has available.

■ Encyclopedias

General and specialized encyclopedias offer quick overviews of topics and easy access to factual information. They also tend to have excellent selective bibliographies, pointing you toward useful sources. You will find a wide variety of encyclopedias in your library's reference collection; you may also have an online encyclopedia, such as *Britannica Online,* available through the Web anywhere on campus. Some specialized encyclopedias include the following:

Encyclopedia of African American History and Culture

Encyclopedia of American Social History

Encyclopedia of Bioethics

Encyclopedia of Educational Research

Encyclopedia of Hispanic Culture in the United States

Encyclopedia of International Relations

Encyclopedia of Philosophy

Encyclopedia of Sociology

Encyclopedia of the United States in the Twentieth Century

Encyclopedia of World Cultures

International Encyclopedia of Communications

McGraw-Hill Encyclopedia of Science and Technology

Political Handbook of the World

■ Statistical Resources

Often statistics are used as evidence in an argument. If your argument depends on establishing that one category is bigger than another, that the majority of people hold a certain opinion, or that one group is more affected by something than another group, statistics can provide the evidence you need. Of course, as with any other source, you need to be sure that your statistics are as reliable as possible and that you are reporting them responsibly.

It isn't always easy to find things counted the way you want. If you embark on a search for numbers to support your argument, be prepared to spend some time locating and interpreting data. Always read the fine print that explains how and when the data were gathered. Some sources for statistics include these:

U.S. Bureau of the Census. This government agency produces a wealth of statistical data, much of it available on CD-ROM or through the Web at <www.census.gov>. A handy compilation of their most useful tables is found in the one-volume annual handbook, *Statistical Abstract of the United States,* which also includes statistics from other government sources.

Other Federal Agencies. Numerous federal agencies gather statistical data. Among these are the National Center for Education Statistics, the National Center for Health Statistics, the National Bureau of Labor Statistics, and the Federal Bureau of Investigation, which annually compiles national crime statistics. One handy place to find a wide variety of federal statistics is a Web site called *FedStats* at <www.fedstats.gov>.

United Nations. Compilations of international data published by the United Nations include the *Demographic Yearbook* and *Statistical Yearbook.* Some statistics are also published by U.N. agencies such as the Food and Health Organization. Some are available from the U.N. Web site at <www.un.org>.

Opinion Polls. Several companies conduct opinion polls, and some of these are available in libraries. One such compilation is the Gallup Poll series, which summarizes public opinion polling from 1935 to the present. Other poll results are reported by the press. Search a database that covers news publications by using your topic and *polls* as keywords to help you locate some summaries of results.

■ Government Publications

Beyond statistics, government agencies compile and publish a wealth of information. For topics that concern public welfare, health, education, politics, foreign relations, earth sciences, the environment, or the economy, government documents may provide just the information you need.

The U.S. federal government is the largest publisher in the world. Its publications are distributed free to libraries designated as document depositories across the country. If your library is not a depository, chances are there is a regional depository somewhere nearby. Local, state, and foreign governments are also potential sources of information.

Federal documents distributed to depository libraries are indexed in *The Monthly Catalog of U.S. Government Documents,* available in many libraries as an electronic database. These include congressional documents such as hearings and committee reports, presidential papers, studies conducted by the Education Department or the Centers for Disease Control, and so on. Many government documents are available through the Internet. If you learn about a government publication through the news media, chances are you will be able to obtain a copy at the Web site of the sponsoring agency or congressional body. In fact, government publications are among the most valuable of resources available on the Web because they are rigorously controlled for content. You know you are looking at a U.S. federal government site when you see the domain suffix *.gov* in the URL.

■ Searching the Web

The World Wide Web is becoming an increasingly important resource for researchers. It is particularly helpful if you are looking for information about organizations, current events, political debates, popular culture, or government-sponsored research and activities. It is not an especially good place to look for literary criticism, historical analysis, or scholarly research articles, which are still more likely to be published in traditional ways. Biologists reporting on an important experiment, for example, are more likely to submit an article about it to a prestigious journal in the field than simply post their results on the Web.

Because anyone can publish whatever they like on the Web, searching for good information can be frustrating. Search engines operate by means of automated programs that gather information about sites and match search terms to whatever is out there, regardless of quality. A search engine may locate thousands of Web documents on a topic, but most are of little relevance and dubious quality. The key is to know in advance what information you need and who might have produced it. For example, if your topic has to do with some aspect of free speech and you know that the American Civil Liberties Union is involved in the issue, a trip to the ACLU home page may provide you with a wealth of information, albeit from a particular perspective. If your state's pollution control agency just issued a report on water quality in the area, you may find the report published at their Web site or the e-mail address of someone who could send it to you. The more you know about your topic before you sit down to surf, the more likely you will use your time productively.

If you have a fairly broad topic and no specific clues about where it might be covered, you may want to start your search using a selective guide to good sites. For example, the University of Texas maintains an excellent directory to sites relating to Latin America. Subject guides that selectively list valuable sites can be found at the *Argus Clearinghouse* at <www.clearinghouse.net>, the University of California's *Infomine* at <http://infomine.ucr.edu>, and the *World Wide Web Virtual Library* project at <www.vlib.org/Home.html>. Reference librarians will also be able to point you to quality sites that relate to your topic.

If you have a fairly specific topic in mind or are looking for a particular organization or document on the Web, a search engine can help you find it. *Google* is one of the best. No matter what search engine you choose, find out how it works, how it ranks results, and how deeply it indexes Web pages. Some search engines will retrieve more results than others simply because of the way the program gathers information from sites. As with databases, there are usually ways to refine a search and improve your results. Many search engines offer an advanced search option that may provide some useful options for refining and limiting a search.

It is important to know what will not be retrieved by a search engine. Because publishing and transmitting texts on the Web is relatively easy, it is becoming more common for libraries to subscribe to databases and electronic journals that are accessed through a Web browser. You may have *Britannica Online* and *Lexis/Nexis* as options on your library's home page. However, the contents of those subscriptions will be available only to your campus community and will not be searched by general Web search engines.

EVALUATING SOURCES

When you begin studying your sources, read first to acquire general familiarity with your subject. Make sure that you are covering both sides of the question—in this case arguments both for and against the existence of zoos—as well as facts and opinions from a variety of sources. In investigating this subject, you will encounter data from biologists, ecologists, zoo directors, anthropologists, animal-rights activists, and ethical philosophers; their varied points of view will contribute to the strength of your claim.

As you read, look for what seem to be the major issues. They will probably be represented in all or most of your sources. For the claim about zoos the major issues may be summarized as follows: (1) the fundamental right wild animals have to liberty; (2) the harm done to animals who are denied this right and kept in captivity. On the other side, these issues will emerge: (1) the lack of concrete evidence that animals suffer or are harmed by being in zoos; (2) the benefits, in terms of entertainment, education, and conservation efforts that the public derives from zoos. The latter two, of course, are the issues you will have to refute. Your note taking should emphasize these important issues.

Record questions as they occur to you in your reading. Why do zoos exist? What are their major goals, and how well do they meet them? What happens to animals who are removed from the wild and placed in zoos? What happens to animals born and reared in captivity? How do these groups compare with their wild counterparts, who are free to live in their natural habitats? Do animals really have a right to liberty? What are the consequences of denying them this right? Are there consequences to humanity?

■ Evaluating Print Sources

The sources you find provide useful information that you need for your paper and help you support your claims. One key to supporting claims effectively is to make sure you have the best evidence available. It is tempting when searching a database or the Web to take the first sources that look good, print them or copy them, and not give them another thought until you are sitting down to compose your argument—only to discover that the sources aren't as valuable as they could be. Sources that looked pretty good at the beginning of your research may turn out to be less useful once you have learned more about the topic. And a source that seems interesting at first glance may turn out to be a rehash or digest of a much more valuable source, something you realize only when you sit down and look at it carefully.

To find the right stuff, be a critical thinker from the start of your research process. Scan and evaluate the references you encounter throughout your search. As you examine options in a database, choose sources that use relevant terms in their titles, seem directed to an appropriate audience, and are published in places that will look good in your Works Cited list. For example, a Senate Foreign Relations Committee report will be more impressive as a source than a comparable article in *Good Housekeeping.* An article from the scholarly journal *Foreign Affairs* will carry more clout than an article from *Reader's Digest,* even if they are on the same subject.

Skim and quickly evaluate each source that looks valuable.

- Is it relevant to your topic?
- Does it provide information you haven't found elsewhere?
- Can you learn anything about the author, and does what you learn inspire confidence?

As you begin to learn more about your topic and develop an outline, you can use sources to help direct your search. If a source mentions an organization, for example, you may use that clue to run a search on the Web for that organization's home page. If a newspaper story refers to a study published in a scientific journal, you may want to seek out that study to see the results of the research firsthand. And if you have a source that includes references to other publications, scan through them, and see which might also prove helpful to you. When you first started your research, chances are you weren't quite sure what you were looking for. Once you are familiar with your topic, you need to concentrate on finding sources that will best support the claims you want to make, and your increasing familiarity with the issue will make it easier to identify the best sources. That may mean a return trip to the library.

Once you have selected some useful sources to support your claims, make a more in-depth evaluation to be sure you have the best evidence available.

- Is it current enough? Have circumstances changed since this text was published?

- Is the author someone I want to call on as an expert witness? Does the author have the experience or credentials to make a solid argument that carries weight with my readers?

- Is it reliable information for my purposes? It may be highly opinionated, but are the basic facts it presents confirmed in other sources? Is the evidence presented in the text convincing?

These questions are not always easy to answer. In some cases, articles will include some information about the author, such as where he or she works. In other cases, no information or even an author's name is given. In that case, it may help to evaluate the publication and its reputation. If you aren't familiar with a publication and don't feel confident making your own judgment, see if it is described in Katz's *Magazines for Libraries,* which evaluates the reputation and quality of periodicals.

■ Evaluating Web Sources

Web sites pose challenges and offer unique opportunities for researchers, for one reason because they are part of a developing genre of writing. When evaluating a Web site, first examine what kind of site you are reading. Is the Web page selling or advertising goods or services (a business site)? Is it advocating a point of view (an advocacy site) or providing relatively neutral information, such as that found in the yellow pages (an informative or educational site)? Is the Web site addressing the interests of people in a particular organization or with common interests (an information-sharing site)? Is it reporting up-to-the-minute news (a news site) or appealing to some aspect of an individual's life and interests (a personal site)? Useful information for a research paper may be obtained from any of these kinds of Web pages, but it is helpful to know what the main purpose of the site is — and who its primary audience is — when determining how productive it will be for your research.

As you weigh the main purpose of the site, evaluate its original context. Does the site originate in a traditional medium, such as a print journal or an encyclopedia? Is the site part of an online journal, in which case its material had to go through a screening process? Or is the site the product of one individual's or organization's desire to create a Web page, which means the work may not have been screened or evaluated by any outside agency? In that case, the information may still be valuable, but you must be even more careful when evaluating it.

Answering preliminary questions like these help you before you begin a more specific evaluation of the site's content. To find answers to many of these questions, make a brief overview of the site itself, by looking, for example, at the clues contained in the Web address. That is, *.com* in the address means a business or commercial site; *.edu,* a site sponsored by a university or college; *.k12* is a site associated with a primary or secondary school; *.gov* indicates that the federal government sponsored the site; and *.org* suggests that the site is part of a nonprofit or noncommercial group. Sites originating outside the United States have URLs that end with a two-letter country abbreviation, such as *.uk* for United Kingdom. Although these address clues can reveal a great deal about the origins and purposes of a Web site, remember that personal Web sites may also contain some of these abbreviations. Institutions such as schools and businesses sometimes sponsor individuals' personal Web sites (which are often unscreened by the institution) as well as official institutional sites. One possible key to determining whether a Web site is a personal page, however, is to look for a tilde (~) plus a name or part of a name in the address. Finally, if you are unsure of the sponsoring organization of a page, try erasing all the information in the URL after the first slash (/) and pressing the "Enter" key. Doing so often brings you to the main page of the organization sponsoring the Web site.

Most Web sites include a way to contact the author or sponsoring organization of the site, usually through e-mail. This is often a quick and easy way to get answers to the preliminary questions. If the site contains an address or phone number as part of its contact information, this means the organization or individual is available and probably willing to stand behind the site's content. If you can't find contact information the site may not be suitable to use as a primary resource. The information is not necessarily invalid, but such clues should alert you that information found on that page needs to be verified.

For the next step—that of more closely evaluating the contents of any Web site—Web researchers generally agree on the importance of five criteria: the authority, accuracy, objectivity, currency, and coverage of the site.[1] These criteria are just as important in evaluating traditional print texts, but electronic texts require special care. To understand how these criteria work, let's look at a specific example.

■ Evaluating a Web Page: One Example

Your latest assignment for a course in argumentation is to research and write on a topic of significance to you and your future. You are a woman thinking about a career in technology, and you want to know how women fare in such careers. You remember hearing that many women

---

[1] Wolfram Memorial Library Web site.

GirlTECH Home Page

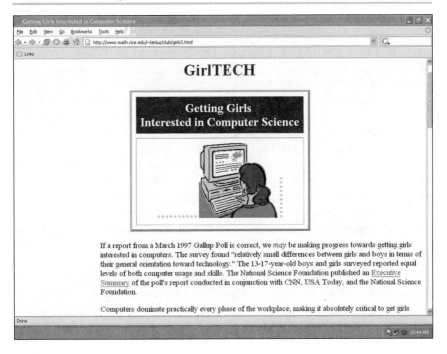

don't choose technology as a career path, despite the opportunities for personal and financial enrichment. You decide to research the subject so that you can write an argument that addresses this issue, maybe one that encourages women to enter computer science. Ultimately, though, your argument will depend on what facts, statistics, and debates you unearth about the broader issue of women following careers in technology. As you research, then, you have at least two competing goals in mind: first, to learn as much as you can about a topic that you find interesting and may affect your professional aspirations, and second, to gather data for a tentative argument you want to make, in this case counteracting the apparent tendency of women to avoid careers in technology.

You begin by using the databases of academic and nonacademic articles typically located through your college's or university's library Web page. These databases direct you to both academic and less formal articles stored in journals that are kept either online or as print materials in your library. You also check the library's catalog for books on the subject. These texts likely will result in a range of sources for your search, and comparing a number of them will give you an idea of what the existing published research about women in technology covers. These kinds of sources— published online or in print—also can provide in-depth coverage of your topic, something that your average Web page found through *Yahoo!* or

Google does not. The different issues covered also will make you realize how important it will be to narrow your topic about women and technology so that you can write an argument on a manageable piece of a complex subject.

After your initial foray into your library's traditional research materials, you want to explore World Wide Web resources. Can women find support on the Web in any online organizations for their choice of a technological career? What resources about this topic are available to someone who may have access to a computer but not to a research library?

You begin searching for answers through at least two of the standard search engines (*Lycos, Ask Jeeves,* or *Yahoo!,* for example). Because each search engine has different strengths and weaknesses, you are likely to find different sources on each. Searches on "Women and Technology" and "Women and Computers" lead to a site titled "Getting Girls Interested in Computer Science" (the home page of which is reproduced here). When the page first comes up, you notice the title underneath the linked name *Cynthia Lanius* in the upper left corner and the heading "Girl-TECH."

Scrolling down, you notice a few paragraphs of text about women in technology (not an in-depth analysis but some potentially useful statistics and resources). You also can see at a glance that Lanius is making use

Cynthia Lanius's Personal Web Page

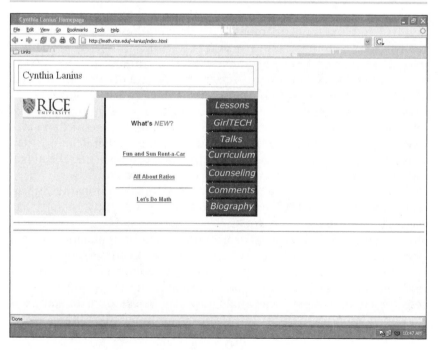

of a documentation style that is possible only in electronic texts. She acknowledges her sources by means of linking directly to electronic versions of them rather than using the more traditional endnotes or parenthetical documentation. Readers who are interested can delve further into the subject by clicking on the links. They can also recognize Lanius as the author of the text on the home page of the site through her use of first person. Hers is the e-mail address they are invited to send comments to, and her linked name is the first thing that viewers see at the top left of the page.

Before you closely examine the page to evaluate its content, pay attention to the site's URL <http://math.rice.edu/~lanius/club/girls3.html>. The *.edu* means that an educational institution sponsors the site, that the institution is Rice University, and even more specifically, that the mathematics department of Rice University sponsors the site. All of this information is determined by erasing the information after *.edu* in the URL. It is also important to note *~lanius* in the URL because it signifies a personal Web page representing the ideas of Cynthia Lanius rather than those of Rice University as an institution. That in itself doesn't disqualify the site as a source of useful information, but it does remind careful readers to examine Cynthia Lanius's credentials and why she created the site. Her exact affiliation with Rice University cannot be told from this opening page and requires further investigation.

A quick review of the whole page shows no sign that it originates from an existing publication or is part of an online journal. This, then, is another reason for the reader to take care in evaluating this site's content. Such a review also reveals that the page is concerned with advocacy as well as with education.

After this preliminary work is completed, you can apply the five criteria for evaluating Web sites: authority, accuracy, objectivity, currency, and coverage.

Authority

You have already begun to wonder about the authority of the author Cynthia Lanius. (The word *author* is the root for *authority*. Think about how these words became connected and how that connection is sometimes abused; not all authors are authorities.) Click on the link Lanius provides at the top of the page, which leads to her home page. This page shows the logo for Rice University, affiliating Lanius with this reputable institution, and also includes a variety of links, including sample math lessons that Lanius created for girls and a variety of reference sources. Most important for an evaluation of her authority, however, is the information about her work experience and the lists of publications, presentations, and awards Lanius provides in her biography. Before her years at Rice University, she taught high school math, at Rice she was Executive Director of the Center for Excellence and Equity in Education, and she is now Technology Integration Specialist for a school district in Texas. The link to some of her presentations shows that Lanius has given numerous speeches on girls, science, math, technology, and education. Clearly, serious organizations and individuals value her ideas and research, which suggests that Lanius's site is potentially useful and that she carries authority as an expert on women and technology.

Lanius's biography also lists the committees she is a member of, with each committee title serving as a link to the group's site. Her site links as well to organizations from which Lanius has received rewards and institutions at which she has worked. This sort of linking makes it possible to verify much of Lanius's information. Obviously you will not be able to verify every detail from every source, but the Web can help you check an authority's credentials and background.

Accuracy

Lanius's GirlTECH Web site includes many different kinds of information: statistics regarding the number of women who received computer science degrees in U.S. universities from 1985 to 1995, statistics that suggest a serious gap between the number of men studying computer science and the number of women pursuing this field, and statistics about the number of boys and girls in high schools taking advanced placement classes and

Lanius's Biography Page

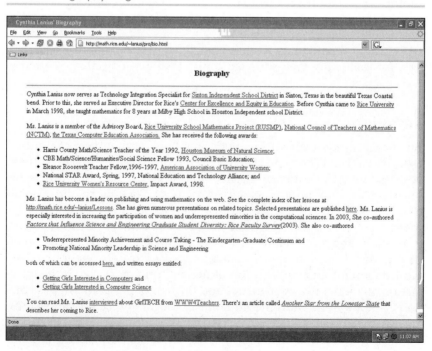

exams in science and math. Since Lanius's Web site—and much of her career—is based on combating statistics such as these, finding out more about these numbers is critical. Statistics come from many sources and are presented (and manipulated) in many ways; understanding their sources and how they compare to other statistics on the same or related issues is imperative. On the GirlTECH home page, Lanius provides links to the National Science Foundation and the College Board, two reliable resources that can help confirm the numbers. As you continue researching, be on the lookout for further statistics and compare them with Lanius's. What larger story about women and technology can you create based on statistical studies and reports?

In the text on the GirlTECH home page, Lanius moves from statistics to her experience working with female high school students. She ends the opening essay with a quote from two of her colleagues at Rice that explains their love of computer science. Such personal testimony cannot be evaluated for accuracy in the same way as can statistics. To evaluate its effectiveness, a thoughtful reader should put himself or herself into the role of a student who feels shut out of technology classes or careers and consider whether the strategy Lanius offers would help alleviate insecurities or difficulties. A reader could also compare Lanius's ideas with those in literature on education and marginalized groups. Most important, though, a reader should recognize that anecdotal information (which may be supported by research but does not represent universal fact) is different from statistical information and must be evaluated using different strategies. Go to the GirlTECH Web site and read through more of its content and the content of some of the links provided. How many kinds of knowledge (facts, opinions, arguments, etc.) are represented? What kinds of strategies will be needed to determine their accuracy?

Objectivity

Objectivity is an especially important and difficult factor to determine for a Web site such as "Getting Girls Interested in Computer Science." The site is concerned both with education and advocacy and is making an argument for a specific issue. The question, then, is not whether the site has any biases; it admits to a clear bias: that of greater inclusion of girls and women in the world of technology. In fact, all sites, even the most neutral ones, have biases; it is not possible to create a perfectly inclusive, objective, value-free text.

For most sites, then, the job of the research writer is to determine the nature of the biases and the degree to which they interfere with the information provided. This process involves analyzing the assumptions, or *warrants,* underlying the argument of a Web page and determining the basis for these warrants.

Lanius's site takes at least three things for granted, that is, it operates from three basic warrants. First, Lanius's site assumes that the number of women in technology-related fields is too low. Second, the site assumes that this low number represents a problem and not simply a difference between the genders that we should accept. Third, the site assumes that early intervention through education can change this trend and help girls see technological fields as options.

The first warrant is easy to analyze. By looking at several studies of women in technological fields (including some of the sites Lanius links to), we can determine that, indeed, the number of women in technological careers is significantly lower than we might expect based on the number of women in the workforce. More difficult is evaluating the objectivity of the second warrant: that this underrepresentation is a problem all educators and, in fact, all people should be concerned about. Such an assumption will provoke a variety of interpretations. Some readers, for example, may believe the low number of women in technological fields to be a reflection of where women's interests lie. Others may view professional career choices as a matter of individual choice and not something that schools or educators should address directly. Still others may assume that any discussion about inclusion of underrepresented groups automatically means quotas or reverse discrimination. It is important for the discriminating reader to understand why Lanius and Rice University would conclude that the low number of women in technological fields is a problem. Similarly, in evaluating the objectivity of Lanius's third warrant, it is important to ask why she believes education is a key to changing this situation.

Only when readers carefully examine issues such as these, while trying to put themselves into Lanius's shoes, can they determine whether an unfair bias makes the information, opinions, and suggestions that Lanius offers tainted or suspect. Such work can be done only when Lanius's work is compared with other research on girls, women, technology, and education, which she, helpfully, has provided access to on her Web site.

Currency

Currency is critical when evaluating Web sites. When a site was first created and when it was last updated influence the way you read the site and how you assess the other four criteria. Take the first criteria of authority, for example.

If you go to the Rice University math department page, you may be surprised to find that Lanius is not listed among the faculty. If you look further, though, you will find her listed under "Resources and Projects." She explains in her biography that while she was formerly on the faculty at Rice, she now works for a public school district. Because GirlTECH is an ongoing project begun at Rice, its site continues to be maintained through the university's site. It is clear from the dates on her publications and presentations that Lanius maintained the site at least through 2003.

Currency plays an equally important role in the second criterion, accuracy. Statistics, for example, change rapidly, and what were cutting-edge numbers a few years ago might now be completely different (for example, the number of Internet users has changed dramatically over the past decade and even in the last few years). It is always useful to analyze how current the statistics and arguments being offered on a Web site may be and to compare the dates of statistics such as the ones Lanius offers to the dates of other studies you encounter. Close analysis helps assure that you can present the most accurate research in your argument and are able to counter arguments based on less current information.

Coverage

Finally, readers of a Web site must evaluate the site's coverage, another difficult issue since no one text or Web site can cover a topic as large and complex as girls and women in technology. One way to gauge the coverage of a Web site is to look carefully at its primary topic and to examine other positions and opinions not represented by the site. Search for these perspectives in other forms of research, both Web-based and print, and think about why the author of the Web site chose not to include them in the text. Are they not of primary importance to the author's ideas? Is it possible that he or she may not be familiar with these alternative perspectives? Is it possible that they are not very reliable? How do you think the author would respond to such perspectives?

Analyzing the variety, quality, and number of links a Web site provides is also important. "Getting Girls Interested in Computer Science" is a successful Web site because it offers a long list of resources and links to other academic centers and professional organizations that promote technological fields for girls and women. It also includes links to online articles describing women in technology and sites that have been specifically created for girls. You may still want to pursue other research that takes the contrary view that the small number of women in technological professions is not the problem that Lanius sees. Nevertheless, this site does provide an excellent, well-rounded coverage of girls, women, and technology.

Conclusion

Evaluating Web sites as sources of information — indeed, evaluating any research text — is a difficult process. The five criteria we've used to evaluate Cynthia Lanius's "Getting Girls Interested in Computer Science" overlap. Starting with any one of the five criteria almost inevitably leads to the others: The accuracy of the information, for example, is clearly related to the authority of the Web site's author, to the biases present in the site, and to the coverage of the information offered. For some sites, one of these criteria will be most important; for others you may have to address all five in detail. You will not be able to analyze every Web site the way we have, but do subject the most important Web sites you encounter to this analysis before you tap them for information central to your work.

WORKING WITH SOURCES

■ Taking Notes

While everyone has methods of taking notes, here are a few suggestions that should be useful to research writers who need to read materials quickly, comprehend and evaluate the sources, use them as part of a research paper assignment, and manage their time carefully.

When taking notes from a source, summarize instead of quoting long passages. Summarizing as you read saves time. If you feel that a direct quote is more effective than anything you could write and provides crucial support for your argument, copy the material word for word. Leave all punctuation exactly as it appears and insert ellipsis points (". . .") if you delete material. Enclose all quotations in quotation marks and copy complete information about your source, including the author's name, the title of the book or article, the journal name if appropriate, page numbers, and publishing information. If you quote an article that appears in an anthology, record complete information about the book itself.

Note Card with
Quotation

> *Hediger*　　　　　　　　　　　　　　　　　　　　**25**
>
> *"The wild animal, with its marked tendency to escape, is notorious for the fact that it is never completely released from that all-important activity, avoiding enemies, even during sleep, but is constantly on alert."*

Note Card with
Summary

> *Hediger*　　　　　　　　　　　　　　　　　　　　**25**
>
> *Animals who live in the wild have to be on the watch for predators constantly.*

If you aren't sure whether you will use a piece of information later, don't copy the whole passage. Instead, make a note of its bibliographic information so that you can find it again if you need it. Taking too many notes, however, is preferable to taking too few, a problem that will force you to go back to the library for missing information.

Record complete bibliographical information for each source that you intend to use in your paper (as well as for those sources you may use). This ensures that you will have all the information necessary to document your paper. Some researchers keep two sets of note cards: one set for the bibliographical information and one set for the notes themselves. Each source then appears on a card by itself, ready to be arranged in alphabetical order for the Works Cited or References page of the paper.

Use the note-taking process as a prewriting activity. Often when you summarize an author's ideas or write down direct quotes, you see or understand the material in new ways. Freewrite about the importance of these quotes, paraphrases, or summaries, or at least about those that seem especially important. If nothing else, take a minute to justify in writing why you chose to record the notes. Doing so will help you clarify and develop your thoughts about your argument.

Note Card with
Statistics

Reiger   *32*
By end of decade, worldwide extinction rate will be one species per hour.
Other statistics, too, in Reiger, "The Wages of Growth," Field and Stream, July 1981:32.

Bibliography
Note Card

Hediger, Heini. The Psychology and Behavior of Animals in Zoos and Circuses. Trans. Geoffrey Sircom. New York: Dover, 1968.

Taking this prewriting step seriously will help you analyze the ideas you record from outside sources. You will then be better prepared for the more formal (and inevitable) work of summarizing, paraphrasing, and composing involved in thinking critically about your topic and writing a research paper. Maybe most important, such work will help with that moment all writers face when they realize they "know what they want to say but can't find the words to say it." Overcoming such moments does not depend on finding inspiration while writing the final draft of a paper. Instead, successfully working through this common form of writer's block depends more on the amount of prewriting and thoughtful consideration of the notes done early in the research process.

As you take notes, also remember to refer to your outline to ensure that you are acquiring sufficient data to support all the points you intend to raise. Of course, you will be revising your outline during the course of your research as issues are clarified and new ideas emerge, but the outline will serve as a rough guide throughout the writing process. Keeping close track of your outline will also prevent you from recording material that is interesting but not relevant.

Relying on the knowledge of others is an important part of doing research; expert opinions and eloquent arguments help support your claims when your own expertise is limited. But remember, this is *your* paper. Your ideas and insights into other people's ideas are just as important as the information you uncover at the library. When writing an argument, do not simply regurgitate the words and thoughts of others in your essay. Work to achieve a balance between providing solid information from expert sources and offering your own interpretation of the argument and the evidence that supports it.

Using word-processing software can invigorate the process of note taking and of outlining (see p. 376). Taking notes using a computer gives you more flexibility than using pen and paper alone. For example, you can save your computer-generated notes and your comments on them in numerous places (at home, school, or work, or on a disk); you can cut and paste the text into various documents; you can add to the notes or modify them and still revert to the originals with ease. (Be sure not to delete or save over your original files, by always using the Save As function when modifying your original files.)

If your computer allows access to the World Wide Web, you can link notes to background material that may be useful once you begin writing drafts of your paper. For example, you could create links to an author's Web page or to any of his or her other works published on the Web. You could create a link to a study or an additional source cited in your notes, or you could link to the work of other researchers who support or argue against the information you recorded.

Because you can record information in any number of ways on your computer, your notes act as tools in the writing process. One of the best ways to start is to open a file for each source; enter the bibliographic information; directly type into the file a series of potentially useful quotations, paraphrases, and summaries; and add your initial ideas about the source. (For each entry, note the correct page references as you go along and indicate clearly whether you are quoting, paraphrasing, or summarizing.) You can then use the capabilities of your computer to aid you in the later stages of the writing process. For example, you can collect all your research notes into one large file in which you group like sources, evaluate whether you have too much information about one issue or one side of an argument, or examine sources that conflict with one another. You can imagine various organizational schemes for your paper based on the central themes and issues of the notes you have taken, and you can more clearly determine which quotes and summaries are essential to your paper and which may not be needed.

When you're ready to begin your first draft, the computer allows you to readily integrate material from your source notes into your research paper by cutting and pasting, thus eliminating the need to retype and reducing the chance of error. You can also combine all the bibliographic materials you have saved in separate files and then use the computer to alphabetize your sources for your final draft.

Although word processors do not dramatically change the research process, they do highlight the fact that taking notes, prewriting, drafting a paper, and creating bibliographies are integrated activities that should build from one another. When you take notes from a journal, book, or Web site, you develop your note-taking abilities so that they help with the entire writing process.

■ Quoting

You may want to quote passages or phrases from your sources if they express an idea in words more effective than your own. In this particular project, you might come across a statement that provides succinct, irrefutable evidence for an issue you wish to support. If the author of this statement is a professional in his or her field, someone with a great deal of authority on the subject, it would be appropriate to quote that author. Suppose, during the course of your research for the zoo paper, you find that many sources agree that zoos don't have the money or space necessary to maintain large enough animal populations to ensure successful captive breeding programs. But so far you only have opinions to that effect. You have been unable to find any concrete documentation of this fact until you come across Ulysses S. Seal's address to the National Zoological Park Symposia for the Public, September 1982. Here is how you could use Seal's words in your paper (using reference citation style of the American Psychological Association):

> Bear in mind that "none of these [zoo] budgets is allocated specifically for species preservation. Zoos have been established primarily as recreational

> institutions and are only secondarily developing programs in conservation, education and research" (Seal, 1982, p. 74).

Notice the use of brackets (not parentheses) in the first sentence, which enclose material that did not appear in the original source but is necessary for clarification. Brackets must be used to indicate any such changes in quoted material. Equally important, however, is that you introduce the author of the quote in such a way as to establish that person's authority on the subject under discussion. This is even more important in argumentation than in other types of writing. In the example above, it is unlikely that anyone except zoo employees—and probably not even those individuals—would know who Seal is simply from seeing his name mentioned in parentheses. Your argument will have more power if you establish the authority of each author from whose work you quote, paraphrase, or summarize. To establish authority, you may refer to the person's position, institutional affiliation, publications, or some other similar "claim to fame."

> According to the late Ulysses S. Seal III (1982), founder of the Conservation Breeding Specialist Group and of a "computer dating service" for mateless animals, "None of these [zoo] budgets is allocated specifically for species preservation. Zoos have been established primarily as recreational institutions and are only secondarily developing programs in conservation, education, and research" (p. 74).

Notice that once the name of the author being cited is mentioned in the writer's own text, it does not have to be repeated in the parentheses. This particular example uses APA style. Later in the chapter, you will see more examples of both APA and MLA styles of documentation.

Writer's Guide: Incorporating Quotations into Your Text

1. The most effective way to lead into the first quotation from a source is to use the author's full name and his or her claim to authority — a few words identifying the person by title, institutional affiliation, or publications. Remember that for nonspecialists, the name of an author you are quoting may have little meaning, and relegating the last name to parentheses at the end of the quotation does not use that author's authority to strengthen your argument. Once you have used the full name once, any future references may use only the last name of the author. If the author's name, full or last only, is used in your lead-in to the quote, you do not have to repeat it in the parentheses that complete the documentation. One additional advantage of mentioning the author or authors is that a reader can tell where your ideas leave off and those from your source begin.

2. There are three primary means of linking a supporting quotation to your own text. Remember that in each case, the full citation for the source will be listed alphabetically by the author's name in the list of works cited at the end of the paper, or by title if no author is given. The number in parentheses is the page of that source on which the quotation appears. The details of what appears in parentheses will be covered later in the discussion of MLA (Modern Language Association) and APA (American Psychological Association) documentation styles.

- You may choose to make a brief quotation a grammatical part of your own sentence. In that case, you do not separate the quotation from your sentence with a comma, unless there is another reason for the comma, and you do not capitalize the first word of the quotation, unless there is another reason for doing so. In this sort of situation, there may be times when you have to change the tense of a verb, in brackets, to make the quote fit smoothly into your text or when you need to make other small changes, always in brackets.

EXAMPLES

APA style

James Rachels (1976), University Professor of Philosophy at the University of Alabama at Birmingham and author of several books on moral philosophy, explains that animals' right to liberty derives from "a more basic right not to have one's interests needlessly harmed" (p. 210).

MLA style

James Rachels, University Professor of Philosophy at the University of Alabama at Birmingham and author of several books on moral philosophy, explains that animals' right to liberty derives from "a more basic right not to have one's interests needlessly harmed" (210).

- You may use a traditional speech tag such as "he says" or "she writes." This is the most common way of introducing a quote. Be sure to put a comma after the tag and begin the quotation with a capital letter. At the end of the quotation, close the quote, add the page number and any other necessary information in parentheses, and then add the period.

EXAMPLES

APA style

James Rachels (1976), University Professor of Philosophy at the University of Alabama at Birmingham and author of several books on moral philosophy, writes, "The right to liberty — the right to be free of external constraints on one's actions — may then be seen as derived from a more basic right not to have one's interests needlessly harmed" (p. 210).

MLA style

James Rachels, University Professor of Philosophy at the University of Alabama at Birmingham and author of several books on moral philosophy, writes, "The right to liberty — the right to be free of external constraints on one's actions — may then be seen as derived from a more basic right not to have one's interests needlessly harmed" (210).

Students are sometimes at a loss as to what sorts of verbs to use in these tag statements. Try using different terms from this list or others like them. Remember that in writing about a printed or electronic text, it is customary to write in present tense unless there is a compelling reason to use past tense.

argues	declares	replies
asks	explains	responds
asserts	implores	states
concludes	insists	suggests
continues	proclaims	
counters	questions	

• You may vary the way you introduce quotations by using a colon to separate the quotation from a *complete sentence* that introduces it.

EXAMPLES

APA style

For example, the Zurich Zoo's Dr. Heini Hediger (1985) protests that it is absurd to attribute human qualities to animals at all, but he nevertheless resorts to a human analogy: "Wild animals in the zoo rather resemble estate owners. Far from desiring to escape and regain their freedom, they are only bent on defending the space they inhabit and keeping it safe from invasion" (p. 9).

MLA style

The late Ulysses S. Seal III, founder of the Conservation Breeding Specialist Group and of a "computer dating service" for mateless animals, acknowledges the subordinate position species preservation plays in budgeting decisions: "Zoos have been established primarily as recreational institutions and are only secondarily developing programs in conservation, education, and research" (74).

3. Long quotations are handled differently from shorter ones. In MLA style, a quotation of more than four lines and in APA style, a quotation of more than forty words are set off as a block quotation. That means that the writer must double-space before and after the quotation — as well as double-spacing the quotation itself — and indent the whole quotation ten additional spaces (MLA) or five spaces (APA) from the left margin. The passage is not placed in quotation marks because the placement on the page indicates that it is a quotation. With block quotations, the parentheses used to provide documentation at the end of the passage are placed after, rather than before, the period. Block quotations should be used even more sparingly than shorter ones.

4. Avoid "floating" quotations. That is, do not jump from a sentence of your own text into a quotation with no connection between the two. Introduce every direct quotation.

5. Avoid back-to-back quotations. There should always be some of your own ideas to justify including a quotation, so some of your own text should always intervene between quoted passages. Quotations should be introduced logically and gracefully in your text. Make sure that the quoted material either supports or illustrates the point you have just made or the point you are about to make and that your writing remains grammatically correct once the quotation is introduced.

Quotations should be introduced logically and gracefully in your text. Make sure that the quoted material either supports or illustrates the point you have just made or the point you are about to make and that your writing remains grammatically correct once the quotation is introduced.

Quotations are an important tool for establishing your claims, but it is important not to overuse them. If you cannot say most of what you want to say in your own words, you probably haven't thought hard enough about what it is you want to say.

■ Paraphrasing

Paraphrasing involves restating the content of an original source in your own words. It is most useful when the material from your source is too long for your paper, can be made clearer to the reader by rephrasing, or is written in a style markedly different from your own.

A paraphrase should be as true to the original source as you can make it: Do not change the tone or the ideas, or even the order in which the ideas are presented. Take care not to allow your own opinions to creep into your paraphrase of someone else's argument. Your readers should always be aware of which arguments belong to you and which belong to outside sources.

Like a quotation, a paraphrase must *always* include documentation, or you will be guilty of plagiarism. Even though you are using your own words, the ideas in a paraphrase belong to someone else, and that person deserves credit for them. One final caveat: When putting a long passage into your own words, beware of picking up certain expressions and turns of phrase from your source. If you do end up using your source's exact words, make sure to enclose them in quotation marks.

Below is a passage from Shannon Brownlee's "First It Was 'Save the Whales,' Now It's 'Free the Dolphins'" (*Discover,* December 1986, pp. 70–72), along with a good paraphrase of the passage and two unacceptable paraphrases. Following APA style, the author's last name and the date of publication are provided in parentheses in the original because they are not mentioned in the text.

ORIGINAL PASSAGE

But are we being good caretakers by holding a dolphin or a sea lion in a tank? Yes, if two conditions are met: that they're given the best treatment possible and, no less important, that they're displayed in a way that educates and informs us. Captive animals must be allowed to serve as ambassadors for their species (Brownlee, 1986, p. 72).

A PARAPHRASE THAT PLAGIARIZES

In "First It Was 'Save the Whales,' Now It's 'Free the Dolphins,'" Shannon Brownlee (1986) argues that it's all right for people to hold animals in captivity as long as (1) the animals are treated as well as possible, and (2) the animals are displayed in a way that educates the public. Brownlee insists that animals be allowed to serve as "ambassadors for their species" (p. 72).

A PARAPHRASE THAT ALTERS THE MEANING OF THE ORIGINAL PASSAGE

According to Shannon Brownlee (1986), a captive animal is being treated fairly as long as it's kept alive and its captivity gives people pleasure. In her essay, "First It Was 'Save the Whales,' Now It's 'Free the Dolphins,'" she argues that people who keep animals in cages are responsible to the animals in only two ways: (1) they should treat their captives as well as possible (even if a small tank is all that can be provided), and (2) they should make sure that the spectators enjoy watching them (p. 72).

A GOOD PARAPHRASE

Shannon Brownlee (1986) holds that two criteria are necessary in order for the captivity of wild animals to be considered worthwhile. First, the animals should be treated as well as possible. Second, their captivity should have educational value for the people who come to look at them. "Captive animals," Brownlee claims, "must be allowed to serve as ambassadors for their species" (p. 72).

■ Summarizing

A summary, like a paraphrase, involves shortening the original passage as well as putting it in your own words. It gives the gist of the passage, including the important points while leaving out details. What makes summarizing difficult is that it requires you to capture often long and complex texts in just a few lines or a short paragraph. To do such work, you must be able to comprehend a variety of materials (see page 26 on "Responding as a Critical Reader" and specifically the section on "Comprehending Arguments" for further advice on this issue). To summarize well, you need to imagine yourself as the author of the piece you are summarizing and be true to the ideas that the author is expressing, even when those ideas conflict with your point of view. You must then move smoothly from being a careful reader to being a writer who, in your own words, recreates another's thoughts.

We summarize for many reasons: to let our boss know the basics of what we have been doing or to tell a friend why she should or should not see a movie. In your classes you are often asked to summarize articles or books, and even when this is not an explicit part of an assignment, the ability to summarize is usually expected. That is, when you are instructed to analyze an essay or to compare and contrast two novels, central to this work is the ability to carefully comprehend and recreate authors' ideas. Summarizing is the cornerstone on which all other critical reading and writing tasks are built.

When writing a research paper, the ability to summarize effectively is especially critical, because sources, though useful for your argument, will simply be too long to include in your text. It is up to you, then, to summarize those points and ideas that are most critical for your argument either because they support that argument or because they represent a counter point of view.

For instance, in the paper at the end of this chapter, "Why Zoos Should Be Eliminated," the statement "It is generally acknowledged that it is difficult to breed zoo animals" is not a direct quotation. The idea comes from Jon Luoma's article in *Audubon* magazine (the writer of this essay acknowledges that this idea comes from Luoma). Returning to the original source makes it clear that neither quoting nor fully paraphrasing would have been suitable choices because the writer was able to reduce the following passage from Luoma's article to one sentence.

> But the successful propagation of entire captive species poses awesome management problems. . . . Sanford Friedman, the Minnesota Zoo's director of biological programs, had explained to me that long-term maintenance of a species in captivity demands solutions to these fundamental problems. "First, we have to learn *how* to breed them. Second, we have to decide *who* to breed. And third, we have to figure out *what* to do with them and their offspring once we've bred them."

This passage is far too long to include in a brief research paper but is easily summarized without losing any of its effectiveness.

When summarizing long or difficult texts, try some of the following strategies to help you comprehend the essential points of the text.

1. Before you summarize, analyze the text following the strategies given in the section on "Responding as a Critical Reader" (p. 26). For example, you should always utilize prereading strategies by looking over the text as a whole before you read it carefully. Such work will often yield clues about the central ideas of the text from the title, the subheadings, and the introduction. Also, use your pen once you begin to read the text so that you link the acts of reading and writing. Underline important ideas, ask questions in the margins about difficult or significant ideas, and highlight

topic sentences. Take a few minutes after reading the essay to jot down the essential ideas and any questions you have about the reading.

2. Reread the introduction and conclusion after you have read the essay once or twice. These two sections should complement each other and offer clues to the most significant issues of the text. An introduction or conclusion is often more than one paragraph; therefore, it is important that you read the first and last few paragraphs of an essay to understand what the author is trying to impress upon the reader. If you are summarizing a book, look especially at the preface, the first and last chapters, and any reviewers' comments. These sections will not tell you everything you need to know to summarize an entire book, but they will help you decide which points matter.

3. For a difficult essay, you may want to list all the subheadings (if they are used) or the topic sentence of each paragraph. These significant guideposts will map the piece as a whole: What do they tell you about the central ideas and the main argument the author is making? After reviewing the subheads or topic sentences, can you reread the essay and engage more easily with its finer points? For a book, you can do the same thing with chapter headings to break down the essential ideas. Remember that when you summarize, you must put another's words into your own (and cite the original text as well), so do not simply let a list of the subheadings or chapter titles stand in for your summary. They likely won't make sense when put together in paragraph form, but they will provide you with valuable ideas regarding the central points of the text.

4. Remember that summarizing requires attention to overall meaning and not to specific details. Therefore, avoid including many specific examples or concrete details from the text you are summarizing and try to let your reader know what these examples and details add up to. Some of the specificity and excitement of the original text will be lost, but when summarizing, the goal is not to recreate all that is interesting about the original text. Rather, the writer's goal is to let the reader know the essential meaning of the original text in a clear, straightforward way.

■ Avoiding Plagiarism

Plagiarism is the use of someone else's words or ideas without adequate acknowledgment—that is, presenting such words or ideas as your own. Putting something in your own words is not in itself a defense against plagiarism; the source of the ideas must be identified as well. Giving credit to the sources you use serves three important purposes: (1) it reflects your own honesty and seriousness as a researcher; (2) it enables the reader to find the source of the reference and read further, sometimes to verify that the source has been correctly used; and (3) it adds the authority of experts to your argument. Deliberate plagiarism is nothing less than cheating and theft, and it is an offense that deserves serious punishment.

Accidental plagiarism can be avoided if you take a little care when researching and writing your papers.

The writer of the zoo paper, for instance, uses and correctly introduces the following direct quotation by James Rachels (para. 4):

As James Rachels (1976) writes:

> Humans have a right to liberty because they have various other interests that will suffer if their freedom is unduly restricted. The right to liberty -- the right to be free of external constraints on one's actions -- may then be seen as derived from a more basic right not to have one's interests needlessly harmed. (p. 210)

If the writer of the zoo paper had chosen to state this idea more briefly, in her own words, the result might have been something like this: "Human beings believe in their fundamental right to liberty because they all agree that they would suffer without it. The right to liberty, then, stems from the right not to suffer unnecessarily." Although the wording has been significantly altered, if this statement appeared as is, undocumented, the author of the paper would be guilty of plagiarism because the ideas are not original. To avoid plagiarism, the author needs to include a reference to James Rachels at the beginning of the summary and a citation of the page number at the end. Taking care to document sources is an obvious way to avoid plagiarism. You should also be careful in taking notes and, when writing your paper, indicating where your ideas end and someone else's ideas begin.

When taking notes, make sure either to quote word-for-word *or* to paraphrase: one or the other, not a little bit of both. If you quote, enclose any language that you borrow from other sources in quotation marks. That way, when you look back at your note cards weeks later, you won't mistakenly assume that the language is your own. If you know that you aren't going to use a particular writer's exact words in your paper, then take the time to summarize that person's ideas right away. That will save you time and trouble later.

When using someone else's ideas in your paper, always let the reader know where that person's ideas begin and end. Here is an example from the zoo paper (para. 11):

> When zoo animals do mate successfully, the offspring is often weakened by inbreeding. According to geneticists, this is because a population of 150 breeder animals is necessary in order to "assure the more or less permanent survival of a species in captivity" (Ehrlich & Ehrlich, 1981, p. 211).

The phrase "according to geneticists" indicates that the material to follow comes from another source, cited parenthetically at the end of the borrowed material. If the student had not included the phrase "according to geneticists," it might look as if she only borrowed the passage in quotation marks, and not the information that precedes that passage.

Material that is considered common knowledge—that is, familiar or at least accessible to the general public—does not have to be documented. The author of *Hamlet,* the date the Declaration of Independence was signed, or the definition of *misfeasance,* while open to dispute (some scholars, for example, claim that William Shakespeare did not write *Hamlet*) are indisputably considered to be common knowledge in our culture. Unfortunately, it is not always clear whether a particular fact *is* common knowledge. Although too much documentation can clutter a paper and distract the reader, it's still better to cite too many sources than to cite too few and risk being accused of dishonesty. In general, if you are unsure whether or not to give your source credit, you should document the material.

■ Including Visuals in Your Paper

In this world of instantaneous Internet access to millions of documents and sites, it is easy to perceive knowledge as free for our use. The fact that information is easy to access does not relieve you of the responsibility of giving credit to those who originated the ideas expressed there. In fact, the ease with which material can be posted to the Internet makes it even more difficult to separate valid information from that which is questionable at best.

Since the Internet is a world of images as well as words, it may give you ideas for livening up your own work with all sorts of visuals. Don't forget, though, that you are obligated to give credit to the source of your visuals along with the ideas and words that you use. A graph or chart may provide just the sort of statistical support that will make a key point in your argument, and it can be easily cut and pasted or scanned into your electronic text, but you must document that graph or chart just as you would text. You should acknowledge the location where you found the visual and as much information as is provided about who produced it. If you use copyrighted graphs or charts in work that you publish either in print or electronic form, you should seek permission for their use. The same is true for photographs and other illustrations, although some books and Web sites offer images that you can use free of charge. You may be surprised to find that something as common as your school's logo is copyrighted and cannot be used on your Web page, for example, without permission.

■ Keeping Research under Control

Your preliminary outline provides guideposts for your research. You will need to revise it as you go along to make room for new ideas and evidence and for the questions that come up as you read. Rather than try to fit each new piece of information into your outline, you can use the numbering or lettering system in your outline to cross-reference your notebooks or file cards.

As much as possible, keep all materials related to the same point in the same place. You might do this by making a separate pile of file cards for each point and its support and questions or by reserving several pages in your notebook for information bearing on each point.

How do you know when you have done enough research? If you have kept your outline updated, you have a visual record of your progress. Check this against the guidelines on pages 394–96. Is each point backed by at least two pieces of support? Do your sources represent a range of authors and of types of data? If a large proportion of your support comes from one book, or if most of your references are to newspaper articles, you probably need to keep working. On the other hand, if your notes cite five different authorities making essentially the same point, you may have collected more data than you need. It can be useful to point out that more than one authority holds a given view and to make notes of examples that are notably different from one another. But it is not necessary to take down all the passages or examples expressing the same idea.

■ To This Point

Before you leave the library or your primary sources and start writing, check to make sure your research is complete.

1. Does your working outline show any gaps in your argument?

2. Have you found adequate data to support your claim?

3. Have you identified the warrants linking your claim with data and ensured that these warrants too are adequately documented?

4. If you intend to quote or paraphrase sources in your paper, do your notes include exact copies of all statements you may want to use and complete references?

5. Have you answered all the relevant questions that have come up during your research?

6. Do you have enough information about your sources to document your paper?

Writer's Guide: Checklist for Research Papers

1. If your assignment required a certain number of sources, have you *used* at least that many and not simply listed that many in your Works Cited page? (Remember that you list only the works you actually quote from, paraphrase, or summarize in your paper.)

2. Have you introduced each direct quotation, identifying the source by name and claim to authority?

3. Have you provided parenthetical documentation for any material that you quoted, paraphrased, or summarized, according to the style that you are using (MLA or APA)?

4. If the author is clearly identified in your sentence, have you omitted the name from the parentheses?

5. If a reader looks for that author's name in the Works Cited page, will he or she find it in proper alphabetical order?

6. If a reader looks for the information cited on the page you give in parentheses, will he or she find it on that page?

7. If there is more than one author, have you acknowledged all of the authors instead of only the first one?

8. If you have a quotation long enough to be handled as a block quote, have you indented it properly; provided the proper documentation, properly punctuated; and left off the quotation marks (except for any that were in the original)?

9. Is any wording in quotation marks *exactly* as it was in the original except for any wording in brackets or any omissions indicated by ellipses?

10. Have you avoided any back-to-back quotations that have none of your text in between?

11. Have you double-spaced the paper throughout, including any block quotations and the entries in the Works Cited page?

12. Have you checked for accuracy every entry on your Works Cited page, using the examples in this book as models?

13. Are the second and following lines in a Work Cited entry indented five spaces more than the first line?

14. Have you edited for any errors in grammar and mechanics?

COMPILING AN ANNOTATED BIBLIOGRAPHY

An annotated bibliography is a list of sources that includes the usual bibliographic information followed by a paragraph describing and evaluating each source. Its purpose is to provide information about each source in a bibliography so that the reader has an overview of the resources related to a given topic.

For each source in an annotated bibliography, the same bibliographic information included in a Works Cited or References list is provided, alphabetized by author. Each reference also has a short paragraph that describes the work, its main focus, and, if appropriate, the methodology used in or the style of the work. An annotation might note special features such as tables or illustrations. Usually an annotation evaluates the source by analyzing its usefulness, reliability, and overall significance for understanding the topic. An annotation might include some information on the credentials of the author or the organization that produced it.

A SAMPLE ANNOTATION USING THE MLA CITATION STYLE

Warner, Marina. "Pity the Stepmother." <u>New York Times</u>. 12 May 1991, late
    ed.: D17. <u>Lexis/Nexis Universe</u> 12 Dec. 1998 <http://web.lexis-nexis
    .com/universe/form/academic/univ_gennews.html>.

The author asserts that many fairy tales feature absent or cruel mothers,
transformed by romantic editors such as the Grimm brothers into stepmothers because the idea of a wicked mother desecrated an ideal. She
argues that figures in fairy tales should be viewed in their historical context and that social conditions often affected the way that motherhood
figured in fairy tales. Warner, a novelist and author of books on the images of Joan of Arc and the Virgin Mary, writes persuasively about the
social roots of a fairy-tale archetype.

A SAMPLE ANNOTATION USING THE APA CITATION STYLE

"Don't Zoos Contribute to the Saving of Species from Extinction?" <u>Animal
    Rights Resource Site</u>. Envirolink Network. 14 Dec. 1998 <http://arrs
    .envirolink.org/Faqs+Ref/ar-faq/Q68.html>.

This Web site provides arguments against the idea that zoos save species
from extinction. Breeding in captivity doesn't always work, and the limited gene pool creates problems. Habitat restoration is difficult, and
until the problems of poaching and pollution are solved, the habitat
will be dangerous for reintroduced species. Meanwhile, the individual
animals living in zoos lose their freedom because of an abstract and
possibly faulty concept. This Web site, part of the Animal Rights Resource Site sponsored by the Envirolink organization, is brief but
outlines the major arguments against zoos' role in preserving species.

MLA SYSTEM FOR CITING PUBLICATIONS

One of the simplest methods of crediting sources is the Modern Language
Association (MLA) in-text system, which is used in the research paper on
fairy tales in this chapter. In the text of your paper, immediately after any
quotation, paraphrase, or anything else you wish to document, simply insert a parenthetical mention of the author's last name and the page number on which the material appeared. You don't need a comma after the
author's name or an abbreviation of the word "page" or "p." For example,
the following sentence appears in the fairy tale paper:

> Famines in the seventeenth century often reduced the peasantry to a diet
> of "bad black bread, acorns, and roots" (Weber 96).

The parenthetical reference tells the reader that the information in this
sentence came from page 96 of the book or article by Eugen Weber that

appears in the Works Cited, at the end of the paper. The complete reference on the Works Cited page provides all the information readers need to locate the original source in the library:

Weber, Eugen. "Fairies and Hard Facts: The Reality of Folktales." Journal of the
  History of Ideas 42 (1981): 93-113.

If the author's name is mentioned in the same sentence, it is also acceptable to place only the page numbers in parentheses; it is not necessary to repeat the author's name. For example,

> Bettelheim sees symbolic meaning in every motif and element in the story,
> and assumes that children interpret these symbolically as well (159-66).

If you are using more than one work by the same author, you will need to provide in the parentheses the title or a recognizable shortened form of the title of the particular work being cited. If the author's name is not mentioned in the sentence, you should include in parentheses the author's last name, the title, and the page number, with a comma between the author's name and the title. If both the author's name and the title of any work being cited are mentioned in the sentence, the parentheses will include only the page number.

Some sources do not name an author. To cite a work with an unknown author, give the title, or a recognizable shortened form, in the text of your paper. If the work does not have numbered pages, often the case in Web pages or nonprint sources, do not include page numbers. For example,

> In some cases Sephardic Jews, "converted" under duress, practiced Chris-
> tianity openly and Judaism in secret until recently ("Search for the Buried
> Past").

The list of works cited includes all material you have used to write your research paper. This list appears at the end of your paper and always starts on a new page. Center the title Works Cited, double-space between the title and the first entry, and begin your list, which should be arranged alphabetically by author. Each entry should start at the left margin; indent all subsequent lines of the entry five spaces. Number each page, and double-space throughout.

Another method of documenting sources is to use notes, either footnotes (at the foot of the page) or endnotes (on a separate page at the end of the paper). The note method is not as commonly used today as the in-text system because reference notes repeat almost all the information already given on the Works Cited page. If footnotes or endnotes are used, most word-processing programs have functions that make the insertion of these notes convenient.

Nevertheless, it is a valid method, so we illustrate it here. Superscript numbers go at the end of the sentence or phrase being referenced:

Roman authors admit to borrowing frequently from earlier Greek writers for their jokes, although no joke books in the original Greek survive today.[1]

The reference note for this citation would be

[1]Alexander Humez and Nicholas Humez, Alpha to Omega (Boston: Godine, 1981) 79.

On the Works Cited page this reference would be:

Humez, Alexander, and Nicholas Humez. Alpha to Omega. Boston: Godine,
     1981.

Notice that the page number for a book citation is given in the note but not the reference and that the punctuation differs. Otherwise the information is the same. Number the notes consecutively throughout your paper.

One more point: *Content notes*, which provide additional information not readily worked into a research paper, are also indicated by superscript numbers. Susan Middleton's paper on fairy tales features four such notes, included on a Notes page before the list of Works Cited.

Following are examples of the citation forms you are most likely to need as you document your research. In general, for both books and magazines, information should appear in the following order: author, title, and publication information. Each item should be followed by a period. When using as a source an essay that appears in this book, follow the citation model for "Material reprinted from another source," unless your instructor indicates otherwise. Consult the *MLA Handbook for Writers of Research Papers*, Fifth Edition, by Joseph Gibaldi (New York: Modern Language Association of America, 1999) for other documentation models and a list of acceptable shortened forms of publishers.

■ Print Sources

A BOOK BY A SINGLE AUTHOR

Gubar, Susan. Racechanges: White Skin, Black Face in American Culture. New
     York: Oxford UP, 1997.

AN ANTHOLOGY OR COMPILATION

Dark, Larry, ed. Prize Stories 1997: The O. Henry Awards. New York: Anchor,
     1997.

A BOOK BY TWO AUTHORS

Alderman, Ellen, and Caroline Kennedy. The Right to Privacy. New York: Vintage,
     1995.

Note: This form is followed even for two authors with the same last name.

Ehrlich, Paul, and Anne Ehrlich. <u>Extinction: The Causes and Consequences of the Disappearance of Species</u>. New York: Random, 1981.

A BOOK BY TWO OR MORE AUTHORS

Heffernan, William A., Mark Johnston, and Frank Hodgins. <u>Literature: Art and Artifact</u>. San Diego: Harcourt, 1987.

If there are more than three authors, name only the first and add "et al." (and others).

A BOOK BY A CORPORATE AUTHOR

Poets & Writers, Inc. <u>The Writing Business: A Poets & Writers Handbook</u>. New York: Poets & Writers, 1985.

A WORK IN AN ANTHOLOGY

Head, Bessie. "Woman from America." <u>Wild Women: Contemporary Short Stories by Women Celebrating Women</u>. Ed. Sue Thomas. Woodstock: Overlook, 1994. 45-51.

AN INTRODUCTION, PREFACE, FOREWORD, OR AFTERWORD

Callahan, John F. Introduction. <u>Flying Home and Other Stories</u>. By Ralph Ellison. Ed. John F. Callahan. New York: Vintage, 1996. 1-9.

MATERIAL REPRINTED FROM ANOTHER SOURCE

Diffie, Whitfield, and Susan Landau. "Privacy: Protections and Threats." <u>Privacy on the Line: The Politics of Wiretapping and Encryption</u>. Cambridge, MA: MIT P, 1998. Rpt. in <u>Elements of Argument: A Text and Reader</u>. Annette T. Rottenberg. 7th ed. Boston: Bedford/St. Martin's, 2003. 554.

A MULTIVOLUME WORK

Skotheim, Robert Allen, and Michael McGiffert, eds. <u>Since the Civil War</u>. Vol. 2 of <u>American Social Thought: Sources and Interpretations</u>. 2 vols. Reading: Addison, 1972.

AN EDITION OTHER THAN THE FIRST

Charters, Ann, ed. <u>The Story and Its Writer: An Introduction to Short Fiction</u>, 5th ed. Boston: Bedford/St. Martin's, 1999.

A TRANSLATION

Allende, Isabel. <u>The House of the Spirits</u>. Trans. Magda Bogin. New York: Knopf, 1985.

A REPUBLISHED BOOK

Weesner, Theodore. <u>The Car Thief</u>. 1972. New York: Vintage-Random, 1987.

Note: The only information about original publication you need to provide is the publication date, which appears immediately after the title.

A BOOK IN A SERIES

Eady, Cornelius. <u>Victims of the Latest Dance Craze</u>. Omnation Press Dialogues on Dance Series 5. Chicago: Omnation, 1985.

AN ARTICLE FROM A DAILY NEWSPAPER

Doctorow, E. L. "Quick Cuts: The Novel Follows Film into a World of Fewer Words." <u>New York Times</u> 15 Mar. 1999, sec. B: 1+.

AN ARTICLE FROM A PERIODICAL

Schulhofer, Stephen. "Unwanted Sex." <u>Atlantic Monthly</u> Oct. 1998: 55-66.

AN UNSIGNED EDITORIAL

"Medium, Message." Editorial. <u>Nation</u> 28 Mar. 1987: 383-84.

ANONYMOUS WORKS

"The March Almanac." <u>Atlantic</u> Mar. 1995: 20.

<u>Citation World Atlas</u>. Maplewood: Hammond, 1987.

AN ARTICLE FROM A JOURNAL WITH SEPARATE PAGINATION FOR EACH ISSUE

Brewer, Derek. "The Battleground of Home: Versions of Fairy Tales." <u>Encounter</u> 54.4 (1980): 52-61.

AN ARTICLE IN A JOURNAL WITH CONTINUOUS PAGINATION THROUGHOUT THE VOLUME

McCafferty, Janey. "The Shadders Go Away." <u>New England Review and Bread Loaf Quarterly</u> 9 (1987): 332-42.

Note that the issue number is not mentioned here; because the volume has continuous pagination throughout the year, only the volume number 9 is needed.

A REVIEW

Walker, David. Rev. of <u>A Wave</u>, by John Ashbery. <u>Field</u> 32 (1985): 63-71.

AN ARTICLE IN A REFERENCE WORK

"Bylina." <u>The Princeton Encyclopedia of Poetry and Poetics</u>. Ed. Alex Preminger. Enlarged ed. Princeton: Princeton UP, 1974.

A GOVERNMENT DOCUMENT

United States. National Endowment for the Arts. <u>1989 Annual Report</u>. Washington: Office of Public Affairs, 1990.

Frequently the Government Printing Office (GPO) is the publisher of federal government documents.

REPORTS

Gura, Mark. <u>The Gorgeous Mosaic Project: A Work of Art by the Schoolchildren of the World</u>. Teacher's packet. East Brunswick: Children's Atelier, 1990. ERIC ED 347 257.

Kassebaum, Peter. Cultural Awareness Training Manual and Study Guide. ERIC, 1992. ED 347 289.

The ERIC number at the end of the entry indicates that this source is available through ERIC (Educational Resource Information Center); some libraries have these available on microfiche. The number indicates which report to look for. Some ERIC documents were published elsewhere, as in the first example. If no other publishing information is given, treat ERIC (with no city given) as the publisher, as shown in the second entry. Reports are also published by NTIS (National Technical Information Service), state geological surveys, organizations, institutes within universities, and so on and may be called "technical reports," or "occasional papers." Be sure to include the source and the unique report number, if given.

AN UNPUBLISHED MANUSCRIPT

Leahy, Ellen. "An Investigation of the Computerization of Information Systems in a Family Planning Program." Unpublished master's degree project. Div. of Public Health, U of Massachusetts, Amherst, 1990.

A LETTER TO THE EDITOR

Flannery, James W. Letter. <u>New York Times Book Review</u> 28 Feb. 1993: 34.

PERSONAL CORRESPONDENCE

Bennett, David. Letter to the author. 3 Mar. 1993.

A CARTOON

Henley, Marian. "Maxine." Cartoon. <u>Valley Advocate</u> 25 Feb. 1993: 39.

■ Electronic Sources

A WEB SITE

<u>Fairy Tales: Origins and Evolution</u>. Ed. Christine Daaé. 12 Dec. 1998 <http://www.darkgoddess.com/fairy>.

Include the title if available; the author's name if available or, if not, a generic description such as "Home page"; the sponsoring organization or institution except in the case of commercial sponsorship; date of access; and URL in angle brackets.

A PAGE WITHIN A WEB SITE

"Don't Zoos Contribute to the Saving of Species from Extinction?" Animal Rights Resource Site. Envirolink Network. 14 Dec. 1998 <http://arrs.envirolink .org/faqs+Ref/ar-faq/Q68.html>.

A BOOK AVAILABLE ON THE WEB

Kramer, Heinrich, and James Sprenger. The Malleus Maleficarum. Trans. Montague Summers. New York: Dover, 1971. 14 Dec. 1998 <http://www .geocities.com/Athens/2962/witchcraze/malleus_2_ii_html>.

In this case the book had been previously published, and information about its original publication was included at the site.

AN ARTICLE FROM AN ELECTRONIC JOURNAL

Minow, Mary. "Filters and the Public Library: A Legal and Policy Analysis." First Monday 2.12 (1 Dec. 1997). 28 Nov. 1998 <http:www .firstmonday.dk/issues/issue2_12/minow/index.html>.

MATERIAL ACCESSED THROUGH A COMPUTER SERVICE

Boynton, Robert S. "The New Intellectuals." Atlantic Monthly Mar. 1995. Atlantic Unbound. America Online. 3 Mar. 1995. Keyword: Atlantic.

A CD-ROM

Corcoran, Mary B. "Fairy Tale." Grolier Multimedia Encyclopedia. CD-ROM. Danbury: Grolier, 1995.

AN ARTICLE FROM A FULL-TEXT DATABASE AVAILABLE THROUGH THE WEB

Warner, Marina. "Pity the Stepmother." New York Times. 12 May 1991, late ed.: D17. Lexis/Nexis Universe 12 Dec. 1998. <http://web.lexis-nexis.com/ universe/form/academic/univ_gennews.html>.

Include the original source information and the name of the database, access date, and URL.

AN ARTICLE FROM A CD-ROM FULL-TEXT DATABASE

"Tribal/DNC Donations." News from Indian Country. (Dec. 1997). Ethnic Newswatch. CD-ROM. Softline. 12 Oct. 1998.

Include the original source information and the name of the database, the designation *CD-ROM,* the publisher of the CD-ROM, and the electronic publication data, if available.

AN ARTICLE FROM AN ELECTRONIC REFERENCE WORK

"Folk Arts." Britannica Online. <u>Encyclopaedia Britannica</u>. 14 Dec. 2002.
    <http://www.eb.com:180>.

A PERSONAL E-MAIL COMMUNICATION

Franz, Kenneth. "Re: Species Reintroduction." E-mail to the author. 12 Oct.
    2001.

AN E-MAIL COMMUNICATION POSTED TO A DISCUSSION LIST

Lee, Constance. "Re: Mothers and Stepmothers." Online posting. 10 Sept. 2002.
    Folklore Discussion List <mglazer@panam.edu>.

If the address of the discussion list archives is known, include that information in angle brackets; if not, place the moderator's e-mail address in
angle brackets.

A POSTING TO A WEB FORUM

DeYoung, Chris. Online posting. 12 Dec. 1998. Issues: Gay Rights. 14 Dec. 1998
    <http://community.cnn.com/cgi-bin/WebX?14@52.7bmLaPoSc49^0@
    .ee7239c/12479>.

Include the author, header (if any) in quotation marks, the designation
Online posting, the date of the posting, the name of the forum, the date of
access, and the URL.

A NEWSGROUP POSTING

Vining, Philip. "Zoos and Infotainment." Online posting. 16 Oct. 2002. 12 Dec.
    2002. <news:alt.animals.ethics.vegetarian>.

Include the author, header in quotation marks, the designation *Online
posting*, the date of posting, the date of access, and the name of the newsgroup.

A SYNCHRONOUS COMMUNICATION

Krishnamurthi, Ashok. Online discussion of cyberlaw and the media. "Reinvent-
    ing Copyright in a Digital Environment." 25 Oct. 2002. MediaMOO. 25 Oct.
    2002 <telnet://purple-crayon.media.mit.edu:8888>.

To cite a synchronous communication from a MUD or a MOO, include
the name of the speaker, a description of the event, the date, the forum,
the date of access, and the electronic address.

■ Other Sources

A LECTURE

Calvino, Italo. "Right and Wrong Political Uses of Literature." Symposium on Eu-
    ropean Politics. Amherst College, Amherst. 25 Feb. 1976.

A FILM

The Voice of the Khalam. Prod. Loretta Pauker. Perf. Leopold Senghor, Okara, Birago Diop, Rubadiri, and Francis Parkes. Contemporary Films/McGraw-Hill, 1971. 16 mm, 29 min.

Other pertinent information to give in film references, if available, is the writer and director (see model for radio/television program for style).

A TELEVISION OR RADIO PROGRAM

The Shakers: Hands to Work, Hearts to God. Narr. David McCullough. Dir. Ken Burns and Amy Stechler Burns. Writ. Amy Stechler Burns, Wendy Tilghman, and Tom Lewis. PBS. WGBY, Springfield. 28 Dec. 1992.

A VIDEOTAPE

Style Wars! Videotape. Prod. Tony Silver and Henry Chalfont. New Day Films, 1985. 69 min.

DVD

Harry Potter and the Sorcerer's Stone. DVD. Prod. Chris Columbus. Warner Bros., 2001. 152 min.

A PERFORMANCE

Quilters: A Musical Celebration. By Molly Newman and Barbara Damashek. Dir. Joyce Devlin. Musical dir. Faith Fung. Mt. Holyoke Laboratory Theatre, South Hadley, MA. 26 Apr. 1991. Based on The Quilters: Women and Domestic Art by Patricia Cooper and Norma Bradley Allen.

AN INTERVIEW

Hines, Gregory. Interview. With D. C. Denison. Boston Globe Magazine 29 Mar. 1987: 2.

Note: An interview conducted by the author of the paper would be documented as follows:

Hines, Gregory. Personal interview. 29 Mar. 1987.

SAMPLE RESEARCH PAPER (MLA STYLE)

The following paper, prepared in the MLA style, was written for an advanced composition course. Told to compose a research paper on a literary topic, Susan Middleton chose to write on fairy tales—a subject literary enough to satisfy her instructor, yet general enough to encompass her own interest in developmental psychology. But as she explored the subject, she found herself reading in a surprising array of disciplines, including folklore, anthropology, and history. Although she initially expected to report on the psychological importance of fairy tales, Middleton at last wrote an argument about the importance of their historical and cultural roots. Her paper, as is typical for literary papers, anchors its argument in the events and details of its chosen text, "Hansel and Gretel." But it also makes effective use of sources to help readers understand that there is more to the tale than a story that sends children happily off to sleep.

When a Fairy Tale Is Not Just a Fairy Tale

By
Susan Middleton

Professor Herrington
English 2A
October 2004

Include a title page if an outline is part of the paper. If no outline is required, include name, instructor's name, course name, and date at the upper left corner of page 1.

Middleton ii

Outline

Topic outline.
Some instruc-
tors require a
thesis state-
ment under
"Outline"
heading and
before the out-
line itself.

I. Introduction:
   A. Dictionary definition of "fairy tale"
   B. Thesis: "Hansel and Gretel" has historical roots
II. Origin and distribution of tale
III. Historical basis of motifs
   A. Physical and economic hardship
      1. Fear of the forest
      2. Poverty and starvation
      3. Child abandonment
      4. Fantasies of finding treasure
   B. Cruel stepmother
   C. Wicked witch
      1. Eating meat associated with cannibalism and upper classes
      2. Elderly caretaker for unwanted children
      3. Witches in community
      4. Witchcraft as remnant of ancient fertility religion
IV. Rebuttals to historical approach
   A. Motivation for telling realistic tales
   B. Psychological interpretations
      1. Fairy tales dreamlike, not literal
      2. Freudian interpretation
V. Conclusion

Middleton 1

When a Fairy Tale Is Not Just a Fairy Tale

"Hansel and Gretel" is a well-known fairy tale, beloved of many children in both Europe and North America.[1] Although it has no fairies in it, it conforms to the definition of "fairy tale" given in <u>Merriam-Webster's Collegiate Dictionary</u>, Tenth Edition: "a story (as for children) involving fantastic forces and beings (as fairies, wizards, and goblins)." As anyone familiar with this tale will remember, Hansel and Gretel are two children on an adventure in the woods, where they encounter a wicked witch in a gingerbread house, who plans to fatten and eat them. Through their ingenuity they outsmart her, burn her up in her own oven, and return home triumphantly with a hoard of riches found in her house.

We think of fairy tales as being lighthearted fantasies that entertain but don't have much relevance to daily life. We often borrow the word to describe a movie with an unlikely plot, or a person not quite grounded in reality: "Oh, he's living in a fairy tale world; he hasn't got his head on his shoulders." In fact, the second definition of "fairy tale" in <u>Webster's</u> is "a made-up story usually designed to mislead."

So what is the meaning of "Hansel and Gretel"? Is it simply a story of make-believe, or something more? Fairy tales are told, read, and heard in the context of a time and place. Today we are exposed to them through illustrated storybooks, cartoons, and film. But in Europe, before technologies in printing made mass publishing possible, folktales were passed on orally. Women were the primary tellers of folktales, though they were later gathered and published by male writers such as Charles Perrault and the Grimm Brothers ("Tales"). They were told by adults mostly for adult audiences, although people often first heard them as children. They served to entertain and to relieve the boredom of repetitive work in the fields during the day and in the home in the evening (Weber 93, 113). In peasant and aboriginal communities, that is often still the case (Taggart 437).

I believe that "Hansel and Gretel" has historical meaning. Embedded in this simple narrative is a record of the

Title centered

Raised, superscript number refers to notes giving information at the end of the paper.

Writer briefly summarizes tale to orient readers.

In-text citation of author and pages; citation appears at the end of the sentence before the period.

Thesis with claim of fact that the writer must support

Middleton 2

experiences and events once common in the lives of the
people who first told and listened to it.

Where did "Hansel and Gretel" come from? We do not
know for certain. In oral form this tale shows wide distribution. Different versions have been recorded all over Europe,
India, Japan, Africa, the Caribbean, Pacific Islands, and among
native North and South Americans ("Hansel and Gretel"). As
with all folktales, there is no agreement among folklorists[2]
about whether all these versions migrated from one place to
another, sprang up independently, or derive from some combination of the two ("Hansel and Gretel"). Most oral versions of
it have been recorded in Europe (Aarne 117). This does not
prove that the tale originated there -- it may simply reflect
the eagerness of people in Europe during the nineteenth and
twentieth centuries to record their own folk history -- but it is
the best guideline for now.

The tale may be very ancient, since folktales can be
passed on faithfully from one generation to another without
change. (The origins of "Cinderella," for example, can be
traced back to China in the ninth century [Thompson,
Folktale 126].) But we can't know that for sure. So, even
though "Hansel and Gretel" may have originated hundreds or
even thousands of years ago, it probably is only safe to compare a tale with the historical period when the tale was first
recorded. For "Hansel and Gretel" this means Europe in the
seventeenth to nineteenth centuries.[3]

Eugen Weber is one historian who sees direct parallels between the characters and motifs in "Hansel and Gretel" (and
other Grimms' fairy tales) and the social and economic conditions in Europe during this period. One of the central themes
in the tale is poverty and abandonment. Recall how the tale
begins: Hansel and Gretel live with their parents near a huge
forest; their father is a woodcutter. The family is facing starvation because there is a famine. Twice their parents abandon
them in the woods to save themselves. The first time the children are able to find their way home, but the second time
they get lost.

Reference to dictionary article — page number not necessary

Square brackets used to represent parentheses within parentheses

Specific support from the tale cited

Middleton 3

As Weber points out, until the middle of the nineteenth century, the forest, especially for northern Europeans, carried the real potential for encountering danger in the form of robbers, wild animals, and getting lost (96-97). Moreover, conditions of poverty, starvation, early death, and danger from unknown adults were common throughout Europe for peasants and the working class (96). The majority of Europeans at the beginning of the eighteenth century were farmers, and the average life expectancy was about twenty-five years (Treasure 660, 667). Famines in the seventeenth century often reduced the peasantry to a diet of "bad black bread, acorns, and roots" (Weber 96). Hansel and Gretel are treated by the witch to a dinner of pancakes and sugar, milk, nuts, and apples (101). This may not sound particularly nourishing to our ears because we assume a healthy dinner must have vegetables and/or meat. But when you're starving, anything is likely to taste good; this would have been a sumptuous meal for Hansel and Gretel.

Consecutive references immediately following an identified source ("Weber") cite only the pages within the source without repeating the source.

Narrative details linked to historical facts

Childhood was thought of differently then than today. "Valued as an extra pair of hands or deplored as an extra mouth to feed, the child belonged to no privileged realm of play and protection from life's responsibilities" (Treasure 664). Social historian John Boswell estimates that anywhere from 10 to 40 percent of children in towns and cities were abandoned during the eighteenth century. Parental motivation included removing the stigma of illegitimate or physically deformed children, being unable to support their children and hoping to give them a better life with strangers, desiring to promote one child's inheritance over another's, or simply lacking interest in raising the child (48, 428).

Source cited after direct quotation

Weber points out that peasants had very little cash and didn't use banks. Hiding and finding treasure -- gold, silver, and jewelry -- was a much more common occurrence two centuries ago than it is today (101), a kind of lottery for the poor. In this light, the riches the children find in the witch's house could reflect the common person's fantasy of striking it rich.

Writer's interpretation of one aspect of the story

Middleton 4

A central motif in the story is the stepmother who wants to abandon the children to keep herself and her husband from starving. (The father, at first reluctant, eventually gives in to his wife's plan.) As Weber and others have noted, stepmothers were not unusual in history. The death rate among childbearing women was much higher in past centuries than it is today. When women died in childbirth, there was strong economic motivation for fathers to remarry. In the seventeenth and eighteenth centuries, 20 to 80 percent of widowers remarried within the year of their wife's death. By the mid-nineteenth century, after life expectancy rose, only 15 percent of widowers did so (94, 112).

Reference to a newspaper

What accounts for the stereotype of the heartless stepmother? Warner argues that mothers, not stepmothers, actually appeared in many of the tales in their original forms, until romantic editors, like the Grimm brothers, "rebelled against this desecration of motherhood and changed mothers into wicked stepmothers" (D17). Weber suggests that stepmothers were assigned the role of doing evil to children for economic reasons: The family would risk losing its good name and perhaps its land if a biological parent killed a child (107). There is also the issue of inheritance from the stepmother's point of view: If her husband dies, her husband's children, not she, would inherit the land and property. Literary and legal evidence of stepmothers plotting to eliminate stepchildren, especially stepsons, shows up in European literature as far back as two millennia ago (Boswell 128).

Transition to new topic: witches

Another major theme in "Hansel and Gretel" is the wicked witch, which also shows up in lots of other fairy tales. One of the common beliefs about witches was that they ate children. According to the words of a purported witch in the Malleus Maleficarum, a treatise on witchcraft published originally around 1486, "[we] cook them in a cauldron until the whole flesh comes away from the bones to make a soup that may be easily drunk" (Kramer and Sprenger, ch. 2, para. 12). The authors of this work were alarmists, describing in sometimes improbable terms the evil behavior of witches, but the question remains: Were there witches in European history, and if so, where did the reputation for eating children come from?

Middleton 5

Weber notes that in fairy tales only evil figures eat meat of any kind, whether animal or human flesh. Before the middle of the nineteenth century the peasantry rarely ate meat, but the aristocracy and bourgeoisie did. This discrepancy may be the origin of the motif in some fairy tales of evil figures of upper-class background wanting to eat children (112, 101). Weber seems to imply that child-eating witches symbolized to the peasantry either resentment of or paranoia about the aristocracy.

Although the witch's cottage in "Hansel and Gretel" is not described as grand or large, there are other allusions to wealth and comfort. The witch puts the two children to bed between clean sheets, a luxury for much of the peasantry, who slept on straw and for whom bed lice were a common reality (Treasure 661-62). And of course there is the hoard of coin money and jewelry the children later discover there. Perhaps more significantly, the witch herself has a lot of power, just as the aristocracy was perceived to have, including the power to deceive and take away life.

David Bakan suggests that the historical basis for the witch is the unmarried elderly woman in the community who took in unwanted, illegitimate children and was often paid to do this (66-67). There is also evidence that witchcraft, ranging from white magic to sorcery (black magic), was practiced by both individual women and men among the peasantry during this time. For example, "the 'cunning folk' were at least as numerous in sixteenth-century England as the parish clergy. Moreover, in their divinatory, medical, and religious functions they were far more important in peasant society than were the official clergy" (Horsley 697). Witches were called on to influence the weather, provide love potions, find lost objects, midwife, identify thieves, and heal illnesses (698). Some services performed by witches were ambiguous: "Apparently some peasants would conjure the storms or weather spirits to avoid striking their own fields -- but to strike someone else's instead," but for the most part the wisewomen and sorcerers were different people (698).

The idea that an organized witch cult, as portrayed by the Catholic Church during the Middle Ages, actually existed

Middleton 6

is dismissed today by most social historians. Jesse Nash thinks we should reconsider the possibility that some of the behavior witches were accused of, including ritual cannibalism and sexual orgies in the woods, actually occurred in some form (12). He sees witchcraft as "a surviving remnant of a religion which was concerned with the fertility of crops, animals, humans, and with the alteration of seasons and with the identification of humans with animals" (13). These practices date back to a matriarchal goddess religion which flourished in Europe 5,000 to 7,000 years ago, before invasion of the patriarchal cultures from India (Marija Gimbutas in Nash 12). This religion included human sacrifice and was based on the concept of maintaining balance in the universe: The goddess of life was at the same time the goddess of death. Woodwives and fairies, who lived in the forest, "were mediators of sacred knowledge to their communities" (16).

Source within a source cited

Nash suggests that in Europe, although Christianity became the official way of thinking about the world, it did not replace the old beliefs entirely, despite strong attempts by the Church to eliminate them. Religious beliefs and practices can persist hidden for generations if need be.[4] The peasants were able to live with and practice both Christianity and paganism in combination for centuries (25).

So we have seen there is validity to the claim that many of the motifs of "Hansel and Gretel" have historical roots. However, one might well ask why people would want to hear stories so close to their own experiences. If oral tales during this time were meant as entertainment mostly for adults, wouldn't they want something to take their minds off their troubles? Weber suggests a couple of motivations for telling fairy tales. One was to experience "the delights of fear" (97). Fairy tales were told along with ghost stories, gossip, jokes, and fables. I suspect it was similar to the thrill some people get today watching scary movies with happy endings.

Having supported her major claim, the writer continues by anticipating and addressing possible rebuttals.

Second, fairy tales helped to explain how the world worked. To most people not able to read, the world of cause and effect was mysterious and could only be explained through symbolism and analogy. Folktales had been used in

Middleton 7

church sermons since the fourteenth century (Weber 110, Zipes 22).

Two sources cited at once

But the industrial age ushered in the scientific revolution, and with it came the concept of explaining the unknown by breaking it down into working parts (Weber 113). Reading became available to large numbers of people. By this time fairy tales were no longer meaningful ways to explain the world for ordinary adults, so they became the province of children's entertainment (113).

Folklorist Alan Dundes thinks it is naive to assume fairy tales have literal meaning. In recent years he and a number of other people have looked to psychology to explain the origin of fairy tales. "Fairy tales are like dreams -- can you find the historic origin of dreams?" (Dundes). In their structure and characters fairy tales do have a number of dreamlike aspects: They rarely state the feelings of the hero directly, and all inner experiences of the hero are projected outward into objects in nature and other people (Tatar 91). The other characters seem not to have separate lives of their own; all their actions and intentions relate to the hero (Brewer 55). Also, magical things happen: Elements of nature speak, granting favors to the hero or threatening success or even life. In one version of "Hansel and Gretel," for example, a white duck talks to the children and carries them across a lake on their way home.

Competing theories presented

Telephone interview—no page numbers

The symbolic nature of fairy tales, however, doesn't deny the validity of examining them for historical origins. As anyone who has recorded their own dreams knows, people and objects from mundane, daily life show up regularly in them. Sometimes these elements are disguised as symbols, but other times they are transparently realistic. Similarly, the talking duck and the gingerbread house in "Hansel and Gretel" may be unreal, but other themes have more literal counterparts in history.

One of the most quoted interpreters of fairy tales is psychologist Bruno Bettelheim, whose The Uses of Enchantment analyzes fairy tales in Freudian terms. In his view, "Hansel and Gretel" represents the task each of us as children must

Middleton 8

face in coming to terms with anxiety -- not the anxiety of facing starvation and being literally abandoned in the woods,
but the ordinary fear of separating from our parents (especially mother) in the process of growing up to become independent adults. Bettelheim sees symbolic meaning in every
motif and element in the story, and assumes that children
interpret these symbolically as well (159-66).

*Partial validity
of competing
theories ac-
knowledged*

Undeniably, there are themes in "Hansel and Gretel" -- as
in many of our most common fairy tales -- that strike deep
psychological chords with both children and adults. The
wicked stepmother is a good example: Children often fantasize
they are really stepchildren or adopted as a way to account
for feeling victimized and abused by their parents. "In real
life this fantasy occurs among children with a very high frequency" (Bakan 76).

*Having quali-
fied her major
claim in light
of other theo-
ries, student
goes on to
reiterate the
support of her
major claim in
her conclusion.*

These themes help to explain the enduring popularity of
fairy tales among middle-class children over the last two centuries. But we cannot treat fairy tales as if they spring full-
blown from the unconscious and tell us nothing about the
past. For the people who told and heard "Hansel and Gretel"
in the seventeenth to nineteenth centuries in Europe, the tale
was describing events and phenomena that happened, if not
to them, then to someone they knew. Everyone in rural communities was likely to have been exposed, whether in person
or by hearsay, to some elderly woman claiming powers to alter
weather patterns, heal the sick, cast spells, midwife, or take
in illegitimate babies. Stepmothers were common, poverty and
famine ongoing, and abandonment and child abuse very real.
In addition to providing entertainment, tales like "Hansel and
Gretel" reassured teller and listener alike that the ordinary
physical hardships, which for most of us today are fictions,
were possible to overcome.

Middleton 9

Notes

Content notes appear at the end of the paper, before Works Cited.

[1] We in the United States know it primarily in printed form, as it has come to us from Germany. Between 1812 and 1857, the Grimm brothers, Jacob and Wilhelm, published several editions of Kinder und Hausmarchen (Children's and Household Tales) (Zipes 6, 41, 79). In addition to "Hansel and Gretel," this book included over 200 other folktales (though not all of them were fairy tales). The anthology increased in popularity until by the turn of the twentieth century it outsold all other books in Germany except the Bible (Zipes 15). To date it has been translated into some seventy languages (Denecke).

[2] Folklorists collect folktales from around the world and analyze them. Tales are categorized according to type (basic plot line) and motifs (elements within the tale). Two widely used references for folklorists are Antti Aarne's Types of the Folklore and Stith Thompson's Motif-index. "Hansel and Gretel" is type 327A in the Aarne classification.

Space included between superscript number and beginning of note

[3] The Grimms were the first to record tale type 327A in 1812 (see note 1). A related tale about Tom Thumb (tale type 327B) was first recorded by Charles Perrault from France in 1697 (Thompson, Folktale 37, 182).

Indent five spaces to superscript number; rest of note is flush left.

[4] Consider the example of Sephardic Jews who "converted" to Christianity under duress in Spain in the fifteenth century. Some of them moved to North America, and their descendants continued to practice Christianity openly and Judaism in secret until recently ("Search for the Buried Past").

Middleton 10

Works Cited

Aarne, Antti. The Types of the Folktale: Classification and
    Bibliography. Trans. and ed. Stith Thompson. 2nd rev.
    ed. FF Communications 184. Helsinki: Suomalainen
    Tiedeakatemia, 1964.

Bakan, David. Slaughter of the Innocents. Toronto: Canadian
    Broadcasting System, 1971.

Bettelheim, Bruno. The Uses of Enchantment: The Meaning
    and Importance of Fairy Tales. 1976. New York: Vintage,
    1977.

Boswell, John. The Kindness of Strangers: The Abandonment
    of Children in Western Europe from Late Antiquity to the
    Renaissance. New York: Pantheon, 1988.

Brewer, Derek. "The Battleground of Home: Versions of Fairy
    Tales." Encounter 54.4 (1980): 52–61.

Denecke, Ludwig. "Grimm, Jacob Ludwig Carl and Wilhelm
    Carl." Encyclopaedia Britannica: Macropaedia. 1992 ed.

Dundes, Alan. Telephone interview. 10 Feb. 1993.

"Fairy tale." Merriam-Webster's Collegiate Dictionary. 10th ed.
    1993.

"Hansel and Gretel." Funk & Wagnalls Standard Dictionary of
    Folklore, Mythology, and Legend. Ed. Maria Leach. New
    York: Funk & Wagnalls, 1949.

Horsley, Richard A. "Who Were the Witches? The Social Roles
    of the Accused in the European Witch Trials." Journal of
    Interdisciplinary History 9 (1979): 689-715.

Kramer, Heinrich, and James Sprenger. The Malleus Malefi-
    carum. Trans. Montague Summers. New York: Dover,
    1971. 14 Dec. 1998. <http://www.geocities.com/Athens/
    2962/witchcraze/malleus_2_ii_html>.

Nash, Jesse. "European Witchcraft: The Hidden Tradition."
    Human Mosaic 21.1-2 (1987): 10-30.

"Search for the Buried Past." The Hidden Jews of New
    Mexico. Prod. Nan Rubin. WFCR, Amherst, MA.
    13 Sept. 1992.

Taggart, James M. " 'Hansel and Gretel' in Spain and Mexico."
    Journal of American Folklore 99 (1986): 435-60.

Sources arranged alphabetically by author's last name or by title

First line flush left in citation, rest indented five spaces

Book

Periodical

Encyclopedia article

Interview

An online book

Radio broadcast

Middleton 11

"The Tales and Their Tellers." Ed. Christine Daaé. <u>Fairy Tales:</u>   *A page within*
<u>Origins and Evolution</u>. 12 Dec. 1998. <http://www   *a Web site*
.darkgoddess.com/fairy/tellers.htm>.

Tatar, Maria. "Folkloristic Phantasies: Grimm's Fairy Tales and   *Article in*
Freud's Family Romance." <u>Fairy Tales as Ways of Know-</u>   *an edited*
<u>ing: Essays on Marchen in Psychology, Society and Liter-</u>   *anthology*
<u>ature</u>. Ed. Michael M. Metzger and Katharina Mommsen.
<u>Germanic Studies in America</u> 41. Berne: Lang, 1981.
75-98.

Thompson, Stith. <u>The Folktale</u>. New York: Holt, 1946.   *Two consecu-*
---. <u>Motif-index of Folk-literature: A Classification of Narra-</u>   *tive works by*
<u>tive Elements in Folktales, Ballads, Myths, Fables, Medi-</u>   *the same*
<u>aeval Romances, Exempla, Fabliaux, Jest-books, and</u>   *author*
<u>Local Legends</u>. Rev. ed. 6 vols. plus index. Bloomington: *Volume in a*
Indiana UP, 1957.   *multivolume*

Treasure, Geoffrey R. R. "European History and Culture: The   *revised edition*
Emergence of Modern Europe, 1500-1648." <u>Encyclopaedia</u>
<u>Britannica: Macropaedia</u>. 1992 ed. 657-83.

Warner, Marina. "Pity the Stepmother." <u>New York Times</u>. 12   *Newspaper*
May 1991, late ed.: D17. <u>Lexis/Nexis Universe</u> 12 Dec.   *online from*
1998. <http://web.lexis-nexis.com/universe/form/   *a computer*
academic/univ_gennews.html>.   *service*

Weber, Eugen. "Fairies and Hard Facts: The Reality of Folktales." <u>Journal of the History of Ideas</u> 42 (1981):
93-113.

Zipes, Jack. <u>The Brothers Grimm: From Enchanted Forests to</u>
<u>the Modern World</u>. New York: Routledge, 1988.

APA SYSTEM FOR CITING PUBLICATIONS

Instructors in the social sciences might prefer the citation system of the American Psychological Association (APA). Like the MLA system, the APA system calls for a parenthetical citation in the text of the paper. Unlike the MLA system, the APA system includes the year of publication in the parenthetical reference. Here is an example:

Even though many South American countries rely on the drug trade for their economic survival, the majority of South Americans disapprove of drug use (Gorriti, 1989, p. 72).

The complete publication information for Gorriti's article will appear at the end of your paper, on a page titled "References." (Sample citations for the "References" page follow.)

If your list of references includes more than one work written by the same author in the same year, cite the first work as *a* and the second as *b*. For example, Gorriti's second article of 1989 would be cited in your paper as (Gorriti, 1989b).

Following are examples of the citation forms you are most likely to use. If you need the format for a type of publication not listed here, consult the *Publication Manual of the American Psychological Association*, Fifth Edition (2001).

■ Print Sources

A BOOK BY A SINGLE AUTHOR

Briggs, J. (1988). *Fire in the crucible: The alchemy of creative genius.* New York: St. Martin's Press.

MULTIPLE WORKS BY THE SAME AUTHOR IN THE SAME YEAR

Gardner, H. (1982a). *Art, mind, and brain: A cognitive approach to creativity.* New York: Basic.

Gardner, H. (1982b). *Developmental psychology: An introduction* (2nd ed.). Boston: Little, Brown.

AN ANTHOLOGY OR COMPILATION

Gioseffi, D. (Ed.). (1988). *Women on war.* New York: Simon & Schuster.

A BOOK BY TWO OR MORE AUTHORS OR EDITORS

Atwan, R., & Roberts, J. (Eds.). (1996). *Left, right, and center: Voices from across the political spectrum.* Boston: Bedford Books.

Note: List the names of *all* the authors or editors, no matter how many.

A BOOK BY A CORPORATE AUTHOR

International Advertising Association. (1977). *Controversy advertising: How advertisers present points of view on public affairs.* New York: Hastings House.

A WORK IN AN ANTHOLOGY

Mukherjee, B. (1988). The colonization of the mind. In Gioseffi, D. (Ed.) *Women on war* (pp. 140-142). New York: Simon & Schuster.

AN INTRODUCTION, PREFACE, FOREWORD, OR AFTERWORD

Hemenway, R. (1984). Introduction. In Z. N. Hurston, *Dust tracks on a road*. Urbana: University of Illinois Press, ix-xxxix.

AN EDITION OTHER THAN THE FIRST

Gumpert, G., & Cathcart, R. (Eds.). (1986). *Inter/media: Interpersonal communication in a media world* (3rd ed.). New York: Oxford University Press.

A TRANSLATION

Sartre, J. P. (1962). *Literature and existentialism*. (B. Frechtman, Trans.). New York: Citadel Press. (Original work published 1949.)

A REPUBLISHED BOOK

James, W. (1969). *The varieties of religious experience: A study in human nature*. London: Collier Books. (Original work published 1902.)

A BOOK IN A SERIES

Berthrong, D. J. (1976). *The Cheyenne and Arapaho ordeal: Reservation and agency life in the Indian territory, 1875-1907. Vol. 136. The civilization of the American Indian series*. Norman: University of Oklahoma Press.

A MULTIVOLUME WORK

Mussen, P. H. (Ed.). (1983). *Handbook of child psychology* (4th ed., Vols. 1–4). New York: Wiley.

AN ARTICLE FROM A DAILY NEWSPAPER

Hottelet, R. C. (1990, March 15). Germany: Why it can't happen again. *Christian Science Monitor,* p. 19.

AN ARTICLE FROM A PERIODICAL

Gorriti, G. A. (1989, July). How to fight the drug war. *Atlantic Monthly,* 70-76.

AN ARTICLE IN A JOURNAL WITH CONTINUOUS PAGINATION THROUGHOUT THE VOLUME

Cockburn, A. (1989). British justice, Irish victims. *The Nation, 249,* 554-555.

AN ARTICLE FROM A JOURNAL WITH SEPARATE PAGINATION FOR EACH ISSUE

Mukerji, C. Visual language in science and the exercise of power: The case of cartography in early modern Europe. *Studies in Visual Communication,* 10(3), 30–45.

AN ARTICLE IN A REFERENCE WORK

Frisby, J. P. (1990). Direct perception. In M. W. Eysenck (Ed.), *Blackwell dictionary of cognitive psychology* (pp. 95-100). Oxford: Basil Blackwell.

A GOVERNMENT PUBLICATION

United States Dept. of Health, Education, and Welfare. (1973). *Current ethical issues in mental health.* Washington, DC: U.S. Government Printing Office.

AN ABSTRACT

Fritz, M. (1990/1991). A comparison of social interactions using a friendship awareness activity. *Education and Training in Mental Retardation, 25,* 352-359. (From *Psychological Abstracts,* 1991, 78, Abstract No. 11474)

When the dates of the original publication and of the abstract differ, give both dates separated by a slash.

AN ANONYMOUS WORK

The status of women: Different but the same. (1992-1993). *Zontian, 73*(3), 5.

If the primary contributors to developing the program are known, begin the reference with those as the author(s) instead of the corporate author. If you are citing a documentation manual rather than the program itself, add the word "manual" before the closing bracket. If there is additional information needed for retrieving the program (such as report and/or acquisition numbers), add this at the end of the entry, in parentheses after the last period.

A REVIEW

Harris, I. M. (1991). [Review of the book *Rediscovering masculinity: Reason, language, and sexuality*]. *Gender and Society,* 5, 259-261.

Give the author of the review, not the author of the book being reviewed. Use this form for a film review also. If the review has a title, place it before the bracketed material, and treat it like an article title.

A LETTER TO THE EDITOR

Pritchett, J. T., & Kellner, C. H. (1993). Comment on spontaneous seizure activity [Letter to the editor]. *Journal of Nervous and Mental Disease, 181,* 138-139.

PERSONAL CORRESPONDENCE

B. Ehrenreich (personal communication, August 7, 1992).

(B. Ehrenreich, personal communication, August 7, 1992.)

Cite all personal communications to you (such as letters, memos, e-mails, and telephone conversations) in text only, *without* listing them among the references. The phrasing of your sentences will determine which of the two above forms to use.

AN UNPUBLISHED MANUSCRIPT

McIntosh, P. (1988). *White privilege and male privilege: A personal account of coming to see correspondences through work in women's studies.* Working Paper 189. Unpublished manuscript, Wellesley College, Center for Research on Women, Wellesley, MA.

PROCEEDINGS OF A MEETING, PUBLISHED

Guerrero, R. (1972/1973). Possible effects of the periodic abstinence method. In W. A. Uricchio & M. K. Williams (Eds.), *Proceedings of a Research Conference on Natural Family Planning* (pp. 96-105). Washington, DC: Human Life Foundation.

If the date of the symposium or conference is different from the date of publication, give both, separated by a slash. If the proceedings are published annually, treat the reference like a periodical article.

■ Electronic Sources

AN ARTICLE FROM AN ONLINE PERIODICAL

Palya, W., Walter, D., Kessel, R., & Lucke, R. (2001). Linear modeling of steady-state behavioral dynamics [Electronic version]. *Journal of the Experimental Analysis of Behavior, 77,* 3-27.

If the article duplicates the version which appeared in a print periodical, use the same basic primary journal reference. See "An Article from a Periodical." If you have viewed the article only in its electronic form, add in brackets [Electronic version].

Riordan, V. (2001, January 1). Verbal-performance IQ discrepancies in children attending a child and adolescent psychiatry clinic. *Child and Adolescent*

Psychiatry On-Line. Retrieved August 9, 2002, from http://www.priory.com/
psych/iq.htm

If the article does not have a corresponding print version, include the
date of access and the URL.

A NONPERIODICAL WEB DOCUMENT

Munro, K. (2001, February). *Changing your body image.* Retrieved February 5,
2002, from http://www.kalimunro.com/article_changing_body
_image.html

In general, follow this format: author's name, the date of publication (if
no publication date is available, use "n.d."), the title of the document in
italics, date of access, and the source's URL.

A CHAPTER OR SECTION IN A WEB DOCUMENT

National Council of Welfare, Canada. (1998). Other issues related to poverty
lines. In *A new poverty line: Yes, no or maybe?* (chap. 5). Retrieved July 9,
2002, from http://www.ncwcnbes.net/htmdocument/reportnewpovline/
chap5.htm

AN E-MAIL

Do not include personal communications such as e-mails in your list of
references. See "Personal Correspondence."

A MESSAGE POSTED TO A NEWSGROUP

Isaacs, K. (2002, January 20). Philosophical roots of psychology [Msg 1]. Message posted to news://sci.psychology.psychotherapy.moderated

Include an online posting in your reference list only if the posting is
archived and is retrievable. Otherwise, cite an online posting as a personal
communication and do not include it in the list of references. Care
should be taken when citing electronic discussions. In general, they are
not scholarly sources.

AN ARTICLE FROM A DATABASE

Lopez, F. G., Melendez, M. C., Sauer, E. M., Berger, E., & Wyssmann, J. (1998).
Internal working models, self-reported problems, and help-seeking attitudes
among college students. *Journal of Counseling Psychology, 45,* 79-83. Retrieved April 1, 2002, from PsycARTICLES database.

To cite material retrieved from a database, follow the format appropriate
to the work retrieved and add the date of retrieval and the name of the
database.

■ Other Sources

A FILM

Wachowski, A., & Wachowski, L. (Writers/Directors). Silver, J. (Producer).
(1999). *The matrix.* [Motion picture]. United States: Warner Bros.

Include the name and the function of the originator or primary contributor (director or producer). Identify the work as a motion picture. Include the country of origin and the studio. If the motion picture is of limited circulation, provide the name and address of the distributor in parentheses at the end of the reference.

A TELEVISION SERIES

Jones, R. (Producer). (1990). *Exploring consciousness.* [Television series].
Boston: WGBH.

SAMPLE RESEARCH PAPER (APA STYLE)

The following paper urges a change in our attitude toward zoos. Arguing the value claim that it is morally wrong for humans to exploit animals for entertainment, the student combines expert opinion gathered from research with her own interpretations of evidence. She is always careful to anticipate and represent the claims of the opposition before going on to refute them.

The student uses the APA style, modified to suit the preferences of her writing instructor. APA style requires a title page with a centered title, author, affiliation, and a short title that can be used as a "running head" on each page. An abstract page follows the title page and includes a one-paragraph abstract or summary of the article. Amanda Repp was told she could omit the title page and abstract recommended by the APA. A full description of APA publication conventions can be found in the *Publication Manual of the American Psychological Association,* Fifth Edition (2001).

Amanda Repp   Zoos   1
English 102-G
Mr. Kennedy
Fall 2004

Why Zoos Should Be Eliminated

Zoos have come a long way from their grim beginnings. Once full of tiny cement-block steel cages, the larger zoos now boast simulated jungles, veldts, steppes, and rain forests, all in an attempt to replicate the natural habitats of the incarcerated animals. The attempt, however admirable, is misguided. It is morally wrong to keep wild animals in captivity, and no amount of replication, no matter how realistic, can compensate for the freedom these creatures are denied.

Peter Batten (1976) argues that a wild animal's life "is spent in finding food, avoiding enemies, sleeping, and in mating or other family activities. . . . Deprivation of any of these fundamentals results in irreparable damage to the individual" (p. 1). The fact that humans may be stronger or smarter than beasts does not give them the right to ambush and exploit animals for the purposes of entertainment.

We humans take our own liberty quite seriously. Indeed, we consider liberty to be one of our inalienable rights. But too many of us apparently feel no obligation to grant the same right to animals, who, because they cannot defend themselves against our sophisticated methods of capture and because they do not speak our language, cannot claim it for themselves.

But the right to liberty is not based on the ability to claim it, or even on the ability to understand what it is. As James Rachels (1976) writes:

> Humans have a right to liberty because they have various other interests that will suffer if their freedom is unduly restricted. The right to liberty -- the right to be free of external constraints on one's actions -- may then be seen as derived from a more basic right not to have one's interests needlessly harmed. (p. 210)

Animals, like people, have interests that are harmed if they are kept in captivity: They are separated from their families and prevented from behaving according to their natural instincts by being removed from the lives they know, which are the lives they were meant to lead.

Some argue that animals' interests are not being harmed when they are kept in zoos or aquariums -- that no damage is being done to the individual -- but their claims are highly disputable. For example, the Zurich Zoo's Dr. Heini Hediger (1985) protests that it is absurd to attribute human qualities to animals at all, but he nevertheless resorts to a human analogy: "Wild animals in the zoo rather resemble estate owners. Far from desiring to escape and regain their freedom, they are only bent on defending the space they inhabit and keeping it safe from invasion" (p. 9). How can Dr. Hediger explain the actions of the leopards and cheetahs I have seen executing figure eights off the walls and floors of their cages for hours on end? I have watched, spellbound by their grace but also horrified; it is impossible to believe that these animals do not want their freedom. An estate owner would not spend his time running frantically around the perimeters of his property. These cats know they are not lords of any estate. The senseless repetition of their actions suggests that the cats know that they are caged and that there is nothing to defend against, no "estate" to protect.

Shannon Brownlee (1986) also believes that there is no concrete evidence that incarcerated animals are suffering or unhappy, but she weakens her own case in her description of Jackie, a dolphin in captivity who "spends the day in a seeming stupor" and "chews on the mackerel half-heartedly" at feeding time (p. 70). Clearly there *is* something wrong with Jackie; this becomes apparent when Brownlee contrasts Jackie's lethargic behavior with that of wild dolphins cavorting in the bay. Brownlee points out that Jackie has never tried to escape through a hole in his enclosure, although he knows it is there. But this fact does not necessarily mean that Jackie enjoys captivity. Instead, it may mean that Jackie's spirit has been broken and that he no longer remembers or cares what his earlier days were like. Granted we have no way of knowing what Jackie is really feeling, but does that give us the right to *assume* that he is not feeling anything?

Summary of an opposing argument

Argument flaw

Refutation of opposing argument based on evidence from personal experience

Summary of a second opposing argument; argument flaw

Challenge to an unstated warrant in the argument

To be fair, Brownlee does not go that far. She does allow Jackie one emotional state, attributing his malaise to boredom. But perhaps if the author were removed from members of her family, as well as all other members of her species, and prevented from engaging in activities that most mattered to her, she would recognize Jackie's problems as something more than boredom. In any case, why should we inflict boredom on Jackie, or any other animal, just because we happen to have the means to do so?

The writer shifts to the second half of her argument.

Having registered these basic objections to zoos -- that keeping any creature in captivity is a fundamental infringement on that creature's right to liberty and dignity -- I want to take a closer look at the zoo as an institution, in order to assess fairly its goals and how it tries to meet them. Most zoo professionals today maintain that zoos exist for two main reasons: to educate humans and to conserve animal species. These are both admirable goals, certainly, but as Seal (1985) notes, "none of these [zoo] budgets is allocated specifically for species preservation. Zoos have been established primarily as recreational institutions and are only secondarily developing programs in conservation, education, and research" (p. 74). The fact is most zoos do not have the money, space, or equipment required to make significant contributions in this area. The bulk of their money goes to the upkeep of the animals and exhibits -- that is, to put it crudely, to the displays.

Clarifying word in square brackets

Another opposing argument, with refutation

On behalf of the education a zoo provides, a common argument is that there is nothing like seeing the real thing. But what you see in the zoo is not a real thing at all. According to a statement from the Animal Rights Resource Site, "The conditions under which animals are kept in zoos typically distorts their behavior significantly" (How will people see). Many zoo and aquarium animals, like Jackie the dolphin, have been domesticated to the point of lethargy, in part because they are being exhibited alone or with only one other member of their species, when what they are used to is traveling in groups and finding their own food, instead of being fed. Anyone who wants to see the real thing would be better off

Summary of two expert opinions that zoos do not help endangered species

Zoos 4

watching some of the excellent programming about nature
and wildlife that appears on public television.

As for conservation, it is clearly a worthwhile effort, but
zoos are not effective agents of species preservation. It is
generally acknowledged that it is difficult to breed zoo animals (Luoma, 1982, p. 104). Animals often do not reproduce
at all--quite possibly because of the artificial, and consequently unsettling, circumstances in which they live. When
zoo animals do mate successfully, the offspring is often weakened by inbreeding. According to geneticists, this is because a
population of 150 breeder animals is necessary in order to
"assure the more or less permanent survival of a species in
captivity" (Ehrlich & Ehrlich, 1981, p. 211). Few zoos have
the resources to maintain populations that size. When zoos
rely on smaller populations for breeding (as many do), the
species' gene pool becomes more and more limited, "vigor and
fecundity tend to decline" (Ehrlich & Ehrlich, 1981, p. 212),
and this can eventually lead to extinction. In other words, we
are not doing these animals any favors by trying to conserve
them in zoos. Indeed, Wilson (1995) writes that "all the zoos
in the world today can sustain a maximum of only 2,000
species of mammals, birds, reptiles, and amphibians, out of
about 24,000 known to exist" (p. 57). Reserves and preserva-
tions, which have room for the larger populations necessary
for successful conservation efforts and which can concentrate
on breeding animals rather than on displaying them, are
much more suitable for these purposes.

For what purposes, then, are zoos suitable? Are they even
necessary? At present, they must house the many generations
of animals that have been bred there, since these animals
have no place else to go. Most animals in captivity cannot go
back to the wild for one of two reasons. The first is that the
creatures would be unable to survive there, since their instincts for finding their own food and protecting themselves
from predators, or even the weather, have been greatly diminished during their time spent in captivity (Morton, 1985,
p. 155). Perhaps this is why Jackie the dolphin chooses to remain in his enclosure.

Author, date, page cited parenthetically

Source with two authors cited parenthetically

Paraphrase with source cited parenthetically

Zoos 5

The other reason animals cannot return to the wild is an even sadder one: In many cases, their natural habitats no longer exist. Thanks to deforesting and clearing of land for homes, highways, factories, and shopping malls -- which are continually being built with no regard for the plant and animal life around them -- ecosystems are destroyed constantly, driving increasing numbers of species from their homes. Air and water pollution and toxic waste, results of the ever-increasing urbanization and industrialization throughout the world, are just some of the agents of this change. It is a problem I wish to address in closing.

The writer closes by proposing a solution of her own.

If zoos were to leave breeding programs to more appropriate organizations and to stop collecting animals, the zoo as an institution would eventually be phased out. Animals would cease to be exhibits and could resume being animals, and the money previously used to run zoos could be put to much better use. Ideally it could be used to investigate why endangered species are endangered, and why so many of the original habitats of these species have disappeared. Most important, it could be used to explore how we can change our habits and reorient our behavior, attitudes, and priorities, so we can begin to address these issues.

The problem of endangered species does not exist in a vacuum; it is a symptom of a much greater predicament. Humankind is responsible for this predicament, and it is up to us to recognize this before it is too late. Saving a selected species here and there will do none of us any good if those species can exist only in isolated, artificial environments, where they will eventually breed themselves into extinction. The money that has been concentrated on such efforts should be devoted instead to educating the public about the endangered planet -- not just its animals -- or, like the animals, none of us will have any place to go.

Zoos   6

References

Batten, P. (1976). *Living trophies.* New York: Crowell.

Brownlee, S. (1986, December). First it was "save the whales," now it's "free the dolphins." *Discover,* 70-72.

Ehrlich, P., & Ehrlich, A. (1981). *Extinction: The causes and consequences of the disappearance of species.* New York: Random House.

Hediger, H. (1985). From cage to territory. In R. Kirchschofer (Ed.), *The world of zoos: A survey and gazetteer* (pp. 9-20). New York: Viking.

How will people see wild animals and learn about them without zoos? (n.d.). In *Animal Rights Resource Site.* Retrieved December 14, 1998, from http://arrs.envirolink .org/faqs+Ref/ar-faq/Q70.html

Luoma, J. (1982, November). Prison or ark? *Audubon,* 102-109.

Morton, E. S. (1985). The realities of reintroducing species to the wild. In J. R. Hoage (Ed.), *Animal extinctions: What everyone should know* (pp. 147-158). National Zoological Park Symposia for the Public series. Washington, DC: Smithsonian Institution.

Rachels, J. (1976). Do animals have a right to liberty? In T. Regan & P. Singer (Eds.), *Animal rights and human obligations* (pp. 205-223). Englewood Cliffs, NJ: Prentice-Hall.

Seal, U. S. (1985). The realities of preserving species in captivity. In J. R. Hoage (Ed.), *Animal extinctions: What everyone should know* (pp. 147-158). National Zoological Park Symposia for the Public series. Washington, DC: Smithsonian Institution.

Wilson, E. (1995, October 30). Wildlife: Legions of the doomed. *Time,* 57-62. Retrieved December 12, 1999, from *Lexis/Nexis Universe.*

References start a new page.

A book with two authors

A work in an anthology

An article from a periodical

For each reference, flush left on first line, and indent five spaces on subsequent lines.

An article online from a database

CHAPTER 11

Presenting an Argument Orally

Speech is the basic skill overlooked by many who urge a return to the Three R's. The ability to speak clearly and persuasively, and to think on one's feet can be as vital to success as reading and writing. Beginning with the job interview, speech classifies a person.[1]

You already know a good deal about the power of persuasive speech. You've not only listened to it from parents, teachers, preachers, coaches, friends, and enemies; you've practiced it yourself with varying degrees of success.

A classics scholar points out that the oratorical techniques we use today were "invented in antiquity and have been used to great effect ever since."[2] But history is not our only guide to the principles of public speaking. Much of what we know about the power of persuasive speech is knowledge based on lifelong experience—things we learn in everyday discourse with different kinds of people who respond to different appeals. Early in life you learned that you did not use the same language or the same approach to argue with your mother or your teacher as you used with your sibling or your friend. You learned, or tried to learn, how to convince people to listen to you and to trust you because you were truthful and knew what you were talking about. And perhaps equally important, if you won the argument, you wanted to make it clear that your victory would not mean hardship for the loser (no obvious gloating).

[1] Fred M. Hechinger, "About Education," *New York Times*, May 11, 1988, sec. B, p. 7.
[2] Mary Lefkowitz, "Classic Oratory," *New York Times*, January 24, 1999, sec. W, p. 15.

Although speeches to a larger, less familiar audience will require much more preparation, many of the rules of argument that guided you in your personal encounters can be made to work for you in more public arenas.

You will often be asked to make oral presentations in your college classes. Many jobs, both professional and nonprofessional, will call for speeches to groups of fellow employees or prospective customers, to community groups, and even government officials. Wherever you live, there will be controversies and public meetings about schooling and political candidates, about budgets for libraries and road repairs and pet control. The ability to rise and make your case before an audience is one that you will want to cultivate as a citizen of a democracy. Great oratory is probably no longer the most powerful influence in our society, and computer networks have usurped the role of oral communication in many areas of public life. But whether it's in person or on television there is still a significant role for a live presenter, a real human being to be seen and heard.

Some of your objectives as a writer will also be relevant to you as a speaker: making the appropriate appeal to an audience, establishing your credibility, finding adequate support for your claim. But other elements of argument will be different: language, organization, and the use of visual and other aids.

Before you begin a brief examination of these elements, keep in mind the larger objectives of the speechmaker. A good introduction to the process of influencing an audience is *the motivated sequence*.[3] This outline, created by a professor of speech communication, lists the five steps that must be taken in order to motivate an audience to adopt a policy, an action, or a belief.

1. Getting attention (attention step)
2. Showing the need: describing the problem (need step)
3. Satisfying the need: presenting the solution (satisfaction step)
4. Visualizing the results (visualization step)
5. Requesting action or approval (action step)

Perhaps you noticed that these steps resemble the steps taken by advertisers. (That list appears in the sample analysis of an ad in Chapter 2.) The resemblance is not accidental. According to the author of the motivated sequence, this is a description of the way "people systematically think their way through to a decision."

As you read the following discussions of audience, credibility, language, organization, support, and visual and aural aids, try to think of occasions in your own experience when you were aware of these elements in spoken argument, formal or informal.

[3] Alan H. Monroe and Douglas Ehninger, *Principles of Speech Communication* (Glenview, Ill.: Scott, Foresman, 1969), p. 261.

THE AUDIENCE

Most speakers who confront a live audience already know something about the members of that audience. They may know why the audience is assembled to hear the particular speaker, their vocations, their level of education, and their familiarity with the subject. They may know whether the audience is friendly, hostile, or neutral to the views that the speaker will express. Analyzing the audience is an essential part of speech preparation. If speakers neglect it, both audience and speaker will suffer. At some time all of us have been trapped as members of an audience, forced to listen to a lecture, a sermon, an appeal for action when it was clear that the speaker had little or no idea what we were interested in or capable of understanding. In such situations the speaker who seems indifferent to the needs of the audience will also suffer because the audience will either cease to listen or reject his claim outright.

In college classes students who make assigned speeches on controversial topics are often encouraged to first survey the class. Questionnaires and interviews can give the speaker important clues to the things he should emphasize or avoid: They will tell him whether he should give both sides of a debatable question, introduce humor, use simpler language, and bring in visual or other aids.

But even where such specific information is not immediately available, speakers are well advised to find out as much as they can about the beliefs and attitudes of their audience from other sources. They will then be better equipped to make the kinds of appeals—to reason and to emotion—that the audience is most responsive to. For example, two young evangelists for a religious group (not students at the university) were invited to visit a speech class and present an argument for joining their group. The visitors knew that the class was learning the principles of persuasive speaking; they had no other information about the listeners. After the speech, the students in the class asked questions about some practices of the religious group which had received unfavorable media attention, but the speakers turned aside all questions, saying they did not engage in argument but were instructed only to describe the rewards of joining their group. Before some other audience, such a strategy might have been emotionally satisfying and ultimately persuasive. For this class, however, which was prepared to look for hard evidence, logic, and valid assumptions, the refusal to answer questions suggested evasion and indifference to the interests of their audience. Class evaluations of the speech revealed, to no one's surprise, that the visitors had failed to motivate their listeners.

If you know something about your audience, ask yourself what impression your clothing, gestures and bodily movements, voice, and general demeanor might convey. It might be worth pointing out here that the visitors cited above arrived dressed in three-piece suits and sporting crew cuts to confront an audience in tee shirts, torn jeans, and long hair. The fact that both speakers and listeners were the same age was not quite enough to overcome an impression of real differences. Make sure, too, that you understand the nature of the occasion—is it too solemn for humor? too formal for personal anecdotes?— and the purpose of the meeting, which can influence your choice of language and the most effective appeal.

CREDIBILITY

The evaluation of audience and the presentation of your own credibility are closely related. In other words, what can you do to persuade this particular audience that you are a reliable exponent of the views you are expressing? Credibility, as you learned in Chapter 1, is another name for *ethos* (the Greek word from which the English word *ethics* is derived) and refers to the honesty, moral character, and intellectual competence of the speaker.

Public figures, whose speeches and actions are reported in the media, can acquire (or fail to acquire) reputations for being endowed with those characteristics. And there is little doubt that a reputation for competence and honesty can incline an audience to accept an argument that would be rejected if offered by a speaker who lacks such a reputation. One study, among many that report similar results, has shown that the same speech will be rated highly by an audience that thinks the Surgeon General of the United States has delivered it but treated with much less regard if they hear it delivered by a college sophomore.

How, then, does a speaker who is unknown to the audience or who boasts only modest credentials convince his listeners that he is a responsible advocate? From the moment the speaker appears before them, members of the audience begin to make an evaluation, based on external signs, such as clothing and mannerisms. But the most significant impression of the speaker's credibility will be based on what the speaker says and how he says it. Does the speaker give evidence that he knows the subject? Does he seem to be aware of the needs and values of the audience? Especially if he is arguing an unpopular claim, does he seem modest and conciliatory?

An unknown speaker is often advised to establish his credentials in the introduction to his speech, to summarize his background and experience as proof of his right to argue the subject he has chosen. A prize-winning and widely reprinted speech by a student begins with these words:

When you look at me, it is easy to see several similarities between us. I have two arms, two legs, a brain, and a heart just like you. These are my hands, and they are just like yours. Like you, I also have wants and desires; I am capable of love and hate. I can laugh and I can cry. Yes, I'm just like you, except for one very important fact—I am an ex-con.[4]

This is a possibly risky beginning—not everybody in the audience will be friendly to an ex-con—but it signifies that the speaker brings some authority to his subject, which is prison reform. It also attests to the speaker's honesty and may rouse sympathy among certain listeners. (To some in the audience, the speaker's allusions to his own humanity will recall another moving defense, the famous speech by Shylock, the Jewish moneylender, in Shakespeare's *The Merchant of Venice*.)

The speaker will often use an admission of modesty as proof of an honest and unassuming character. He presents himself not as an expert but as one well aware of his limitations. Such an appeal can generate sympathy in the audience (if they believe him) and a sense of identification with the speaker.

The professor of classics quoted earlier has analyzed the speech of a former senator who defended President Clinton at his impeachment trial. She found that the speaker "made sure his audience understood that he was one of them, a friend, on their level, not above them. He denied he was a great speaker and spoke of his friendship with Mr. Clinton." As the writer points out, this confession brings to mind the speech by Mark Antony in *Julius Caesar*:

> I am no orator, as Brutus is,
> But (as you know me all) a plain blunt man
> That loves my friend; (3.2.226–28)

The similarity of these attempts at credibility, separated by almost four hundred years (to say nothing of the fact that Aristotle wrote about *ethos* 2,500 years ago) tells us a good deal about the enduring influence of *ethos* or character on the speaker's message.

ORGANIZATION

Look at the student speech at the end of this chapter. The organization of this short speech—the usual length of speeches delivered in the classroom—is easily mastered and works for all kinds of claims.

At the end of the first paragraph the speaker states what he will try to prove, that a vegetarian diet contributes to prevention of chronic diseases. In the third paragraph the speaker gives the four points that he will

---

[4]Richard M. Duesterbeck, "Man's Other Society," in Wil Linkugel, R. R. Allen, and Richard Johannesen, eds., *Contemporary American Speeches* (Belmont, Calif.: Wadsworth, 1965), p. 264.

develop in his argument for vegetarianism. Following the development of these four topics, the conclusion urges the audience to take action, in this case, to stop eating meat.

This basic method of organizing a short speech has several virtues. First, the claim or thesis statement that appears early in a short speech, if the subject is well chosen, can engage the interest of the audience at once. Second, the list of topics guides the speaker in planning and developing his speech. Moreover, it tells the audience what to listen for as they follow the argument.

A well-planned speech has a clearly defined beginning, middle, and end. The beginning, which offers the introduction, can take a number of forms, depending on the kind of speech and its subject. Above all, the introduction must win the attention of the audience, especially if they have been required to attend, and encourage them to look forward to the rest of the speech. The authors of the motivated sequence suggest seven basic attention-getters: (1) referring to the subject or occasion, (2) using a personal reference, (3) asking a rhetorical question, (4) making a startling statement of fact or opinion, (5) using a quotation, (6) telling a humorous anecdote, (7) using an illustration.[5]

The speeches by the ex-con and the vegetarian provide examples of two of the attention-getters cited above—using a personal reference and asking a rhetorical question. In another kind of argument, a claim of fact, the student speaker uses a combination of devices to introduce her claim that culturally deprived children are capable of learning:

> In Charles Schulz's popular cartoon depiction of happiness, one of his definitions has special significance for the American school system. The drawing shows Linus, with his eyes closed in a state of supreme bliss, a broad smile across two-thirds of his face and holding a report card upon which is a big bold "A." The caption reads: "Happiness is finding out you're not so dumb after all." For once, happiness is not defined as a function of material possessions, yet even this happiness is practically unattainable for the "unteachables" of the city slums. Are these children intellectually inferior? Are they unable to learn? Are they not worth the time and the effort to teach? Unfortunately, too many people have answered "yes" to these questions and promptly dismissed the issue.[6]

The middle or body of the speech is, of course, the longest part. It will be devoted to development of the claim that appeared at the beginning. The length of the speech and the complexity of the subject will determine how much support you provide. Some points will be more important than others and should therefore receive more extended treatment. Unless the order is chronological, it makes sense for the speaker to arrange

---

[5] Monroe and Ehninger, p. 206.

[6] Carolyn Kay Geiman, "Are They Really 'Unteachables'?" in Linkugel, Allen, and Johannesen, p. 123.

the supporting points in emphatic order, that is, the most important at the end because this may be the one that listeners will remember.

The conclusion should be brief; some rhetoricians suggest that the ending should constitute 5 percent of the total length of the speech. For speeches that contain several main points with supporting data, you may need to summarize. Or you may return to one of the attention-getters mentioned earlier. One writer recommends this as "the most obvious method" of concluding speeches, "particularly appropriate when the introduction has included a quotation, an interesting anecdote, a reference to an occasion or a place, an appeal to the self-interest of the audience, or a reference to a recent incident."[7]

An example of such an ending appears in a speech given by Bruce Babbitt, Secretary of the Interior, in 1996. Speaking to an audience of scientists and theologians, the Secretary defended laws that protected the environment. This is how the speech began:

> A wolf's green eyes, a sacred blue mountain, the words from Genesis, and the answers of children all reveal the religious values manifest in the 1977 Endangered Species Act.

(The children Babbitt refers to had written answers to a question posed at an "eco-expo" fair, "Why Save the Environment?")

And this is the ending of the speech:

> I conclude here tonight by affirming that those religious values remain at the heart of the Endangered Species Act, that they make themselves manifest through the green eyes of the grey wolf, through the call of the whooping crane, through the splash of the Pacific salmon, through the voices of America's children.
>
> We are living between the flood and the rainbow: between the threats to creation on the one side and God's covenant to protect life on the other.
>
> Why should we save endangered species?
>
> Let us answer this question with one voice, the voice of the child at that expo, who scrawled her answer at the very bottom of the sheet:
> "Because we can."[8]

The speaker must also ensure the smooth flow of his argument throughout. Coherence, or the orderly connections between ideas, is even more important in speech than in writing because the listener cannot go back to uncover these connections. The audience listens for expressions that serve as guideposts—words, phrases, and sentences to indicate which direction the argument will take. The student speech on vegetarianism uses these words among others: *next, then, finally, here, first*

[7]James C. McCroskey, *An Introduction to Rhetorical Communication* (Englewood Cliffs, N.J.: Prentice-Hall, 1968), p. 204.

[8]Calvin McLeod Logue and Jean DeHart, eds., *Representative American Speeches, 1995–1996* (New York: Wilson, 1996), p. 70ff.

of all, whereas, in addition, secondly, in fact, now, in conclusion. Other expressions can also help the listener to follow the development. Each of the following examples from real speeches makes a bridge from a previous idea to a new one: "Valid factual proof, right? No, wrong!" "Consider an illustration of this misinformation." "But there is another way." "Up to this point, I've spoken only of therapy." "And so we face this new challenge." "How do we make this clear?" "Now, why is this so important?"

LANGUAGE

It should be observed that each kind of rhetoric has its own appropriate style. That of written prose is not the same as that of spoken oratory.
—Aristotle

In the end, your speech depends on the language. No matter how accurate your analysis of the audience, how appealing your presentation of self, how deep your grasp of the material, if the language does not clearly and emphatically convey your argument, the speech will probably fail. Fortunately, the effectiveness of language does not depend on long words or complex sentence structure; quite the contrary. Most speeches, especially those given by beginners to small audiences, are distinguished by an oral style that respects the rhythms of ordinary speech and sounds spontaneous.

The vocabulary you choose, like the other elements of spoken discourse we have discussed, is influenced by the kind of audience you confront. A student audience may be entertained or moved to identification with you and your message if you use the slang of your generation; an assembly of elderly church members at a funeral may not be so generous. Use words that both you and your listeners are familiar with, language that convinces the audience you are sharing your knowledge and opinions, neither speaking down to them nor over their heads. As one writer puts it, "You never want to use language that makes the audience appear ignorant or stupid."

Make sure, too, that the words you use will not be considered offensive by some members of your audience. Today we are all sensitive, sometimes hypersensitive, to terms we once used freely if not wisely. One word, improperly used, can cause some listeners to reject the whole speech.

The short speeches you give will probably not be devoted to elaborating grand abstractions, but it is not only abstract terms that need definition. When you know your subject very well, you forget that others can be ignorant of it. Think whether the subject is one that the particular audience you are addressing is not likely to be familiar with. If this is the case, then explain even the basic terms. In one class a student who had chosen to discuss a subject about which he was extremely knowledgeable, betting on horse races, neglected to define clearly the words *exacta, subfecta, trifecta, parimutuel,* and others, leaving his audience fairly befuddled.

Wherever it is appropriate, use concrete language with details and examples that create images and cause the listener to feel as well as think. One student speaker used strong words to good effect in providing some unappetizing facts about hot dogs: "In fact, the hot dog is so adulterated with chemicals, so contaminated with bacteria, so puffy with gristle, fat, water, and lacking in protein, that it is nutritionally worthless."[9]

Another speech on a far more serious subject offered a personal experience with vivid details. The student speaker was a hemophiliac making a plea for blood donations.

> I remember the three long years when I couldn't even walk because repeated hemorrhages had twisted my ankles and knees to pretzel-like forms. I remember being pulled to school in a wagon while other boys rode their bikes and pushed to my table. I remember sitting in the dark empty classroom by myself during recess while the others went out in the sun to run and play. And I remember the first terrible day at the big high school when I came on crutches and built-up shoes carrying my books in a sack around my neck.[10]

As a rule, the oral style demands simpler sentences. That is because the listener must grasp the grammatical construction without the visual clues of punctuation available on the printed page. Simpler means shorter and more direct. Use subject-verb constructions without a string of phrases or clauses preceding the subject or interrupting the natural flow of the sentence. Use the active voice frequently. In addition to assuring clarity for the audience, such sentences are easier for the speaker to remember and to say. (The sentences in the paragraph above are long, but notice that the sentence elements of subject, verb, and subordinate clause are arranged in the order dictated by natural speech.)

Simpler, however, does not mean less impressive. A speech before any audience may be simply expressed without loss of emotional or intellectual power. "The Nature of Prejudice" in Chapter 3 is a noteworthy example. First delivered as a speech to an audience of experts, it nevertheless reflects the characteristics of conversation. One of the most eloquent short speeches ever delivered in this country is the surrender speech in 1877 by Chief Joseph of the Nez Percé Tribe, which clearly demonstrates the power of simple words and sentences.

> I am tired of fighting. Our chiefs are killed. Looking Glass is dead. Toohulsote is dead. The old men are all dead. It is the young men who

[9] Donovan Ochs and Anthony Winkler, *A Brief Introduction to Speech* (New York: Harcourt, Brace, Jovanovich, 1979), p. 74.
[10] Ralph Zimmerman, "Mingled Blood," in Linkugel, Allen, and Johannesen, p. 200.

say no and yes. He who led the young men is dead. It is cold and we have no blankets. The little children are freezing to death. My people, some of them, have run away to the hills and have no blankets, no food. No one knows where they are—perhaps they are freezing to death. I want to have time to look for my children and see how many of them I can find. Maybe I shall find them among the dead. Hear me, my chiefs. I am tired. My heart is sad and sick. From where the sun now stands I will fight no more forever.[11]

If you are in doubt about the kind of language in which you should express yourself, you might follow Lincoln's advice: "Speak so that the most lowly can understand you, and the rest will have no difficulty."

A popular stylistic device—repetition and balance or parallel structure—can emphasize and enrich parts of your message. Look back to the balanced sentences of the passage from the student speaker on hemophilia, sentences beginning with "I remember." Almost all inspirational speeches, including religious exhortation and political oratory, take advantage of such constructions, whose rhythms evoke an immediate emotional response. It is one of the strengths of Martin Luther King Jr.'s "I Have a Dream." Keep in mind that the ideas in parallel structures must be similar and that, for maximum effectiveness, they should be used sparingly in a short speech. Not least, the subject should be weighty enough to carry this imposing construction.

SUPPORT

The support for a claim is essentially the same for both spoken and written arguments. Factual evidence, including statistics, and expert opinion, as well as appeals to needs and values, are equally important in oral presentations. But time constraints will make a difference. In a speech the amount of support that you provide will be limited to the capacity of listeners to digest and remember information that they cannot review. This means that you must choose subjects that can be supported adequately in the time allotted. The speech by Secretary Babbitt, for example, on saving the environmental protection laws, developed material on animals, national lands, water, his own history, religious tradition, and the history of environmental legislation, to name only the most important. It would have been impossible to defend his proposition in a half-hour speech. Although his subject was far more limited, the author of the argument for vegetarianism could not do full justice to his claim for lack of time. Meat-eaters would find that some of their questions remain unanswered, and

[11]M. Gidley, *Kopet: A Documentary Narrative of Chief Joseph's Last Years.* (Chicago: Contemporary Books, 1981), p. 31.

even those listeners friendly to the author's claim might ask for more evidence from authoritative sources.

While both speakers and writers use logical, ethical, and emotional appeals in support of their arguments, the forms of presentation can make a significant difference. The reasoning process demanded of listeners must be relatively brief and straightforward, and the supporting evidence readily assimilated. The ethical appeal or credibility of the speaker is affected not only by what he says but by his appearance, bodily movements, and vocal expressions. And the appeal to the sympathy of the audience can be greatly enhanced by the presence of the speaker. Take the excerpt from the speech of the hemophiliac. The written descriptions of pain and heartbreak are very moving, but place yourself in the audience, looking at the victim and imagining the suffering experienced by the human body standing in front of you. No doubt the effect would be deep and long-lasting, perhaps more memorable even than the written word.

Because the human instrument is so powerful, it must be used with care. You have probably listened to speakers who used gestures and voice inflections that had been dutifully rehearsed but were obviously contrived and worked, unfortunately, to undermine rather than support the speaker's message and credibility. If you are not a gifted actor, avoid gestures, body language, and vocal expressions that are not truly felt.

Some speech theorists treat support or proofs as *nonartistic* and *artistic*. The nonartistic support—factual data, expert opinion, examples—is considered objective and verifiable. Its acceptability should not depend on the character and personality of the speaker. It is plainly different from the artistic proof, which is subjective, based on the values and attitudes of the listener, and therefore more difficult for the speaker to control. This form of support is called artistic because it includes creative strategies within the power of the speaker to manipulate. In earlier parts of this chapter we have discussed the artistic proofs, ways of establishing credibility, and recognizing the values of the audience.

PRESENTATION AIDS

■ Charts, Graphs, Handouts

Some speeches, though not all, will be enhanced by visual and other aids: charts, graphs, maps, models, objects, handouts, recordings, and computer technology. These aids, however, no matter how visually or aurally exciting, should not overwhelm your own oral presentation. The objects are not the stars of the show. They exist to make your spoken argument more persuasive.

Charts and graphs, large enough and clear enough to be seen and understood, can illuminate speeches that contain numbers of any kind, especially statistical comparisons. You can make a simple chart yourself, on paper for use with an easel or a transparency for use with a slide projector. Enlarged illustrations or a model of a complicated machine—say, the space shuttle—would help a speaker to explain its function. You already know that photographs or videos are powerful instruments of persuasion, above all in support of appeals for humanitarian aid, for both people and animals.

Court cases have been won or lost on the basis of diagrams or charts that purport to prove the innocence or guilt of a defendant. Such aids do not always speak for themselves. No matter how clear they are to the designer, they may be misinterpreted or misunderstood by a viewer. Some critics have argued that the jury in the O. J. Simpson case failed to understand the graphs of DNA relationships that experts for the prosecution displayed during the trial. Before you show any diagrams or charts of any complexity to your audience, ask friends if they find them easy to understand.

The use of a handout also requires planning. It's probably unwise to put your speech on hold while the audience reads or studies a handout that requires time and concentration. Confine the subject matter of handouts to material that can be easily grasped as you discuss or explain it.

■ Audio

Audio aids may also enliven a speech or even be indispensable to its success. One student played a recording of a scene from *Romeo and Juliet*, spoken by a cast of professional actors, to make a point about the relationship between the two lovers. Another student chose to define several types of popular music, including rap, goth, heavy metal, and techno. But he used only words, and the lack of any musical demonstration meant that the distinctions remained unclear.

■ Video

With sight, sound, and movement, a video can illustrate or reinforce the main points of a speech. A speech warning people not to drink and drive will have a much greater effect if enhanced by a video showing the tragic and often gruesome outcome of car accidents caused by drunk driving. Schools that teach driver's education frequently rely on these bone-chilling videos to show their students that getting behind the wheel is a serious responsibility, not a game. If you want to use video, check to make sure that a VCR and television are available to you. Most schools have an audio-visual department that manages the delivery, setup, and return of all equipment.

■ Multimedia

Multimedia presentation software programs enable you to combine several different media such as text, charts, sound, and still or moving pictures into one unit. In the business world, multimedia presentations are commonly used in situations where you have a limited amount of time to persuade or teach a fairly large audience. For instance, the promotion director of a leading teen magazine is trying to persuade skeptical executives that a magazine Web site would increase sales and advertising revenue. Since the magazine is sold through newsstand and subscription, some executives question whether the cost of creating and maintaining a Web site outweighs the benefits. Using multimedia presentation software, the promotion director can integrate: demographic charts and graphs showing that steadily increasing numbers of teenagers surf the Web, a segment from a television news program reporting that many teens shop online (an attraction for advertisers), and downloaded pages from a competitor's Web site to demonstrate that others are already reaping the benefits of the Internet. With several studies reporting that people today are increasingly "visual" in their learning styles, multimedia software may be the most effective aid for an important presentation.

Though effective when done well, technically complicated presentations require large amounts of time and careful planning. First you must ensure that your computer is powerful enough to adeptly handle presentation software such as Microsoft PowerPoint, Lotus Freelance, Harvard Graphics, Adobe Persuasion, Cintel Charisma, and Asymetrix Compel. Then you need to familiarize yourself with the program. Most presentation software programs come equipped with helpful tutorials. If the task of creating your own presentation from scratch seems overwhelming, you can use one of the many preformatted presentation templates: You will simply need to customize the content. Robert Stephens, the founder of the Geek Squad, a Minneapolis-based business that provides on-site emergency response to computer problems, gives the following tips for multimedia presentations:

1. In case of equipment failure, always bring two of everything.

2. Back up your presentation not only on floppy disk, but on CD-ROM, or a Zip drive.

3. Avoid live visits to the Internet. Because connections can fail or be painfully slow, and sites can move or disappear, if you must visit the Internet in your presentation, download the appropriate pages onto your hard drive ahead of time. It will still look like a live visit.

4. In the end, technology cannot replace creativity. Make sure that you are using multimedia to reinforce not replace your main points.[12]

---

[12] Robert Stephens as paraphrased in "When Your Presentation Crashes . . . Who You Gonna Call?" by Eric Matson, *Fast Company*, February/March 1997, p. 130.

Make sure that any necessary apparatus will be available at the right time. If you have never used the devices you need for your presentation, practice using them before the speech. Few things are more disconcerting for the speechmaker and the audience than a speaker who is fumbling with his materials, unable to find the right picture or to make a machine work.

SAMPLE PERSUASIVE SPEECH

The following speech was delivered by C. Renzi Stone to his public speaking class at the University of Oklahoma. Told to prepare a persuasive speech, Stone chose to speak about the health benefits of vegetarianism. Note his attention-grabbing introduction.

Live Longer and Healthier: Stop Eating Meat!

C. RENZI STONE

What do Steve Martin, Dustin Hoffman, Albert Einstein, Jerry Garcia, Michael Stipe, Eddie Vedder, Martina Navratilova, Carl Lewis, and 12 million other Americans all have in common? All of these well-known people were or are vegetarians. What do they know that we don't? Consuming a regimen of high-fat, high-protein flesh foods is a sure-fire prescription for disaster, like running diesel fuel through your car's gasoline engine. In the book *Why Do Vegetarians Eat Like That?* David Gabbe asserts that millions of people today are afflicted with chronic diseases that can be directly linked to the consumption of meat. Eating a vegetarian diet can help prevent many of those diseases.

In 1996, 12 million Americans identified themselves as vegetarians. That number is twice as many as in the decade before. According to a recent National Restaurant Association poll found in *Health* magazine, one in five diners say they now go out of their way to choose restaurants that serve at least a few meatless entrees. Obviously, the traditionally American trait of a meat-dominated society has subsided in recent years.

In discussing vegetarianism today, first I will tell how vegetarians are perceived in society. Next, I will introduce several studies validating my claim that a meatless diet is extraordinarily healthy. I will then show how a veggie diet can strengthen the immune system and make the meatless body a shield from unwanted diseases such as cancer and heart disease. Maintaining a strict vegetarian diet can also lead to a longer life. Finally, I will put an image into the audience's mind of a meatless society that relies on vegetables for the main course at breakfast, lunch, and dinner.

Moving to my first point, society generally holds two major misperceptions about vegetarians. First of all, society often perceives vegetarians as a radical group of people with extreme principles. In this view, vegetarians are seen as a monolithic group of people who choose to eat vegetables because they are opposed to the killing of animals for food. The second major misconception is that because vegetarians do not eat meat, they do not get the proper amounts of essential vitamins and minerals often found in meat.

Here is my response to these misconceived notions. First of all, vegetarians are not a homogeneous group of radicals. Whereas many vegetarians in the past did join the movement on the principle that killing animals is wrong, many join the movement today mainly for its health benefits. In addition, there are many different levels of vegetarianism. Some vegetarians eat nothing but vegetables. Others don't eat red meat but do occasionally eat chicken and fish.

Secondly, contrary to popular opinion, vegetarians get more than enough vitamins and minerals in their diet and generally receive healthier nourishment than meat eaters. In fact, in an article for *Health* magazine, Peter Jaret states that vegetarians actually get larger amounts of amino acids due to the elimination of saturated fats which are often found in meat products. Studies show that the health benefits of a veggie lifestyle contribute to increased life expectancy and overall productivity.

Hopefully you now see that society's perceptions of vegetarians are outdated and just plain wrong. You are familiar with many of the problems associated with a meat-based diet, and you have heard many of the benefits of a vegetarian diet. Now try to imagine how you personally can improve your life by becoming a vegetarian.

Can you imagine a world where people retire at age eighty and lead productive lives into their early 100s? Close your eyes and think about celebrating your seventieth wedding anniversary, seeing your great-grandchildren get married, and witnessing 100 years of world events and technological innovations. David Gabbe's book refers to studies that have shown a vegetarian diet can increase your life expectancy up to fifteen years. A longer life is within your reach, and the diet you eat has a direct impact on your health and how you age.

In conclusion, vegetarianism is a healthy life choice, not a radical cult. By eliminating meat from their diet, vegetarians reap the benefits of a vegetable-based diet that helps prevent disease and increase life expectancy. People, take heed of my advice. There are many more sources of information available for those who want to take a few hours to research the benefits of the veggie lifestyle. If you don't believe my comments, discover the whole truth for yourself.

Twelve million Americans know the health benefits that come with being a vegetarian. Changing your eating habits can be just as easy as making your bed in the morning. Sure, it takes a few extra minutes and some thought, but your body will thank you in the long run.

You only live once. Why not make it a long stay?

APPENDIX

Classic Arguments

A Modest Proposal

JONATHAN SWIFT

I t is a melancholy object to those who walk through this great town[1] or travel in the country, when they see the streets, the roads, and cabin doors, crowded with beggars of the female sex, followed by three, four, or six children, all in rags and importuning every passenger for an alms. These mothers, instead of being able to work for their honest livelihood, are forced to employ all their time in strolling to beg sustenance for their helpless infants, who, as they grow up, either turn thieves for want of work, or leave their dear native country to fight for the Pretender in Spain, or sell themselves to the Barbados.[2]

I think it is agreed by all parties that this prodigious number of children in the arms, or on the backs, or at the heels of their mothers, and frequently of their fathers, is in the present deplorable state of the kingdom a very great additional grievance; and therefore whoever could find out a fair, cheap, and easy method of making these children sound, useful members of the commonwealth would deserve so well of the public as to have his statue set up for a preserver of the nation.

But my intention is very far from being confined to provide only for the children of professed beggars; it is of a much greater extent, and shall take in the whole number of infants at a certain age who are born of parents in effect as little able to support them as those who demand our charity in the streets.

As to my own part, having turned my thoughts for many years upon this important subject, and maturely weighed the several schemes of other projectors,[3] I have always found them grossly mistaken in their computation. It is true, a child just dropped from its dam may be supported by her milk for a solar year, with little other nourishment; at most

---

[1] Dublin. — EDS. [All notes are the editors'.]

[2] The Pretender was James Stuart, who was exiled to Spain. Many Irish men had joined an army attempting to return him to the English throne in 1715. Others had become indentured servants, agreeing to work for a set number of years in Barbados or other British colonies in exchange for their transportation out of Ireland.

[3] Planners.

This essay is acknowledged by almost all critics to be the most powerful example of irony in the English language. (*Irony* means saying one thing but meaning another.) In 1729 Jonathan Swift (1667–1745), prolific satirist and dean of St. Patrick's Cathedral in Dublin, was moved to write in protest against the terrible poverty in which the Irish were living under British rule. Notice that the essay is organized according to one of the patterns outlined in Part Two of this book (see Presenting the Stock Issues, Chapter 9, p. 383). First, Swift establishes the need for a change, then he offers his proposal, and finally, he lists its advantages.

not above the value of two shillings, which the mother may certainly get, or the value in scraps, by her lawful occupation of begging; and it is exactly at one year that I propose to provide for them in such a manner as instead of being a charge upon their parents or the parish, or wanting food and raiment for the rest of their lives, they shall on the contrary contribute to the feeding, and partly to the clothing, of many thousands.

There is likewise another great advantage in my scheme, that it will 5 prevent those voluntary abortions, and that horrid practice of women murdering their bastard children, alas, too frequent among us, sacrificing the poor innocent babes, I doubt, more to avoid the expense than the shame, which would move tears and pity in the most savage and inhuman breast.

The number of souls in this kingdom being usually reckoned one million and a half, of these I calculate there may be about two hundred thousand couples whose wives are breeders; from which number I subtract thirty thousand couples who are able to maintain their own children, although I apprehend there cannot be so many under the present distress of the kingdom; but this being granted, there will remain an hundred and seventy thousand breeders. I again subtract fifty thousand for those women who miscarry, or whose children die by accident or disease within the year. There only remain an hundred and twenty thousand children of poor parents annually born. The question therefore is, how this number shall be reared and provided for, which, as I have already said, under the present situation of affairs, is utterly impossible by all the methods hitherto proposed. For we can neither employ them in handicraft or agriculture; we neither build houses (I mean in the country) nor cultivate land. They can very seldom pick up a livelihood by stealing till they arrive at six years old, except where they are of towardly parts;[4] although I confess they learn the rudiments much earlier, during which time they can however be looked upon only as probationers, as I have been informed by a principal gentleman in the county of Cavan, who protested to me that he never knew above one or two instances under the age of six, even in a part of the kingdom so renowned for the quickest proficiency in that art.

I am assured by our merchants that a boy or a girl before twelve years old is no salable commodity; and even when they come to this age they will not yield above three pounds, or three pounds and a half a crown at most on the Exchange; which cannot turn to account either to the parents or the kingdom, the charge of nutriment and rags having been at least four times that value.

I shall now therefore humbly propose my own thoughts, which I hope will not be liable to the least objection.

I have been assured by a very knowing American of my acquaintance in London, that a young healthy child well nursed is at a year old a most

[4] Innate talents.

delicious, nourishing, and wholesome food, whether stewed, roasted, baked, or boiled; and I make no doubt that it will equally serve in a fricassee or a ragout.[5]

I do therefore humbly offer it to public consideration that of the hundred and twenty thousand children, already computed, twenty thousand may be reserved for breed, whereof only one fourth part to be males, which is more than we allow to sheep, black cattle, or swine; and my reason is that these children are seldom the fruits of marriage, a circumstance not much regarded by our savages, therefore one male will be sufficient to serve four females. That the remaining hundred thousand may at a year old be offered in sale to the persons of quality and fortune through the kingdom, always advising the mother to let them suck plentifully in the last month, so as to render them plump and fat for a good table. A child will make two dishes at an entertainment for friends; and when the family dines alone, the fore or hind quarter will make a reasonable dish, and seasoned with a little pepper or salt will be very good boiled on the fourth day, especially in winter. 10

I have reckoned upon a medium that a child just born will weigh twelve pounds, and in a solar year if tolerably nursed increaseth to twenty-eight pounds.

I grant this food will be somewhat dear, and therefore very proper for landlords, who, as they have already devoured most of the parents, seem to have the best title to the children.

Infant's flesh will be in season throughout the year, but more plentiful in March, and a little before and after. For we are told by a grave author, an eminent French physician,[6] that fish being a prolific diet, there are more children born in Roman Catholic countries about nine months after Lent than at any other season; therefore, reckoning a year after Lent, the markets will be more glutted than usual, because the number of popish infants is at least three to one in this kingdom; and therefore it will have one other collateral advantage, by lessening the number of Papists among us.

I have already computed the charge of nursing a beggar's child (in which list I reckon all cottagers, laborers, and four-fifths of the farmers) to be about two shillings per annum, rags included; and I believe no gentleman would repine to give ten shillings for the carcass of a good fat child, which, as I have said, will make four dishes of excellent nutritive meat, when he hath only some particular friend or his own family to dine with him. Thus the squire will learn to be a good landlord, and grow popular among the tenants; the mother will have eight shillings net profit, and be fit for work till she produces another child.

---

[5] Stew.

[6] A reference to Swift's favorite French writer, François Rabelais (1494?–1553), who was actually a broad satirist known for his coarse humor.

Those who are more thrifty (as I must confess the times require) may   15
flay the carcass; the skin of which artificially[7] dressed will make admirable
gloves for ladies, and summer boots for fine gentlemen.

As to our city of Dublin, shambles[8] may be appointed for this purpose
in the most convenient parts of it, and butchers we may be assured will
not be wanting; although I rather recommend buying the children alive,
and dressing them hot from the knife as we do roasting pigs.

A very worthy person, a true lover of his country, and whose virtues
I highly esteem, was lately pleased in discoursing on this matter to offer
a refinement upon my scheme. He said that many gentlemen of his kingdom, having of late destroyed their deer, he conceived that the want of
venison might be well supplied by the bodies of young lads and maidens,
not exceeding fourteen years of age nor under twelve, so great a number
of both sexes in every county being now ready to starve for want of work
and service; and these to be disposed of by their parents, if alive, or otherwise by their nearest relations. But with due deference to so excellent a
friend and so deserving a patriot, I cannot be altogether in his sentiments;
for as to the males, my American acquaintance assured me from frequent
experience that their flesh was generally tough and lean, like that of our
schoolboys, by continual exercise, and their taste disagreeable; and to
fatten them would not answer the charge. Then as to the females, it
would, I think with humble submission, be a loss to the public, because
they soon would become breeders themselves; and besides, it is not improbable that some scrupulous people might be apt to censure such a
practice (although indeed very unjustly) as a little bordering upon cruelty; which, I confess, hath always been with me the strongest objection
against any project, how well soever intended.

But in order to justify my friend, he confessed that this expedient was
put into his head by the famous Psalmanazar,[9] a native of the island Formosa, who came from thence to London above twenty years ago, and in
conversation told my friend that in his country when any young person
happened to be put to death, the executioner sold the carcass to persons
of quality as a prime dainty; and that in his time the body of a plump girl
of fifteen, who was crucified for an attempt to poison the emperor, was
sold to his Imperial Majesty's prime minister of state, and other great
mandarins of the court, in joints from the gibbet, at four hundred
crowns. Neither indeed can I deny that if the same use were made of several plump young girls in this town, who without one single groat to their
fortunes cannot stir abroad without a chair, and appear at the playhouse

---

[7] With art or craft.

[8] Butcher shops or slaughterhouses.

[9] Georges Psalmanazar was a Frenchman who pretended to be Japanese and wrote an
entirely imaginary *Description of the Isle Formosa.* He had become well known in gullible
London society.

and assemblies in foreign fineries which they never will pay for, the king-dom would not be the worse.

Some persons of a desponding spirit are in great concern about that vast number of poor people who are aged, diseased, or maimed, and I have been desired to employ my thoughts what course may be taken to ease the nation of so grievous an encumbrance. But I am not in the least pain upon that matter, because it is very well known that they are every day dying and rotting by cold and famine, and filth and vermin, as fast as can be reasonably expected. And as to the younger laborers, they are now in almost as hopeful a condition. They cannot get work, and conse-quently pine away for want of nourishment to a degree that if any time they are accidentally hired to common labor, they have not strength to perform it; and thus the country and themselves are happily delivered from the evils to come.

I have too long digressed, and therefore shall return to my subject. I   20 think the advantages by the proposal which I have made are obvious and many, as well as of the highest importance.

For first, as I have already observed, it would greatly lessen the number of Papists, with whom we are yearly overrun, being the principal breeders of the nation as well as our most dangerous enemies; and who stay at home on purpose to deliver the kingdom to the Pretender, hoping to take their advantage by the absence of so many good Protestants, who have chosen rather to leave their country than to stay at home and pay tithes against their conscience to an Episcopal curate.

Secondly, the poorer tenants will have something valuable of their own, which by law may be made liable to distress,[10] and help to pay their landlord's rent, their corn and cattle being already seized and money a thing unknown.

Thirdly, whereas the maintenance of an hundred thousand children, from two years old and upwards, cannot be computed at less than ten shillings a piece per annum, the nation's stock will be thereby increased fifty thousand pounds per annum, besides the profit of a new dish intro-duced to the tables of all gentlemen of fortune in the kingdom who have any refinement in taste. And the money will circulate among ourselves, the goods being entirely of our own growth and manufacture.

Fourthly, the constant breeders, besides the gain of eight shillings sterling per annum by the sale of their children, will be rid of the charge of maintaining them after the first year.

Fifthly, this food would likewise bring great custom to taverns, where   25 the vintners will certainly be so prudent as to procure the best receipts for dressing it to perfection, and consequently have their houses frequented by all the fine gentlemen, who justly value themselves upon their knowl-edge in good eating; and a skillful cook, who understands how to oblige his guests, will contrive to make it as expensive as they please.

---

[10]Subject to possession by lenders.

Sixthly, this would be a great inducement to marriage, which all wise nations have either encouraged by rewards or enforced by laws and penalties. It would increase the care and tenderness of mothers toward their children, when they were sure of a settlement for life to the poor babes, provided in some sort by the public, to their annual profit instead of expense. We should see an honest emulation among the married women, which of them could bring the fattest child to the market. Men would become as fond of their wives during the time of their pregnancy as they are now of their mares in foal, their cows in calf, or sows when they are ready to farrow; nor offer to beat or kick them (as is too frequent a practice) for fear of a miscarriage.

Many other advantages might be enumerated. For instance, the addition of some thousand carcasses in our exportation of barreled beef, the propagation of swine's flesh, and improvements in the art of making good bacon, so much wanted among us by the great destruction of pigs, too frequent at our tables, which are no way comparable in taste or magnificence to a well-grown, fat, yearling child, which roasted whole will make a considerable figure at a lord mayor's feast or any other public entertainment. But this and many others I omit, being studious of brevity.

Supposing that one thousand families in this city would be constant customers for infants' flesh, besides others who might have it at merry meetings, particularly weddings and christenings, I compute that Dublin would take off annually about twenty thousand carcasses, and the rest of the kingdom (where probably they will be sold somewhat cheaper) the remaining eighty thousand.

I can think of no one objection that will possibly be raised against this proposal, unless it should be urged that the number of people will be thereby much lessened in the kingdom. This I freely own, and it was indeed one principal design in offering it to the world. I desire the reader will observe, that I calculate my remedy for this one individual kingdom of Ireland and for no other that ever was, is, or I think ever can be upon earth. Therefore let no man talk to me of other expedients: of taxing our absentees at five shillings a pound: of using neither clothes nor household furniture except what is of our own growth and manufacture: of utterly rejecting the materials and instruments that promote foreign luxury: of curing the expensiveness of pride, vanity, idleness, and gaming in our women: of introducing a vein of parsimony, prudence, and temperance: of learning to love our country, in the want of which we differ even from Laplanders and the inhabitants of Topinamboo:[11] of quitting our animosities and factions, nor acting any longer like the Jews, who were murdering one another at the very moment their city was taken:[12] of being a little cautious not to sell our country and conscience for nothing:

[11] District of Brazil.

[12] During the Roman siege of Jerusalem (A.D. 70), prominent Jews were charged with collaborating with the enemy and put to death.

of teaching landlords to have at least one degree of mercy toward their tenants: lastly, of putting a spirit of honesty, industry, and skill into our shopkeepers; who, if a resolution could now be taken to buy only our native goods, would immediately unite to cheat and exact upon us in the price, the measure, and the goodness, nor could ever yet be brought to make one fair proposal of just dealing, though often and earnestly invited to it.

Therefore I repeat, let no man talk to me of these and the like expedients, till he hath at least some glimpse of hope that there will ever be some hearty and sincere attempt to put them in practice.

But as to myself, having been wearied out for many years with offering vain, idle, visionary thoughts, and at length utterly despairing of success, I fortunately fell upon this proposal, which, as it is wholly new, so it hath something solid and real, of no expense and little trouble, full in our own power, and whereby we can incur no danger in disobliging England. For this kind of commodity will not bear exportation, the flesh being of too tender a consistence to admit a long continuance in salt, although perhaps I could name a country which would be glad to eat up our whole nation without it.

After all, I am not so violently bent upon my own opinion as to reject any offer proposed by wise men, which shall be found equally innocent, cheap, easy, and effectual. But before something of that kind shall be advanced in contradiction to my scheme, and offering a better, I desire the author or authors will be pleased maturely to consider two points. First, as things now stand, how they will be able to find food and raiment for an hundred thousand useless mouths and backs. And secondly, there being a round million of creatures in human figure throughout this kingdom, whose sole subsistence put into a common stock would leave them in debt two millions of pounds sterling, adding those who are beggars by profession to the bulk of farmers, cottagers, and laborers, with their wives and children who are beggars in effect; I desire those politicians who dislike my overture, and may perhaps be so bold to attempt an answer, that they will first ask the parents of these mortals whether they would not at this day think it a great happiness to have been sold for food at a year old in this manner I prescribe, and thereby have avoided such a perpetual scene of misfortunes as they have since gone through by the oppression of landlords, the impossibility of paying rent without money or trade, the want of common sustenance, with neither house nor clothes to cover them from the inclemencies of the weather, and the most inevitable prospect of entailing the like of greater miseries upon their breed forever.

I profess, in the sincerity of my heart, that I have not the least personal interest in endeavoring to promote this necessary work, having no other motive than the public good of my country, by advancing our trade, providing for infants, relieving the poor, and giving some pleasure to the rich. I have no children by which I can propose to get a single penny; the youngest being nine years old, and my wife past childbearing.

DISCUSSION QUESTIONS

1. What implicit assumption about the treatment of the Irish underlies Swift's proposal? Do expressions such as "just dropped from its dam" (para. 4) and "whose wives are breeders" (para. 6) give the reader a clue?

2. In this essay Swift assumes a persona; that is, for the purposes of the proposal he makes, he pretends to be a different person. Describe the characteristics of that person. Point out the places in the essay that reveal them.

3. In several places, however, Swift reveals himself as the outraged witness of English cruelty and indifference. Note the language that seems to reflect his own feelings.

4. Throughout the essay Swift recites lists of facts, many of them in the form of statistics. How do these facts contribute to the persuasiveness of his argument? How do they affect the reader?

5. What social practices and attitudes of both the Irish and the English does Swift condemn?

6. Does Swift offer any solutions for the problems he attacks? How do you know?

7. When this essay first appeared in 1729, some readers took it seriously and accused Swift of monstrous cruelty. Can you think of reasons that these readers failed to recognize the ironic intent?

WRITING SUGGESTIONS

8. Try an ironical essay of your own. Choose a subject that clearly lends itself to such treatment. As Swift did, use logic and restraint in your language.

9. Choose a problem for which you think you have a solution. Defend your solution by using the stock issues as your pattern of organization.

Civil Disobedience

HENRY DAVID THOREAU

I heartily accept the motto, — "That government is best which governs least"; and I should like to see it acted up to more rapidly and systematically. Carried out, it finally amounts to this, which also I believe, — "That government is best which governs not at all"; and when men are prepared for it, that will be the kind of government which they will have. Government is at best but an expedient; but most governments are usually, and all governments are sometimes, inexpedient. The objections which have been brought against a standing army, and they are many and weighty, and deserve to prevail, may also at last be brought against a standing government. The standing army is only an arm of the standing government. The government itself, which is only the mode which the people have chosen to execute their will, is equally liable to be abused and perverted before the people can act through it. Witness the present Mexican war, the work of comparatively a few individuals using the standing government as their tool; for, in the outset, the people would not have consented to this measure.

This American government, — what is it but a tradition, though a recent one, endeavoring to transmit itself unimpaired to posterity, but each instant losing some of its integrity? It has not the vitality and force of a single living man; for a single man can bend it to his will. It is a sort of wooden gun to the people themselves. But it is not the less necessary for this; for the people must have some complicated machinery or other, and hear its din, to satisfy that idea of government which they have. Governments show thus how successfully men can be imposed on, even impose on themselves, for their own advantage. It is excellent, we must all allow. Yet this government never of itself furthered any enterprise, but by the alacrity with which it got out of its way. *It* does not keep the country free. *It* does not settle the West. *It* does not educate. The character inherent in the American people has done all that has been accomplished; and it would have done somewhat more, if the government had not sometimes got in its way. For government is an expedient by which men would fain succeed in letting one another alone; and, as has been said, when it is most expedient, the governed are most let alone by it. Trade and commerce, if they were not made of India-rubber, would never manage to

Henry David Thoreau (1817–1862), philosopher and writer, is best known for *Walden*, an account of his solitary retreat to Walden Pond, near Concord, Massachusetts. Here he remained for more than two years in an effort to "live deliberately, to front only the essential facts of life." "Civil Disobedience" was first given as a lecture in 1848 and published in 1849. It was widely read and influenced both Mahatma Gandhi in the passive-resistance campaign he led against the British in India and Martin Luther King Jr. in the U.S. civil rights movement.

bounce over the obstacles which legislators are continually putting in their way; and, if one were to judge these men wholly by the effects of their actions, and not partly by their intentions, they would deserve to be classed and punished with those mischievous persons who put obstructions on the railroads.

But, to speak practically and as a citizen, unlike those who call themselves no-government men, I ask for, not at once no government, but *at once* a better government. Let every man make known what kind of government would command his respect, and that will be one step toward obtaining it.

After all, the practical reason why, when the power is once in the hands of the people, a majority are permitted, and for a long period continue, to rule, is not because they are most likely to be in the right, nor because this seems fairest to the minority, but because they are physically the strongest. But a government in which the majority rule in all cases cannot be based on justice, even as far as men understand it. Can there not be a government in which majorities do not virtually decide right and wrong, but conscience?—in which majorities decide only those questions to which the rule of expediency is applicable? Must the citizen ever for a moment, or in the least degree, resign his conscience to the legislator? Why has every man a conscience, then? I think that we should be men first, and subjects afterward. It is not desirable to cultivate a respect for the law, so much as for the right. The only obligation which I have a right to assume, is to do at any time what I think right. It is truly enough said, that a corporation has no conscience; but a corporation of conscientious men is a corporation *with* a conscience. Law never made men a whit more just; and, by means of their respect for it, even the well-disposed are daily made the agents of injustice. A common and natural result of an undue respect for law is, that you may see a file of soldiers, colonel, captain, corporal, privates, powder-monkeys, and all, marching in admirable order over hill and dale to the wars, against their wills, aye, against their common sense and consciences, which makes it very steep marching indeed, and produces a palpitation of the heart. They have no doubt that it is a damnable business in which they are concerned; they are all peaceably inclined. Now, what are they? Men at all? or small moveable forts and magazines, at the service of some unscrupulous man in power? Visit the Navy-Yard, and behold a marine, such a man as an American government can make, or such as it can make a man with its black arts,—a mere shadow and reminiscence of humanity, a man laid out alive and standing, and already, as one may say, buried under arms with funeral accompaniments, though it may be, —

Not a drum was heard, nor a funeral note,
As his corse to the rampart we hurried;
Not a soldier discharged his farewell shot
O'er the grave where our hero we buried.

The mass of men serve the state thus, not as men mainly, but as ma- 5
chines, with their bodies. They are the standing army, and the militia,
jailers, constables, posse comitatus, &c. In most cases there is no free exercise whatever of the judgment or of the moral sense; but they put themselves on a level with wood and earth and stones; and wooden men can
perhaps be manufactured that will serve the purpose as well. Such command no more respect than men of straw, or a lump of dirt. They have
the same sort of worth only as horses and dogs. Yet such as these even are
commonly esteemed good citizens. Others, — as most legislators, politicians, lawyers, ministers, and office-holders, — serve the State chiefly with
their heads; and, as they rarely make any moral distinctions, they are as
likely to serve the Devil, without *intending* it, as God. A very few, as heroes, patriots, martyrs, reformers in the great sense, and *men*, serve the
state with their consciences also, and so necessarily resist it for the most
part, and they are commonly treated as enemies by it. A wise man will
only be useful as a man, and will not submit to be "clay," and "stop a hole
to keep the wind away," but leave that office to his dust at least: —

> I am too high-born to be propertied,
> To be a secondary at control,
> Or useful serving-man and instrument
> To any sovereign state throughout the world.

He who gives himself entirely to his fellow-men appears to them useless and selfish; but he who gives himself partially to them is pronounced
a benefactor and philanthropist.

How does it become a man to behave toward this American government today? I answer that he cannot without disgrace be associated with
it. I cannot for an instant recognize that political organization as *my* government which is the *slave's* government also.

All men recognize the right of revolution; that is, the right to refuse
allegiance to, and to resist, the government, when its tyranny or its inef-
ficiency are great and unendurable. But almost all say that such is not the
case now. But such was the case, they think, in the Revolution of '75. If
one were to tell me that this was a bad government because it taxed certain foreign commodities brought to its ports, it is most probable that I
should not make an ado about it, for I can do without them. All machines
have their friction; and possibly this does enough good to counterbalance
the evil. At any rate, it is a great evil to make a stir about it. But when the
friction comes to have its machine, and oppression and robbery are organized, I say, let us not have such a machine any longer. In other words,
when a sixth of the population of a nation which has undertaken to be
the refuge of liberty are slaves, and a whole country is unjustly overrun
and conquered by a foreign army, and subjected to military law, I think
that it is not too soon for honest men to rebel and revolutionize. What

makes this duty the more urgent is the fact, that the country so overrun is not our own, but ours is the invading army.

Paley, a common authority with many on moral questions, in his chapter on the "Duty of Submission to Civil Government," resolves all civil obligation into expediency; and he proceeds to say, "that so long as the interest of the whole society requires it, that is, so long as the established government cannot be resisted or changed without public inconveniency, it is the will of God that the established government be obeyed, and no longer. . . . This principle being admitted, the justice of every particular case of resistance is reduced to a computation of the quantity of the danger and grievance on the one side, and of the probability and expense of redressing it on the other." Of this, he says, every man shall judge for himself. But Paley appears never to have contemplated those cases to which the rule of expediency does not apply, in which a people, as well as an individual, must do justice, cost what it may. If I have unjustly wrested a plank from a drowning man, I must restore it to him though I drown myself. This, according to Paley, would be inconvenient. But he that would save his life, in such a case, shall lose it. This people must cease to hold slaves, and to make war on Mexico, though it cost them their existence as a people.

In their practice, nations agree with Paley; but does any one think 10 that Massachusetts does exactly what is right at the present crisis?

> A drab of state, a cloth-'o-silver slut,
> To have her train borne up, and her soul trail in the dirt.

Practically speaking, the opponents to a reform in Massachusetts are not a hundred thousand politicians at the South, but a hundred thousand merchants and farmers here, who are more interested in commerce and agriculture than they are in humanity, and are not prepared to do justice to the slave and to Mexico, *cost what it may.* I quarrel not with far-off foes, but with those who, near at home, cooperate with, and do the bidding of, those far away, and without whom the latter would be harmless. We are accustomed to say, that the mass of men are unprepared; but improvement is slow, because the few are not materially wiser or better than the many. It is not so important that many should be as good as you, as that there be some absolute goodness somewhere; for that will leaven the whole lump. There are thousands who are *in opinion* opposed to slavery and to the war, who yet in effect do nothing to put an end to them; who, esteeming themselves children of Washington and Franklin, sit down with their hands in their pockets, and say that they know not what to do, and do nothing; who even postpone the question of freedom to the question of free-trade, and quietly read the prices-current along with the latest advice from Mexico, after dinner, and, it may be, fall asleep over them both. What is the price-current of an honest man and patriot today? They hesitate, and they regret, and sometimes they petition; but they do nothing in earnest and with effect. They will wait, well disposed, for others to remedy the evil, that they may no longer have it to regret. At most, they give only a cheap vote, and a feeble countenance and God-speed, to the right, as it goes by them. There are nine hundred and ninety-nine patrons of virtue to one virtuous man; but it is easier to deal with the real possessor of a thing than with the temporary guardian of it.

All voting is a sort of gaming, like checkers or backgammon, with a slight moral tinge to it, a playing with right and wrong, with moral questions; and betting naturally accompanies it. The character of the voters is not staked. I cast my vote, perchance, as I think right; but I am not vitally concerned that that right should prevail. I am willing to leave it to the majority. Its obligation, therefore, never exceeds that of expediency. Even voting *for the right* is *doing* nothing for it. It is only expressing to men feebly your desire that it should prevail. A wise man will not leave the right to the mercy of chance, nor wish it to prevail through the power of the majority. There is but little virtue in the action of masses of men. When the majority shall at length vote for the abolition of slavery, it will be because they are indifferent to slavery, or because there is but little slavery left to be abolished by their vote. *They* will then be the only slaves. Only *his* vote can hasten the abolition of slavery who asserts his own freedom by his vote.

I hear of a convention to be held at Baltimore, or elsewhere, for the selection of a candidate for the presidency, made up chiefly of editors, and men who are politicians by profession; but I think, what is it to any independent, intelligent, and respectable man what decision they may come to? Shall we not have the advantage of his wisdom and honesty, nevertheless? Can we not count upon some independent votes? Are there not many individuals in the country who do not attend conventions? But no: I find that the respectable man, so called, has immediately drifted from his position, and despairs of his country, when his country has more reason to despair of him. He forthwith adopts one of the candidates thus selected as the only *available* one, thus providing that he is himself *available* for any purposes of the demagogue. His vote is of no more worth than that of any unprincipled foreigner or hireling native, who may have been bought. O for a man who is *a man*, and, as my neighbor says, has a bone in his back which you cannot pass your hand through! Our statistics are at fault: The population has been returned too large. How many *men* are there to a square thousand miles in this country? Hardly one. Does not America offer any inducement for men to settle here? The American has dwindled into an Odd Fellow, — one who may be known by the development of his organ of gregariousness, and a manifest lack of intellect and cheerful self-reliance; whose first and chief concern, on coming into the world, is to see that the Almshouses are in good repair; and, before yet he has lawfully donned the virile garb, to collect a fund for the support of the widows and orphans that may be; who, in short, ventures to live only by the aid of the Mutual Insurance company, which has promised to bury him decently.

It is not a man's duty, as a matter of course, to devote himself to the eradication of any, even the most enormous wrong; he may still properly have other concerns to engage him; but it is his duty, at least, to wash his hands of it, and, if he gives it no thought longer, not to give it practically his support. If I devote myself to other pursuits and contemplations, I must first see, at least, that I do not pursue them sitting upon another man's shoulders. I must get off him first, that he may pursue his contemplations too. See what gross inconsistency is tolerated. I have heard some of my townsmen say, "I should like to have them order me out to help put down an insurrection of the slaves, or to march to Mexico;—see if I would go"; and yet these very men have each, directly by their allegiance, and so indirectly, at least, by their money, furnished a substitute. The soldier is applauded who refuses to serve in an unjust war by those who do not refuse to sustain the unjust government which makes the war; is applauded by those whose own act and authority he disregards and sets at nought; as if the State were penitent to that degree that it hired one to scourge it while it sinned, but not to that degree that it left off sinning for a moment. Thus, under the name of Order and Civil Government, we are all made at last to pay homage to and support our own meanness. After the first blush of sin, comes its indifference; and from immoral it becomes, as it were, *un*moral, and not quite unnecessary to that life which we have made.

The broadest and most prevalent error requires the most disinterested virtue to sustain it. The slight reproach to which the virtue of patriotism is commonly liable, the noble are most likely to incur. Those who, while they disapprove of the character and measures of a government, yield to it their allegiance and support, are undoubtedly its most conscientious supporters, and so frequently the most serious obstacles to reform. Some are petitioning the State to dissolve the Union, to disregard the requisitions of the President. Why do they not dissolve it themselves,—the union between themselves and the State,—and refuse to pay their quota into its treasury? Do not they stand in the same relation to the State, that the State does to the Union? And have not the same reasons prevented the State from resisting the Union which have prevented them from resisting the State?

How can a man be satisfied to entertain an opinion merely, and enjoy 15 *it*? Is there any enjoyment in it, if his opinion is that he is aggrieved? If you are cheated out of a single dollar by your neighbor, you do not rest satisfied with knowing that you are cheated, or with saying that you are cheated, or even with petitioning him to pay you your due; but you take effectual steps at once to obtain the full amount, and see that you are never cheated again. Action from principle, the perception and the performance of right, changes things and relations; it is essentially revolutionary, and does not consist wholly with anything which was. It not only divides states and churches, it divides families; ay, it divides the *individual*, separating the diabolical in him from the divine.

Unjust laws exist: Shall we be content to obey them, or shall we endeavor to amend them, and obey them until we have succeeded, or shall we transgress them at once? Men generally, under such a government as this, think that they ought to wait until they have persuaded the majority to alter them. They think that, if they should resist, the remedy would be worse than the evil. But it is the fault of the government itself that the remedy *is* worse than the evil. *It* makes it worse. Why is it not more apt to anticipate and provide for reform? Why does it not cherish its wise minority? Why does it cry and resist before it is hurt? Why does it not encourage its citizens to be on the alert to point out its faults, and *do* better than it would have them? Why does it always crucify Christ, and excommunicate Copernicus and Luther, and pronounce Washington and Franklin rebels?

One would think, that a deliberate and practical denial of its authority was the only offence never contemplated by government; else, why has it not assigned its definite, its suitable and proportionate penalty? If a man who has no property refuses but once to earn nine shillings for the State, he is put in prison for a period unlimited by any law that I know, and determined only by the discretion of those who placed him there; but if he should steal ninety times nine shillings from the State, he is soon permitted to go at large again.

If the injustice is part of the necessary friction of the machine of government, let it go, let it go: Perchance it will wear smooth, — certainly the machine will wear out. If the injustice has a spring, or a pulley, or a rope, or a crank, exclusively for itself, then perhaps you may consider whether the remedy will not be worse than the evil; but if it is of such a nature that it requires you to be the agent of injustice to another, then, I say, break the law. Let your life be a counter friction to stop the machine. What I have to do is to see, at any rate, that I do not lend myself to the wrong which I condemn.

As for adopting the ways which the State has provided for remedying the evil, I know not of such ways. They take too much time, and a man's life will be gone. I have other affairs to attend to. I came into this world, not chiefly to make this a good place to live in, but to live in it, be it good or bad. A man has not everything to do, but something; and because he cannot do *everything*, it is not necessary that he should do *something* wrong. It is not my business to be petitioning the Governor or the Legislature any more than it is theirs to petition me; and, if they should not hear my petition, what should I do then? But in this case the State has provided no way: Its very Constitution is the evil. This may seem to be harsh and stubborn and unconciliatory; but it is to treat with the utmost kindness and consideration the only spirit that can appreciate or deserves it. So is all change for the better, like birth and death, which convulse the body.

I do not hesitate to say, that those who call themselves Abolitionists 20
should at once effectually withdraw their support, both in person and
property, from the government of Massachusetts, and not wait till they
constitute a majority of one, before they suffer the right to prevail
through them. I think that it is enough if they have God on their side,
without waiting for that other one. Moreover, any man more right than
his neighbors, constitutes a majority of one already.

I meet this American government, or its representative, the State government, directly, and face to face, once a year — no more — in the person
of its tax-gatherer; this is the only mode in which a man situated as I am
necessarily meets it; and it then says distinctly, Recognize me; and the
simplest, the most effectual, and, in the present posture of affairs, the in-
dispensablest mode of treating with it on this head, of expressing your
little satisfaction with and love for it, is to deny it then. My civil neighbor, the tax-gatherer, is the very man I have to deal with, — for it is, after
all, with men and not with parchment that I quarrel, — and he has voluntarily chosen to be an agent of the government. How shall he ever
know well what he is and does as an officer of the government, or as a
man, until he is obliged to consider whether he shall treat me, his neighbor, for whom he has respect, as a neighbor and well-disposed man, or as
a maniac and disturber of the peace, and see if he can get over this ob-
struction to his neighborliness without a ruder and more impetuous
thought or speech corresponding with his action? I know this well, that
if one thousand, if one hundred, if ten men whom I could name, — if ten
honest men only, — aye, if *one* HONEST man, in this State of Massachusetts,
ceasing to hold slaves, were actually to withdraw from this copartnership,
and be locked up in the county jail therefor, it would be the abolition of
slavery in America. For it matters not how small the beginning may seem
to be: What is once well done is done forever. But we love better to talk
about it: That we say is our mission. Reform keeps many scores of newspapers in its service, but not one man. If my esteemed neighbor, the
State's ambassador, who will devote his days to the settlement of the
question of human rights in the Council Chamber, instead of being
threatened with the prisons of Carolina, were to sit down the prisoner of
Massachusetts, that State which is so anxious to foist the sin of slavery
upon her sister, — though at present she can discover only an act of in-
hospitality to be the ground of a quarrel with her, — the Legislature would
not wholly waive the subject the following winter.

Under a government which imprisons any unjustly, the true place for
a just man is also a prison. The proper place today, the only place which
Massachusetts has provided for her freer and less desponding spirits, is in
her prisons, to be put out and locked out of the State by her own act, as
they have already put themselves out by their principles. It is there that
the fugitive slave, and the Mexican prisoner on parole, and the Indian
come to plead the wrongs of his race, should find them; on that separate,
but more free and honorable ground, where the State places those who

are not *with* her, but *against* her,—the only house in a slave State in which a free man can abide with honor. If any think that their influence would be lost there, and their voices no longer afflict the ear of the State, that they would not be as an enemy within its walls, they do not know by how much truth is stronger than error, nor how much more eloquently and effectively he can combat injustice who has experienced a little in his own person. Cast your whole vote, not a strip of paper merely, but your whole influence. A minority is powerless while it conforms to the majority; it is not even a minority then; but it is irresistible when it clogs by its whole weight. If the alternative is to keep all just men in prison, or give up war and slavery, the State will not hesitate which to choose. If a thousand men were not to pay their tax-bills this year, that would not be a violent and bloody measure, as it would be to pay them, and enable the State to commit violence and shed innocent blood. This is, in fact, the definition of a peaceable revolution, if any such is possible. If the tax-gatherer, or any other public officer, asks me, as one has done, "But what shall I do?" my answer is, "If you really wish to do any thing, resign your office." When the subject has refused allegiance, and the officer has resigned his office, then the revolution is accomplished. But even suppose blood should flow. Is there not a sort of blood shed when the conscience is wounded? Through this wound a man's real manhood and immortality flow out, and he bleeds to an everlasting death. I see this blood flowing now.

I have contemplated the imprisonment of the offender, rather than the seizure of his goods,—though both will serve the same purpose,—because they who assert the purest right, and consequently are most dangerous to a corrupt State, commonly have not spent much time in accumulating property. To such the State renders comparatively small service, and a slight tax is wont to appear exorbitant, particularly if they are obliged to earn it by special labor with their hands. If there were one who lived wholly without the use of money, the State itself would hesitate to demand it of him. But the rich man,—not to make any invidious comparison,—is always sold to the institution which makes him rich. Absolutely speaking, the more money, the less virtue; for money comes between a man and his objects, and obtains them for him; and it was certainly no great virtue to obtain it. It puts to rest many questions which he would otherwise be taxed to answer; while the only new question which it puts is the hard but superfluous one, how to spend it. Thus his moral ground is taken from under his feet. The opportunities of living are diminished in proportion as what are called the "means" are increased. The best thing a man can do for his culture when he is rich is to endeavor to carry out those schemes which he entertained when he was poor. Christ answered the Herodians according to their condition. "Show me the tribute-money," said he;—and one took a penny out of his pocket;— if you use money which has the image of Cæsar on it, and which he has made current and valuable, that is, *if you are men of the State*, and gladly enjoy the advantages of Cæsar's government, then pay him back some of his own when he demands it; "Render therefore to Cæsar that which is Cæsar's, and to God those things which are God's,"—leaving them no wiser than before as to which was which; for they did not wish to know.

When I converse with the freest of my neighbors, I perceive that, whatever they may say about the magnitude and seriousness of the question, and their regard for the public tranquility, the long and the short of the matter is, that they cannot spare the protection of the existing government, and they dread the consequences to their property and families of disobedience to it. For my own part, I should not like to think that I ever rely on the protection of the State. But, if I deny the authority of the State when it presents its tax-bill, it will soon take and waste all my property, and so harass me and my children without end. This is hard. This makes it impossible for a man to live honestly, and at the same time comfortably, in outward respects. It will not be worth the while to accumulate property; that would be sure to go again. You must hire or squat somewhere, and raise but a small crop, and eat that soon. You must live within yourself, and depend upon yourself always tucked up and ready for a start, and not have many affairs. A man may grow rich in Turkey even, if he will be in all respects a good subject of the Turkish government. Confucius said: "If a state is governed by the principles of reason, poverty and misery are subjects of shame; if a state is not governed by the principles of reason, riches and honors are the subjects of shame." No: Until I want the protection of Massachusetts to be extended to me in some distant southern port, where my liberty is endangered, or until I am bent solely on building up an estate at home by peaceful enterprise, I can afford to refuse allegiance to Massachusetts, and her right to my property and life. It costs me less in every sense to incur the penalty of disobedience to the State, than it would to obey. I should feel as if I were worth less in that case.

Some years ago, the State met me in behalf of the Church, and commanded me to pay a certain sum toward the support of a clergyman whose preaching my father attended, but never I myself. "Pay," it said, "or be locked up in the jail." I declined to pay. But, unfortunately, another man saw fit to pay it. I did not see why the schoolmaster should be taxed to support the priest, and not the priest the schoolmaster; for I was not the State's schoolmaster, but I supported myself by voluntary subscription. I did not see why the lyceum should not present its tax-bill, and have the State to back its demand, as well as the Church. However, at the request of the selectmen, I condescended to make some such statement as this in writing:—"Know all men by these presents, that I, Henry Thoreau, do not wish to be regarded as a member of any incorporated society which I have not joined." This I gave to the town clerk; and he has it. The State, having thus learned that I did not wish to be regarded as a member of that church, has never made a like demand on me since;

though it said that it must adhere to its original presumption that time. If I had known how to name them, I should then have signed off in detail from all the societies which I never signed on to; but I did not know where to find a complete list.

I have paid no poll-tax for six years. I was put into a jail once on this account, for one night; and, as I stood considering the walls of solid stone, two or three feet thick, the door of wood and iron, a foot thick, and the iron grating which strained the light, I could not help being struck with the foolishness of that institution which treated me as if I were mere flesh and blood and bones, to be locked up. I wondered that it should have concluded at length that this was the best use it could put me to, and had never thought to avail itself of my services in some way. I saw that, if there was a wall of stone between me and my townsmen, there was a still more difficult one to climb or break through, before they could get to be as free as I was. I did not for a moment feel confined, and the walls seemed a great waste of stone and mortar. I felt as if I alone of all my townsmen had paid my tax. They plainly did not know how to treat me, but behaved like persons who are underbred. In every threat and in every compliment there was a blunder; for they thought that my chief desire was to stand the other side of that stone wall. I could not but smile to see how industriously they locked the door on my meditations, which followed them out again without let or hindrance, and *they* were really all that was dangerous. As they could not reach me, they had resolved to punish my body; just as boys, if they cannot come at some person against whom they have a spite, will abuse his dog. I saw that the State was half-witted, and it was timid as a lone woman with her silver spoons, and that it did not know its friends from its foes, and I lost all my remaining respect for it, and pitied it.

Thus the State never intentionally confronts a man's sense, intellectual or moral, but only his body, his senses. It is not armed with superior wit or honesty, but with superior physical strength. I was not born to be forced. I will breathe after my own fashion. Let us see who is the strongest. What force has a multitude? They only can force me who obey a higher law than I. They force me to become like themselves. I do not hear of *men* being *forced* to live this way or that by masses of men. What sort of life were that to live? When I meet a government which says to me, "Your money or your life," why should I be in haste to give it my money? It may be in a great strait, and not know what to do: I cannot help that. It must help itself; do as I do. It is not worth the while to snivel about it. I am not responsible for the successful working of the machinery of society. I am not the son of the engineer. I perceive that, when an acorn and a chestnut fall side by side, the one does not remain inert to make way for the other, but both obey their own laws, and spring and grow and flourish as best they can, till one, perchance, overshadows and destroys the other. If a plant cannot live according to its nature, it dies; and so a man.

The night in prison was novel and interesting enough. The prisoners in their shirt-sleeves were enjoying a chat and the evening air in the doorway, when I entered. But the jailer said, "Come, boys, it is time to lock up"; and so they dispersed, and I heard the sound of their steps returning into the hollow apartments. My roommate was introduced to me by the jailer, as "a first-rate fellow and a clever man." When the door was locked, he showed me where to hang my hat, and how he managed matters there. The rooms were white-washed once a month; and this one, at least, was the whitest, most simply furnished, and probably the neatest apartment in the town. He naturally wanted to know where I came from, and what brought me there; and, when I had told him, I asked him in my turn how he came there, presuming him to be an honest man, of course; and, as the world goes, I believe he was. "Why," said he, "they accuse me of burning a barn; but I never did it." As near as I could discover, he had probably gone to bed in a barn when drunk, and smoked his pipe there; and so a barn was burnt. He had the reputation of being a clever man, had been there some three months waiting for his trial to come on, and would have to wait as much longer; but he was quite domesticated and contented, since he got his board for nothing, and thought that he was well-treated.

He occupied one window, and I the other; and I saw, that if one stayed there long, his principal business would be to look out the window. I had soon read all the tracts that were left there, and examined where former prisoners had broken out, and where a grate had been sawed off, and heard the history of the various occupants of that room; for I found that even here there was a history and a gossip which never circulated beyond the walls of the jail. Probably this is the only house in the town where verses are composed, which are afterward printed in a circular form, but not published. I was shown quite a long list of verses which were composed by some young men who had been detected in an attempt to escape, who avenged themselves by singing them.

I pumped my fellow-prisoner as dry as I could, for fear I should never 30
see him again; but at length he showed me which was my bed, and left me to blow out the lamp.

It was like travelling into a far country, such as I had never expected to behold, to lie there for one night. It seemed to me that I never had heard the town-clock strike before, nor the evening sounds of the village; for we slept with the windows open, which were inside the grating. It was to see my native village in the light of the Middle Ages, and our Concord was turned into a Rhine stream, and visions of knights and castles passed before me. They were the voices of old burghers that I heard in the streets. I was an involuntary spectator and auditor of whatever was done and said in the kitchen of the adjacent village-inn, —a wholly new and rare experience to me. It was a closer view of my native town. I was fairly inside of it. I never had seen its institutions before. This is one of its peculiar institutions; for it is a shire town. I began to comprehend what its inhabitants were about.

In the morning, our breakfasts were put through the hole in the door, in small oblong-square tin pans, made to fit, and holding a pint of chocolate, with brown bread, and an iron spoon. When they called for the vessels again, I was green enough to return what bread I had left; but my comrade seized it, and said that I should lay that up for lunch or dinner. Soon after, he was let out to work at haying in a neighboring field, whither he went every day, and would not be back till noon; so he bade me good-day, saying that he doubted if he should see me again.

When I came out of prison,—for some one interfered, and paid that tax,—I did not perceive that great changes had taken place on the common, such as he observed who went in a youth, and emerged a tottering and gray-headed man; and yet a change had to my eyes come over the scene,—the town, and State, and country,—greater than any that mere time could effect. I saw yet more distinctly the State in which I lived. I saw to what extent the people among whom I lived could be trusted as good neighbors and friends; that their friendship was for summer weather only; that they did not greatly propose to do right; that they were a distinct race from me by their prejudices and superstitions, as the Chinamen and Malays are; that, in their sacrifices to humanity, they ran no risks, not even to their property; that, after all, they were not so noble but they treated the thief as he had treated them, and hoped, by a certain outward observance and a few prayers, and by walking in a particular straight though useless path from time to time, to save their souls. This may be to judge my neighbors harshly; for I believe that many of them are not aware that they have such an institution as the jail in their village.

It was formerly the custom in our village, when a poor debtor came out of jail, for his acquaintances to salute him, looking through their fingers, which were crossed to represent the grating of a jail window, "How do ye do?" My neighbors did not thus salute me, but first looked at me, and then at one another, as if I had returned from a long journey. I was put into jail as I was going to the shoemaker's to get a shoe which was mended. When I was let out the next morning, I proceeded to finish my errand, and having put on my mended shoe, joined a huckleberry party, who were impatient to put themselves under my conduct; and in half an hour,—for the horse was soon tackled,—was in the midst of a huckleberry field, on one of our highest hills, two miles off, and then the State was nowhere to be seen.

This is the whole story of "My Prisons." 35

I have never declined paying the highway tax, because I am as desirous of being a good neighbor as I am of being a bad subject; and, as for supporting schools, I am doing my part to educate my fellow-countrymen now. It is for no particular item in the tax-bill that I refuse to pay it. I simply wish to refuse allegiance to the State, to withdraw and stand aloof from it effectually. I do not care to trace the course of my dollar, if I could, till it buys a man, or a musket to shoot one with, —the dollar is innocent, —but I am concerned to trace the effects of my allegiance. In fact, I quietly declare war with the State, after my fashion, though I will still make what use and get what advantage of her I can, as is usual in such cases.

If others pay the tax which is demanded of me, from a sympathy with the State, they do but what they have already done in their own case, or rather they abet injustice to a greater extent than the State requires. If they pay the tax from a mistaken interest in the individual taxed, to save his property or prevent his going to jail, it is because they have not considered wisely how far they let their private feelings interfere with the public good.

This, then, is my position at present. But one cannot be too much on his guard in such a case, lest his action be biased by obstinacy, or an undue regard for the opinions of men. Let him see that he does only what belongs to himself and to the hour.

I think sometimes, Why, this people mean well; they are only ignorant; they would do better if they knew how: why give your neighbors this pain to treat you as they are inclined to? But I think again, this is no reason why I should do as they do, or permit others to suffer much greater pain of a different kind. Again, I sometimes say to myself, When many millions of men, without heat, without ill will, without personal feelings of any kind, demand of you a few shillings only, without the possibility, such is their constitution, of retracing or altering their present demand, and without the possibility, on your side, of appeal to any other millions, why expose yourself to this overwhelming brute force? You do not resist cold and hunger, the winds and the waves, thus obstinately; you quietly submit to a thousand similar necessities. You do not put your head into the fire. But just in proportion as I regard this as not wholly a brute force, partly a human force, and consider that I have relations to those millions as to so many millions of men, and not of mere brute or inanimate things, I see that appeal is possible, first and instantaneously, from them to the Maker of them, and, secondly, from them to themselves. But, if I put my head deliberately into the fire, there is no appeal to fire or to the Maker of fire, and I have only myself to blame. If I could convince myself that I have any right to be satisfied with men as they are, and to treat them according, and not according, in some respects, to my requisitions and expectations of what they and I ought to be, then, like a good Mussulman and fatalist, I should endeavor to be satisfied with things as they are, and say it is the will of God. And, above all, there is this difference between resisting this and a purely brute or natural force, that I can resist this with some effect; but I cannot expect, like Orpheus, to change the nature of the rocks and trees and beasts.

I do not wish to quarrel with any man or nation. I do not wish to split 40 hairs, to make fine distinctions, or set myself up as better than my neighbors. I seek rather, I may say, even an excuse for conforming to the laws of the land. I am but too ready to conform to them. Indeed, I have reason to suspect myself on this head; and each year, as the tax-gatherer comes round, I find myself disposed to review the acts and position of the general and State governments, and the spirit of the people, to discover a pretext for conformity.

> We must affect our country as our parents;
> And if at any time we alienate
> Our love or industry from doing it honor,
> We must respect effects and teach the soul
> Matter of conscience and religion,
> And not desire of rule or benefit.

I believe that the State will soon be able to take all my work of this sort out of my hands, and then I shall be no better a patriot than my fellow-countrymen. Seen from a lower point of view, the Constitution, with all its faults, is very good; the law and the courts are very respectable; even this State and this American government are, in many respects, very admirable and rare things, to be thankful for, such as a great many have described them; but seen from a point of view a little higher, they are what I have described them; seen from a higher still, and the highest, who shall say what they are, or that they are worth looking at or thinking of at all?

However, the government does not concern me much, and I shall bestow the fewest possible thoughts on it. It is not many moments that I live under a government, even in this world. If a man is thought-free, fancy-free, imagination-free, that which *is not* never for a long time appearing *to be* to him, unwise rulers or reformers cannot fatally interrupt him.

I know that most men think differently from myself; but those whose lives are by profession devoted to the study of these or kindred subjects, content me as little as any. Statesmen and legislators, standing so completely within the institution, never distinctly and nakedly behold it. They speak of moving society, but have no resting-place without it. They may be men of a certain experience and discrimination, and have no doubt invented ingenious and even useful systems, for which we sincerely thank them; but all their wit and usefulness lie within certain not very wide limits. They are wont to forget that the world is not governed by policy and expediency. Webster never goes behind government, and so cannot speak with authority about it. His words are wisdom to those legislators who contemplate no essential reform in the existing government; but for thinkers, and those who legislate for all time, he never once glances at the subject. I know of those whose serene and wise speculations on this theme would soon reveal the limits of his mind's range and hospitality. Yet, compared with the cheap professions of most reformers, and the still cheaper wisdom and eloquence of politicians in general, his are almost the only sensible and valuable words, and we thank Heaven for him. Comparatively, he is always strong, original, and, above all, practical. Still his quality is not wisdom, but prudence. The lawyer's truth is not Truth, but consistency, or a consistent expediency. Truth is always in harmony with herself, and is not concerned chiefly to reveal the justice that may consist with wrong-doing. He well deserves to be called, as he has been called, the Defender of the Constitution. There are really no blows to be given by him but defensive ones. He is not a leader, but a follower. His leaders are the men of '87. "I have never made an effort," he says, "and never propose to make an effort; I have never countenanced an effort, and never mean to countenance an effort, to disturb the arrangement as originally made, by which the various States came into the Union." Still thinking of the sanction which the Constitution gives to slavery, he says, "Because it was a part of the original compact, — let it stand." Notwithstanding his special acuteness and ability, he is unable to take a fact out of its merely political relations, and behold it as it lies absolutely to be disposed of by the intellect, — what, for instance, it behooves a man to do here in America today with regard to slavery, but ventures, or is driven, to make some such desperate answer as the following, while professing to speak absolutely, and as a private man, — from which what new and singular code of social duties might be inferred? "The manner," says he, "in which the governments of those States where slavery exists are to regulate it, is for their own consideration, under their responsibility to their constituents, to the general laws of propriety, humanity, and justice, and to God. Associations formed elsewhere, springing from a feeling of humanity, or any other cause, have nothing whatever to do with it. They have never received any encouragement from me, and they never will."[1]

They who know of no purer sources of truth, who have traced up its stream no higher, stand, and wisely stand, by the Bible and the Constitution, and drink at it there with reverence and humility; but they who behold where it comes trickling into this lake or that pool, gird up their loins once more, and continue their pilgrimage toward its fountainhead.

No man with a genius for legislation has appeared in America. They are rare in the history of the world. There are orators, politicians, and eloquent men, by the thousand; but the speaker has not yet opened his mouth to speak, who is capable of settling the much-vexed questions of the day. We love eloquence for its own sake, and not for any truth which it may utter, or any heroism it may inspire. Our legislators have not yet learned the comparative value of free-trade and of freedom, of union, and of rectitude, to a nation. They have no genius or talent for comparatively humble questions of taxation and finance, commerce and manufactures and agriculture. If we were left solely to the wordy wit of legislators in

---

[1] These extracts have been inserted since the Lecture was read.

Congress for our guidance, uncorrected by the seasonable experience and the effectual complaints of the people, America would not long retain her rank among the nations. For eighteen hundred years, though perchance I have no right to say it, the New Testament has been written; yet where is the legislator who has wisdom and practical talent enough to avail himself of the light which it sheds on the science of legislation?

The authority of government, even such as I am willing to submit to, — for I will cheerfully obey those who know and can do better than I, and in many things even those who neither know nor can do so well, — is still an impure one: To be strictly just, it must have the sanction and consent of the governed. It can have no pure right over my person and property but what I concede to it. The progress from an absolute to a limited monarchy, from a limited monarchy to a democracy, is a progress toward a true respect for the individual. Even the Chinese philosopher was wise enough to regard the individual as the basis of the empire. Is a democracy, such as we know it, the last improvement possible in government? Is it not possible to take a step further towards recognizing and organizing the rights of man? There will never be a really free and enlightened State, until the State comes to recognize the individual as a higher and independent power, from which all its own power and authority are derived, and treats him accordingly. I please myself with imagining a State at last which can afford to be just to all men, and to treat the individual with respect as a neighbor; which even would not think it inconsistent with its own repose, if a few were to live aloof from it, not meddling with it, nor embraced by it, who fulfilled all the duties of neighbors and fellowmen. A State which bore this kind of fruit, and suffered it to drop off as fast as it ripened, would prepare the way for a still more perfect and glorious State, which also I have imagined, but not yet anywhere seen. 45

DISCUSSION QUESTIONS

1. Summarize briefly Thoreau's reasons for arguing that civil disobedience is sometimes a *duty*.

2. Thoreau, like Martin Luther King Jr. in "Letter from Birmingham Jail" (p. 571), speaks of "unjust laws" (para. 16). Do they agree on the positions that citizens should take in response to these laws? Are Thoreau and King guided by the same principles?

3. What examples of government policy and action does Thoreau use to prove that civil disobedience is a duty? Explain why they are—or are not—effective.

4. Why do you think Thoreau provides such a detailed account of one day in prison? (Notice that King does not give a description of his confinement.) What observation about the community struck Thoreau when he emerged from jail?

WRITING SUGGESTIONS

5. Argue that civil disobedience to a school policy or action is justified. (Examples might include failure to establish an ethnic studies department, refusal to allow ROTC on campus, refusal to suspend a professor accused of sexual harassment.) Be specific about the injustice of the policy or action and the values that underlie the resistance.

6. Under what circumstances might civil disobedience prove to be dangerous and immoral? Can you think of cases of disobedience when *conscience*, as Thoreau uses the term, did not appear to be the guiding principle? Try to identify what you think is the true motivation for the resistance.

The Crisis

CARRIE CHAPMAN CATT

I have taken for my subject, "The Crisis," because I believe that a crisis has come in our movement which, if recognized and the opportunity seized with vigor, enthusiasm and will, means the final victory of our great cause in the very near future. I am aware that some suffragists do not share this belief; they see no signs nor symptoms today which were not present yesterday; no manifestations in the year 1916 which differ significantly from those in the year 1910. To them, the movement has been a steady, normal growth from the beginning and must so continue until the end. I can only defend my claim with the plea that it is better to *imagine* a crisis where none exists than to fail to recognize one when it comes; for a crisis is a culmination of events which calls for new considerations and new decisions. A failure to answer the call may mean an opportunity lost, a possible victory postponed.

The object of the life of an organized movement is to secure its aim. Necessarily, it must obey the law of evolution and pass through the stages of agitation and education and finally through the stage of realization. As one has put it: "A new idea floats in the air over the heads of the people and for a long, indefinite period evades their understanding but, by and by, when through familiarity, human vision grows clearer, it is caught out of the clouds and crystalized into law." Such a period comes to every movement and is its crisis. In my judgment, that crucial moment, bidding us to renewed consecration and redoubled activity has come to our cause. I believe our victory hangs within our grasp, inviting us to pluck it out of the clouds and establish it among the good things of the world.

If this be true, the time is past when we should say: "Men and women of America, look upon that wonderful idea up there; see, one day it will come down." Instead, the time has come to shout aloud in every city, village and hamlet, and in tones so clear and jubilant that they will reverberate from every mountain peak and echo from shore to shore: "The

---

Carrie Chapman Catt (1859–1947) was an outspoken advocate of women's suffrage and the founder of the League of Women Voters. This speech was given in September 1916 in Atlantic City, New Jersey, at a special convention of the National American Woman Suffrage Association, of which she was president. Her powerful speech is one of the one hundred most important speeches in American history. In it she presents the war in Europe taking place at that time as an opportunity to push for women's right to vote. European women had proven to be such effective "war assets" that it would be hard for them to ever be relegated to the inferior positions they had occupied before the war. American women could hardly be satisfied with less.

Woman's Hour has struck."[1] Suppose suffragists as a whole do not believe a crisis has come and do not extend their hands to grasp the victory, what will happen? Why, we shall all continue to work and our cause will continue to hang, waiting for those who possess a clearer vision and more daring enterprise. On the other hand, suppose we reach out with united earnestness and determination to grasp our victory while it still hangs a bit too high? Has any harm been done? None!

Therefore, fellow suffragists, I invite your attention to the signs which point to a crisis and your consideration of plans for turning the crisis into victory.

First: We are passing through a world crisis. All thinkers of every land   5 tell us so; and that nothing after the great war will be as it was before. Those who profess to know, claim that 100 millions of dollars are being spent on the war every day and that 2 years of war have cost 50 billions of dollars or 10 times more than the total expense of the American Civil War. Our own country has sent 35 millions of dollars abroad for relief expenses.

Were there no other effects to come from the world's war, the transfer of such unthinkably vast sums of money from the usual avenues to those wholly abnormal would give so severe a jolt to organized society that it would vibrate around the world and bring untold changes in its wake.

But three and a half millions of lives have been lost. The number becomes the more impressive when it is remembered that the entire population of the American Colonies was little more than three and one-half millions. These losses have been the lives of men within the age of economic production. They have been taken abruptly from the normal business of the world and every human activity from that of the humblest, unskilled labor to art, science and literature has been weakened by their loss. Millions of other men will go to their homes, blind, crippled and incapacitated to do the work they once performed. The stability of human institutions has never before suffered so tremendous a shock. Great men are trying to think out the consequences but one and all proclaim that no imagination can find color or form bold enough to paint the picture of the world after the war. British and Russian, German and Austrian, French and Italian agree that it will lead to social and political revolution throughout the entire world. Whatever comes, they further agree that the war presages a total change in the status of women.

A simple-minded man in West Virginia, when addressed upon the subject of woman suffrage in that state, replied, "We've been so used to

---

[1] This phrase refers to the frustration of woman's rights activists in the post–Civil War period who were told to defer the demand for woman suffrage because this was "the Negro's hour." [All notes are by Karlyn Kohrs Campbell, the editor of *Man Cannot Speak for Her* (Greenwood, 1989).]

keepin' our women down, 'twould seem queer not to." He expressed what greater men feel but do not say. Had the wife of that man spoken in the same clear-thinking fashion, she would have said, "We women have been so used to being kept down that it would seem strange to get up. Nature intended women for doormats." Had she so expressed herself, these two would have put the entire anti-suffrage argument in a nutshell.

In Europe, from the Polar Circle to the Aegean Sea, women have risen as though to answer that argument. Everywhere they have taken the places made vacant by men and in so doing, they have grown in self-respect and in the esteem of their respective nations. In every land, the people have reverted to the primitive division of labor and while the men have gone to war, women have cultivated the fields in order that the army and nation may be fed. No army can succeed and no nation can endure without food; those who supply it are a war power and a peace power.

Women by the thousands have knocked at the doors of munition fac- 10 tories and, in the name of patriotism, have begged for the right to serve their country there. Their services were accepted with hesitation but the experiment once made, won reluctant but universal praise. An official statement recently issued in Great Britain announced that 660,000 women were engaged in making munitions in that country alone. In a recent convention of munition workers, composed of men and women, a resolution was unanimously passed informing the government that they would forego vacations and holidays until the authorities announced that their munition supplies were sufficient for the needs of the war and Great Britain pronounced the act the highest patriotism. Lord Derby addressed such a meeting and said, "When the history of the war is written, I wonder to whom the greatest credit will be given; to the men who went to fight or to the women who are working in a way that many people hardly believed that it was possible for them to work." Lord Sydenham added his tribute. Said he, "It might fairly be claimed that women have helped to save thousands of lives and to change the entire aspect of the war. Wherever intelligence, care and close attention have been needed, women have distinguished themselves." A writer in the *London Times* of July 18, 1916, said: "But, for women, the armies could not have held the field for a month; the national call to arms could not have been made or sustained; the country would have perished of inanition and disorganization. If, indeed, it be true that the people have been one, it is because the genius of women has been lavishly applied to the task of reinforcing and complementing the genius of men. The qualities of steady industry, adaptability, good judgement and concentration of mind which men do not readily associate with women have been conspicuous features."

On fields of battle, in regular and improvised hospitals, women have given tender and skilled care to the wounded and are credited with the restoration of life to many, many thousands. Their heroism and self-sacrifice have been frankly acknowledged by all the governments; but their endurance, their skill, the practicality of their service, seem for the first time, to have been recognized by governments as "war power." So, thinking in war terms, great men have suddenly discovered that women are "war assets". Indeed, Europe is realizing, as it never did before, that women are holding together the civilization for which men are fighting. A great search-light has been thrown upon the business of nation-building and it has been demonstrated in every European land that it is a partnership with equal, but different responsibilities resting upon the two partners.

It is not, however, in direct war work alone that the latent possibilities of women have been made manifest. In all the belligerent lands, women have found their way to high posts of administration where no women would have been trusted two years ago and the testimony is overwhelming that they have filled their posts with entire satisfaction to the authorities. They have dared to stand in pulpits (once too sacred to be touched by the unholy feet of a woman) and there, without protest, have appealed to the Father of All in behalf of their stricken lands. They have come out of the kitchen where there was too little to cook and have found a way to live by driving cabs, motors and streetcars. Many a woman has turned her hungry children over to a neighbor and has gone forth to find food for both mothers and both families of children and has found it in strange places and occupations. Many a drawing-room has been closed and the maid who swept and dusted it is now cleaning streets that the health of the city may be conserved. Many a woman who never before slept in a bed of her own making, or ate food not prepared by paid labor, is now sole mistress of parlor and kitchen.

In all the warring countries, women are postmen [sic], porters, railway conductors, ticket, switch and signal men. Conspicuous advertisements invite women to attend agricultural, milking and motor-car schools. They are employed as police in Great Britain and women detectives have recently been taken on the government staff. In Berlin, there are over 3,000 women streetcar conductors and 3,500 women are employed on the general railways. In every city and country, women are doing work for which they would have been considered incompetent two years ago.

The war will soon end and the armies will return to their native lands. To many a family, the men will never come back. The husband who returns to many a wife, will eat no bread the rest of his life save of her earning.

What, then, will happen after the war? Will the widows left with families to support cheerfully leave their well-paid posts for those commanding lower wages? Not without protest! Will the wives who now must support crippled husbands give up their skilled work and take up the occupations which were open to them before the war? Will they resignedly say: "The woman who has a healthy husband who can earn for her, has a right to tea and raisin cake, but the woman who earns for herself and a husband who has given his all to his country, must be content with butterless bread"? Not without protest! On the contrary, the economic axiom, denied and evaded for centuries, will be blazoned on every 15 factory, counting house and shop: "Equal pay for equal work"; and common justice will slowly, but surely enforce that law. The European woman has risen. She may not realize it yet, but the woman "doormat" in every land has unconsciously become a "doorjamb"! She will have become accustomed to her new dignity by the time the men come home. She will wonder how she ever could have been content lying across the threshold now that she discovers the upright jamb gives so much broader and more normal a vision of things. The men returning may find the new order a bit queer but everything else will be strangely unfamiliar too, and they will soon grow accustomed to all the changes together. The "jamb" will never descend into a "doormat" again.

The male and female anti-suffragists of all lands will puff and blow at the economic change which will come to the women of Europe. They will declare it to be contrary to Nature and to God's plan and that somebody ought to do something about it. Suffragists will accept the change as the inevitable outcome of an unprecedented world's cataclysm over which no human agency had any control and will trust in God to adjust the altered circumstances to the eternal evolution of human society. They will remember that in the long run, all things work together for good, for progress and for human weal.

The economic change is bound to bring political liberty. From every land, there comes the expressed belief that the war will be followed by a mighty, oncoming wave of democracy for it is now well known that the conflict has been one of governments, of kings and Czars, Kaisers and Emperors; not of peoples. The nations involved have nearly all declared that they are fighting to make an end of wars. New and higher ideals of governments and of the rights of the people under them, have grown enormously during the past two years. Another tide of political liberty, similar to that of 1848, but of a thousandfold greater momentum, is rising from battlefield and hospital, from camp and munitions factory, from home and church which, great men of many lands, tell us, is destined to sweep over the world. On the continent, the women say, "It is certain that the vote will come to men and women after the war, perhaps not immediately but soon. In Great Britain, which was the storm centre of the suffrage movement for some years before the war, hundreds of bitter, active opponents have confessed their conversion on account of the war services of women. Already, three great provinces of Canada, Manitoba, Alberta, and Saskatchawan [sic], have given universal suffrage to their women in sheer generous appreciation of their war work. Even Mr. Asquith, world renouned [sic] for his immovable opposition to the Parliamentary suffrage for British women, has given evidence of a change of view.[2] Some months ago, he announced his amazement at the utterly

[2]Herbert Henry Asquith (1852–1928), British prime minister (1908–1916) and leader of the Liberal party until 1925, when he was raised to the peerage; he opposed woman suffrage.

unexpected skill, strength and resource developed by the women and his gratitude for their loyalty and devotion. Later, in reply to Mrs. Henry Fawcett, who asked if woman suffrage would be included in a proposed election bill, he said that when the war should end, such a measure would be considered without prejudice carried over from events prior to the war.[3] A public statement issued by Mr. Asquith in August, was couched in such terms as to be interpreted by many as a pledge to include women in the next election bill.

In Great Britain, a sordid appeal which may prove the last straw to break the opposition to woman suffrage, has been added to the enthusiastic appreciation of woman's patriotism and practical service and to the sudden comprehension that motherhood is a national asset which must be protected at any price. A new voters' list is contemplated. A parliamentary election should be held in September but the voters are scattered far and wide. The whole nation is agitated over the questions involved in making a new register. At the same time, there is a constant anxiety over war funds, as is prudent in a nation spending 50 millions of dollars per day. It has been proposed that a large poll tax be assessed upon the voters of the new lists, whereupon a secondary proposal of great force has been offered and that is, that twice as much money would find its way into the public coffers were women added to the voters' list. What nation, with compliments fresh spoken concerning women's patriotism and efficiency, could resist such an appeal?

So it happens that above the roar of cannon, the scream of shrapnel and the whirr of aeroplanes, one who listens may hear the cracking of the fetters which have long bound the European woman to outworn conventions. It has been a frightful price to pay but the fact remains that a womanhood, well started on the way to final emancipation, is destined to step forth from the war. It will be a bewildered, troubled and grief-stricken womanhood with knotty problems of life to solve, but it will be freer to deal with them than women have ever been before.

"The Woman's Hour has struck." It has struck for the women of Europe and for those of all the world. The significance of the changed status of European women has not been lost upon the men and women of our land; our own people are not so unlearned in history, nor so lacking in National pride that they will allow the Republic to lag long behind the Empire, presided over by the descendant of George the Third. If they possess the patriotism and the sense of nationality which should be the inheritance of an American, they will not wait until the war is ended but will boldly lead in the inevitable march of democracy, our own American specialty. Sisters, let me repeat, the Woman's Hour has struck! 20

---

[3] Millicent Garrett Fawcett, the leading figure in the National Union of Women's Suffrage Societies, which began in 1867 and stood apart from the more militant suffrage organizations.

Second: As the most adamantine rock gives way under the constant dripping of water, so the opposition to woman suffrage in our own country has slowly disintegrated before the increasing strength of our movement. Turn backward the pages of our history! Behold, brave Abbie Kelley rotten-egged because she, a woman, essayed to speak in public.[4] Behold the Polish Ernestine Rose startled that women of free America drew aside their skirts when she proposed that they should control their own property.[5] Recall the saintly Lucretia Mott and the legal-minded Elizabeth Cady Stanton, turned out of the [W]orld's Temperance Convention in London and conspiring together to free their sex from the world's stupid oppressions.[6] Remember the gentle, sweet-voiced Lucy Stone, egged because she publicly claimed that women had brains capable of education.[7] Think upon Dr. Elizabeth Blackwell, snubbed and boycotted by other women because she proposed to study medicine.[8] Behold Dr. Antoinette Brown Blackwell, standing in sweet serenity before an Assembly of howling clergymen, angry that she, a woman dared to attend a Temperance Convention as a delegate. Revere the intrepid Susan B. Anthony mobbed from Buffalo to Albany because she demanded fair play for women. These are they who builded with others the foundation of political liberty for American women.

Those who came after only laid the stones in place. Yet, what a wearisome task even that has been! Think of the wonderful woman who has wandered from village to village, from city to city, for a generation compelling men and women to listen and to reflect by her matchless eloquence. Where in all the world's history has any movement among men produced so invincible an advocate as our own Dr. Anna Howard Shaw? Those whom she has led to the light are Legion. Think, too, of the con-

---

[4] Abigail ("Abby") Kelley [Foster] (1810–1887), abolitionist and woman's rights lecturer, spoke first in 1838 to a mixed audience in Philadelphia's Pennsylvania Hall. A powerful agitator, she was attacked as a Jezebel and faced angry mobs outraged at a woman speaking effectively to mixed audiences against slavery.

[5] An allusion to the 1836 effort to petition the New York Legislature to amend the Married Woman's Property Act.

[6] Lucretia Coffin Mott and other women were not seated as delegates at the World Anti-Slavery Convention in 1840. Cady Stanton was present but not a delegate.

[7] Lucy Stone (1818–1893), the first Massachusetts woman to take [earn] a college degree (Oberlin, 1847). She became a lecturer for the American Anti-Slavery Society, but also spoke on woman's rights prior to the emergence of a movement, fearlessly facing hostile audiences. Defying convention, she kept her own name after her marriage to Henry Blackwell in 1855. She became the leader of the New England wing of the suffrage movement, a founder of the American Woman Suffrage Association and of the *Woman's Journal* (1870), which after 1872 she and her husband, and later her daughter, Alice Stone Blackwell, edited.

[8] Elizabeth Blackwell (1821–1910), the first woman of modern times to graduate in medicine. She received her degree in 1849 from Geneva College, and founded the New York Infirmary for Women and Children in 1857, and the Woman's Medical College of the New York Infirmary in 1868.

secration, the self-denial, the never-failing constancy of that other noble soul set in a frail but unflinching body,—the heroine we know as Alice Stone Blackwell![9] A woman who never forgets, who detects the slightest flaw in the weapons of her adversary, who knows the most vulnerable spot in his armor, president over the *Woman's Journal* and, like a lamp in lighthouse, the rays of her intelligence, far-sightedness and clear-thinking have enlightened the world concerning our cause. The names of hundreds of other brave souls spring to memory when we pause to review the long struggle.

The hands of many suffrage master-masons have long been stilled; the names of many who laid the stones have been forgotten. That does not matter. The main thing is that the edifice of woman's liberty nears completion. It is strong, indestructible. All honor to the thousands who have helped in the building.

The four Cornerstones of the foundations were laid long years ago. We read upon the first: "We demand for women education, for not a high school or college is open to her"; upon the second, "We demand for women religious liberty for in few churches is she permitted to pray or speak"; upon the third, "We demand for women the right to own property and an opportunity to earn an honest living. Only six, poorly-paid occupations are open to her, and if she is married, the wages she earns are not hers"; upon the fourth, "We demand political freedom and its symbol, the vote."

The stones in the foundation have long been overgrown with the 25 moss and mould of time, and some there are who never knew they were laid. Of late, four capstones at the top have been set to match those in the base, and we read upon the first: "The number of women who are graduated from high schools, colleges and universities is legion"; upon the second, "The Christian Endeavor, that mighty, undenominational church militant, asks the vote for the women and the Methodist Episcopal Church, and many another, joins that appeal"; upon the third, "Billions of dollars worth of property are earned [and] owned by women; more than 8 millions of women are wage-earners. Every occupation is open to them"; upon the fourth: "Women vote in 12 States; they share in the determination of 91 electoral votes."

After the capstones and cornice comes the roof. Across the empty spaces, the roof-tree has been flung and fastened well in place. It is not made of stone but of two *planks*—planks in the platform of the two majority parties, and these are well supported by planks in the platforms of all minority parties.

---

[9] Daughter of Lucy Stone and Henry Blackwell (1857–1950). Following graduation from Boston University in 1881, she bore the main burdens of editing the *Woman's Journal*, the country's leading woman's rights newspaper founded by her parents, for the next thirty-five years.

And we who are the builders of 1916, do we see a crisis? Standing upon these planks which are stretched across the top-most peak of this edifice of woman's liberty, what shall we do? Over our heads, up there in the clouds, but tantalizing [sic] near, hangs the roof of our edifice, — the vote. What is our duty? Shall we spend time in admiring the capstones and cornice? Shall we lament the tragedies which accompanied the laying of the cornerstones? Or, shall we, like the builders of old, chant, "Ho! all hands, all hands, heave to! All hands, heave to!" and while we chant, grasp the overhanging roof and with a long pull, a strong pull and a pull together, fix it in place forevermore?

Is the crisis real or imaginary? If it be real, it calls for action, bold, immediate and decisive.

Let us then take measure of our strength. Our cause has won the endorsement of all political parties. Every candidate for the presidency is a suffragist. It has won the endorsement of most churches; it has won the hearty approval of all great organizations of women. It has won the support of all reform movements; it has won the progressives of every variety. The majority of the press in most States is with us. Great men in every political party, church and movement are with us. The names of the greatest men and women of art, science, literature and philosophy, reform, religion and politics are on our lists.

We have not won the reactionaries of any party, church or society, and 30 we never will. From the beginning of things, there have been Antis. The Antis drove Moses out of Egypt; they crucified Christ who said, "Love thy neighbor as thyself" [Matt. 19:19, 22:39]; they have persecuted Jews in all parts of the world; they poisoned Socrates, the great philosopher; they cruelly persecuted Copernicus[10] and Galileo,[11] the first great scientists; they burned Giordano Bruno at the stake because he believed the world was round;[12] they burned Savonarola who warred upon church corruption;[13]

[10]Nicholas Copernicus (1473–1543), Polish astronomer, whose great work, the foundation of modern astronomy, was *De revolutionibus orbium coelestium* (1543), dedicated to Pope Paul III.

[11]Galileo Galilei (1564–1642), Italian astronomer, mathematician, and physicist, who constructed the first complete astronomical telescope, and whose investigations confirmed the Copernican theory of the solar system. In 1616 that theory was denounced as dangerous to faith, but in 1632 Galileo published a work which supported it, and was tried in 1633 by the Inquisition and forced to recant all beliefs and writings holding that the earth and other planets revolved about the sun.

[12]Giordano Bruno (1548–1600), Italian philosopher. His major metaphysical works were *De la causa, principio, et uno* (1584) and *De l'infinito, universo et mondi* (1584). Tried for heresy in Venice in 1591 by the Inquisition, he was imprisoned, then burned to death at Rome.

[13]Girolamo Savonarola (1452–1498), Italian religious reformer, prior of San Marco, the Dominican house in Florence. He was excommunicated by Pope Alexander VI for disobedience after he continued to preach against the scandalously corrupt papal court. Under torture he supposedly confessed to being a false prophet and was hanged for schism and heresy.

they burned Eufame McIlyane [sic] because she used an anaesthetic;[14] they burned Joan d'Arc for a heretic; they have sent great men and women to Siberia to eat their hearts out in isolation; they burned in effigy William Lloyd Garrison; they egged Abbie Kelley and Lucy Stone and mobbed Susan B. Anthony. Yet, in proportion to the enlightenment of their respective ages, these Antis were persons of intelligence and honest purpose. They were merely deaf to the call of Progress and were enraged because the world insisted upon moving on. Antis male and female there still are and will be to the end of time. Give to them a prayer of forgiveness for they know not what they do; and prepare for the forward march.

We have not won the ignorant and illiterate and we never can. They are too undeveloped mentally to understand that the institutions of today are not those of yesterday nor will be those of tomorrow.

We have not won the forces of evil and we never will. Evil has ever been timorous and suspicious of all change. It is an instinctive act of self-preservation which makes it fear and consequently oppose votes for women. As the Hon. Champ Clark said the other day: "Some good and intelligent people are opposed to woman suffrage; but all the ignorant and evil-minded are against it."[15]

These three forces are the enemies of our cause.

Before the vote is won, there must and will be a gigantic final conflict between the forces of progress, righteousness and democracy and the forces of ignorance, evil and reaction. That struggle may be postponed, but it cannot be evaded or avoided. There is no question as to which side will be the victor.

Shall we play the coward, then, and leave the hard knocks for our 35 daughters, or shall we throw ourselves into the fray, bare our own shoulders to the blows, and thus bequeath to them a politically liberated womanhood? We have taken note of our gains and of our resources, and they are all we could wish. Before the final struggle, we must take cognizance of our weaknesses. Are we prepared to grasp the victory? Alas, no! Our movement is like a great Niagara with a vast volume of water tumbling over its ledge but turning no wheel. Our organized machinery is set for the propagandistic stage and not for the seizure of victory. Our supporters are spreading the argument for our cause; they feel no sense of responsibility for the realization of our hopes. Our movement lacks cohesion, organization, unity and consequent momentum.

Behind us, in front of us, everywhere about us are suffragists, — millions of them, but inactive and silent. They have been "agitated and

[14]Euphemia MacCalyean was sentenced to be burned in Scotland on June 15, 1591, for attempting to relieve her pains in giving birth to twins and for other charges related to witchcraft.

[15]James Beauchamp Clark (1850–1921), member U.S. House of Representatives (1893–1895, 1897–1921). He became Democratic leader (1907) and Speaker (1911–1919), and in 1912 was the leading Democratic candidate for the presidency until William Jennings Bryan shifted his support to Woodrow Wilson.

educated" and are with us in belief. There are thousands of women who have at one time or another been members of our organization but they have dropped out because, to them the movement seemed negative and pointless. Many have taken up other work whose results were more immediate. Philanthropy, charity, work for corrective laws of various kinds, temperance, relief for working women and numberless similar public services have called them. Others have turned to the pleasanter avenues of clubwork, art or literature.

There are thousands of other women who have never learned of the earlier struggles of our movement. They found doors of opportunity open to them on every side. They found well-paid posts awaiting the qualified woman and they have availed themselves of all these blessings; almost without exception they believe in the vote but they feel neither gratitude to those who opened the doors through which they have entered to economic liberty nor any sense of obligation to open other doors for those who come after.

There are still others who, timorously looking over their shoulders to see if any listeners be near, will tell us they hope we will win and win soon but they are too frightened of Mother Grundy to help.[16] There are others too occupied with the small things of life to help. They say they could find time to vote but not to work for the vote. There are men, too, millions of them, waiting to be called. These men and women are our reserves. They are largely unorganized and untrained soldiers with little responsibility toward our movement. Yet these reserves must be mobilized. The final struggle needs their numbers and the momentum those numbers will bring. Were never another convert made, there are suffragists enough in this country, if combined, to make so irresistible a driving force that victory might be seized at once.

How can it be done? By a simple change of mental attitude. If we are to seize the victory, that change must take place in this hall, here and now!

The old belief, which has sustained suffragists in many an hour of discouragement, "woman suffrage is bound to come," must give way to the new, "The Woman's Hour has struck." The long drawn out struggle, the cruel hostility which, for years was arrayed against our cause, have accustomed suffragists to the idea of indefinite postponement but eventual victory. The slogan of a movements sets its pace. The old one counseled patience; it said, there is plenty of time; it pardoned sloth and half-hearted effort. It set the pace of an educational campaign. The "Woman's Hour has struck" sets the pace of a crusade which will have its way. It says: "Awake, arise, my sisters, let your hearts be filled with joy, — the time of victory is here. Onward March."

If you believe with me that a crisis has come to our movement, — if you believe that the time for final action is now, if you catch the rosy tints of the coming day, what does it mean to you? Does it not give you a thrill

40

---

[16]Public opinion personified.

of exaltation; does the blood not course more quickly through your veins; does it not bring a new sense of freedom, of joy and of determination? Is it not true that you who wanted a little time ago to lay down the work because you were weary with long service, now, under the compelling influence of a changed mental attitude, are ready to go on until the vote is won. The change is one of spirit! Aye, and the spiritual effect upon you will come to others. Let me borrow an expression from Hon. John Finlay: What our great movement needs now is a "mobilization of spirit", — the jubilant, glad spirit of victory. Then let us sound a bugle call here and now to the women of the Nation: "The Woman's Hour has struck." Let the bugle sound from the suffrage headquarters of every State at the inauguration of a State campaign. Let the call go forth again and again and yet again. Let it be repeated in every article written, in every speech made, in every conversation held. Let the bugle blow again and yet again. The political emancipation of our sex call[s] you, women of America, arise! Are you content that others shall pay the price of your liberty?

Women in schools and counting house, in shops and on the farm, women in the home with babes at their breasts and women engaged in public careers will hear. The veins of American women are not filled with milk and water. They are neither cowards nor slackers. They will come. They only await the bugle call to learn that the final battle is on.

DISCUSSION QUESTIONS

1. What are the signs Catt sees that suggest America's crisis point in the fight for women's suffrage might turn into victory?
2. In what ways has World War I changed the role of women in Europe?
3. What does Catt predict will happen to women's status in Europe once the war is over?
4. Explain Catt's metaphor of woman as doormat or as doorjamb.
5. Explain the metaphor of the construction of a building that Catt uses to describe the suffrage movement.
6. In what ways does Catt appeal to the emotions of those listening to her speech in 1916?
7. What other effective argumentative strategies does Catt use in the speech?
8. How does she use language effectively to strengthen her speech?

WRITING SUGGESTIONS

9. Argue that Catt's speech is a blend of appeal to the reason and to the emotions of her audience.
10. How does she use her analysis of what is happening in Europe to appeal to an American audience?
11. Explain how Catt's speech, given in 1916, still has relevance in the early twentieth century.

Letter from Birmingham Jail

MARTIN LUTHER KING JR.

A Call for Unity: A Letter
from Eight White Clergymen

April 12, 1963

We the undersigned clergymen are among those who, in January, issued "An Appeal for Law and Order and Common Sense," in dealing with racial problems in Alabama. We expressed understanding that honest convictions in racial matters could properly be pursued in the courts, but urged that decisions of those courts should in the meantime be peacefully obeyed.

Since that time there had been some evidence of increased forebearance and a willingness to face facts. Responsible citizens have undertaken to work on various problems which cause racial friction and unrest. In Birmingham, recent public events have given indication that we all have opportunity for a new constructive and realistic approach to racial problems.

However, we are now confronted by a series of demonstrations by some of our Negro citizens, directed and led in part by outsiders. We recognize the natural impatience of people who feel that their hopes are slow in being realized. But we are convinced that these demonstrations are unwise and untimely.

We agree rather with certain local Negro leadership which has called for honest and open negotiation of racial issues in our area. And we believe this kind of facing of issues can best be accomplished by citizens of our own metropolitan area, white and Negro, meeting with their knowledge and experience of the local situation. All of us need to face that responsibility and find proper channels for its accomplishment.

Just as we formerly pointed out that "hatred and violence have no   5
sanction in our religious and political traditions," we also point out that such actions as incite to hatred and violence, however technically peaceful those actions may be, have not contributed to the resolution of our local problems. We do not believe that these days of new hope are days when extreme measures are justified in Birmingham.

Martin Luther King Jr. (1929–1968) was a clergyman, author, distinguished civil rights leader, and winner of the Nobel Prize for peace in 1964 for his contributions to racial harmony and his advocacy of nonviolent response to aggression. He was assassinated in 1968. In "Letter from Birmingham Jail," he appears as a historian and philosopher. He wrote the letter from a jail cell on April 16, 1963, after his arrest for participation in a demonstration for civil rights for African Americans. The letter was a reply to eight Alabama clergymen who, in the first letter reprinted here, had condemned demonstrations in the streets. Kings essay is from *A Testament of Hope* (1986).

We commend the community as a whole, and the local news media and law enforcement officials in particular, on the calm manner in which these demonstrations have been handled. We urge the public to continue to show restraint should the demonstrations continue, and the law enforcement officials to remain calm and continue to protect our city from violence.

We further strongly urge our own Negro community to withdraw support from these demonstrations, and to unite locally in working peacefully for a better Birmingham. When rights are consistently denied, a cause should be pressed in the courts and in negotiations among local leaders, and not in the streets. We appeal to both our white and Negro citizenry to observe the principles of law and order and common sense.

> (Signed)
> C.C.J. Carpenter, D.D., L.L.D., Bishop of Alabama; Joseph A. Durick, D.D., Auxiliary Bishop, Diocese of Mobile-Birmingham; Rabbi Milton L. Grafman, Temple Emanu-El, Birmingham, Alabama; Bishop Paul Hardin, Bishop of the Alabama–West Florida Conference of the Methodist Church; Bishop Nolan B. Harmon, Bishop of the North Alabama Conference of the Methodist Church; George M. Murray, D.D., L.L.D., Bishop Coadjutor, Episcopal Diocese of Alabama; Edward V. Ramage, Moderator, Synod of the Alabama Presbyterian Church in the United States; Earl Stallings, Pastor, First Baptist Church, Birmingham.

King's Reply from Birmingham Jail

My dear Fellow Clergymen,

While confined here in the Birmingham city jail, I came across your recent statement calling our present activities "unwise and untimely." Seldom, if ever, do I pause to answer criticism of my work and ideas. If I sought to answer all of the criticisms that cross my desk, my secretaries would be engaged in little else in the course of the day, and I would have no time for constructive work. But since I feel that you are men of genuine good will and your criticisms are sincerely set forth, I would like to answer your statement in what I hope will be patient and reasonable terms.

I think I should give the reason for my being in Birmingham, since you have been influenced by the argument of "outsiders coming in." I have the honor of serving as president of the Southern Christian Leadership Conference, an organization operating in every southern state, with headquarters in Atlanta, Georgia. We have some eighty-five affiliate organizations all across the South—one being the Alabama Christian Movement for Human Rights. Whenever necessary and possible we share staff, educational, and financial resources with our affiliates. Several months ago our local affiliate here in Birmingham invited us to be on call to engage in a nonviolent direct-action program if such were deemed necessary. We readily consented and when the hour came we lived up to our promises. So I am here, along with several members of my staff, because we were invited here. I am here because I have basic organizational ties here.

Beyond this, I am in Birmingham because injustice is here. Just as the eighth-century prophets left their little villages and carried their "thus saith the Lord" far beyond the boundaries of their hometowns; and just as the Apostle Paul left his little village of Tarsus and carried the gospel of Jesus Christ to practically every hamlet and city of the Graeco-Roman world, I too am compelled to carry the gospel of freedom beyond my particular hometown. Like Paul, I must constantly respond to the Macedonian call for aid.

Moreover, I am cognizant of the interrelatedness of all communities and states. I cannot sit idly by in Atlanta and not be concerned about what happens in Birmingham. Injustice anywhere is a threat to justice everywhere. We are caught in an inescapable network of mutuality, tied in a single garment of destiny. Whatever affects one directly affects all indirectly. Never again can we afford to live with the narrow, provincial "outside agitator" idea. Anyone who lives in the United States can never be considered an outsider anywhere in this country.

You deplore the demonstrations that are presently taking place in   5
Birmingham. But I am sorry that your statement did not express a similar concern for the conditions that brought the demonstrations into being. I am sure that each of you would want to go beyond the superficial social analyst who looks merely at effects, and does not grapple with underlying causes. I would not hesitate to say that it is unfortunate that so-called demonstrations are taking place in Birmingham at this time, but I would say in more emphatic terms that it is even more unfortunate that the white power structure of this city left the Negro community with no other alternative.

In any nonviolent campaign there are four basic steps: (1) collection of the facts to determine whether injustices are alive, (2) negotiation, (3) self-purification, and (4) direct action. We have gone through all of these steps in Birmingham. There can be no gainsaying of the fact that racial injustice engulfs this community.

Birmingham is probably the most thoroughly segregated city in the United States. Its ugly record of police brutality is known in every section of this country. Its unjust treatment of Negroes in the courts is a notorious reality. There have been more unsolved bombings of Negro homes and churches in Birmingham than any city in this nation. These are the hard, brutal, and unbelievable facts. On the basis of these conditions Negro leaders sought to negotiate with the city fathers. But the political leaders consistently refused to engage in good faith negotiation.

Then came the opportunity last September to talk with some of the leaders of the economic community. In these negotiating sessions certain promises were made by the merchants—such as the promise to remove the humiliating racial signs from the stores. On the basis of these promises Reverend Shuttlesworth and the leaders of the Alabama Christian Movement for Human Rights agreed to call a moratorium on any type of demonstrations. As the weeks and months unfolded we realized that we were the victims of a broken promise. The signs remained. Like so many experiences of the past we were confronted with blasted hopes, and the dark shadow of a deep disappointment settled upon us. So we had no alternative except that of preparing for direct action, whereby we would present our very bodies as a means of laying our case before the conscience of the local and national community. We were not unmindful of the difficulties involved. So we decided to go through a process of self-purification. We started having workshops on nonviolence and repeatedly asking ourselves the questions, "Are you able to accept blows without retaliating?" "Are you able to endure the ordeals of jail?" We decided to set our direct-action program around the Easter season, realizing that with the exception of Christmas, this was the largest shopping period of the year. Knowing that a strong economic withdrawal program would be the by-product of direct action, we felt that this was the best time to bring pressure on the merchants for the needed changes. Then it occurred to us that the March election was ahead and so we speedily decided to postpone action until after election day. When we discovered that Mr. Connor was in the run-off, we decided again to postpone action so that the demonstrations could not be used to cloud the issues. At this time we agreed to begin our nonviolent witness the day after the run-off.

This reveals that we did not move irresponsibly into direct actions. We too wanted to see Mr. Connor defeated; so we went through postponement after postponement to aid in this community need. After this we felt that direct action could be delayed no longer.

You may well ask, "Why direct action? Why sit-ins, marches, etc.? 10 Isn't negotiation a better path?" You are exactly right in your call for negotiation. Indeed, this is the purpose of direct action. Nonviolent direct action seeks to create such a crisis and establish such creative tension that a community that has constantly refused to negotiate is forced to confront the issue. It seeks so to dramatize the issue that it can no longer be ignored. I just referred to the creation of tension as a part of the work of the nonviolent resister. This may sound rather shocking. But I must confess that I am not afraid of the word tension. I have earnestly worked and preached against violent tension, but there is a type of constructive nonviolent tension that is necessary for growth. Just as Socrates felt that it was necessary to create a tension in the mind so that individuals could rise from the bondage of myths and half-truths to the unfettered realm of creative analysis and objective appraisal, we must see the need of having nonviolent gadflies to create the kind of tension in society that will help men to rise from the dark depths of prejudice and racism to the majestic heights of understanding and brotherhood. So the purpose of the direct action is to create a situation so crisis-packed that it will inevitably open the door to negotiation. We, therefore, concur with you in your call for negotiation. Too long has our beloved Southland been bogged down in the tragic attempt to live in monologue rather than dialogue.

One of the basic points in your statement is that our acts are untimely. Some have asked, "Why didn't you give the new administration time to act?" The only answer that I can give to this inquiry is that the new administration must be prodded about as much as the outgoing one before it acts. We will be sadly mistaken if we feel that the election of Mr. Boutwell will bring the millennium to Birmingham. While Mr. Boutwell is much more articulate and gentle than Mr. Connor, they are both segregationists, dedicated to the task of maintaining the status quo. The hope I see in Mr. Boutwell is that he will be reasonable enough to see the futility of massive resistance to desegregation. But he will not see this without pressure from the devotees of civil rights. My friends, I must say to you that we have not made a single gain in civil rights without determined legal and nonviolent pressure. History is the long and tragic story of the fact that privileged groups seldom give up their privileges voluntarily. Individuals may see the moral light and voluntarily give up their unjust posture; but as Reinhold Niebuhr has reminded us, groups are more immoral than individuals.

We know through painful experience that freedom is never voluntarily given by the oppressor; it must be demanded by the oppressed. Frankly, I have never yet engaged in a direct-action movement that was "well-timed," according to the timetable of those who have not suffered unduly from the disease of segregation. For years now I have heard the words "Wait!" It rings in the ear of every Negro with a piercing familiarity. This "Wait" has almost always meant "Never." It has been a tranquilizing thalidomide, relieving the emotional stress for a moment, only to give birth to an ill-formed infant of frustration. We must come to see with the distinguished jurist of yesterday that "justice too long delayed is justice denied." We have waited for more than 340 years for our constitutional and God-given rights. The nations of Asia and Africa are moving with jetlike speed toward the goal of political independence, and we still creep at horse and buggy pace toward the gaining of a cup of coffee at a lunch counter. I guess it is easy for those who have never felt the stinging darts of segregation to say, "Wait." But when you have seen vicious mobs lynch your mothers and fathers at will and drown your sisters and brothers at whim; when you see hate-filled policemen curse, kick, brutalize, and even kill your black brothers and sisters with impunity; when you see the vast majority of your 20 million Negro brothers smothering in an airtight cage of poverty in the midst of an affluent society; when you suddenly find your tongue twisted and your speech stammering as you seek to explain to your six-year-old daughter why she can't go to the public amusement park that has just been advertised on television, and see tears welling up in her little eyes when she is told that Funtown is closed to colored children, and see the depressing clouds of inferiority begin to form in her little mental sky, and see her begin to distort her little personality by unconsciously developing a bitterness toward white people; when you have to concoct an answer for a five-year-old son asking in agonizing pathos: "Daddy, why do white people treat colored people so mean?"; when you take a cross-country drive and find it necessary to sleep night after night in the uncomfortable corners of your automobile because no motel will accept you; when you are humiliated day in and day out by nagging signs reading "white" and "colored"; when your first name becomes "nigger" and your middle name becomes "boy" (however old you are) and your last name becomes "John," and when your wife and mother are never given the respected title "Mrs."; when you are harried by day and haunted by night by the fact that you are a Negro, living constantly at tiptoe stance never quite knowing what to expect next, and plagued with inner fears and outer resentments; when you are forever fighting a degenerating sense of "nobodiness"; then you will understand why we find it difficult to wait. There comes a time when the cup of endurance runs over, and men are no longer willing to be plunged into an abyss of injustice where they experience the blackness of corroding despair. I hope, sirs, you can understand our legitimate and unavoidable impatience.

You express a great deal of anxiety over our willingness to break laws. This is certainly a legitimate concern. Since we so diligently urge people to obey the Supreme Court's decision of 1954 outlawing segregation in the public schools, it is rather strange and paradoxical to find us consciously breaking laws. One may well ask, "How can you advocate breaking some laws and obeying others?" The answer is found in the fact that there are two types of laws: There are *just* and there are *unjust* laws. I would agree with Saint Augustine that "An unjust law is no law at all."

Now what is the difference between the two? How does one determine when a law is just or unjust? A just law is a man-made code that squares with the moral law or the law of God. An unjust law is a code that is out of harmony with the moral law. To put it in the terms of Saint Thomas Aquinas, an unjust law is a human law that is not rooted in eternal and natural law. Any law that uplifts human personality is just. Any law that degrades human personality is unjust. All segregation statutes are unjust because segregation distorts the soul and damages the personality. It gives the segregator a false sense of superiority, and the segregated a false sense of inferiority. To use the words of Martin Buber, the great Jewish philosopher, segregation substitutes an "I-it" relationship for the "I-thou" relationship, and ends up relegating persons to the status of things. So segregation is not only politically, economically, and sociologically unsound, but it is morally wrong and sinful. Paul Tillich has said that sin is separation. Isn't segregation an existential expression of man's tragic separation, an expression of his awful estrangement, his terrible sinfulness? So I can urge men to disobey segregation ordinances because they are morally wrong.

Let us turn to a more concrete example of just and unjust laws. An 15 unjust law is a code that a majority inflicts on a minority that is not binding on itself. This is difference made legal. On the other hand, a just law is a code that a majority compels a minority to follow that it is willing to follow itself. This is sameness made legal.

Let me give another explanation. An unjust law is a code inflicted upon a minority which that minority had no part in enacting or creating because they did not have the unhampered right to vote. Who can say that the legislature of Alabama which set up the segregation laws was democratically elected? Throughout the state of Alabama all types of conniving methods are used to prevent Negroes from becoming registered voters, and there are some counties without a single Negro registered to vote despite the fact that the Negro constitutes a majority of the population. Can any law set up in such a state be considered democratically structured?

These are just a few examples of unjust and just laws. There are some instances when a law is just on its face and unjust in its application. For instance, I was arrested Friday on a charge of parading without a permit. Now there is nothing wrong with an ordinance which requires a permit for a parade, but when the ordinance is used to preserve segregation and to deny citizens the First Amendment privilege of peaceful assembly and peaceful protest, then it becomes unjust.

I hope you can see the distinction I am trying to point out. In no sense do I advocate evading or defying the law as the rabid segregationist would do. This would lead to anarchy. One who breaks an unjust law must do it *openly, lovingly* (not hatefully as the white mothers did in New Orleans when they were seen on television screaming, "nigger, nigger, nigger"), and with a willingness to accept the penalty. I submit that an individual who breaks a law that conscience tells him is unjust, and willingly accepts the penalty by staying in jail to arouse the conscience of the community over its injustice, is in reality expressing the very highest respect for law.

Of course, there is nothing new about this kind of civil disobedience. It was seen sublimely in the refusal of Shadrach, Meshach, and Abednego to obey the laws of Nebuchadnezzar because a higher moral law was involved. It was practiced superbly by the early Christians who were willing to face hungry lions and the excruciating pain of chopping blocks, before submitting to certain unjust laws of the Roman Empire. To a degree academic freedom is a reality today because Socrates practiced civil disobedience.

We can never forget that everything Hitler did in Germany was 20 "legal" and everything the Hungarian freedom fighters did in Hungary was "illegal." It was "illegal" to aid and comfort a Jew in Hitler's Germany. But I am sure that if I had lived in Germany during that time I would have aided and comforted my Jewish brothers even though it was illegal. If I lived in a Communist country today where certain principles dear to the

Christian faith are suppressed, I believe I would openly advocate disobeying these antireligious laws. I must make two honest confessions to you, my Christian and Jewish brothers. First, I must confess that over the last few years I have been gravely disappointed with the white moderate. I have almost reached the regrettable conclusion that the Negro's great stumbling block in the stride toward freedom is not the White Citizen's Councilor or the Ku Klux Klanner, but the white moderate who is more devoted to "order" than to justice; who prefers a negative peace which is the absence of tension to a positive peace which is the presence of justice; who constantly says, "I agree with you in the goal you seek, but I can't agree with your methods of direct action"; who paternalistically feels that he can set the timetable for another man's freedom; who lives by the myth of time and who constantly advises the Negro to wait until a "more convenient season." Shallow understanding from people of good will is more frustrating than absolute misunderstanding from people of ill will. Lukewarm acceptance is much more bewildering than outright rejection.

I had hoped that the white moderate would understand that law and order exist for the purpose of establishing justice, and that when they fail to do this they become dangerously structured dams that block the flow of social progress. I had hoped that the white moderate would understand that the present tension of the South is merely a necessary phase of the transition from an obnoxious negative peace, where the Negro passively accepted his unjust plight, to a substance-filled positive peace, where all men will respect the dignity and worth of human personality. Actually, we who engage in nonviolent direct action are not the creators of tension. We merely bring to the surface the hidden tension that is already alive. We bring it out in the open where it can be seen and dealt with. Like a boil that can never be cured as long as it is covered up but must be opened with all its pus-flowing ugliness to the natural medicines of air and light, injustice must likewise be exposed, with all of the tension its exposing creates, to the light of human conscience and the air of national opinion before it can be cured.

In your statement you asserted that our actions, even though peaceful, must be condemned because they precipitate violence. But can this assertion be logically made? Isn't this like condemning the robbed man because his possession of money precipitated the evil act of robbery? Isn't this like condemning Socrates because his unswerving commitment to truth and his philosophical delvings precipitated the misguided popular mind to make him drink the hemlock? Isn't this like condemning Jesus because His unique God-consciousness and never-ceasing devotion to His will precipitated the evil act of crucifixion? We must come to see, as federal courts have consistently affirmed, that it is immoral to urge an individual to withdraw his efforts to gain his basic constitutional rights because the quest precipitates violence. Society must protect the robbed and punish the robber.

I had also hoped that the white moderate would reject the myth of time. I received a letter this morning from a white brother in Texas which said: "All Christians know that the colored people will receive equal rights eventually, but it is possible that you are in too great of a religious hurry. It has taken Christianity almost two thousand years to accomplish what it has. The teachings of Christ take time to come to earth." All that is said here grows out of a tragic misconception of time. It is the strangely irrational notion that there is something in the very flow of time that will inevitably cure all ills. Actually time is neutral. It can be used either destructively or constructively. I am coming to feel that the people of ill will have used time much more effectively than the people of good will. We will have to repent in this generation not merely for the vitriolic words and actions of the bad people, but for the appalling silence of the good people. We must come to see that human progress never rolls in on wheels of inevitability. It comes through the tireless efforts and persistent work of men willing to be co-workers with God, and without this hard work time itself becomes an ally of the forces of social stagnation. We must use time creatively, and forever realize that the time is always ripe to do right. Now is the time to make real the promise of democracy, and transform our pending national elegy into a creative psalm of brotherhood. Now is the time to lift our national policy from the quicksand of racial injustice to the solid rock of human dignity.

You spoke of our activity in Birmingham as extreme. At first I was rather disappointed that fellow clergymen would see my nonviolent efforts as those of the extremist. I started thinking about the fact that I stand in the middle of two opposing forces in the Negro community. One is a force of complacency made up of Negroes who, as a result of long years of oppression, have been so completely drained of self-respect and a sense of "somebodiness" that they have adjusted to segregation, and of a few Negroes in the middle class who, because of a degree of academic and economic security, and because at points they profit by segregation, have unconsciously become insensitive to the problems of the masses. The other force is one of bitterness and hatred, and comes perilously close to advocating violence. It is expressed in the various black nationalist groups that are springing up over the nation, the largest and best known being Elijah Muhammad's Muslim movement. This movement is nourished by the contemporary frustration over the continued existence of racial discrimination. It is made up of people who have lost faith in America, who have absolutely repudiated Christianity, and who have concluded that the white man is an incurable "devil." I have tried to stand between these two forces, saying that we need not follow the "do-nothingism" of the complacent or the hatred and despair of the black nationalist. There is the more excellent way of love and nonviolent protest. I'm grateful to God that, through the Negro church, the dimension of nonviolence entered our struggle. If this philosophy had not emerged, I am convinced that by now many streets of the South would be flowing with floods of blood. And I am further convinced that if our white brothers dismiss us as "rabble-rousers" and "outside agitators" those of us who are working through the channels of nonviolent direct action and refuse to support our nonviolent efforts, millions of Negroes, out of frustration and despair, will seek solace and security in black nationalist ideologies, a development that will lead inevitably to a frightening racial nightmare.

Oppressed people cannot remain oppressed forever. The urge for free- 25 dom will eventually come. This is what happened to the American Negro. Something within has reminded him of his birthright of freedom; something without has reminded him that he can gain it. Consciously and unconsciously, he has been swept in by what the Germans call the *Zeitgeist*, and with his black brothers of Africa, and his brown and yellow brothers of Asia, South America, and the Caribbean, he is moving with a sense of cosmic urgency toward the promised land of racial justice. Recognizing this vital urge that has engulfed the Negro community, one should readily understand public demonstrations. The Negro has many pent-up resentments and latent frustrations. He has to get them out. So let him march sometime; let him have his prayer pilgrimages to the city hall; understand why he must have sit-ins and freedom rides. If his repressed emotions do not come out in these nonviolent ways, they will come out in ominous expressions of violence. This is not a threat; it is a fact of history. So I have not said to my people "get rid of your discontent." But I have tried to say that this normal and healthy discontent can be channelized through the creative outlet of nonviolent direct action. Now this approach is being dismissed as extremist. I must admit that I was initially disappointed in being so categorized.

But as I continued to think about the matter I gradually gained a bit of satisfaction from being considered an extremist. Was not Jesus an extremist in love—"Love your enemies, bless them that curse you, pray for them that despitefully use you." Was not Amos an extremist for justice—"Let justice roll down like waters and righteousness like a mighty stream." Was not Paul an extremist for the gospel of Jesus Christ—"I bear in my body the marks of the Lord Jesus." Was not Martin Luther an extremist—"Here I stand; I can do none other so help me God." Was not John Bunyan an extremist—"I will stay in jail to the end of my days before I make a butchery of my conscience." Was not Abraham Lincoln an extremist—"This nation cannot survive half slave and half free." Was not Thomas Jefferson an extremist—"We hold these truths to be self-evident, that all men are created equal." So the question is not whether we will be extremist but what kind of extremist will we be. Will we be extremists for hate or will we be extremists for love? Will we be extremists for the preservation of injustice—or will we be extremists for the cause of justice? In that dramatic scene on Calvary's hill, three men were crucified. We must not forget that all three were crucified for the same crime—the crime of extremism. Two were extremists for immorality, and thusly fell below their environment. The other, Jesus Christ, was an extremist for love, truth, and goodness, and thereby rose above his environment. So, after all, maybe the South, the nation, and the world are in dire need of creative extremists.

I had hoped that the white moderate would see this. Maybe I was too optimistic. Maybe I expected too much. I guess I should have realized that few members of a race that has oppressed another race can understand or appreciate the deep groans and passionate yearnings of those that have been oppressed and still fewer have the vision to see that injustice must be rooted out by strong, persistent, and determined action. I am thankful, however, that some of our white brothers have grasped the meaning of this social revolution and committed themselves to it. They are still all too small in quantity, but they are big in quality. Some like Ralph McGill, Lillian Smith, Harry Golden, and James Dabbs have written about our struggle in eloquent, prophetic, and understanding terms. Others have marched with us down nameless streets of the South. They have languished in filthy roach-infested jails, suffering the abuse and brutality of angry policemen who see them as "dirty nigger-lovers." They, unlike so many of their moderate brothers and sisters, have recognized the urgency of the moment and sensed the need for powerful "action" antidotes to combat the disease of segregation.

Let me rush on to mention my other disappointment. I have been so greatly disappointed with the white church and its leadership. Of course, there are some notable exceptions. I am not unmindful of the fact that each of you has taken some significant stands on this issue. I commend you, Reverend Stallings, for your Christian stance on this past Sunday, in welcoming Negroes to your worship service on a nonsegregated basis. I commend the Catholic leaders of this state for integrating Springhill College several years ago.

But despite these notable exceptions I must honestly reiterate that I have been disappointed with the church. I do not say that as one of the negative critics who can always find something wrong with the church. I say it as a minister of the gospel, who loves the church; who was nurtured in its bosom; who has been sustained by its spiritual blessings, and who will remain true to it as long as the cord of life shall lengthen.

I had the strange feeling when I was suddenly catapulted into the 30 leadership of the bus protest in Montgomery several years ago that we would have the support of the white church. I felt that the white ministers, priests, and rabbis of the South would be some of our strongest allies. Instead, some have been outright opponents, refusing to understand the freedom movement and misrepresenting its leaders; all too many others have been more cautious than courageous and have remained silent behind the anesthetizing security of the stained-glass windows.

In spite of my shattered dreams of the past, I came to Birmingham with the hope that the white religious leadership of this community would see the justice of our cause, and with deep moral concern, serve as the channel through which our just grievances would get to the power structure. I had hoped that each of you would understand. But again I have been disappointed. I have heard numerous religious leaders of the South call upon their worshipers to comply with a desegregation decision because it is the *law,* but I have longed to hear white ministers say, "Follow this decree because integration is morally *right* and the Negro is your brother." In the midst of blatant injustices inflicted upon the Negro, I have watched white churches stand on the sideline and merely mouth pious irrelevancies and sanctimonious trivialities. In the midst of a mighty struggle to rid our nation of racial and economic injustice, I have heard so many ministers say, "Those are social issues with which the gospel has no real concern," and I have watched so many churches commit themselves to a completely otherworldly religion which made a strange distinction between body and soul, the sacred and the secular.

So here we are moving toward the exit of the twentieth century with a religious community largely adjusted to the status quo, standing as a taillight behind other community agencies rather than a headlight leading men to higher levels of justice.

I have traveled the length and breadth of Alabama, Mississippi, and all the other southern states. On sweltering summer days and crisp autumn mornings I have looked at her beautiful churches with their lofty spires pointing heavenward. I have beheld the impressive outlay of her massive religious education buildings. Over and over again I have found myself asking: "What kind of people worship here? Who is their God? Where were their voices when the lips of Governor Barnett dripped with words of interposition and nullification? Where were they when Governor Wallace gave the clarion call for defiance and hatred? Where were their voices of support when tired, bruised, and weary Negro men and women decided to rise from the dark dungeons of complacency to the bright hills of creative protest?"

Yes, these questions are still in my mind. In deep disappointment, I have wept over the laxity of the church. But be assured that my tears have been tears of love. There can be no deep disappointment where there is not deep love. Yes, I love the church; I love her sacred walls. How could I do otherwise? I am in the rather unique position of being the son, the grandson, and the great-grandson of preachers. Yes, I see the church as the body of Christ. But, oh! How we have blemished and scarred that body through social neglect and fear of being nonconformists.

There was a time when the church was very powerful. It was during 35 that period when the early Christians rejoiced when they were deemed worthy to suffer for what they believed. In those days the church was not merely a thermometer that recorded the ideas and principles of popular opinion; it was a thermostat that transformed the mores of society. Wherever the early Christians entered a town the power structure got disturbed and immediately sought to convict them for being "disturbers of the peace" and "outside agitators." But they went on with the conviction that they were "a colony of heaven," and had to obey God rather than man. They were small in number but big in commitment. They were too God-intoxicated to be "astronomically intimidated." They brought an end to such ancient evils as infanticide and gladiatorial contest.

Things are different now. The contemporary church is often a weak, ineffectual voice with an uncertain sound. It is so often the archsupporter of the status quo. Far from being disturbed by the presence of the church, the power structure of the average community is consoled by the church's silent and often vocal sanction of things as they are.

But the judgment of God is upon the church as never before. If the church of today does not recapture the sacrificial spirit of the early church, it will lose its authentic ring, forfeit the loyalty of millions, and be dismissed as an irrelevant social club with no meaning for the twentieth century. I am meeting young people every day whose disappointment with the church has risen to outright disgust.

Maybe again, I have been too optimistic. Is organized religion too inextricably bound to the status quo to save our nation and the world? Maybe I must turn my faith to the inner spiritual church, the church within the church, as the true *ecclesia* and the hope of the world. But again I am thankful to God that some noble souls from the ranks of organized religion have broken loose from the paralyzing chains of conformity and joined us as active partners in the struggle for freedom. They have left their secure congregations and walked the streets of Albany, Georgia, with us. They have gone through the highways of the South on tortuous rides for freedom. Yes, they have gone to jail with us. Some have been kicked out of their churches, and lost support of their bishops and fellow ministers. But they have gone with the faith that right defeated is stronger than evil triumphant. These men have been the leaven in the lump of the race. Their witness has been the spiritual salt that has preserved the true meaning of the gospel in these troubled times. They have carved a tunnel of hope through the dark mountain of disappointment.

I hope the church as a whole will meet the challenge of this decisive hour. But even if the church does not come to the aid of justice, I have no despair about the future. I have no fear about the outcome of our struggle in Birmingham, even if our motives are presently misunderstood. We will reach the goal of freedom in Birmingham and all over the nation, because the goal of America is freedom. Abused and scorned though we may be, our destiny is tied up with the destiny of America. Before the Pilgrims landed at Plymouth we were here. Before the pen of Jefferson etched across the pages of history the majestic words of the Declaration of Independence, we were here. For more than two centuries our foreparents labored in this country without wages; they made cotton king; and they built the homes of their masters in the midst of brutal injustice and shameful humiliation—and yet out of a bottomless vitality they continued to thrive and develop. If the inexpressible cruelties of slavery could not stop us, the opposition we now face will surely fail. We will win our freedom because the sacred heritage of our nation and the eternal will of God are embodied in our echoing demands.

I must close now. But before closing I am impelled to mention one 40 other point in your statement that troubled me profoundly. You warmly commended the Birmingham police force for keeping "order" and "preventing violence." I don't believe you would have so warmly commended the police force if you had seen its angry violent dogs literally biting six unarmed, nonviolent Negroes. I don't believe you would so quickly commend the policemen if you would observe their ugly and inhuman treatment of Negroes here in the city jail; if you would watch them push and curse old Negro women and young Negro girls; if you would see them slap and kick old Negro men and young boys; if you will observe them, as they did on two occasions, refuse to give us food because we wanted to sing our grace together. I'm sorry that I can't join you in your praise for the police department.

It is true that they have been rather disciplined in their public handling of the demonstrators. In this sense they have been rather publicly "nonviolent." But for what purpose? To preserve the evil system of segregation. Over the last few years I have consistently preached that nonviolence demands that the means we use must be as pure as the ends we seek. So I have tried to make it clear that it is wrong to use immoral means to attain moral ends. But now I must affirm that it is just as wrong, or even more so, to use moral means to preserve immoral ends. Maybe Mr. Connor and his policemen have been rather publicly nonviolent, as Chief Pritchett was in Albany, Georgia, but they have used the moral means of nonviolence to maintain the immoral end of flagrant racial injustice. T. S. Eliot has said that there is no greater treason than to do the right deed for the wrong reason.

I wish you had commended the Negro sit-inners and demonstrators of Birmingham for their sublime courage, their willingness to suffer, and their amazing discipline in the midst of the most inhuman provocation. One day the South will recognize its real heroes. They will be the James Merediths, courageously and with a majestic sense of purpose facing jeering and hostile mobs and the agonizing loneliness that characterizes the life of the pioneer. They will be old, oppressed, battered Negro women, symbolized in a seventy-two-year-old woman of Montgomery, Alabama, who rose up with a sense of dignity and with her people decided not to ride the segregated buses, and responded to one who inquired about her tiredness with ungrammatical profundity: "My feet is tired, but my soul is rested." They will be the young high school and college students, young ministers of the gospel, and a host of their elders courageously and nonviolently sitting-in at lunch counters and willingly going to jail for conscience's sake. One day the South will know that when these disinherited children of God sat down at lunch counters they were in reality standing up for the best in the American dream and the most sacred values in our Judeo-Christian heritage, and thusly, carrying our whole nation back to those great wells of democracy which were dug deep by the Founding Fathers in the formulation of the Constitution and the Declaration of Independence.

Never before have I written a letter this long (or should I say a book?). I'm afraid that it is much too long to take your precious time. I can assure you that it would have been much shorter if I had been writing from a comfortable desk, but what else is there to do when you are alone for days in the dull monotony of a narrow jail cell other than write long letters, think strange thoughts, and pray long prayers?

If I have said anything in this letter that is an overstatement of the truth and is indicative of an unreasonable impatience, I beg you to forgive me. If I have said anything in this letter that is an understatement of the truth and is indicative of my having a patience that makes me patient with anything less than brotherhood, I beg God to forgive me.

I hope this letter finds you strong in the faith. I also hope that circumstances will soon make it possible for me to meet each of you, not as an integrationist or a civil rights leader, but as a fellow clergyman and a Christian brother. Let us all hope that the dark clouds of racial prejudice will soon pass away and the deep fog of misunderstanding will be lifted from our fear-drenched communities and in some not too distant tomorrow the radiant stars of love and brotherhood will shine over our great nation with all of their scintillating beauty.

Yours for the cause of Peace and Brotherhood,
Martin Luther King Jr.

DISCUSSION QUESTIONS

1. King uses figurative language in his letter. Find some particularly vivid passages, and evaluate their effect in the context of this letter.

2. Explain King's distinction between just and unjust laws. Are there dangers in attempting to make such a distinction?

3. What characteristics of mind and behavior does King exhibit in the letter? Select the specific passages that provide proof.

4. Why does King say that "the white moderate" (para. 27) is a greater threat to African American progress than the outspoken racist? Is his explanation convincing?

5. How does King justify his philosophy of nonviolence in the face of continued aggression against Americans who are of African descent?

WRITING SUGGESTIONS

6. Can you think of a law against which defiance would be justified? Explain why the law is unjust and why refusal to obey is morally defensible.

7. In paragraph 19 King lists the grievances of African Americans in this country. King's catalog is similar to the lists in the Declaration of Independence. Can you think of any other group that might compile a list of grievances? If so, choose a group, and draw up such a list making sure that your list is as clear and specific as those you have read.

APPENDIX

Arguing about Literature

Writing a paper about a work of literature—a novel, a short story, a poem, or a play—is not so different from writing about matters of public policy. In both cases you make a claim about something you have read and demonstrate the validity of that claim by providing support. In papers about literature, support consists primarily of evidence from examples and details in the work itself and your own interpretation of the language, the events, and the characters. In addition, you can introduce expert scholarly opinion and history and biography where they are relevant.

First, a note about the differences between imaginative literature and argumentative essays. Although the strategies for writing papers about them may be similar, strategies for reading and understanding the works under review will be different. Suppose you read an essay by a psychologist who wants to prove that lying to children, even with the best intentions, can have tragic consequences. The claim of the essay will be directly stated, perhaps even in the first sentence. But if an author writes a short story or a play about the same subject, he or she will probably not state the central idea directly but will *show* rather than *tell*. The theme will emerge through a narrative of dramatic events, expressions of thoughts and feelings by the characters, a depiction of relationships, descriptions of a specific setting, and other elements of fiction. In other words, you will derive the idea or the theme indirectly. This is one reason that a work of fiction can lend itself to multiple interpretations. But it is also the reason that literature, with its evocation of the mysteries of real life, exerts a perpetual fascination.

Different kinds of literary works emphasize different elements. In the following discussion the elements of fiction, poetry, and drama are briefly summarized. The discussion will suggest ways of reading imaginative literature for both pleasure and critical analysis.

THE ELEMENTS OF FICTION

The basic elements of imaginative prose—a short story, a novel, or a play—are *theme, conflict,* and *character.* Other elements such as language, plot, point of view, and setting also influence the effectiveness of any work, but without a central idea, a struggle between opposing forces, and interesting people, it's unlikely that the work will hold our attention. (On the other hand, literature is full of exceptions, and you will certainly find examples that defy the rules.)

The theme is the central idea. It answers the question, What is the point of this story or play? Does the author give us some insight into a personal dilemma? Does he or she show how social conditions shape human behavior? Do we learn how certain traits of character can influence a human life? The answers to these questions apply not only to the specific situation and invented characters in a particular story. In the most memorable works the theme—the lesson to be drawn, the truth to be learned—embodies an idea that is much larger than the form the story assumes. For example, in "The Use of Force," the short story by William Carlos Williams in this appendix (p. 546), the title refers to the *subject* but not the theme. The author wanted to say something *about* the use of force. His theme is a complicated and unwelcome insight into human nature, with implications for all of us, not just the doctor who is the principal actor in the story.

Conflict is present in some form in almost all imaginative writing. It creates suspense and introduces moral dilemmas. External conflicts occur between individuals and between individuals and natural forces. Internal conflicts take place in the minds and hearts of the characters who must make difficult choices between competing goals and values—between right and wrong, pleasure and duty, freedom and responsibility. These two kinds of conflict are not exclusive of each other. A story of war, for example, may include suspenseful physical encounters between opposing forces, but the characters may also be compelled to make painful choices about their actions. In the best works, conflicts are important, not trivial. They may reveal uncommon virtues or shortcomings in the characters, alter their relationships with other people, and even change the course of their lives.

Conflicts exist only because characters—human beings, or in some satires, animals—engage in them. In contests with forces of nature, as in Hemingway's *The Old Man and the Sea,* it is the courage and persistence of a human being that gives meaning to the story. Memorable fictional characters are not easy to create. As readers we demand that characters be interesting, plausible, consistent, and active, physically and mentally. We must care about them, which is not the same as liking them. To care about characters means retaining enough curiosity about them to keep reading and to regret their departure when the story has come to an end. However different and unfamiliar their activities, we should feel that the characters are real. Even in science fiction we insist that the creatures exhibit human characteristics that we can recognize and identify with. But fictional characters should also be distinguishable from one another. Stereotypes are tiresome and unconvincing.

We learn about characters primarily from their speech and their actions but also from what the author and other characters reveal about them. Remembering that characters often withhold information or conceal their motives, even from themselves, we must often depend on our own knowledge and experience to interpret their behavior and judge their plausibility.

THE ELEMENTS OF DRAMA

Drama shares with fiction the elements we have discussed earlier—theme, conflict, and character. But because a play is meant to be performed, it differs from a written story in significant ways. These differences impose limits on the drama, as opposed to the novel, which can do almost anything.

First, stage action is restricted. Violent action—a war scene, for example—must usually take place offstage, and certain situations—such as the hunt for Moby Dick in Melville's novel—would be hard to reproduce in a theater. This means that a play emphasizes internal rather than external conflict.

Second, the author of a play, unlike the author of a short story or a novel, cannot comment on the action, the characters, or the significance of the setting. (It is true that a narrator sometimes appears on stage as a kind of Greek chorus to offer observation on the action, but this is uncommon.) A much greater burden must therefore rest on what the characters say. They must reveal background, explain offstage events, interpret themselves and others, and move the plot forward largely through speech. If the author of a novel lacks skill in reproducing plausible speech, he can find ways to avoid dialogue, but the playwright has no such privilege. She must have an ear for the rhythms and idioms of language that identify particular characters.

Another element which assumes more importance in a play than in a novel is plot. The dramatist must confine an often complicated and event-filled story to two or three hours on the stage. And, as in any listening experience, the audience must be able to follow the plot without the luxury of going back to review.

As you read a long play, you may find it helpful to keep in mind a simple diagram that explains the development of the plot, whether comedy or tragedy. The Freytag pyramid, created in 1863 by a German critic, shows that almost every three- or five-act play begins in a problem or conflict which sets in motion a series of events, called *the rising action*. At some point there is a *climax*, or turning point, followed by *the falling action*, which reverses the fortunes of the main characters and leads to a conclusion that may be happy or unhappy.

Shakespeare's *Macbeth* is an almost perfect example of the pyramid. The rising action in this tragedy is one of continued success for the main characters. The climax is a crisis on the battlefield, after which the fortunes of Macbeth and Lady Macbeth decline, ending in failure and death. In a comedy, the developments are reversed. The rising action is a series of stumbles and mishaps; then in the climax the hero finds the money or rescues the heroine, and the falling action ushers in a number of welcome surprises that culminate in a happy ending. (Think of a Jim Carrey comedy.) Typically the rising action in any play takes longer and thus creates suspense.

Reading a play is not the same as seeing one on stage. Many playwrights, like novelists, describe their settings and their characters in elaborate detail. In *Long Day's Journey into Night*, Eugene O'Neill's autobiographical play, descriptions of the living-room in which the action occurs and of the mother and father, who appear in the first act, cover more than three pages in small print. When you read, you fill the imaginary stage with your own interpretations of the playwright's descriptions, derived perhaps from places or persons in your own experience. You may forget that the playwright is dependent on directors, set designers, and actors, with other philosophies and approaches to stagecraft, to interpret his or her work. It can come as a surprise to see the stage version of the play you have read and interpreted very differently.

All playwrights want their plays to be performed. Still, the best plays are read far more frequently than they are produced on stage. Fortunately, reading them is a literary experience with its own rewards.

THE ELEMENTS OF POETRY

There are several kinds of poetry, among them epic, dramatic, and lyric. Epic poetry celebrates the heroic adventures of a human or superhuman character in a long, event-filled narrative. Milton's *Paradise Lost* is the preeminent example in English, but you may also be familiar with *The Iliad, The Odyssey*, and *The Aeneid*, the epics of ancient Greece and Rome. Dramatic poetry also tells a story, sometimes through monologue, as in Robert Browning's "My Last Duchess," where the Duke recounts the reasons why he murdered his wife; sometimes through dialogue, as in Robert Frost's "The Death of the Hired Man." These stories are often told in blank verse, unrhymed five-beat lines. Playwrights of the past, Shakespeare among others, adopted this poetic form.

Modern poems are much more likely to be lyrics—poetry derived from song. (The term *lyric* comes from the word for an ancient musical instrument, the lyre.) The lyric is most frequently an expression of the poet's feeling rather than an account of events. The characteristics that make poetry harder to read than prose are the very characteristics that define it: compression and metaphor. A lyric poem is highly concentrated. It focuses on what is essential in an experience, the details that illuminate it vividly against the background of our ordinary lives. Metaphor is a form of figurative language, a way of saying one thing to mean something else. It is a simile which omits the "like" or "as": for example, "A mighty fortress is our God." The poet chooses metaphoric images that appeal to our senses in order to reinforce the literal meaning. In a famous poem Thomas Campion compared the beauty of his sweetheart's face to that of a garden.

> There is a garden in her face
> Where roses and white lilies grow,
> A heavenly paradise is that place,
> Wherein all pleasant fruits do flow.

A poem, like an essay, tries to prove something. Like a short story, its message is indirect, expressed in the language of metaphor. It seldom urges a practical course of action. What it tries to prove is that a feeling or a perception—a response to love or death, or the sight of a snowy field on a dark night—is true and real.

The lyric poet's subjects are common ones—love, joy, sorrow, nature, death—but he or she makes uncommon use of words, imagery, and rhythm. These are the elements you examine as evidence of the poet's theme and depth of feeling.

Precisely because the poem will condense her experience, the poet must choose words with immediate impact. For example, in a poem about an encounter with a snake, Emily Dickinson writes,

> But never met this Fellow
> Attended, or alone
> Without a tighter breathing
> And Zero at the bone—

Although we have never seen this use of "zero" before, it strikes us at once as the perfect choice to suggest a kind of chilling fear.

In the best poems images transform the most commonplace experiences. Here is the first quatrain of Shakespeare's sonnet number 73, about loving deeply what will not live forever.

> That time of year thou mayest in me behold
> When yellow leaves or none or few do hang
> Upon those boughs which shake against the cold
> Bare ruined choirs where late the sweet birds sang.

Nowhere does Shakespeare mention that he is growing old. Instead, here and in subsequent stanzas he creates images of dead or dying things—autumn trees, the coming of night, dying fires—that convey feelings of cold and desolation. The final couplet expresses the theme directly:

Thus thou perceivs't, which makes thy love more strong,
To love that well which thou must leave ere long.

It is the imagery, however, that brings the theme to life and enables us to understand and share the poet's feeling.

Rhythm, defined as measured and balanced movement, is almost as important as language. As children, even before we fully understand all the words, we derive pleasure from the sounds of Mother Goose and the Dr. Seuss rhymes. Their sound patterns reflect the musical origin of poetry and the fact that poetry was meant to be chanted rather than read. Listen to the rhythm of these opening lines from Andrew Marvell's "To His Coy Mistress"—"Had we but world enough and time,/This coyness, lady, were no crime"—and hear the lilting four-beat meter that suggests song. If you look through an anthology of poetry written before the twentieth century, you will see even from the appearance of the poems on the page that the cadence or rhythm of most poems creates an orderly pattern. Edgar Allan Poe's "The Raven" is a familiar example of poems in which rhyme and rhythm come together to produce a harmonious design.

Measured movement in poetry is less common today. Free verse breaks with this ancient convention. (The very regularity of "The Raven" is now a subject for parody.) The poet of free verse invents his own rhythms, governed by meaning, free association, and a belief in poetry as a democratic art, one capable of reaching all people. In "Song of Myself," Walt Whitman (1819–1892), one of America's most influential poets, writes in a new voice that resembles the sound of spoken language:

A child said *What is the grass?* fetching it to me with full hands,
How could I answer the child? I do not know what it is any more
    than he.
I guess it must be the flag of my disposition, out of hopeful green stuff
    woven.

Notice, however, that the phrase "out of hopeful green stuff woven" is the language of poetry, not prose.

Much twentieth-century poetry dispenses altogether with both rhyme and formal rhythms, but the lyric remains unmistakably alive. Perhaps you have read poems by William Carlos Williams or e. e. cummings, who have used new rhythms to create their own distinctive versions of the lyric.

THE CULTURAL CONTEXT

Even those works that are presumed to be immortal and universal are products of a particular time in history and a particular social and political context. These works may therefore represent points of view with which we are unsympathetic. Today, for example, some women are uncomfortable with Shakespeare's *The Taming of the Shrew*, which finds comic possibilities in the subjugation of a woman to her husband's will. Jews may be offended by the characterization of Shylock in *The Merchant of Venice* as a Jewish money-lender who shows little mercy to his debtor. Some African Americans have resented the portrayal of Jim, the slave in *Huckleberry Finn*. Even *Peter Pan* has provoked criticism for its depiction of American Indians. In your own reading you may find fault with an author's attitude toward his subject; defending your own point of view against that of the author can be a satisfying literary exercise. To bring fresh, perhaps controversial, interpretations into an analysis may, indeed, enliven discussion and even revive interest in older works that no longer move us. But remember that the evidence will be largely external, based on social and political views that will themselves need explanation.

There is, after all, a danger in allowing our ideas about social and political correctness to take over and in imposing our values on those of another time, place, or culture. Literature, like great historical writing, enables us to enter worlds very different from our own. The worlds we read about in novels and plays may be governed by different moral codes, different social conventions, different religious values, many of which we reject or don't understand. Characters in these stories, even those cast as heroes and heroines, sometimes behave in ways we consider ignorant or self-serving. (Russell Baker, the humorist, observed that it was unfortunate that the writers of the past were not so enlightened as we are.) But reading has always offered an experience otherwise unavailable, a ready escape from our own lives into the lives of others, whose ways, however strange, we try to understand, whether or not we approve.

CHOOSING WHAT TO WRITE ABOUT

Your paper can take one of several different approaches. It is worth emphasizing that comedy and tragedy generally share the same literary elements. A tragedy, of course, ends in misfortune or death. A comedy typically ends with a happy resolution of all problems.

1. You may analyze or explain the meaning or theme of a work that is subject to different interpretations. For example, a famous interpretation of *Hamlet* in 1910[1] suggested that Hamlet was unable to avenge his father's murder because of guilt over his own Oedipal love for his mother. Or, having seen a distorted movie version of a familiar book (unfortunately, there are plenty of examples) you can explain what you think is the real theme of the book and how the movie departs from it.

[1] Ernest Jones, *Hamlet and Oedipus* (New York: Norton, 1949).

Some stories and plays, although based in reality, seem largely symbolic. "The Lottery," a widely read short story by Shirley Jackson, describes a ritual that hints at other meanings than those usually attributed to lotteries. *Waiting for Godot*, a play by Samuel Beckett, is a work that has inspired a dozen interpretations; the name *Godot*, with the embedded word *God*, suggests several. But exercise caution in writing about symbols. Saul Bellow, the Nobel Prize-winning novelist, has written an essay, "Deep Readers of the World, Beware!" that explains the dangers. He reminds us that "a true symbol is substantial, not accidental. You cannot avoid it, you cannot remove it."

2. You may analyze the conflicts in a story or play. The conflicts that make interesting papers are those that not only challenge our understanding (as with Iago's villainy in *Othello*) but encourage us to reflect on profound moral issues. For example, how does Mark Twain develop the struggle in Huckleberry Finn between his southern prejudices and his respect for Jim's humanity? How does John Proctor, the hero of Arthur Miller's *The Crucible*, resolve the moral dilemmas that lead him to choose death rather than a freedom secured by lies?

3. You may choose to write about an especially vivid or contradictory character, describing his traits in such a way as to make clear why he is worth a detailed examination. The protagonist of *The Stranger* by Albert Camus, for example, is a murderer who, although he tells us little or nothing about himself and is therefore difficult to understand, eventually earns our sympathy.

4. You may concentrate on the setting if it has special significance for the lives of the characters and what they do, as in Joseph Conrad's *Heart of Darkness* and Tennessee Williams's *A Streetcar Named Desire*. Setting may include time or historical period as well as place. Ask if the story or play would have taken shape in quite the same way in another time and place.

5. You may examine the language or style. No analysis of a poem would be complete without attention to the language, but the style of a prose work can also contribute to the impact on the reader. Hemingway's clean, economical style has often been studied, as has Faulkner's dense, complicated prose, equally powerful but very different. But you should probably not attempt an analysis of style unless you are sure you can discuss the uses of diction, grammar, syntax, and rhythm.

GUIDELINES FOR WRITING THE PAPER

1. Decide on a limited topic as the subject for your paper. The most interesting topics, of course, are those that are not so obvious: original interpretations, for example, that arise from a genuine personal response. Don't be afraid to disagree with a conventional reading of the literary work, but be sure you can find sufficient evidence for your point of view.

2. Before you begin to write, make a brief outline of the points that will support your thesis. You may find that you don't have enough evidence to make a good case to a skeptical reader. Or you may find that you have too much for a short paper and that your thesis, therefore, is too broad.

3. The evidence that you provide can be both internal and external. Internal evidence is found in the work itself: an action that reveals motives and consequences, statements by the characters about themselves and others, comments by the author about her characters, and interpretation of the language. External evidence comes from outside the work: a comment by a literary critic, information about the historical period or the geographical location of the work, or data about the author's life and other works he has written.

If possible, use more than one kind of evidence. The most important proof, however, will come from a careful selection of material from the work itself.

4. One temptation to avoid is using quotations from the work or from a critic so abundantly that your paper consists of a string of quotations and little else. Remember that the importance of your paper rests on your interpretations of the evidence. Your own analysis should constitute the major part of the paper. The quotations should be introduced only to support important points.

5. Organize your essay according to the guidelines you have followed for an argumentative essay on a public issue (see Chapter 9, pp. 373–93). Two of the organizational plans that work best are defending the main idea and refuting the opposing view—that is, a literary interpretation with which you disagree. In both cases the simplest method is to state your claim—the thesis you are going to defend—in the first paragraph and then line up evidence point by point in order of importance. If you feel comfortable beginning your paper in a different way, you may start with a paragraph of background: the reasons that you have chosen to explore a particular topic or a description of your personal response to the work—for example, where you first saw a play performed, how a story or poem affected you. (H. L. Mencken, the great American social critic, said discovering *Huckleberry Finn* was "the most stupendous event of my whole life!" What a beginning for an essay!)

It is always useful to look at book or movie reviews in good newspapers and magazines for models of organization and development that suggest a wide range of choices for your own paper.

Read the following short story, and reflect on it for a few moments. Then turn back to the following questions. Were you surprised at the actions of the doctor? What is the author saying about the use of force? Do you agree? What kinds of conflicts has he dramatized? Are some more important than others? How do the characterizations of the people in the story contribute to the theme?

Thinking about the answers to these questions will give you a clearer perspective on the essay written by a student that follows the story. After reading the essay, you may see other elements of fiction that might have been analyzed in a critical paper.

The Use of Force

WILLIAM CARLOS WILLIAMS

They were new patients to me, all I had was the name, Olson. Please come down as soon as you can, my daughter is very sick.

When I arrived I was met by the mother, a big startled looking woman, very clean and apologetic who merely said, Is this the doctor? and let me in. In the back, she added, You must excuse us, doctor, we have her in the kitchen where it is warm. It is very damp here sometimes.

The child was fully dressed and sitting on her father's lap near the kitchen table. He tried to get up, but I motioned for him not to bother, took off my overcoat and started to look things over. I could see that they were all very nervous, eyeing me up and down distrustfully. As often, in such cases, they weren't telling me more than they had to, it was up to me to tell them; that's why they were spending three dollars on me.

The child was fairly eating me up with her cold, steady eyes, and no expression to her face whatever. She did not move and seemed, inwardly, quiet; an unusually attractive little thing, and as strong as a heifer in appearance. But her face was flushed, she was breathing rapidly, and I realized that she had a high fever. She had magnificent blonde hair, in profusion. One of those picture children often reproduced in advertising leaflets and the photogravure sections of the Sunday papers.

She's had a fever for three days, began the father and we don't know 5 what it comes from. My wife has given her things, you know, like people

---

William Carlos Williams (1883–1963) wrote poems, novels, plays, and short stories. A pediatrician in the industrial city of Rutherford, New Jersey, much of his work, including "The Use of Force" (*The Farmers' Daughters*, 1938), depicts the daily hardships of his impoverished patients.

do, but it don't do no good. And there's been a lot of sickness around. So we tho't you'd better look her over and tell us what is the matter.

As doctors often do I took a trial shot at it as a point of departure. Has she had a sore throat?

Both parents answered me together, No . . . No, she says her throat don't hurt her.

Does your throat hurt you? added the mother to the child. But the little girl's expression didn't change nor did she move her eyes from my face.

Have you looked?

I tried to, said the mother, but I couldn't see.   10

As it happens we had been having a number of cases of diphtheria in the school to which this child went during that month and we were all, quite apparently, thinking of that, though no one had as yet spoken of the thing.

Well, I said, suppose we take a look at the throat first. I smiled in my best professional manner and asking for the child's first name I said, come on, Mathilda, open your mouth and let's take a look at your throat.

Nothing doing.

Aw, come on, I coaxed, just open your mouth wide and let me take a look. Look, I said opening both hands wide. I haven't anything in my hands. Just open up and let me see.

Such a nice man, put in the mother. Look how kind he is to you. 15
Come on, do what he tells you to. He won't hurt you.

At that I ground my teeth in disgust. If only they wouldn't use the word "hurt" I might be able to get somewhere. But I did not allow myself to be hurried or disturbed but speaking quietly and slowly I approached the child again.

As I moved my chair a little nearer suddenly with one cat-like movement both her hands clawed instinctively for my eyes and she almost reached them too. In fact she knocked my glasses flying and they fell, though unbroken, several feet away from me on the kitchen floor.

Both the mother and father almost turned themselves inside out in embarrassment and apology. You bad girl, said the mother, taking her and shaking her by one arm. Look what you've done. The nice man . . .

For heaven's sake, I broke in. Don't call me a nice man to her. I'm here to look at her throat on the chance that she might have diphtheria and possibly die of it. But that's nothing to her. Look here, I said to the child, we're going to look at your throat. You're old enough to understand what I'm saying. Will you open it now by yourself or shall we have to open it for you?

Not a move. Even her expression hadn't changed. Her breaths how- 20
ever were coming faster and faster. Then the battle began. I had to do it. I had to have a throat culture for her own protection. But first I told the parents that it was entirely up to them. I explained the danger but said

that I would not insist on a throat examination so long as they would take the responsibility.

If you don't do what the doctor says you'll have to go to the hospital, the mother admonished her severely.

Oh yeah? I had to smile to myself. After all, I had already fallen in love with the savage brat, the parents were contemptible to me. In the ensuing struggle they grew more and more abject, crushed, exhausted while she surely rose to magnificent heights of insane fury of effort bred of her terror of me.

The father tried his best, and he was a big man but the fact that she was his daughter, his shame at her behavior and his dread of hurting her made him release her just at the critical moment several times when I had almost achieved success, till I wanted to kill him. But his dread also that she might have diphtheria made him tell me to go on, go on though he himself was almost fainting, while the mother moved back and forth behind us raising and lowering her hands in an agony of apprehension.

Put her in front of you on your lap, I ordered, and hold both her wrists.

But as soon as he did the child let out a scream. Don't, you're hurt- 25 ing me. Let go of my hands. Let them go I tell you. Then she shrieked terrifyingly, hysterically. Stop it! Stop it! You're killing me!

Do you think she can stand it, doctor! said the mother.

You get out, said the husband to his wife. Do you want her to die of diphtheria?

Come on now, hold her, I said.

Then I grasped the child's head with my left hand and tried to get the wooden tongue depressor between her teeth. She fought, with clenched teeth, desperately! But now I also had grown furious—at a child. I tried to hold myself down but I couldn't. I know how to expose a throat for inspection. And I did my best. When finally I got the wooden spatula behind the last teeth and just the point of it into the mouth cavity, she opened up for an instant, but before I could see anything she came down again and gripping the wooden blade between her molars she reduced it to splinters before I could get it out again.

Aren't you ashamed, the mother yelled at her. Aren't you ashamed to 30 act like that in front of the doctor?

Get me a smooth-handled spoon of some sort, I told the mother. We're going through with this. The child's mouth was already bleeding. Her tongue was cut and she was screaming in wild hysterical shrieks. Perhaps I should have desisted and come back in an hour or more. No doubt it would have been better. But I have seen at least two children lying dead in bed of neglect in such cases, and feeling that I must get a diagnosis now or never I went at it again. But the worst of it was that I too had got beyond reason. I could have torn the child apart in my own fury and enjoyed it. It was a pleasure to attack her. My face was burning with it.

The damned little brat must be protected against her own idiocy, one says to one's self at such times. Others must be protected against her. It is social necessity. And all these things are true. But a blind fury, a feeling of adult shame, bred of a longing for muscular release are the operatives. One goes on to the end.

In a final unreasoning assault I overpowered the child's neck and jaws. I forced the heavy silver spoon back of her teeth and down her throat till she gagged. And there it was—both tonsils covered with membrane. She had fought valiantly to keep me from knowing her secret. She had been hiding that sore throat for three days at least and lying to her parents in order to escape just such an outcome as this.

Now truly she *was* furious. She had been on the defensive before but now she attacked. Tried to get off her father's lap and fly at me while tears of defeat blinded her eyes.

Rampolla 1

Jennifer Rampolla
Professor Harrington
English 102-C
May 2, 2005

Title indicates subject
Introduction

Conflicts in "The Use of Force"

"The Use of Force" tells us something about human nature that probably comes as no surprise: The impulse to use violence against a helpless but defiant opponent can be thrilling and irresistible. But the conflict which produces this insight is not a shoot-out between cops and robbers, not a fight for survival against a dangerous enemy, but a struggle between a grown man and a sick child.

The theme

Theme emerges through conflicts

Naming the major conflicts (external and internal)

In this story two major conflicts are dramatized, one external or physical, the other internal or psychological. The conflicts seem obvious. Even the blunt, unadorned language means to persuade us that nothing is concealed. But below the surface, some motives remain unacknowledged, and we guess at them only because we know how easily people deceive themselves.

A concealed conflict (to be explained later)

Body

External conflict developed

The external conflict is vividly depicted, a physical struggle between doctor and child, complete with weapon -- a metal spoon. The outcome is hardly in doubt; the doctor will win. One critic calls this story primarily "an accomplishment (external conflict) story" (Madden 16). But the internal conflict that accompanies a difficult choice is the real heart of the story. The doctor must decide between waiting for a more opportune time to examine the child or exercising brute force to subdue her now. When he decides on brute force, he seems aware of his motives.

Evidence: comment from a critic

Internal conflict developed

Evidence: Quotation

But the worst of it was that I too had got beyond reason. I could have torn the child apart in my own fury and enjoyed it. It was a pleasure to attack her.

Concealed conflict, based on the characters and their relationship

This shocking revelation is not, however, the whole story. Why has he got beyond reason? Why does he take pleasure in attacking a child? The answer lies not only in what we know about the antagonists but in what we can assume about their relationship to each other.

Rampolla 2

The child is brilliantly portrayed in a few grim encounters with the doctor. She is strong, stubborn, secretive, and violent. Despite her size and age, she is a match for the doctor, a challenge that at first excites him.

Description of the child

> I had to smile to myself. After all, I had already fallen in love with the savage brat. . . . In the ensuing struggle . . . she surely rose to magnificent heights of insane fury. . . .

Evidence: Quotation

The picture of the doctor is somewhat harder to read. Sixty years ago (when this story was written) the doctor in a working-class community occupied a position of unusual power and authority. He would not be accustomed to challenges at any level. Clearly the differences in social and economic status between the doctor and his clients are another source of conflict that influences his use of force. Like many people in positions of power, the doctor is torn by contradictory emotions toward those below him. On the one hand, he despises those who are deferential to him, in this case the child's parents. On the other hand, it is unthinkable that a child should dare to oppose him, not only in refusing to obey his instructions but in trying, like a desperate small animal, to attack him. It is even more unthinkable that she should prevail in any contest. He confesses to "a feeling of adult shame." If we look for it, there is also a hint of sexual conflict. The child is blond and beautiful; the doctor says he is in love with her. (Would this story have worked in quite the same way if the child had been a boy?) The doctor attempts to rationalize his use of force, but he knows that it is not the child's welfare that finally compels him to overcome her resistance. In the end, reason gives way to pride and vanity.

Description of the doctor

Unexpressed social conflict

Evidence: External, from history

Evidence: Quotation

Perhaps another concealed conflict?

The doctor's real motivation

Most of us respond to this story with a mixture of feelings -- anger at the pleasure the doctor takes in his use of force, confusion and even fear at the realization that doctors may not always behave like gentle and loving helpers, and pity for the little girl with whom it is easy to identify. The author doesn't spell out the moral implications of the doctor's

Conclusion

The reader's mixed reaction

Rampolla 3

Sympathy for the child

internal conflict. But perhaps it is significant that the author gives the last words to the little girl: "Tears of defeat blinded her eyes." I think he has chosen this ending in order to direct our sympathy to the victim, an unhappy child who struggled hopelessly to protect herself. Although we know that the doc-tor has performed a necessary and merciful act, we are left to wonder if it matters that he has done it for the wrong reason.

Reaction to the theme

Rampolla 4

Work Cited

Madden, David. <u>Studies in the Short Story</u>. New York: Holt, 1980.

Trifles

SUSAN GLASPELL

CHARACTERS

GEORGE HENDERSON, county attorney
HENRY PETERS, sheriff
LEWIS HALE, a neighboring farmer
MRS. PETERS
MRS. HALE

SCENE: *The kitchen in the now abandoned farmhouse of John Wright, a gloomy kitchen, and left without having been put in order—unwashed pans under the sink, a loaf of bread outside the breadbox, a dish towel on the table—other signs of incompleted work. At the rear the outer door opens and the Sheriff comes in followed by the County Attorney and Hale. The Sheriff and Hale are men in middle life, the County Attorney is a young man; all are much bundled up and go at once to the stove. They are followed by the two women— the Sheriff's wife first; she is a slight wiry woman, a thin nervous face. Mrs. Hale is larger and would ordinarily be called more comfortable looking, but she is disturbed now and looks fearfully about as she enters. The women have come in slowly, and stand close together near the door.*

COUNTY ATTORNEY *(rubbing his hands):* This feels good. Come up to the fire, ladies.

MRS. PETERS *(after taking a step forward):* I'm not—cold.

SHERIFF *(unbuttoning his overcoat and stepping away from the stove as if to mark the beginning of official business):* Now, Mr. Hale, before we move things about, you explain to Mr. Henderson just what you saw when you came here yesterday morning.

COUNTY ATTORNEY: By the way, has anything been moved? Are things just as you left them yesterday?

SHERIFF *(looking about):* It's just about the same. When it dropped below zero last night I thought I'd better send Frank out this morning to make a fire for us—no use getting pneumonia with a big case on, but I told him not to touch anything except the stove—and you know Frank.

Susan Glaspell (1876–1948) was an American playwright and novelist. In 1916 she wrote *Trifles* for the Provincetown Players, a Provincetown, Massachusetts, theater troupe founded by Glaspell and her husband. Based on her recollection of a real murder case that she covered as a journalist in Iowa, *Trifles* was so successful that Glaspell decided to rewrite it as a short story, "A Jury of Her Peers."

COUNTY ATTORNEY: Somebody should have been left here yesterday.

SHERIFF: Oh—yesterday. When I had to send Frank to Morris Center for that man who went crazy—I want you to know I had my hands full yesterday. I knew you could get back from Omaha by today and as long as I went over everything here myself—

COUNTY ATTORNEY: Well, Mr. Hale, tell just what happened when you came here yesterday morning.

HALE: Harry and I had started to town with a load of potatoes. We came along the road from my place and as I got here I said, "I'm going to see if I can't get John Wright to go in with me on a party telephone." I spoke to Wright about it once before and he put me off, saying folks talked too much anyway, and all he asked was peace and quiet—I guess you know about how much he talked himself; but I thought maybe if I went to the house and talked about it before his wife, though I said to Harry that I didn't know as what his wife wanted made much difference to John—

COUNTY ATTORNEY: Let's talk about that later, Mr. Hale. I do want to talk about that, but tell now just what happened when you got to the house.

HALE: I didn't hear or see anything; I knocked at the door, and still it was all quiet inside. I knew they must be up, it was past eight o'clock. So I knocked again, and I thought I heard somebody say, "Come in." I wasn't sure, I'm not sure yet, but I opened the door—this door *(indicating the door by which the two women are still standing)* and there in that rocker—*(pointing to it)* sat Mrs. Wright. *(They all look at the rocker.)*

COUNTY ATTORNEY: What—was she doing?

HALE: She was rockin' back and forth. She had her apron in her hand and was kind of—pleating it.

COUNTY ATTORNEY: And how did she—look?

HALE: Well, she looked queer.

COUNTY ATTORNEY: How do you mean—queer?

HALE: Well, as if she didn't know what she was going to do next. And kind of done up.

COUNTY ATTORNEY: How did she seem to feel about your coming?

HALE: Why, I don't think she minded—one way or other. She didn't pay much attention. I said, "How do, Mrs. Wright, it's cold, ain't it?" And she said, "Is it?"—and went on kind of pleating at her apron. Well, I was surprised; she didn't ask me to come up to the stove, or to set down, but just sat there, not even looking at me, so I said, "I want to see John." And then she—laughed. I guess you would call it a laugh. I thought of Harry and the team outside, so I said a little sharp: "Can't I see John?" "No," she says, kind o' dull like. "Ain't he home?" says I. "Yes," says she, "he's home." "Then why can't I see him?" I asked her, out of patience. "'Cause he's dead," says she. *"Dead?"* says I. She just nodded her head, not getting a bit excited, but rockin' back and forth. "Why—where is he?" says I, not knowing what to say. She just pointed upstairs—like that *(himself pointing to the room above)*. I started for the stairs, with the idea of going up there. I walked from there to here—then I says, "Why, what did he die of?" "He died of a rope round his neck," says she, and just went on pleatin' at her apron. Well, I went out and called Harry. I thought I might—need help. We went upstairs and there he was lyin'—

COUNTY ATTORNEY: I think I'd rather have you go into that upstairs, where you can point it all out. Just go on now with the rest of the story.

HALE: Well, my first thought was to get that rope off. It looked . . . *(stops; his face twitches)* . . . but Harry, he went up to him, and he said, "No, he's dead all right, and we'd better not touch anything." So we went back downstairs. She was still sitting that same way. "Has anybody been notified?" I asked. "No," says she, unconcerned. "Who did this, Mrs. Wright?" said Harry. He said it businesslike—and she stopped pleatin' of her apron. "I don't know," she says. "You don't *know?*" says Harry. "No," says she. "Weren't you sleepin' in the bed with him?" says Harry. "Yes," says she, "but I was on the inside." "Somebody slipped a rope round his neck and strangled him and you didn't wake up?" says Harry. "I didn't wake up," she said after him. We must 'a' looked as if we didn't see how that could be, for after a minute she said, "I sleep sound." Harry was going to ask her more questions but I said maybe we ought to let her tell her story first to the coroner, or the sheriff, so Harry went fast as he could to Rivers' place, where there's a telephone.

COUNTY ATTORNEY: And what did Mrs. Wright do when she knew that you had gone for the coroner?

HALE: She moved from the rocker to that chair over there *(pointing to a small chair in the corner)* and just sat there with her hands held together and looking down. I got a feeling that I ought to make some conversation, so I said I had come in to see if John wanted to put in a telephone, and at that she started to laugh, and then she stopped and looked at me—scared. *(The County Attorney, who has had his notebook out, makes a note.)* I dunno, maybe it wasn't scared. I wouldn't like to say it was. Soon Harry got back, and then Dr. Lloyd came and you, Mr. Peters, and so I guess that's all I know that you don't.

COUNTY ATTORNEY *(looking around):* I guess we'll go upstairs first—and then out to the barn and around there. *(To the Sheriff.)* You're convinced that there was nothing important here—nothing that would point to any motive?

SHERIFF: Nothing here but kitchen things. *(The County Attorney, after again looking around the kitchen, opens the door of a cupboard closet. He gets up on a chair and looks on a shelf. Pulls his hand away, sticky.)*

COUNTY ATTORNEY: Here's a nice mess. *(The women draw nearer.)*

MRS. PETERS *(to the other woman):* Oh, her fruit; it did freeze. *(To the Lawyer.)* She worried about that when it turned so cold. She said the fire'd go out and her jars would break.

SHERIFF *(rises):* Well, can you beat the woman! Held for murder and worryin' about her preserves.

COUNTY ATTORNEY: I guess before we're through she may have something more serious than preserves to worry about.

HALE: Well, women are used to worrying over trifles. *(The two women move a little closer together.)*

COUNTY ATTORNEY *(with the gallantry of a young politician):* And yet, for all their worries, what would we do without the ladies? *(The women do not unbend. He goes to the sink, takes a dipperful of water from the pail, and pouring it into a basin, washes his hands. Starts to wipe them on the roller towel, turns it for a cleaner place.)* Dirty towels! *(Kicks his foot against the pans under the sink.)* Not much of a housekeeper, would you say, ladies?

MRS. HALE *(stiffly):* There's a great deal of work to be done on a farm.

COUNTY ATTORNEY: To be sure. And yet *(with a little bow to her)* I know there are some Dickson county farmhouses which do not have such roller towels. *(He gives it a pull to expose its full length again.)*

MRS. HALE: Those towels get dirty awful quick. Men's hands aren't always as clean as they might be.

COUNTY ATTORNEY: Ah, loyal to your sex, I see. But you and Mrs. Wright were neighbors. I suppose you were friends, too.

MRS. HALE *(shaking her head):* I've not seen much of her of late years. I've not been in this house—it's more than a year.

COUNTY ATTORNEY: And why was that? You didn't like her?

MRS. HALE: I liked her all well enough. Farmers' wives have their hands full, Mr. Henderson. And then—

COUNTY ATTORNEY: Yes—?

MRS. HALE *(looking about):* It never seemed a very cheerful place.

COUNTY ATTORNEY: No—it's not cheerful. I shouldn't say she had the homemaking instinct.

MRS. HALE: Well, I don't know as Wright had, either.

COUNTY ATTORNEY: You mean that they didn't get on very well?

MRS. HALE: No, I don't mean anything. But I don't think a place'd be any cheerfuller for John Wright's being in it.

COUNTY ATTORNEY: I'd like to talk more of that a little later. I want to get the lay of things upstairs now. *(He goes to the left where three steps lead to a stair door.)*

SHERIFF: I suppose anything Mrs. Peters does'll be all right. She was to take in some clothes for her, you know, and a few little things. We left in such a hurry yesterday.

COUNTY ATTORNEY: Yes, but I would like to see what you take, Mrs. Peters, and keep an eye out for anything that might be of use to us.

MRS. PETERS: Yes, Mr. Henderson. *(The women listen to the men's steps on the stairs, then look about the kitchen.)*

MRS. HALE: I'd hate to have men coming into my kitchen, snooping around and criticizing. *(She arranges the pans under sink which the lawyer had shoved out of place.)*

MRS. PETERS: Of course it's no more than their duty.

MRS. HALE: Duty's all right, but I guess that deputy sheriff that came out to make the fire might have got a little of this on. *(Gives the roller towel a pull.)* Wish I'd thought of that sooner. Seems mean to talk about her for not having things slicked up when she had to come away in such a hurry.

MRS. PETERS *(who has gone to a small table in the left rear corner of the room, and lifted one end of a towel that covers a pan):* She had bread set. *(Stands still.)*

MRS. HALE *(eyes fixed on a loaf of bread beside the breadbox, which is on a low shelf at the other side of the room. Moves slowly toward it.):* She was going to put this in there. *(Picks up loaf, then abruptly drops it. In a manner of returning to familiar things.)* It's a shame about her fruit. I wonder if it's all gone. *(Gets up on the chair and looks.)* I think there's some here that's all right, Mrs. Peters. Yes—here; *(holding it toward the window)* this is cherries, too. *(Looking again.)* I declare I believe that's the only one. *(Gets down, bottle in her hand. Goes to the sink and wipes it off on the outside.)* She'll feel awful bad after all her hard work in the hot weather. I remember the afternoon I put up my cherries last summer. *(She puts the bottle on the big kitchen table, center of the room. With a sigh, is about to sit down in the rocking-chair. Before she is seated realizes what chair it is; with a slow look at it, steps back. The chair which she has touched rocks back and forth.)*

MRS. PETERS: Well, I must get those things from the front room closet. *(She goes to the door at the right, but after looking into the other room, steps back.)* You coming with me, Mrs. Hale? You could help me carry them. *(They go in the other room; reappear, Mrs. Peters carrying a dress and skirt, Mrs. Hale following with a pair of shoes.)* My, it's cold in there. *(She puts the clothes on the big table, and hurries to the stove.)*

MRS. HALE *(examining the skirt):* Wright was close. I think maybe that's why she kept so much to herself. She didn't even belong to the Ladies' Aid. I suppose she felt she couldn't do her part, and then you don't enjoy things when you feel shabby. I heard she used to wear pretty clothes and be lively, when she was Minnie Foster, one of the town girls singing in the choir. But that—oh, that was thirty years ago. This all you want to take in?

MRS. PETERS: She said she wanted an apron. Funny thing to want, for there isn't much to get you dirty in jail, goodness knows. But I suppose just to make her feel more natural. She said they was in the top drawer in this cupboard. Yes, here. And then her little shawl that always hung behind the door. *(Opens stair door and looks.)* Yes, here it is. *(Quickly shuts door leading upstairs.)*

MRS. HALE *(abruptly moving toward her):* Mrs. Peters?

MRS. PETERS: Yes, Mrs. Hale?

MRS. HALE: Do you think she did it?

MRS. PETERS *(in a frightened voice):* Oh, I don't know.

MRS. HALE: Well, I don't think she did. Asking for an apron and her little shawl. Worrying about her fruit.

MRS. PETERS *(starts to speak, glances up, where footsteps are heard in the room above. In a low voice):* Mr. Peters says it looks bad for her. Mr. Henderson is awful sarcastic in a speech and he'll make fun of her sayin' she didn't wake up.

MRS. HALE: Well, I guess John Wright didn't wake when they was slipping that rope under his neck.

MRS. PETERS: No, it's strange. It must have been done awful crafty and still. They say it was such a—funny way to kill a man, rigging it all up like that.

MRS. HALE: That's just what Mr. Hale said. There was a gun in the house. He says that's what he can't understand.

MRS. PETERS: Mr. Henderson said coming out that what was needed for the case was a motive; something to show anger, or—sudden feeling.

MRS. HALE *(who is standing by the table):* Well, I don't see any signs of anger around here. *(She puts her hand on the dish towel which lies on the table, stands looking down at table, one-half of which is clean, the other half messy.)* It's wiped to here. *(Makes a move as if to finish work, then turns and looks at loaf of bread outside the breadbox. Drops towel. In that voice of coming back to familiar things.)* Wonder how they are finding things upstairs. I hope she had it a little more red-up up there. You know, it seems kind of *sneaking*. Locking her up in town and then coming out here and trying to get her own house to turn against her!

MRS. PETERS: But, Mrs. Hale, the law is the law.

MRS. HALE: I s'pose 'tis. *(Unbuttoning her coat.)* Better loosen up your things, Mrs. Peters. You won't feel them when you go out. *(Mrs. Peters takes off her fur tippet, goes to hang it on hook at back of room, stands looking at the under part of the small corner table.)*

MRS. PETERS: She was piecing a quilt. *(She brings the large sewing basket and they look at the bright pieces.)*

MRS. HALE: It's a log cabin pattern. Pretty, isn't it? I wonder if she was goin' to quilt it or just knot it? *(Footsteps have been heard coming down the stairs. The Sheriff enters followed by Hale and the County Attorney.)*

SHERIFF: They wonder if she was going to quilt it or just knot it! *(The men laugh, the women look abashed.)*

COUNTY ATTORNEY *(rubbing his hands over the stove):* Frank's fire didn't do much up there, did it? Well, let's go out to the barn and get that cleared up. *(The men go outside.)*

MRS. HALE *(resentfully):* I don't know as there's anything so strange, our takin' up our time with little things while we're waiting for them to get the evidence. *(She sits down at the big table smoothing out a block with decision.)* I don't see as it's anything to laugh about.

MRS. PETERS *(apologetically):* Of course they've got awful important things on their minds. *(Pulls up a chair and joins Mrs. Hale at the table.)*

MRS. HALE *(examining another block):* Mrs. Peters, look at this one. Here, this is the one she was working on, and look at the sewing! All the rest of it has been so nice and even. And look at this! It's all over the place! Why, it looks as if she didn't know what she was about! *(After she has said this they look at each other, then start to glance back at the door. After an instant Mrs. Hale has pulled at a knot and ripped the sewing.)*

MRS. PETERS: Oh, what are you doing, Mrs. Hale?

MRS. HALE *(mildly):* Just pulling out a stitch or two that's not sewed very good. *(Threading a needle.)* Bad sewing always made me fidgety.

MRS. PETERS *(nervously):* I don't think we ought to touch things.

MRS. HALE: I'll just finish up this end. *(Suddenly stopping and leaning forward.)* Mrs. Peters?

MRS. PETERS: Yes, Mrs. Hale?

MRS. HALE: What do you suppose she was so nervous about?

MRS. PETERS: Oh—I don't know. I don't know as she was nervous. I sometimes sew awful queer when I'm just tired. *(Mrs. Hale starts to say something, looks at Mrs. Peters, then goes on sewing.)* Well, I must get these things wrapped up. They may be through sooner than we think. *(Putting apron and other things together.)* I wonder where I can find a piece of paper, and string. *(Rises.)*

MRS. HALE: In that cupboard, maybe.

MRS. PETERS *(looking in cupboard):* Why, here's a bird-cage. *(Holds it up.)* Did she have a bird, Mrs. Hale?

MRS. HALE: Why, I don't know whether she did or not—I've not been here for so long. There was a man around last year selling canaries cheap, but I don't know as she took one; maybe she did. She used to sing real pretty herself.

MRS. PETERS *(glancing around):* Seems funny to think of a bird here. But she must have had one, or why would she have a cage? I wonder what happened to it?

MRS. HALE: I s'pose maybe the cat got it.

MRS. PETERS: No, she didn't have a cat. She's got that feeling some people have about cats—being afraid of them. My cat got in her room and she was real upset and asked me to take it out.

MRS. HALE: My sister Bessie was like that. Queer, ain't it?

MRS. PETERS *(examining the cage):* Why, look at this door. It's broke. One hinge is pulled apart.

MRS. HALE *(looking too):* Looks as if someone must have been rough with it.

MRS. PETERS: Why, yes. *(She brings the cage forward and puts it on the table.)*

MRS. HALE: I wish if they're going to find any evidence they'd be about it. I don't like this place.

MRS. PETERS: But I'm awful glad you came with me, Mrs. Hale. It would be lonesome for me sitting here alone.

MRS. HALE: It would, wouldn't it? *(Dropping her sewing.)* But I tell you what I do wish, Mrs. Peters. I wish I had come over sometimes when *she* was here. I—*(looking around the room)*—wish I had.

MRS. PETERS: But of course you were awful busy, Mrs. Hale—your house and your children.

MRS. HALE: I could've come. I stayed away because it weren't cheerful—and that's why I ought to have come. I—I've never liked this place. Maybe because it's down in a hollow and you don't see the road. I dunno what it is, but it's a lonesome place and always was. I wish I had come over to see Minnie Foster sometimes. I can see now—*(Shakes her head.)*

MRS. PETERS: Well, you mustn't reproach yourself, Mrs. Hale. Somehow we just don't see how it is with other folks until—something turns up.

MRS. HALE: Not having children makes less work—but it makes a quiet house, and Wright out to work all day, and no company when he did come in. Did you know John Wright, Mrs. Peters?

MRS. PETERS: Not to know him; I've seen him in town. They say he was a good man.

MRS. HALE: Yes—good; he didn't drink, and kept his word as well as most, I guess, and paid his debts. But he was a hard man, Mrs. Peters. Just to pass the time of day with him—*(Shivers.)* Like a raw wind that gets to the bone. *(Pauses, her eye falling on the cage.)* I should think she would 'a' wanted a bird. But what do you suppose went with it?

MRS. PETERS: I don't know, unless it got sick and died. *(She reaches over and swings the broken door, swings it again, both women watch it.)*

MRS. HALE: You weren't raised round here, were you? *(Mrs. Peters shakes her head.)* You didn't know—her?

MRS. PETERS: Not till they brought her yesterday.

MRS. HALE: She—come to think of it, she was kind of like a bird her-self—real sweet and pretty, but kind of timid and—fluttery. How—

she—did—change. *(Silence: then as if struck by a happy thought and relieved to get back to everyday things.)* Tell you what, Mrs. Peters, why don't you take the quilt in with you? It might take up her mind.

MRS. PETERS: Why, I think that's a real nice idea, Mrs. Hale. There couldn't possibly be any objection to it could there? Now, just what would I take? I wonder if her patches are in here—and her things. *(They look in the sewing basket.)*

MRS. HALE: Here's some red. I expect this has got sewing things in it. *(Brings out a fancy box.)* What a pretty box. Looks like something somebody would give you. Maybe her scissors are in here. *(Opens box. Suddenly puts her hand to her nose.)* Why—*(Mrs. Peters bends nearer, then turns her face away.)* There's something wrapped up in this piece of silk.

MRS. PETERS: Why, this isn't her scissors.

MRS. HALE *(lifting the silk):* Oh, Mrs. Peters—it's—*(Mrs. Peters bends closer.)*

MRS. PETERS: It's the bird.

MRS. HALE *(jumping up):* But, Mrs. Peters—look at it! Its neck! Look at its neck! It's all—other side *to.*

MRS. PETERS: Somebody—wrung—its—neck. *(Their eyes meet. A look of growing comprehension, of horror. Steps are heard outside. Mrs. Hale slips box under quilt pieces, and sinks into her chair. Enter Sheriff and County Attorney. Mrs. Peters rises.)*

COUNTY ATTORNEY *(as one turning from serious things to little pleasantries):* Well, ladies, have you decided whether she was going to quilt it or knot it?

MRS. PETERS: We think she was going to—knot it.

COUNTY ATTORNEY: Well, that's interesting, I'm sure. *(Seeing the bird-cage.)* Has the bird flown?

MRS. HALE *(putting more quilt pieces over the box):* We think the—cat got it.

COUNTY ATTORNEY *(preoccupied):* Is there a cat? *(Mrs. Hale glances in a quick covert way at Mrs. Peters.)*

MRS. PETERS: Well, not *now.* They're superstitious, you know. They leave.

COUNTY ATTORNEY *(to Sheriff Peters, continuing an interrupted conversation):* No sign at all of anyone having come from the outside. Their own rope. Now let's go up again and go over it piece by piece. *(They start upstairs.)* It would have to have been someone who knew just the—*(Mrs. Peters sits down. The two women sit there not looking at one another, but as if peering into something and at the same time holding back. When they talk now it is in the manner of feeling their way over strange ground, as if afraid of what they are saying, but as if they cannot help saying it.)*

MRS. HALE: She liked the bird. She was going to bury it in that pretty box.

MRS. PETERS *(in a whisper):* When I was a girl—my kitten—there was a boy took a hatchet, and before my eyes—and before I could get there—*(Covers her face an instant.)* If they hadn't held me back I would have—*(catches herself, looks upstairs where steps are heard, falters weakly)*—hurt him.

MRS. HALE *(with a slow look around her):* I wonder how it would seem never to have had any children around. *(Pause.)* No, Wright wouldn't like the bird—a thing that sang. She used to sing. He killed that, too.

MRS. PETERS *(moving uneasily):* We don't know who killed the bird.

MRS. HALE: I knew John Wright.

MRS. PETERS: It was an awful thing was done in this house that night, Mrs. Hale. Killing a man while he slept, slipping a rope around his neck that choked the life out of him.

MRS. HALE: His neck. Choked the life out of him. *(Her hand goes out and rests on the bird-cage.)*

MRS. PETERS *(with rising voice):* We don't know who killed him. We don't *know.*

MRS. HALE *(her own feeling not interrupted):* If there'd been years and years of nothing, then a bird to sing to you, it would be awful—still, after the bird was still.

MRS. PETERS *(something within her speaking):* I know what stillness is. When we homesteaded in Dakota, and my first baby died—after he was two years old, and me with no other then—

MRS. HALE *(moving):* How soon do you suppose they'll be through looking for the evidence?

MRS. PETERS: I know what stillness is. *(Pulling herself back.)* The law has got to punish crime, Mrs. Hale.

MRS. HALE *(not as if answering that):* I wish you'd seen Minnie Foster when she wore a white dress with blue ribbons and stood up there in the choir and sang. *(A look around the room.)* Oh, I *wish* I'd come over here once in a while! That was a crime! That was a crime! Who's going to punish that?

MRS. PETERS *(looking upstairs):* We mustn't—take on.

MRS. HALE: I might have known she needed help! I know how things can be—for women. I tell you, it's queer, Mrs. Peters. We live close together and we live far apart. We all go through the same things—it's all just a different kind of the same thing. *(Brushes her eyes, noticing the bottle of fruit, reaches out for it.)* If I was you I wouldn't tell her her fruit was gone. Tell her it *ain't.* Tell her it's all right. Take this in to prove it to her. She—she may never know whether it was broke or not.

MRS. PETERS *(takes the bottle, looks about for something to wrap it in; takes petticoat from the clothes brought from the other room, very nervously begins winding this around the bottle. In a false voice):* My, it's a good thing the men couldn't hear us. Wouldn't they just laugh! Getting all stirred up over a little thing like a—dead canary. As if that could have anything to do with—with—wouldn't they *laugh! (The men are heard coming down stairs.)*

MRS. HALE *(under her breath):* Maybe they would—maybe they wouldn't.

COUNTY ATTORNEY: No, Peters, it's all perfectly clear except a reason for doing it. But you know juries when it comes to women. If there was some definite thing. Something to show—something to make a story about—a thing that would connect up with this strange way of doing it—*(The women's eyes meet for an instant. Enter Hale from outer door.)*

HALE: Well, I've got the team around. Pretty cold out there.

COUNTY ATTORNEY: I'm going to stay here a while by myself. *(To the Sheriff.)* You can send Frank out for me, can't you? I want to go over everything. I'm not satisfied that we can't do better.

SHERIFF: Do you want to see what Mrs. Peters is going to take in? *(The Lawyer goes to the table, picks up the apron, laughs.)*

COUNTY ATTORNEY: Oh, I guess they're not very dangerous things the ladies have picked out. *(Moves a few things about, disturbing the quilt pieces which cover the box. Steps back.)* No, Mrs. Peters doesn't need supervising. For that matter a sheriff's wife is married to the law. Ever think of it that way, Mrs. Peters?

MRS. PETERS: Not—just that way.

SHERIFF *(chuckling):* Married to the law. *(Moves toward the other room.)* I just want you to come in here a minute, George. We ought to take a look at these windows.

COUNTY ATTORNEY *(scoffingly):* Oh, windows!

SHERIFF: We'll be right out, Mr. Hale. *(Hale goes outside. The Sheriff follows the County Attorney into the other room. Then Mrs. Hale rises, hands tight together, looking intensely at Mrs. Peters, whose eyes make a slow turn, finally meeting Mrs. Hale's. A moment Mrs. Hale holds her, then her own eyes point the way to where the box is concealed. Suddenly Mrs. Peters throws back quilt pieces and tries to put the box in the bag she is wearing. It is too big. She opens box, starts to take bird out, cannot touch it, goes to pieces, stands there helpless. Sound of a knob turning in the other room. Mrs. Hale snatches the box and puts it in the pocket of her big coat. Enter County Attorney and Sheriff.)*

COUNTY ATTORNEY *(facetiously):* Well, Henry, at least we found out that she was not going to quilt it. She was going to—what is it you call it, ladies?

MRS. HALE *(her hand against her pocket):* We call it—knot it, Mr. Henderson.

CURTAIN.

To His Coy Mistress

ANDREW MARVELL

Had we but world enough, and time,
This coyness, lady, were no crime.
We would sit down, and think which way
To walk, and pass our long love's day.
Thou by the Indian Ganges' side   5
Should'st rubies find; I by the tide
Of Humber[1] would complain. I would
Love you ten years before the Flood;
And you should, if you please, refuse
Till the conversion of the Jews.   10
My vegetable love should grow
Vaster than empires, and more slow.
An hundred years should go to praise
Thine eyes, and on thy forehead gaze;
Two hundred to adore each breast;   15
But thirty thousand to the rest:
An age at least to every part,
And the last age should show your heart.
For, lady, you deserve this state,
Nor would I love at lower rate.   20
   But at my back I always hear
Time's wingèd chariot hurrying near;
And yonder all before us lie
Deserts of vast eternity.
Thy beauty shall no more be found,   25
Nor in thy marble vault shall sound
My echoing song; then worms shall try
That long-preserved virginity;
And your quaint honor turn to dust,
And into ashes all my lust.   30

[1] An estuary in England. — All notes are the editors'.

Andrew Marvell (1621–1678) was a longtime member of the British Parliament and a writer of political satires. Today, however, he is remembered for two splendid poems, "The Garden" and the one that appears here. "To His Coy Mistress" is a noteworthy expression of an idea familiar in the love poems of many languages—*carpe diem*, Latin for "seize the day," the idea that life is fleeting and love and other pleasures should be enjoyed while the lovers are still young and beautiful.

The grave's a fine and private place,
But none, I think, do there embrace.
    Now, therefore, while thy youthful hue
Sits on thy skin like morning dew,
And while thy willing soul transpires   35
At every pore with instant fires,
Now let us sport us while we may;
And now, like amorous birds of prey,
Rather at once our time devour,
Than languish in his slow-chapped² power.   40
Let us roll all our strength and all
Our sweetness up into one ball;
And tear our pleasures with rough strife
Thorough³ the iron gates of life.
Thus, though we cannot make our sun   45
Stand still, yet we will make him run.

²Slow-jawed.
³Through.

Acknowledgments (continued from page ii)

Radley Balko. "Absolutely. Government Has No Business Interfering with What You Eat." Published in *Time* magazine, June 7, 2004. Copyright © 2004 by Radley Balko. Reprinted by permission of the author.

Kelly Brownell and Marion Nestle. "Not If Blaming the Victim Is Just an Excuse to Let Industry Off the Hook." From *Time* magazine, June 7, 2004. Copyright © 2004 by Kelly Brownell and Marion Nestle. Reprinted by permission of the authors.

Warren Burger. "The Right to Bear Arms." Originally published in *Parade*, January 14, 1990. Copyright © 1990 Warren E. Burger. Reprinted with permission from *Parade* and the Estate of Warren Burger. All rights reserved.

"A Call for Unity: A Letter from Eight White Clergymen." Reprinted with permission.

Peggy Carlson. "Why We Don't Need Animal Experimentation." Reprinted with permission by the Physicians Committee for Responsible Medicine (PCRM), 5100 Wisconsin Ave., Suite 400, Washington, DC 20016; www.perm.org.

Carrie Chapman Catt. "The Crisis." From *Man Cannot Speak for Her*, Volume I: *A Critical Study of Early Feminist Rhetoric*, ed. by Karlyn Kohrs Campbell, Greenwood Press. Copyright © 1989 by Karlyn Kohrs Campbell. Reprinted with permission of Greenwood Publishing Group, Inc., Westport, CT.

"Chance of reading on vacation." Imodium ad. Reprinted with permission of McNeil Consumer & Specialty Pharmaceuticals Division of McNeil-PPC, Inc.

Mona Charen. "The Misleading Debate on Stem Cell Research." From *Townhall.com*, August 20, 2004. Copyright © 2004 by News America Syndicate. Reprinted by permission of Mona Charen and Creator's Syndicate, Inc.

Jo Ann Citron. "Will It Be Marriage or Civil Union?" Originally published in *The Gay & Lesbian Review Worldwide*, March/April 2004, v. 11, i2, p. 10(2). Copyright © 2004 The Gay & Lesbian Review Worldwide. Reprinted by permission of the author.

"Cool Gear." The Advertising Archives #30517377.

John Patrick Diggins. "The Pursuit of Whining: Affirmative Action circa 1776." Originally published in *The New York Times*, September 25, 1995. Copyright © 1995 by The New York Times Company. Reprinted by permission.

Sandra Feldman. "The Childswap Society." From the January 1998 "Where We Stand" monthly column of the American Federation of Teachers. Reprinted with permission.

Stanley Fish. "Colleges Caught in Vise." From *The New York Times*, September 18, 2003. Copyright © 2003 The New York Times Company. Reprinted by permission.

David Gelernter. "Computers and the Pursuit of Happiness." Reprinted by permission of the author.

Nathan Glazer. "Do We Need the Census Race Question?" From *The Public Interest*, No 149 (Fall 2002), pp. 21–31. © 2002 by National Affairs, Inc. Reprinted with permission.

Bernard Goldberg. "Connecting the Dots . . . to Terrorism." From *Bias: A CBS Insider Exposes How the Media Distorts the News*. Copyright © Regnery Publishing. Reprinted by permission of the publisher.

Paul Goodman. "A Proposal to Abolish Grading." From *Compulsory Miseducation* by Paul Goodman. Copyright © 1964 by Horizon Press, New York. Reprinted by Permission of Sally Goodman.

E. J. Graff. "Real Marriage, Real Life." From *The American Prospect*, Volume 14, Number 4, April 1, 2003. The American Prospect, 11 Beacon Street, Suite 1120, Boston, MA 02108. Reprinted with permission. All rights reserved.

Jennifer Grossman. "Food for Thought (and for Credit)." From *The New York Times*, September 2, 2003, p. 23, col. 1. Copyright © 2003 The New York Times Company. Reprinted with permission.

Elisha Dov Hack. "College Life vs. My Moral Code." Originally published in *The New York Times*, September 9, 1997. Copyright © 1997 by The New York Times Company. Reprinted by permission.

Richard Hayes. "Supersize Your Child?" Originally titled "Selective Science." From *Tom Paine.com*. February 12, 2004. Copyright © 2004 Tompaine.com. Reprinted with permission of Institute for America's Future, Inc. www.tompaine.com.

Adolf Hitler. "On Nation and Race." From *Mein Kampf* by Adolf Hitler, translated by Ralph Manheim. Copyright © 1943 and renewed 1971 by Houghton Mifflin Company. Reprinted by permission of Houghton Mifflin Company. All rights reserved. Canadian Rights: Used by permission of The Random House Group Ltd.

The Hunger Site home page. Used with permission of CharityUSA.com LLC, owner of The Hunger Site, The Breast Cancer Site, The Rainforest Site, and GreaterGood.com.

"Jihad News" by Gary Varvel cartoon used by permission of Gary Varvel and Creators Syndicate, Inc.

GLOSSARY

Abstract language: language expressing a quality apart from a specific object or event; opposite of *concrete language*

Ad hominem: "against the man"; attacking the arguer rather than the *argument* or issue

Ad populum: "to the people"; playing on the prejudices of the *audience*

Anecdotal evidence: stories or examples used to illustrate a *claim* but that do not prove it with scientific certainty

Appeal to tradition: a proposal that something should continue because it has traditionally existed or been done that way

Argument: a process of reasoning and advancing proof about issues on which conflicting views may be held; also, a statement or statements providing *support* for a *claim*

Audience: those who will hear an *argument;* more generally, those to whom a communication is addressed

Authoritative warrant: a *warrant* based on the credibility or trustworthiness of the source

Backing: the assurances on which a *warrant* or assumption is based

Begging the question: making a statement that assumes that the issue being argued has already been decided

Claim: the conclusion of an argument; what the arguer is trying to prove

Claim of fact: a *claim* that asserts something exists, has existed, or will exist, based on data that the *audience* will accept as objectively verifiable

Claim of policy: a *claim* asserting that specific courses of action should be instituted as solutions to problems

Claim of value: a *claim* that asserts some things are more or less desirable than others

Cliché: a worn-out expression or idea, no longer capable of producing a visual image or provoking thought about a subject

Concrete language: language that describes specific, generally observable, persons, places, or things; in contrast to *abstract language*

Connotation: the overtones that adhere to a word through long usage

Credibility: the audience's belief in the arguer's trustworthiness; see also *ethos*

Data: facts or figures from which a conclusion may be inferred; see *evidence*

Deduction: reasoning by which we establish that a conclusion must be true because the statements on which it is based are true; see also *syllogism*

Definition: an explanation of the meaning of a term, concept, or experience; may be used for clarification, especially of a *claim*, or as a means of developing an *argument*

Definition by negation: defining a thing by saying what it is not

Empirical evidence: *support* verifiable by experience or experiment

Enthymeme: a *syllogism* in which one of the premises is implicit

Ethos: the qualities of character, intelligence, and goodwill in an arguer that contribute to an *audience's* acceptance of the *claim*

Euphemism: a pleasant or flattering expression used in place of one that is less agreeable but possibly more accurate

Evidence: *facts* or opinions that support an issue or *claim;* may consist of *statistics,* reports of personal experience, or views of experts

Extended definition: a *definition* that uses several different methods of development

Fact: something that is believed to have objective reality; a piece of information regarded as verifiable

Factual evidence: *support* consisting of *data* that are considered objectively verifiable by the audience

Fallacy: an error of reasoning based on faulty use of *evidence* or incorrect *inference*

False analogy: assuming without sufficient proof that if objects or processes are similar in some ways, then they are similar in other ways as well

False dilemma: simplifying a complex problem into an either/or dichotomy

Faulty emotional appeals: basing an argument on feelings, especially pity or fear—often to draw attention away from the real issues or conceal another purpose

Faulty use of authority: failing to acknowledge disagreement among experts or otherwise misrepresenting the trustworthiness of sources

Hasty generalization: drawing conclusions from insufficient evidence

Induction: reasoning by which a general statement is reached on the basis of particular examples

Inference: an interpretation of the *facts*

Major premise: see *syllogism*

Minor premise: see *syllogism*

MLA: the Modern Language Association, a professional organization for college teachers of English and foreign languages

Motivational appeal: an attempt to reach an *audience* by recognizing their *needs* and *values* and how these contribute to their decision making

Motivational warrant: a type of *warrant* based on the *needs* and *values* of an *audience*

Need: in the hierarchy of Abraham Maslow, whatever is required, whether psychological, or physiological, for the survival and welfare of a human being

Non sequitur: "it does not follow"; using irrelevant proof to buttress a *claim*

Paraphrase: to restate the content of an original source in your own words

Picturesque language: words that produce images in the minds of the *audience*

Plagiarism: the use of someone else's words or ideas without adequate acknowledgment

Policy: a course of action recommended or taken to solve a problem or guide decisions

Post hoc: mistakenly inferring that because one event follows another they have a causal relation; from *post hoc ergo propter hoc* ("after this, therefore because of this"); also called "doubtful cause"

Proposition: see *claim*

Qualifier: a restriction placed on the *claim* may not always be true as stated

Quote: to repeat exactly words from a printed, electronic, or spoken source

Refutation: an attack on an opposing view to weaken it, invalidate it, or make it less credible

Reservation: a restriction placed on the *warrant* to indicate that unless certain conditions are met, the warrant may not establish a connection between the *support* and the *claim*

Slanting: selecting *facts* or words with *connotations* that favor the arguer's bias and discredit alternatives

Slippery slope: predicting without justification that one step in a process will lead unavoidably to a second, generally undesirable step

Slogan: an attention-getting expression used largely in politics or advertising to promote support of a cause or product

Statistics: information expressed in numerical form

Stipulative definition: a *definition* that makes clear that it will explore a particular area of meaning of a term or issue

Straw man: disputing a view similar to, but not the same as, that of the arguer's opponent

Style: choices in words and sentence structure that make a writer's language distinctive

Substantive warrant: a *warrant* based on beliefs about the reliability of *factual evidence*

Support: any material that serves to prove an issue or *claim;* in addition to *evidence,* it includes appeals to the *needs* and *values* of the *audience*

Syllogism: a formula of deductive *argument* consisting of three propositions: a major premise, a minor premise, and a conclusion

Thesis: the main idea of an essay

Toulmin model: a conceptual system of argument devised by the philosopher Stephen Toulmin; the terms *claim, support, warrant, backing, qualifier,* and *reservation* are adapted from this system

Two wrongs make a right: diverting attention from the issue by introducing a new point, e.g., by responding to an accusation with a counteraccusation that makes no attempt to refute the first accusation

Values: conceptions or ideas that act as standards for judging what is right or wrong, worthwhile or worthless, beautiful or ugly, good or bad

Warrant: a general principle or assumption that establishes a connection between the *support* and the *claim*

INDEX OF SUBJECTS

INDEX OF AUTHORS AND TITLES

Need more help with writing and research?
Visit our Web sites.

We have a wide variety of Web sites designed to help students with their most common writing concerns. You'll find advice from experts, models you can rely on, and exercises that will tell you right away how you're doing. And it's all free and available any hour of the day.

Need help with grammar problems?
Exercise Central   (bedfordstmartins.com/exercisecentral)

Want to see what papers for your other courses look like?
Model Documents Gallery   (bedfordstmartins.com/modeldocs)

Stuck somewhere in the research process? (Maybe at the beginning?)
The Bedford Research Room   (bedfordstmartins.com/researchroom)

Wondering whether a Web site is good enough to use in your paper?
Tutorial for Evaluating Online Sources
(bedfordstmartins.com/onlinesourcestutorial)

Having trouble figuring out how to cite a source?
Research and Documentation Online   (bedfordstmartins.com/resdoc)

Confused about plagiarism?
The St. Martin's Tutorial on Avoiding Plagiarism
(bedfordstmartins.com/plagiarismtutorial)

Want to get more out of your word processor?
Using Your Word Processor   (bedfordstmartins.com/wordprocessor)

Trying to improve the look of your paper?
Using Your Word Processor to Design Documents
(bedfordstmartins.com/docdesigntutorial)

Need to create slides for a presentation?
Preparing Presentation Slides Tutorial
(bedfordstmartins.com/presentationslidetutorial)

Interested in creating a Web site?
Web Design Tutorial   (bedfordstmartins.com/webdesigntutorial)